THE IRISH
Presbyterian
HYMNBOOK

THE IRISH
Presbyterian
HYMNBOOK

Words Edition

CANTERBURY
PRESS
Norwich

The Irish Presbyterian Hymnbook is published on behalf of
The Trustees of the Presbyterian Church In Ireland
by Canterbury Press Norwich.

Canterbury Press Norwich, St Mary's Works,
St Mary's Plain, Norwich NR3 3BH,
a division of SCM-Canterbury Press Ltd, a subsidiary of
Hymns Ancient & Modern Ltd, a registered charity.

The Irish Presbyterian Hymnbook Words Edition.

First published September 2004
© *Compilation*, The Trustees of the Presbyterian Church in Ireland

A catalogue record of this book is available from the British Library.

ISBN 1-85311-611-4

Music engraving and typesetting:
Andrew Parker, Ferndown, Dorset BH22 8BB United Kingdom
Printing and binding:
William Clowes Ltd, Copland Way, Ellough, Beccles, Suffolk
NR34 7TL United Kingdom

CONTENTS

THE IRISH PSALTER

THE HYMNS AND SONGS

Hymn No.

CREATION
MORNING	1
EVENING	8
GOD'S WORLD	17
THE ENVIRONMENT	37
SEASONS OF THE YEAR	41
HARVEST	50

THE FALL
THE HUMAN CONDITION	61

GOD THROUGH THE YEARS
HIS FAITHFULNESS	77
HIS GUIDANCE	103
HIS PROVIDENCE	109
NEW YEAR OLD YEAR	131

THE TEMPLE
DEDICATION OF BUILDINGS	137
THE PEOPLE OF GOD	140
THE TRINITY	157
WORSHIP	164
PRAISE	199
PRAYER	247
THE BIBLE	261
DEDICATION OF GIFTS OFFERINGS	278
CLOSE OF SERVICE	280

CHRIST PROMISED
HIS FIRST ADVENT	290

JESUS CHRIST
HIS BIRTH	305
HIS LIFE AND MINISTRY	341
HEALING	364
BAPTISM	370
THE LORD'S SUPPER	379
HIS PASSION AND DEATH	395
HIS RESURRECTION	428
HIS ASCENSION	445

THE HOLY SPIRIT
    HIS WORK IN INDIVIDUAL LIVES   457
    HIS WORK IN THE LIFE OF THE CHURCH   470
    ORDINATION AND COMMISSIONING   481

THE GROWTH OF THE CHURCH
    IN INDIVIDUAL LIVES   485
    CONFIRMATION   531
    DEDICATION   535
    DISCIPLESHIP   555
    IN SOCIETY   MARRIAGE   575
    HOME AND FAMILY   585
    THE COMMUNITY   588
    IN THE NATION   603
    AMONG THE NATIONS   614
    MISSION   627

THE LAST THINGS
    CHRIST'S RETURN   644
    HEAVEN   654
    FUNERAL HYMNS   661
    THE CHURCH TRIUMPHANT   665

INDEXES

PREFACE

As our denomination has emerged from its once exclusively psalm-singing tradition, three hymnbooks, apart from the supplement *Glory to God* produced in 1994, have to date served our requirements. The first produced in 1898 was succeeded by the *Revised Church Hymnary* in 1927, which although replaced in 1973 by the *Church Hymnary* (3rd edition), continues to be used in about forty percent of our congregations. In the year 1995 the General Assembly of our Church decided not to co-operate with the Church Hymnary Trust in its preparation of *Church Hymnary* (4th edition).

This left our denomination in somewhat of a dilemma. Were we now to be left without Presbyterian hymnbooks — albeit hymnbooks which, through the passage of time, had become dated both in language and style, and which obviously could not take on board any of the excellent new materials becoming available? This was exacerbated by the decision of Oxford University Press to discontinue the production of the *Revised Church Hymnary* and their declared intention that when *Church Hymnary* (4th edition) was published the *Church Hymnary* (3rd edition) would also be discontinued.

A common suggestion at the time was that we adopt, from a proliferation of available hymnbooks in existence, one that would meet the requirements of our denomination. Members of Assembly were asked to channel their recommendations of such hymnals through the General Board to the Public Worship Committee. In all, seventeen such hymnals were given serious consideration and although many of these are excellent denominational or inter-denominational hymnbooks, none was thought entirely suitable to meet the needs and theological emphasis of our denomination.

Hence the decision of the General Assembly in 2001 to ask the Public Worship Committee to proceed towards the production of a hymnbook by the Presbyterian Church in Ireland *for* the Presbyterian Church in Ireland. Surely a most significant decision in the life of any denomination! For this specific purpose, the Public Worship Committee was enlarged by a further ten members with particular theological or musical expertise. Informally this enlarged committee became know as the Hymnal Committee.

One of its first tasks was to draw up criteria to govern the size and character of the new hymnbook. Eventually four sub-committees, each with conveners, were appointed to deal with the compilation and selection of materials (words and music) in the following areas:

1 **Existing Materials**
2 **Contemporary Materials**
3 **Psalmody and Liturgical Materials**
4 **Children's and Young People's Materials.**

A list of suggested materials, although not definitive, had been drawn up and presented to the General Assembly in 2000. It now became the task of the Hymnal Committee to consider responses of congregations to this list, and arrive at what was considered to be the best items for inclusion, bearing in mind the limitations of a core book. In addition the best versions of hymns had to be sought out and then, of course, married to what were considered the best tunes and indeed tune arrangements. The next task was to allocate the materials according to subject headings, and cross reference these, if appropriate, to other subject headings. It was also important to ensure that our contemporary and inclusive gender criteria were applied.

After much careful consideration and valuable advice from the General Assembly's Financial Secretary, Clive Knox, and his assistant Jonathan Kelly, four publishers were asked to tender for the publication of the new book. Eventually, SCM-Canterbury Press Ltd was appointed, and Gordon Knights, its Chief Executive, has been in constant contact with the committee, particularly in the area of copyright. His guidance, and that of his colleague Andrew Parker, has been invaluable.

The remit of the Existing Materials Sub-Committee was to sift through what was deemed the best in the two hymnbooks currently in use (i.e. *Revised Church Hymnary* and *Church Hymnary* (3rd edition)) and indeed any other hymnbook, and apply our criteria to this list in order to make these materials more acceptable and meaningful to contemporary worshippers. The aim was that all members of our congregations, young and not so young, will be enabled to sing with meaning and clarity. It should be noted that this kind of revision of hymns is nothing new. Throughout history hymns have been revised, adapted and rewritten. Indeed, many of the hymns we regard as classics are in reality very different from their original texts. Taken all this into consideration, plus the fact that the majority of hymns within the new Hymn Book are within this category, this proved a huge challenge.

The task of the Contemporary Materials Sub-Committee, although very different, proved none the less demanding. Changes that have taken place in theological understanding and worship styles clearly cannot and must not be ignored; nor can the vast post-war surge in hymn-writing, with its plethora of materials, much of which is excellent as a vehicle of praise and worship to God. The continuing rich outpouring of contemporary worship songs is surely a sign of vitality in the life of the Church, and is thus to be welcomed. However, there have emerged an enormous amount of materials, some of which will have lasting value and much will not. The remit of this committee was to sift through a plethora of materials and come up with what was deemed to be suitable for inclusion in the new hymnbook, always bearing in mind the theological emphasis of our denomination. In order to take advantage of this continuing output of contemporary materials, it is the considered opinion of the Public Worship Committee that there will need to be a supplement to this core book produced about every five to seven years.

Then we come to the Psalms and Liturgical Materials Sub-Committee. The feedback from a questionnaire that went out to all congregations through presbyteries in 1999 left us in no doubt that we were to keep the *Irish Psalter* as we have had it attached to both *Revised Church Hymnary* and *Church Hymnary* (3rd edition). However, the question emerged — what about the large volume of psalms now available in the vernacular? These must surely not be missed out! Hence the remit of the Psalms and Liturgical Materials Sub-Committee was to sift through the psalms in this medium and come up with a suitable selection for the new hymnbook, ensuring that careful attention was paid to the meaning of each psalm in its context.

This brings us to the fourth and final group — The Children and Young People's Materials Sub-Committee. Ever since the new hymnbook was first talked about, it was the desire of those involved that it would become a core hymnbook to suit the whole Church, and that it would be family-orientated to suit all preferences, occasions, seasons and stages in development. This must surely include children and young people, whom we recognise as not just the Church of tomorrow, but a very important part of the Church of today! There has emerged from this sub-committee a really splendid selection of Children and Young People's hymns, second to none of any available denominational hymn book. Indeed, it is one of the great strengths of this hymnbook, with its selection including many of the great old favourites from away back, as well as those from more recent times.

The Hymnal Committee is well aware that the launch of a new denominational hymnbook is not without its potential for conflict and differences of opinion. Indeed it would be well nigh impossible to get a hymnbook to please everybody! Realistically we face the fact that tensions exist between those who see themselves as guardians of traditional church music and those who see themselves as advocates of the more informal contemporary style. It has been the desire and intention of the committee to bring the best of both traditions together under the one cover — which, after much discussion, it was decided should be called the *Irish Presbyterian Hymnbook*.

We are conscious that the launch of this new hymnbook coincides with a time of unprecedented change in society, in the world and indeed public worship. These changes in attitude, with all their accompanying tensions have, on the one hand, led to widespread secularism and materialism with strong overtones of scepticism. On the other hand, there have been the strong influences of charismatic and ecumenical experimentation. All this is exacerbated by the reality or threat of international, national or provincial terrorism and also the huge implications of such realities as global warming, genetic engineering and environmental pollution. This is something of the background canvas of the real world at the time of the launch of this new hymnbook. It therefore behoves us as a church to provide worshippers with a tool that will enable them to express their worship to Almighty God in language and sentiments that they can understand, and with which they can fully identify.

It was A. W. Tozier who usefully declared, 'after the sacred Scriptures, the next best companion for the soul is a good Hymnal.' In this new hymnbook strenuous efforts have been made to represent the crucial elements of biblical revelation as far as possible within the limits of our expertise and resources. Indeed, at a glance it can be seen that the ordering of materials follows the biblical pattern. We commence with Creation, then stage by stage reach the Doctrine of the Last Things via The Fall; God through the Ages; The Temple; Christ Promised; Jesus Christ; The Holy Spirit; The Growth of the Church; In Society. What better pattern to follow than that of Holy Scripture?

It is clearly impossible to undertake a project of this magnitude without the help of a host of people. Of course, one immediately thinks of the members of the Hymnal Committee, and in particular the conveners of the four sub-committees mentioned above. John F. Murdoch convened the sub-committee on Existing Materials. His encyclopedic knowledge of hymns (words and music); his attention to detail, and his enthusiastic endurance to the end of the exercise leaves the Church at large very much in his debt. Then there are the conveners of the other three sub-committees, Harry Morrow (Contemporary Materials), Mark Spratt (Psalmody and Liturgical materials) and Oswald McAuley (Children's Materials). These men had the demanding task of compiling their respective materials for acceptance or rejection by the full committee. They then had to prepare the materials that were decided upon for the publisher. Finally, they had to proof-read and re-read their respective materials, often within very rigid time-tables. This demanded not just hours, but days upon days of their valuable time! For this latter task of proof-reading they were ably assisted by Joan Cowle, Margaret Crooks, Olive Marshall, Hastings McIntyre, John Murdock and Bill Saunderson.

The task of preparing this new hymnbook was undertaken under two Clerks of the General Assembly — Sam Hutchinson and Donald Watts, two Conveners of the Communications Board — Ivor Smith and Alistair Kennedy and two Chairmen of the Public Worship Committee — Barkley Wallace and John Murdock. All six men have, within their capacities, been most supportive and have given much valuable advice and encouragement. Mention must also be made to the General Assembly's Information Officer, Stephen Lynas, whose help, particularly in the area of graphics and presentation in electronic format has been invaluable, as has that of his secretary Ann McCully. The Minister's Secretary in Hillhall, Maree Gillespie and son John Richardson both spent many hours on the computer preparing lists and scripts. Hillhall Church provided the accommodation where much of the work was carried out, and Sally Richardson was always in the background to provide much appreciated refreshments. Nor does the contribution of Lorraine Smyth, and Louise and Pat McIvor's offer of help in communicating with the wider Church on the issue of the official and regional launches, go unnoticed.

It has been the constant prayer of the committee throughout its preparation that this new hymnbook will bring much blessing to our people in their praise of Almighty God. At a time when there is perhaps too much of the practice of 'doing our own thing' as congregations, it has the potential to be a great unifying influence on our denomination. This will be enhanced as we sing out of the same book the Psalms, Hymns, and Spiritual Songs contained within its covers. It has consistently been our concern that it will be attractive in presentation, comprehensive in content, accessible in indexing and affordable in price. Our prayer is that it will be taken up with enthusiasm by our congregations, and that it will enable those who gather for worship to offer that worship in a vibrant, meaningful and relevant way. Thus may it be used in the salvation of souls, the encouragement of believers, the upbuilding of God's Kingdom and in the bringing of glory to the One to whom all Glory is due — the Lord Jesus Christ — the sole King and Head of the Church.

Jack Richardson
Convener, Public Worship Committee

NOTES ON THE WORDS

Charged with the production of a new hymnbook for the Presbyterian Church in Ireland, in giving careful attention to the matter of words, the Committee has sought to be true to the principles with which it was presented:

1 Updated language

The use of 'thee' and 'thy', '-eth' and '-est', associated with a form of words no longer in fashion in ecclesiastical use, has been largely eliminated, often with the straightforward and quite seamless substitution of 'You' and 'Your', but at times with the alteration or rearrangement of some familiar lines, and always within the limitations imposed by owners of copyright.

However, in some instances, notably *Be Thou my Vision* and *Thine be the glory,* the original form, being so well-known and well-loved, has been retained alongside an alternative, i.e. *Lord, be my vision* and *Glory to Jesus.* In the case of *My faith looks up to Thee* it was decided to leave well alone, since the degree of alteration necessary would have made a valued hymn unrecognisable.

2 All-inclusive language

Strenuous attempts have been made to circumvent the problem caused to present-day worshippers by the apparently male-orientated bias of earlier hymnody; so that 'Good Christian men' has become 'Good Christians all', 'Rise up, O men of God' has become 'Rise up, O Church of God', and 'O brother man, fold to thy heart thy brother' will be found in a new form as 'Fold to your heart your sister and your brother'.

On occasion however, where contingent alteration proved extensive and too complicated 'men' and 'mankind' have been allowed to remain, in the hope that they will be understood in their general and generic sense.

3 Old and New together

   i Enduring respect for psalms and paraphrases in their original form has been honoured, and they appear in their totality, as has been customary, as a first section of the book. However, opportunity has been taken to introduce in the main section some updated versions, in the hope that in

PREFACE

this form old treasures of what was the earliest hymnbook both of Christianity and of Presbyterianism may be opened anew for today's worshippers.

ii   The results of a Churchwide survey were taken into account in the selection of material from *Church Hymnary*, (3rd edition) and in the restoration from *Revised Church Hymnary* of hymns which had been omitted in that publication. *What a friend we have in Jesus* and *Lord Jesus, where Your people meet* will again be available in the standard hymnbook, and the words of older writers such as John Newton and Frances Ridley Havergal are to be found alongside the work of more recent authors like Fred Kaan and Timothy Dudley-Smith.   Examples tried and tested and considered of lasting worth from *Glory to God*, the Church's supplement which provided a bridge between the old and the contemporary, have been retained.

4   Contemporary language

Contemporary language will be found married in a substantial number of items to contemporary music.   The abundance of material which has been produced in more recent years presented a difficulty of choice which was given specific focus by the decision to exclude 'choruses' and for the most part to avoid songs consisting of only one verse, and by the desire to incorporate examples of contemporary praise wherever possible in the various categories suggested by the overall Biblical progression of the book.

5   Language of the Young

It was recognised that since publication of *Church Hymnary*, (3rd edition) the section it included for use with children has become largely outdated.   This new publication has taken full advantage of the wealth of material which has become familiar in children's worship and, while preserving theological content, will allow younger members of the Church family to praise God in language and through concepts which relate more directly to their everyday experience.

6   Contemporary themes

By the same token other sections of the hymnbook have been introduced or expanded to reflect issues of today's world, so that in words that are sung in worship it is possible to express from a wider selection the concerns of world peace, the environment, family life and social responsibility.

In all its work it has been the prime aim of the Committee, through the vehicle of words, at its best imperfect, to enable the worshipping community with understanding and with enthusiasm to declare the incomparable 'worth-ship' of a perfect God.

John F. Murdoch

COPYRIGHT

The Publishers thank the owners or controllers of copyright for permission to use the hymns and tunes throughout this collection. An obelus or dagger denotes that the text has been altered with permission, where the text is in copyright. As is customary nowadays, acknowledgements are given on-page with the material.

Every effort have been made to trace copyright owners or controllers, to seek permission to use text and music, and to make alterations as necessary. The Publishers apologise to those who have not been traced at the time of going to press, and whose rights have inadvertently not been acknowledged. Any ommissions or inaccuracies of permissions or copyright details will be corrected in future printings.

REPRODUCTION OF COPYRIGHT MATERIAL

For permission to reproduce copyright hymns and music from this collection, whether in permanent or temporary form, by whatever means, application must be made to the respective owners or controllers at the contact addresses shown on-page.

THE PSALMS OF DAVID IN METRE

1

1 That man hath perfect
blessedness
who walketh not astray
in counsel of ungodly men,
nor stands in sinners' way,
nor sitteth in the scorner's chair:
2 but placeth his delight
upon God's law, and meditates
on his law day and night.

3 He shall be like a tree that hath
been planted by a river,
which in its season yields its fruit,
and his leaf fadeth never:
and all he doth shall prosper
well.
4 The wicked are not so;
but like they are unto the chaff,
which wind drives to and fro.

5 In judgment therefore shall not
stand
such as ungodly are;
nor in the assembly of the just
shall wicked men appear.
6 Because the way of godly men
unto the Lord is known;
whereas the way of wicked men
shall quite be overthrown.

2

1 Why rage the heathen? and vain
things
why do the people mind?
2 Kings of the earth do set
themselves,
and princes are combined,
to plot against the Lord, and his
anointed, saying thus,
3 let us asunder break their bands,
and cast their cords from us.

4 He that in heaven sits shall
laugh;
the Lord shall scorn them all.
5 Then shall he speak to them in
wrath,
in rage he vex them shall.
6 Yet, I, my King appointed have
upon my holy hill;
on Zion mount his throne is set,
established by my will.

7 The sure decree I will declare:
the Lord hath said to me,
thou art mine only Son; this day
I have begotten thee.
8 Ask of me, and for heritage
the heathen I'll make thine;
and for possession I to thee
will give earth's utmost line.

9 Thou with a rod of iron shalt
beat down and break them all;
them, as potter's vessel, thou
shalt dash in pieces small.
10 Now, therefore, kings, be wise; be
taught
ye judges of the earth:
11 serve ye the Lord in holy fear;
join trembling with your mirth.

12 Kiss ye the Son, lest in his ire
ye perish from the way,
for suddenly his wrath may
burn:
blest all that on him stay.

3

1 O Lord, how are my foes
increased!
against me many rise.
2 Many say of my soul, For him
in God no succour lies.
3 Yet thou my shield and glory art,
the uplifter of mine head.
4 I cried, and from his holy hill
the Lord me answer made.

5 I laid me down and slept, I
waked;
for God sustained me.
6 I will not fear though thousands
ten
set round against me be.
7 Arise, O Lord; save me, my God;
for thou hast struck my foes
upon the cheek; the wicked's
teeth
hast broken by thy blows.

8 Salvation surely doth belong
unto the Lord alone;
thy blessing, Lord, for evermore
thy people is upon.

4

1 Give ear unto me when I call,
God of my righteousness;
have mercy, hear my prayer;
thou hast
enlarged me in distress.
2 O ye the sons of men! how long

will ye love vanities?
How long my glory turn to
    shame,
and will ye follow lies?
3 But know, that for himself the
       Lord
the godly man doth choose:
the Lord, when I on him do call,
to hear will not refuse.
4 Fear, and sin not; talk with your
       heart
on bed, and silent be.
5 Offerings present of
       righteousness,
and in the Lord trust ye.

6 O who will show us any good?
is that which many say:
but of thy countenance the light,
Lord, lift on us alway.
7 Upon my heart bestowed by thee,
more gladness I have found
than they, even then, when corn
    and wine
did most with them abound.
8 I will both lay me down in peace,
and quiet sleep will take;
because thou only me to dwell
in safety, Lord, dost make.

5

1 Give ear unto my words, O Lord,
my meditation weigh.
2 Hear my loud cry, my King, my
       God;
for I to thee will pray.
3 Lord, thou shalt early hear my
       voice:
I early will direct
my prayer to thee; and, looking
    up,
an answer will expect.

4 For thou art not a God that doth
in wickedness delight;
neither shall evil dwell with
    thee,
5 nor fools stand in thy sight.
All evil-doers thou dost hate,
6 cutt'st off that liars be:
the bloody and deceitful man
abhorred is by thee.

7 But I into thy house will come
in thine abundant grace;
and I will worship in thy fear
toward thy holy place.
8 Lord, lead me in thy
       righteousness,

for foes do lie in wait:
thy way, wherein I am to walk,
before my face make straight.
9 For in their mouth there is no
       truth,
their inward part is vile;
their throat's an open sepulchre,
their tongue is full of guile.
10 O God, condemn them; let them
       be
by their own counsel quelled:
them for their many sins cast out,
for they 'gainst thee rebelled.
11 But let all joy that trust in thee,
for aye lift up their voice,
for them thou sav'st: in thee let
    all
that love thy name rejoice.
12 For, Lord, unto the righteous man
thou wilt thy blessing yield:
with favour thou wilt compass
    him
about, as with a shield.

6

FIRST VERSION

1 Lord, in thy wrath rebuke me
       not;
nor in thy hot rage chasten me.
2 Lord, pity me, for I am weak:
heal me, for my bones vexed be.
3 My soul is also vexed sore;
but, Lord, how long stay wilt thou
    make?
4 Return, O Lord, my soul set free;
O save me for thy mercies' sake.

5 Because those that deceased are
of thee shall no remembrance
    have;
and who is he that will to thee
give praises lying in the grave?
6 I with my groaning weary am,
and all the night till morn
    appears,
through grief I make my bed to
    swim,
and water all my couch
    with tears.
7 Mine eye, consumed with grief,
       grows old,
because of all mine enemies.
8 Hence from me, evil-doers all;
for God hath heard my weeping
    cries.
9 God hath my supplication heard;
by him my prayer received shall
    be.

10 Shamed and sore vexed be all
  my foes,
turned back and shamed
  suddenly.

6 SECOND VERSION

1 In thy great indignation, Lord,
  do thou rebuke me not;
nor on me lay thy chastening
  hand
in thy displeasure hot.
2 Lord, pity me, for I am weak;
  have mercy upon me:
and heal thou me, O Lord,
  because
my bones much vexed be.

3 My soul is vexed sore: but, Lord,
  how long stay wilt thou make?
4 Return, O Lord, my soul set free,
  save for thy mercy's sake.
5 Because of thee in death there
  shall
no more remembrance be:
of those that in the grave do lie,
  who shall give thanks to thee?

6 I with my groaning weary am;
  all night till morn appears,
through grief I make my bed to
  swim,
my couch to flow with tears.
7 By reason of my vexing grief
  mine eye consumed is;
it waxeth old, because of all
  that are mine enemies.

8 But now, depart from me all ye
  that work iniquity:
because the Lord hath heard
  my voice
when I did mourn and cry.
9 Unto my supplication's voice
  the Lord hath lent his ear;
when to the Lord my prayer
  I make,
he graciously will hear.

10 Let all be troubled and asham'd,
  that enemies are to me;
let them turn back, and suddenly
  ashamed let them be.

7

1 O Lord my God, in thee do I
  my confidence repose;
save and deliver me from all
  my persecuting foes;
2 lest that the enemy my soul
  should, like a lion, tear,

in pieces rending it, while there
  is no deliverer.
3 O Lord my God, if it be so
  that I committed this;
if it be so that in my hands
  iniquity there is;
4 if I rewarded ill to him
  that was at peace with me;
(yea, even the man that
  without cause
my foe was I did free;)

5 Then let the foe pursue and take
  my soul, and my life thrust
down to the earth, and let him
  lay
mine honour in the dust.
6 Rise in thy wrath, Lord,
  raise thyself,
for my foes raging be;
and, to the judgment which thou
  hast
commanded, wake for me.

7 Of nations the assembled host
  around thee shall draw nigh;
and over them do thou return
  unto thy place on high.
8 Jehovah shall the people judge;
  my judge, Jehovah, be,
after my righteousness and mine
  integrity in me.

9 O let the wicked's mischief end;
  the righteous fortify;
because the righteous God
  art thou
who heart and reins dost try.
10 In God, who saves the upright in
  heart,
is my defence and stay.
11 God is a righteous judge, and
  God
is angry every day.

12 If he do not repent and turn,
  then he his sword will whet;
his bow he hath already bent,
  and hath it ready set:
13 he also hath for him prepared
  the instruments of death;
against the persecutors he
  his shafts ordained hath.

14 Behold, he with iniquity
  doth travail as in birth;
a mischief he conceived hath,
  and falsehood shall bring forth.
15 He made a pit, and digged it
  deep,
another there to take;

but he is fallen into the ditch
which he himself did make.
16 On his own head shall be
returned
the mischief he hath wrought;
the violence that he hath done,
shall on himself be brought.
17 According to his righteousness
the Lord I'll magnify;
and praise will sing unto his
name,
who is the Lord most high.

8 FIRST VERSION

1 How excellent in all the earth,
Lord, our Lord, is thy name!
who hast thy glory far advanced
above the starry frame.
2 From infants' and from sucklings'
mouth
thou power didst ordain,
because of foes, that so thou
might'st
the vengeful foe restrain.
3 When I look up unto thy
heavens,
which thine own fingers framed,
unto the moon and to the stars,
which were by thee ordained;
4 then say I, What is man, that he
remembered is by thee?
Or what the son of man,
that thou
so kind to him should'st be?
5 For thou a little lower hast
him than the angels made;
with glory and with dignity
thou crowned hast his head.
6 Of thy hands' works thou madest
him lord,
all 'neath his feet didst lay,
7 all sheep and oxen, yea, and
beasts
that in the field do stray;
8 Fowl of the air, fish of the sea,
all that pass through the same.
9 How excellent in all the earth,
Lord, our Lord, is thy name!

8 SECOND VERSION

1 O Lord, our Lord, how excellent
in all the earth thy name!
who hast thy glory set above
the starry frame.
2 From infants' and from sucklings'
mouths

is strength by thee ordained,
that so the avenger may be
quelled,
the foe restrained.
3 When I behold thy spacious
heavens,
the work of thine own hand,
the moon and stars in order set
by thy command;
4 O, what is man, that thou
should'st him
in kind remembrance bear?
Or what the son of man, that
thou
for him should'st care?
5 For thou a little lower hast
him than the angels made;
with honour and with glory thou
hast crowned his head.
6 Lord of thy works thou hast him
made:
all unto him must yield,
all sheep and oxen, yea, and
beasts
which roam the field,
7 Fowl of the air, fish of the sea,
all that pass through the same.
O Lord, our Lord, in all the earth
how great thy name!

9

1 Lord, thee I'll praise with all my
heart,
thy wonders all proclaim.
2 In thee, most High, I'll greatly joy,
and sing unto thy name.
3 When back my foes were turned,
they fell,
and perished at thy sight:
4 for thou maintain'st my right and
cause;
enthroned sitt'st judging right.
5 The heathen thou rebuked hast,
the wicked overthrown;
thou hast put out their names,
that they
may never more be known.
6 The desolations are complete
that fell the foe upon;
their cities thou hast razed quite,
their memory is gone.
7 The Lord for ever doth endure;
for judgment sets his throne;
8 in righteousness to judge the
world,
justice to give each one.

9 So shall the Lord a refuge be
   for those that are oppressed;
   a refuge will he be for them,
   what time they are distressed.

10 And they that know thy name
      in thee
   their confidence will place:
   for thou hast not forsaken them
   that truly seek thy face.

11 O sing ye praises to the Lord
   that dwells in Zion hill;
   among the people everywhere
   his deeds declare ye still.

12 When he enquireth after blood,
   he doth remember them:
   the afflicted he doth not forget
   that call upon his name.

13 Lord, pity me; behold the grief
   which I from foes sustain;
   even thou, who from the gates
      of death
   dost raise me up again:

14 That I in Zion's daughter's gates
   may all thy praise relate;
   and that I may exult with joy
   in thy salvation great.

15 Sunk are the heathen in the pit
   which they themselves prepared;
   and in the net which they
      have hid
   their own feet fast are snared.

16 The Lord is by the judgment
      known
   which he himself hath wrought:
   the sinners' hands do make
      the snares
   wherewith themselves are
      caught.

17 The wicked shall be turned back
   into death's dark abode;
   and all the nations that forget
   the great and mighty God.

18 For they that needy are shall not
   forgotten be alway;
   the expectation of the poor
   shall not be lost for aye.

19 Arise, Lord, let not man prevail;
   judge heathen in thy sight;

20 that they may know themselves
      but men,
   the nations, Lord, affright.

10

1 Wherefore is it that thou, O Lord,
   dost stand from us afar?
   and wherefore hidest thou thyself
   when times so troublous are?

2 The wicked in his loftiness
   doth persecute the poor:
   in the devices they have framed
   let them be taken sure.

3 The wicked of his heart's desire
   doth talk with boastful word;
   the covetous renounceth, yea,
   he doth despise the Lord.

4 The wicked in his haughtiness
   upon God doth not call;
   and in the counsels of his heart
   there is no God at all.

5 His ways at all times grievous
      are;
   thy judgments from his sight
   removed are: at all his foes
   he puffeth with despite.

6 Within his heart he thus
      hath said,
   I shall not moved be;
   and no adversity at all
   shall ever come to me.

7 His mouth with cursing, fraud,
      and wrong,
   is filled abundantly;
   and underneath his tongue
      there is
   mischief and vanity.

8 He closely sits in villages;
   he slays the innocent:
   against the poor that pass him by
   his cruel eyes are bent.

9 He lion-like lurks in his den;
   he waits the poor to take,
   and when he draws him in
      his net,
   his prey he doth him make.

10 Himself he humbleth very low,
   he croucheth down withal,
   that so a multitude of poor
   may by his strong ones fall.

11 He thus hath said within
      his heart,
   God hath it quite forgot;
   he hides his countenance, and he
   for ever sees it not.

12 O Lord, do thou arise; O God,
   lift up thine hand on high:
   put not the meek afflicted ones
   out of thy memory.

13 Why is it that the wicked man
   doth God thus still despise?
   Because that God will it require
   he in his heart denies.

14 Thou hast it seen; for wrong
      and wrath
   thou seest to repay:

the poor commits himself to thee;
thou art the orphan's stay.

15 The arm break of the
    wicked man,
and of the evil one;
do thou seek out his wickedness,
until thou findest none.

16 The Lord is king through ages all,
even to eternity;
the heathen people from his land
are perished utterly.

17 O Lord, of those that humble are
thou the desire didst hear;
thou wilt prepare their heart,
    and thou
to hear wilt bend thine ear;

18 to judge the fatherless and those
that are oppressed sore;
that man, who is but of the earth,
may them oppress no more.

11

1 I in the Lord do put my trust;
how is it then that ye
say to my soul, Even as a bird,
unto your mountain flee?

2 For, lo, the wicked bend
    their bow,
their shafts on string they fit,
that those who upright are
    in heart
they privily may hit.

3 If the foundations be destroyed,
what hath the righteous done?

4 God in his holy temple is,
in heaven is his throne.
His eyes behold, his eyelids try

5 men's sons. The just he proves:
but his soul hates the wicked
    man,
and him that violence loves.

6 Snares, fire and brimstone,
    furious storms,
on sinners he shall rain:

7 this, as the portion of their cup,
doth unto them pertain.
Because the Lord most righteous
    doth
in righteousness delight;
they shall his countenance behold
who are in heart upright.

12

1 Help, Lord, because the godly
    man
doth daily fade away;

and from among the sons of men
the faithful do decay.

2 Unto his neighbour every one
doth utter vanity:
they with a double heart do
    speak,
and lips of flattery.

3 God shall cut off all flattering
    lips,
tongues that speak proudly thus,

4 our tongues prevail; our lips are
    ours:
who is lord over us?

5 For the oppression of the poor,
for him in need that sighs,
to save him from his scornful
    foes,
God saith, I will arise.

6 Jehovah's words are words most
    pure;
they are like silver tried
in earthen furnace, seven times
that hath been purified.

7 Lord, thou shalt them preserve
    and keep
for ever from this race.

8 On all sides walk the wicked,
    when
vile men are high in place.

13   FIRST VERSION

1 How long wilt thou forget me,
    Lord?
Shall it for ever be?
O how long shall it be that thou
wilt hide thy face from me?

2 How long take counsel in my
    soul,
still sad in heart, shall I?
How long exalted over me
shall be mine enemy?

3 O Lord my God, consider well,
and answer to me make:
mine eyes enlighten, lest the
    sleep
of death me overtake.

4 Lest that mine enemy should say,
against him I prevail;
and those that trouble me rejoice,
when I am moved and fail.

5 But I have all my confidence
upon thy mercy set;
my heart within me shall rejoice
in thy salvation great.

6 Unto Jehovah then will I
sing praises cheerfully,

because he hath his bounty
shown
to me abundantly.

13 SECOND VERSION

1 How long wilt thou forget me?
O Lord, for evermore?
For ever wilt thou let me
thine absent face deplore?
How long in fruitless wailing
shall I consume the day?
And thus how long prevailing
my vaunting foe bear sway?

2 O, do not thou forsake me!
Enlighten thou my gloom;
lest fatal sleep o'ertake me,
the death-sleep of the tomb;
lest then my foe insulting
should boast of his success,
and impious men exulting
triumph in my distress.

3 Lord, in my tribulation
I trust thy mercy still,
and surely thy salvation
my heart with joy shall fill.
Thine aid thou didst afford me,
thy praises I will sing;
and for his mercies toward me
will bless my God and king.

14

1 That there is not a God, the fool
doth in his heart conclude:
they are corrupt, their works are
vile,
not one of them doth good.

2 The Lord upon the sons of men
from heaven did look abroad,
to see if any understood,
and did seek after God.

3 Corrupt they altogether are,
they all aside are gone;
and there is none that doeth
good,
yea, sure there is not one.

4 These workers of iniquity
do they not know at all,
that they my people eat as bread,
nor on Jehovah call?

5 There feared they much; for God
is with
the whole race of the just.

6 You shame the counsel of the
poor,
because the Lord's his trust.

7 Let Israel's help from Zion come:

when back the Lord shall bring
his captives, Jacob shall rejoice,
and Israel shall sing.

15

1 Within thy tabernacle, Lord,
who shall abide with thee?
and in thy high and holy hill
who shall a dweller be?

2 The man that walketh uprightly,
and worketh righteousness,
and as he thinketh in his heart,
so doth he truth express.

3 Who doth not slander with his
tongue,
nor to his friend doth hurt;
nor yet against his neighbour
doth
take up an ill report.

4 In whose eyes vile men are
despised;
but those the Lord that fear
he honoureth; and changeth not,
though to his hurt he swear.

5 His coin puts not to usury,
nor take reward will he
against the guiltless. Who doth
thus
shall never moved be.

16

1 Lord, keep me, for I trust in thee;
to God this was my cry,

2 thou art my Lord, and above thee
not any good have I.

3 To saints on earth, the excellent,
there my delight's all placed;

4 their sorrows shall be multiplied
to other gods that haste:

Of their drink-offerings of blood
no offering will I make;
their very names into my lips
I will not even take.

5 Of mine inheritance and cup
the Lord's the portion sure;
the lot that fallen is to me
thou dost maintain secure.

6 Unto me happily the lines
in pleasant places fell;
yea, the inheritance I have
in beauty doth excel.

7 I bless the Lord, because he doth
by counsel me conduct,
and in the seasons of the night
my reins do me instruct.

8 Before me still the Lord I set:
since it is so that he
doth ever stand at my right hand,
I shall not moved be.

9 Because of this my heart is glad,
and joy shall be expressed
even by my glory; and my flesh
in confidence shall rest.

10 Because my soul unto the grave
shall not be left by thee;
and thou wilt not thine Holy One
corruption give to see.

11 Thou wilt me show the path of
life:
of joy there is full store
before thy face; in thy right hand
are pleasures evermore.

17

1 Lord, hear the right, regard my
cry,
unto my prayer give heed,
that doth not in hypocrisy
from feigned lips proceed.

2 And from before thy presence let
my judgment come to me;
turn thou thine eyes to upright
things,
look thou on equity.

3 My heart thou provest, and by
night
dost visit and me try,
but findest nought; for my intent
my mouth doth not belie.

4 As for men's works, I, by the
word
that from thy lips doth flow,
have kept myself out of the paths
wherein destroyers go.

5 Hold up my goings, Lord, me
guide
in those thy paths divine,
so that my footsteps may not slide
out of those ways of thine.

6 I called have on thee, O God,
because thou wilt me hear:
that thou may'st hearken to my
speech,
to me incline thine ear.

7 Thy wondrous loving-kindness
show,
thou that, by thy right hand,
sav'st them that trust in thee
from those
that up against them stand.

8 As the apple of the eye me keep;
in thy wings' shade me hide

9 from wasting deadly foes, who
me
beset on every side.

10 In their own fat they are
inclosed;
their mouth speaks loftily.

11 Our steps they compass, and to
earth
down bowing set their eye.

12 He like unto a lion is
that's greedy of his prey,
or lion young, which lurking doth
in secret places stay.

13 Arise, and disappoint my foe,
and cast him down, O Lord:
and from the wicked man my
soul
deliver by thy sword.

14 From worldly men, Lord, by thy
hand
let me delivered be,
who only in this present life
their part and portion see;

Whom with thy treasure thou
dost fill:
they many sons receive;
and of their great abundance they
unto their children leave.

15 But as for me, I thine own face
in righteousness will see;
and with thy likeness, when I
wake,
I satisfied shall be.

18

1 Thee will I love, O Lord, my
strength.

2 My fortress is the Lord,
my rock, and he that doth to me
deliverance afford:
my God, my strength, whom I
will trust,
a buckler unto me,
the horn of my salvation sure,
and my high tower, is he.

3 Unto the Lord, who worthy is
of praises, will I cry;
and then shall I preserved be
safe from mine enemy.

4 The cords of death encompassed
me,
sin's floods made me afraid;

5 bands of the grave were round
me drawn,
death's snares were on me laid.

6 I in distress called on the Lord,
   cry to my God did I;
   he from his temple heard my
      voice,
   to his ears came my cry.
7 Earth as affrighted then did
      shake,
   trembling upon it seized:
   the hills' foundations moved
      were,
   because he was displeased.
8 Up from his nostrils came a
      smoke,
   and from his mouth there came
   devouring fire, and coals by it
   were turned into flame.
9 He also bowed down the
      heavens,
   and thence he did descend;
   and thickest clouds of darkness
      did
   under his feet attend.
10 And he upon a cherub rode,
   and thereon he did fly;
   yea, on the swift wings of the
      wind
   his flight was from on high.
11 He darkness made his secret
      place:
   about him, for his tent,
   dark waters were, and thickest
      clouds
   of the airy firmament.
12 And at the brightness of that
      light,
   which was before his eye,
   his thick clouds passed away,
      hailstones
   and coals of fire did fly.
13 Jehovah also in the heavens
   did thunder in his ire;
   and there the Highest gave his
      voice,
   hailstones and coals of fire.
14 Yea, he his arrows sent abroad,
   and them he scattered;
   his lightnings also he shot out,
   and them discomfited.
15 The waters' channels then were
      seen,
   the world's foundations vast
   at thy rebuke discovered were,
   and at thy nostrils' blast.
16 And from above the Lord sent
      down,
   and took me from below;
   from many waters he me drew,
   which would me overflow.

17 He rescued me from my strong
      foes,
   and such as did me hate;
   because he saw that they for me
   too strong were and too great.
18 They came upon me in the day
   of my calamity;
   but even then the Lord himself
   a stay was unto me.
19 Unto a place of liberty
   and room he hath me brought;
   because he took delight in me,
   he my deliverance wrought.
20 According to my righteousness
   he did me recompense;
   he me repaid according to
   my hands' pure innocence.
21 For I the Lord's ways kept, nor
      from
   my God turned wickedly.
22 His judgments were before me, I
   his laws put not from me.
23 Sincere before him was my heart,
   upright with him was I;
   and watchfully I kept myself
   from mine iniquity.
24 According to my righteousness
   the Lord did me requite;
   after the cleanness of my hands
   appearing in his sight.
25 Thou to the gracious showest
      grace,
   to just men just thou art;
26 pure to the pure, but froward still
   to men of froward heart.
27 For thou wilt the afflicted save
   in grief that low do lie;
   but wilt bring down the
      countenance
   of those whose looks are high.
28 For thou thyself wilt light my
      lamp,
   that it shall shine full bright:
   the Lord my God will also make
   my darkness to be light.
29 By thee through troops of men I
      break,
   and them discomfit all;
   and, by my God assisting me,
   I overleap a wall.
30 As for God, perfect is his way;
   Jehovah's word is tried;
   he is a buckler to all those
   who do in him confide.
31 Who but the Lord is God? but he
   who is a rock and stay?

32 'Tis God that girdeth me with strength,
and perfect makes my way.

33 He made my feet swift as the hinds',
on my heights made me stand;
34 my hands he taught to war, my arms
a bow of brass did bend.

35 The shield of thy salvation thou
upon me didst bestow:
thy right hand held me up, and great
thy kindness made me grow.

36 And in my way my steps thou hast
enlarged under me,
that I go safely, and my feet
are kept from sliding free.
37 Mine enemies I did pursue,
and them did overtake;
nor did I turn again till I
an end of them did make.

38 I wounded them, they could not rise;
they 'neath my feet did fall.
39 Thou girdedst me with strength for war;
my foes thou brought'st down all:
40 and thou hast given me the necks
of all mine enemies,
that I might utterly destroy
those who against me rise.

41 They in their trouble cried for help,
but there was none to save;
yea, they did cry unto the Lord,
but he no answer gave.
42 Then did I beat them small as dust
before the wind that flies;
and I did cast them out like dirt
upon the street that lies.

43 Thou mad'st me free from people's strife,
the heathen's head to be:
a people whom I have not known
shall service do to me.
44 At hearing they shall me obey,
to me they shall submit.
45 Strangers for fear shall fade away
who in their strongholds sit.

46 Jehovah lives, blessed be my Rock;
God, who me saves, praised be.
47 God doth avenge me, and subdue

the people under me.
48 He saves me from mine enemies;
yea, thou hast lifted me
above my foes, and from the man
of violence set me free.

49 Therefore to thee will I give thanks
the heathen folk among;
and to thy name, O Lord, I will
give praises in a song.
50 He great deliverance gives his king:
he mercy doth extend
to David, his anointed one,
and his seed without end.

19 FIRST VERSION

1 The heavens God's glory do declare,
the skies his hand-works preach:
2 day utters speech to day, and night
to night doth knowledge teach.
3 There is no speech nor tongue to which
their voice doth not extend:
4 their line is gone through all the earth,
their words to the world's end.

5 There he a tabernacle hath
erected for the sun;
who comes like bridegroom from his tent,
like strong man joys to run.
6 From heaven's end he goeth forth,
circling to the end again;
and there is nothing from his heat
that hidden doth remain.

7 God's law is perfect, and converts
the soul in sin that lies:
God's testimony is most sure,
and makes the simple wise.
8 The statutes of the Lord are right,
and do rejoice the heart:
the Lord's command is pure, and doth
light to the eyes impart.

9 Unspotted is the fear of God,
and doth endure for ever:
the judgments of the Lord are true
and righteous altogether.
10 They more than gold, yea, much fine gold,

to be desired are:
than honey, honey from the comb
that droppeth, sweeter far.

11 Moreover, they thy servant warn
how he his life should frame:
a great reward provided is
for them that keep the same.
12 Who can his errors understand?
from secret faults me cleanse:
13 thy servant keep thou also back
from all presumptuous sins;

and do not suffer them to have
dominion over me:
I shall be righteous then, and
clear
from great transgression be.
14 The words which from my mouth
proceed,
the thoughts sent from my heart,
accept, O Lord, for thou my
strength
and my Redeemer art.

19 SECOND VERSION

1 The lofty heavens proclaim
the majesty of God;
the firmament displays
his handiwork abroad:
day unto day doth utter speech,
and night to night doth
knowledge teach.

2 Aloud they do not speak,
they utter forth no word,
nor into language break;
yet is their witness heard:
their line through all the earth
extends,
their words to earth's remotest
ends.

3 In them he hath prepared
a dwelling for the sun;
which, as a mighty man,
exults his race to run;
and, bridegroom-like in his array,
comes from his chamber, bringing
day.

4 His daily going forth
is from the end of heaven;
the firmament to him
is for his circuit given.
He to its end returns again;
hid from his heat can nought
remain.

5 The Lord's law is complete;
it makes the soul arise:
the Lord's decree is sure;

it makes the simple wise:
the statutes of the Lord are right
imparting to the heart delight.

6 The Lord's command is pure;
light on the eyes it pours:
the Lord's fear is unstained;
for ever it endures:
the judgments of the Lord are
true,
and altogether righteous, too.

7 More to be prized than gold,
yea, much fine gold, they are;
than honey from the comb
that droppeth, sweeter far.
They also warn thy servant,
Lord;
in keeping them is great reward.

8 Who can his errors know?
From secret faults me cleanse:
keep thou thy servant back
from all presumptuous sins:
let them not triumph over me;
then shall I pure and upright be.

9 Yea, then I shall be free
from much and heinous sin.
O let the words I speak,
and all my thoughts within,
be acceptable, Lord, to thee,
who strength and Saviour art
to me.

20

1 Jehovah hear thee in the day
when trouble he doth send;
and let the name of Jacob's God
thee from all ill defend.
2 O let him help send from above,
out of his sanctuary;
from Zion, his own holy hill,
let him give strength to thee.
3 Let him remember all thy gifts,
accept thy sacrifice:
4 grant thee thine heart's wish, and
fulfil
thy thoughts and counsel wise.
5 In thy salvation we will joy;
in our God's name we will
display our banners: and the
Lord
thy prayers all fulfil.

6 Now know I God his king doth
save:
he from his holy heaven
will hear him, with the saving
strength
by his own right hand given.

7 In chariots some put confidence,
on horses some rely;
but we the Lord's name mention
will,
who is our God most high.

8 We rise and upright stand, when
they
are bowed down and fall.

9 Deliver, Lord; O let the King
us hear, when we do call.

21

1 Jehovah, in thy strength the king
shall very joyful be:
and in thy saving help rejoice
how fervently shall he!

2 Thou hast bestowed upon him
all that his heart would have;
and thou from him didst not
withhold
whate'er his lips did crave.

3 For thou with blessings dost him
meet
of goodness manifold;
and thou hast set upon his head
a crown of purest gold.

4 When he desired life of thee,
thou life to him didst give;
even such a length of days, that
he
for evermore should live.

5 In that salvation wrought by thee
his glory is made great;
honour and comely majesty
thou hast upon him set.

6 Because that thou for evermore
most blessed hast him made;
and thou hast with thy
countenance
made him exceeding glad.

7 Because the king upon the Lord
his confidence doth lay;
and through the grace of the Most
High
shall not be moved away.

8 Thine hand shall all those men
find out
that enemies are to thee;
even thy right hand shall find
out those
of thee that haters be.

9 Like fiery oven thou shalt them
make,
when kindled is thine ire;
the Lord in wrath shall swallow
them,
devour them shall the fire.

10 Their fruit from earth thou shalt
destroy,
their seed men from among:

11 for they beyond their might
'gainst thee
did mischief plot and wrong.

12 Thou therefore shalt make them
turn back,
when thou thy shafts shalt place
upon thy strings, made ready all
to fly against their face.

13 In thy almighty strength, O Lord,
do thou exalted be:
so shall we sing with joyful
hearts,
thy power praise shall we.

22

1 My God, my God, wherefore is it
thou hast forsaken me?
Why from my help so far, and
from
my cry of agony?

2 All day, my God, to thee I cry,
yet am not heard by thee;
and in the season of the night
I cannot silent be.

3 But thou art holy, thou that dost
inhabit Israel's praise.

4 Our fathers hoped in thee, they
hoped,
and thou didst them release.

5 When unto thee they sent their
cry,
to them deliverance came:
because they put their trust in
thee,
they were not put to shame.

6 But as for me, a worm I am,
and as no man am prized;
reproach of men I am, and by
the people am despised.

7 All that me see laugh me to
scorn;
shoot out the lip do they;
they nod and shake their heads
at me,
and, mocking, thus do say,

8 He trusted in the Lord, that he
would free him by his might;
let him deliver him, since he
had in him such delight.

9 But thou art he out of the womb
that didst me safely take;
when I was on my mother's
breasts,
thou me to trust didst make.

10 And I was cast upon thy care,
even from my birth till now;
and from my mother's womb my God
and my support art thou.
11 Be not far off, for trouble's near,
and none to help is found.
12 Bulls many compass me, strong bulls
of Bashan me surround.

13 Their mouths they opened wide on me,
upon me gape did they,
like to a lion ravening
and roaring for his prey.
14 Like water I'm poured out, my bones
all out of joint do part:
amidst my bowels, as the wax,
so melted is my heart.

15 My strength is like a potsherd dried;
my tongue it cleaveth fast
unto my jaws; and to the dust
of death thou brought me hast.
16 For dogs have compassed me about:
the wicked, that did meet
in their assembly, me enclosed;
they pierced my hands and feet.

17 I all my bones may tell; they do
upon me look and stare.
18 Upon my vesture lots they cast,
my clothes among them share.
19 But be not far, O Lord, my strength;
haste to give help to me.
20 From sword my soul, from power of dogs
my darling, set thou free.

21 From the devouring lion's mouth
my life do thou defend;
to save from horns of unicorns
thou dost me answer send.
22 Among those that my brethren are
I will declare thy name;
amidst the congregation I
thy praises will proclaim.

23 Praise ye the Lord who do him fear;
him glorify all ye
the seed of Jacob; fear him all
that Israel's children be.
24 For he despised not nor abhorred
the afflicted's misery;

nor from him hid his face, but heard,
when he to him did cry.
25 Within the congregation great
my praise shall be of thee;
my vows before them that him fear
shall be performed by me.
26 The meek shall eat, and shall be filled;
they also praise shall give
unto the Lord that do him seek:
your heart shall ever live.

27 All ends of the earth remember shall,
and turn unto the Lord;
the kindreds of the nations all
thee homage shall accord.
28 Because the kingdom to the Lord
doth appertain as his;
likewise among the nations all,
the Governor he is.

29 Earth's fat ones eat, and worship shall:
all who to dust descend
shall bow to him; none of them can
his soul from death defend.
30 A seed shall service do to him;
unto the Lord it shall
a generation reckoned be,
even to ages all.

31 They shall come forth, and shall declare
his truth and righteousness
unto a people yet unborn,
and that he hath done this.

23

1 The Lord's my shepherd, I'll not want.
2 He makes me down to lie
in pastures green: he leadeth me
the quiet waters by.
3 My soul he doth restore again;
and me to walk doth make
within the paths of righteousness,
even for his own name's sake.

4 Yea, though I walk in death's dark vale,
yet will I fear none ill;
for thou art with me, and thy rod
and staff me comfort still.
5 My table thou hast furnished
in presence of my foes;

my head thou dost with oil
      anoint,
and my cup overflows.

6 Goodness and mercy all my life
shall surely follow me:
and in God's house for evermore
my dwelling-place shall be.

24

1 The earth belongs unto the Lord,
and all that it contains;
the world that is inhabited,
and all that there remains.
2 For the foundations of the same
he on the seas did lay,
and he hath it established
upon the floods to stay.

3 Who is the man that shall ascend
into the hill of God?
Or who within his holy place
shall have a firm abode?
4 Whose hands are clean, whose
      heart is pure,
and unto vanity
who hath not lifted up his soul,
nor sworn deceitfully.

5 This is the man who shall receive
the blessing from the Lord;
the God of his salvation shall
him righteousness accord.
6 This is the generation who
do after him enquire;
they Jacob are, who seek thy face
with their whole hearts' desire.

7 Ye gates, lift up your heads on
      high;
ye doors that last for aye,
be lifted up, that so the King
of glory enter may.
8 But who of glory is the King?
The mighty Lord is this;
even that same Lord that great in
      might
and strong in battle is.

9 Ye gates, lift up your heads; ye
      doors,
doors that do last for aye,
be lifted up, that so the King
of glory enter may.
10 But who is he that is the King
of glory? who is this?
The Lord of hosts, and none but
      he,
the King of glory is.

25 FIRST VERSION

1 To thee I lift my soul;
2 O Lord, I trust in thee:
my God, let me not be ashamed,
nor foes exult o'er me.
3 Let none that wait on thee
be put to shame at all;
but those that without cause
      transgress,
let shame upon them fall.

4 Show me thy ways, O Lord;
thy paths O teach thou me:
5 and do thou lead me in thy truth,
therein my teacher be:
for thou art God that dost
to me salvation send,
and I upon thee all the day
expecting do attend.

6 Thy tender mercies, Lord,
to mind do thou recall,
and loving-kindnesses, for they
have been through ages all.
7 My sins and faults of youth
do thou, O Lord, forget:
after thy mercy think on me,
and for thy goodness great.

8 God good and upright is;
the way he'll sinners show.
9 The meek in judgement he will
      guide,
and make his path to know.
10 The whole paths of the Lord
are truth and mercy sure,
to those that do his covenant
      keep,
and testimonies pure.

11 Now, for thine own name's sake,
O Lord, I thee entreat
to pardon mine iniquity;
for it is very great.
12 What man is he that fears
the Lord, and doth him serve?
Him shall he teach the way that
      he
shall choose, and still observe.

13 His soul shall dwell at ease;
and his posterity
shall flourish still, and of the
      earth
inheritors shall be.
14 With those that fear him is
the secret of the Lord;
the knowledge of his covenant
he will to them afford.

15 Mine eyes upon the Lord
continually are set;
for he it is that shall bring forth
my feet out of the net.
16 Turn unto me thy face,
and to me mercy show;
because that I am desolate,
and am brought very low.

17 My heart's griefs are increased:
me from distress relieve.
18 See mine affliction and my pain,
and all my sins forgive.
19 Consider thou my foes,
because they many be;
and it a cruel hatred is
which they do bear to me.

20 O do thou keep my soul,
do thou deliver me;
and let me never be ashamed,
because I trust in thee.
21 Let truth and right me keep,
for I on thee attend.
22 Redemption, Lord, to Israel
from all his troubles send.

25 SECOND VERSION

1 To thee I lift my soul, O Lord;
2 my God, I trust in thee:
let me not be ashamed; let not
my foes exult o'er me.
3 Yea, let thou none ashamed be
that do on thee attend:
ashamed let them be, O Lord,
who without cause offend.

4 Thy ways, Lord, show; teach me
thy paths;
5 lead me in truth, teach me:
for of my safety thou art God;
all day I wait on thee.
6 Thy mercies that most tender are
to mind, O Lord, recall,
and loving-kindnesses; for they
have been through ages all.

7 Let not the errors of my youth,
nor sins, remembered be:
in mercy, for thy goodness' sake,
O Lord, remember me.
8 Since good and upright is the
Lord,
the way he'll sinners show;
9 the meek in judgment he will
guide,
and make his path to know.

10 The whole paths of the Lord our
God
are truth and mercy sure,

to such as keep his covenant,
and testimonies pure.
11 Now, for thine own name's sake,
O Lord,
I humbly thee entreat
to pardon mine iniquity;
for it is very great.

12 Who fears the Lord? him shall he
teach
the way that he shall choose.
13 His soul shall dwell at ease; his
seed
the earth, as heirs, shall use.
14 The secret of the Lord is with
such as do fear his name;
and he his holy covenant
will manifest to them.

15 Towards the Lord my waiting
eyes
continually are set;
for he it is that shall bring forth
my feet out of the net.
16 O turn thee unto me, my God,
and mercy to me show;
for I am lone and desolate,
and am brought very low.

17 Enlarged the griefs are of mine
heart;
me from distress relieve.
18 See mine affliction and my pain,
and all my sins forgive.
19 Consider thou mine enemies,
because they many be;
and it a cruel hatred is
which they do bear to me.

20 O do thou keep my soul; O God,
do thou deliver me:
let me not be ashamed; for I
do put my trust in thee.
21 Let truth and uprightness me
keep,
for I on thee attend.
22 Redemption, Lord, to Israel
from all his troubles send.

26

1 Judge me, O Lord, for I have
walked
in mine integrity:
I trusted also in the Lord;
slide therefore shall not I.
2 Examine me, and do me prove;
try heart and reins, O God:
3 for thy love is before mine eyes,
thy truth's paths I have trod.

4   With persons vain I have not sat,
    nor with dissemblers gone:
5   the assembly of ill men I hate;
    to sit with such I shun.
6   Mine hands in innocence, O
        Lord,
    I'll wash and purify;
    so to thine holy altar go,
    and compass it will I:

7   That I with voice of thanksgiving
    may publish and declare,
    and tell of all thy mighty works,
    that great and wondrous are.
8   The habitation of thy house,
    Lord, I have loved well;
    yea, in that place I do delight
    where doth thine honour dwell.

9   With sinners gather not my soul,
    and such as blood would spill:
10 whose hands devices
        mischievous,
    whose right hand bribes do fill.
11 But as for me, I will walk on
    in mine integrity:
    do thou redeem me, and, O Lord,
    be merciful to me.

12 My foot upon an even place
    doth stand with steadfastness:
    within the congregations I
    Jehovah's name will bless.

27   FIRST VERSION

1   The Lord's my light and saving
        health,
    who shall make me dismayed?
    My life's strength is the Lord; of
        whom
    then shall I be afraid?
2   What time mine enemies and
        foes,
    most wicked persons all,
    to eat my flesh against me rose,
    they stumbled and did fall.
3   Against me though an host
        encamp,
    my heart yet fearless is:
    though war against me rise, I will
    be confident in this.
4   One thing I of the Lord desired,
    and will seek to obtain,
    that all days of my life I may
    within God's house remain;

    That I the beauty of the Lord
    behold may and admire,
    and that I in his holy place
    may reverently enquire.

5   For he in his pavilion shall
    me hide in evil days;
    in secret of his tent me hide,
    and on a rock me raise.

6   And now even at this present
        time
    mine head shall lifted be
    above all those that are my foes,
    and round encompass me:
    then offerings of joyfulness
    into his house I'll bring;
    and I will sing unto the Lord,
    yea, I will praises sing.

7   O Lord, give ear unto my voice,
    when I do cry to thee;
    upon me also mercy have,
    and do thou answer me.
8   When thou didst say, Seek ye my
        face,
    then unto thee reply
    thus did my heart, Above all
        things
    thy face, Lord, seek will I.

9   Far from me hide not thou thy
        face;
    put not away from thee
    thy servant in thy wrath: thou
        hast
    an helper been to me.
    O God, who my salvation art,
    leave me not, nor forsake;
10 though father, mother, both me
        leave,
    the Lord me up will take.

11 O Lord, instruct me in thy way,
    to me a leader be
    in a plain path, because of those
    that hatred bear to me.
12 Give me not to mine enemies'
        will;
    for witnesses that lie
    against me risen are, and such
    as breathe out cruelty.

13 I fainted had, unless that I
    believed had to see
    the Lord's own goodness in the
        land
    of them that living be.
14 Wait on the Lord, and be thou
        strong,
    and he shall strength afford
    unto thine heart; yea, do thou
        wait,
    I say, upon the Lord.

27 SECOND VERSION

1 Jehovah is my light,
and my salvation he;
who then shall me affright?
The Lord is unto me
my life's sure stronghold, ever
near;
of whom then shall I stand in
fear?

2 When wicked men, my foes
and adversaries all,
to eat my flesh arose,
they stumbled and did fall.
Though hosts surround, I will not
quail;
in this I trust, though war assail.

3 For one thing did I pray,
this I'll seek to obtain,
that all my life I may
in the Lord's house remain;
Jehovah's beauty to admire,
and in his temple to inquire.

4 Within his tent he will
me hide in evil days,
me in his tent conceal,
and on a rock me raise.
And now my head shall lifted be
above my foes that compass me.

5 Into his courts with joy
I'll sacrifices bring;
songs shall my lips employ,
praise to the Lord I'll sing.
Lord, hear me when I cry to thee;
on me have mercy; answer me.

6 Thou saidst, Seek ye my face;
then did my heart reply,
In thine abundant grace,
thy face, Lord, seek will I.
In wrath hide not thy face from
me,
nor put thy servant far from thee.

7 My help of old art thou,
to thee I me betake;
O God, my Saviour, now
leave me not, nor forsake.
When father, mother, both me
leave,
the Lord himself will me receive.

8 Teach me, O Lord, thy way;
me in a plain path guide,
for foes my steps survey:
me give not to their pride:
for false accusers 'gainst me rise,
and such as breathe out cruelties.

9 I fainted had unless
I had believed to see
the Lord's own graciousness
'mong them that living be.
Wait on the Lord; be strong of
heart;
yea, wait, and he shall strength
impart.

28 FIRST VERSION

1 To thee I'll cry, O Lord, my rock;
hold not thy peace to me;
lest like those who to death go
down
I by thy silence be.

2 The voice hear of my humble
prayers,
when unto thee I cry;
when to thy holy oracle
I lift mine hands on high.

3 With ill men draw me not away
that work iniquity;
that speak peace to their friends,
while in
their hearts doth mischief lie.

4 Give them according to their
deeds,
and evil of their way;
after the work of their own hands
do thou to them repay.

5 God shall not build, but them
destroy,
who would not understand
the Lord's own works, nor did
regard
the doing of his hand.

6 For ever blessed be the Lord,
for graciously he heard
the voice of my petitions, and
my prayers did regard.

7 The Lord's my strength and
shield; my heart
upon him did rely;
and I am helped: hence my heart
doth joy exceedingly;
and with my song I will him
praise.

8 Their strength is God alone:
he also is the saving strength
of his anointed one.

9 O thine own people do thou
save.
Bless thine inheritance;
them also do thou feed, and them
for evermore advance.

28 SECOND VERSION

1 To thee, Jehovah, will I cry,
my rock; O, be not silent now!
Lest, if thou hold thy peace, I be
like those who in the pit lie low.

2 O, hear my supplication's voice,
when unto thee for help I cry,
when to thy holy oracle
I lift my pleading hands on high.

3 O, with the wicked draw me not
away, nor with the men of sin;
who to their neighbours speak of
peace,
but evil is their heart within.

4 Give them according to their
deed,
their evil doings all reward;
give them according to their
works,
return them their desert, O Lord.

5 Since they Jehovah's mighty acts,
and doings of his hands disdain,
he will destroy them in his
wrath,
and never build them up again.

6 blest be Jehovah! He hath heard
my supplication's voice in
heaven;
Jehovah is my strength and
shield;
I trusted him, he help hath given.

7 And therefore shall my heart
exult,
my song shall of his praises be.
He is their strength; the saving
strength
of his anointed one is he.

8 O, save the nation of thy love,
O, bless thy chosen heritage;
feed them and lead them as a
flock,
lift thou them up from age to age.

29 FIRST VERSION

1 Give ye unto the Lord, ye sons
that of the mighty be,
all strength and glory to the Lord
with cheerfulness give ye.

2 O give ye glory to the Lord,
and his great name adore;
and in the beauty of holiness
bow down the Lord before.

3 The Lord's voice on the waters
is;
the God of majesty

doth thunder, and on multitudes
of waters sitteth he.

4 A mighty voice it is that comes
out from the Lord most high;
the voice of the great Lord is full
of glorious majesty.

5 The voice of the Eternal doth
asunder cedars tear;
Jehovah doth the cedars break
that Lebanon doth bear.

6 He makes them like a calf to skip,
even that great Lebanon,
and, like to a young unicorn,
the mountain Sirion.

7 The Lord's voice cleaves the
flames of fire;

8 the desert it doth shake:
the Lord doth make the
wilderness
of Kadesh all to quake.

9 The Lord's voice makes the hinds
to calve,
it makes the forest bare:
and in his temple every one
his glory doth declare.

10 The Lord sat on the flood; the
Lord
sits King, and ever shall.

11 The Lord will give his people
strength,
and with peace bless them all.

29 SECOND VERSION

1 Give ye to Jehovah, O sons of the
mighty,
give ye to Jehovah the glory and
power;
give ye to Jehovah the honour
and glory;
in beauty of holiness kneel and
adore.

2 The voice of Jehovah comes
down on the waters;
in thunder the God of the glory
draws nigh:
lo, over the waves of the wide
flowing waters
Jehovah as King is enthronèd on
high!

3 The voice of Jehovah is mighty, is
mighty;
the voice of Jehovah in majesty
speaks:
the voice of Jehovah the cedars is
breaking;
Jehovah the cedars of Lebanon
breaks.

4   Like young heifers sporting, they
       skip when he speaketh;
    lo, Lebanon leaps at the sound of
       his name!
    Like son of the unicorn Sirion is
       skipping;
    the voice of Jehovah divideth the
       flame.

5   The voice of Jehovah — it
       shaketh the desert;
    the desert of Kadesh it shaketh
       with fear:
    the hind of the field into travail-
       pangs casteth:
    the voice of Jehovah the forest
       strips bare.

6   Each one, in his temple, his glory
       proclaimeth.
    He sat on the flood; he is King on
       his throne.
    Jehovah all strength to his people
       imparteth;
    Jehovah with peace ever blesseth
       his own.

30   FIRST VERSION

1   Lord, I will thee extol, for thou
    hast lifted me on high,
    and over me thou to rejoice
    madest not mine enemy.
2   O thou who art the Lord my God,
    I in distress to thee
    with loud cries lifted up my
       voice,
    and thou hast healed me.

3   O Lord, my soul thou hast
       brought up
    and rescued from the grave;
    that I to death should not go
       down,
    alive thou didst me save.
4   O ye that are his holy ones,
    sing praise unto the Lord;
    and unto him give thanks, when
       ye
    his holiness record.

5   For but a moment lasts his
       wrath;
    life in his favour lies:
    weeping may for a night endure,
    at morn doth joy arise.
6   In my prosperity I said
    that nothing shall me move:
7   O Lord, thou hast my mountain
       made
    to stand strong by thy love.

    Thou didst thy face hide; then
       was I
    sore troubled and dismayed:
8   I cried to thee, O Lord, to thee
    I supplication made:
9   what profit is there in my blood,
    when I to death go down?
    Shall dust give praises unto thee?
    Shall it thy truth make known?

10 Hear, Lord, have mercy; help me,
       Lord;
11 thou didst from sackcloth free;
    my grief to dancing thou hast
       turned,
    with gladness girded me;
12 That sing thy praise my glory
       may,
    and never silent be.
    O Lord my God, for evermore
    I will give thanks to thee.

30   SECOND VERSION

1   Lord, I will thee extol;
    for thou hast set me free,
    and over me to rule
    madest not mine enemy.
    To thee, O Lord my God, I cried;
    and thou hast health and
       strength supplied.

2   Thou hast my soul restored,
    when I was near the grave;
    and from the pit, O Lord,
    alive thou didst me save.
    O ye his saints, sing to the Lord;
    with thanks his holiness record.

3   Soon in his anger past;
    life in his favour lies:
    tears for a night may last,
    at morn shall joy arise.
    I said in my prosperity,
    I surely never moved shall be.

4   My mountain, by thy grace,
    thou madest to stand in power;
    thou didst withdraw thy face,
    and I was troubled sore.
    To thee, O Lord, with cries I
       prayed;
    I to the Lord petition made.

5   What shall my blood avail,
    when I to grave go down?
    Shall dust thy praises tell;
    shall it thy truth make known?
    Hear me, O Lord, and mercy
       send;
    thy help to me, O Lord, extend.

6 My mourning thou at last
hast into dancing turned:
and thou for sackcloth hast
with gladness me adorned;
that sing to thee my glory may.
Lord, thee my God I'll praise
for aye.

31

1 In thee, O Lord, I put my trust;
shamed let me never be:
according to thy righteousness
do thou deliver me.
2 Bow down thine ear to me, with
speed
send me deliverance:
to save me, my strong rock be
thou,
and my house of defence.

3 Because thou art my rock, and
thee
I for my fortress take;
do thou me therefore lead and
guide,
even for thine own name's sake.
4 And, since thou art my strength,
do thou
pull me out of the net,
which they in subtlety for me
so privily have set.

5 Into thy hand I do commit
my spirit; thou art he,
O thou, Jehovah, God of truth,
who hast redeemed me.
6 Those that do lying vanities
regard I have abhorred:
but as for me, my confidence
is fixed upon the Lord.

7 I'll in thy mercy greatly joy:
for thou my miseries
considered hast; thou hast my
soul
known in adversities;
8 and thou hast not inclosed me
within the enemy's hand;
and by thee have my feet been
made
in a large place to stand.

9 O Lord, upon me mercy have,
for trouble is on me:
mine eye, my belly, and my soul,
with grief consumed be.
10 Because my life with grief is
spent,
my years with sighs and groans:
my strength doth fail; and for my
sin

consumed are my bones.

11 I through my foes all was a scorn,
and to my neighbours near
a great reproach have I become,
and to my friends a fear:
12 and when they saw me walk
abroad,
they from my presence fled;
I like a broken vessel am,
forgotten as one dead.

13 For slanders I of many heard;
fear compassed me, while they
against me did consult, and plot
to take my life away.
14 But as for me, O Lord, my trust
upon thee I have laid;
and I to thee, Thou art my God,
have confidently said.

15 My times are wholly in thy hand:
do thou deliver me
from their hands that mine
enemies
and persecutors be.
16 Thy countenance to shine do thou
upon thy servant make;
and unto me salvation give,
for thy great mercies' sake.

17 Let me not be ashamed, O Lord,
for on thee called I have:
let wicked men be shamed, let
them
be silent in the grave.
18 To silence put the lying lips,
that grievous things do say,
and hard reports, in pride and
scorn,
on righteous men do lay.

19 How great's thy goodness thou
for them
that fear thee keep'st in store,
and wrought'st for them that
trust in thee
the sons of men before!
20 In secret of thy presence thou
shalt hide them from man's
pride:
from strife of tongues thou closely
shalt,
as in a tent, them hide.

21 All praise and thanks be to the
Lord:
for he hath magnified
his wondrous love to me within
a city fortified.
22 For, From thine eyes cut off I am,
I in my haste had said;

my voice yet heard'st thou, when
to thee
with cries my moan I made.

23 O love the Lord, all ye his saints;
because the Lord doth guard
the faithful, and he plenteously
proud doers doth reward.

24 Be of good courage, and he
strength
unto your heart shall send,
all ye whose hope and confidence
upon the Lord depend.

32

1 O blessed is the man to whom
is freely pardoned
all the transgression he hath
done,
whose sin is covered.

2 blest is the man to whom the
Lord
imputeth not his sin,
and in whose spirit is no guile,
nor fraud is found therein.

3 When I from speaking did
refrain,
and silent was my tongue,
my bones then waxed old,
because
I cried out all day long.

4 Because on me both day and
night
thine hand did heavy lie,
so that my moisture turned is
in summer's drought thereby.

5 I thereupon have unto thee
my sin acknowledged,
and likewise mine iniquity
I have not covered:
I will confess unto the Lord
my trespasses, said I;
and of my sin thou freely didst
forgive the iniquity.

6 For this shall every godly one
his prayer make to thee;
in such a time he shall thee seek,
as found thou mayest be.
Surely, when floods of waters
great
do swell up to the brim,
they shall not overwhelm his
soul,
nor once come near to him.

7 Thou art my hiding-place, thou
shalt
from trouble keep me free:

thou with songs of deliverance
about shalt compass me.

8 I will instruct thee, and thee
teach
the way that thou shalt go;
and, with mine eye upon thee
set,
I will direction show.

9 Then be not like the horse or
mule,
which do not understand;
whose mouth, that they may
come to thee,
a bridle must command.

10 Unto the man that wicked is
his sorrows shall abound;
but him that trusteth in the Lord
mercy shall compass round.

11 Ye righteous, in the Lord be glad,
in him do ye rejoice:
all ye that upright are in heart,
for joy lift up your voice.

33

1 Ye righteous, in the Lord rejoice;
it comely is and right,
that upright men with thankful
voice
should praise the Lord of might.

2 Jehovah praise with harp, to him
sing with the psaltery;
upon a ten-stringed instrument
make ye sweet melody.

3 A new song to him sing, and play
with loud noise skilfully;

4 for right's the Lord's word, all his
work
is done in verity.

5 To judgment and to righteousness
a love he beareth still;
the loving-kindness of the Lord
the earth throughout doth fill.

6 The heavens by Jehovah's word
did their beginning take;
and by the breathing of his
mouth
he all their hosts did make.

7 The waters of the seas he brings
together as an heap;
and in storehouses, as it were,
he layeth up the deep.

8 Let earth, and all that live
therein,
with reverence fear the Lord;
let all the world's inhabitants
dread him with one accord.

9   For he did speak the word, and
       done
    it was without delay;
    established it firmly stood,
    whatever he did say.

10 The Lord the counsel brings to
       nought
    which heathen folk do take;
    and what the people do devise
    of none effect doth make.

11 O but the counsel of the Lord
    doth stand for ever sure;
    and of his heart the purposes
    from age to age endure.

12 That nation blessed is, whose
       God
    Jehovah is, and those
    a blessed people are, whom for
    his heritage he chose.

13 The Lord from heaven looks; he
       sees
    all sons of men full well:

14 he views all from his dwelling-
       place
    that in the earth do dwell.

15 He forms their hearts alike, and
       all
    their doings he observes.

16 Great hosts save not a king, much
       strength
    no mighty man preserves.

17 An horse for safety and defence
    is a deceitful thing;
    and by the greatness of his
       strength
    can no deliverance bring.

18 Behold, on those that do him fear
    the Lord doth set his eye;
    even those who on his mercy do
    with confidence rely;

19 from death to free their soul, in
       dearth
    life unto them to yield.

20 Our soul doth wait upon the
       Lord;
    he is our help and shield.

21 Since in his holy name we trust,
    our heart shall joyful be.

22 Lord, let thy mercy be on us,
    as we do hope in thee.

34

1   God will I bless all times; his
       praise
    my mouth shall still express.

2   My soul shall boast in God: the
       meek

shall hear with joyfulness.

3   Extol the Lord with me, let us
    his name together praise;

4   I sought the Lord, he heard, and
       did
    above all fears me raise.

5   They looked to him and
       lightened were:
    their faces were not shamed;

6   this poor man cried, God heard,
       and him
    from all distress redeemed.

7   The angel of the Lord encamps,
    and round encompasseth
    all those about that do him fear,
    and them delivereth.

8   O taste and see that God is good:
    who trusts in him is blessed.

9   Fear God his saints: none that
       him fear
    shall be with want oppressed.

10 The lions young may hungry be,
    and they may lack their food:
    but they that truly seek the Lord
    shall not lack any good.

11 O children, hither do ye come,
    and unto me give ear;
    I shall you teach to understand
    how ye the Lord should fear.

12 What man is he that life desires,
    to see good would live long?

13 Thy lips refrain from speaking
       guile,
    and from ill words thy tongue.

14 Depart from ill, do good, seek
       peace,
    pursue it earnestly.

15 God's eyes are on the just; his
       ears
    are open to their cry.

16 The face of God is set against
    those that do wickedly,
    that he may quite out from the
       earth
    cut off their memory.

17 The righteous cry unto the Lord,
    he unto them gives ear;
    and they out of their troubles all
    by him delivered are.

18 The Lord is ever nigh to them
    in heart that broken be;
    those who in spirit contrite are
    he saveth graciously.

19 The troubles that afflict the just
    in number many be;
    but yet at length out of them all
    the Lord doth set him free.

20 He carefully his bones doth keep,
whatever may befall;
that not so much as one of them
can broken be at all.

21 Ill shall the wicked slay;
condemned
shall be who hate the just.

22 The Lord redeems his servants'
souls;
none perish that him trust.

35

1 Plead, Lord, with those that
plead; and fight
with those that fight with me.

2 Of shield and buckler take thou
hold,
stand up mine help to be.

3 Draw also out the spear, and stop
my persecutors' way;
and in thy mercy, to my soul,
I'm thy salvation, say.

4 Let them confounded be and
shamed
that for my soul have sought:
who plot my hurt turned back be
they,
and to confusion brought.

5 Let them be like unto the chaff
that flies before the wind;
and let the angel of the Lord
pursue them hard behind.

6 With darkness cover thou their
way,
and let it slippery prove;
and let the angel of the Lord
pursue them from above.

7 For without cause have they for
me
in secret hid their snare;
and they a pit without a cause
did for my soul prepare.

8 Let ruin seize him unawares;
his net he hid withal
himself let catch; and in the
same
destruction let him fall.

9 My soul in God shall joy, and
glad
in his salvation be:

10 and all my bones shall say, O
Lord,
Who is like unto thee,

Who dost the poor set free from
him
that is for him too strong;

the poor and needy from the
man
that spoils and does him wrong?

11 False witnesses arose; 'gainst me
things that I knew not laid:

12 they to the spoiling of my soul
me ill for good repaid.

13 But as for me, when they were
sick,
in sackcloth sad I mourned;
my humbled soul did fast, my
prayer
into my bosom turned.

14 I bore myself as for a friend,
or brother dear to me;
as one who for a mother mourns,
I bowed down heavily.

15 But in my trouble they rejoiced,
and they together met;
the abjects vile together did
themselves against me set.
I knew it not; they did me tear,
and quiet would be not.

16 with mocking hypocrites at feasts
they gnashed their teeth at me.

17 How long, Lord, look'st thou on?
from those
destructions they intend
rescue my soul, from lions young
my darling do defend.

18 I will give thanks to thee, O Lord,
within the assembly great;
and where much people
gathered are
thy praises forth will set.

19 Let not my wrongful enemies
proudly rejoice o'er me;
nor let them wink with scornful
eye,
who hate me causelessly.

20 For peace they do not speak at
all:
but crafty plots prepare
against all those within the land
that meek and quiet are.

21 Their mouths they open wide at
me,
they say, Ha, ha! we see:

22 Lord, thou hast seen, hold not thy
peace;
Lord, be not far from me.

23 Stir up thyself; wake, that thou
may'st
judgement to me afford,
even to my cause, O thou that art
my only God and Lord.

24 O Lord my God, do thou me
judge
after thy righteousness;
and let them not their joy o'er
me
triumphantly express:
25 nor let them say within their
hearts,
Ah, we would have it thus;
nor suffer them to say, Lo, he
is swallowed up by us.

26 Shamed and confounded be they
all
that at my hurt are glad;
let those against me that do boast
with shame and scorn be clad.
27 Let them who love my righteous
cause
with gladness shout, nor cease
to say, The Lord be magnified,
who loves his servant's peace.

28 Thy righteousness shall also be
declared by my tongue;
the praises that belong to thee
speak shall it all day long.

36

1 The wicked man's transgression
speaks
within my heart and says,
Undoubtedly the fear of God
is not before his eyes.
2 Because himself he flattereth
in his own blinded eyes
the hatefulness shall not be found
of his iniquities.

3 Words from his mouth
proceeding are,
fraud and iniquity:
he to be wise, and to do good,
hath left off utterly.
4 He mischief, lying on his bed,
most cunningly doth plot:
he sets himself in ways not good,
ill he abhorreth not.

5 Thy mercy, Lord, is in the
heavens;
thy truth doth reach the clouds;
6 thy justice is like mountains
great;
thy judgments deep as floods:
Lord, thou preservest man and
beast.

7 How precious is thy grace!
Therefore in shadow of thy wings
men's sons their trust shall place.

8 They with the fatness of thy
house
shall be well satisfied;
from rivers of thy pleasure thou
wilt drink to them provide.
9 Because of life the fountain pure
remains alone with thee;
and in that purest light of thine
we clearly light shall see.

10 Thy loving-kindness unto them
continue that thee know;
and still on men upright in heart
thy righteousness bestow.
11 And suffer not the foot of pride
to trample upon me;
and by the hand of wicked men
thrust forth let me not be.

12 There fallen to the earth are they
that work iniquities:
cast down they are, and never
shall
be able to arise.

37

1 For evil doers fret thou not
thyself unquietly;
nor do thou envy bear to those
that work iniquity.
2 For, even like unto the grass,
soon be cut down shall they;
and, like the green and tender
herb,
they wither shall away.

3 Set thou thy trust upon the Lord,
and be thou doing good;
and so thou in the land shalt
dwell,
and verily have food.
4 Delight thyself in God; he'll give
thine heart's desire to thee.
5 Thy way to God commit, him
trust,
it bring to pass shall he.

6 And, like unto the light, he shall
thy righteousness display;
and he thy judgment shall bring
forth,
like noon-tide of the day.
7 rest in the Lord, and patiently
wait for him: do not fret
for him who, prospering in his
way,
success in sin doth get.

8 Let anger cease within thy heart,
and wrath forsake thou too:
fret not thyself in any wise,
that evil thou should'st do.

9　For those that evil-doers are
shall be cut off and fall:
but those that wait upon the Lord
the earth inherit shall.

10　For yet a little while, and then
the wicked shall not be;
his place thou shalt consider well,
but it thou shalt not see.

11　But by inheritance the earth
the meek ones shall possess:
they also shall delight themselves
in an abundant peace.

12　The wicked gnashes with his
teeth,
and plots the just to slay;

13　the Lord shall laugh at him,
because
at hand he sees his day.

14　The wicked have drawn out the
sword,
and bent their bow, to slay
the poor and needy, and to kill
men of an upright way.

15　But their own sword, which they
have drawn,
shall enter their own heart;
their bows which they bent
shall break,
and into pieces part.

16　A little that a just man hath
is more and better far
than is the wealth of many such
as vile and wicked are.

17　For sinners' arms shall broken
be;
the Lord the just sustains.

18　The Lord doth know the just
man's ways;
their heritage remains.

19　They shall not be ashamed when
they
the evil time do see;
and when the days of famine are
they satisfied shall be.

20　But wicked men, Jehovah's foes,
as fat of lambs, decay;
they shall consume, yea, into
smoke
they shall consume away.

21　The wicked borrows, but the
same
again he doth not pay:
whereas the righteous mercy
shows,
and gives his own away.

22　For such as blessed be of him
the earth inherit shall;

and they that cursed are of him
shall be destroyed all.

23　A good man's footsteps by the
Lord
are ordered aright;
and in the way wherein he walks
he greatly doth delight.

24　Although he fall, yet shall he not
be cast down utterly;
because the Lord with his own
hand
upholds him mightily.

25　I have been young, and now am
old,
yet have I never seen
the just man left, nor that his
seed
for bread have beggars been.

26　He's ever merciful, and lends:
his seed is blest therefore.

27　Depart from evil, and do good,
and dwell for evermore.

28　For God loves judgment, and his
saints
leaves not in any case;
they are kept ever: but cut off
shall be the sinner's race.

29　The just inherit shall the land,
and ever in it dwell.

30　The just man's mouth doth
wisdom speak;
his tongue doth judgment tell.

31　His God's law is within his
heart;
his steps slide not away.

32　The wicked man doth watch the
just,
and seeketh him to slay.

33　Yet him the Lord will not forsake,
nor leave him in his hands:
the righteous will he not
condemn,
when he in judgement stands.

34　Wait on the Lord, and keep his
way,
and thee exalt shall he
earth to inherit; when cut off
the wicked thou shalt see.

35　I saw the wicked great in power
spread like a green bay-tree:

36　he passed, yea, was not: him I
sought,
but found he could not be.

37　Mark thou the perfect, and
behold
the man of uprightness;
because that surely of this man
the latter end is peace.

38 But those men that transgressors are
shall be destroyed together;
the latter end of wicked men
shall be cut off for ever.
39 But the salvation of the just
is from the Lord above;
he in the time of their distress
their stay and strength doth
prove.
40 The Lord shall help and rescue
them;
he shall them free and save
from wicked men; because in
him
their confidence they have.

38

1 In thy great indignation, Lord,
do thou rebuke me not;
nor on me lay thy chastening
hand,
in thy displeasure hot.
2 For in me fast thine arrows stick,
thine hand doth press me sore:
3 and in my flesh there is no
health,
nor soundness any more.

This grief I have, because thy
wrath
is forth against me gone;
and in my bones there is no rest,
for sin that I have done.
4 Because gone o'er mine head my
sins
and my transgressions be;
and, as a weighty burden, they
too heavy are for me.

5 My wounds corrupt and noisome
are;
my folly makes it so.
6 I troubled am, and much bowed
down;
all day I mourning go.
7 For a disease that loathsome is
so fills my loins with pain,
that in my weak and weary flesh
no soundness doth remain.

8 So very feeble and infirm,
and sorely crushed am I,
that, through disquiet of my
heart,
I make loud moan and cry.
9 O Lord, before thine eyes is all
that is desired by me:
and of my heart the secret groans
not hidden are from thee.

10 My heart doth pant incessantly,
my strength doth quite decay;
as for mine eyes, their wonted
light
is from me gone away.
11 My lovers and my friends do
stand
far distant from my sore;
and those do stand aloof that
were
kinsmen and kind before.
12 Yea, they that seek my life lay
snares;
who seek to do me wrong
speak mischief, and deceitful
things
imagine all day long.
13 But, as one deaf that heareth not,
I suffered all to pass;
I as a dumb man did become,
whose mouth not opened was:
14 As one that hears not, in whose
mouth
are no reproofs at all.
15 For, Lord, I hope in thee; my
God,
thou'lt hear me when I call.
16 For I said, Hear me, lest they
should
rejoice o'er me with pride;
and o'er me magnify themselves,
what time my foot doth slide.

17 Because I ready am to halt,
my grief I ever see:
18 for I'll declare my sin, and grieve
for mine iniquity.
19 But yet my foes are full of life,
and strong are they beside;
and they that hate me wrongfully
are greatly multiplied.
20 And they for good that render ill
as enemies me withstood;
yea, even for this, because that I
do follow what is good.
21 Forsake me not, O Lord; my God,
far from me never be.
22 O Lord, thou my salvation art,
haste to give help to me.

39 FIRST VERSION

1 I said, I will look to my ways,
lest with my tongue I sin:
in sight of wicked men my mouth
with bridle I'll keep in.
2 With silence I as dumb became,
I did myself restrain

even from good; but then the
more
increased was my pain.

3 My heart within me waxed hot,
and, while I mused long,
a fire within me kindled was;
then spake I with my tongue.

4 Mine end and measure of my
days,
O Lord, unto me show
what is the same; that I thereby
how frail I am may know.

5 Lo, thou my days an handbreadth
mad'st;
mine age is nought with thee:
sure each man in his best estate
is wholly vanity.

6 Sure each man walks in a vain
show;
they vex themselves in vain:
he heaps up wealth, and doth not
know
to whom it shall pertain.

7 And now, O Lord, what wait I
for?
My hope is fixed on thee.

8 Free me from all my trespasses,
the fool's scorn make not me.

9 Dumb am I, opening not my
mouth,
because this work is thine.

10 O, take thy stroke away from me;
by thy hand's blow I pine.

11 When with rebukes thou dost
correct
man for iniquity,
like moth thou dost his beauty
waste:
each man is vanity.

12 Regard my cry, Lord, at my tears
and prayers not silent be:
I sojourn as my fathers all,
and stranger am with thee.

13 O spare thou me, that I my
strength
recover may again,
before that hence I do depart,
and here no more remain.

39 SECOND VERSION

1 I will of my ways be heedful,
that I sin not with my tongue;
for my mouth a curb is needful,
while the wicked round me
throng.

2 Thus I said, and dumb remainèd;
from my lips no sound was
heard;
from good words I even
refrainèd,
but my inmost soul was stirred.

3 Long my heart was in me
burning,
ere the smothered flame
out-brake,
and, the enkindled words
returning,
thus impatiently I spake:

4 Teach me, Lord, the number
meting
of my days, how brief it is;
make me see and know how
fleeting,
vain and sad a life is this.

5 Life a span is at the longest;
mine is nothing, Lord, to thee;
in his best estate and strongest
man is only vanity.

6 Yea, he fleeting past us goeth
in a shadow brief and vain,
heaping riches; but none
knoweth
who shall gather them again.

7 And where, Lord, is my reliance?
All my hope is fixed on thee.
From my sin, and the defiance
of the foolish, save thou me!

8 I, because it was thy pleasure,
murmured not, nor silence broke;
yet remove thy plague: o'er
measure
grievous is thy heavy stroke.

9 When for sin or slighted duty
man corrected is by thee,
but a moth-worn robe his beauty,
and but vanity is he.

10 See my tears, regard my danger;
be not deaf unto my prayer;
for a sojourner and stranger
am I, as my fathers were.

11 Spare me, yet a little spare me,
to recover strength, before
thy dread summons hence shall
bear me
to be seen on earth no more!

40

1 I waited for the Lord my God,
and patiently did bear;
at length to me he did incline
my voice and cry to hear.

2 He took me from a fearful pit,
and from the miry clay,
and on a rock he set my feet,
establishing my way.

3 He put a new song in my mouth,
our God to magnify:
many shall see it, and shall fear,
and on the Lord rely.

4 O blessed is the man whose trust
upon the Lord relies;
respecting not the proud, nor
such
as turn aside to lies.

5 O Lord my God, full many are
the wonders thou hast done;
thy gracious thoughts to us-ward
far
above all thoughts are gone.
None can them reckon unto thee;
if I would them declare,
if I would speak of them, they
more
than can be numbered are.

6 No sacrifice nor offering
didst thou at all desire;
mine ears thou op'st; sin-offering
thou
and burnt didst not require:

7 then to the Lord these were my
words,
I come, behold and see;
within the volume of the book
it written is of me:

8 To do thy will I take delight,
O thou my God that art:
yea, that most holy law of thine
I have within my heart.

9 Within the congregation great
I righteousness did preach:
lo, thou dost know, O Lord, that I
refrained not my speech.

10 I never did within my heart
conceal thy righteousness;
I thy salvation have declared,
and shown thy faithfulness:
thy kindness, which most loving
is,
concealed have not I,
nor from the congregation great
have hid thy verity.

11 Thy tender mercies, Lord, from
me
O do thou not restrain;
thy loving-kindness, and thy
truth,
let them me still maintain.

12 For ills past reckoning compass
me,
and mine iniquities
such hold upon me taken have,
I cannot lift mine eyes:

More they than hairs upon my
head,
thence is my heart dismayed;

13 be pleased, O Lord, to rescue me;
Lord, hasten to mine aid.

14 Shamed and confounded be they
all
that seek my soul to kill;
yea, let them backward driven be
and sham'd, that wish me ill.

15 For a reward of this their shame
confounded let them be,
who in this manner scoffing say,
Aha, aha! to me.

16 Let all who seek thy face rejoice,
and still be glad in thee;
who thy salvation love, say still,
the Lord exalted be.

17 I'm poor and needy, yet the Lord
of me a care doth take;
thou art my Saviour and my
help;
my God, no tarrying make.

41

1 Blessed is he that carefully
considereth the poor;
the Lord in time of trouble him
deliverance will secure.

2 He will him keep, yea save alive;
on earth he blessed shall live;
and to his enemies' desire
thou wilt him never give.

3 The Lord will strengthen when
on bed
of weakness he doth mourn;
and in his sickness sore, O Lord,
thou all his bed wilt turn.

4 I said, O Lord, do thou extend
thy mercy unto me;
O do thou heal my soul, because
I have offended thee.

5 Those that to me are enemies
of me do evil say,
when shall he die, that so his
name
may perish quite away?

6 To see me if he comes, he speaks
vain words: but then his heart
doth gather mischief, which he
tells,
when forth he doth depart.

7   My haters jointly whispering
    against me hurt devise;
8   mischief, say they, cleaves fast to
    him;
    he lies and shall not rise.
9   Yea, even mine own familiar
    friend,
    on whom I did rely,
    who ate my bread, even he his
    heel
    against me lifted high.
10 But, Lord, be merciful to me,
    and up again me raise,
    that I may justly them requite
    according to their ways.
11 By this I know that certainly
    I favoured am by thee;
    because my hateful enemy
    doth not exult o'er me.
12 But as for me, thou me uphold'st
    in mine integrity;
    and me before thy countenance
    thou sett'st continually.
13 The Lord, the God of Israel,
    be blest for ever then,
    from age to age eternally.
    Amen, yea, and amen.

42

1   As pants the hart for water-
    brooks,
    my soul pants, Lord, for thee;
2   for God, the living God, I thirst;
    God's courts when shall I see?
3   My tears have unto me been
    meat
    both in the night and day,
    while unto me continually,
    Where is thy God? they say.

4   My soul is poured out in me,
    when this I think upon;
    because that with the multitude
    I heretofore had gone;
    with them into God's house I
    went,
    with voice of joy and praise;
    yea, with the multitude that kept
    the solemn holy days.

5   O why art thou cast down, my
    soul?
    Why in me so dismayed?
    Trust God, for I shall praise him
    yet;
    his countenance is mine aid.
6   My God, my soul's cast down in
    me:
    remember thee I will

from Jordan's land, and
    Hermon's heights,
    even from Mizar hill.

7   At voice of thy great water-spouts
    deep unto deep doth call;
    thy breaking waves pass over me,
    yea, and thy billows all.
8   His loving-kindness yet the Lord
    command will in the day;
    his song is with me in the night;
    to God, my life, I'll pray.
9   I'll say to God my rock, O why
    dost thou forget me so?
    For the oppression of my foes
    why do I mourning go?
10 'Tis as a sword within my bones,
    when me my foes upbraid;
    even when by them, Where is
    thy God?
    is daily to me said.
11 O why art thou cast down, my
    soul?
    Why thus with grief opprest
    art thou disquieted in me?
    In God still hope and rest:
    for yet I know I shall him praise,
    who graciously to me
    the health is of my countenance,
    yea, mine own God is he.

43

1   Against a wicked race, O God,
    plead thou my cause, judge me;
    from the unjust and crafty man
    O do thou set me free.
2   For thou the God art of my
    strength;
    why thrust me then away?
    And for the oppression of the foe
    why mourn I all the day?
3   O send thy light forth and thy
    truth;
    let them be guides to me,
    and bring me to thine holy hill,
    even where thy dwellings be.
4   Then will I to God's altar go,
    to God my chiefest joy:
    yea, God, my God, thy name to
    praise
    my harp I will employ.

5   Why art thou then cast down, my
    soul?
    What should discourage thee?
    And why with vexing thoughts
    art thou
    disquieted in me?

Still trust in God; for him to
praise
good cause I yet shall have:
he of my countenance is the
health,
my God that doth me save.

44

1 O God, we with our ears have
heard,
our fathers have us told,
the work that in their days thou
didst
even in the days of old.
2 Thy hand did drive the heathen
out,
and plant them in their place;
the nations all thou didst afflict,
but them thou didst increase.

3 For neither got their sword the
land,
nor did their arm them save;
but thy right hand, arm,
countenance;
for God them favour gave.
4 Thou art my King: for Jacob,
Lord,
deliverances command.
5 Through thee we shall push
down our foes,
that do against us stand:

We, through thy name, shall
tread down those
that risen against us have.
6 For in my bow I shall not trust,
nor shall my sword me save.
7 But from our foes thou hast us
saved,
our haters put to shame.
8 In God we all the day do boast,
and ever praise thy name.

9 But now we are cast off by thee,
thou puttest us to shame;
and when our armies forth do go,
thou goest not with them.
10 Thou mak'st us from the enemy
to turn back in dismay;
and they, who hate us, for
themselves
our spoils do take away.

11 Like sheep for meat thou gavest
us,
'mong heathen cast we be.
12 Thou didst for nought thy people
sell;
their price enriched not thee.

13 Unto our neighbours a reproach
we have been made by thee;
derision and a scorn to those
that round about us be.
14 A by-word also thou dost us
among the heathen make;
the people, in contempt and
spite,
at us their heads do shake.
15 Before me my confusion doth
abide continually,
and of my countenance the
shame
doth wholly cover me.

16 For voice of him that doth
reproach,
and speaketh blasphemy;
because of the avenging foe,
and cruel enemy.
17 All this is come on us, yet we
have not forgotten thee;
nor falsely in thy covenant
behaved ourselves have we.
18 Back from thy way turned not our
hearts,
from thee we have not strayed;
19 though crushed by thee in
dragons' haunts,
and covered with death's shade.
20 If we God's name forgot, or
stretched
to a strange god our hands,
21 shall not God search this out? for
he
heart's secrets understands.

22 Yea, for thy sake we're killed all
day,
counted as slaughter-sheep.
23 Rise, Lord, cast us not ever off;
awake, why dost thou sleep?
24 O wherefore hidest thou thy
face?
forgett'st our cause distressed,
25 and our oppression? For our soul
down to the dust is pressed.

Our body also on the earth
fast cleaving hold doth take.
26 Rise for our help, and us redeem,
even for thy mercies' sake.

45   FIRST VERSION

1 My heart brings forth a goodly
thing;
my words that I indite
concern the King: my tongue's a
pen
of one that swift doth write.

2   Thou fairer art than sons of men:
into thy lips is store
of grace infused; God therefore
    thee
hath blessed for evermore.

3   O thou that art the mighty One,
thy sword gird on thy thigh;
even with thy glory excellent,
and with thy majesty.

4   For meekness, truth, and
    righteousness,
ride prosperously in state;
and thee thine own right hand
    shall teach
things terrible and great.

5   Thine arrows sharply pierce the
    heart
of the enemies of the King;
and under thy dominion they
the people down do bring.

6   For ever and for ever is,
O God, thy throne of might;
the sceptre of thy kingdom is
a sceptre that is right.

7   Thou lovest right and hatest ill;
hence God, thy God, even he
above thy fellows hath with oil
of joy anointed thee.

8   Of aloes, myrrh, and cassia
a smell thy garments had,
out of the ivory palaces,
whereby they made thee glad.

9   Among thy women honourable
kings' daughters were at hand:
upon thy right hand did the
    queen
in gold of Ophir stand.

10   O daughter, hearken and regard,
and do thine ear incline;
likewise forget thy father's house,
and people that are thine.

11   And so thy beauty by the King
greatly desired shall be;
because he is thy Lord, do thou
him worship reverently.

12   The daughter there of Tyre shall
    be
with gifts and offerings great:
those of the people that are rich
thy favour shall entreat.

13   Behold, the daughter of the King
all glorious is within;
and with embroideries of gold
her garments wrought have been.

14   She shall be brought unto the
    King
in robes with needle wrought;
her fellow-virgins following
shall unto thee be brought.

15   They shall be brought with
    gladness great,
and mirth on every side,
into the palace of the King,
and there they shall abide.

16   Thy fathers' place thy sons shall
    fill
whom thou to thee shalt take,
and in all places of the earth
them noble princes make.

17   Thy name remembered I will
    make
through ages all to be:
the people therefore evermore
shall praises give to thee.

45   SECOND VERSION

1   My heart inditing is
good matter in a song:
I speak the things that I have
    made,
which to the King belong:
my tongue shall be as quick,
his honour to indite,
as is the pen to any scribe
that useth fast to write.

2   Thou fairer art than men;
grace in thy lips doth flow:
and therefore blessings evermore
on thee doth God bestow.

3   Thy sword gird on thy thigh,
thou that art great in might:
appear in dreadful majesty,
and in thy glory bright.

4   For meekness, truth, and right,
ride prosperously in state;
and thy right hand shall teach to
    thee
things terrible and great.

5   Thy shafts shall pierce their
    hearts
that foes are to the King;
whereby into subjection thou
the people down shalt bring.

6   Thy royal seat, O Lord,
for ever shall remain:
the sceptre of thy kingdom doth
all righteousness maintain.

7   Thou lovest right, hat'st ill;
hence God, thy God, even he
above thy fellows hath with oil
of joy anointed thee.

8   Of myrrh and spices sweet
a smell thy garments had,
out of the ivory palaces,
whereby they made thee glad.

9   And in thy glorious train
kings' daughters waiting stand;
and thy fair queen in Ophir gold
doth stand at thy right hand.

10   O daughter, take good heed,
incline, and give good ear;
thou must forget thy kindred all,
and father's house most dear.

11   Thy beauty by the King
shall then desired be;
and do thou humbly worship
     him,
because thy Lord is he.

12   The daughter then of Tyre
there with a gift shall be;
and all the wealthy of the land
shall make their suit to thee.

13   The daughter of the King
all glorious is within;
and with embroideries of gold
her garments wrought have been.

14   She cometh to the King
in robes with needle wrought;
the virgins that do follow her
shall unto thee be brought.

15   They shall be brought with joy,
and mirth on every side,
into the palace of the King,
and there they shall abide.

16   And in thy fathers' stead,
thy children thou shalt take
and in all places of the earth
them noble princes make.

17   I will show forth thy name
to generations all:
therefore the people evermore
to thee give praises shall.

46   FIRST VERSION

1   God is our refuge and our
     strength,
in straits a present aid;

2   therefore, although the earth
     remove,
we will not be afraid:
though hills amidst the seas be
     cast;

3   though waters roaring make,
and troubled be; yea, though the
     hills
by swelling seas do shake.

4   A river is, whose streams make
     glad
the city of our God,
the holy place, wherein the Lord
most high hath his abode.

5   God in the midst of her doth
     dwell;
nothing shall her remove:
God unto her an helper will,
and that right early, prove.

6   The heathen raged tumultuously,
the kingdoms moved were:
the Lord God uttered his voice,
the earth did melt for fear.

7   The Lord of hosts is on our side
our safety to maintain:
the God of Jacob doth for us
a refuge high remain.

8   Come, and behold what
     wondrous works
have by the Lord been wrought;
come, see what desolations he
upon the earth hath brought.

9   Unto the ends of all the earth
wars into peace he turns:
the bow he breaks, the spear he
     cuts,
in fire the chariot burns.

10   Be still, and know that I am God;
among the heathen I
will be exalted; I on earth
will be exalted high.

11   The Lord of hosts is on our side
our safety to maintain;
the God of Jacob doth for us
a refuge high remain.

46   SECOND VERSION

1   God is our sure defence, our aid
in time of tribulation;
our heart shall never be
     dismayed,
though fail the earth's
     foundation,
o'er hills though foaming floods
     ascend,
though billows roar, and ocean
     rend
the mountain-peaks asunder.

2   A river by the holy shrine,
a pure and peaceful river,
makes glad the seat of power
     divine:
she stands unmoved for ever;
for God is in the midst of her,
a help, a stay, a comforter;
he comes at break of morning.

3   In Jacob's God our strength is
       found,
  when heathen hosts assemble;
  he speaks in thunder; at the
      sound
  earth melts and nations tremble:
  the Lord of hosts a refuge stands.
  And lo! the wonders of his
      hands,
  the wrath, the desolation!

4   He lulls the war, he burns the car,
  the bow and spear he breaketh;
  be still, he cries, for I arise;
  the Lord, the Lord awaketh,
  o'er all the earth a God most
      high:
  the Lord of hosts, our help, is
      nigh,
  our strength, the God of Jacob.

47

1   All people, clap your hands; to
      God
  with voice of triumph shout:
2   for dreadful is the Lord most
      high,
  great King the earth throughout.
3   Subdue the people under us
  assuredly shall he;
  under our feet the nations all
  brought down by him shall be.

4   The lot of our inheritance
  choose out for us doth he,
  even Jacob's glory, whom he
      loved,
  and called his own to be.
5   God is with shouts gone up, the
      Lord
  with trumpets sounding high.
6   Sing praise to God, sing praise,
      sing praise,
  praise to our King sing ye.

7   For God is king of all the earth;
  with knowledge praise express.
8   God rules the nations; God sits
      on
  his throne of holiness.
9   The princes of the people are
  assembled willingly;
  even of the God of Abraham
  they who the people be.

  Because the shields that do
      defend
  the earth are only his:
  they unto God belong, and he
  exalted greatly is.

48

1   Great is the Lord, and greatly he
  is to be praised still,
  within the city of our God,
  upon his holy hill.
2   Mount Zion stands most
      beautiful,
  the joy of all the land;
  the city of the mighty King
  upon the north doth stand.

3   The Lord within her palaces
  is for a refuge known.
4   For, lo, the kings that gathered
      were
  together by have gone.
5   But when they did behold the
      same,
  they wondering would not stay;
  but, being troubled at the sight,
  they thence did haste away.

6   Great terror there took hold on
      them,
  with fear possessed they were;
  their grief came like a woman's
      pain,
  when she a child doth bear.
7   Thou Tarshish ships with east
  wind break'st:
8   as we have heard it told,
  so, in the city of the Lord,
  our eyes did it behold.

  In our God's city, which his hand
  for ever stablish will.
9   We of thy loving-kindness
      thought,
  Lord, in thy temple still.
10   O God, according to thy name,
  through all the earth's thy praise;
  and thy right hand, O God, is full
  of righteousness always.

11   Because thy judgements are
      made known,
  let Zion mount rejoice;
  of Judah let the daughters all
  send forth a cheerful voice.
12   Walk about Zion, and go round;
  the high towers thereof tell:
13   consider ye her palaces,
  and mark her bulwarks well;

  That ye may tell posterity.
14   For this God doth abide
  our God for evermore; he will
  even unto death us guide.

49 FIRST VERSION

1 Hear this, all people, and give
ear,
all in the world that dwell,
2 both low and high, both rich and
poor;
3 my mouth shall wisdom tell:
my heart shall knowledge
meditate.
4 I will incline mine ear
to parables, and on the harp
my sayings dark declàre.

5 Amidst those days that evil be,
why should I fearing doubt?
When my pursuers' wickedness
doth compass me about.
6 Whoe'er they be that in their
wealth
their confidence do place,
and who do boast themselves
because
their riches grow apace;

7 Yet none of these his brother can
redeem by any way;
nor can he unto God for him
sufficient ransom pay;
8 that he should still for ever live
and not corruption see:
9 their soul's redemption costly is,
nor can it ever be.

10 Because he sees that wise men
die,
that fools and brutish all
do perish, and, when dead, their
wealth
doth unto others fall.
11 Their inward thought is that their
homes
and dwelling places all
shall stand for evermore; their
lands
by their own names they call.

12 But yet in honour shall not man
abide continually;
but passing hence may be
compared
unto the beasts that die.
13 Thus brutish folly plainly is
their wisdom and their way;
yet their posterity approve
what they do fondly say.

14 Like sheep they in the grave are
laid,
and death shall them devour;
and in the morning upright men

shall over them have power:
their beauty from their dwelling
shall
consume within the grave.
15 But from death's hand God will
me free,
for he shall me receive.

16 Be not afraid then when a man
enriched thou dost see;
nor when the glory of his house
increaseth wondrously.
17 For he shall carry nothing hence,
when death his days doth end;
nor shall his glory after him
into the grave descend.

18 Although he his own soul did
bless,
whilst he on earth did live;
(and when thou to thyself dost
well,
men will thee praises give;)
19 he to his fathers' race shall go;
they never shall see light.
20 Man honoured wanting
knowledge is
like beasts that perish quite.

49 SECOND VERSION

1 Ye dwellers all on earth, give ear,
both rich and poor, and high and
low!
For musings deep I will declare,
and wisdom from my tongue
shall flow.
Mine ear I bend to mystic lays;
dark sayings on my harp
expound.
Why should I fear in evil days,
when sinners hem me in
around?

2 Mark those who on their wealth
rely,
and glory in their store's
increase;
not one a brother's life can buy,
nor from his God procure him
peace.
The soul's redemption is so dear,
that no man can sufficient have
to purchase life for ever here,
or 'scape corruption in the grave.

3 Men see the fool and wise man
fall,
and all their hoards to others
passed;
yet by their names their lands
they call,

and think their house will ever
last.
But man's vain honour soon
decays,
even as the brutish herd they
die;
and though their seed their
sayings praise,
their way is only vanity.

4 Like sheep they in the grave are
laid,
where hungry death shall on
them prey;
their glories in the dust shall
fade,
and just men rise more blest than
they.
But God my soul from death will
free,
and home receive me to himself:
then fear thou not, if one thou see
surpassing thee in place or pelf:

5 For though his life more blest he
thought,
and others did his path
commend,
he to his grave shall carry
nought,
nor shall his pomp to him
descend.
No; to his fathers he must pass,
and lie in darkness out of sight,
Man, foolish man, in honoured
place,
is like the beasts, which perish
quite.

50 FIRST VERSION

1 The mighty God, the Lord,
speaks, and to earth doth call
even from the rising of the sun
to where he hath his fall.
2 From out of Zion hill,
where beauty dwells enshrined,
God in his glorious majesty
and mighty power hath shined.
3 Our God shall surely come,
keep silence shall not he:
before him fire shall waste, great
storms
shall round about him be.
4 Unto the heavens above
he shall send forth his call,
and likewise to the earth, that he
may judge his people all.
5 Together let my saints
unto me gathered be,

those that by sacrifice have made
a covenant with me.
6 And then the heavens shall
his righteousness declare:
because the Lord himself is he
by whom men judged are.

7 My people Israel, hear:
speak will I from on high;
against thee I will testify;
God, even thy God, am I.
8 I for thy sacrifice
no blame on thee will lay:
nor for burnt-offerings, which to
me
thou offeredst every day.

9 I'll take no calf nor goats
from house or fold of thine:
10 beasts of the forest, cattle all
on thousand hills, are mine.
11 The fowls on mountains high
are all to me well known;
wild beasts which in the fields do
lie,
even they are all mine own.

12 Then, if I hungry were,
I would not tell it thee;
because the world, and fulness all
thereof, belongs to me.
13 Will I eat flesh of bulls?
Or goats' blood drink will I?
14 Thanks offer thou to God, and
pay
thy vows to the Most High.

15 And call upon me when
in trouble thou shalt be;
I will deliver thee, and thou
shalt glory give to me.
16 But to the wicked man
God saith, Why dost thou dare
my covenant in thy mouth to
take,
my statutes to declare?

17 Yet thou instruction wise
perversely hated hast,
likewise my words behind thy
back
thou in contempt dost cast.
18 Thou didst to him consent,
when thou a thief hast seen;
and with the vile adulterers
thou hast partaker been.

19 Thou giv'st thy mouth to ill;
thy tongue deceit doth frame;
20 thou sitt'st, and 'gainst thy
brother speak'st,
thy mother's son dost shame.

21 Because I silence kept,
while thou these things hast
wrought;
that I was altogether like
thyself hath been thy thought:

Yet I will thee reprove,
and set before thine eyes,
arrayed in order, thy misdeeds,
and thine iniquities.

22 Now, ye that God forget,
consider this with care;
lest I, when there is none to save,
do you in pieces tear.

23 He doth me glorify
who offers to me praise;
and him I'll God's salvation
show
that orders right his ways.

50 SECOND VERSION

1 The mighty God, the Lord, doth
speak,
and to the earth doth call,
even from the rising of the sun
to where he hath his fall.

2 From out of Zion, his own hill,
where beauty dwells enshrined,
God in his glorious majesty
and mighty power hath shined.

3 Our God assuredly shall come,
keep silence shall not he;
before him fire shall waste, great
storms
shall round about him be.

4 He to the heavens above shall
call,
and to the earth below,
that of his people he to all
his judgment just may show.

5 Let all my saints together now
unto me gathered be,
those that by sacrifice have made
a covenant with me.

6 And then the heavens shall
declare
his righteousness abroad;
because the Lord himself doth
come;
none else is judge but God.

7 Hear, O my people, I will speak,
and I will testify
against thee, O mine Israel;
God, even thy God, am I.

8 Not for thy sacrifices I
reprove thee ever will,

nor for burnt-offerings, which
have been
before me offered still.

9 I'll take no bullock nor he-goats
from house nor folds of thine:
10 beasts of the forest, cattle all
on thousand hills, are mine.
11 The fowls are all to me well
known
that mountains high do yield;
and I do challenge as mine own
the wild beasts of the field.

12 If I were hungry, I would not
to thee for need complain;
for earth, with all its fulness, doth
to me of right pertain.
13 That I to eat the flesh of bulls
take pleasure dost thou think?
Or that I need, to quench my
thirst,
the blood of goats to drink?

14 Nay, rather unto me, thy God,
thanksgiving offer thou;
to the Most High perform thy
word,
and fully pay thy vow:
15 and in the day of thy distress
do thou unto me cry;
I will deliver thee, and thou
my name shalt glorify.

16 But to the wicked man God saith,
How is it thou dost dare
my covenant in thy mouth to
take,
my statutes to declare?
17 And yet all good instruction thou
perversely hated hast,
likewise my words behind thy
back
thou in contempt dost cast.

18 When thou a thief didst see, with
him
thou didst consent to sin,
and with the vile adulterers
thou hast partaker been.
19 Thy mouth to evil thou dost give,
thy tongue deceit doth frame.
20 Thou sitt'st, and 'gainst thy
brother speak'st,
thy mother's son to shame.

21 These things thou wickedly hast
done,
and I have silent been;
thou thought'st that I was like
thyself,
and did approve thy sin:

but I will sharply thee reprove,
and set before thine eyes,
arrayed in order, thy misdeeds
and thine iniquities.

22 Consider this, and be afraid,
ye that forget the Lord,
lest I in pieces tear you all,
when none can help afford.

23 He truly doth me glorify
who offers to me praise;
and him I'll God's salvation show
that orders right his ways.

51

1 After thy loving-kindness, Lord,
have mercy upon me:
for thy compassions great, blot out
all mine iniquity.

2 Me cleanse from sin, and
throughly wash
from mine iniquity;

3 for my transgressions I confess;
my sin I ever see.

4 'Gainst thee, thee only, have I
sinned,
in thy sight done this ill;
that when thou speak'st thou
may'st be just,
and clear in judging still.

5 Behold, I in iniquity
was formed the womb within;
my mother also me conceived
in guiltiness and sin.

6 Behold, thou in the inward parts
with truth delighted art;
and wisdom thou shalt make me
know
within the hidden part.

7 Do thou with hyssop sprinkle me,
I shall be cleansed so;
yea, wash thou me, and then I
shall
be whiter than the snow.

8 Of gladness and of joyfulness
make me to hear the voice,
that so these very bones which
thou
hast broken may rejoice.

9 All mine iniquities blot out,
thy face hide from my sin.

10 Create a clean heart, Lord, renew
a right spirit me within.

11 Cast me not from thy sight, nor
take
thy Holy Spirit away.

12 restore me thy salvation's joy;
with thy free Spirit me stay.

13 Then will I teach thy ways unto
those that transgressors be;
and those that sinners are shall
then
be turned unto thee.

14 O God, of my salvation God,
from guilt of blood me free:
then of thy righteousness my
tongue
shall sing aloud to thee.

15 My closed lips, O Lord, by thee
let them be opened;
then shall thy praises by my
mouth
abroad be published.

16 Thou sacrifice desirest not,
else would I give it thee;
nor wilt thou with burnt-offering
at all delighted be.

17 A broken spirit is to God
a pleasing sacrifice:
a broken and a contrite heart,
Lord, thou wilt not despise.

18 In thy good pleasure do thou
good
to Zion, thine own hill:
the walls of thy Jerusalem
build up of thy good will.

19 Then righteous offerings shall
thee please,
and offerings burnt which they,
with whole burnt-offerings, and
with calves,
shall on thine altar lay.

52

1 Why boast thyself, O mighty man,
of mischief and of wrong?
The goodness of Almighty God
endureth all day long.

2 Thy tongue doth mischief still
devise,
and falsely doth revile;
like to a razor whetted sharp,
for ever working guile.

3 Ill more than good thou lov'st,
lies more
than speaking righteousness:

4 thou lovest all-devouring words,
tongue of deceitfulness.

5 So God shall thee destroy for aye,
remove thee, pluck thee out
quite from thy tent, and from the
land
of living men thee root.

6   The righteous shall it see and
     fear,
   and laugh at him they shall:
7   lo, this the man is that did not
   make God his strength at all:
   but he in his abundant wealth
   his confidence did place;
   and he took strength unto himself
   from his own wickedness.

8   But I am in the house of God
   like a green olive tree;
   I in God's mercy put my trust
   unto eternity.
9   And I for ever will thee praise,
   because thou hast done this;
   before thy saints I on thy name
   will wait, for good it is.

53

1   That there is not a God, the fool
   doth in his heart conclude:
   they are corrupt, their works are
     vile,
   not one of them doth good.
2   Upon the sons of men did God
   from heaven cast his eyes,
   to see if any one there was
   that sought God, and was wise.

3   Corrupt they altogether are,
   they all are backward gone;
   and there is none that doeth
     good,
   no, not so much as one.
4   These workers of iniquity,
   do they not know at all,
   that they my people eat as bread,
   and on God do not call?

5   Even there they were afraid, and
     stood
   with trembling all dismayed,
   whereas there was no cause at all
   why they should be afraid.
   For God his bones that thee
     besieged
   hath scattered all abroad;
   thou hast confounded them, for
     they
   despised are of God.

6   Let Israel's help from Zion come:
   when back the Lord shall bring
   his captives, Jacob shall rejoice,
   and Israel shall sing.

54

1   Save me, O God, by thy great
     name,
   and judge me by thy strength:
2   hear thou my prayer, O God;
     give ear
   unto my words at length.
3   For they that strangers are to me
   do up against me rise;
   oppressors seek my soul, and
     God
   set not before their eyes.

4   Lo, God an helper is to me,
   and therefore I am bold;
   the Lord hath taken part with
     those
   that do my soul uphold.
5   Unto my foes their wickedness
   he surely shall repay:
   O for thy truth's sake cut them
     off,
   and sweep them clean away.

6   I with a willing mind will give
   a sacrifice to thee;
   thy name, O Lord, because 'tis
     good,
   shall be extolled by me.
7   Because he hath delivered me
   from all adversities;
   and its desire mine eye hath seen
   upon mine enemies.

55

1   Hear thou my prayer, O God,
   hide not
   from my entreating voice:
2   attend and hear me, in my plaint
   I mourn and make a noise;
3   for voice of enemies, and for
   vile men's oppression great:
   on me they cast iniquity,
   and they in wrath me hate.

4   Sore pained within me is my
     heart:
   death's terrors on me fall.
5   On me comes trembling, fear and
     dread
   me overwhelmed withal.
6   O that I like a dove had wings,
   said I, then would I flee
   far hence, that I might find a
     place
   where I in rest might be.

7   Lo, then far off I wander would,
   and in the desert stay;

8   from stormy wind and tempest I
would haste to 'scape away.
9   O Lord, on them destruction
bring,
do thou their tongues divide;
for in the city violence
and strife have I descried.
10   They day and night upon the
walls
do compass it around:
there mischief is, and sorrow
there
in midst of it is found.
11   Abundant wickedness there is
within its inward part;
and from its streets deceitfulness
and guile do not depart.

12   He was no foe that me
reproached,
for that I could abide;
no hater that against me rose,
else I from him might hide.
13   'Twas thou, a man, mine equal,
guide,
who mine acquaintance wast:
14   we joined sweet counsels: to
God's house
amidst the throng we passed.

15   Let death them seize, and to the
grave
alive let them depart;
for wickedness is in their house
and evil in their heart.
16   I call on God; the Lord me saves.
17   I make my plaint and sigh
at evening, morning, and at
noon;
and he regards my cry.

18   He hath my soul delivered,
that it in peace might be
from battle that against me was;
for many were with me.
19   The Lord shall hear and them
afflict
(of old abideth he),
even them who have no fear of
God,
and changes never see.

20   'Gainst those that were at peace
with him
he hath put forth his hand:
the covenant that he had made,
by breaking he profaned.
21   More smooth than butter were
his words,
while in his heart was war:

his speeches were more soft than
oil,
and yet drawn swords they are.

22   Cast thou thy burden on the
Lord,
and he shall thee sustain;
yea, he shall cause the righteous
man
unmoved to remain.
23   But thou, O God, in judgment
just
those men shalt overthrow,
and in destruction's dungeon
dark
at last shalt lay them low;

The bloody and deceitful men
shall not live half their days:
but upon thee with confidence
I will depend always.

56

1   Show mercy, Lord, to me, for man
would swallow me outright;
he me oppresseth, while he doth
all day against me fight.
2   All day they would me swallow
up
who hate me spitefully;
for they be many that do fight
against me, O Most High.

3   When I'm afraid I'll trust in thee:
4   in God I'll praise his word;
I will not fear what flesh can do,
my trust is in the Lord.
5   All day they wrest my words;
their thoughts
'gainst me are all for ill.
6   They meet, they lurk, they mark
my steps,
waiting my soul to kill.

7   But shall they by iniquity
escape thy judgments so?
O God, with indignation down
do thou the people throw.
8   Thou tellest all my wanderings,
not one dost overlook;
into thy bottle put my tears:
are they not in thy book?

9   My foes shall, when I cry, turn
back;
I know God is for me.
10   In God his word I'll praise; his
word
in God shall praised be.
11   In God I trust; I will not fear
what man can do to me.

2 Thy vows upon me are, O God:
   I'll render praise to thee.

3 Thou, who from death didst save
      my soul,
   my feet from falling free,
   to walk before God in the light
   of those that living be.

57 FIRST VERSION

1 Be merciful to me, O God;
   be merciful to me;
   because my soul her confidence
   doth wholly place in thee.
   Yea, in the shadow of thy wings
   my refuge I will place,
   until these sad calamities
   do wholly overpass.

2 My cry I will cause to ascend
   to God who is most high;
   to God, who doth all things for
      me
   perform most perfectly.

3 From heaven he shall send
      down, and me
   from his reproach defend
   that would devour me: God his
      truth
   and mercy forth shall send.

4 My soul among fierce lions is,
   I firebrands live among,
   men's sons, whose teeth are
      spears and darts,
   a sharp sword is their tongue.

5 Be thou exalted very high
   above the heavens, O God;
   let thou thy glory be advanced
   o'er all the earth abroad.

6 My soul's bowed down; for they
      a net
   have laid, my steps to snare:
   into the pit which they have
      digged
   for me, they fallen are.

7 My heart is fixed, my heart is
      fixed,
   O God; I'll sing and praise.

8 My glory wake; wake psaltery,
      harp:
   myself I'll early raise.

9 I'll praise thee 'mong the people,
      Lord;
   'mong nations sing will I:

10 for great to heaven thy mercy is,
   thy truth is to the sky.

11 O Lord, exalted be thy name
   above the heavens to stand:

do thou thy glory far advance
above both sea and land.

57 SECOND VERSION

1 Thy mercy, Lord, to me extend;
   on thy protection I depend,
   and to thy wings for shelter haste
   until this storm be overpast.

2 To him I will in trouble cry,
   the sovereign Judge and God
      most high,
   who wonders hath for me begun,
   and will not leave his work
      undone.

3 For he from heaven shall quell
      the power
   of him who would my life
      devour;
   forth shall his truth and mercy
      send,
   and my distracted soul defend.

4 For I with cruel men converse,
   like hungry lions wild and fierce;
   with men whose teeth are spears,
      their words
   envenomed darts and two-edged
      swords.

5 Be thou, O God, exalted high:
   and, as thy glory fills the sky,
   so be it o'er the earth displayed,
   and thou, as there, be here
      obeyed!

6 To take me they their net
      prepared;
   my sinking soul almost
      despaired;
   but they are fallen, by thy decree,
   into the pit they dug for me.

7 O God, my heart is fixed, 'tis
      bent,
   its thankful tribute to present;
   and with my heart my voice I'll
      raise
   to thee, my God, in songs of
      praise.

8 Awake my glory; harp and lute,
   no longer let your strings be
      mute;
   and I, my tuneful part to take,
   will with the early dawn awake.

9 Thy praises, Lord, I will resound
   to all the listening nations round;
   thy mercy highest heaven
      transcends,
   thy truth beyond the clouds
      extends.

10 Be thou, O God, exalted high!
And, as thy glory fills the sky,
so be it o'er the earth displayed,
and thou, as there, be here
obeyed.

58

1 Do ye, O congregation, then,
indeed speak righteousness?
O ye that are the sons of men,
judge ye with uprightness?
2 Yea, even within your very
hearts
ye wickedness have done;
ye of your hands the violence
weigh out the earth upon.

3 Estranged the ungodly are,
even from the very womb;
they, speaking falsehood, stray as
soon
as to the world they come.
4 Unto a serpent's poison like
their poison doth appear;
yea, they are like the adder deaf,
that closely stops her ear;

5 That so she may not hear the
voice
of one that charm her would,
no, not though he most cunning
were,
and charm most wisely could.
6 Their teeth, O God, within their
mouth
break thou in pieces small;
the great teeth break thou out, O
Lord,
of these young lions all.

7 Let them like waters melt away,
which downward still do flow:
in pieces cut his arrows all,
when he shall bend his bow.
8 Like to a snail that melts away,
let each of them be gone:
like woman's birth untimely, that
hath never seen the sun.

9 He shall them take away before
your pots the thorns can find,
both living, and in fury great,
as with a stormy wind.
10 The righteous when he
vengeance sees
shall be most joyful then;
the righteous one shall wash his
feet
in blood of wicked men.

11 So men shall say, The righteous
man
reward shall never miss:
and verily upon the earth
a God to judge there is.

59

1 My God, deliver me from those
that are mine enemies;
and be thou my defence from
those
that up against me rise.
2 From workers of iniquity
do thou deliver me;
and give me safety from the men
of blood and cruelty.

3 For, lo, they for my soul lay wait:
the mighty do combine
against me, Lord; not for my
fault,
nor any sin of mine.
4 They run, and, without fault in
me,
themselves do ready make:
awake to meet me with thy help;
and do thou notice take.

5 Awake, Jehovah, God of hosts,
thou God of Israel,
to visit heathen all: spare none
that wickedly rebel.
6 At eventide they come again;
they make great noise and sound,
like to a dog, and often walk
the city all around.

7 Behold, they belch out with their
mouth,
and in their lips are swords:
for thus they say, Who now is he
that heareth these our words?
8 But thou, O Lord, shalt laugh at
them,
and all the heathen mock.
9 While he's in power I'll wait on
thee;
for God is my high rock.

10 He of my mercy that is God
betimes shall me prevent;
upon mine enemies God shall let
me see mine heart's content.
11 Them slay not, lest my folk
forget;
but scatter them abroad
by thy strong power; and bring
them down,
O thou our shield and God.

12 For their mouth's sin, and for the
  words
   that from their lips do fly,
  let them be taken in their pride;
   because they curse and lie.
13 In wrath consume them, them
  consume,
   that so they may not be:
  and that in Jacob God doth rule
   to earth's ends let them see.

14 At eventide they come again,
   they make great noise and sound
  like to a dog, and often walk
   the city all around.
15 They also wander up and down,
   that food they may obtain;
  and if they are not satisfied,
   they all night long remain.

16 But of thy power I'll sing aloud;
   at morn thy mercy praise:
  for thou to me my refuge wast,
   and tower, in troublous days.
17 O God, thou art my strength, I
  will
   sing praises unto thee;
  for God is my defence, a God
   of mercy unto me.

60

1 O God, thou hast rejected us,
   and scattered us abroad;
  thou justly hast displeased been;
   return to us, O God.
2 The earth to tremble thou hast
  made;
   therein didst breaches make:
  do thou thereof the breaches heal,
   because the land doth shake.

3 Hard things thou hast thy people
  shown,
   distress upon them sent;
  and thou hast caused us to drink
   wine of astonishment.
4 And yet a banner thou hast given
   to those who thee do fear;
  that it by them, because of truth,
   displayed may appear.

5 That thy beloved people may
   delivered be from thrall,
  save with the power of thy right
  hand,
   and hear me when I call.
6 God in his holiness did speak,
   my joy shall be complete;
  I Shechem will divide, by line
   the vale of Succoth mete.

7 Gilead I claim as mine by right;
   Manasseh mine shall be;
  Ephraim is of mine head the
   strength;
  Judah gives laws for me;
8 Moab my washpot is; my shoe,
   Edom, I'll cast o'er thee;
  Philistia, through thy borders all
   cry out because of me.

9 O who is he will bring me to
   the city fortified?
  O who is he that to the land
   of Edom will me guide?
10 O God, who hast rejected us,
   wilt thou not help us so?
  Even thou, O God, who dost no
   more
  forth with our armies go?

11 Help us from trouble; for the
   help
  is vain which man bestows:
12 through God we shall do
   valiantly;
  he shall tread down our foes.

61   FIRST VERSION

1 O God, give ear unto my cry;
   unto my prayer attend.
2 From the utmost corner of the
   land
  my cry to thee I'll send.
  What time my heart is
   overwhelmed
  and in perplexity,
  do thou me lead unto the Rock
   that higher is than I.

3 For thou hast for my refuge been
   a shelter by thy power;
  and for defence against my foes
   thou hast been a strong tower.
4 Within thy tabernacle I
   for ever will abide;
  and under covert of thy wings
   with confidence me hide.

5 For thou the vows that I did
   make,
  O Lord, my God, didst hear:
  thou hast given me the heritage
   of those thy name that fear.
6 A life prolonged for many days
   thou to the king shalt give;
  as many generations are
   the years which he shall live.

7 He in God's presence his abode
   for evermore shall have;
  O do thou truth and mercy both

THE IRISH PSALTER

prepare, that may him save.
8 And so will I perpetually
sing praise unto thy name;
that having made my vows, I
may
each day perform the same.

61 SECOND VERSION

1 Lord, hear my voice, my prayer
attend;
from earth's remotest bound I
send
my supplicating cry.
When troubles great o'erwhelm
my breast,
then lead me on the rock to rest
that higher is than I.

2 In thee my soul has shelter
found,
and thou hast been from foes
around
the tower of my defence.
My home shall thy pavilion be;
to covert of thy wings I'll flee,
and find deliverance.

3 For thou, O Lord, my vows hast
heard;
on me the heritage conferred
of those that fear thy name.
Long life thou to the king wilt
give;
through generations he shall live,
from age to age the same.

4 Before the Lord shall he abide;
O do thou truth and grace
provide
to guard him in the way.
So I thy praises will make known,
and humbly bending at thy
throne,
my vows will daily pay.

62

1 My soul with expectation doth
depend on God indeed:
my strength and my salvation do
from him alone proceed.
2 He only my salvation is,
and my strong rock is he:
he only is my sure defence;
much moved I shall not be.
3 How long rush ye upon a man,
and him to slay seek all?
To crush him like a tottering
fence,
and as a bowing wall?

4 Only to cast him down they plot;
in lies they take delight;
and while they with the mouth
do bless,
they curse with inward spite.
5 Only on God do thou, my soul,
still patiently attend;
my expectation and my hope
on him alone depend.
6 He only my salvation is,
and my strong rock is he;
he only is my sure defence:
I shall not moved be.

7 In God my glory placed is,
and my salvation sure;
in God the rock is of my strength,
my refuge most secure.
8 Ye people place your confidence
in him continually;
before him pour ye out your
heart;
God is our refuge high.

9 Surely mean men are vanity,
and great men are a lie;
in balance laid, they wholly are
more light than vanity.
10 Do ye not in oppression trust,
in robbery be not vain;
set not your hearts on riches,
when
increased is your gain.

11 God hath it spoken once to me,
yea, this I heard again,
that power to Almighty God
alone doth appertain.
12 Yea, mercy also unto thee
belongs, O Lord, alone:
for thou according to his work
rewardest every one.

63

1 Lord, thee my God, I'll early
seek:
my soul doth thirst for thee;
my flesh longs in a dry parched
land,
wherein no waters be:
2 that I thy power may behold,
and brightness of thy face,
as I have seen thee heretofore
within thy holy place.
3 Since better is thy love than life,
my lips thee praise shall give.
4 I in thy name will lift my hands,
and bless thee while I live.

5 Even as with marrow and with
 fat
my soul shall filled be;
then shall my mouth with joyful
 lips
sing praises unto thee.

6 When I do thee upon my bed
remember with delight,
I meditate on thee throughout
the watches of the night.

7 In shadow of thy wings I'll joy;
for thou my help hast been.

8 My soul thee follows hard; and
 me
thy right hand doth sustain.

9 To lowest depths of earth shall go
those who my soul would slay;

10 They by the sword shall perish
 all,
of foxes be the prey.

11 Yet shall the king in God rejoice,
and each one glory shall
that swears by him; but stopped
 shall be
the mouth of liars all.

64

1 Unto the voice of my complaint,
O God, give thou an ear;
my life save from the enemy,
of whom I stand in fear.

2 Me from their secret counsel hide
who evil-doers be;
from noisy tumult of the men
that work iniquity:

3 Who do their tongues with
 malice whet,
and make them cut like swords;
in whose bent bows are arrows
 set,
even sharp and bitter words:

4 That they may at the perfect man
in secret aim their shot:
yea, suddenly they dare at him
to shoot, and fear it not.

5 In ill encourage they themselves,
and close their snares do lay:
together conference they have;
Who shall them see? they say.

6 They have searched out
 iniquities,
a perfect search they keep:
of each of them the inward
 thought,
and heart, is very deep.

7 God shall an arrow shoot at
 them,
and wound them suddenly:

8 so their own tongue shall them
 confound;
all who them see shall fly.

9 And on all men a fear shall fall,
God's works they shall declare;
for they shall wisely notice take
what these his doings are.

10 The righteous in the Lord shall
 joy,
and in him trust he shall;
and they that upright are in heart
shall greatly glory all.

65

1 Praise waits for thee in Zion,
 Lord:
to thee vows paid shall be.

2 O thou that hearer art of prayer,
all flesh shall come to thee.

3 Iniquities, I must confess,
prevail against me do:
but as for our transgressions all,
them purge away shalt thou.

4 Blessed is the man whom thou
 dost choose,
and makest approach to thee,
that he within thy courts, O Lord,
may still a dweller be:
we surely shall be satisfied
with thy abundant grace,
and with the goodness of thy
 house,
even of thy holy place.

5 O God, who our salvation art,
thou, in thy righteousness,
by fearful works unto our prayers
thine answer dost express:
therefore the ends of all the
 earth,
and those upon the sea
who dwell afar, their confidence,
O Lord, will place in thee.

6 Who, being girt with power, sets
 fast
by his great strength the hills.

7 Who noise of seas, noise of their
 waves,
and people's tumult, stills.

8 Those in the utmost parts that
 dwell
are at thy signs afraid:
the outgoings of the morn and
 eve
by thee are joyful made.

9 Earth thou dost visit, watering it;
thou mak'st it rich to grow
with God's full flood; thou corn
provid'st,
when thou prepar'st it so.
10 Its ridges thou dost water well,
its furrows down dost press;
thou mak'st it soft with plenteous
rain,
its springing thou dost bless.

11 So thou the year most liberally
dost with thy goodness crown;
and all thy paths abundantly
on us drop fatness down.
12 They drop upon the pastures
wide,
that in the desert lie;
the little hills on every side
rejoice right pleasantly.

13 With flocks the pastures clothed
be,
the vales with corn are clad;
and now they shout and sing to
thee,
for thou hast made them glad.

66

1 All lands to God, in joyful
sounds,
aloft your voices raise.
2 Sing forth the honour of his
name,
and glorious make his praise.
3 Say unto God, How terrible
in all thy works art thou!
Through thy great power thy foes
to thee
shall be constrained to bow.

4 All on the earth shall worship
thee,
they shall thy praise proclaim
in songs: they shall sing
cheerfully
unto thy holy name.

5 Come, and the works that God
hath wrought
with admiration see:
in dealing with the sons of men
most terrible is he.

6 Into dry land the sea he turned,
and they a passage had;
even marching through the flood
on foot,
there we in him were glad.
7 He ruleth ever by his power;
his eyes the nations see:

O let not the rebellious ones
in pride exalted be.

8 Ye people, bless our God; aloud
the voice speak of his praise;
9 our soul in life who safe
preserves,
our foot from sliding stays.
10 For thou didst prove and try us,
Lord,
as men do silver try;
11 brought'st us into the net, and
mad'st
bands on our loins to lie.

12 Thou hast made men ride o'er
our heads;
through fire and flood we
passed;
but yet into abundance great
thou hast us brought at last.
13 I'll bring burnt-offerings to thy
house;
to thee my vows I'll pay,
14 which my lips uttered, my mouth
spake,
when trouble on me lay.

15 Burnt-sacrifices of fat sheep,
incense of rams I'll bring;
of bullocks and of goats I will
present an offering.
16 All that fear God, come, hear, I'll
tell
what he did for my soul.
17 I with my mouth unto him cried,
my tongue did him extol.

18 If in my heart I sin regard,
the Lord me will not hear:
19 but surely God me heard, and to
my prayer's voice gave ear.
20 O let the Lord, our gracious God,
for ever blessed be,
who turned not my prayer from
him,
nor yet his grace from me.

67 FIRST VERSION

1 Lord, bless and pity us,
shine on us with thy face:
2 that the earth thy way, and
nations all
may know thy saving grace.
3 Let people praise thee, Lord;
let people all thee praise.
4 O let the nations all be glad,
in songs their voices raise:

Thou'lt justly people judge,
on earth rule nations all.

5 Let people praise thee, Lord; let them
praise thee, both great and small.
6 The earth her fruit hath given;
our God shall blessing send.
7 God shall us bless; men shall him fear
unto earth's utmost end.

67 SECOND VERSION

1 O God, be merciful to us,
and bless us, in thy grace;
and do thou cause to shine on us
the brightness of thy face:
2 that so thy way upon the earth
to all men may be known;
also among the nations all
thy saving health be shown.

3 Let people give thee praise, O God;
let people all thee praise.
4 O let the nations joyful be,
in songs their voices raise.
For justly thou shalt people judge,
and nations rule on earth.
5 Let people give thee praise, O God;
let all praise thee with mirth.

6 The earth her increase yielded hath;
God, our God, bless us shall.
7 God shall us bless; and of the earth
the ends shall fear him all.

68

1 Let God arise, and scattered
let all his enemies be;
and let all those that do him hate
before his presence flee.
2 As smoke is driven, so drive thou them;
as fire melts wax away,
before God's grace let wicked men
so perish and decay.

3 But let the righteous all be glad,
exult before God's sight;
yea, let them filled with gladness be,
and joy with all their might.
4 Sing praise to God, prepare his way,
whose name is JAH adored,

who through the desert rideth forth;
exult before the Lord.

5 Because the Lord a father is
unto the fatherless;
God is the widow's judge, within
his place of holiness.
6 God sets the lonely in a home,
and frees the chained from bands;
but those against him who rebel
inhabit parched lands.

7 O God, what time thou didst go forth
before thy people's face;
and when through the great wilderness
thy glorious marching was;
8 then at God's presence shook the earth,
then drops from heaven fell;
this Sinai shook before the Lord,
the God of Israel.

9 O God, thou to thine heritage
didst send a plenteous rain,
whereby thou, when it weary was,
didst it refresh again.
10 Thy congregation then did make
their habitation there:
of thine own goodness for the poor,
O God, thou didst prepare.

11 The Lord himself did give the word,
the word abroad did spread;
great was the company of them
the same who published.
12 Kings of great armies foiled were,
and forced to flee away;
and women, who remained at home,
distributed the prey.

13 Though ye have lain among the pots,
like doves ye shall appear,
whose wings with silver, and with gold
whose feathers covered are.
14 When there the Almighty scattered kings,
like Salmon's snow 'twas white.
15 A hill of God is Bashan's hill,
a towering hill for height.

16 Why do ye frown, ye mountains high,
upon the hill of God?

Here God desires to dwell, the Lord
for aye will make abode.

17 God's chariots twenty thousand are,
thousands on thousands strong;
Sinai is in the holy place,
the Lord is them among.

18 Thou hast, O Lord, most glorious,
ascended up on high;
and in triumph victorious led
captive captivity:
thou hast received gifts for men,
for such as did rebel;
yea, even for them, that God the Lord
in midst of them might dwell.

19 Blessed be the Lord, who is to us
of our salvation God;
who daily with us benefits
us plenteously doth load.

20 He of salvation is the God,
who is our God most strong;
and unto God the Lord from death
the issues do belong.

21 But surely God shall wound the head
of those that are his foes;
the hairy scalp of him that still
on in his trespass goes.

22 The Lord hath said, I will bring back
again from Bashan hill;
yea, from the dark depths of the sea
bring back again I will.

23 That in the blood of enemies
thy foot imbrued may be,
and of thy dogs dipped in the same
the tongues thou mayest see.

24 Thy goings they have seen, O God;
the steps of majesty
of my God, and my mighty King,
within the sanctuary.

25 Before went singers, after them
the players took their way;
in midst of damsels that with skill
did on the timbrels play.

26 Within the congregations great
bless God with one accord;
ye who from Israel's fountain are,
bless ye the mighty Lord.

27 Their ruler, little Benjamin,
and Judah's princes high,
the chiefs of Zabulon, are there,
and chiefs of Naphtali.

28 Thy God commands thy strength; make strong
what thou wrought'st for us, Lord.

29 For thy house at Jerusalem
kings shall thee gifts afford.

30 The beast that dwelleth in the reeds,
the bulls that fiercely look,
with herd of calves, the people all,
do thou, O Lord, rebuke,
till every one submit himself,
and silver pieces bring:
the people that delight in war
disperse, O God and King.

31 Those that be princes great shall then
come from Egyptian lands;
and Ethiopia to God
shall soon stretch out her hands.

32 O all ye kingdoms of the earth,
sing praises to this King;
for he is Lord that ruleth all,
unto him praises sing.

33 To him that rides on heavens of heavens,
which he of old did found;
lo, he sends out his voice, a voice
in might that doth abound.

34 Strength unto God do ye ascribe,
because his majesty
is over Israel, his strength
is in the clouds most high.

35 Dread art thou from thy temple, Lord;
Israel's own God is he,
who gives his people strength and pow'r:
O let God blessed be.

69

1 Save me, O God, because the floods
do so environ me,
that even unto my very soul
come in the waters be.

2 I downward in deep mire do sink,
where standing there is none:
into deep waters I am come,
where floods have o'er me gone.

3 I weary with my crying am,
my throat is also dried;
mine eyes do fail, while for my
    God
I waiting do abide.
4 Those men who do without a
    cause
bear hatred unto me
are more in number than the
    hairs
upon my head that be:

Strong are they who without a
    cause
me hate and would me slay;
and therefore what I never took
I forced am to repay.
5 Lord, thou my folly know'st, my
    sins
not covered are from thee.
6 Let none who wait on thee be
    shamed,
Lord God of hosts, in me.

O thou who God of Israel art,
let none that wait on thee
confounded be at any time,
or made ashamed in me.
7 For I have borne reproach for
    thee;
my face is clothed with shame.
8 To brethren strange, to mother's
    sons
an alien I became.

9 Because the zeal did eat me up
which to thine house I bear;
and the reproaches cast at thee
upon me fallen are.
10 My tears and fasting mourned
    my soul,
and that was made my shame:
11 I put on sackcloth, and to them
a byword I became.

12 The men that in the gate do sit
against me evil spake;
they also that vile drunkards
    were
of me their song did make.
13 But, in a time of favour, Lord,
I make my prayer to thee;
in truth of thy salvation, Lord,
and mercy great, hear me.

14 Deliver me out of the mire,
from sinking do me keep;
free me from those that do me
    hate,
and from the waters deep.
15 Let not the flood o'er me prevail,
whose water overflows;

nor deep me swallow, nor the pit
her mouth upon me close.
16 Hear me, O Lord, because thy
    love
and kindness are most good;
turn unto me, according to
thy mercies' multitude.
17 Nor from thy servant hide thy
    face:
I'm troubled, soon attend.
18 Draw near my soul, and it
    redeem;
me from my foes defend.

19 To thee is my reproach well
    known,
my shame, and my disgrace:
those that mine adversaries be
are all before thy face.
20 My heart is broken by reproach,
I'm full of grief and pain:
for pity and for comforters
I looked, but looked in vain.
21 They also bitter gall did give
unto me for my meat:
they gave me vinegar to drink,
what time my thirst was great.
22 Before them let their table prove
a snare; and do thou make
their welfare and prosperity
a trap themselves to take.
23 Let thou their eyes so darkened
    be,
that sight may them forsake;
and let their loins be made by
    thee
continually to shake.
24 Thine anger pour thou out on
    them,
let thy wrath seize them all;
25 be desolation in their tents,
their homes to ruin fall.

26 Because they persecute the man
whom thou didst smite before;
and mocking tell the grief of
    those
whom thou hast wounded sore.
27 Do thou add sin unto their sin,
and, for their wickedness,
do thou not let them come at all
into thy righteousness.

28 Out of the book of life let them
be razed and blotted quite;
among the righteous and the just
their names do thou not write.
29 But now become exceeding poor
and sorrowful am I:

by thy salvation, O my God,
let me be set on high.

30 The name of God I with a song
most cheerfully will praise;
and I, in giving thanks to him,
his name will highly raise.

31 This to the Lord a sacrifice
more grateful far shall prove
than bullock, ox, or any beast
that hath both horn and hoof.

32 When this the humble men shall
see,
it joy to them shall give:
all ye that after God do seek,
your heart shall ever live.

33 For God the poor hears, and will
not
his prisoners contemn.

34 Let heaven, and earth, and seas
him praise,
and all that move in them.

35 For God will Judah's cities build,
and he will Zion save,
that they may dwell therein, and
it
in sure possession have.

36 And they that are his servants'
seed
inherit shall the same;
and they shall have their
dwelling there
that love his blessed name.

70 FIRST VERSION

1 O God, to save me haste;
with speed, Lord, succour me.

2 Let them that for my soul do seek
shamed and confounded be:

3 turned back be they, and shamed,
that in my hurt delight.
Turned back be they, Ha, ha! that
say,
their shaming to requite.

4 In thee let all be glad,
and joy that seek for thee:
let them who thy salvation love
say still, God praised be.

5 I poor and needy am;
come, Lord, and make no stay:
my help thou and deliverer art;
O Lord, make no delay.

70 SECOND VERSION

1 Make haste, O God, me to
preserve;
with speed, Lord, succour me.

2 Let them that for my soul do seek
shamed and confounded be:
let them be turned back, and
shamed,
that in my hurt delight.

3 Turned back be they, Ha, ha! that
say,
their shaming to requite.

4 O Lord, in thee let all be glad,
and joy that seek for thee:
let them who thy salvation love
say still, God praised be.

5 But I both poor and needy am;
come, Lord, and make no stay:
my help thou and deliverer art;
O Lord, make no delay.

71

1 O Lord, my hope and confidence
are placed alone in thee;
O never let thy servant then
put to confusion be.

2 And let me, in thy righteousness,
from thee deliverance have;
and set me free, incline thine ear
unto me, and me save.

3 Be thou my dwelling-rock, to
which
I ever may resort:
thou gav'st commandment me to
save
thou art my rock and fort.

4 Free me, my God, from wicked
hands,
hands cruel and unjust:

5 for thou, O Lord God, art my
hope,
and from my youth my trust.

6 Thou from my birth didst hold
me up;
thou didst me safely bring
out of my mother's womb; and I
still praise to thee will sing.

7 To many I a wonder am:
thou art my refuge strong.

8 Filled let my mouth be with thy
praise
and honour all day long.

9 O do not cast me off, when me
old age doth overtake;
and in the time of failing strength
do thou not me forsake.

10 For those that are mine enemies
against me speak with hate;
and they together counsel take
that for my soul lay wait.

1 They said, God leaves him; him
    pursue
and take: none will him save.
2 Be thou not far from me, my
    God:
thy speedy help I crave.
3 Confound, consume them, that
    unto
my soul are enemies:
clothed be they with reproach
    and shame
that do my hurt devise.

4 But as for me, with confidence
still hope in thee will I;
and yet with praises more and
    more
I will thee magnify.
5 Thy justice and thy saving help
my mouth abroad shall show,
even all the day; for I thereof
the numbers do not know.

6 And I will constantly go on
in strength of God the Lord;
and thine own righteousness,
    even thine
alone, I will record.
7 For even from my youth, O God,
by thee I have been taught;
and hitherto I have declared
the wonders thou hast wrought.

8 Forsake me not, O God, when I
old and gray-headed grow:
till to this age thy strength, thy
    power
to all to come, I show.
9 And thy most perfect
    righteousness,
O Lord, is very high,
who hast so great things done: O
    God,
who is like unto thee?

10 Thou, Lord, who great
    adversities,
and sore, to me didst show,
shalt me revive, and bring again
from depths of earth below.
11 My greatness and my power thou
    wilt
increase, and far extend:
on every side against all grief
thou wilt me comfort send.

22 Thee, even thy truth, I'll also
    praise,
my God, with psaltery:
thou Holy One of Israel,
with harp I'll sing to thee.

23 My lips shall much rejoice in
    thee,
when I thy praises sound;
my soul, which thou redeemed
    hast,
in joy shall much abound.
24 My tongue thy justice shall
    proclaim,
continuing all day long;
for they confounded are, and
    shamed,
that seek to do me wrong.

72

1 O Lord, thy judgments give the
    king,
his son thy righteousness.
2 With right he shall thy people
    judge,
thy poor with uprightness.
3 The lofty mountains shall bring
    forth
unto the people peace;
likewise the little hills the same
shall do by righteousness.

4 The people's poor ones he shall
    judge,
the needy's children save;
and those shall he in pieces break
who them oppressed have.
5 They shall thee fear, while sun
    and moon
do last, through ages all.
6 Like rain on mown grass he shall
    drop,
or showers on earth that fall.

7 The just shall flourish in his days,
and prosper in his reign:
he shall, while doth the moon
    endure,
abundant peace maintain.
8 His large and great dominion
    shall
from sea to sea extend:
it from the river shall reach forth
unto earth's utmost end.

9 They in the wilderness that dwell
bow down before him must;
and they that are his enemies
shall lick the very dust.
10 The kings of Tarshish, and the
    isles,
to him shall presents bring;
and unto him shall offer gifts
Sheba's and Seba's king.

11 Yea, all the mighty kings on earth
before him down shall fall;
and all the nations of the world
do service to him shall.
12 For he the needy shall preserve,
when he to him doth call;
also the poor, and him that hath
no help of man at all.

13 The poor man and the indigent
in mercy he shall spare;
he shall preserve alive the souls
of those that needy are.
14 Both from deceit and violence
their soul he shall set free;
and in his sight most precious
and dear their blood shall be.

15 Yea, he shall live, and given to
him
shall be of Sheba's gold:
for him still shall they pray, and
he
all day shall be extolled.
16 Of corn an handful in the earth
on tops of mountains high,
with prosperous fruit shall shake,
like trees
on Lebanon that be.

The city shall be flourishing,
her citizens abound
in number shall, like to the grass
that grows upon the ground.
17 His name for ever shall endure;
last like the sun it shall:
men shall be blessed in him, and
blessed
all nations shall him call.

18 Now blessed be the Lord our
God,
the God of Israel,
for he alone doth wondrous
works,
in glory that excel.
19 And blessed be his glorious name
to all eternity:
the whole earth let his glory fill.
Amen, so let it be.

73

1 Yea, God is good to Israel,
to each pure-hearted one.
2 But as for me, my steps nigh
slipped,
my feet were almost gone.
3 For I was envious, and grudged
the foolish folk to see,
when I perceived wicked men
enjoy prosperity.

4 For still their strength continues
firm;
their death of bands is free.
5 Not troubled they like other men
nor plagued, as others be.
6 Therefore their pride, like to a
chain,
them compasseth about:
and, as a garment, violence
doth cover them throughout.

7 Their eyes stand out with fat;
they have
more than their hearts could
seek;
8 they mock, and loftily of wrong
and of oppression speak.
9 They set their mouth even in the
heavens
in proud and haughty talk;
their boastful and reviling tongue
upon the earth doth walk.

10 His people oftentimes for this
look back, and turn about;
since waters of so full a cup
to these are poured out.
11 And thus they say, How can it be
that God these things doth know
Or, Can there in the Highest be
knowledge of things below?

12 Lo these the wicked are, and yet
they prosper at their will
in worldly things; they do
increase
in wealth and riches still.
13 I verily have done in vain
my heart to purify;
to no effect in innocence
my hands made clean have I.

14 For daily, and all day throughout,
great plagues I suffered have;
yea, every morning I anew
did chastisement receive.
15 If in this manner foolishly
to speak I would intend,
the generation of thy sons,
behold, I should offend.

16 But when I thought this thing to
know,
it was too hard for me,
17 till to God's sanctuary I went;
then I their end did see.
18 Upon a slippery place them set
assuredly thou hast;
and down into destruction thou
dost suddenly them cast.

19 How in a moment suddenly
to ruin brought are they!

With fearful terrors utterly
they are consumed away.
20 Even like unto a dream, when
one
from sleeping doth arise;
so thou, O Lord, when thou
awak'st
their image shalt despise.

21 Thus I was grieved in my heart,
and in my reins oppressed.
22 So rude was I, and ignorant,
and in thy sight a beast.
23 And yet, O Lord, I do abide
continually with thee:
thou dost me take by my right
hand,
and still upholdest me.

24 Thou with thy counsel, while I
live,
wilt me conduct and guide;
and to thy glory afterward
receive me to abide.
25 Whom have I in the heavens
high
but thee, O Lord, alone?
And in the earth whom I desire
besides thee there is none.

26 My flesh and heart do faint and
fail;
but God doth fail me never;
for of my heart God is the
strength;
my portion sure for ever.
27 For, lo, they that are far from thee
for ever perish shall;
them that forsake thee wantonly
thou hast destroyed all.

28 But surely it is good for me
that I draw near to God;
in God I trust that all thy works
I may declare abroad.

74 FIRST VERSION

1 O God, why hast thou cast us off?
is it for evermore?
Against thy pasture-sheep why
doth
thine anger smoke so sore?
2 The congregation of thy choice
in thy remembrance hold,
the people who have purchased
been
by thee in days of old;

The tribe of thine inheritance,
which thou redeemed hast,
this Zion hill, wherein thou hadst
thy dwelling in the past.

3 To these long desolations, Lord,
thy feet lift, tarry not,
for all the ill thy foes within
thy holy place have wrought.

4 In midst of thine own meeting-
place
thine enemies do roar:
their ensigns they set up for signs
of triumph thee before.
5 It seemed as if one lifted up
his axe thick trees upon —
6 and now with hammer and with
axe
they break its carvings down.

7 They fired have thy holy place,
and have defiled the same,
by casting down unto the ground
the place where dwelt thy name.
8 Thus said they in their hearts, Let
us
destroy them out of hand:
they burnt up all the synagogues
of God within the land.

9 Our signs we do not now behold;
there is not us among
a prophet more, nor any one
that knows the time how long.
10 How long then shall the foe, O
God,
reproachfully exclaim?
And shall the adversary thus
always blaspheme thy name?

11 Thy hand, even thy right hand of
might,
to stretch forth why delay?
O from thy bosom pluck it out,
and sweep them quite away.
12 For certainly God is my king,
even from the times of old,
working in midst of all the earth
salvation manifold.

13 The sea, by thy great power, to
part
asunder thou didst make;
and thou the dragons' heads, O
Lord,
didst in the waters break.
14 The heads of the leviathan
thou brakest, and didst give
him to be meat unto the folk
that in the desert live.

15 Thou clav'st the fountain and the
flood;
didst dry the rivers great;
16 both day and night are thine;
thou didst
the light and sun create.

17 By thee the borders of the earth
were settled everywhere:
the summer and the winter both
by thee created were.
18 How that the foe hath thee
reproached,
O keep it in record;
and that the foolish people have
blasphemed thy name, O Lord.
19 Unto the multitude do not
thy turtle's soul deliver:
the congregation of thy poor
do not forget for ever.
20 Unto thy covenant have respect;
for earth's dark places be
full of the habitations dread
of horrid cruelty.
21 O let not those that be oppressed
return again with shame:
let those that poor and needy are
give praise unto thy name.
22 Do thou, O God, arise and plead
the cause that is thine own:
remember how thou art
reproached
still by the foolish one.
23 Forget not thou the voice of them
that foes are unto thee;
the tumult of thine enemies
ascends continually.

74 SECOND VERSION

1 O God, why hast thou cast us off?
why doth for ever smoke
thy wrath against thy chosen race,
sheep of thy flock?
2 Thy church, by thee redeemed of
old,
in love remember still;
the tribe of thy inheritance,
this Zion hill.
3 Here thou hast dwelt; lift up thy
feet,
to these sad ruins haste,
thy holy place with wicked hands
by foes laid waste.
4 Thy enemies in triumph shout,
where saints were wont to pray;
their ensigns on thy temple's
walls
for signs display.
5 It seemed as if one cut down
trees,
but now the carved work falls;
with axes and with hammers
now
they break the walls.

6 They have thy temple set on fire,
in dust they have defiled
thy holy place, where dwelt thy
name,
thy house despoiled.
7 They, to destroy us all at once,
did in their hearts conspire;
through all the land God's
synagogues
they've burnt with fire.
8 Our signs we see not; there is
now
no prophet us among;
nor is there any one who knows
the time how long.
9 O Lord, how long shall those
blaspheme
thy name who thee withstand?
Why hide thyself? Make bare thy
hand,
even thy right hand.
10 Because God is my King of old,
salvation worketh he
through all the earth, and by his
strength
divides the sea.
11 Thou broken hast the dragons'
heads,
and as their meat didst give
Leviathan to those who did
in deserts live.
12 Fountain and flood thou didst
divide,
mad'st mighty rivers dry;
the day is thine, the night is
thine,
the sun and sky.
13 Thou hast established by decree
all borders of the earth;
to summer and to winter thou
hast given birth.
14 O Lord, do thou this keep in
mind,
how enemies defame,
and how the foolish people have
blasphemed thy name.
15 Thy turtle dove deliver not
to crowds which it beset,
and thy poor flock for evermore
do not forget.
16 Unto thy covenant have respect,
for everywhere we see
the earth's dark habitations filled
with cruelty.
17 O let not those that are oppressed
return again with shame;

but let the poor and needy ones
still praise thy name.

18 Arise, O God, plead thine own
    cause;
keep thou in memory
how every day the foolish man
reproacheth thee.

19 Of them that up against thee rise
the tumult ever grows;
forget not thou the voice of them
that are thy foes.

75

1 To thee, O God, do we give
    thanks,
we do give thanks to thee;
because thy wondrous works
    declare
thy great name near to be.

2 I shall the time appointed take,
the moment fixed upon;
and I shall judgment uprightly
render to every one.

3 Dissolved is the land, with all
that in the same do dwell;
but I the pillars thereof do
bear up, and stablish well.

4 I to the foolish people said,
Do not deal foolishly;
and unto those that wicked are,
lift not your horn on high.

5 Lift not your horn on high, nor
    speak

6 with stubborn neck. But know
that not from east, nor west, nor
    south,
doth exaltation flow.

7 But God is judge; he puts down
    one,
and sets another up.

8 For in the hand of God most high
of red wine is a cup:

'Tis full of mixture, he pours
    forth,
and makes the wicked all
wring out the bitter dregs
    thereof;
yea, and they drink them shall.

9 But I for ever will declare,
I Jacob's God will praise.

10 All horns of wicked men I'll
    break
but just men's horns will raise.

76

1 In Judah God is known, his name
is great in Israel;

2 in Salem is his holy place,
in Zion he doth dwell.

3 There arrows of the bow he
    brake,
the shield, the sword, the war.

4 More glorious thou than hills of
    prey,
more excellent by far.

5 Those that were stout of heart are
    spoiled,
they slept their sleep outright;
and none of those their hands
    did find,
that were the men of might.

6 When thy rebuke, O Jacob's God,
had forth against them passed,
their horses and their chariots
    were
into a dead sleep cast.

7 Thou, even thou, art to be feared,
and what man then is he
that may stand up before thy
    sight,
if once thou angry be?

8 From heaven thou madest
    judgment heard;
the earth was still with fear,

9 when God to judgment rose, to
    save
all meek on earth that were.

10 Surely the very wrath of man
unto thy praise redounds:
thou to the remnant of his wrath
wilt set restraining bounds.

11 Vow to the Lord your God, and
    pay:
all ye that near him be,
bring gifts and presents unto
    him;
for to be feared is he.

12 For he the spirit shall cut off
of those that princes be:
unto the kings that are on earth
most terrible is he.

77

1 My voice I will lift up to God,
I'll cry to God nor spare;
my voice I will lift up to God,
and he will hear my prayer.

2 In day of woe I sought the Lord;
by night in ceaseless grief

my hand was stretched out to
   him;
my soul refused relief.

3   I to remembrance God do call,
   and then I sigh and mourn;
   I with myself commune, my heart
   with grief is overborne.

4   Thou dost deny mine eyelids
      sleep,
   withhold the rest I seek;
   my trouble is so great that I
   unable am to speak.

5   I thought on days and years of
      old,
   recalled my song by night;

6   I with my heart communed, my
      soul
   made earnest search for light.

7   For ever will the Lord cast off,
   and gracious be no more?

8   For ever is his mercy gone?
   Fails his word evermore?

9   Is't so that to be gracious
   the Lord forgotten hath;
   and that his tender mercies he
   hath shut up in his wrath?

10   Then said I, This my weakness is;
   but call to mind will I
   the years of the right hand of him
   who is the Lord most high.

11   Yea, I remember will the works
   performed by the Lord:
   the wonders done of old by thee
   I surely will record.

12   Upon thy doings I will muse,
   on thy works meditate;

13   most holy is thy way, O God:
   what God like thee is great?

14   Thou art the God that wonders
      dost
   by thy right hand most strong:
   thy mighty power thou hast
      declared
   the nations all among.

15   To thine own people with thine
      arm
   thou didst redemption bring;
   to Jacob's sons, and to the tribes
   of Joseph that do spring.

16   The waters did thee see, O God,
   the waters did thee see;
   the depths thereof were troubled
      all,
   for fear aside did flee.

17   The clouds in water forth were
      poured,

sound loudly did the sky;
and swiftly through the world
      abroad
thine arrows fierce did fly.

18   Thy thunder's voice along the
      heaven
   a mighty noise did make;
   thy lightnings lighten did the
      world,
   earth trembled and did shake.

19   Thy way is in the sea, and in
   the waters great thy path;
   thy footsteps hidden are, O Lord;
   none knowledge thereof hath.

20   Thy people thou didst safely lead,
   like to a flock of sheep;
   by Moses' hand and Aaron's thou
   didst them conduct and keep.

78

1   Attend, my people, to my law;
   thereto give thou an ear;
   the words that from my mouth
      proceed
   attentively do hear.

2   My mouth shall speak a parable,
   and sayings dark of old;

3   the same which we have heard
      and known,
   and us our fathers told.

4   We also will them not conceal
   from their posterity;
   but to the race that is to come
   declare them faithfully.
   The praises of the Lord our God,
   and his almighty strength,
   the wondrous works that he hath
      done,
   we will show forth at length.

5   His testimony and his law
   in Israel he did place,
   and charged our fathers it to
      show
   to their succeeding race;

6   that so that race which was to
      come
   might well them learn and
      know;
   and sons unborn, who should
      arise,
   might to their sons them show:

7   That they might set their hope in
      God,
   and suffer not to fall
   his mighty works out of their
      mind,

8 but keep his precepts all:
and might not, like their fathers, be
a stiff rebellious race;
a race not right in heart; with God
whose spirit faithless was.

9 The sons of Ephraim nor bows
nor other arms did lack;
yet, when the day of battle came,
faint-hearted they turned back.

10 They brake God's covenant, and refused
in his commands to go;

11 his works and wonders they forgot,
which he to them did show.

12 Things marvellous he brought to pass;
their fathers them beheld
within the land of Egypt done,
yea, even in Zoan's field.

13 The sea asunder he did cleave,
he led them through the deep;
and made the waters stand on high,
as though they were an heap.

14 With cloud by day, with light of fire
all night, he did them guide.

15 He in the desert clave the rocks,
and drink as floods supplied.

16 He from the rock brought streams, like floods
made waters down to run;

17 yet sinned they still, in desert they
provoked the Highest One.

18 For in their heart they tempted God,
and, speaking with mistrust,
they greedily did meat require
to satisfy their lust.

19 Against the Lord himself they spake,
and, murmuring, said thus,
A table in the wilderness
can God prepare for us?

20 Behold, he smote the rock, and streams
forth gushed and waters wide:
but can he give his people bread,
and flesh for them provide?

21 The Lord did hear, and waxed wroth;
so kindled was a flame

'gainst Jacob, and 'gainst Israel
up indignation came.

22 For they believed not God, nor trust
in his salvation had;

23 though clouds above he did command,
and heaven's doors open made,

24 and manna rained on them, and gave
them corn of heaven to eat.

25 Man angels' food did eat; to them
he to the full sent meat.

26 And in the heaven he did cause
an eastern wind to blow;
and by his power he did direct
the southern wind to go.

27 Then flesh as thick as dust he made
to rain down them among;
and feathered fowls, like to the sand
which lies the shore along.

28 At his command amidst their camp
these showers of flesh down fell,
all round about the tabernacles
and tents where they did dwell.

29 So they did eat abundantly,
and had of meat their fill;
for he did give to them what was
their own desire and will.

30 They from their lust had not estranged
their heart and their desire;
but while the meat was in their mouths,
which they did so require,

31 God's wrath upon them came, and slew
the fattest of them all;
so that the choice of Israel,
o'erthrown by death, did fall.

32 Yet after all the Lord had done
they still went on in sin;
nor did believe, although his works
so wonderful had been.

33 Wherefore their days in vanity
he did consume and waste;
and by his wrath their wretched years
away in grief did haste.

34 But when he slew them, then they did

to seek him show desire;
yea, they returned, and after God
right early did enquire.
35 And thus that God had been
their Rock
they did remember then;
even that the high almighty God
had their Redeemer been.

36 Yet with their mouth they
flattered him,
and with their tongues they lied;
37 their heart not steadfast was;
they from
his covenant turned aside.

38 But, full of pity, he forgave
their sin, them did not slay,
nor stirred up all his wrath, but
oft
his anger turned away.

39 For that they were but fading
flesh
to mind he did recall;
a wind that passeth soon away,
nor doth return at all.

40 How often did they him provoke
within the wilderness!
And in the desert did him grieve
with their rebelliousness!

41 Yea, turning back, they tempted
God,
and limits they did place
upon the High and Holy One,
the God of Israel's race.

42 They did not call to mind his
power,
nor yet the day when he
delivered them out of the hand
of their fierce enemy;

43 When wonders he in Egypt
wrought,
and signs in Zoan's field;
44 their rivers turned he into blood,
their streams no drink did yield.

45 He sent the fly which them
devoured,
the frog which did them spoil;
46 He gave the worm their increase
all,
the locust all their toil.

47 Their vines with hail, their
sycamores
he with the frost did blast;
48 hail on their beasts, hot
thunderbolts
upon their flocks, he cast.

49 Fierce anger he let loose on them,
and indignation strong,

distress and trouble, angels sent
of evil them among.

50 He for his wrath made way; their
soul
from death he did not save;
but over to the pestilence
their life in judgment gave.

51 In Egypt he the first-born all
did smite down everywhere;
among the tents of Ham, even
those
chief of their strength that were.

52 But his own people, like to sheep,
thence to go forth he made;
and he, amidst the wilderness,
them, as a flock, did lead.

53 And he in safety led them on,
so that they did not fear;
whereas their enemies by the sea
quite overwhelmed were.

54 Unto his holy border then
the Lord his people led,
even to the mount which his
right hand
for them had purchased.

55 The nations which in Canaan
dwelt,
by his almighty hand
before his people's face he drove
out of their native land;

Which for inheritance to them
by line he did divide,
and made the tribes of Israel
within their tents abide.

56 Yet God most high they did
provoke,
and him they tempted still;
his testimonies to observe
did not incline their will;

57 But like their fathers turned back,
and dealt unfaithfully:
aside they turned, like a bow
that shoots deceitfully.

58 For they to anger did provoke
him with their places high;
and with their graven images
moved him to jealousy.

59 When God heard this he waxed
wroth,
and much loathed Israel then:
60 so Shiloh's tent he left, the tent
which he had pitched with men.

61 And he his strength delivered
into captivity;
he left his glory in the hand
of his proud enemy.

62 His people also he gave o'er
unto the sword's fierce rage:
and hotly did his anger burn
against his heritage.
63 The fire consumed their choice
young men;
their maids no marriage had;
64 and when their priests fell by the
sword,
their wives no mourning made.

65 But then the Lord arose, as one
who from his sleep awakes;
and like a strong man who from
wine
a shout of triumph makes.
66 Upon his enemies' backs he
made
his heavy stroke to fall;
to a perpetual reproach
and shame he put them all.

67 Moreover, he the tabernacle
of Joseph did refuse;
the mighty tribe of Ephraim
he would in no wise choose:
68 but he the tribe of Judah chose
to be the rest above;
and of mount Zion he made
choice,
which he so much did love.

69 He also like unto the heights
did build his sanctuary,
like to the earth which he did
found
to perpetuity.
70 Of David, that his servant was,
he also choice did make,
and even from the folds of sheep
was pleased him to take:

71 From waiting on the ewes with
young,
he brought him forth to feed
Israel, his inheritance,
his people, Jacob's seed.
72 And so in his integrity
of heart he did them feed;
and with a wise and skilful hand
them prudently did lead.

79

1 O God, into thy heritage
the heathen entrance made;
thy holy place they have defiled;
on heaps Jerusalem laid.
2 Thy servants' bodies they have
cast
to fowls of heaven for meat;

and of thy saints have thrown the
flesh
to beasts of earth to eat.
3 Their blood about Jerusalem
like water they have shed;
and there was none to bury them
when they were slain and dead.
4 Unto our neighbours a reproach
most base become are we;
a scorn and laughing-stock to
those
that round about us be.

5 How long, Lord, shall thine anger
last?
Wilt thou still keep the same?
And shall thy fervent jealousy
burn like unto a flame?
6 Thy fury on the heathen pour
that have thee never known,
and on those kingdoms which thy
name
have never called upon.

7 For these are they who have
devoured
thy servant Jacob's race;
and they all waste and desolate
have made his dwelling-place.
8 Against us count not former sins,
thy tender mercies show;
let them prevent us speedily:
we are brought very low.

9 For thy name's glory help us,
Lord,
who hast our Saviour been:
deliver us; for thy name's sake
O purge away our sin.
10 Why say the heathen, Where's
their God?
Let him to them be known,
when those who shed thy
servants' blood
are in our sight o'erthrown.

11 O let the prisoner's sighs ascend
before thy sight on high;
preserve thou in thy mighty
power
those that are doomed to die.
12 And to our neighbours' bosom let
it sevenfold rendered be,
even the reproach wherewith
they have
O Lord, reproached thee.

13 So we, thy folk, and pasture-
sheep,
shall give thee thanks always;
and unto generations all
we will show forth thy praise.

80

1 Hear, Israel's Shepherd! like a flock
  thou that dost Joseph guide;
shine forth, O thou that dost between
  the cherubim abide.
2 In Ephraim's, and Benjamin's, and in Manasseh's sight,
do thou for our salvation come;
  stir up thy strength and might.
3 Turn us again, O Lord our God, and upon us vouchsafe
to make thy countenance to shine,
  and so we shall be safe.
4 O Lord of hosts, almighty God, how long shall kindled be
thy wrath against the prayer made
  by thine own folk to thee?
5 Thou tears of sorrow givest them instead of bread to eat;
yea, tears instead of drink thou giv'st
  to them in measure great.
6 Thou makest us a strife unto our neighbours round about;
our enemies among themselves
  at us do laugh and flout.
7 Turn us again, O God of hosts, and upon us vouchsafe
to make thy countenance to shine,
  and so we shall be safe.
8 A vine from Egypt thou didst bring
  by thine outstretched hand:
and thou didst cast the heathen out
  to plant it in their land.
9 A place thou didst prepare for it, where it might grow and stand;
thou madest it deep root to take,
  and cover all the land.
10 The mountains veiled were with its shade,
  as with a covering;
the goodly cedars with the boughs
  which out of it did spring.
11 Upon the one hand to the sea her boughs she forth did send;
upon the other to the flood
  her branches did extend.
12 Why hast thou then thus broken down

and torn her hedge away;
so that all passers-by do pluck,
and make of her a prey?
13 The boar that from the forest comes
  treads down and wastes it still;
the wild beast also of the field
  devours it at his will.
14 O God of hosts, we thee beseech, return now unto thine;
look down from heaven in love, behold,
  and visit this thy vine:
15 This vine tree, which thine own right hand
  hath planted us among;
and that same branch, which for thyself
  thou hast made to be strong.
16 Burnt up it is with flaming fire, 'tis utterly cut down;
they quickly to destruction go
  when once thy face doth frown.
17 O let thy hand be still upon the man of thy right hand,
the Son of man, whom for thyself
  thou madest strong to stand.
18 So henceforth we will not go back, nor turn from thee at all:
O do thou quicken us, and we
  upon thy name will call.
19 Turn us again, Lord God of hosts, and upon us vouchsafe
to make thy countenance to shine,
  and so we shall be safe.

81

1 Sing loud to God our strength; with joy
  to Jacob's God do sing.
2 Take up a psalm, the pleasant harp,
  timbrel and psaltery bring.
3 Blow trumpets at new moon, and when
  our feast appointed is:
4 a charge to Israel, and a law of Jacob's God, was this.
5 To Joseph this an ordinance he made, when Egypt's land
he travelled through, where speech I heard
  I did not understand.
6 His shoulder I from burdens took, his hands from pots did free.
7 Thou didst in trouble on me call, and I delivered thee:

In secret place of thunder I
to thee did answer make;
and at the streams of Meribah
of thee a proof did take.
8 O thou, my people, give an ear,
I'll testify to thee;
to thee, O Israel, if thou wilt
but hearken unto me.

9 In midst of thee there shall not be
any strange god at all;
nor unto any god unknown
thou bowing down shalt fall.
10 I am the Lord thy God, who did
from Egypt land thee guide;
I'll fill thy mouth abundantly,
do thou it open wide.

11 My people would not hear my
voice,
Israel my counsel spurned;
12 I gave them up to their hard
hearts,
to their own ways they turned.
13 O that my people had me heard,
Israel my ways had chose!
14 I had their enemies soon
subdued,
my hand turned on their foes.

15 The haters of the Lord to him
submission should have feigned;
but as for them, their time should
have
for evermore remained.
16 He should have also fed them
with
the finest of the wheat;
of honey from the rock thy fill
I should have made thee eat.

82

1 In gods' assembly God doth
judge;
he judgeth gods among.
2 How long, accepting persons vile,
will ye give judgment wrong?
3 The fatherless and needy judge;
the poor and suffering right;
4 the destitute and needy free;
them rid of ill men's might.

5 They know not, nor will
understand,
in darkness they walk on:
all the foundations of the earth
out of their course have gone.
6 I said that ye are gods, and are
sons of the Highest all:
7 but ye shall die like men, and as
one of the princes fall.

8 O God, do thou raise up thyself,
the earth to judgment call:
for thou, as thine inheritance,
shalt take the nations all.

83

1 Keep not, O God, we thee
entreat,
O keep not silence now:
no longer hold thy peace, O God,
at rest no more be thou.
2 For, lo, thine enemies a noise
tumultuously have made;
and they that haters are of thee
have lifted up the head.

3 Against thy chosen people they
do crafty counsel take;
and they against thy hidden ones
do consultations make.
4 Come, let us cut them off, said
they,
no nation let them be;
nor let the name of Israel
be held in memory.

5 For with joint heart they plot, in
league
against thee they combine:
6 the tents of Edom, Ishmaelites,
Moab's and Hagar's line;
7 Gebal, and Ammon, Amalek,
Philistines, those of Tyre,
8 and Assur joined with them; to
help
Lot's children they conspire.

9 Do to them as to Midian,
Jabin at Kison strand,
10 and Sis'ra, which at En-dor fell,
as dung to fat the land.
11 Like Oreb and like Zeeb make
their noble men to fall;
to Zeba and Zalmunna like,
make thou their princes all;

12 Who said, For our inheritance
God's dwellings let us take;
13 like stubble whirled before the
blast,
my God, do thou them make.
14 As fire consumes the wood, as
flame
doth mountains set on fire,
15 chase and affright them with the
storm
and tempest of thine ire.

16 Their faces fill with shame, O
Lord,
that they may seek thy name.

17   Let them confounded be and
vexed,
and perish in their shame:
18   that men may know, that thou, to
whom
alone doth appertain
the name Jehovah, dost most
high
o'er all the earth remain

84

1   How lovely is thy dwelling-place,
O Lord of hosts, to me!
The tabernacles of thy grace
how pleasant, Lord, they be!
2   My thirsty soul longs veh'mently,
yea faints, thy courts to see;
my very heart and flesh cry out,
O living God, for thee.

3   Behold, the sparrow findeth out
an house wherein to rest;
the swallow also for herself
provided hath a nest;
even thine own altars, where she
safe
her young ones forth may bring,
O thou almighty Lord of hosts,
who art my God and King.

4   Blest are they in thy house that
dwell,
they ever give thee praise.
5   Blest is the man whose strength
thou art,
in whose heart are thy ways:
6   who as they pass through Baca's
vale
make it a place of springs;
also the rain that falleth down
rich blessing to it brings.

7   So they from strength unwearied
go
still forward unto strength,
until in Zion they appear
before the Lord at length.
8   Lord God of hosts, my prayer
hear;
O Jacob's God, give ear.
9   See, God our shield, look on the
face
of thine anointed dear.

10   For in thy courts one day excels
a thousand; rather in
my God's house will I keep a
door,
than dwell in tents of sin.
11   For God the Lord's a sun and
shield:

he'll grace and glory give;
and will withhold no good from
them
that uprightly do live.

12   O thou that art the Lord of hosts,
that man is truly blest,
who with assured confidence
on thee alone doth rest.

85   FIRST VERSION

1   Thou hast been favourable, Lord,
to thy beloved land;
Jacob's captivity thou hast
recalled with mighty hand.
2   Thou pardoned thy people hast
all their iniquities;
thou all their trespasses and sins
hast covered from thine eyes.

3   Thou hast thine anger all
withdrawn,
turned from thy furiousness;
4   O God of our salvation, turn,
and cause thy wrath to cease.
5   Shall thy displeasure thus endure
against us without end?
Wilt thou to generations all
thine anger still extend?

6   That in thee may thy people joy,
wilt thou not us revive?
7   Show us thy mercy, Lord, to us
do thy salvation give.
8   I'll hear what God the Lord will
speak:
to his folk he'll speak peace,
and to his saints; but let them not
return to foolishness.

9   Surely to them that fear the Lord
is his salvation near;
that glory in our land again
a dweller may appear.
10   Truth meets with mercy,
righteousness
and peace kiss mutually:
11   truth springs from earth, and
righteousness
looks down from heaven high.

12   Yea, what is good the Lord shall
give;
our land shall yield increase:
13   justice, to set us in his steps,
shall go before his face.

PSALMS

85 SECOND VERSION

1 Lord, thine heart in love hath
        yearned
   on thy lost and fallen land;
   Israel's race is homeward turned,
   thou hast freed thy captive band:
2 thou hast borne thy people's sin,
   covered all their deeds of ill;
   all thy wrath is gathered in,
   and thy burning anger still.

3 Turn us, stay us, now once more,
   God of all our health and peace;
   let thy cloud of wrath fleet o'er,
   from thine own thy fury cease.
4 Wilt thou ne'er the storm assuage
   on the realm of thy desire,
   lengthening out from age to age
   thy consuming jealous ire?

5 Wilt thou not in mercy turn?
   Turn, and be our life again,
   that thy people's heart may burn
   with the gladness of thy reign.
6 Show us now thy tender love;
   thy salvation, Lord, impart;
   I the voice divine would prove,
   listening in my silent heart:

7 Listening what the Lord will
        say —
   'Peace' to all that own his will:
   to his saints that love his way,
   'Peace', and 'turn no more to ill'.
8 Ye that fear him, nigh at hand
   now his saving health ye find,
   that the glory in our land,
   as of old, may dwell enshrined.

9 Mercy now and justice meet,
   peace and truth for aye embrace;
   truth from earth is springing
        sweet,
   justice looks from her high place.
10 Nor will God his goodness stay,
   nor our land her bounteous store:
   marking out her Maker's way,
   Righteousness shall go before.

86

1 O Lord, do thou bow down thine
        ear,
   and hear me graciously;
   because I sore afflicted am,
   and am in poverty.
2 Because I'm holy, let my soul
   by thee preserved be:
   O thou, my God, thy servant
        save,
   that puts his trust in thee.

3 Since unto thee all day I cry,
   be merciful to me.
4 Rejoice thy servant's soul; for,
        Lord,
   I lift my soul to thee.
5 For thou art very gracious, Lord,
   and ready to forgive;
   and rich in mercy, all that call
   upon thee to relieve.

6 Hear, Lord, my prayer; unto the
        voice
   of my request attend:
7 in troublous times I'll call on
        thee,
   for thou wilt answer send.
8 Lord, there is none among the
        gods
   that may compare with thee;
   and to the works which thou hast
        done
   no works can likened be.

9 All nations whom thou mad'st
        shall come
   and worship reverently
   before thy face; and they, O Lord,
   thy name shall glorify.
10 Because thou art exceeding great,
   and works by thee are done
   which are to be admired; and
        thou
   art God thyself alone.

11 Teach me thy way, and in thy
        truth,
   O Lord, then walk will I;
   unite my heart, that I thy name
   may fear continually.
12 O Lord my God, with all my
        heart
   to thee I will give praise;
   and I the glory will ascribe
   unto thy name always:

13 Because thy mercy toward me
   in greatness doth excel;
   and thou delivered hast my soul
   out from the lowest hell.
14 O God, the proud against me
        rise,
   the violent have met,
   who for my soul have sought;
        and thee
   before them have not set.

15 But thou, Lord, art a gracious
        God,
   and most compassionate;
   long-suffering, and slow to wrath,
   in truth and mercy great.

16 O turn to me thy countenance,
and mercy on me have;
thy servant strengthen, and the son
of thine own handmaid save.

17 Show me a sign for good, that they
who do me hate may see,
and be ashamed: because thou, Lord,
didst help and comfort me.

87

1 Upon the hills of holiness
he his foundation sets.
2 God, more than Jacob's dwellings all,
delights in Zion's gates.
3 Things glorious are said of thee,
thou city of the Lord.
4 Rahab and Babel I as those
that know me will record:

Lo, Tyrus, and with it the land
where dwells the Philistine,
and likewise Ethiopia;
this one was born therein.
5 Of Zion shall be said, This man
and that man born was there;
and he that is the Lord most high
himself shall stablish her.

6 When God the people writes,
he'll count
that this man born was there.
7 The singers as the players say,
my well-springs in thee are.

88

1 Lord God, my Saviour, day and night
before thee cried have I.
2 Before thee let my prayer come;
give ear unto my cry.
3 For troubles great do fill my soul;
my life draws nigh the grave.
4 I'm counted with those that go down
to death, and no strength have.

5 Free midst the dead, like to the slain
that in the grave do lie;
cut off from thy hand, whom no more
thou hast in memory.
6 Thou hast me laid in lowest pit,
in deeps and darksome caves;

7 thy wrath lies hard on me, thou hast
me pressed with all thy waves.

8 Thou hast put far from me my friends,
made me their scorn to know;
and I am so shut up that I
no longer forth can go.
9 By reason of my deep distress,
mine eye doth waste away;
to thee, Lord, I call, and stretch
my hands out every day.

10 Wilt thou show wonders to the dead?
shall they rise and thee bless?
11 Shall in the grave thy love be told?
in death thy faithfulness?
12 Shall thy great wonders in the dark,
or shall thy righteousness
be known to any in the land
of deep forgetfulness?

13 But, Lord, to thee I cried; my prayer
at morn shall come to thee.
14 Why, Lord, dost thou cast off my soul,
and hide thy face from me?
15 Distressed am I, and from my youth
I ready am to die;
thy terrors I have borne, and am
distracted fearfully.

16 By thy fierce wrath I'm overwhelmed,
cut off by dread of thee;
17 like floods thy terrors round me close,
all day they compass me.
18 My friends thou hast put far from me,
and him that did me love;
and those that mine acquaintance were
to darkness didst remove.

89

1 God's mercies I will ever sing;
and with my mouth I shall
thy faithfulness make to be known
to generations all.
2 For mercy shall be built, said I,
for ever to endure;

thy faithfulness even in the
heavens
thou wilt establish sure.

3 I with my chosen one have made
a covenant graciously;
and to my servant whom I loved,
to David sworn have I;

4 that I thy seed establish shall
for ever to remain,
and will to generations all
thy throne build and maintain.

5 The praises of thy wonders, Lord,
the heavens shall express;
the assembly of the holy ones
shall praise thy faithfulness.

6 For who in heaven with the Lord
may once himself compare?
Who is like God among the sons
of those that mighty are?

7 Great fear in meeting of the
saints
is due unto the Lord;
and he above all round him
should
with reverence be adored.

8 O Lord, the God of hosts, who
can
to thee compared be?
The mighty One, the Lord, whose
truth
doth round encompass thee.

9 Even in the swelling of the sea
thou over it dost reign;
and when the waves thereof do
rise,
thou stillest them again.

10 Rahab in pieces thou didst break,
like one that slaughtered is;
and with thy mighty arm thou
hast
dispersed thine enemies.

11 The heavens are thine, thou for
thine own
the earth dost also take;
the world, and fulness of the
same,
thou by thy power didst make.

12 The north and south from thee
alone
their first beginning had;
both Tabor mount and Hermon
hill
shall in thy name be glad.

13 Thou hast an arm that's full of
power:
thy hand is great in might;

and thy right hand exceedingly
exalted is in height.

14 Justice and judgment of thy
throne
are made the dwelling-place;
mercy, accompanied with truth,
shall go before thy face.

15 O greatly blessed the people are
the joyful sound that know;
in brightness of thy face, O Lord,
they ever on shall go.

16 They in thy name shall all the
day
rejoice exceedingly;
and in thy righteousness shall
they
exalted be on high.

17 Because the glory of their
strength
doth only stand in thee;
and in thy favour shall our horn
and power exalted be.

18 For to the Lord belongs our
shield,
that doth us safety bring;
and unto Israel's Holy One
the man that is our king.

19 In vision to thy holy one
thou saidst, I help upon
a strong one laid; out of the folk
I raised a chosen one;

20 even David, I have found him
out
a servant unto me;
and with my holy oil my King
anointed him to be.

21 With whom my hand shall
stablished be;
mine arm shall make him strong.

22 From him the foe shall not exact,
nor son of mischief wrong.

23 I will beat down before his face
all his malicious foes;
I will them greatly plague who
do
with hatred him oppose.

24 My mercy and my faithfulness
with him yet still shall be;
and in my name his horn and
power
men shall exalted see.

25 His hand of might shall reach
afar,
I'll set it in the sea;
and his right hand established
shall in the rivers be.

26 Thou art my Father and my God,
he unto me shall cry;
the rock of my salvation thou
on whom I do rely.
27 I'll make him my first-born, more
high
than kings of any land.
28 My love I'll ever keep for him,
my covenant fast shall stand.

29 His seed I by my power will
make
for ever to endure;
and, as the days of heaven, his
throne
shall stable be and sure.
30 But if his children shall forsake
my laws, and go astray,
and in my judgments shall not
walk,
but wander from the way:

31 If they my statutes do profane,
my laws do not respect;
32 I'll visit then their faults with
rods,
their sins with stripes correct.
33 Yet I'll not take my love from
him,
nor false my promise make.
34 My covenant I'll not break, nor
change
what with my mouth I spake.

35 Once by my holiness I sware,
to David I'll not lie;
36 his seed and throne shall, as the
sun,
before me last for aye.
37 Like to the moon established
it shall for ever be:
the witness which is in the
heaven
doth witness faithfully.

38 But, wroth with thine anointed,
thou
renounced and loathed him hast;
39 his covenant made void, his
crown
to earth profaned cast.
40 His hedges all hast broken down,
his strong-holds down hast torn.
41 He is a spoil to passers-by,
to neighbours all a scorn.

42 Thou hast set up his foes' right
hand;
made all his enemies glad:
43 turned his sword's edge, and him
to stand
in battle hast not made.

44 His glory thou hast made to
cease,
his throne to earth down cast;
45 thou shortened hast his days of
youth,
with shame him covered hast.

46 How long, Lord, wilt thou hide
thyself?
for ever, in thine ire?
and shall thine indignation hot
burn like unto a fire?
47 Remember, Lord, how short a
time
I shall on earth remain:
O wherefore is it so that thou
hast made all men in vain?

48 What man is he that liveth here,
and death shall never see?
Or from the power of the grave
what man his soul shall free?
49 Thy former loving-kindnesses,
O Lord, where be they now?
Those which in truth and
faithfulness
to David sworn hast thou?

50 Mind, Lord, thy servant's sad
reproach:
I in my bosom bear
the scornings of the people all,
who strong and mighty are:
51 and that thine enemies, O Lord,
have cast reproach upon,
have cast reproach upon the
steps
of thine anointed one.

52 All blessing to the Lord our God
let be ascribed then:
for evermore so let it be.
Amen, yea, and amen.

90   FIRST VERSION

1 Lord, thou hast been our
dwelling-place
in generations all.
2 Before thou ever hadst brought
forth
the mountains great or small;
ere ever thou hadst formed the
earth,
and all the world abroad;
thou even from everlasting art
to everlasting God.

3 Thou, Lord, unto destruction dost
man that is mortal turn;
and unto them thou sayest,
Again,

ye sons of men, return.

4 Because a thousand years appear
   no more before thy sight
   than yesterday when it is past,
   or than a watch by night.

5 As with an overflowing flood
   thou carriest them away:
   they like a sleep are, like the
       grass
   that grows at morn are they.

6 At morn it flourishes and grows,
   cut down at even doth fade.

7 For by thine anger we're
       consumed,
   thy wrath makes us afraid.

8 Our sins thou and iniquities
   dost in thy presence place,
   and sett'st our secret faults before
   the brightness of thy face.

9 For in thine anger all our days
   do pass on to an end;
   and as a tale that hath been told,
   so we our years do spend.

10 Threescore and ten years do sum
       up
   our days and years, we see;
   or if, by reason of more strength,
   in some fourscore they be,
   yet doth the strength of such old
       men
   but grief and labour prove;
   for it is soon cut off, and we
   fly hence and soon remove.

11 Who knows thine anger's power,
       and keeps
   thy fear before his eyes?

12 To count our days so teach thou
       us
   that our hearts may be wise.

13 Turn yet again to us, O Lord,
   how long thus shall it be?
   Let it repent thee now for those
   that servants are to thee.

14 O with thy tender mercies, Lord,
   us early satisfy;
   so we rejoice shall all our days,
   and still be glad in thee.

15 According as the days have been
   wherein we grief have had,
   and years wherein we ill have
       seen,
   so do thou make us glad.

16 O let thy work and power appear
   thy servants' face before;
   and show unto their children
       dear

thy glory evermore:

17 and let the beauty of the Lord
   our God be us upon;
   and our hands' works establish
       thou,
   establish them each one.

90   SECOND VERSION

1 Lord, thou hast been a dwelling-
       place,
   a rest in tribulations,
   to us, thine own redeemed race,
   through all our generations.
   Thou, ere the mountains sprang
       to birth,
   or ever thou hadst formed the
       earth,
   art God from everlasting.

2 Thou turnest man again to clay;
   by thee that doom was spoken;
   as with a torrent borne away,
   gone like a sleep when broken.
   A thousand years are in thy sight
   but as a watch amid the night,
   or yesterday departed.

3 At morn we flourish like the
       grass,
   when green and fresh it groweth;
   which, withered ere the evening
       pass,
   the sweeping sickle moweth.
   Thus do thy chastisements
       consume
   our blasted hopes, our early
       bloom;
   we fade at thy displeasure.

4 Lo! thou hast set before thine
       eyes
   all our misdeeds and errors;
   our secret sins from darkness rise
   to thy confronting terrors.
   At thy rebuke, cut short by death,
   our life is like the transient
       breath,
   that told a bygone story.

5 Our days are three-score years
       and ten;
   ten more man's strength may
       borrow;
   but if the span be lengthened
       then
   that strength is toil and sorrow;
   for soon arrives the closing hour:
   but who discerns thy fearful
       power,
   proportioned to thine anger?

6　Lord, teach us so to count our
　　　days,
that we may prize them duly,
and set our heart on wisdom's
　　　ways,
that we may praise thee truly.
Return, thy servants' griefs
　　　behold,
and with thy mercy, as of old,
O, satisfy us early!

7　restore us comfort for our fears,
joy for our long affliction;
our children give through
　　　changing years
increasing benediction.
Thy glorious beauty, Lord, reveal;
and with thy prospering favour
　　　seal
thy servants and their labours.

91

1　He that doth in the secret place
of the Most High reside,
under the shade of him that is
the Almighty shall abide.

2　I of the Lord my God will say,
He is my refuge still,
he is my fortress and my God,
and in him trust I will.

3　Assuredly he shall thee save,
and give deliverance
both from the fowler's snare and
　　　from
the noisome pestilence.

4　His feathers shall thee hide; thy
　　　trust
under his wings shall be:
his faithfulness shall be a shield
and buckler unto thee.

5　Thou shalt not need to be afraid
for terrors of the night;
nor for the arrow that doth fly
by day, while it is light;

6　nor for the pestilence that walks
in darkness secretly;
nor for destruction that doth
　　　waste
at noon-day openly.

7　A thousand at thy side shall fall,
on thy right hand shall lie
ten thousand dead; yet unto thee
it shall not once come nigh.

8　Thou with thine eyes shalt only
　　　look,
and a beholder be;
and thou the merited reward
of wicked men shalt see.

9　For thou, O Lord, art constantly
my refuge and mine aid;
thou hast the Lord who is most
　　　high
thy habitation made.

10　No plague shall near thy
　　　dwelling come;
no ill shall thee befall:

11　for thee to keep in all thy ways
his angels charge he shall.

12　They in their hands shall bear
　　　thee up,
still waiting thee upon;
lest thou at any time should'st
　　　dash
thy foot against a stone.

13　Upon the adder thou shalt tread,
and on the lion strong;
thy feet on dragons trample shall,
and on the lions young.

14　Because on me he set his love,
deliver him will I;
because my great name he hath
　　　known,
I will him set on high.

15　He'll call on me, I'll answer him;
I will be with him still
in trouble, to deliver him,
and honour him I will.

16　And length of days to his desire
I will on him bestow;
and, in my love, I unto him
will my salvation show.

92

1　To render thanks unto the Lord
it is a comely thing,
and to thy name, O thou Most
　　　High,
due praise aloud to sing:

2　thy loving-kindness to show forth
when shines the morning light;
and to declare thy faithfulness
with pleasure every night,

3　upon a ten-stringed instrument,
and on the psaltery,
upon the harp with solemn
　　　sound
and grave sweet melody.

4　For thou, Lord, by thy mighty
　　　deeds
hast gladness to me brought;
and I will triumph in the works
which by thy hands are wrought.

5　How great and wondrous, Lord,
　　　thy works!

thy thought how deep it is!
6 A brutish man discerneth not,
fools understand not this.
7 When even like unto the grass
springs up the wicked race,
and workers of iniquity
do flourish all apace.

'Tis that cut off and quite
destroyed
they may for ever be:
8 but thou, O Lord, art throned on
high,
unto eternity.
9 For, lo, thine enemies, O Lord,
thine enemies perish shall;
the workers of iniquity
shall be dispersed all.

10 But, like the unicorn's, my horn
exalted is by thee:
anointed also with fresh oil
I am abundantly.
11 Mine eye shall also my desire
see on mine enemies;
mine ears shall of the wicked
hear,
that do against me rise.

12 But like the palm-tree flourishing
shall be the righteous one;
he shall like to the cedar grow
that is in Lebanon.
13 Those that within the house of
God
are planted by his grace,
they shall grow up, and flourish
all
in our God's holy place.

14 And in old age, when others fade,
they fruit still forth shall bring;
they shall be fat and full of sap,
and aye be flourishing;
15 to show that upright is the Lord:
he is a rock to me;
and he from all unrighteousness
is altogether free.

93

1 The Lord doth reign, and clothed
is he
with majesty most bright;
the Lord hath clothed himself, he
hath
him girt about with might.
The world is also stablished,
that it cannot depart.
2 Thy throne is fixed of old, and
thou
from everlasting art.

3 The floods, O Lord, have lifted
up,
have lifted up their voice;
the floods have lifted up their
waves,
and made a mighty noise.
4 But yet the Lord, who is on high,
is more of might by far
than noise of many waters is,
than great sea-billows are.

5 Thy testimonies every one
in faithfulness excel;
and holiness for ever, Lord,
thine house becometh well.

93

SECOND VERSION

1 The Lord is king and weareth
a robe of glory bright,
he clothed with strength
appeareth,
and girt with powerful might.
2 The earth he hath so grounded
that moved it cannot be;
his throne long since was
founded,
more old than time is he.

3 The waters highly flowing
have raised their voice, O Lord;
the seas their fury showing
with billows loud have roared.
4 But God in strength excelleth
strong seas and powerful deeps;
with him still pureness dwelleth,
and firm his truth he keeps.

94

1 O Lord, the God to whom alone
all vengeance doth belong;
thou, who the God of vengeance
art,
shine forth, avenging wrong.
2 Lift up thyself, thou of the earth
the sovereign judge that art;
and unto those that haughty are
a recompense impart.

3 How long, Jehovah, shall the men
who evil-doers be,
how long shall they who wicked
are
thus triumph haughtily?
4 How long shall grievous things
by them
be uttered and told?
And all that work iniquity
to boast themselves be bold?

5 Thy folk they break in pieces,
 Lord,
 thine heritage oppress:
6 the widow and the stranger slay,
 and kill the fatherless:
7 yet say, The Lord shall not
 perceive,
 nor God of Jacob know.
8 Ye brutish people! understand;
 fools! when wise will ye grow?
9 Shall he who plants the ear of
 man
 to hear unable be?
 and he who fashioneth the eye,
 shall he not clearly see?
10 He who the nations doth correct,
 shall he reproof not show?
 he that doth knowledge teach to
 man,
 shall he himself not know?
11 Man's thoughts to be but vanity
 the Lord doth well discern.
12 Blessed is the man thou
 chastenest, Lord,
 and mak'st thy law to learn:
13 that thou mayest give him rest
 from days
 of sad adversity,
 until the pit be digged for those
 that work iniquity.
14 Because the Lord will not cast off
 those that his people be,
 nor yet his own inheritance
 forsake at all will he:
15 but judgment unto righteousness
 shall yet return again;
 and all shall follow after it
 that are right-hearted men.
16 Who will rise up for me against
 those that do wickedly?
 Who will stand up for me 'gainst
 those
 that work iniquity?
17 Unless the Lord had been my
 help,
 my soul in death had lain;
18 but if I say, My foot doth slip,
 thy love doth me sustain.
19 Amidst the multitude of cares
 whereby I am oppressed,
 thy comforts, Lord, refresh my
 soul,
 thy mercies give me rest.
20 Shall of iniquity the throne
 have fellowship with thee,
 which mischief, cunningly
 contrived,

doth by a law decree?
21 Against the righteous souls they
 join,
 they guiltless blood condemn.
22 But of my refuge God's the rock,
 and my defence from them.
23 On them their own iniquity
 the Lord shall cause to fall,
 and in their sin shall cut them
 off;
 our God destroy them shall.

95 FIRST VERSION

1 O come, and let us to the Lord
 in songs our voices raise,
 with joyful noise let us the rock
 of our salvation praise.
2 Let us before his presence come
 with praise and thankful voice;
 let us sing psalms to him with
 grace,
 and make a joyful noise.
3 The Lord's a great God and great
 King,
 above all gods he is.
4 Depths of the earth are in his
 hand,
 the strength of hills is his.
5 To him the spacious sea belongs,
 for he the same did make;
 the dry land also from his hands
 its form at first did take.
6 O come and let us worship him,
 let us bow down withal,
 and on our knees before the Lord
 our Maker let us fall.
7 For he's our God, the people we
 of his own pasture are,
 and of his hand the sheep;
 today,
 if ye his voice will hear,
8 Then harden not your hearts, as
 in
 the wilderness of old,
 when Meribah and Massah did
 trial and strife behold.
9 When me your fathers tempted,
 proved,
 and did my working see.
10 Even for the space of forty years
 this race hath grieved me.

 I said, This people errs in heart,
 my ways they do not know;
11 so in my wrath I sware, that to
 my rest they should not go.

95 SECOND VERSION

1. O come, let us sing to the Lord,
in God our salvation rejoice,
in psalms of thanksgiving record
his praise, with one spirit, one
voice.
For Jehovah is king — and he
reigns
the God of all gods on his throne;
the strength of the hills he
maintains,
the ends of the earth are his own.

2. The sea is Jehovah's; he made
the tide its dominion to know:
the land is Jehovah's; he laid
its solid foundations below.
O come let us worship and kneel
before our Creator, our God;
the people who serve him with
zeal,
the flock whom he guides with
his rod.

3. To-day, if his voice ye will hear,
he speaks from above to you still;
'O turn not aside; but forbear
to harden your hearts to my will.
as once on the wilderness way
of old my long-suffering you
tried;
the day of temptation, the day
when God's righteous wrath ye
defied.

4. 'Your fathers against me
rebelled;
and forty years long was I
grieved,
my works while they daily
beheld,
but, tempting their God,
disbelieved.
Their heart had from me gone
astray,
and I sware in my wrath, that
unblest
the people that knew not my way
should ne'er enter into my rest.'

96

1. O sing a new song to the Lord:
sing all the earth to God.
2. To God sing, bless his name,
show still
his saving health abroad.
3. Among the nations of the earth
his glory do declare;

and unto all the people show
his works that wondrous are.

4. For great's the Lord, and greatly
he
is to be magnified;
yea, worthy to be feared is he
above all gods beside.
5. For all the gods are idols dumb
which blinded nations fear;
but our God is the Lord, by
whom
the heavens created were.

6. Great honour is before his face,
and majesty divine;
strength is within his holy place,
and there doth beauty shine.
7. Do ye ascribe unto the Lord,
of people every tribe,
glory do ye unto the Lord
and mighty power ascribe.

8. Give ye the glory to the Lord
that to his name is due;
come ye into his courts, and bring
an offering with you.
9. In beauty of his holiness
O do the Lord adore;
likewise let all the earth
throughout
tremble his face before.

10. 'Mong heathen say, Jehovah
reigns;
the world shall steadfast be
so that it move not; he shall
judge
the people righteously.
11. Let heavens be glad before the
Lord,
and let the earth rejoice;
let seas and all their fulness roar,
and make a mighty noise.

12. Let fields rejoice, and everything
that springeth of the earth;
then of the forest all the trees
shall shout aloud with mirth
13. before the Lord; because he
comes,
to judge the earth comes he;
he'll judge the world with
righteousness,
the people faithfully.

97

1 God reigneth, let the earth be
    glad,
  and isles rejoice each one.
2 Dark clouds him compass; and in
    right
  and judgment dwells his throne.
3 Fire goes before him, and his foes
  it burns up round about:
4 his lightnings lighten did the
    world;
  earth saw, and shook throughout.
5 Hills at the presence of the Lord,
  like wax, did melt away;
  even at the presence of the Lord
  of all the earth, I say.
6 The heavens declare his
    righteousness,
  all men his glory see.
7 All who serve graven images,
  confounded let them be.

  Who do of idols boast themselves,
  let shame upon them fall:
  ye that are called gods, see that
  ye do him worship all.
8 Zion did hear, and joyful was,
  glad Judah's daughters were;
  they much rejoiced, O Lord,
    because
  thy judgments did appear.
9 For thou, O Lord, art high above
  all things on earth that are;
  above all other gods thou art
  exalted very far.
10 Hate ill, all ye that love the Lord:
  his saints' souls keepeth he;
  and from the hands of wicked
    men
  he sets them safe and free.
11 For every one that righteous is
  sown is a joyful light,
  and gladness sown is for all those
  that are in heart upright.
12 Ye righteous, in the Lord rejoice;
  express your thankfulness,
  when ye into your memory
  do call his holiness.

98   FIRST VERSION

1 O sing a new song to the Lord,
  for wonders he hath done:
  his right hand and his holy arm
  him victory hath won.
2 Jehovah his salvation hath
  now caused to be known;

his justice in the heathen's sight
he openly hath shown.
3 He mindful of his grace and truth
  to Israel's house hath been;
  and the salvation of our God
  all ends of the earth have seen.
4 Let all the earth unto the Lord
  send forth a joyful noise;
  lift up your voice aloud to him,
  sing praises, and rejoice.
5 With harp, with harp, and voice
    of psalms,
  unto Jehovah sing:
6 with trumpets, cornets, gladly
    sound
  before the Lord the King.
7 Let seas and all their fulness
    roar;
  the world, and dwellers there;
8 let floods clap hands, and let the
    hills
  together joy declare
9 Before the Lord; because he
    comes,
  to judge the earth comes he;
  he'll judge the world with
    righteousness,
  the nations uprightly.

98   SECOND VERSION

1 Sing a new song to Jehovah,
  for he wondrous things hath
    wrought;
  his right hand and arm most holy
  victory to him have brought.
2 Lo! the Lord his great salvation
  openly hath now made known;
  in the sight of every nation
  he his righteousness has shown.
3 Mindful of his truth and mercy
  he to Israel's house hath been;
  and the Lord our God's salvation
  all the ends of earth have seen.
4 All the earth sing to Jehovah!
  shout aloud! sing and rejoice!
  With the harp sing to Jehovah!
  with the harp and tuneful voice.
5 Sound the trumpet and the
    cornet,
  shout before the Lord the King;
  sea, and all its fulness, thunder;
  earth, and all its people, sing.
6 Let the rivers in their gladness
  clap their hands with one accord;
  let the mountains sing together
  joyfully before the Lord.

7   For to judge the earth he cometh;
    and with righteousness shall he
    judge the world, and all the
        nations
    with most perfect equity.

99

1   Jehovah is enthroned as king,
    let all the people quake;
    he sits between the cherubim,
    let earth be moved and shake.
2   In Zion is Jehovah great,
    above all people high;
3   thy great dread name, which holy
        is,
    O let them magnify.

4   The king's strength also
        judgment loves;
    thou settlest equity:
    just judgment thou dost execute
    in Jacob righteously.
5   The Lord our God exalt on high,
    and reverently do ye
    before his footstool bow
        yourselves:
    the Holy One is he.

6   Moses and Aaron 'mong his
        priests,
    Samuel 'mong those who prayed;
    these called upon the Lord, and
        he
    unto them answer made.
7   Within the pillar of the cloud
    he to his people spake;
    his testimonies they observed,
    his statute did not break.

8   Thou answer'dst them, O Lord
        our God;
    thou wast a God that gave
    pardon to them, though on their
        deeds
    thou wouldest vengeance have.
9   Do ye exalt the Lord our God,
    and at his holy hill
    do ye him worship: for the Lord
    our God is holy still.

100   FIRST VERSION

1   All people that on earth do dwell,
    sing to the Lord with cheerful
        voice;
2   him serve with mirth, his praise
        forth tell,
    come ye before him and rejoice.
3   Know that the Lord is God
        indeed;

without our aid he did us make:
we are his folk, he doth us feed,
and for his sheep he doth us take.

4   O enter then his gates with
        praise,
    approach with joy his courts
        unto:
    praise, laud, and bless his name
        always,
    for it is seemly so to do.
5   Because the Lord our God is
        good,
    his mercy is for ever sure;
    his truth at all times firmly stood,
    and shall from age to age endure.

100   SECOND VERSION

1   O all ye lands, unto the Lord
    make ye a joyful noise.
2   Serve God with gladness, and
        before
    him come with cheerful voice.
3   Know ye the Lord that he is God;
    us for himself he made:
    we are his people, and the sheep
    within his pasture fed.

4   O enter then his gates with
        thanks,
    his courts with voice of praise;
    give thanks to him with
        joyfulness,
    and bless his name always.
5   Because the Lord our God is
        good,
    his mercy faileth never;
    and unto generations all
    his truth endureth ever.

101

1   I mercy will and judgment sing,
    Lord, I will sing to thee.
2   With wisdom in a perfect way
    shall my behaviour be.
    O when in kindness unto me
    wilt thou be pleased to come?
    I with a perfect heart will walk
    within my house at home.

3   I will endure no wicked thing
    before mine eyes to be;
    I hate their work that turn aside,
    it shall not cleave to me.
4   A stubborn and a froward heart
    depart quite from me shall;
    a person given to wickedness
    I will not know at all.

5 I'll cut him off that slandereth
his neighbour privily:
the haughty heart I will not bear,
nor him whose look is high.
6 I'll mark the faithful of the land,
that they may dwell with me;
who walketh in a perfect way
to me shall servant be.

7 Who of deceit a worker is
in my house shall not dwell;
and in my presence shall he not
remain that lies doth tell.
8 Each morn the wicked of the land
shall be cut off by me;
to root out from God's city all
that work iniquity.

102 FIRST VERSION

1 O Lord, unto my prayer give ear,
my cry let come to thee;
2 and in the day of my distress
hide not thy face from me.
Give ear to me; what time I call,
to answer me make haste:
3 for, as an hearth, my bones are
burnt,
my days, like smoke, do waste.

4 My heart within me smitten is,
like grass is withered;
because for very grief I do
forget to eat my bread.
5 By reason of my cries and groans
my bones cleave to my skin.
6 Like pelican in wilderness
forsaken I have been:

I like an owl 'mid ruins am,
that nightly there doth moan;
7 I watch, like sparrow that doth sit
on the house-top alone.
8 My bitter enemies all the day
reproaches cast on me;
and, being mad at me, with rage
against me sworn they be.

9 For I did ashes eat as bread,
and, in my sorrow deep,
my drink I also mingled have
with tears that I did weep.
10 Thine indignation and thy wrath
did cause this grief and pain;
for thou hast lifted me on high,
and cast me down again.

11 My days are like unto a shade,
which doth declining pass;
and I am dried and withered,
even like unto the grass.

12 But thou, O Lord, dost sit
enthroned,
eternal is thy sway;
and thy remembrance shall
endure
from age to age alway.

13 Thou shalt arise and mercy have
upon thy Zion yet;
the time to favour her is come,
the time that thou hast set.
14 For in her rubbish and her stones
thy servants pleasure take;
yea, they the very dust thereof
do favour for her sake.

15 So shall the heathen people fear
the Lord's most holy name;
and all the kings upon the earth
thy glory and thy fame.
16 For Zion by thy mighty Lord
built up again shall be,
and in his glorious majesty
to men appear shall he.

17 The prayer of the destitute
he surely will regard;
their prayer he will not despise,
by him it shall be heard.
18 For generations yet to come
shall men these things record;
so shall a people yet to be
created praise the Lord.

19 For from his holy height the Lord
hath downward cast his eye;
and he upon the earth beneath
hath looked from heaven high;
20 that of the mournful prisoner
the groanings he might hear,
to set them free that unto death
by men appointed are:

21 That they in Zion may declare
the Lord's most holy name,
and publish in Jerusalem
the praises of the same
22 when all the people gathered are
in troops with one accord,
and kingdoms are assembled all
to serve the mighty Lord.

23 My wonted strength and force he
hath
abated in the way,
my days he also shortened hath:
24 thus therefore did I say,
My God, in mid-time of my days
take thou me not away:
from age to age eternally
thy years endure and stay.

The firm foundation of the earth
of old time thou hast laid:
the heavens also are the work
which thine own hands have
    made.
Thou shalt for evermore endure,
but they shall perish all;
yea, every one of them wax old,
like to a garment, shall:

Thou, as a vesture, shalt them
    change,
and they shall changed be;
but thou the same art, and thy
    years
are to eternity.
The children of thy servants shall
continually endure;
and in thy sight, O Lord, their
    seed
shall be established sure.

02 SECOND VERSION

Lord, hear my prayer, and let my
    cry
have speedy access unto thee;
in day of my calamity
O hide not thou thy face from
    me.
Hear when I call to thee; that day
an answer speedily return:
my days, like smoke, consume
    away,
and, as an hearth, my bones do
    burn.

My heart is smitten like the grass
when withered by the scorching
    heat,
because in grief my days I pass,
and quite forget my bread to eat.
By reason of my smart within,
and my most bitter cries and
    groans,
my flesh consumed is, my skin
all parched doth cleave unto my
    bones.

The pelican of wilderness,
the owl of ruins drear, I match;
and, like a bird companionless
upon the housetop, I keep watch.
I all day long am made a scorn,
reproached by my malicious foes;
they mad with rage 'gainst me
    have sworn,
the men against me that arose.

For I have ashes eaten up,
as if to me they had been bread;

and with my drink I in my cup
of bitter tears a mixture made.
10 Because thy wrath was not
    appeased,
nor thou thine anger didst
    restrain;
for though thou hadst me high
    upraised,
thou hast me now cast down
    again.

11 My days are like a shade alway,
which doth declining swiftly
    pass;
and I am withered away,
even like unto the fading grass.
12 But thou, O Lord, shalt still
    endure,
from all changes thou art free,
and to all generations sure
shall thy remembrance ever be.

13 Thou shalt arise, and mercy yet
thou to mount Zion shalt extend:
the time is come for favour set,
the time when thou shalt blessing
    send.
14 Thy saints take pleasure in her
    stones,
her very dust to them is dear.
15 All heathen lands and kingly
    thrones
on earth thy glorious name shall
    fear.

16 For God in glory shall appear,
to build up Zion and repair.
17 He shall regard and lend his ear
unto the needy's humble prayer:
the afflicted's prayer he will not
    scorn.
18 All times shall this be on record:
and generations yet unborn
shall praise and magnify the
    Lord.

19 He from his holy place looked
    down,
the earth he viewed from heaven
    on high;
20 to hear the prisoner's mourning
    groan,
and free them that are doomed to
    die;
21 that Zion, and Jerusalem too,
his name and praise may well
    record,
22 when people and the kingdoms
    do
assemble all to praise the Lord.

23 My strength he weakened in the
        way,
    my days of life he shortened.
24 My God, O take me not away
    in mid-time of my days, I said:
    Thy years throughout all ages
        last.
25 Of old thou hast established
    the earth's foundation firm and
        fast:
    thy mighty hands the heavens
        have made.
26 They perish shall, as garments
        do,
    but thou shalt evermore endure;
    as vestures, thou shalt change
        them so;
    and they shall all be changed
        sure:
27 but from all changes thou art
        free;
    thy countless years do last for aye.
28 Thy servants, and their seed who
        be,
    established shall before thee stay.

103

1   O thou my soul, bless God the
        Lord;
    and all that in me is
    be stirred up his holy name
    to magnify and bless.
2   Bless, O my soul, the Lord thy
        God,
    and not forgetful be
    of all his gracious benefits
    he hath bestowed on thee.
3   All thine iniquities who doth
    most graciously forgive:
    who thy diseases all and pains
    doth heal, and thee relieve.
4   Who doth redeem thy life, that
        thou
    to death mayest not go down;
    who thee with loving-kindness
        doth
    and tender mercies crown:
5   Who with abundance of good
        things
    doth satisfy thy mouth;
    so that, even as the eagle's age,
    renewed is thy youth.
6   God righteous judgment executes
    for all oppressed ones.
7   His ways to Moses he made
        known,
    his acts to Israel's sons.

8   The Lord our God is merciful,
    and he is gracious,
    long-suffering, and slow to wrath,
    in mercy plenteous.
9   He will not chide continually,
    nor keep his anger still.
10 With us he dealt not as we
        sinned,
    nor did requite our ill.
11 For as the heaven in its height
    the earth surmounteth far,
    so great to those that do him fear
    his tender mercies are:
12 As far as east is distant from
    the west, so far hath he
    from us removed, in his love,
    all our iniquity.
13 Such pity as a father hath
    unto his children dear,
    like pity shows the Lord to such
    as worship him in fear.
14 For he remembers we are dust,
    and he our frame well knows.
15 Frail man, his days are like the
        grass,
    as flower in field he grows:
16 For over it the wind doth pass,
    and it away is gone;
    and of the place where once it
        was
    it shall no more be known.
17 But unto them that do him fear
    God's mercy never ends;
    and to their children's children
        still
    his righteousness extends:
18 To such as keep his covenant,
    and mindful are alway
    of his commandments just and
        good,
    that they may them obey.
19 The Lord prepared hath his
        throne
    in heavens firm to stand;
    and every thing that being hath
    his kingdom doth command.
20 O ye his angels, that excel
    in strength, bless ye the Lord;
    ye who obey what he commands,
    and hearken to his word.
21 O bless and magnify the Lord,
    ye glorious hosts of his;
    ye ministers that do fulfil
    whate'er his pleasure is.

O bless the Lord, all ye his works,
wherewith the world is stored
in his dominions every where.
My soul, bless thou the Lord.

04 FIRST VERSION

1 Bless God, my soul. O Lord my
God,
thou art exceeding great;
with honour and with majesty
thou clothed art in state.
2 With light, as with a robe, thyself
thou coverest about;
and, like unto a curtain, thou
the heavens stretchest out.

3 Who of his chambers doth the
beams
within the waters lay;
who doth the clouds his chariot
make,
on wings of wind make way.
4 Who flaming fire his ministers,
his angels spirits, doth make:
5 who earth's foundations firm did
lay,
that it should never shake.

6 Thou didst it cover with the
deep,
as with a garment spread:
the waters stood above the hills,
above the mountains' head.
7 But at the voice of thy rebuke
they fled and would not stay;
they at thy thunder's dreadful
voice
did haste them fast away.

8 They by the hills ascend, their
way
back by the vales they take,
descending to the very place
which thou for them didst make.
9 Thou hast a bound unto them set,
o'er which they may not go,
that they may not return again
the earth to overflow.

10 He through the valley sendeth
springs,
'mong hills their course they
take:
11 beasts of the field all drink of
them,
their thirst wild asses slake.
12 The birds of heaven their
dwelling make
where these do flow along,
and from among the leafy boughs
with joy give forth their song.

13 He from his chambers watereth
the hills when they are dried:
with fruit and increase of thy
works
the earth is satisfied.
14 For cattle he makes grass to grow,
herb for man's use to spring,
that from the bosom of the earth
he bread for him may bring;

15 And wine that to the heart of
man
doth cheerfulness impart,
oil that doth make his face to
shine,
bread strengthening his heart.
16 The trees of God are full of sap;
the cedars that do stand
on Lebanon, which planted were
by his almighty hand.

17 Birds of the air upon their boughs
do choose their nests to make;
as for the stork, the fir tree she
doth for her dwelling take.
18 The lofty mountains for wild
goats
a place of refuge be:
the conies also to the rocks
do for their safety flee.

19 He sets the moon in heaven,
thereby
the seasons to discern:
from him the sun his certain time
of going down doth learn.
20 Thou darkness mak'st, 'tis night,
then beasts
of forests creep abroad.
21 The lions young roar for their
prey,
and seek their meat from God.

22 The sun doth rise, and home they
flock,
down in their dens they lie.
23 Man goeth to his work, and doth
his toil till evening ply.
24 O Lord, how manifold thy works!
In wisdom wonderful
thou every one of them hast
made;
earth's of thy riches full:

25 So is this great and spacious sea,
wherein things creeping are,
which numbered cannot be; and
beasts
both great and small are there.
26 There ships go, there leviathan,
which thou mad'st there to play;

27 all wait on thee, that in due time
    their food receive they may.

28 That which thou givest unto
        them
    they gather for their food;
    thy bounteous hand thou openest,
    they filled are with good.

29 Thou hid'st thy face, they
        troubled are;
    their breath thou tak'st away,
    then do they die, and to their
        dust
    return again do they.

30 Thy quickening spirit thou
        send'st forth,
    and they created be;
    and then the earth's decayed face
    renewed is by thee.

31 The glory of Jehovah shall
    endure while ages run;
    the Lord Almighty shall rejoice
    in all that he hath done.

32 Earth, as affrighted, trembleth all,
    if he on it but look;
    and if the mountains he but
        touch,
    they presently do smoke.

33 I to the Lord most high will sing,
    so long as I shall live;
    and while I being have I shall
    to my God praises give.

34 Of him my meditation shall
    sweet thoughts to me afford;
    and as for me, I will rejoice
    and triumph in the Lord.

35 From earth let sinners be
        consumed,
    let ill men no more be.
    O thou my soul, bless thou the
        Lord.
    Praise to the Lord give ye.

104 SECOND VERSION

1   My soul, praise the Lord;
    thou, Lord, mine own God,
    art glorious, enrobed
    in beauty and might;

2   the heavens, like a curtain,
    thou spreadest abroad;
    as raiment, around thee
    enfoldest the light.

3   For chamber-beams sure,
    dark waters he binds;
    of clouds dim and deep
    his chariot doth frame,

    on stormy blasts riding,
    on wings of all winds;

4   his angels are spirits,
    his servants a flame.

5   Foundations secure
    he laid for the globe,
    that stable and firm
    it ever should last;

6   the waste ocean gathering
    o'er all as a robe:
    o'er all the high mountains
    the surging waves passed.

7   At thy dread rebuke
    they flee and they fail;
    thy thunder is heard,
    they speed here and there;

8   they burst the ridge over,
    they rush down the vale;
    where thou hast appointed,
    they haste to repair.

9   Thine own word hath set
    their border and bound;
    they roar and they toss,
    but cannot pass o'er:
    the word of Jehovah
    a sure fence is found;
    the flood o'er the mountains
    returneth no more.

10 He unto the vales
    the springs doth convey;
    and onward they wind
    their course through the hills;

11 whereat the wild asses
    their thirst oft allay,
    and beasts of the forest
    thereof drink their fills.

12 By these pleasant springs,
    the fowls of the air
    inhabit the trees,
    the margin along;
    and, as in their gladness
    they move here and there
    among the green branches,
    praise God with their song.

13 His rain on the hills
    he pours from on high;
    with fruit of thy works
    the earth is replete;

14 his grass to the cattle
    he doth not deny,
    and gives for man's service
    the green herb as meat.

15 From earth, store of food
    he brings for man's sake;
    rich oil, gladsome wine,
    heart-strengthening bread.

5 His trees full of moisture
the great God did make;
his cedars he planted
on Lebanon's head.

7 Secure in those shades
the bird builds her nest;
the firs to the stork
a house have supplied;
8 the hills are a refuge
for wild goats to rest;
the crags of the rough rocks
for conies to hide.

9 The moon he hath set
for seasons to run;
the times he ordained
her change ever shows;
and so, his course circling,
the glorious sun
his hour of descending
as constantly knows.

0 When darkness doth come
by thy will and power,
then prowl forth abroad
the beasts of the wood.
1 The lions range roaring
their prey to devour;
and yet it is thou, Lord,
who givest them food.

2 As riseth the sun,
they all get them in;
withdrawn from his light,
to couch in their den;
3 but man forth proceedeth
his toil to begin;
till night come to call him
to take rest again.

4 How manifold, Lord,
the works of thy hand!
Surpassing our thoughts
their numbers are found!
Thy outspread creation
in wisdom is planned,
and full of thy riches
the wide world around.

5 So in the great sea
thy works are displayed,
where creeping things move,
unnumbered in sort;
6 and there the ships wander,
and there thou hast made
Leviathan, hugest
of monsters, to sport.

7 All these wait on thee
their food to receive;
that thou, in due time,
their portion may'st give:

28 and, when it doth please thee
their wants to relieve,
full gladly they gather
thy bounty and live.

  Thou openest thine hand;
how full their supply!
29 Thou hidest thy face;
confounded they mourn:
when thou from them takest
their spirit, they die,
and to their dust, changing,
again they return.

30 Thou send'st forth thy breath,
and they are new made;
and earth, as at first,
looks vernal and bright.
31 In glory for ever
the Lord is arrayed;
and in his creation
our God will delight.

32 He looks on the earth,
it reels to and fro;
he touches the hills,
with smoke they are crowned.
33 Through life to Jehovah
mine anthems shall flow;
while yet I have being
his praise I will sound.

34 With dear thoughts of him
my heart shall run o'er;
with God all my joy
in treasure is stored.
35 The sinners are wasted;
earth sees them no more;
the rebels — where are they?
My soul, praise the Lord.

105

1 Give thanks to God, call on his
  name;
to men his deeds make known.
2 Sing ye to him, sing psalms;
  proclaim
his wondrous works each one.
3 To glory in his holy name,
unite with one accord:
and let the heart of every one
rejoice that seeks the Lord.

4 The Lord Almighty and his
  strength
with steadfast hearts seek ye:
his blessed and his gracious face
seek ye continually.
5 Think on the works that he hath
  done.
Which admiration breed;

his wonders, and the judgments all
which from his mouth proceed;

6 O ye that are of Abraham's race,
his servant faithful known;
and ye that Jacob's children are,
whom he chose for his own.

7 Because he, and he only, is
the mighty Lord our God;
and his most righteous judgments are
in all the earth abroad.

8 His covenant he remembered hath,
that it may ever stand:
to thousand generations he
his promise did command.

9 Which covenant he firmly made
with faithful Abraham,
and unto Isaac by his oath
he did renew the same:

10 And unto Jacob, for a law,
he made it firm and sure,
a covenant to Israel,
which ever should endure:

11 he said, I will give Canaan's land
for heritage to you;

12 while they were strangers there, and few,
in number very few:

13 While yet they went from land to land
without a sure abode;
and while through sundry kingdoms they
did wander far abroad;

14 yet, notwithstanding, suffered he
no man to do them wrong;
yea, for their sakes, he did reprove
kings, who were great and strong.

15 Thus did he say, Touch ye not those
that mine anointed be,
nor do the prophets any harm
that do pertain to me.

16 He called for famine on the land,
he brake the staff of bread:

17 but yet he sent a man before,
by whom they should be fed;

Even Joseph, whom unnaturally
sell for a slave did they;

18 whose feet with fetters they did hurt,
and he in irons lay;

19 until the time that his word came
to give him liberty;

the word and purpose of the Lord
did him in prison try.

20 Then sent the king and did command
that he enlarged should be:
he that the people's ruler was
did send to set him free.

21 To be the Lord of all his house
he raised him as most fit;
to him of all that he possessed
he did the charge commit:

22 That he might at his pleasure bind
the princes of the land;
and also teach his senators
wisdom to understand.

23 And down into the land of Ham,
to Egypt, Israel came;
and for a season Jacob then
did sojourn in the same.

24 And he did greatly by his power
increase his people there;
and stronger than their enemies
they by his blessing were.

25 Their heart he turned then to hate
his people bitterly,
with those that this own servant were
to deal in subtlety.

26 His servant Moses he did send,
Aaron his chosen one:

27 by these his signs and wonders great
in Ham's land were made known.

28 Darkness he sent, and made it dark;
his word they did obey.

29 He turned their waters into blood,
and he their fish did slay.

30 The land in plenty brought forth frogs
in chambers of their kings.

31 His word all sorts of flies and lice
in all their border brings.

32 For showers hail and flaming fire
into their land he sent:

33 and he their vines and fig-trees smote;
trees of their coasts he rent.

34 He spake, and caterpillars came,
locusts did much abound;

35 which in their land all herbs consumed,

and all fruits of their ground.
He smote all first-born in their
land,
chief of their strength each one.
With gold and silver brought
them forth,
weak in their tribes were none.

Egypt was glad when forth they
went,
their fear on them did light.
He spread a cloud for covering,
and fire to shine by night.
They asked, he sent the quail,
and bread
of heaven on them bestowed;
the rock he opened, waters
gushed,
streams in the desert flowed.

For on his holy promise he,
and servant Abraham, thought.
With joy his people, his elect
with gladness, forth he brought.
And unto them the pleasant
lands
he of the heathen gave;
that of the people's labour they
inheritance might have.

That they his statutes might
observe
according to his word;
and that they might his laws
obey.
Give praise unto the Lord.

06

Give praise and thanks unto the
Lord,
for bountiful is he;
his tender mercy doth endure
unto eternity.
God's mighty works who can
express?
or show forth all his praise?
Blessed are they that judgment
keep
and justly do always.

Remember me, Lord, with that
love
which thou to thine dost bear;
with thy salvation, O my God,
to visit me draw near:
that I thy chosen's good may see,
and in their joy rejoice;
and may with thine inheritance
triumph with cheerful voice.

6 We with our fathers sinned have,
and of iniquity
too long we have the workers
been;
we have done wickedly.
7 The wonders great, which thou,
O Lord,
didst work in Egypt's land,
our fathers, though they them
beheld,
yet did not understand:

And they thy mercies' multitude
kept not in memory;
but at the sea, even the Red sea,
rebelled most grievously.
8 Nevertheless he saved them,
even for his own name's sake;
that so he might to be well
known
his mighty power make.

9 The Red Sea also he rebuked,
and then dried up it was:
through depths, as through the
wilderness,
he safely made them pass.
10 From hands of those that hated
them
he did his people save;
and from the foeman's cruel
hand
to them redemption gave.

11 The waters overwhelmed their
foes;
not one was left alive.
12 Then they believed his word, and
praise
to him in songs did give.
13 But soon did they his mighty
works
forget unthankfully,
and on his counsel and his will
did not wait patiently;

14 They lusted in the wilderness,
in desert God did tempt.
15 He gave them what they sought,
but to
their soul he leanness sent.
16 They envied Moses in the camp,
and grudged his rule to see;
Aaron, Jehovah's hole one,
they viewed with jealousy.

17 Therefore the earth did open
wide,
and Dathan did devour,
and all Abiram's company
did cover in that hour.

THE IRISH PSALTER

18 Likewise among their company
a fire was kindled then;
and so the hot consuming flame
burnt up these wicked men.

19 Upon the hill of Horeb they
an idol-calf did frame,
a molten image they did make,
and worshipped the same.

20 And changed the High and Holy One,
who all their glory was,
into the likeness of an ox
that feedeth upon grass.

21 They did forget the mighty God,
who had their saviour been,
by whom such great things
brought to pass
they had in Egypt seen.

22 He in the land of Ham wrought signs,
things terrible did he,
when he his mighty hand and arm
stretched out at the Red Sea.

23 Then said he, he would them destroy,
had not, his wrath to stay,
his chosen Moses stood in breach,
that them he should not slay.

24 Yea, they despised the pleasant land,
believed not his word:

25 but in their tents they murmured,
not hearkening to the Lord.

26 To slay them in the desert then
he lifted up his hand:

27 'mong nations to o'erthrow their seed,
and scatter in each land.

28 They unto Baal-peor did
themselves associate;
the sacrifices of the dead
they impiously ate.

29 Thus by inventions of their own
they did provoke his ire;
and then upon them suddenly
the plague brake in as fire.

30 Then Phinehas stood up and judged,
and so the plague did cease;

31 to ages all this counted was
to him for righteousness.

32 And at the waters, where they strove,
they did him angry make,
in such sort, that it fared ill

with Moses for their sake:

33 because against his spirit they
rebelled most grievously,
so that he uttered with his lips
words unadvisedly.

34 Nor, as the Lord commanded them,
did they the nations slay

35 but with the heathen mingled were,
and learned of them their way.

36 their idols they did serve, and these
became to them a snare;

37 they unto demons sacrificed
their sons and daughters there.

38 In their own children's guiltless blood
their hands they did imbrue,
whom to Canaan's idols they
for sacrifices slew:
so was the land defiled with blood.

39 Stained by their works were they
and by inventions of their own
they wantonly did stray.

40 For this against his people burned
the anger of the Lord;
and he his own inheritance
in righteousness abhorred.

41 He gave them to the heathen's power;
their foes did them command:

42 their enemies them oppressed, they were
made subject to their hand.

43 He many times delivered them,
yet still they did rebel
with counsels vain, and by their sin
into destruction fell.

44 Yet their affliction he beheld,
when he did hear their cry:

45 and he for them his covenant
did call to memory;

After his mercies' multitude

46 he did repent, and make
them to be pitied of all those
who did them captive take.

47 Save, Lord our God, and gather us
the heathen from among,
that we thy holy name may praise
in a triumphant song.

48 Blessed be Jehovah, Israel's God,

to all eternity:
let all the people say, Amen.
Praise to the Lord give ye.

107

1 Praise ye the Lord, for he is good,
his mercies lasting be;
2 let his redeemed say so, whom he
from hand of foes did free;
3 and gathered them out of the lands,
from north, south, east, and west.
4 They strayed in desert's pathless way,
no city found to rest.

5 Their soul with thirst and hunger faints:
when troubles sore them press,
6 thy cry unto the Lord, and he
them frees from their distress.
7 Them also in a way to walk
that right is he did guide,
that they might to a city go,
wherein they might abide.

8 O that men to the Lord would give
praise for his goodness then,
and for his works of wonder done
unto the sons of men!
9 For he the soul that longing is
doth fully satisfy;
with goodness he the hungry soul
doth fill abundantly.

10 Such as shut up in darkness deep,
and in death's shade abide,
whom strongly hath affliction bound,
and irons fast have tied:
11 because against the words of God
they wrought rebelliously;
and they the counsel did contemn
of him that is most High:

12 With labour he brought down their hearts,
they fell, and help none gave;
13 in trouble to the Lord they cried,
from straits he did them save.
14 He out of darkness did them bring,
and from death's shade them take;
their bands, wherewith they had been bound,
he did asunder break.

15 O that men to the Lord would give
praise for his goodness then,
and for his works of wonder done
unto the sons of men!
16 Because the mighty gates of brass
in pieces he did tear,
by him in sunder also cut
the bars of iron were.

17 Fools, for their trespasses and sins,
do sore affliction bear;
18 all kinds of meat their soul abhors;
they to death's gates draw near.
19 In grief they cry to God; he saves
them from their miseries.
20 He sends his word, them heals, and them
from their destruction frees.

21 O that men to the Lord would give
praise for his goodness then,
and for his works of wonder done
unto the sons of men!
22 And let them sacrifice to him
offerings of thankfulness;
and let them show abroad his works
in songs of joyfulness.

23 Who go to sea in ships, and in
great waters trading be,
24 the Lord's works these within the deep
and his great wonders see.
25 For he commands, and forth in haste
the stormy tempest flies,
which makes the sea with rolling waves
aloft to swell and rise.

26 They mount to heaven, then to the depths
they do go down again;
their soul doth faint and melt away
with trouble and with pain.
27 They reel and stagger like one drunk,
at their wit's end they be:
28 in trouble to the Lord they cry,
from straits he sets them free.

29 The storm is changed into a calm
at his command and will;
so that the waves, which raged before,

now quiet are and still.

30 Then are they glad, because at rest
and quiet now they be:
so to the haven he them brings,
which they desired to see.

31 O that men to the Lord would give
praise for his goodness then,
and for his works of wonder done
unto the sons of men!

32 Among the people gathered
let them exalt his name;
among assembled elders spread
his most renowned fame.

33 He turneth springs to thirsty ground,
floods to a wilderness;

34 for sins of those that dwell therein,
fat land to barrenness.

35 He turns to pools the wilderness
long parched with drought and burned;
by him the ground dried up before
to water-springs is turned.

36 And there, for dwelling, he a place
doth to the hungry give,
that they a city may prepare
where they in peace may live.

37 There sow they fields, and vineyards plant,
which yield fruits of increase;

38 his blessing makes them multiply,
lets not their herds decrease.

39 Again they are diminished,
and brought to low estate,
by pressure of calamity,
and by affliction great.

40 On princes he doth pour contempt,
and causeth them to stray,
and wander in a wilderness,
wherein there is no way.

41 Yet setteth he the poor on high
from all their miseries,
and even like unto a flock
he maketh families.

42 They that are righteous shall rejoice,
when they the same shall see;
and, as ashamed, stop her mouth
shall all iniquity.

43 Whoso is wise, and will these things

observe, and them record,
even they shall understand the love
and kindness of the Lord.

108

1 My heart is fixed, O God; I'll sing,
and with my glory praise.
2 Awake up psaltery and harp;
myself I'll early raise.
3 I'll praise thee 'mong the people Lord;
'mong nations sing will I:
4 for above heaven thy mercy's great,
thy truth doth reach the sky.

5 Be thou above the heavens, O God,
exalted gloriously;
thy glory all the earth above
be lifted up on high.
6 That those who thy beloved are
delivered may be,
O do thou save with thy right hand,
and answer give to me.

7 God in his holiness did speak,
My joy shall be complete;
Shechem I will divide, by line
the vale of Succoth mete.
8 Gilead I claim as mine by right;
Manasseh mine shall be;
Ephraim is of my head the strength;
Judah gives laws for me;

9 Moab my wash-pot is; my shoe
I'll over Edom throw;
over Philistia my shout
of triumph forth shall go.
10 O who is he will bring me to
the city fortified?
O who is he that to the land
of Edom will me guide?

11 O God, who hast rejected us,
wilt thou not help us so?
Even thou, O God, who dost no more
forth with our armies go.
12 From trouble help thou us, for vain
the help from man that flows.
13 Through God we shall do valiantly;
he shall tread down our foes.

09

O thou the God of all my praise,
do thou not hold thy peace;
for mouths of wicked men to
speak
against me do not cease:
the mouths of vile deceitful men
against me opened be;
and with a false and lying tongue
they have accused me.

They did beset me round with
words
of hatred and of spite;
and, though to them no cause I
gave,
against me they did fight.
They for my love became my
foes:
I set myself to pray.
Evil for good, hatred for love,
to me they did repay.

Set thou the wicked over him;
and upon his right hand
against him in the judgment let
the adversary stand.
And when by thee he shall be
judged,
let him condemned be;
and let his prayer sin become,
when he shall call on thee.

Few be his days, and in his room
his charge another take.
His children let be fatherless,
his wife a widow make.
His children let be vagabonds,
and beg continually;
and from their places desolate
seek bread for their supply.

Let covetous extortioners
catch all he hath away:
of all for which he laboured hath
let strangers make a prey.
Let there be none to pity him,
let there be none at all
that on his children fatherless
will let his mercy fall.

Let his posterity from earth
cut off for ever be,
and in the next age let their
name
be blotted out by thee.
Let God his father's wickedness
still to remembrance call;
and never let his mother's sin
be blotted out at all.

15 But let them all before the Lord
appear continually,
that he may wholly from the
earth
cut off their memory.
16 Because he mercy minded not,
but persecuted still
the poor and needy, that he
might
the broken-hearted kill.

17 As he in cursing pleasure took,
so doth it to him fall;
as he delighted not to bless,
he is not blest at all.
18 As cursing he like clothes puts on,
into his bowels so,
like water, and into his bones,
like oil, it down doth go.

19 Like to the garment let it be
which doth himself array,
and for a girdle, wherewith he
is girt about alway.
20 From God let this be their
reward
that enemies are to me,
and their reward that speak
against
my soul maliciously.

21 But for thine own name's sake,
deal thou,
O God the Lord, with me:
since good thy loving-kindness is,
from trouble set me free.
22 For I am poor and indigent,
afflicted sore am I,
my heart within me also is
wounded exceedingly.

23 I pass like a declining shade,
I'm like the locust tossed:
24 my knees through fasting
weakened are,
my flesh hath fatness lost.
25 I also am a vile reproach
unto them made to be;
and they that do upon me look
do shake their heads at me.

26 O thou, who art the Lord my
God,
an helper be to me;
and, for thy tender mercy's sake,
do thou my Saviour be.
27 That thereby they may know that
this
is thy almighty hand;
and that thou, Lord, hast done
the same
they may well understand.

28   Although they curse with spite,
        yet, Lord,
    bless thou with loving voice:
    let them asham'd be when they
        rise;
    thy servant let rejoice.

29   Let thou mine adversaries fierce
    with shame be clothed all;
    and, as a mantle, over them
    let their confusion fall.

30   But as for me, I with my mouth
    will greatly praise the Lord;
    and I among the multitude
    his praises will record.

31   For at the right hand of the poor
    shall stand the Lord most high,
    to save him from all those that
        would
    condemn his soul to die.

110   FIRST VERSION

1   Jehovah said unto my Lord,
    sit thou at my right hand,
    until I make thy foes a stool,
    whereon thy feet may stand.

2   The Lord shall out of Zion send
    the rod of thy great power:
    in midst of all thine enemies
    be thou the governor.

3   A willing people in thy day
    of power shall come to thee,
    in holy beauties from morn's
        womb;
    thy youth like dew shall be.

4   The Lord himself hath made an
        oath,
    and will repent him never,
    of the order of Melchizedek
    thou art a priest for ever.

5   The glorious and mighty Lord,
    that sits at thy right hand,
    shall, in his day of wrath, strike
        through
    kings that do him withstand.

6   Among the nations he shall
        judge,
    the places fill with dead;
    and over broad and spacious
        lands
    he shall strike down the head.

7   The brook that runneth in the
        way
    with drink shall him supply;
    and, for this cause, in triumph he
    shall lift his head on high.

110   SECOND VERSION

1   Unto my Lord Jehovah said:
    At my right hand I throne thee,
    till, at thy feet in triumph laid,
    thy foes their ruler own thee.
    From Zion hill the Lord shall
        send
    thy sceptre, till before thee bend
    the knees of proud rebellion.

2   Thy saints, to greet thy day of
        might,
    in holy raiment muster:
    as dewdrops in the morning light
    thy youths around thee cluster.
    The Lord hath sworn and made
        decree,
    thou, like Melchizedek, shalt be
    a kingly priest for ever.

3   The Lord at thy right hand shall
        bring
    on rulers desolation;
    the Lord shall smite each
        heathen king,
    and judge each rebel nation.
    He, swiftly marching in his
        wrath,
    shall quaff the brook upon his
        path,
    and lift his head in glory.

111

1   Praise ye the Lord: with my
        whole heart
    the Lord's praise I'll declare,
    where the assemblies of the just
    and congregations are.

2   The doings of Jehovah are
    exceeding great in might;
    sought out they are of every one
    that doth therein delight.

3   His work most honourable is,
    most glorious and pure,
    and his untainted righteousness
    for ever doth endure.

4   His works most wondrous he
        hath made
    remembered still to be;
    the Lord is most compassionate,
    and merciful is he.

5   He giveth meat unto all those
    that truly do him fear;
    and evermore his covenant
    he in his mind will bear.

6   He did the power of his works
    unto his people show,

when he the heathen's heritage
upon them did bestow.

7 His hands' works all are truth
and right,
all his commands are sure;
8 and, done in truth and
uprightness,
they evermore endure.
9 He sent redemption to his folk,
his covenant set for aye:
holy and reverend is his name,
to be adored alway.

10 Wisdom's beginning is God's
fear:
and wise in heart are they
who his most holy precepts keep:
his praise endures for aye.

112

1 Praise ye the Lord. The man is
blessed
that fears the Lord aright,
he who in his commandments all
doth greatly take delight.
2 His seed shall power have on
earth
and great prosperity:
the children of the upright man
shall ever blessed be.

3 Riches and wealth shall ever be
within his house in store;
and his unspotted righteousness
endures for evermore.
4 Unto the upright light doth rise,
though he in darkness be:
compassionate, and merciful,
and righteous is he.

5 A good man doth his favour
show,
and doth to others lend:
he in the judgment will his cause
maintain unto the end.
6 Surely there is not anything
that ever shall him move:
the righteous man's memorial
shall everlasting prove.

7 When he shall evil tidings hear,
he shall not be afraid:
his heart is fixed, his confidence
upon the Lord is stay'd.
8 His heart is firmly stablished,
afraid he shall not be,
until upon his enemies
he his desire shall see.

9 He hath dispersed his wealth
abroad,

and given to the poor;
his horn in honour shall be
raised,
his righteousness endure.
10 The wicked shall it see, and fret,
his teeth gnash, melt away:
what wicked men do most desire
shall utterly decay.

113

1 Praise ye the Lord: who serve
the Lord,
O praise, the Lord's name praise.
2 The Lord's name, blessed let it be
from this time forth always.
3 From rising sun to where he sets
the Lord's name's to be praised.
4 'Bove nations all the Lord is high,
'bove heavens his glory raised.

5 Unto the Lord our God that
dwells
on high, who can compare?
6 Himself that humbleth things to
see
in heaven and earth that are.
7 He lifts the helpless from the
dust,
the poor from low estate;
8 That he may him with princes
set,
his people's princes great.

9 The barren woman house to keep
he maketh, and to be
of sons a mother full of joy.
Praise to the Lord give ye.

114 FIRST VERSION

1 When Israel out of Egypt went,
and did his dwelling change,
when Jacob's house went out
from those
that were of language strange,
2 Judah became his holy place,
Israel his own domain;
3 the sea beheld, and quickly fled,
Jordan turned back again.

4 Like rams the mountains, and
like lambs
the hills skipped to and fro.
5 O sea, why fledd'st thou? Jordan,
back
why wast thou driven so?
6 Ye mountains great, wherefore
was it
that ye did skip like rams?
And wherefore was it, little hills,
that ye did leap like lambs?

7 O at the presence of the Lord,
earth, tremble thou for fear,
what time the presence of the
    God
of Jacob doth appear:
8 who in the desert from the rock
did pools of water bring;
and by his power did turn the
    flint
into a water-spring.

114 SECOND VERSION

1 When Israel had from Egypt
    gone,
Jacob from men of speech
    unknown;
then Judah was his holy place,
and his dominion Israel's race.
2 The sea, affrighted, saw and fled;
back Jordan driven was with
    dread;
the lofty mountains skipped like
    rams,
and all the little hills like lambs.
3 What ailed thee, that thou
    fledd'st, O sea?
Thou, Jordan, that thou back didst
    flee?
Ye mountains, that ye skipped
    like rams?
and all ye little hills like lambs?
4 Earth, tremble, for the Lord is
    near:
before the God of Jacob, fear;
who from the rock did water
    bring,
and made the flint a water-
    spring.

115 FIRST VERSION

1 Not unto us, Lord, not to us,
but do thou glory take
unto thy name, even for thy
    truth,
and for thy mercy's sake.
2 O wherefore should the heathen
    say,
where is their God now gone?
3 But our God in the heavens is,
what pleased him he hath done.

4 Their idols silver are and gold,
work of men's hands they be.
5 Mouths have they, but they do
    not speak;
and eyes, but do not see;
6 ears have they, but they do not
    hear;

noses, yet smell they not;
7 hands, feet, but handle not, nor
    walk;
nor speak they through their
    throat.
8 Like them their makers are, and
    all
on them their trust that build.
9 O Israel, trust thou in the Lord,
he is their help and shield.
10 O Aaron's house, trust in the
    Lord,
their help and shield is he.
11 Who fear the Lord, trust in the
    Lord,
their help and shield is he.
12 The Lord of us hath mindful
    been,
and he will bless us still:
he will the house of Israel bless,
bless Aaron's house he will.
13 Both small and great, that fear
    the Lord,
he will them surely bless.
14 The Lord will you, you and your
    seed,
yet more and more increase.
15 O blessed are ye of the Lord,
who made the earth and heaven.
16 The heavens are for the Lord, but
    earth
he to men's sons hath given.
17 The dead praise not the Lord, nor
    those
in grave that silent be;
18 him praise will we henceforth for
    aye.
Praise to the Lord give ye.

115 SECOND VERSION

1 Not ours the glory make,
Lord, give not us the fame;
but for thy truth and mercy's
    sake
ascribe it to thy name!
2 To say, Where is their God,
why should the heathen dare?
Since he in heaven hath his
    abode,
and works his pleasure there.

3 Men's hands their idols make
of silver and of gold;
mouths have they, but they
    cannot speak;
eyes, but they nought behold.
4 Their ears are senseless too;
their nostrils smelling not;

their hands and feet nor feel nor
go,
nor speak they through their
throat.

5 All those who them adore,
or form them, like them be;
O Israel, trust God evermore,
for our defence is he.

6 On God, who shields the just,
let Aaron's house depend;
let those who fear him in him
trust,
for he will such defend.

7 God hath remembered us,
and will his mercy show;
on Israel, and on Aaron's house,
he blessings will bestow.

8 Of high and low degree,
all those that him adore
he keeps; and you and yours
shall he
increase yet more and more.

9 Blest of the Lord are ye,
who made both earth and
heaven;
heaven for himself created he,
but earth to men hath given.

10 Their voice they cannot raise,
who down to silence go;
but we, from this time forth, his
praise
for evermore will show.

116

1 I love the Lord, because my voice
and prayers he did hear.

2 I, while I live, will call on him,
who bowed to me his ear.

3 The cords of death on every side
encompassed me around;
the sorrows of the grave me
seized,
I grief and trouble found.

4 Then on the Lord's name did I
call,
and unto him did say,
Deliver thou my soul, O Lord,
I do thee humbly pray.

5 Our God is very merciful,
gracious and just the Lord:

6 he saves the meek: I was brought
low,
he did me help afford.

7 O thou my soul, do thou return
unto thy quiet rest;
for largely unto thee the Lord

his bounty hath expressed.

8 For my distressed soul from
death
delivered was by thee:
thou didst my mourning eyes
from tears,
my feet from falling, free.

9 I in the land of those that live
will walk the Lord before.

10 I did believe, I therefore spake:
I was afflicted sore.

11 I said, when I was in my haste,
that all men liars be.

12 What shall I render to the Lord
for all his gifts to me?

13 I'll of salvation take the cup,
and on the Lord's name call;

14 I'll pay my vows unto the Lord
before his people all.

15 Dear in his sight is his saints'
death.

16 Thy servant, Lord, am I;
thy servant sure, thine
handmaid's son:
my bands thou didst untie.

17 Thank-offerings I to thee will
give,
and on the Lord's name call.

18 I'll pay my vows now to the Lord
before his people all,

19 within the courts of the Lord's
house,
within the midst of thee,
O city of Jerusalem.
Praise to the Lord give ye.

117 FIRST VERSION

1 O all ye nations of the earth
give praise unto the Lord;
and all ye people magnify
his name with one accord.

2 For great to us-ward ever are
his loving-kindnesses:
his truth endures for evermore.
the Lord O do ye bless.

117 SECOND VERSION

1 From all that dwell below the
skies,
O let Jehovah's praise arise!
and let his glorious name be sung
in every land, by every tongue!

2 Great are the mercies of the Lord,
and truth eternal is his word;
ye nations, sound from shore to
shore
Jehovah's praise for evermore!

118

1 O praise the Lord, for he is good;
his mercy lasteth ever.
2 Let those who are of Israel say,
His mercy faileth never.
3 Now let the house of Aaron say,
His mercy lasteth ever.
4 Let those that fear the Lord now
say,
His mercy faileth never.

5 I in distress called on the Lord;
the Lord did answer me:
he in a large place did me set,
from trouble made me free.
6 The Lord himself is on my side,
I will not be afraid;
for any thing that man can do
I shall not be dismayed.
7 The Lord doth take my part with
them
that help to succour me;
therefore on those that do me
hate
I my desire shall see.
8 'Tis better in the Lord to trust
than trust in man's defence;
9 better trust in the Lord than
make
princes our confidence.

10 The nations, joining all in one,
did compass me about:
but in the Lord's most holy name
I shall them all root out.
11 They compassed me about; I say,
They compassed me about:
but in the Lord's most holy name
I shall them all root out.

12 Like bees they compassed me
about;
they're quenched like thorns that
flame:
for I will surely them destroy,
in the Lord's holy name.
13 Thou hast sore thrust that I might
fall,
the Lord hath succoured me:
14 the Lord my Saviour is become,
my strength and song is he.

15 In dwellings of the just the voice
of joy and health shall be;
the right hand of the mighty Lord
doth ever valiantly.
16 The right hand of the mighty
Lord
exalted is on high;

the right hand of the mighty Lord
doth ever valiantly.
17 I shall not die, but live, and shall
Jehovah's works make known.
18 The Lord hath me chastised sore,
but not to death brought down.
19 O set ye open unto me
the gates of righteousness;
then will I enter into them,
and I the Lord will bless.

20 This is the gate of God, by it
the just shall enter in.
21 Thee will I praise, for thou me
heard'st,
and hast my safety been.
22 That stone is made head corner-
stone,
which builders did despise:
23 this is the doing of the Lord,
and wondrous in our eyes.

24 This day the Lord hath made, in
it
we'll joy triumphantly.
25 Save, Lord, I pray thee; Lord, I
pray
send thou prosperity.
26 Blessed in the Lord's great name
is he
that cometh us among;
we bless you from the house
which doth
unto the Lord belong.

27 God is the Lord, who unto us
hath made light to arise:
bind ye unto the altar's horns
with cords the sacrifice.
28 Thou art my God, I'll thee exalt;
my God, I will thee praise.
29 Praise ye the Lord, for he is good:
his mercy lasts always.

119

ALEPH THE FIRST PART

1 Blessed are they that undefiled,
and straight are in the way;
who in the Lord's most holy law
do walk, and do not stray.
2 Blessed are they who to observe
his statutes are inclined;
and who do seek the living God
with their whole heart and mind.

3 Such in his ways do walk, and
they
do no iniquity.
4 Thou hast commanded us to keep
thy precepts carefully.

5 O that thy statutes to observe
thou would'st my ways direct!
6 Then shall I not be shamed when I
thy precepts all respect.

7 Then with integrity of heart
thee will I praise and bless,
when I the judgments all have learned
of thy pure righteousness.
8 That I will keep thy statutes all
firmly resolved have I:
O do not then, most gracious God,
forsake me utterly.

119

BETH The Second Part

9 By what means shall a young man learn
his way to purify?
If he according to thy word
thereto attentive be.
10 Unfeignedly thee have I sought
with all my soul and heart:
O let me not from the right path
of thy commands depart.

11 Thy word I in my heart have hid,
that I offend not thee.
12 O Lord, thou ever blessed art,
thy statutes teach thou me.
13 The judgements of thy mouth each one
my lips declared have:
14 more joy thy testimonies' way
than riches all me gave.

15 Thy holy precepts I will make
my meditation still:
and have respect unto thy ways
most carefully I will.
16 Upon thy statutes my delight
shall constantly be set:
and, by thy grace, I never will
thy holy word forget.

119

GIMEL The Third Part

17 With me thy servant, in thy grace,
deal bountifully, Lord;
that by thy favour I may live,
and duly keep thy word.
18 Open mine eyes, that of thy law
the wonders I may see.
19 I am a stranger on the earth,
hide not thy laws from me.

20 My soul within me breaks, and doth
much fainting still endure,
through longing that it hath all times
unto thy judgements pure.
21 Thou hast rebuked the cursed proud,
who from thy precepts swerve.
22 Reproach and shame remove from me,
for I thy laws observe.

23 Though princes in assembly sit,
and counsel 'gainst me take,
thy statutes I, thy servant, still
my meditation make.
24 My comfort, and my heart's delight,
thy testimonies be;
and they, in all my doubts and fears,
are counsellors to me.

119

DALETH The Fourth Part

25 My soul to dust cleaves; quicken me,
according to thy word.
26 My ways I showed, and me thou heard'st;
teach me thy statutes, Lord.
27 The way of thy commandments teach,
and make me well to know;
so all thy works that wondrous are
I shall to others show.

28 My soul doth melt, and drop away,
for heaviness and grief:
to me, according to thy word,
give strength and send relief.
29 O let the way of falsehood far
from me removed be;
and graciously thy holy law
do thou grant unto me.

30 I chosen have the perfect way
of truth and verity:
thy judgments that most righteous are
before me laid have I.
31 I to thy testimonies cleave;
shame do not on me cast.
32 I'll run thy precepts' way, for thou
my heart enlarged hast.

THE IRISH PSALTER

119

HE THE FIFTH PART

33 Teach me, O Lord, the perfect
way
of thy precepts divine,
and to observe it to the end
I shall my heart incline.
34 Give understanding unto me,
so keep thy law shall I;
yea, even with my whole heart I
shall
observe it carefully.
35 In thy law's path make me to go;
for I delight therein.
36 My heart unto thy testimonies,
and not to greed, incline.
37 Turn thou away my sight and
eyes
from viewing vanity;
and in thy good and holy way
be pleased to quicken me.
38 Confirm to me thy gracious word,
which I did gladly hear;
to me thy servant, Lord, who am
devoted to thy fear.
39 Turn thou away my feared
reproach;
for good thy judgments be.
40 Lo, for thy precepts I have
longed;
in thy truth quicken me.

119

VAU THE SIXTH PART

41 Let thy sweet mercies also come
and visit me, O Lord:
let thy salvation come to me,
according to thy word.
42 So shall I have wherewith I may
give him an answer just,
who spitefully reproacheth me;
for in thy word I trust.
43 The word of truth out of my
mouth
take thou not utterly;
for on thy righteous judgments
still
doth all my hope rely.
44 So shall I keep for evermore
thy law continually.
45 Because I have thy precepts
sought,
I'll walk at liberty.
46 I'll speak thy word to kings, and I
shall not be moved with shame;

47 and in thy laws I will delight,
for I have loved the same.
48 To thy commandments, which I
loved,
my hands lift up I will;
and I will also meditate
upon thy statutes still.

119

ZAIN THE SEVENTH PART

49 The promise keep in mind,
which thou
didst to thy servant make,
the word, which as my ground of
hope
thou causedst me to take.
50 By this, in time of my distress,
great comfort I have known;
for in my straits I am revived
by this thy word alone.
51 The arrogant and proud in heart
did greatly me deride;
yet from thy good and holy law
I have not turned aside.
52 Thy righteous judgments, which
of old
thou didst make known, O Lord,
I have remembered, and to me
they comfort did afford.
53 Horror took hold on me, because
ill men thy law forsake.
54 I in my house of pilgrimage
thy laws my songs do make.
55 Thy name by night, Lord, I did
mind,
and I have kept thy law.
56 And this I had, because thy word
I kept, and stood in awe.

119

CHETH THE EIGHTH PART

57 Thou my sure portion art alone,
which I did choose, O Lord;
I have resolved, and said, that I
would keep thy holy word.
58 With my whole heart I did
entreat
thy face and favour free:
according to thy gracious word
be merciful to me.
59 I thought upon my former ways,
and did my life well try;
and to thy testimonies pure
my feet then turned I.
60 I did not stay, nor linger long,

as those that slothful are;
but hastily thy laws to keep
myself I did prepare.

61 Bands of the wicked me beset,
thy law I did not slight.
62 I'll rise at midnight thee to
praise,
even for thy judgments right.
63 I am companion to all those
who fear, and thee obey.
64 O Lord, thy mercy fills the earth:
teach me thy laws, I pray.

119

TETH THE NINTH PART

65 Well hast thou with thy servant
dealt,
as thou didst promise give.
66 Good judgment me, and
knowledge teach,
for I thy word believe.
67 Ere I afflicted was I strayed;
but now I keep thy word.
68 Good art thou, and thou doest
good:
teach me thy statutes, Lord.

69 The men that are puffed up with
pride
against me forged a lie;
but as for me, thy precepts keep
with all my heart will I.
70 Their hearts, through worldly
ease and wealth,
as fat as grease they be;
but in thy holy law I take
delight continually.
71 It hath been very good for me
that I afflicted was,
that I might well instructed be,
and learn thy holy laws.
72 The word that cometh from thy
mouth
is better unto me
than many thousands and great
sums
of gold and silver be.

119

JOD THE TENTH PART

73 Thy hands have made and
fashioned me;
teach me thy laws, O Lord.
74 They who thee fear see me with
joy,
for I trust in thy word.

75 That righteous are thy judgments,
Lord,
I know, and do confess;
and that thou hast afflicted me
in truth and faithfulness.
76 O let thy kindness merciful,
I pray thee, comfort me,
as to thy servant promised was
in faithfulness by thee.
77 And let thy tender mercies come
to me, that I may live;
because thy holy laws to me
sweet delectation give.

78 O let the proud ashamed be;
for they without a cause
with me have falsely dealt; but I
will muse upon thy laws.
79 Let such as fear thee, and have
known
thy statutes, turn to me.
80 In thy laws let my heart be
sound,
that shamed I may not be.

119

CAPH THE ELEVENTH PART

81 My soul for thy salvation faints;
yet I thy word believe,
82 mine eyes fail for thy word: I say,
When wilt thou comfort give?
83 For like a bottle I'm become,
that in the smoke is set:
but still thy righteous statutes,
Lord,
I never do forget.

84 How many are thy servant's
days?
when wilt thou execute
just judgment on these wicked
men
that do me persecute?
85 The proud have digged pits for
me,
which is against thy laws.
86 Thy words all faithful are: help
me,
pursued without a cause.

87 They so consumed me, that on
earth
my life they scarce did leave:
thy precepts yet forsook I not,
but close to them did cleave.
88 After thy loving-kindness, Lord,
me quicken and preserve:
the testimony of thy mouth
so shall I still observe.

119

LAMED The Twelfth Part

89 Thy word for ever is, O Lord,
in heaven settled fast;
90 and unto generations all
thy faithfulness doth last:
the earth thou hast established,
and it abides by thee.
91 This day they stand as thou
ordain'dst;
for all thy servants be.

92 Unless in thy most perfect law
my soul delights had found,
I should have perished at the
time
my troubles did abound.
93 Thy precepts I will ne'er forget;
they quickening to me brought.
94 Lord, I am thine; O save thou
me:
thy precepts I have sought.

95 For me the wicked have laid
wait,
me seeking to destroy:
but I thy testimonies true
consider will with joy.
96 An end of all perfection here
have I beheld, O God;
but thy command no limit hath,
it is exceeding broad.

119

MEM The Thirteenth Part

97 O how I love thy law! it is
my study all the day:
98 it makes me wiser than my foes;
for it doth with me stay.
99 Than all my teachers now I have
more understanding far;
because my meditation still
thy testimonies are.

10 0In understanding I excel
even those that aged be;
because thy precepts to observe
I have sought earnestly.
101 My feet from each ill way I
stayed,
that I may keep thy word.
102 I from thy judgments have not
swerved;
for thou hast taught me, Lord.

103 How sweet unto my taste, O
Lord,
are all thy words of truth!

Yea, I do find them sweeter far
than honey to my mouth.
104 I through thy precepts, that are
pure,
do understanding get;
I therefore every way that's false
with all my heart do hate.

119

NUN The Fourteenth Part

105 Thy word is to my feet a lamp,
and to my path a light.
106 Sworn have I, and I will perform,
to keep thy judgments right.
107 I am afflicted very much
and chastened sore, O Lord:
in mercy raise and quicken me,
according to thy word.

108 The free-will-offerings of my
mouth
accept, I thee beseech:
and unto me thy servant, Lord,
thy judgments clearly teach.
109 Though still my soul be in my
hand,
thy laws I'll not forget.
110 I erred not from them, though for
me
the wicked snares did set.

111 I of thy testimonies have
above all things made choice,
to be my heritage for aye;
for they my heart rejoice.
112 I carefully inclined have
my heart still to attend;
that thy statutes may perform
alway unto the end.

119

SAMECH The Fifteenth Part

113 I hate the men of double mind,
but love thy law do I.
114 My shield and hiding-place thou
art:
I on thy word rely.
115 All ye that evil-doers are
from me depart away;
for the commandments of my
God
I purpose to obey.

116 According to thy faithful word
uphold and stablish me,
that I may live, and of my hope
ashamed never be.
117 Hold thou me up, so shall I be

in peace and safety still;
and to thy statutes have respect
continually I will.

118 Thou tread'st down all that love
to stray;
false their deceit doth prove.
119 Vile men, like dross, thou putt'st
away;
therefore thy law I love.
120 For fear of thee my very flesh
doth tremble, all dismayed;
and of thy righteous judgments,
Lord,
my soul is much afraid.

119

AIN The Sixteenth Part

121 To all men I have judgment
done,
performing justice right;
then let me not be left unto
my fierce oppressors' might.
122 For good unto thy servant, Lord,
thy servant's surety be:
from the oppression of the proud
do thou deliver me.

123 Mine eyes do fail with looking
long
for thy salvation great,
while for thy word of
righteousness
I earnestly do wait.
124 In mercy with thy servant deal,
thy statutes to me show.
125 I am thy servant, wisdom give,
that I thy laws may know.

126 'Tis time to work, Lord; for they
have
made void thy law divine.
127 Therefore thy precepts more I
love
than gold, yea, gold most fine.
128 Concerning all things thy
commands
I therefore judge are right;
and every false and wicked way
is hateful in my sight.

119

PE The Seventeenth Part

129 Thy statutes, Lord, are wonderful,
my soul them keeps with care.
130 The entrance of thy words gives
light,
makes wise who simple are.

131 My mouth I also opened have,
and panted earnestly;
for after thy commandments I
have longed exceedingly.

132 Look on me, Lord, and merciful
do thou unto me prove,
as thou art wont to do to those
thy name who truly love.
133 O let my footsteps in thy word
aright still ordered be:
let no iniquity obtain
dominion over me.

134 From man's oppression save
thou me;
so keep thy laws I will.
135 Thy face make on thy servant
shine:
teach me thy statutes still.
136 Rivers of waters from mine eyes
ran down, because I saw
that wicked men go on in sin,
and do not keep thy law.

119

TSADDI The Eighteenth Part

137 O Lord, thou ever righteous art;
thy judgments upright be.
138 Ordained thy testimonies are
in faithfulness by thee.
139 My zeal hath even consumed me,
because mine enemies
thy holy words forgotten have,
and do thy laws despise.

140 Thy word is very pure, on it
thy servant's love is set.
141 Small and despised I am, yet I
thy laws do not forget.
142 Thy righteousness is
righteousness
which ever doth endure;
thy holy law, Lord, also is
the very truth most pure.

143 Distress and anguish have me
found,
fast hold on me they take:
yet in my trouble my delight
I thy commandments make.
144 Eternal righteousness is in
thy testimonies all:
give understanding unto me,
and ever live I shall.

119

KOPH THE NINETEENTH PART

145 With my whole heart I cried,
     Lord, hear;
     I will thy word obey.
146 I cried to thee; Save me, and I
     will keep thy laws alway.
147 I of the morning did prevent
     the dawning with my cry,
     for all my hope and confidence
     did on thy word rely.

148 Mine eyes did wakefully prevent
     the watches of the night,
     that in thy word with careful
          mind
     then meditate I might.
149 After thy loving-kindness hear
     my voice, that calls on thee:
     according to thy judgment, Lord,
     revive and quicken me.

150 The men who mischief seek draw
          nigh,
     they from thy law are far:
151 but thou art near, O Lord; and
          truth
     all thy commandments are.
152 From thine own testimonies, long
     hath this been known to me,
     that thou hast founded them to
          last
     unto eternity.

119

RESH THE TWENTIETH PART

153 On my affliction do thou look,
     and me in safety set:
     deliver me, O Lord, for I
     thy law do not forget
154 After thy word revive thou me;
     save me, and plead my cause.
155 Salvation is from sinners far;
     for they seek not thy laws.

156 O Lord, both great and manifold
     thy tender mercies be:
     according to thy judgments just
     revive and quicken me.
157 My persecutors many are,
     and foes that do combine;
     yet from thy testimonies pure
     my heart doth not decline.

158 I saw transgressors, and was
          grieved;
     for they keep not thy word.
159 Behold, thy precepts I have
          loved,

in love me quicken, Lord.
160 The sum of thy most holy word
     is only truth most pure:
     thy righteous judgments every
          one
     for evermore endure.

119

SCHIN THE TWENTY-FIRST PART

161 Princes have persecuted me,
     although no cause they saw:
     but still of thy most holy word
     my heart doth stand in awe.
162 I at thy word rejoice, as one
     of spoil that finds great store.
163 Thy law I love; but lying all
     I hate and do abhor.

164 Seven times a-day it is my care
     to give due praise to thee;
     because of all thy judgments,
          Lord,
     which righteous ever be.
165 Great peace have they who love
          thy law;
     offence they shall have none.
166 I hoped for thy salvation, Lord,
     and thy commands have done.

167 My soul thy testimonies pure
     observed carefully;
     on them my heart is set, and
          them
     I love exceedingly.
168 Thy testimonies and thy laws
     I kept with special care;
     for all my works and ways each
          one
     before thee open are.

119

TAU THE TWENTY-SECOND PART

169 O let my earnest prayer and cry
     come near before thee, Lord:
     give understanding unto me,
     according to thy word.
170 Let my request before thee come:
     after thy word me free.
171 My lips shall utter praise, when
          thou
     hast taught thy laws to me.

172 My tongue of thy most blessed
          word
     shall speak, and it confess;
     for truly thy commandments all
     are perfect righteousness.
173 O let thy hand be help to me:

thy precepts are my choice.
174 I longed for thy salvation, Lord,
and in thy law rejoice.

175 O let my soul live, and it shall
give praises unto thee;
and let thy judgments righteous
be helpful unto me.
176 I, like a lost sheep, went astray;
thy servant seek, and find:
for thy commands I suffered not
to slip out of my mind.

120

1 I in my strait cried to the Lord,
and he gave ear to me.
2 From lying lips, and guileful
tongue,
O Lord, my soul set free.
3 What shall be given unto thee?
What heaped on thee, false
tongue?
4 The burning coals of juniper,
sharp arrows of the strong.
5 Woe's me that I in Mesech am
a sojourner so long:
that I beside the tents do dwell
to Kedar that belong.
6 My soul with him that hateth
peace
hath long a dweller been.
7 I am for peace; but when I speak,
for battle they are keen.

121

1 I to the hills will lift mine eyes,
from whence doth come mine
aid.
My safety cometh from the Lord,
who heaven and earth hath
made.
2 Thy foot he'll not let slide, nor
will
he slumber that thee keeps.
Behold, he that keeps Israel,
he slumbers not, nor sleeps.

3 The Lord thee keeps, the Lord
thy shade
on thy right hand doth stay:
the moon by night thee shall not
smite,
nor yet the sun by day.
4 The Lord shall keep thy soul; he
shall
preserve thee from all ill.
Henceforth thy going out and in
God keep for ever will.

122

1 I joyed when To the house of
God,
go up, they said to me.
2 Jerusalem, within thy gates
our feet shall standing be.
3 Jerusalem, as a city, is
compactly built together:
4 unto that place the tribes go up,
the tribes of God go thither, —

A statute this for Israel, —
to God's name thanks to pay.
5 For thrones of judgment, even
the thrones
of David's house there stay.
6 Pray that Jerusalem may have
peace and felicity:
let them that love thee and thy
peace
have still prosperity.

7 Therefore I wish that peace may
still
within thy walls remain,
and ever may thy palaces
prosperity retain.
8 Now, for my friends' and
brethren's sakes,
Peace be in thee, I'll say.
9 And for the house of God the
Lord,
I'll seek thy good alway.

123

1 O thou that dwellest in the
heavens,
I lift mine eyes to thee.
2 Behold, as servants' eyes are
turned
their master's hand to see,
and as upon her mistress' hand
a handmaid's eyes attend;
our eyes are on the Lord our
God,
till he us mercy send.

3 O Lord, be gracious unto us,
unto us gracious be;
because replenished with
contempt
exceedingly are we.
4 Our soul is filled with scorn of
those
that at their ease abide,
and with the insolent contempt
of those that swell in pride.

124 FIRST VERSION

1 Had not the Lord been on our side,
   may Israel now say;
2 Had not the Lord been on our side,
   when men rose us to slay;
3 alive they had us swallowed then
   in rage beyond control;
4 the waters had us overwhelmed,
   the stream gone o'er our soul.

5 Then had the waters swelling high
   over our soul made way.
6 Blessed be the Lord, who to their teeth
   us gave not for a prey.
7 Our soul's escaped, as a bird
   out of the fowler's snare;
   the snare asunder broken is,
   and we escaped are.

8 Our sure and all-sufficient help
   is in Jehovah's name;
   his name who did the heaven create,
   and who the earth did frame.

124 SECOND VERSION

1 Now Israel may say, and that truly,
   If that the Lord had not our cause maintained,
2 if that the Lord had not our right sustained,
   when cruel men who us desired to slay
   rose up in wrath, to make of us their prey;

3 Then certainly they had devoured us all,
   and swallowed quick, for ought that we could deem;
   such was their rage, as we might well esteem.
4 And as fierce floods before them all things drown,
   so had they brought our soul to death quite down.

5 The raging streams, with their proud swelling waves,
   had then our soul o'erwhelmed in the deep.
6 But blessed be God, who doth us safely keep,
   and gave us not a living prey to be

unto their teeth and bloody cruelty.

7 Even as a bird out of the fowler's snare
   escapes away, so is our soul set free:
   rent is their net, and thus escaped we.
8 Therefore our help is in the Lord's great name,
   who heaven and earth by his great power did frame.

125

1 They in the Lord that firmly trust
   shall be like Zion hill,
   which at no time can be removed,
   but stand for ever will.
2 As round about Jerusalem
   the mountains stand alway,
   the Lord his folk doth compass so,
   from henceforth and for aye.

3 For ill men's rod upon the lot
   of just men shall not lie;
   lest righteous men stretch forth their hands
   unto iniquity.
4 Do thou to all those that be good
   thy blessing, Lord, impart;
   thy blessing give thou unto all
   who upright are in heart.

5 But as for such as turn aside
   after their crooked way,
   with ill men God shall send them forth:
   on Israel peace shall stay.

126

1 When Zion's bondage God turned back,
   as men that dreamed were we.
2 Then filled with laughter was our mouth,
   our tongue with melody.
   They 'mong the heathen said, The Lord
   great things for them hath wrought.
3 The Lord hath done great things for us,
   whence joy to us is brought.

4 As streams of water in the south,
   our bondage, Lord, recall.
5 Who sow in tears, a reaping time
   of joy enjoy they shall.

6   The man who, bearing precious
seed,
in going forth doth mourn,
he doubtless, bringing back his
sheaves,
rejoicing shall return.

127

1   Except the Lord do build the
house,
the builders lose their pain:
except the Lord the city keep,
the watchmen watch in vain.
2   'Tis vain for you to rise betimes,
or late from rest to keep,
to feed on sorrows' bread; so
gives
he his beloved sleep.

3   Lo, children are God's heritage,
the womb's fruit his reward.
4   The sons of youth as arrows are,
for strong men's hands prepared.
5   O happy is the man that hath
his quiver filled with those;
they unashamed in the gate
shall speak unto their foes.

128

1   Blest is each one that fears the
Lord,
and walketh in his ways;
2   for of thy labour thou shalt eat,
and prosper all thy days.
3   Thy wife shall as a fruitful vine
by thy house' sides be found;
thy children like to olive-plants
about thy table round.

4   Behold, the man that fears the
Lord,
thus blessed shall he be.
5   The Lord shall out of Zion give
his blessing unto thee:
thou shalt Jerusalem's good
behold
whilst thou on earth dost dwell.
6   Thou shalt thy children's
children see,
and peace on Israel.

129

1   Oft did they vex me from my
youth,
may Israel now declare;
2   oft did they vex me from my
youth,
yet not victorious were.

3   The ploughers ploughed upon
my back,
they long their furrows made;
4   The righteous Lord hath cut the
cords
the wicked round me laid.

5   Let Zion's haters back be turned,
into confusion thrown;
6   as grass on housetops let them be,
which fades ere it be grown:
7   whereof enough to fill his hand
the mower cannot find;
nor can the man his bosom fill,
whose work is sheaves to bind.

8   Nor is it said by passers by,
God's blessing on you rest:
we in the Lord's most holy name
pray that ye may be blest.

130

1   Lord, from the depths to thee I
cried.
2   My voice, Lord, do thou hear:
unto my supplication's voice
give an attentive ear.
3   Lord, who shall stand, if thou, O
Lord,
should'st mark iniquity?
4   But yet with thee forgiveness is,
that feared though mayest be.

5   I wait for God, my soul doth wait,
my hope is in his word.
6   More than they that for morning
watch,
my soul waits for the Lord;
yea, even more than they that
watch
the morning light to see.
7   Let Israel in Jehovah hope,
for with him mercies be;

Redemption also plenteous
is ever found with him.
8   And from all his iniquities
he Israel shall redeem.

131

1   My heart not haughty is, O Lord,
mine eyes not lofty be;
nor do I deal in matters great,
or things too high for me.
2   I surely have myself behaved
with spirit calm and mild,
as child of mother weaned; my
soul
is like a weaned child.

3 Upon the Lord let all the hope
   of Israel placed be,
   even from the time that present
   is
   unto eternity.

132 FIRST VERSION

1 David, and his afflictions all,
   O Lord, remember thou;
2 how he unto the Lord did swear,
   to Jacob's Strong One vow.
3 I will not come into my house,
   nor on my bed repose;
4 no slumber on mine eyes shall
   fall
   nor sleep mine eyelids close;

5 Till for the Lord a place I find,
   where he may make abode,
   a place of habitation meet
   for Jacob's mighty God.
6 That in the land of Ephratah
   it lay we understood;
   we found it in the forest-fields,
   the city of the wood.

7 We'll to his tabernacles go,
   and at his footstool bow.
8 Arise, O Lord, into thy rest,
   the ark of thy strength, and thou.
9 O let thy priests be clothed, Lord,
   with truth and righteousness;
   and let all those that are thy
   saints
   shout loud for joyfulness.

10 For thine own servant David's
    sake,
    do not deny thy grace;
    nor of thine own anointed one
    turn thou away the face.
11 The Lord in truth to David
    sware,
    he will not turn from it,
    I of thy body's fruit will make
    upon thy throne to sit.

12 My covenant if thy sons will
    keep,
    and laws to them made known,
    their children then shall also sit
    for ever on thy throne.
13 For God of Zion hath made
    choice;
    there he desires to dwell.
14 This is my rest, here still I'll stay;
    for I do like it well.

15 Her food I'll greatly bless; her
    poor
    with bread will satisfy.

16 Her priests I'll with salvation
    clothe,
    her saints shall shout for joy.
17 And there will I make David's
    horn
    to bud forth pleasantly:
    for him that mine anointed is
    a lamp ordained have I.

18 As with a garment I will clothe
    with shame his enemies all:
    but yet the crown that he doth
    wear
    upon him flourish shall.

132 SECOND VERSION

1 David, and all his anxious care,
   do thou, O Lord, remember now;
   how he unto the Lord did swear,
   to Jacob's Mighty One did vow:
2 Into my house I will not go,
   nor will I on my bed repose;
   sleep to mine eyes I will not
   know,
   slumber shall not mine eyelids
   close;

3 Till I a place find for the Lord,
   a house for Jacob's Strong One
   build.
   Of it at Ephratah we heard,
   we found it in the forest-field.
4 We'll go into his courts, and bow
   before the footstool of his grace.
   Arise, thine ark of strength, and
   thou,
   O Lord, into thy resting-place.

5 O clothe thy priests with
   righteousness,
   and let thy saints glad shoutings
   make;
   avert not thine anointed's face,
   for thine own servant David's
   sake.
6 The Lord hath unto David sworn
   in truth, he will not turn from it,
   I of the sons unto thee born
   will make upon thy throne to sit.

7 If they my covenant will obey,
   and testimonies I make known,
   their children I will bless, and
   they
   shall sit for ever on thy throne.
8 The Lord hath chosen Zion hill;
   for there he hath desired to
   dwell.
   This is my rest, and here I will
   abide; for I do like it well.

9 I'll her provision richly bless;
with bread her poor I'll satisfy:
her priests I'll clothe with
righteousness;
her saints shall shout aloud for
joy.

10 To bud I'll there make David's
horn,
and for my king a lamp I'll trim;
his enemies I'll clothe with scorn,
but flourish shall his crown
on him.

133

1 Behold, how good a thing it is,
and how becoming well,
together such as brethren are
in unity to dwell!

2 Like precious ointment on the
head,
that down the beard did flow,
even Aaron's beard, and to the
skirts
did of his garments go.

3 As Hermon's dew, the dew that
doth
on Zion hills descend:
for there the blessing God
commands,
life that shall never end.

134

1 Behold, bless ye the Lord, all ye
that his attendants are,
who in Jehovah's temple be,
and praise him nightly there.

2 Your hands within the holy place
lift up, and bless his name.

3 From Zion hill the Lord thee
bless,
who heaven and earth did frame.

135

1 Praise ye the Lord, the Lord's
name praise;
his servants, praise ye God:

2 Who stand in God's house, in the
courts
of our God make abode.

3 Praise ye the Lord, for he is good;
unto him praises sing:
sing praises to his name, because
it is a pleasant thing.

4 For Jacob to himself the Lord
did choose of his own will,
for his peculiar treasure he
hath chosen Israel.

5 Because I know assuredly
the Lord is very great,
and that our Lord above all gods
in glory hath his seat.

6 What things soever pleased the
Lord,
that in the heaven did he,
and in the earth, the seas, and all
the places deep that be.

7 He from the ends of earth doth
make
the vapours to ascend;
for rain he lightnings makes, and
wind
doth from his treasures send.

8 Of Egypt's land the first-born all,
both man and beast, smote he;

9 sent Pharaoh and his servant
signs,
Egypt, in midst of thee.

10 He smote great nations, great
kings slew:

11 Sihon the Am'rite king,
and Og of Bashan, and to nought
did Canaan's kingdoms bring:

12 And for a goodly heritage
their pleasant land he gave,
an heritage which Israel,
his chosen folk, should have.

13 Thy name, O Lord, shall still
endure,
and thy memorial
with honour shall continued be
to generations all.

14 Because the righteous God will
judge
his people righteously;
concerning those that do him
serve
himself repent will he.

15 The idols of the nations are
of silver and of gold,
and from the hands of men they
take
their fashion and their mould.

16 Mouths have they, but they do
not speak;
eyes, but they do not see;

17 ears have they, but hear not; and
in
their mouth no breathings be.

18 Their makers like them are; and
all
their trust in them that place.

19 Bless ye the Lord, O Israel's
house;
O bless him, Aaron's race.

20 O bless the Lord, of Levi's house
    ye who his servants be;
    and all ye that the Lord do fear,
    his holy name bless ye.
21 From Zion, his own holy hill,
    blessed let Jehovah be,
    who dwelleth at Jerusalem.
    Praise to the Lord give ye.

136 FIRST VERSION

1 Give thanks to God, for good is
    he:
    for mercy hath he ever.
2 Thanks to the God of gods give
    ye:
    for his grace faileth never.
3 Thanks give the Lord of lords
    unto:
    for mercy hath he ever:
4 who only wonders great can do:
    for his grace faileth never.

5 The heavens by wisdom
    fashioned he;
    for mercy hath he ever:
6 and stretched the earth above the
    sea;
    for his grace faileth never.
7 To him that made great lights to
    shine;
    for mercy hath he ever:
8 the sun to rule till day decline;
    for his grace faileth never:
9 The moon and stars to rule by
    night;
    for mercy hath he ever:
10 who Egypt's first-born all did
    smite;
    for his grace faileth never:
11 and Israel brought out from their
    land;
    for mercy hath he ever:
12 with outstretched arm, and with
    strong hand;
    for his grace faileth never:
13 By whom the Red Sea parted
    was;
    for mercy hath he ever:
14 who through its midst made
    Israel pass;
    for his grace faileth never:
15 but Pharaoh and his hosts he
    drowned;
    for mercy hath he ever:
16 paths for his own in desert
    found;
    for his grace faileth never:

17 To him great kings who
    overthrew;
    for he hath mercy ever:
18 yea, famous kings in battle slew;
    for his grace faileth never:
19 Sihon, king of the Amorites;
    for he hath mercy ever:
20 and Og, king of the Bashanites;
    for his grace faileth never.

21 Their land as heritage to have,
    (for mercy hath he ever,)
22 his servant Israel right he gave;
    for his grace faileth never.
23 In our low state who on us
    thought;
    for he hath mercy ever:
24 and from our foes our freedom
    wrought;
    for his grace faileth never.
25 Who giveth food to all that live;
    for he hath mercy ever.
26 Thanks to the God of heaven
    give;
    for his grace faileth never.

136 SECOND VERSION

1 Praise God, for he is kind:
    his mercy lasts for aye.
2 Give thanks with heart and mind
    to God of gods alway:
        for certainly
        his mercies dure
        most firm and sure
        eternally.

3 The Lord of lords praise ye,
    whose mercies ever stand.
4 Great wonders only he
    doth work with mighty hand:
        for certainly, ...

5 Give praise to his great name,
    who, by his wisdom high,
    the heaven above did frame,
    and built the lofty sky:
        for certainly, ...

6 To him who did outstretch
    the earth so great and wide;
    above the waters' reach
    who made it to abide:
        for certainly, ...

7 Great lights who made of old;
    for his grace lasteth aye:
8 the sun, which we behold,
    to rule the lightsome day:
        for certainly, ...

9   Also the moon so clear,
    which shineth in our sight;
    the stars that do appear,
    to rule the darksome night:
    for certainly, ...

10 Who smote Egyptian foes,
    that did his message scorn;
    and in his anger rose,
    and slew all their first-born:
    for certainly, ...

11 Thence Israel out he brought;
    his mercies ever stand:
12 with outstretched arm he
        wrought,
    and with a mighty hand:
    for certainly, ...

13 The sea he clave in twain;
    for his grace lasteth still:
14 and through the parted main
    led his own Israel:
    for certainly, ...

15 But cast down Pharaoh then
    beneath the Red Sea's wave,
    and all his mighty men
    unto destruction gave:
    for certainly, ...

16 Who, in his faithfulness,
    his chosen people led
    through the great wilderness,
    and in his love them fed:
    for certainly, ...

17 To him great kings who smote;
    for his grace hath no bound:
18 who slew, and spared not,
    kings famous and renowned:
    for certainly, ...

19 Sihon the Am'rites' prince;
    for his grace lastest aye:
20 and mighty Og, who once
    in Bashan's land had sway:
    for certainly, ...

21 By lot he gave their land,
    for his grace faileth never,
22 into his Israel's hand,
    an heritage for ever:
    for certainly, ...

23 Who also on us thought
    when in our low estate:
24 and from the hand us brought
    of those who did us hate:
    for certainly, ...

25 Who to all flesh gives food;
    for his grace faileth never.
26 Give thanks to God most good,
    the God of heaven, for ever:
    for certainly, ...

137

1   By Babel's streams we sat and
        wept,
    when Zion we thought on.
2   In midst thereof we hung our
        harps
    the willow trees upon.
3   For there a song required they,
    who did us captive bring:
    our spoilers called for mirth, and
        said,
    A song of Zion sing.

4   O how the Lord's song shall we
        sing
    within a foreign land?
5   If thee, Jerusalem, I forget,
    skill part from my right hand.
6   My tongue to my mouth's roof let
        cleave,
    if I do thee forget,
    Jerusalem, and thee above
    my chief joy do not set.

7   Remember Edom's children,
        Lord,
    who in Jerusalem's day,
    Even unto its foundation raze,
    yea, raze it quite, did say.
8   O thou unto destruction doomed,
    daughter of Babylon;
    happy the man that doth to thee
    as thou to us hast done.

9   Yea, happy surely shall he be,
    thy tender little ones
    who shall lay hold upon, and
        them
    shall dash against the stones.

138

1   Thee will I praise with all my
        heart,
    I will sing praise to thee
2   before the gods: and worship will
    toward thy sanctuary.
    I'll praise thy name, even for thy
        truth,
    and kindness of thy love;
    for thou thy word hast magnified
    all thy great name above.

3 Thou didst me answer in the day
    when I did cry to thee;
  and thou with strength my
    fainting soul
  didst strengthen inwardly.
4 All kings upon the earth that are
  shall give thee praise, O Lord:
  what time they from thy mouth
    shall hear
  thy true and faithful word.

5 Yea, in the righteous ways of God
  with gladness they shall sing:
  for great's the glory of the Lord,
  who is for ever king.
6 The Lord is high, yet he regards
  all those that lowly be;
  whereas the proud and lofty ones
  afar off knoweth he.

7 Though I in midst of trouble
    walk,
  I life from thee shall have:
  'gainst my foes' wrath thou'lt
    stretch thine hand;
  thy right hand shall me save.
8 All that which me concerns the
    Lord
  will surely perfect make:
  Lord, still thy mercy lasts; do not
  thine own hands' works forsake.

139   FIRST VERSION

1 O Lord, thou hast me searched
  and known.
2 Thou knowest my sitting down,
  and rising up; yea, all my
    thoughts
  afar to thee are known.
3 My footsteps, and my lying down,
  thou compassest always;
  thou also most entirely art
  acquaint with all my ways.

4 For in my tongue, before I speak,
  not any word can be,
  but altogether, lo, O Lord,
  it is well known to thee.
5 Behind, before, thou hast beset,
  and laid on me thine hand.
6 Such knowledge is too strange for
    me,
  too high to understand.

7 Where from thy Spirit shall I go?
  or from thy presence fly?
8 Ascend I heaven, lo, thou art
    there;
  there, if in hell I lie.
9 Take I the wings of morn, and
    dwell

in utmost parts of sea;
10 even there, Lord, shall thy hand
    me lead,
  thy right hand hold shall me.

11 If I do say that darkness shall
  me cover from thy sight,
  then surely shall the very night
  about me be as light.
12 Yea, darkness hideth not from
    thee,
  but night doth shine as day:
  to thee the darkness and the light
  are both alike alway.

13 Because thou hast possessed my
    reins,
  and thou didst cover me,
  when I within my mother's
    womb
  inclosed was by thee.
14 Thee will I praise, for fearfully
  and strangely made I am:
  thy works are wonderful, and
    well
  my soul doth know the same.

15 When I was made in secret place,
  my substance thou didst see;
  when in the lowest parts of earth
  I was wrought curiously.
16 While yet unformed my
    substance was,
  thine eyes on it did look;
  my days, while yet not one had
    dawned,
  were written in thy book.

17 How precious also are thy
    thoughts,
  O gracious God, to me!
  and in their sum how passing
    great
  and numberless they be!
18 If I should count them, than the
    sand
  they more in number be:
  what time soever I awake,
  I ever am with thee.

19 Thou, Lord, wilt sure the wicked
    slay:
  hence from me bloody men.
20 Thy foes against thee loudly
    speak,
  and take thy name in vain.
21 Do not I hate all those, O Lord,
  that hatred bear to thee?
  With those that up against thee
    rise
  can I but grieved be?

22 With perfect hatred them I hate,
my foes I them do hold.
23 Search me, O God, and know my
heart,
try me, my thoughts unfold:
24 and see if any wicked way
there be at all in me;
and in thine everlasting way
to me a leader be.

139 SECOND VERSION

1 Lord, thou has search'd me, and
hast known
my rising up and lying down;
and from afar thy searching eye
beholds my thoughts that secret
lie.
2 Thou know'st my path and lying
down,
and all my ways to thee are
known;
for in my tongue no word can be,
but lo! O Lord, 'tis known to thee.
3 Behind, before me, thou dost
stand,
and lay on me thy mighty hand.
Such knowledge is for me too
strange,
'tis high beyond my utmost
range.
4 O, whither shall my footsteps fly,
beyond thy Spirit's searching
eye?
To what retreat shall I repair,
and find not still thy presence
there?
5 If I to heaven shall ascend,
thy presence there will me
attend;
if in the grave I make my bed,
lo! there I find thy presence
dread.
6 If on the morning wings I flee,
and dwell in utmost parts of sea,
ev'n there thy hand shall guide
my way,
and thy right hand shall be my
stay.
7 Or if I say, to shun thine eye,
in shades of darkness I will lie,
around me then the very night
will shine as shines the noonday
light.
8 From thee the shades can nought
disguise;
the night is day before thine
eyes;

the darkness is to thee as bright
as are the beams of noonday
light.
9 My very reins belong to thee;
thou in the womb didst cover
me;
and I to thee will praise proclaim,
for fearful, wondrous is my
frame.
10 Thy works are wonderful, I
know;
and when, in depths of earth
below,
this complicated frame was
made,
'twas all before thine eyes
displayed.
11 My substance, yet unformed by
thee,
thy searching eye did clearly see:
my days were written, every one,
within thy books, ere yet begun.
12 Thy thoughts, O God, to me are
dear;
how vast their numbers do
appear!
More than the sand my
reckonings make;
I'm still with thee when I awake.
13 Thou wilt the wicked slay, O
God;
depart from me, ye men of blood,
who speak of thee for ends
profane,
thy foes who take thy name in
vain.
14 Do not I hate thy haters, Lord?
and thy assailants hold abhorred?
A perfect hatred them I show,
and count each one to me a foe.
15 Search me, O God, my heart
discern,
try me, my very thoughts to
learn;
see if in evil paths I stray,
and guide me in the eternal way.

140

1 Lord, from the ill and froward
man
give me deliverance,
and do thou safe preserve me
from
the man of violence:
2 who in their heart things
mischievous

do meditate alway:
and they for war together are
assembled every day.

3 Even like unto a serpent's tongue
their tongues they sharp do
make;
and underneath their lips there
lies
the poison of a snake.

4 Lord, keep me from the wicked's
hands,
from violent men me save;
who utterly to overthrow
my goings purposed have.

5 The proud have hid a snare and
cords,
for me have spread a net;
close by the path they have it
spread,
and gins for me have set.

6 Then to the Lord thus did I say,
My God art thou, O Lord;
then hear my supplication's
voice,
and help to me afford.

7 Jehovah, Lord, thou who the
strength
of my salvation art,
thou to my head in day of war
protection dost impart.

8 Unto the wicked man, O Lord,
his wishes do not grant;
nor further thou his ill device,
lest they themselves should
vaunt.

9 As for the head of those that do
about encompass me,
even by the mischief of their lips
let thou them covered be.

10 Let burning coals upon them fall,
them cast into the flame,
and pits so deep, that they no
more
may rise out of the same.

11 A man of evil tongue shall not
on earth established be:
mischief shall hunt the violent
and waste him utterly.

12 The Lord, I know, will judge the
poor,
maintain the afflicted's right.

13 The righteous shall extol thy
name:
the just dwell in thy sight.

141

1 O Lord, I unto thee do cry,
do thou make haste to me,
and give an ear unto my voice,
when I cry unto thee.

2 As incense let my prayer be
directed in thine eyes;
and the uplifting of my hands
as the evening sacrifice.

3 Set, Lord, a watch before my
mouth,
keep of my lips the door.

4 My heart incline thou not unto
the ills I should abhor,
to practise wicked works with
men
that work iniquity;
and of their dainties let me not
with them partaker be.

5 Let him that righteous is me
smite,
it shall a kindness be;
let him reprove, I shall it count
a precious oil to me;
such oil my head shall not
refuse;
for yet shall come the day
when I, in their calamities,
to God for them shall pray.

6 When down the sides of rugged
rocks
their judges shall be cast,
then shall they hear my words;
for they
shall sweet be to their taste.

7 About the grave's devouring
mouth
our bones are scattered round,
as wood which men do cut and
cleave
lies scattered on the ground.

8 But unto thee, O God the Lord,
mine eyes uplifted be:
my soul do not leave destitute;
my trust is set on thee.

9 Lord, keep me safely from the
snares
which they for me prepare;
and from the subtle gins of those
that evil-doers are.

10 Let workers of iniquity
into their own nets fall,
whilst I do, by thy help, escape
the danger of them all.

142

1 I with my voice cried to the Lord,
  with it made my request:
2 poured out to him my plaint, to him
  my trouble I expressed.
3 When overwhelmed my spirit is,
  then knowest thou my way;
  where I did walk a snare for me
  they privily did lay.

4 Look on the right hand, and behold,
  there's none to know me there;
  all refuge hath me failed, and none
  doth for my soul take care.
5 I cried to thee; I said, Thou art
  a refuge, Lord, to me;
  thou art my portion in the land
  of those that living be.

6 Because I am brought very low,
  attend my cry:
  Me from my persecutors save,
  who stronger are than I.
7 From prison bring my soul, that I
  thy name may glorify:
  the just shall compass me, when thou
  with me deal'st bounteously.

143   FIRST VERSION

1 Lord, hear my prayer, regard my cries;
  and in thy faithfulness
  give thou an answer unto me,
  and in thy righteousness.
2 Thy servant also bring thou not
  in judgment to be tried:
  because no living man can be
  in thy sight justified.

3 Because the foe pursues my soul,
  my life to earth doth tread;
  in darkness he hath made me dwell,
  as those that are long dead.
4 My spirit, then, is overwhelmed
  with sore perplexity;
  within me is my very heart
  amazed wondrously.

5 I call to mind the days of old,
  I think upon thy deeds;
  on all the work I meditate
  which from thy hand proceeds.
6 My hands to thee I stretch; my soul
  thirsts as dry land for thee.

7 Haste, Lord, to hear, my spirit fails:
  hide not thy face from me;

  Lest like to them I do become
  that go down to the dust.
8 At morn let me thy kindness hear;
  for in thee do I trust.
  Teach me the way that I should walk:
  I lift my soul to thee.
9 Lord, free me from my foes; I flee
  to thee to cover me.

10 Because thou art my God, to do
  thy will do me instruct;
  good is thy Spirit, in a land
  that plain is me conduct.
11 Revive and quicken me, O Lord,
  even for thine own name's sake;
  and do thou, in thy righteousness,
  my soul from trouble take.

12 And of thy mercy slay my foes;
  let all destroyed be
  that do afflict my soul: for I
  a servant am to thee.

143   SECOND VERSION

1 O Lord, my prayer hear,
  and to my suppliant cry
  in faithfulness give ear,
  in righteousness reply.
2 In judgment call not me
  thy servant to be tried,
  no living man can be
  in thy sight justified.

3 The foe my soul hath sought,
  my life to earth doth bring;
  to darkness me hath brought,
  as those that long are dead.
4 My spirit therefore vexed
  o'erwhelmed is me within;
  my heart in me perplexed,
  and desolate hath been.

5 Yet I to mind recall
  what ancient days record,
  thy works I ponder all,
  I muse on them O Lord.
6 To thee I stretch my hands,
  do thou my helper be;
  behold as thirsty lands
  my soul doth long for thee.

7 Lord, let my prayer prevail,
  to answer it make speed;
  my spirit quite doth fail:
  hide not thy face in need;

lest I be like to those
that do in darkness sit,
or him that downward goes
into the dreadful pit.

8   Because I trust in thee,
O Lord, cause me to hear
thy loving-kindness free,
when morning doth appear:
make me to know the way
wherein my path should be;
because my soul each day
I do lift up to thee.

9   O Lord, deliver me
from all who me oppose:
to thee, my God, I flee,
to hide me from my foes.

10   No God have I but thee,
teach me to do thy will:
thy Spirit's good, lead me
in a plain pathway still.

11   Lord, for thine own name's sake,
be pleased to quicken me;
in righteousness O take
my soul from misery.

12   In mercy cut off those
that enemies are to me;
slay of my soul the foes:
I servant am to thee.

144

1   O blessed ever be the Lord,
who is my strength and might,
who doth instruct my hands to war,
my fingers teach to fight.

2   My goodness, fortress, my high tower,
deliverer, and shield,
in whom I trust: who under me
my people makes to yield.

3   Lord, what is man, that thou of him
dost so much knowledge take?
Or son of man, that thou of him
so great account dost make?

4   Man is like vanity; his days,
as shadows, pass away.

5   Lord, bow thy heavens, come down, touch thou
the hills, and smoke shall they.

6   Cast forth thy lightning, scatter them;
thine arrows shoot, them rout.

7   Thine hand send from above, me save;
from great depths draw me out;

and from the hand of children strange,

8   Whose mouth speaks vanity;
and their right hand a right hand is
that works deceitfully.

9   A new song I to thee will sing,
Lord, on a psaltery;
I on a ten-stringed instrument
will praises sing to thee.

10   Even he it is that unto kings
doth his salvation send;
who his own servant David doth
from hurtful sword defend.

11   O free me from strange children's hand,
whose mouth speaks vanity:
and their right hand a right hand is
that works deceitfully.

12   That like to well-grown plants our sons
in time of youth may be;
our daughters like to pillars carved
in palace fair to see.

13   That all our garners may be full,
store of all kinds may yield;
and that our flocks may thousands bear,
ten thousands in the field.

14   That strong our oxen be for work,
that no inbreaking be,
nor going forth; and that our streets
from outcry may be free.

15   Blest is the people that is found
in such a case as this;
yea, greatly is the people blest,
whose God Jehovah is.

145   FIRST VERSION

1   I'll thee extol, my God, O King;
I'll bless thy name always.

2   Thee will I bless each day, and will
thy name for ever praise.

3   Great is the Lord, much to be praised;
his greatness search exceeds.

4   Race unto race shall praise thy works,
and show thy mighty deeds.

5   I of thy glorious majesty
the honour will record;
I'll speak of all thy mighty works,

which wondrous are, O Lord.
6 Men of thine acts the might shall
show,
thine acts that dreadful are;
and I, thy glory to advance,
thy greatness will declare.

7 The memory of thy goodness
great
they largely shall express;
with songs of praise they shall
extol
thy perfect righteousness.
8 Jehovah very gracious is,
in him compassions flow;
in mercy he is very great,
and is to anger slow.

9 The Lord most bountiful extends
his goodness unto all:
and over all that he hath made
his tender mercies are.
10 Thee all thy works shall praise, O
Lord,
and thee thy saints shall bless;
11 they shall thy kingdom's glory
show,
thy power by speech express:

12 To make the sons of men to know
his acts done mightily,
and of his kingdom excellent
the glorious majesty.
13 Thy kingdom shall endure for
aye,
thy reign through ages all.
14 God raiseth all that are bowed
down,
upholdeth all that fall.

15 The eyes of all things wait on
thee,
the giver of all good;
and thou in time convenient dost
bestow on them their food.
16 Thy bounteous hand thou
openest,
and dost in kindness give
enough to satisfy the wants
of all on earth that live.

17 The Lord is just in all his ways,
holy in his works all.
18 He's near to all that call on him,
in truth that on him call.
19 He will accomplish the desire
of those that do him fear:
he also will deliver them,
and he their cry will hear.

20 The Lord preserves all who him
love,
that nought can them annoy:

but he all those that wicked are
will utterly destroy.
21 My mouth the praises of the Lord
shall constantly proclaim;
and let all flesh for ever give
praise to his holy name.

145 SECOND VERSION

1 O Lord, thou art my God and
King;
thee will I magnify and praise:
I will thee bless, and gladly sing
unto thy holy name always.
2 Each day I rise I will thee bless,
and praise thy name time
without end.
3 Much to be praised, and great
God is;
his greatness none can
comprehend.

4 Race shall thy works praise unto
race,
the mighty acts show done by
thee.
5 I will speak of the glorious grace,
and honour of thy majesty;
thy wondrous works I will record.
6 By men the might shall be
extolled
of all thy dreadful acts, O Lord;
and I thy greatness will unfold.

7 They utter shall abundantly
the memory of thy goodness
great;
and shall sing praises cheerfully,
whilst they thy righteousness
relate.
8 The Lord is very gracious,
and he doth great compassion
show;
in mercy he is plenteous,
but unto wrath and anger slow.

9 Good unto all men is the Lord:
o'er all his works his mercy is.
10 Thy works all praise to thee
afford;
thy saints, O Lord, thy name shall
bless.
11 The glory of thy kingdom show
shall they, and of thy power tell;
12 that so men's sons his deeds may
know,
his kingdom's glories that excel.
13 Thy kingdom hath none end at
all,
it doth through ages all remain.

14 The Lord upholdeth all that fall,
   the cast-down raiseth up again.
15 The eyes of all things, Lord,
      attend,
   and on thee wait that here do
      live,
   and thou, in season due, dost
      send
   sufficient food them to relieve.
16 Yea, thou thine hand dost open
      wide,
   and everything dost satisfy
   that lives and doth on earth
      abide,
   of thy great liberality.
17 The Lord is just in his ways all,
   and holy in his works each one.
18 He's near to all that on him call,
   who call in truth on him alone.
19 The Lord will the desire fulfil
   of such as truly do him fear:
   in time of need them save he
      will,
   for he their earnest cry will hear.
20 The Lord keeps all in
      faithfulness,
   that bear to him a loving heart:
   but workers all of wickedness
   destroy will he, and quite
      subvert.
21 My mouth the praises of the Lord
   shall therefore constantly
      proclaim:
   and let all flesh with one accord
   for ever bless his holy name.

146

1 Praise ye the Lord: him praise,
   my soul.
2 I'll praise God while I live;
   while I have being to my God
   in songs I'll praises give.
3 Trust not in princes, nor man's
      son,
   in whom there is no stay:
4 his breath departs, to 's earth he
      turns;
   that day his thoughts decay.

5 O happy is that man and blest,
   whom Jacob's God doth aid;
   whose hope upon the Lord doth
      rest,
   and on his God is stayed:
6 who made the earth and heavens
      high,
   who made the swelling deep,

and all that is within the same;
who truth doth ever keep:
7 Who righteous judgment
      executes
   for those oppressed that be,
   who to the hungry giveth food,
   and sets the prisoners free.
8 The Lord doth give the blind
      their sight,
   the bowed down doth raise:
   the Lord doth dearly love all
      those
   who walk in upright ways.
9 The stranger's shield, the
      widow's stay,
   the orphan's help is he:
   but yet by him the wicked's way
   turned upside down shall be.
10 The Lord shall reign for
      evermore:
   thy God, O Zion, he
   to generations all shall reign.
   Praise to the Lord give ye.

147   FIRST VERSION

1 Praise ye the Lord; for it is good
   praise to our God to sing:
   for it is pleasant, and to praise
   is a becoming thing.
2 The Lord builds up Jerusalem,
   and he it is alone
   that the dispersed of Israel
   doth gather into one.
3 Those that are broken in their
      heart
   and grieved in their minds
   he healeth, and their painful
      wounds
   he tenderly up-binds.
4 He counts the number of the
      stars;
   he names them every one.
5 Great is our Lord, and of great
      power;
   his wisdom search can none.
6 The Lord lifts up the meek; and
      casts
   the wicked to the ground.
7 Sing to the Lord, and give him
      thanks;
   on harp his praises sound;
8 who covereth the heaven with
      clouds,
   who for the earth below
   prepareth rain, who maketh grass
   upon the mountains grow.

9 He gives the beast his food, he feeds
the ravens young that cry.
10 His pleasure not in horse's strength,
nor in man's legs doth lie.
11 But in all those that do him fear
the Lord doth pleasure take;
in those that to his mercy do
in hope themselves betake.

12 The Lord praise, O Jerusalem;
Zion, thy God confess:
13 for thy gates' bars he maketh strong,
thy sons in thee doth bless.
14 He in thy borders maketh peace;
with fine wheat filleth thee.
15 He sends forth his command on earth,
his word runs speedily.

16 Hoar-frost, like ashes, scattereth he;
like wool he snow doth give:
17 like morsels casteth forth his ice;
who in its cold can live?
18 He sendeth forth his mighty word,
and melteth them again;
his wind he makes to blow, and then
the waters flow amain.

19 The doctrine of his holy word
to Jacob he doth show;
his statutes and his judgments he
gives Israel to know.
20 Of other nations unto none
such favour shown hath he:
and they his judgments have not known.
Praise to the Lord give ye.

147 SECOND VERSION

1 Praise God! 'tis good and pleasant,
and comely to adore;
Jehovah builds up Salem,
her outcasts doth restore.
2 He heals the broken-hearted,
and makes the wounded live;
the starry hosts he numbers,
and names to all doth give.

3 Our Lord is great and mighty;
his wisdom none can know;
the Lord doth raise the lowly
and sinners overthrow.
4 O thank and praise Jehovah!
Praise him on harp with mirth,

the heaven with clouds who covers,
and sends his rain on earth.
5 He clothes with grass the mountains,
and gives the beasts their food;
he hears the crying ravens,
and feeds their tender brood.
6 In horse's strength delights not,
nor speed of man loves he;
the Lord loves all who fear him,
and to his mercy flee.

7 O Salem, praise Jehovah,
thy God, O Zion, praise;
for he thy gates has strengthened,
and blessed thy sons with grace.
8 With peace he'll bless thy borders,
the finest wheat afford;
he sends forth his commandment,
and swiftly speeds his word.

9 Like wool the snow he giveth,
spreads hail o'er all the land,
hoar-frost like ashes scatters;
who can his cold withstand?
10 Then forth his word he sendeth,
he makes his wind to blow;
the snow and ice are melted,
again the waters flow.

11 He shows his word to Jacob,
to Israel's seed alone;
his statutes and his judgments
the heathen have not known.
Praise ye the Lord!

148 FIRST VERSION

1 Praise ye the Lord. From heavens him praise;
in heights praise to him be.
2 All ye his angels, praise ye him;
his hosts all, praise him ye.
3 O praise ye him, both sun and moon,
praise him, all stars of light.
4 Ye heavens of heavens him praise, and floods
above the heavens' height.

5 Let all the creatures praise the name
of the almighty Lord:
for he commanded, and they were
created by his word.
6 He also, for all times to come,
hath them established sure;

he hath appointed them a law,
which ever shall endure.

7 Praise ye Jehovah from the earth,
dragons, and every deep:
8 fire, hail, snow, vapour, stormy
wind,
his word that fully keep:
9 all hills and mountains, fruitful
trees,
and all ye cedars high:
10 beasts, and all cattle, creeping
things,
and all ye birds that fly:

11 Kings of the earth, all tribes of
men,
princes, earth's judges all:
12 young men, and youthful
maidens too,
old men, and children small.
13 Let them the Lord's name praise,
for it
alone is excellent:
his glory reacheth far above
the earth and firmament.

14 A horn he raiseth for his folk,
to all his saints a praise,
to Israel's seed so near to him.
Jehovah's glory raise.

148   SECOND VERSION

1 From heaven the Lord confess,
in heights his glory raise.
2 Him let all angels bless,
him all his armies praise.
3 Him glorify
Sun, moon, and stars;
4 ye higher spheres,
and cloudy sky.

5 Jehovah gave you birth,
him therefore glorious make;
to being ye came forth,
when he the word but spake.
6 And from that place,
where fixed you be
by his decree,
you cannot pass.

7 Praise him from earth below,
ye dragons, and ye deeps:
8 fire, hail, clouds, wind, and snow,
which in command he keeps.
9 Praise ye his name,
hills great and small,
trees low and tall,
10 beasts wild and tame.

All things that creep or fly,
11 kings, tribes of every tongue,

all princes mean or high,
12 both men and virgins young;
even young and old,
13 exalt his name;
for much his fame
should be extolled.

Jehovah's name be praised
above both earth and sky;
14 for he his saints hath raised,
and set their horn on high:
even those that be
of Israel's race,
near to his grace.
the Lord praise ye.

149   FIRST VERSION

1 Praise ye the Lord: unto him sing
a new song, and his praise
in the assembly of his saints
in sweet psalms do ye raise.
2 Let Israel in his Maker joy,
and to him praises sing:
let all that Zion's children are
be joyful in their King.

3 O let them unto his great name
give praises in the dance;
let them with timbrel and with
harp
in songs his praise advance.
4 For God doth pleasure take in
those
that his own people be;
and he with his salvation sure
the meek will beautify.

5 And in his glory excellent
let all his saints rejoice:
let them to him upon their beds
aloud lift up their voice.
6 Let in their mouth aloft be raised
the high praise of the Lord,
and let them have in their right
hand
a sharp two-edged sword;

7 To execute the vengeance due
upon the heathen all,
and make deserved punishment
upon the people fall.
8 With chains as prisoners to bind
their kings that them command;
yea, and with iron fetters strong,
the nobles of their land.

9 On them the judgment to
perform
found written in his word:
an honour this to all his saints.
O do ye praise the Lord.

149 SECOND VERSION

1 O praise ye the Lord!
Prepare your glad voice,
new songs with his saints
assembled to sing;
before his Creator
let Israel rejoice,
and children of Zion
be glad in their King.

2 And let them his name
extol in the dance;
with timbrel and harp
his praises express;
who always takes pleasure
his saints to advance,
and with his salvation
the humble to bless.

3 His saints shall sing loud
with glory and joy,
and rest undismayed;
with songs in the night
the praise of Jehovah
their lips shall employ;
a sword in their right hand
two-edged for the fight;

4 The heathen to judge,
their pride to consume,
to fetter their kings,
their princes to bind;
to execute on them
the long-decreed doom;
such honour for ever
the holy shall find. Hallelujah.

150

1 Praise ye the Lord. God's praise
within
his sanctuary raise;
and to him in the firmament
of his power give ye praise.
2 Because of all his mighty acts,
with praise him magnify:
O praise him, as he doth excel
in glorious majesty.
3 Praise him with trumpet's
sound; his praise
with psaltery advance:
4 with timbrel, harp, stringed
instruments,
and organs in the dance.
5 Praise him on cymbals loud; him
praise
on cymbals sounding high.
6 Let each thing breathing praise
the Lord.
Praise to the Lord give ye.

DOXOLOGIES
FOR USE AT THE END
OF A PSALM
OR PORTION THEREOF

1

To Father, Son, and Holy Ghost,
the God whom earth and heaven
adore,
be glory, as it was of old,
is now, and shall be evermore.
AMEN.

2

To Father, Son, and Holy Ghost,
the God whom we adore,
be glory, as it was, and is,
and shall be evermore. AMEN.

3

To Thee be glory, Lord,
whom heaven and earth adore,
to Father, Son, and Holy Ghost,
one God for evermore. AMEN.

4

PSALM 124, *second version*

Glory to God the Father, God the
Son,
And unto God the Spirit, Three
in One.
From age to age let saints his
name adore,
his power and love proclaim
from shore to shore,
and spread his fame, till time
shall be no more. AMEN.

5

PSALM 136, *first version*

To Father, Son, and Holy Ghost,
whose mercy faileth never,
be praise and glory, as it was,
is now, and shall be ever. AMEN.

6

PSALM 136, *second version*
PSALM 148, *second version*

To God the Father, Son,
and Spirit ever bless'd,
eternal Three in One,
all worship be address'd,
as heretofore
it was, is now,
and still shall be
for evermore. AMEN.

7

PSALM 143, *second version*

Now glory be to God
the Father, and the Son,
and to the Holy Ghost,
all-glorious Three in One.
And his most holy name
let all his saints adore,
as it hath been, is now,
and shall be evermore. AMEN.

8

To Thee, Almighty Father;
Incarnate Son to Thee;
to Thee, Anointing Spirit, —
all praise and glory be. AMEN.

TRANSLATIONS
AND PARAPHRASES
IN VERSE

1

GENESIS i

1 Let heav'n arise, let earth appear,
   said the Almighty Lord:
   the heav'n arose, the earth
      appear'd,
   at his creating word.

2 Thick darkness brooded o'er the
      deep:
   God said, 'Let there be light:'
   the light shone forth with smiling
      ray,
   and scatter'd ancient night.

3 He bade the clouds ascend on
      high;
   the clouds ascend, and bear
   a wat'ry treasure to the sky,
   and float upon the air.

4 The liquid element below
   was gather'd by his hand;
   the rolling seas together flow,
   and leave the solid land.

5 With herbs, and plants, and
      fruitful trees,
   the new-form'd globe he crown'd,
   ere there was rain to bless the
      soil,
   or sun to warm the ground.

6 Then high in heav'n's
      resplendent arch
   he plac'd two orbs of light,
   he set the sun to rule the day,
   the moon to rule the night.

7 Next, from the deep, th' Almighty
      King
   did vital beings frame;
   fowls of the air of ev'ry wing,
   and fish of ev'ry name.

8 To all the various brutal tribes
   he gave their wondrous birth;
   at once the lion and the worm
   sprung from the teeming earth.

9 Then, chief o'er all his works
      below,
   at last was Adam made;
   his maker's image bless'd his
      soul,
   and glory crown'd his head.

10 Fair in the Almighty Maker's eye
   the whole creation stood.
   he view'd the fabric he had
      rais'd;
   his word pronounc'd it good.

2

GENESIS xxviii. 20-22

1 O God of Bethel! by whose hand
   thy people still are fed;
   who through this weary
      pilgrimage
   hast all our fathers led:

2 Our vows, our pray'rs, we now
      present
   before thy throne of grace:
   God of our fathers! be the God
   of their succeeding race.

3 Through each perplexing path of
      life
   our wand'ring footsteps guide;
   give us each day our daily bread,
   and raiment fit provide.

4 O spread thy cov'ring wings
        around,
   till all our wand'rings cease,
   and at our Father's lov'd abode
   our souls arrive in peace.

5 Such blessings from thy gracious
        hand
   our humble pray'rs implore;
   and thou shalt be our chosen
        God,
   and portion evermore.

3

Job i. 21

1 Naked as from the earth we
        came,
   and enter'd life at first;
   naked we to the earth return,
   and mix with kindred dust.

2 Whate'er we fondly call our own
   belongs to heav'n's great Lord;
   the blessings lent us for a day
   are soon to be restor'd.

3 'Tis God that lifts our comforts
        high,
   or sinks them in the grave:
   he gives; and, when he takes
        away,
   he takes but what he gave.

4 Then, ever blessed be his name!
   his goodness swell'd our store;
   his justice but resumes its own;
   'tis ours still to adore.

4

Job iii. 17-20

1 How still and peaceful is the
        grave!
   where, life's vain tumults past,
   th' appointed house, by Heav'n's
        decree,
   receives us all at last.

2 The wicked there from troubling
        cease,
   their passions rage no more;
   and there the weary pilgrim rests
   from all the toils he bore.

3 There rest the pris'ners, now
        releas'd
   from slav'ry's sad abode;
   no more they hear th' oppres-
        sor's voice,
   or dread the tyrant's rod.

4 There servants, masters, small
        and great,

partake the same repose;
and there, in peace, the ashes
        mix
of those who once were foes.

5 All, levell'd by the hand of
        Death,
   lie sleeping in the tomb;
   till God in judgment calls them
        forth,
   to meet their final doom.

5

Job v. 6-12

1 Though trouble springs not from
        the dust,
   nor sorrow from the ground;
   yet ills on ills, by Heav'n's
        decree,
   in man's estate are found.

2 As sparks in close succession rise,
   so man, the child of woe,
   is doom'd to endless cares and
        toils
   through all his life below.

3 But with my God I leave my
        cause;
   from him I seek relief;
   to him, in confidence of pray'r,
   unbosom all my grief.

4 Unnumber'd are his wondrous
        works,
   unsearchable his ways;
   'tis his the mourning soul to
        cheer,
   the bowed down to raise.

6

Job viii. 11-22

1 The rush may rise where waters
        flow,
   and flags beside the stream;
   but soon their verdure fades and
        dies
   before the scorching beam:

2 So is the sinner's hope cut off;
   or, if it transient rise,
   'tis like the spider's airy web,
   from ev'ry breath that flies.

3 Fix'd on his house he leans; his
        house
   and all its props decay:
   he holds it fast; but, while he
        holds,
   the tott'ring frame gives way.

4 Fair, in his garden, to the sun,

his boughs with verdure smile;
and, deeply fix'd, his spreading
   roots
unshaken stand a while.

5 But forth the sentence flies from
    Heav'n,
that sweeps him from his place;
which then denies him for its
   lord
nor owns it knew his face.

6 Lo! this the joy of wicked men,
who Heav'n's high laws despise:
they quickly fall; and in their
   room
as quickly others rise.

7 But, for the just, with gracious
   care,
God will his pow'r employ;
he'll teach their lips to sing his
   praise,
and fill their hearts with joy.

7

JOB ix. 2-10

1 How should the sons of Adam's
   race
be pure before their God?
If he contends in righteousness,
we sink beneath his rod.

2 If he should mark my words and
   thoughts
with strict inquiring eyes,
could I for one of thousand faults
the least excuse devise?

3 Strong is his arm, his heart is
   wise;
who dares with him contend?
Or who, that tries th' unequal
   strife,
shall prosper in the end?

4 He makes the mountains feel his
   wrath,
and their old seats forsake;
the trembling earth deserts her
   place,
and all her pillars shake.

5 He bids the sun forbear to rise;
th' obedient sun forbears:
his hand with sackcloth spreads
   the skies,
and seals up all the stars.

6 He walks upon the raging sea;
flies on the stormy wind:
none can explore his wondrous
   way,
or his dark footsteps find.

8

JOB xiv. 1-15

1 Few are thy days, and full of woe,
O man, of woman born!
Thy doom is written, 'Dust thou
   art,
and shalt to dust return.'

2 Behold the emblem of thy state
in flow'rs that bloom and die,
or in the shadow's fleeting form,
that mocks the gazer's eye.

3 Guilty and frail, how shalt thou
   stand
before thy sov'reign Lord?
Can troubled and polluted
   springs
a hallow'd stream afford?

4 Determin'd are the days that fly
successive o'er thy head;
the number'd hour is on the
   wing
that lays thee with the dead.

5 Great God! afflict not in thy
   wrath
the short allotted span,
that bounds the few and weary
   days
of pilgrimage to man.

6 All nature dies, and lives again:
the flow'r that paints the field,
the trees that crown the
   mountain's brow,
and boughs and blossoms yield.

7 Resign the honours of their form
at Winter's stormy blast,
and leave the naked leafless
   plain
a desolated waste.

8 Yet soon reviving plants and
   flow'rs
anew shall deck the plain;
the woods shall hear the voice of
   Spring,
and flourish green again.

9 But man forsakes this earthly
   scene,
ah! never to return:
shall any foll'wing spring revive
the ashes of the urn?

10 The mighty flood that rolls along
its torrents to the main,
can ne'er recall its waters lost
from that abyss again.

11 So days, and years, and ages past,
descending down to night,

can henceforth never more
      return
back to the gates of light;
12 and man, when laid in lonesome
      grave,
shall sleep in Death's dark
      gloom,
until th' eternal morning wake
the slumbers of the tomb.
13 O may the grave become to me
the bed of peaceful rest,
whence I shall gladly rise at
      length,
and mingle with the blest!
14 Cheer'd by this hope, with
      patient mind,
I'll wait Heav'n's high decree,
till the appointed period come,
when death shall set me free

9

JOB xxvi. 6, to the end

1 Who can resist th' Almighty arm
that made the starry sky?
or who elude the certain glance
of God's all-seeing eye?
2 From him no cov'ring vails our
      crimes;
hell opens to his sight;
and all Destruction's secret
      snares
lie full disclos'd in light.
3 Firm on the boundless void of
      space
he pois'd the steady pole,
and in the circle of his clouds
bade secret waters roll.
4 While nature's universal frame
its Maker's pow'r reveals,
his throne, remote from mortal
      eyes,
an awful cloud conceals.
5 From where the rising day
      ascends,
to where it sets in night,
he compasses the floods with
      bounds,
and checks their threat'ning
      might.
6 The pillars that support the sky
tremble at his rebuke;
through all its caverns quakes the
      earth,
as though its centre shook.
7 He brings the waters from their
      beds,
although no tempest blows,

and smites the kingdom of the
      proud
without the hand of foes.
8 With bright inhabitants above
he fills the heav'nly land,
and all the crooked serpent's
      breed
dismay'd before him stand.
9 Few of his works can we survey;
these few our skill transcend:
but the full thunder of his pow'r
what heart can comprehend?

10

PROVERBS i. 20-31

1 In streets, and op'nings of the
      gates,
where pours the busy crowd,
thus heav'nly Wisdom lifts her
      voice,
and cries to men aloud:
2 How long, ye scorners of the
      truth,
scornful will ye remain?
How long shall fools their folly
      love,
and hear my words in vain?
3 O turn, at last, at my reproof!
and, in that happy hour,
his bless'd effusions on your
      heart
my Spirit down shall pour.
4 But since so long, with earnest
      voice,
to you in vain I call,
since all my counsels and
      reproofs
thus ineffectual fall;
5 The time will come, when
      humbled low,
in Sorrow's evil day,
your voice by anguish shall be
      taught,
but taught too late, to pray.
6 When, like the whirlwind, o'er
      the deep
comes Desolation's blast;
pray'rs then extorted shall be
      vain,
the hour of mercy past.
7 The choice you made has fix'd
      your doom;
for this is Heav'n's decree,
that with the fruits of what he
      sow'd
the sinner fill'd shall be.

11

PROVERBS iii. 13-17

1   O happy is the man who hears
    instruction's warning voice;
    and who celestial Wisdom makes
    his early, only choice.
2   For she has treasures greater far
    than east or west unfold;
    and her rewards more precious
      are
    than all their stores of gold.
3   In her right hand she holds to
      view
    a length of happy days;
    riches, with splendid honours
      join'd,
    are what her left displays.
4   She guides the young with
      innocence,
    in pleasure's paths to tread,
    a crown of glory she bestows
    upon the hoary head.
5   According as her labours rise,
    so her rewards increase;
    her ways are ways of
      pleasantness,
    and all her paths are peace.

12

PROVERBS vi. 6-12

1   Ye indolent and slothful! rise,
    view the ant's labours, and be
      wise;
    she has no guide to point her
      way,
    no ruler chiding her delay:
2   yet see with what incessant cares
    she for the winter's storm
      prepares;
    in summer she provides her
      meat,
    and harvest finds her store
      complete.
3   But when will slothful man
      arise?
    how long shall sleep seal up his
      eyes?
    Sloth more indulgence still
      demands;
    sloth shuts the eyes, and folds the
      hands.
4   But mark the end; want shall
      assail,
    when all your strength and
      vigour fail;

want, like an armed man, shall
  rush
the hoary head of age to crush.

13

PROVERBS viii. 22, to the end

1   Keep silence, all ye sons of men,
    and hear with rev'rence due;
    eternal Wisdom from above
    thus lifts her voice to you:
2   I was th' Almighty's chief delight
    from everlasting days,
    ere yet his arm was stretched
      forth
    the heav'ns and earth to raise.
3   Before the sea began to flow,
    and leave the solid land,
    before the hills and mountains
      rose,
    I dwelt at his right hand.
4   When first he rear'd the arch of
      heav'n,
    and spread the clouds on air,
    when first the fountains of the
      deep
    he open'd, I was there.
5   There I was with him, when he
      stretch'd
    his compass o'er the deep,
    and charg'd the ocean's swelling
      waves
    within their bounds to keep.
6   With joy I saw th' abode
      prepar'd
    which men were soon to fill:
    them from the first of days I
      lov'd,
    unchang'd, I love them still.
7   Now therefore hearken to my
      words,
    ye children, and be wise:
    happy the man that keeps my
      ways;
    the man that shuns them dies.
8   Where dubious paths perplex the
      mind,
    direction I afford;
    life shall be his that follows me,
    and favour from the Lord.
9   But he who scorns my sacred
      laws
    shall deeply wound his heart,
    he courts destruction who
      contemns
    the counsel I impart.

PARAPHRASES

14

ECCLESIASTES vii. 2-6

1 While others crowd the house of
     mirth,
  and haunt the gaudy show,
  let such as would with Wisdom
     dwell,
  frequent the house of woe.
2 Better to weep with those who
     weep,
  and share th' afflicted's smart,
  than mix with fools in giddy joys
  that cheat and wound the heart.

3 When virtuous sorrow clouds the
     face,
  and tears bedim the eye,
  the soul is led to solemn thought,
  and wafted to the sky.
4 The wise in heart revisit oft
  grief's dark sequester'd cell:
  the thoughtless still with levity
  and mirth delight to dwell.

5 The noisy laughter of the fool
  is like the crackling sound
  of blazing thorns, which quickly
     fall
  in ashes to the ground.

15

ECCLESIASTES ix. 4-6, 10

1 As long as life its term extends,
  hope's blest dominion never
     ends;
  for while the lamp holds on to
     burn,
  the greatest sinner may return.
2 Life is the season God hath giv'n
  to fly from hell, and rise to
     heav'n;
  that day of grace fleets fast away,
  and none its rapid course can
     stay.

3 The living know that they must
     die;
  but all the dead forgotten lie:
  their mem'ry and their name is
     gone,
  alike unknowing and unknown.
4 Their hatred and their love is
     lost,
  their envy bury'd in the dust;
  they have no share in all that's
     done
  beneath the circuit of the sun.

5 Then what thy thoughts design to
     do,
  still let thy hands with might
     pursue;
  since no device nor work is
     found.
  Nor wisdom underneath the
     ground.
6 In the cold grave, to which we
     haste,
  there are no acts of pardon past:
  but fix'd the doom of all remains,
  and everlasting silence reigns.

16

ECCLESIASTES xii. 1

1 In life's gay morn, when sprightly
     youth
  with vital ardour glows,
  and shines in all the fairest
     charms
  which beauty can disclose;
2 deep on thy soul, before its
     pow'rs
  are yet by vice enslav'd,
  be thy Creator's glorious name
  and character engrav'd.

3 For soon the shades of grief shall
     cloud
  the sunshine of thy days;
  and cares, and toils, in endless
     round,
  encompass all thy ways.
4 Soon shall thy heart the woes of
     age
  in mournful groans deplore,
  and sadly muse on former joys,
  that now return no more.

17

ISAIAH i. 10-19

1 Rulers of Sodom! hear the voice
  of heav'n's eternal Lord;
  men of Gomorrah! bend your ear
  submissive to his word.
2 'Tis thus he speaks: To what
     intent
  are your oblations vain?
  Why load my altars with your
     gifts,
  polluted and profane?

3 Burnt-off'rings long may blaze to
     heav'n,
  and incense cloud the skies;
  the worship and the worshipper
  are hateful in my eyes.

4   Your rites, your fasts, your
       pray'rs, I scorn,
and pomp of solemn days:
I know your hearts are full of
       guile,
and crooked are your ways.

5   But cleanse your hands, ye guilty
       race,
and cease from deeds of sin;
learn in your actions to be just,
and pure in heart within.

6   Mock not my name with honours
       vain,
but keep my holy laws;
do justice to the friendless poor,
and plead the widow's cause.

7   Then though your guilty souls are
       stain'd
with sins of crimson dye,
yet, through my grace, with snow
       itself
in whiteness they shall vie.

18

ISAIAH ii. 2-6

1   Behold! the mountain of the Lord
in latter days shall rise
on mountain tops above the hills,
and draw the wond'ring eyes.

2   To this the joyful nations round,
all tribes and tongues shall flow;
Up to the hill of God, they'll say,
and to his house we'll go.

3   The beam that shines from Sion
       hill
shall lighten ev'ry land;
the King who reigns in Salem's
       tow'rs
shall all the world command.

4   Among the nations he shall
       judge;
his judgements truth shall guide;
his sceptre shall protect the just,
and quell the sinner's pride.

5   No strife shall rage, nor hostile
       feuds
disturb those peaceful years;
to ploughshares men shall beat
       their swords,
to pruning-hooks their spears.

6   No longer hosts encount'ring
       hosts
shall crowds of slain deplore:
they hang the trumpet in the
       hall,
and study war no more.

7   Come then, O house of Jacob!
       come
to worship at his shrine;
and, walking in the light of God,
with holy beauties shine.

19

ISAIAH ix. 2-8

1   The race that long in darkness
       pin'd
have seen a glorious light;
the people dwell in day, who
       dwelt
in death's surrounding night.

2   To hail thy rise, thou better Sun!
the gath'ring nations come,
joyous, as when the reapers bear
the harvest treasures home.

3   For thou our burden hast
       remov'd,
and quell'd th' oppressor's sway,
quick as the slaughter'd
       squadrons fell
in Midian's evil day.

4   To us a Child of hope is born;
to us a Son is giv'n;
him shall the tribes of earth obey,
him all the hosts of heav'n.

5   His name shall be the Prince of
       Peace,
for evermore ador'd,
the Wonderful, the Counsellor,
the great and mighty Lord.

6   His pow'r increasing still shall
       spread,
his reign no end shall know;
justice shall guard his throne
       above,
and peace abound below.

20

ISAIAH xxvi. 1-7

1   How glorious Sion's courts
       appear,
the city of our God!
His throne he hath establish'd
       here,
here fix'd his lov'd abode.

2   Its walls, defended by his grace,
no pow'r shall e'er o'erthrow,
salvation is its bulwark sure
against th' assailing foe.

3   Lift up the everlasting gates,
the doors wide open fling;
enter, ye nations, who obey

the statutes of our King.
4 Here shall ye taste unmingled
    joys,
and dwell in perfect peace,
ye, who have known Jehovah's
    name,
and trusted in his grace.

5 Trust in the Lord, for ever trust,
and banish all your fears;
strength in the Lord Jehovah
    dwells
eternal as his years.
6 What though the wicked dwell
    on high,
his arm shall bring them low;
low as the caverns of the grave
their lofty heads shall bow.

7 Along the dust shall then be
    spread
their tow'rs, that brave the skies:
on them needy's feet shall tread,
and on their ruins rise.

21

Isaiah xxxiii. 13-18

1 Attend, ye tribes that dwell
    remote,
ye tribes at hand, give ear;
th' upright in heart alone have
    hope
the false in heart have fear.
2 The man who walks with God in
    truth,
and ev'ry guile disdains;
who hates to lift oppression's rod,
and scorns its shameful gains;

3 Whose soul abhors the impious
    bribe
that tempts from truth to stray,
and from th' enticing snares of
    vice
who turns his eyes away:
4 his dwelling, 'midst the strength
    of rocks,
shall ever stand secure;
his Father will provide his bread,
his water shall be sure.

5 For him the kingdom of the just
afar doth glorious shine;
and he the King of kings shall see
in majesty divine.

22

Isaiah xl. 27, to the end

1 Why pour'st thou forth thine
    anxious plaint,
despairing of relief,
as if the Lord o'erlook'd thy
    cause,
and did not heed thy grief?
2 Hast thou not known, hast thou
    not heard,
that firm remains on high
that everlasting throne of Him
who form'd the earth and sky?

3 Art thou afraid his pow'r shall
    fail
when comes thy evil day?
and can an all-creating arm
grow weary or decay?
4 Supreme in wisdom as in pow'r
the Rock of ages stands;
though him thou canst not see,
    nor trace
the working of his hands.

5 He gives the conquest to the
    weak,
supports the fainting heart;
and courage in the evil hour
his heav'nly aids impart.
6 Mere human pow'r shall fast
    decay,
and youthful vigour cease;
but they who wait upon the Lord
in strength shall still increase.

7 They with unweary'd feet shall
    tread
the path of life divine;
with growing ardour onward
    move,
with growing brightness shine.
8 On eagles' wings they mount,
    they soar,
their wings are faith and love,
till, past the cloudy regions here,
they rise to heav'n above.

23

Isaiah xlii. 1-13

1 Behold my Servant! see him rise
exalted in my might!
Him have I chosen, and in him
I place supreme delight.
2 On him, in rich effusion pour'd,
my Spirit shall descend;

my truths and judgments he
    shall show
to earth's remotest end.

3   Gentle and still shall be his voice,
    no threats from him proceed;
    the smoking flax he shall not
        quench,
    nor break the bruised reed.
4   The feeble spark to flames he'll
        raise;
    the weak will not despise;
    judgment he shall bring forth to
        truth,
    and make the fallen rise.

5   The progress of his zeal and
        pow'r
    shall never know decline,
    till foreign lands and distant isles
    receive the law divine.
6   He who erected heav'n's bright
        arch,
    and bade the planets roll,
    who peopled all the climes of
        earth,
    and form'd the human soul,

7   Thus saith the Lord, Thee have I
        rais'd,
    my Prophet thee install;
    in right I've rais'd thee, and in
        strength
    I'll succour whom I call.
8   I will establish with the lands
    a covenant in thee,
    to give the Gentile nations light,
    and set the pris'ners free:

9   Asunder burst the gates of brass;
    the iron fetters fall;
    and gladsome light and liberty
    are straight restor'd to all.
10   I am the Lord, and by the name
    of great Jehovah known;
    no idol shall usurp my praise,
    nor mount into my throne.

11   Lo! former scenes, predicted
        once,
    conspicuous rise to view;
    and future scenes, predicted now,
    shall be accomplish'd too.
12   Sing to the Lord in joyful strains!
    let earth his praise resound,
    ye who upon the ocean dwell,
    and fill the isles around!

13   O city of the Lord! begin
    the universal song;
    and let the scatter'd villages
    the cheerful notes prolong.

14   Let Kedar's wilderness afar
    lift up its lonely voice;
    and let the tenants of the rock
    with accents rude rejoice;

15   Till 'midst the stream of distant
        lands
    the islands sound his praise;
    and all combin'd, with one
        accord,
    Jehovah's glories raise.

24

ISAIAH xlix. 13-17

1   Ye heav'ns, send forth your song
        of praise!
    earth, raise your voice below!
    Let hills and mountains join the
        hymn,
    and joy through nature flow.
2   Behold how gracious is our God!
    hear the consoling strains,
    in which he cheers our drooping
        hearts,
    and mitigates our pains.

3   Cease ye, when days of darkness
        come,
    in sad dismay to mourn,
    as if the Lord could leave his
        saints
    forsaken or forlorn.
4   Can the fond mother e'er forget
    the infant whom she bore?
    and can its plaintive cries be
        heard,
    nor move compassion more?

5   She may forget: nature may fail
    a parent's heart to move;
    But Sion on my heart shall dwell
    in everlasting love.
6   Full in my sight, upon my hands
    I have engrav'd her name:
    my hands shall build her ruin'd
        walls,
    and raise her broken frame.

25

ISAIAH liii

1   How few receive with cordial
        faith
    the tidings which we bring?
    How few have seen the arm
        reveal'd
    of heav'n's eternal King?
2   The Saviour comes! no outward
        pomp

bespeaks his presence nigh;
no earthly beauty shines in him
to draw the carnal eye.

3   Fair as a beauteous tender flow'r
amidst the desert grows,
so slighted by a rebel race
the heav'nly Saviour rose.

4   Rejected and despis'd of men,
behold a man of woe!
Grief was his close companion
        still
through all his life below.

5   Yet all the griefs he felt were
        ours,
ours were the woes he bore:
pangs, not his own, his spotless
        soul
with bitter anguish tore.

6   We held him as condemn'd by
        Heav'n,
and outcast from his God,
while for our sins he groan'd, he
        bled,
beneath his Father's rod.

7   His sacred blood hath wash'd our
        souls
from sin's polluted stain;
his stripes have heal'd us, and
        his death
reviv'd our souls again.

8   We all, like sheep, had gone
        astray
in ruin's fatal road:
on him were our transgressions
        laid;
he bore the mighty load.

9   Wrong'd and oppress'd, how
        meekly he
in patient silence stood!
Mute, as the peaceful, harmless
        lamb,
when brought to shed its blood.

10 Who can his generation tell?
from prison see him led!
With impious show of law
        condemn'd,
and number'd with the dead.

11 'Midst sinners low in dust he lay;
the rich a grave supply'd:
unspotted was his blameless life;
unstain'd by sin he dy'ed.

12 Yet God shall raise his head on
        high,
though thus he brought him low;
his sacred off'ring, when
        complete,
shall terminate his woe.

13 For, saith the Lord, my pleasure
        then
shall prosper in his hand;
his shall a num'rous offspring be,
and still his honours stand.

14 His soul, rejoicing, shall behold
the purchase of his pain;
and all the guilty whom he sav'd
shall bless Messiah's reign.

15 He with the great shall share the
        spoil,
and baffle all his foes;
though rank'd with sinners, here
        he fell,
a conqueror he rose.

16 He dy'd to bear the guilt of men,
that sin might be forgiv'n:
he lives to bless them and
        defend,
and plead their cause in heav'n

26

Isaiah lv

1   Ho! ye that thirst, approach the
        spring
where living waters flow:
free to that sacred fountain all
without a price may go.

2   How long to streams of false
        delight
will ye in crowds repair?
how long your strength and
        substance waste
on trifles, light as air?

3   My stores afford those rich
        supplies
that health and pleasure give:
incline your ear, and come to me;
the soul that hears shall live.

4   With you a cov'nant I will make,
that ever shall endure;
the hope which gladden'd
        David's heart
my mercy hath made sure.

5   Behold he comes! your leader
        comes,
with might and honour crown'd;
a witness who shall spread my
        name
to earth's remotest bound.

6   See! nations hasten to his call
from ev'ry distant shore;
isles, yet unknown, shall bow to
        him,
and Israel's God adore.

7 Seek ye the Lord while yet his
ear
is open to your call;
while offer'd mercy still is near,
before his footstool fall.
8 Let sinners quit their evil ways,
their evil thoughts forego,
and God, when they to him
return,
returning grace will show.
9 He pardons with o'erflowing
love:
for, hear the voice divine!
My nature is not like to yours,
nor like your ways are mine:
10 But far as heav'n's resplendent
orbs
beyond earth's spot extend,
as far my thoughts, as far my
ways,
your ways and thoughts
transcend.
11 And as the rains from heav'n
distil,
nor thither mount again,
but swell the earth with fruitful
juice,
and all its tribes sustain:
12 So not a word that flows from me
shall ineffectual fall;
but universal nature prove
obedient to my call.
13 With joy and peace shall then be
led
the glad converted lands;
the lofty mountains then shall
sing,
the forests clap their hands.
14 Where briers grew 'midst barren
wilds,
shall firs and myrtles spring;
and nature, through its utmost
bounds,
eternal praises sing.

27

ISAIAH lvii. 15, 16

1 Thus speaks the high and lofty
One;
ye tribes of earth, give ear;
the words of your Almighty King
with sacred rev'rence hear;
2 amidst the majesty of heav'n
my throne is fix'd on high;
and through eternity I hear
the praises of the sky:

3 Yet, looking down, I visit oft
the humble hallow'd cell;
and with the penitent who
mourn
'tis my delight to dwell;
4 the downcast spirit to revive,
the sad in soul to cheer;
and from the bed of dust the man
to heart contrite to rear.
5 With me dwells no relentless
wrath
against the human race;
the souls which I have form'd
shall find
a refuge in my grace.

28

ISAIAH lviii. 5-9

1 Attend, and mark the solemn fast
which to the Lord is dear;
disdain the false unhallow'd
mask
which vain dissemblers wear.
2 Do I delight in sorrow's dress?
saith he who reigns above;
the hanging head and rueful
look,
will they attract my love?
3 Let such as feel oppression's load
thy tender pity share:
and let the helpless, homeless
poor,
be thy peculiar care.
4 Go, bid the hungry orphan be
with thy abundance blest;
invite the wand'rer to thy gate,
and spread the couch of rest.
5 Let him who pines with piercing
cold
by thee be warm'd and clad;
be thine the blissful task to make
the downcast mourner glad.
6 Then, bright as morning, shall
come forth,
in peace and joy, thy days;
and glory from the Lord above
shall shine on all thy ways.

29

LAMENTATIONS iii. 37-40

1 Amidst the mighty, where is he
who saith, and it is done?
Each varying scene of changeful
life
is from the Lord alone.

2   He gives in gladsome bow'rs to
      dwell,
  or clothes in sorrow's shroud;
  his hand hath form'd the light,
      his hand
  hath form'd the dark'ning cloud.

3   Why should a living man
      complain
  beneath the chast'ning rod?
  Our sins afflict us; and the cross
  must bring us back to God.

4   O sons of men! with anxious care
  your hearts and ways explore;
  return from paths of vice to God:
  return, and sin no more!

30

HOSEA vi. 1-4

1   Come, let us to the Lord our God
  with contrite hearts return;
  our God is gracious, nor will
      leave
  the desolate to mourn.

2   His voice commands the tempest
      forth,
  and stills the stormy wave;
  and though his arm be strong to
      smite,
  'tis also strong to save.

3   Long hath the night of sorrow
      reigned,
  the dawn shall bring us light:
  God shall appear, and we shall
      rise
  with gladness in his sight.

4   Our hearts, if God we seek to
      know,
  shall know him, and rejoice;
  his coming like the morn shall be,
  like morning songs his voice.

5   As dew upon the tender herb,
  diffusing fragrance round;
  as show'rs that usher in the
      spring,
  and cheer the thirsty ground:

6   So shall his presence bless our
      souls,
  and shed a joyful light;
  that hallow'd morn shall chase
      away
  the sorrows of the night.

31

MICAH vi. 6-9

1   Thus speaks the heathen: How
      shall man
  the Pow'r Supreme adore?
  With what accepted off'rings
      come
  his mercy to implore?

2   Shall clouds of incense to the
      skies
  with grateful odour speed?
  or victims from a thousand hills
  upon the altar bleed?

3   Does justice nobler blood
      demand
  to save the sinner's life?
  Shall, trembling, in his offspring's
      side
  the father plunge the knife?

4   No: God rejects the bloody rites
  which blindfold zeal began;
  his oracles of truth proclaim
  the message brought to man.

5   He what is good hath clearly
      shown,
  O favour'd race! to thee;
  and what doth God require of
      those
  who bend to him the knee?

6   Thy deeds, let sacred justice rule;
  thy heart, let mercy fill;
  and, walking humbly with thy
      God,
  to him resign thy will

32

HABAKKUK iii. 17, 18

1   What though no flow'rs the fig-
      tree clothe,
  though vines their fruit deny,
  the labour of the olive fail,
  and fields no meat supply?

2   Though from the fold, with sad
      surprise,
  my flock cut off I see;
  though famine pine in empty
      stalls,
  where herds were wont to be?

3   Yet in the Lord will I be glad,
  and glory in his love:
  in him I'll joy, who will the God
  of my salvation prove.

4   He to my tardy feet shall lend
  the swiftness of the roe;

till, rais'd on high, I safely dwell
beyond the reach of woe.

5 God is the treasure of my soul,
the source of lasting joy;
a joy which want shall not
impair,
nor death itself destroy.

33

MATTHEW vi. 9-14

1 Father of all! we bow to thee,
who dwell'st in heav'n ador'd;
but present still through all thy
works,
the universal Lord.
2 For ever hallow'd be thy name
by all beneath the skies;
and may thy kingdom still
advance,
till grace to glory rise.

3 A grateful homage may we yield,
with hearts resign'd to thee;
and as in heav'n thy will is done,
on earth so let it be.
4 From day to day we humbly own
the hand that feeds us still:
give us our bread, and teach to
rest
contented in thy will.

5 Our sins before thee we confess;
O may they be forgiven!
As we to others mercy show,
we mercy beg from Heav'n.
6 Still let thy grace our life direct;
from evil guard our way;
and in temptation's fatal path
permit us not to stray.

7 For thine the pow'r, the kingdom
thine;
all glory's due to thee:
thine from eternity they were,
and thine shall ever be.

34

MATTHEW xi. 25, to the end

1 Thus spoke the Saviour of the
world,
and rais'd his eyes to heav'n:
To thee, O Father! Lord of all,
eternal praise be given.
2 Thou to the pure and lowly heart
hast heav'nly truth reveal'd;
which from the self-conceited
mind
thy wisdom hath conceal'd.

3 Ev'n so! thou, Father, hast
ordain'd
thy high decree to stand;
nor men nor angels may
presume
the reason to demand.
4 Thou only know'st the Son: from
thee
my kingdom I receive;
and none the Father know but
they
who in the Son believe.

5 Come then to me, all ye who
groan,
with guilt and fears opprest;
resign to me the willing heart,
and I will give you rest.
6 Take up my yoke, and learn of
me
the meek and lowly mind;
and thus your weary troubled
souls
repose and peace shall find.

7 For light and gentle is my yoke;
the burden I impose
shall ease the heart, which
groan'd before
beneath a load of woes.

35

MATTHEW xxvi. 26-29

1 'Twas on that night, when
doom'd to know
the eager rage of ev'ry foe,
that night in which he was
betray'd,
the Saviour of the world took
bread:
2 and, after thanks and glory giv'n
to him that rules in earth and
heav'n,
that symbol of his flesh he broke,
and thus to all his foll'wers
spoke:

3 My broken body thus I give
for you, for all; take, eat, and
live;
and oft the sacred rite renew,
that brings my wondrous love to
view.
4 Then in his hands the cup he
rais'd,
and God anew he thank'd and
prais'd;
while kindness in his bosom
glow'd,

and from his lips salvation
   flow'd.

5 My blood I thus pour forth, he
      cries,
   to cleanse the soul in sin that
      lies;
   in this the covenant is seal'd,
   and Heav'n's eternal grace
      reveal'd.

6 With love to man this cup is
      fraught,
   let all partake the sacred
      draught;
   through latest ages let it pour,
   in mem'ry of my dying hour.

36

LUKE i. 46-56

1 My soul and spirit, fill'd with joy,
   my God and Saviour praise,
   whose goodness did from poor
      estate
   his humble handmaid raise.

2 Me bless'd of God, the God of
      might,
   all ages shall proclaim;
   from age to age his mercy lasts,
   and holy is his name.

3 Strength with his arm th'
      Almighty show'd;
   the proud his looks abas'd;
   he cast the mighty to the ground,
   the meek to honour rais'd.

4 The hungry with good things
      were fill'd,
   the rich with hunger pin'd:
   he sent his servant Isr'el help,
   and call'd his love to mind;

5 Which to our fathers' ancient race
   his promise did ensure,
   to Abrah'm and his chosen seed,
   for ever to endure.

37

LUKE ii. 8-15

1 While humble shepherds
      watch'd their flocks
   in Bethleh'm's plains by night,
   an angel sent from heav'n
      appear'd,
   and fill'd the plains with light.

2 Fear not, he said, (for sudden
      dread
   had seiz'd their troubled mind;)
   glad tidings of great joy I bring
   to you, and all mankind.

3 To you, in David's town, this day
   is born, of David's line,
   the Saviour, who is Christ the
      Lord;
   and this shall be the sign:

4 the heav'nly Babe you there shall
      find
   to human view display'd,
   all meanly wrapt in swaddling-
      bands,
   and in a manger laid.

5 Thus spake the seraph; and
      forthwith
   appeared a shining throng
   of angels, praising God; and thus
   address'd their joyful song:

6 All glory be to God on high,
   and to the earth be peace;
   good-will is shown by Heav'n to
      men,
   and never more shall cease.

38

LUKE ii. 25-33

1 Just and devout old Simeon
      liv'd;
   to him it was reveal'd,
   that Christ, the Lord, his eyes
      should see
   ere death his eyelids seal'd.

2 For this consoling gift of Heav'n
   to Israel's fallen state,
   from year to year with patient
      hope
   the aged saint did wait.

3 Nor did he wait in vain; for lo!
   revolving years brought round,
   in season due, the happy day,
   which all his wishes crown'd.

4 When Jesus, to the temple
      brought
   by Mary's pious care,
   as Heav'n's appointed rites
      requir'd,
   to God was offer'd there,

5 Simeon into those sacred courts
   a heav'nly impulse drew;
   he saw the Virgin hold her Son,
   and straight his Lord he knew.

6 With holy joy upon his face
   the good old father smil'd;
   then fondly in his wither'd arms
   he clasp'd the promis'd child:

7 And while he held the heav'n-
      born Babe,
   ordain'd to bless mankind,

thus spoke, with earnest look, and heart
exulting, yet resign'd:

8 Now, Lord! according to thy word,
   let me in peace depart;
   mine eyes have thy salvation seen,
   and gladness fills my heart.

9 At length my arms embrace my Lord,
   now let their vigour cease:
   at last my eyes my Saviour see,
   now let them close in peace.

10 This great salvation, long prepar'd,
   and now disclos'd to view,
   hath prov'd thy love was constant still,
   and promises were true.

11 That Sun I now behold, whose light
   shall heathen darkness chase;
   and rays of brightest glory pour
   around thy chosen race.

39

LUKE iv. 18, 19

1 Hark, the glad sound, the Saviour comes!
   The Saviour promised long;
   let ev'ry heart exult with joy,
   and ev'ry voice be song!

2 On him the Spirit, largely shed,
   exerts its sacred fire;
   wisdom and might, and zeal and love,
   his holy breast inspire.

3 He comes! the pris'ners to relieve,
   in Satan's bondage held;
   the gates of brass before him burst,
   the iron fetters yield.

4 He comes! from dark'ning scales of vice
   to clear the inward sight;
   and on the eye-balls of the blind
   to pour celestial light.

5 He comes! the broken hearts to bind,
   the bleeding souls to cure;
   and with the treasures of his grace
   t' enrich the humble poor.

6 The sacred year has now revolv'd,
   accepted of the Lord,
   when Heav'n's high promise is fulfill'd,
   and Isr'el is restor'd.

7 Our glad hosannas, Prince of Peace!
   thy welcome shall proclaim;
   and heaven's exalted arches ring
   with thy most honour'd name.

40

LUKE xv. 13-25

1 The wretched prodigal behold
   in mis'ry lying low,
   whom vice had sunk from high estate,
   and plung'd in want and woe.

2 While I, despis'd and scorn'd, he cries,
   starve in a foreign land,
   the meanest in my father's house
   is fed with bounteous hand:

3 I'll go, and with a mourning voice,
   fall down before his face:
   Father! I've sinn'd 'gainst Heav'n and thee,
   nor can deserve thy grace.

4 He said, and hasten'd to his home,
   to seek his father's love:
   that father sees him from afar,
   and all his bowels move.

5 He ran, and fell upon his neck,
   embrac'd and kiss'd his son:
   the grieving prodigal bewail'd
   the follies he had done.

6 No more, my father, can I hope
   to find paternal grace;
   my utmost wish is to obtain
   a servant's humble place.

7 Bring forth the fairest robe for him,
   the joyful father said;
   To him each mark of grace be shown,
   and ev'ry honour paid.

8 A day of feasting I ordain;
   let mirth and song abound:
   my son was dead, and lives again!
   was lost, and now is found!

9 Thus joy abounds in paradise
   among the hosts of heav'n,
   soon as the sinner quits his sins,
   repents, and is forgiv'n.

41

John iii. 14-19

1 As when the Hebrew prophet
      rais'd
   the brazen serpent high,
   the wounded look'd and straight
      were cur'd,
   the people ceas'd to die:
2 so from the Saviour on the cross
   a healing virtue flows;
   who looks to him with lively faith
   is sav'd from endless woes.

3 For God gave up his Son to
      death,
   so gen'rous was his love,
   that all the faithful might enjoy
   eternal life above.
4 Not to condemn the sons of men
   the Son of God appear'd;
   no weapons in his hand are seen
   nor voice of terror heard:

5 He came to raise our fallen state,
   and our lost hopes restore:
   faith leads us to the mercy-seat,
   and bids us fear no more.
6 But vengeance just for ever lies
   on all the rebel race,
   who God's eternal Son despise,
   and scorn his offer'd grace.

42

John xiv. 1-7

1 Let not your hearts with anxious
      thoughts
   be troubled or dismay'd;
   but trust in Providence divine,
   and trust my gracious aid.
2 I to my Father's house return;
   there num'rous mansions stand,
   and glory manifold abounds
   through all the happy land.

3 I go your entrance to secure,
   and your abode prepare;
   regions unknown are safe to you,
   when I, your friend, am there.
4 Thence shall I come, when ages
      close,
   to take you home with me;
   there we shall meet to part no
      more,
   and still together be.

5 I am the way, the truth, the life:
   no son of human race,
   but such as I conduct and guide,
   shall see my Father's face.

43

John xiv. 25-28

1 You now must hear my voice no
      more;
   my Father calls me home;
   but soon from heav'n the Holy
      Ghost,
   your Comforter, shall come.
2 That heav'nly Teacher, sent from
      God,
   shall your whole soul inspire;
   your minds shall fill with sacred
      truth,
   your hearts with sacred fire.

3 Peace is the gift I leave with you;
   my peace to you bequeath;
   peace that shall comfort you
      through life,
   and cheer your souls in death.
4 I give not as the world bestows,
   with promise false and vain;
   nor cares, nor fears, shall wound
      the heart
   in which my words remain.

44

John xix. 30

1 Behold the Saviour on the cross,
   a spectacle of woe!
   See from his agonizing wounds
   the blood incessant flow;
2 till death's pale ensigns o'er his
      cheek
   and trembling lips were spread;
   till light forsook his closing eyes,
   and life his drooping head!

3 'Tis finish'd — was his latest
      voice;
   these sacred accents o'er,
   he bow'd his head, gave up the
      ghost,
   and suffer'd pain no more.
4 'Tis finish'd — The Messiah dies
   for sins, but not his own;
   the great redemption is complete,
   and Satan's pow'r o'erthrown.

5 'Tis finish'd — All his groans are
      past;
   his blood, his pain, and toils,
   have fully vanquished our foes,

and crown'd him with their
    spoils.
6   'Tis finish'd — Legal worship
        ends,
    and gospel ages run;
    all old things now are past away,
    and a new world begun.

45

ROMANS ii. 4-8

1   Ungrateful sinners! whence this
        scorn
    of God's long-suff'ring grace?
    and whence this madness that
        insults
    th' Almighty to his face?
2   Is it because his patience waits,
    and pitying bowels move,
    you multiply transgressions more,
    and scorn his offer'd love?
3   Dost thou not know, self-blinded
        man!
    his goodness is design'd
    to wake repentance in thy soul,
    and melt thy harden'd mind?
4   And wilt thou rather chuse to
        meet
    th' Almighty as thy foe,
    and treasure up his wrath in
        store
    against the day of woe?
5   Soon shall that fatal day approach
    that must thy sentence seal,
    and righteous judgments, now
        unknown,
    in awful pomp reveal;
6   while they, who full of holy deeds
    to glory seek to rise,
    continuing patient to the end,
    shall gain th' immortal prize.

46

ROMANS iii. 19-22

1   Vain are the hopes the sons of
        men
    upon their works have built;
    their hearts by nature are
        unclean,
    their actions full of guilt.
2   Silent let Jew and Gentile stand,
    without one vaunting word;
    and, humbled low, confess their
        guilt
    before heav'n's righteous Lord.

3   No hope can on the law be built
    of justifying grace;
    the law, that shows the sinner's
        guilt,
    condemns him to his face.
4   Jesus! how glorious is thy grace!
    when in thy name we trust,
    our faith receives a righteousness
    that makes the sinner just.

47

ROMANS vi. 1-7

1   And shall we then go on to sin,
    that grace may more abound?
    Great God, forbid that such a
        thought
    should in our breast be found!
2   When to the sacred font we came,
    did not the rite proclaim,
    that, wash'd from sin, and all its
        stains,
    new creatures we became?
3   With Christ the Lord we dy'd to
        sin;
    with him to life we rise,
    to life, which now begun on
        earth,
    is perfect in the skies.
4   Too long enthrall'd to Satan's
        sway,
    we now are slaves no more;
    for Christ hath vanquish'd death
        and sin,
    our freedom to restore.

48

ROMANS viii. 31, to the end

1   Let Christian faith and hope
        dispel
    the fears of guilt and woe;
    the Lord Almighty is our friend,
    and who can prove a foe?
2   He who his Son, most dear and
        lov'd
    gave up for us to die,
    shall he not all things freely give
    that goodness can supply?
3   Behold the best, the greatest gift,
    of everlasting love!
    behold the pledge of peace below,
    and perfect bliss above!
4   Where is the judge who can
        condemn,
    since God hath justify'd?

who shall charge those with guilt
    or crime
for whom the Saviour dy'd?

5   The Saviour dy'd, but rose again
    triumphant from the grave;
and pleads our cause at God's
    right hand,
    omnipotent to save.

6   Who then can e'er divide us
    more
from Jesus and his love,
or break the sacred chain that
    binds
the earth to heaven above?

7   Let troubles rise, and terrors
    frown,
and days of darkness fall;
through him all dangers we'll
    defy,
and more than conquer all.

8   Nor death nor life, nor earth nor
    hell,
nor time's destroying sway,
can e'er efface us from his heart,
or make his love decay.

9   Each future period that will bless
as it had bless'd the past;
he lov'd us from the first of time,
he loves us to the last.

49

1 CORINTHIANS xiii

1   Though perfect eloquence
    adorn'd
my sweet persuading tongue,
though I could speak in higher
    strains
than ever angel sung;

2   though prophecy my soul
    inspir'd,
and made all myst'ries plain:
yet, were I void of Christian love,
these gifts were all in vain.

3   Nay, though my faith with
    boundless pow'r
ev'n mountains could remove,
I still am nothing, if I'm void
of charity and love.

4   Although with lib'ral hand I gave
my goods the poor to feed,
nay, gave my body to the flames,
still fruitless were the deed.

5   Love suffers long; love envies
    not;
but love is ever kind;

she never boasteth of herself,
nor proudly lifts the mind.

6   Love harbours no suspicious
    thought,
is patient to the bad;
griev'd when she hears of sins
    and crimes,
and in the truth is glad.

7   Love no unseemly carriage
    shows,
nor selfishly confin'd;
she glows with social tenderness,
and feels for all mankind.

8   Love beareth much, much she
    believes,
and still she hopes the best;
love meekly suffers many a
    wrong,
though sore with hardship
    press'd.

9   Love still shall hold an endless
    reign
in earth and heav'n above,
when tongues shall cease, and
    prophets fail,
and ev'ry gift but love.

10 Here all our gifts imperfect are;
but better days draw nigh,
when perfect light shall pour its
    rays,
and all those shadows fly.

11 Like children here we speak and
    think,
amus'd with childish toys;
but when our pow'rs their
    manhood reach,
we'll scorn our present joys.

12 Now dark and dim, as through a
    glass,
are God and truth beheld;
then shall we see as face to face,
and God shall be unveil'd.

13 Faith, Hope, and Love, now
    dwell on earth,
and earth by them is blest;
but Faith and Hope must yield to
    Love,
of all the graces best.

14 Hope shall to full fruition rise,
and Faith be sight above:
these are the means, but this the
    end;
for saints for ever love.

50

1 Corinthians xv. 52, to the end

1 When the last trumpet's awful
    voice
this rending earth shall shake,
when op'ning graves shall yield
    their charge,
and dust to life awake;

2 those bodies that corrupted fell
shall incorrupted rise,
and mortal forms shall spring to
    life
immortal in the skies.

3 Behold what heav'nly prophets
    sung
is now at last fulfill'd,
that Death should yield his
    ancient reign,
and, vanquish'd, quit the field.

4 Let Faith exalt her joyful voice,
and thus begin to sing;
O Grave! where is thy triumph
    now?
and where, O Death! thy sting?

5 Thy sting was sin, and conscious
    guilt,
'twas this that arm'd thy dart;
the law gave sin its strength and
    force
to piece the sinner's heart:

6 but God, whose name be ever
    bless'd!
disarms that foe we dread,
and makes us conqu'rors when
    we die,
through Christ our living head.

7 Then stedfast let us still remain,
though dangers rise around,
and in the work prescrib'd by
    God
yet more and more abound;

8 assur'd that though we labour
    now,
we labour not in vain,
but, through the grave of
    Heav'n's great Lord
th' eternal crown shall gain.

51

2 Corinthians v. 1-11

1 Soon shall this earthly frame,
    dissolv'd,
in death and ruins lie;
but better mansions wait the just,
prepar'd above the sky.

2 An house eternal, built by God,
shall lodge the holy mind;
when once those prison-walls
    have fall'n
by which 'tis now confin'd.

3 Hence, burden'd with a weight of
    clay,
we groan beneath the load,
waiting the hour which sets us
    free,
and brings us home to God.

4 We know, that when the soul,
    uncloth'd,
shall from this body fly,
'twill animate a purer frame
with life that cannot die.

5 Such are the hopes that cheer the
    just:
these hopes their God hath
    giv'n;
his Spirit is the earnest now,
and seals their souls for heav'n.

6 We walk by faith of joys to come,
faith grounded on his word;
but while this body is our home,
we mourn an absent Lord.

7 What faith rejoices to believe,
we long and pant to see;
we would be absent from the
    flesh,
and present, Lord! with thee.

8 But still, or here, or going hence,
to this our labours tend,
that, in his service spent, our life
may in his favour end.

9 For, Lo! before the Son, as judge,
th' assembled world shall stand,
to take the punishment or prize
from his unerring hand.

10 Impartial retributions then
our different lives await;
our present actions, good or bad,
shall fix our future fate.

52

Philippians ii. 6-12

1 Ye who the Name of Jesus bear,
his sacred steps pursue;
and let that mind which was in
    him
be also found in you.

2 Though in the form of God he
    was,
his only Son declar'd,
nor to be equally ador'd,
as robb'ry did regard;

3 His greatness he for us abas'd,
   for us his glory vail'd;
   in human likeness dwelt on
   earth,
   his majesty conceal'd:
4 nor only as a man appears,
   but stoops a servant low,
   submits to death, nay, bears the
   cross,
   in all its shame and woe.

5 Hence God this gen'rous love to
   men
   with honours just hath crown'd,
   and rais'd the name of Jesus far
   above all names renown'd:
6 that at this name, with sacred
   awe,
   each humble knee should bow,
   of hosts immortal in the skies,
   and nations spread below:

7 That all the prostrate pow'rs of
   hell
   might tremble at his word,
   and ev'ry tribe, and ev'ry tongue
   confess that he is Lord.

53

1 THESSALONIANS iv. 13, to the end

1 Take comfort, Christians, when
   your friends
   in Jesus fall asleep;
   their better being never ends;
   why then dejected weep?
2 Why inconsolable, as those
   to whom no hope is giv'n?
   Death is the messenger of peace,
   and calls the soul to heav'n.

3 As Jesus dy'd, and rose again
   victorious from the dead;
   so his disciples rise, and reign
   with their triumphant Head.
4 The time draws nigh, when from
   the clouds
   Christ shall with shouts descend,
   and the last trumpet's awful
   voice
   the heavens and earth shall rend.

5 Then they who live shall
   changed be,
   and they who sleep shall wake;
   the graves shall yield their
   ancient charge,
   and earth's foundations shake.
6 The saints of God, from death set
   free,
   with joy shall mount on high;

the heav'nly hosts with praises
   loud
shall meet them in the sky.

7 Together to their Father's house
   with joyful hearts they go;
   and dwell for ever with the Lord,
   beyond the reach of woe.
8 A few short years of evil past,
   we reach the happy shore,
   where death-divided friends at
   last
   shall meet, to part no more

54

2 TIMOTHY i. 12

1 I'm not asham'd to own my Lord,
   or to defend his cause,
   maintain the glory of his cross,
   and honour all his laws.
2 Jesus, my Lord! I know his
   name,
   his name is all my boast:
   nor will he put my soul to shame,
   nor let my hope be lost.

3 I know that safe with him
   remains,
   protected by his pow'r,
   what I've committed to his trust,
   till the decisive hour.
4 Then will he own his servant's
   name
   before his Father's face,
   and in the New Jerusalem
   appoint my soul a place.

55

2 TIMOTHY iv. 6-8, 18

1 My race is run; my warfare's
   o'er;
   the solemn hour is nigh,
   when, offer'd up to God, my soul
   shall wing its flight on high.
2 With heav'nly weapons I have
   fought
   the battles of the Lord;
   finish'd my course, and kept the
   faith,
   depending on his word.

3 Henceforth there is laid up for
   me
   a crown which cannot fade;
   the righteous Judge at that great
   day
   shall place it on my head.
4 Nor hath the Sov'reign Lord
   decreed

this prize for me alone;
but for all such as love like me
th' appearance of his Son.

5 From ev'ry snare and evil work
his grace shall me defend,
and to his heav'nly kingdom safe
shall bring me in the end.

56

Titus iii. 3-9

1 How wretched was our former
state,
when, slaves to Satan's sway,
with hearts disorder'd and
impure,
o'erwhelm'd in sin we lay!

2 But, O my soul! for ever praise,
for ever love his name,
who turn'd thee from the fatal
paths
of folly, sin, and shame.

3 Vain and presumptuous is the
trust
which in our works we place,
salvation from a higher source
flows to the human race.

4 'Tis from the mercy of our God
that all our hopes begin;
his mercy sav'd our souls from
death,
and wash'd our souls from sin.

5 His Spirit, through the Saviour
shed,
its sacred fire imparts,
refines our dross, and love divine
rekindles in our hearts.

6 Thence rais'd from death, we live
anew;
and, justify'd by grace,
we hope in glory to appear,
and see our Father's face.

7 Let all who hold this faith and
hope
in holy deeds abound;
thus faith approves itself sincere,
by active virtue crown'd.

57

Hebrews iv. 14, to the end

1 Jesus, the Son of God, who once
for us his life resign'd,
now lives in heav'n, our great
High Priest,
and never-dying friend.

2 Through life, through death, let

us to him
with constancy adhere;
faith shall supply new strength,
and hope
shall banish ev'ry fear.

3 To human weakness not severe
is our High Priest above;
his heart o'erflows with
tenderness,
his bowels melt with love.

4 With sympathetic feelings
touch'd,
he knows our feeble frame;
he knows what sore temptations
are,
for he has felt the same.

5 But though he felt temptation's
pow'r,
unconquer'd he remain'd;
nor, 'midst the frailty of our
frame,
by sin was ever stain'd,

6 As, in the days of feeble flesh,
he pour'd forth cries and tears;
so, though exalted, still he feels
what ev'ry Christian bears.

7 Then let us, with a filial heart,
come boldly to the throne
of grace supreme, to tell our
griefs,
and all our wants make known:

8 That mercy we may there obtain
for sins and errors past,
and grace to help in time of need,
while days of trial last.

58

ANOTHER VERSION OF THE SAME PASSAGE

1 Where high the heav'nly temple
stands,
the house of God not made with
hands,
a great High Priest our nature
wears,
the guardian of mankind
appears.

2 He who for men their surety
stood,
and pour'd on earth his precious
blood,
pursues in heav'n his mighty
plan,
the Saviour and the friend of
man.

3 Though now ascended up on
high,

he bends on earth a brother's
eye;
partaker of the human name,
he knows the frailty of our frame.

4 Our fellow-suff'rer yet retains
a fellow-feeling of our pains;
and still remembers in the skies
his tears, his agonies, and cries.

5 In ev'ry pang that rends the
heart,
the Man of sorrows had a part;
he sympathizes with our grief,
and to the suff'rer sends relief.

6 With boldness, therefore, at the
throne,
let us make all our sorrows
known;
and ask the aids of heav'nly
pow'r
to help us in the evil hour.

59

HEBREWS xii. 1-13

1 Behold what witnesses unseen
encompass us around;
men, once like us, with suff'ring
try'd,
but now with glory crown'd.

2 Let us, with zeal like theirs
inspir'd,
begin the Christian race,
and, freed from each
encumb'ring weight,
their holy footsteps trace.

3 Behold a witness nobler still,
who trod affliction's path,
Jesus, at once the finisher
and author of our faith.

4 He for the joy before him set,
so gen'rous was his love,
endur'd the cross, despis'd the
shame,
and now he reigns above.

5 If he the scorn of wicked men
with patience did sustain,
becomes it those for whom he
dy'd
to murmur or complain?

6 Have ye like him to blood, to
death,
the cause of truth maintain'd?
and is your heav'nly Father's
voice
forgotten or disdain'd?

7 My son, saith he, with patient
mind

endure the chast'ning rod;
believe, when by afflictions try'd,
that thou art lov'd by God.

8 His children thus most dear to
him,
their heav'nly Father trains,
through all the hard experience
led
of sorrows and of pains.

9 We know he owns us for his sons,
when we correction share;
nor wander as a bastard race,
without our Father's care.

10 A father's voice with rev'rence
we
on earth have often heard;
the Father of our spirits now
demands the same regard.

11 Parents may err; but he is wise,
nor lifts the rod in vain;
his chast'nings serve to cure the
soul
by salutary pain.

12 Affliction, when it spreads
around,
may seem a field of woe;
yet there, at last, the happy fruits
of righteousness shall grow.

13 Then let our hearts no more
despond,
our hands be weak no more;
still let us trust our Father's love,
his wisdom still adore.

60

HEBREWS xiii. 20, 21

1 Father of peace, and God of love!
we own thy pow'r to save,
that pow'r by which our
Shepherd rose
victorious o'er the grave.

2 Him from the dead thou
brought'st again,
when, by his sacred blood,
confirmed and seal'd for
evermore,
th' eternal cov'nant stood.

3 O may thy Spirit seal our souls,
and mould them to thy will,
that our weak hearts no more
may stray,
but keep thy precepts still;

4 That to perfection's sacred height
we nearer still may rise,
and all we think, and all we do,
be pleasing in thine eyes.

61

1 Peter i. 3-5

1 Bless'd be the everlasting God,
the Father of our Lord;
be his abounding mercy prais'd,
his majesty adored.

2 When from the dead he rais'd his Son,
and call'd him to the sky,
he gave our souls a lively hope
that they should never die.

3 To an inheritance divine
he taught our hearts to rise;
'tis uncorrupted, undefil'd,
unfading in the skies.

4 Saints by the pow'r of God are kept
till the salvation come:
we walk by faith as strangers here,
but Christ shall call us home.

62

2 Peter iii. 3-14

1 Lo! in the last of days behold
a faithless race arise;
their lawless lust their only rule;
and thus the scoffer cries;

2 Where is the promise, deem'd so true,
that spoke the Saviour near?
E'er since our fathers slept in dust,
no change has reach'd our ear.

3 Years roll'd on years successive glide,
since first the world began,
and on the tide of time still floats,
secure, the bark of man.

4 Thus speaks the scoffer; but his words
conceal the truth he knows,
that form the water's dark abyss
the earth at first arose.

5 But when the sons of men began
with one consent to stray,
at Heav'n's command a deluge swept
the godless race away.

6 A diff'rent fate is now prepar'd
for Nature's trembling frame;
soon shall her orbs be all enwrapt
in one devouring flame.

7 Reserv'd are sinners for the hour
when to the gulf below,
arm'd with the hand of sov'reign pow'r,
the Judge consigns his foe.

8 Though now, ye just! the time appears
protracted, dark, unknown,
an hour, a day, a thousand years,
to heav'n's great Lord are one.

9 Still all may share his sov'reign grace,
in ev'ry change secure;
the meek, the suppliant contrite race,
shall find his mercy sure.

10 The contrite race he counts his friends,
forbids the suppliant's fall;
condemns reluctant, but extends
the hope of grace to all.

11 Yet as the night-wrapt thief who lurks
to seize th' expected prize,
thus steals the hour when Christ shall come,
and thunder rend the skies.

12 Then at the loud, the solemn peal,
the heav'ns shall burst away;
the elements shall melt in flame,
at Nature's final day.

13 Since all this frame of things must end,
as Heav'n has so decreed.
How wise our inmost thoughts to guard,
and watch o'er ev'ry deed;

14 expecting calm th' appointed hour,
when, Nature's conflict o'er,
a new and better world shall rise,
where sin is known no more.

63

1 John iii. 1-4

1 Behold th' amazing gift of love
the Father hath bestow'd
on us, the sinful sons of men,
to call us sons of God!

2 Conceal'd as yet this honour lies,
by this dark world unknown,
a world that knew not when he came,
ev'n God's eternal Son.

3 High is the rank we now possess;
but higher we shall rise;
though what we shall hereafter be
is hid from mortal eyes:
4 Our souls, we know, when he appears,
shall bear his image bright;
for all his glory, full disclos'd,
shall open to our sight.
5 A hope so great, and so divine,
may trials well endure;
and purge the soul from sense and sin,
as Christ himself is pure.

64

REVELATION i. 5-9

1 To him that lov'd the souls of men,
and wash'd us in his blood,
to royal honours rais'd our head,
and made us priests to God;
2 to him let ev'ry tongue be praise,
and ev'ry heart be love!
all grateful honours paid on earth,
and nobler songs above!
3 Behold, on flying clouds he comes!
his saints shall bless the day;
while they that pierc'd him sadly mourn
in anguish and dismay.
4 I am the First, and I the Last;
time centres all in me;
th' Almighty God, who was, and is,
and evermore shall be.

65

REVELATION v. 6, to the end

1 Behold the glories of the Lamb
amidst his Father's throne;
prepare new honours for his name,
and songs before unknown.
2 Lo! elders worship at his feet;
the church adores around,
with vials full of odours rich,
and harps of sweetest sound.
3 These odours are the pray'rs of saints,
these sounds the hymns they raise;

God bends his ear to their requests,
he loves to hear their praise.
4 Who shall the Father's record search,
and hidden things reveal?
Behold the Son that record takes,
and opens ev'ry seal!
5 Hark how th' adoring hosts above
with songs surround the throne!
ten thousand thousand are their tongues;
but all their hearts are one.
6 Worthy the Lamb that dy'd, they cry,
to be exalted thus;
Worthy the Lamb, let us reply,
for he was slain for us.
7 To him be pow'r divine ascrib'd,
and endless blessings paid;
salvation, glory, joy, remain
for ever on his head!
8 Thou hast redeem'd us with thy blood,
and set the pris'ners free;
thou mad'st us kings and priests to God,
and we shall reign with thee.
9 From ev'ry kindred, ev'ry tongue,
thou brought'st thy chosen race;
and distant lands and isles have shar'd
the riches of thy grace.
10 Let all that dwell above the sky,
or on the earth below,
with fields, and floods, and ocean's shores,
to thee their homage show.
11 To Him who sits upon the throne,
the God whom we adore,
and to the Lamb that once was slain,
be glory evermore.

66

REVELATION vii. 13, to the end

1 How bright these glorious spirits shine!
whence all their white array?
How came they to the blissful seats
of everlasting day?
2 Lo, these are they from suff'rings great,
who came to realms of light,

and in the blood of Christ have wash'd
those robes which shine so bright.

3 Now, with triumphal palms, they stand
before the throne on high,
and serve the God they love, amidst
the glories of the sky.

4 His presence fills each heart with joy,
tunes ev'ry mouth to sing:
by day, by night, the sacred courts
with glad hosannas ring.

5 Hunger and thirst are felt no more,
nor suns with scorching ray;
God is their sun, whose cheering beams
diffuse eternal day.

6 The Lamb which dwells amidst the throne
shall o'er them still preside,
feed them with nourishment divine,
and all their footsteps guide.

7 'Mong pastures green he'll lead his flock,
where living streams appear;
and God the Lord from every eye
shall wipe off ev'ry tear.

67

REVELATION xxi. 1-9

1 Lo! what a glorious sight appears
to our admiring eyes!
The former seas have pass'd away,
the former earth and skies.

2 From heav'n the New Jerus'lem comes,
all worthy of its Lord;
see all things now at last renew'd,
and paradise restor'd!

3 Attending angels shout for joy,
and the bright armies sing;
Mortals! behold the sacred seat
of your descending King!

4 The God of glory down to men
removes his bless'd abode;
he dwells with men; his people they,
and he his people's God.

5 His gracious hand shall wipe the tears

from ev'ry weeping eye:
and pains and groans, and grief and fears,
and death itself, shall die.

6 Behold, I change all human things!
saith he, whose words are true;
lo! what was old is pass'd away,
and all things are made new!

7 I am the First, and I the Last,
through endless years the same;
I AM, is my memorial still,
and my eternal name.

8 Ho, ye that thirst! to you my grace
shall hidden streams disclose,
and open full the sacred spring,
whence life for ever flows.

9 Bless'd is the man that overcomes;
I'll own him for a son;
a rich inheritance rewards
the conquests he hath won.

10 But bloody hands and hearts unclean,
and all the lying race,
the faithless, and the scoffing crew,
who spurn at offer'd grace;

11 They, seiz'd by justice, shall be doom'd
in dark abyss to lie,
and in the fiery burning lake
the second death shall die.

12 O may we stand before the Lamb,
when earth and seas are fled,
and hear the Judge pronounce our name,
with blessings on our head!

HYMNS

1

1 When all thy mercies, O my God!
my rising soul surveys,
transported with the view, I'm lost
in wonder, love, and praise.

2 O how shall words, with equal warmth,
the gratitude declare
that glows within my ravish'd heart!
but Thou canst read it there.

3   Thy providence my life sustain'd,
    and all my wants redrest,
    when in the silent womb I lay,
    and hung upon the breast.

4   To all my weak complaints and
        cries
    thy mercy lent an ear,
    ere yet my feeble thoughts had
        learn'd
    to form themselves in pray'r.

5   Unnumber'd comforts to my soul
    thy tender care bestow'd,
    before my infant heart conceiv'd
    from whom those comforts
        flow'd.

6   When in the slipp'ry paths of
        youth
    with heedless steps I ran;
    thine arm, unseen, convey'd me
        safe,
    and led me up to man:

7   Through hidden dangers, toils,
        and deaths,
    it gently clear'd my way;
    and through the pleasing snares
        of vice,
    more to be fear'd than they.

8   When worn with sickness, oft
        hast thou
    with health renew'd my face;
    and, when in sins and sorrows
        sunk,
    reviv'd my soul with grace.

9   Thy bounteous hand with
        worldly bliss
    hath made my cup run o'er;
    and, in a kind and faithful friend,
    hath doubled all my store.

10 Ten thousand thousand precious
        gifts
    my daily thanks employ;
    nor is the least a cheerful heart,
    that tastes those gifts with joy.

11 Through ev'ry period of my life
    thy goodness I'll proclaim;
    and after death, in distant worlds,
    resume the glorious theme.

12 When nature fails, and day and
        night
    divide thy works no more,
    my ever grateful heart, O Lord,
    thy mercy shall adore.

13 Through all eternity to thee
    a joyful song I'll raise;
    for oh! eternity's too short
    to utter all thy praise.

2

1   The spacious firmament on high,
    with all the blue ethereal sky,
    and spangled heav'ns, a shining frame,
    their great Original proclaim.
    The unweary'd sun, from day to day,
    does his Creator's pow'r display;
    and publishes to ev'ry land
    the work of an Almighty hand.

2   Soon as the ev'ning shades prevail,
    the moon takes up the wondrous tale,
    and, nightly to the list'ning earth,
    repeats the story of her birth;
    while all the stars that round her burn,
    and all the planets in their turn,
    confirm the tidings as they roll,
    and spread the truth from pole to pole.

3   What though in solemn silence all
    move round the dark terrestrial ball?
    What though no real voice, nor sound,
    amidst their radiant orbs be found?
    In Reason's ear they all rejoice,
    and utter forth a glorious voice;
    for ever singing, as they shine,
    'The hand that made us is divine!'

3

1   When rising from the bed of death,
    o'erwhelm'd with guilt and fear,
    I see my Maker face to face,
    O how shall I appear!

2   If yet while pardon may be found,
    and mercy may be sought,
    my heart with inward horror shrinks,
    and trembles at the thought;

3   When thou, O Lord! shalt stand
        disclos'd
    in majesty severe,
    and sit in judgement on my soul,
    O how shall I appear!

4   But thou hast told the troubled mind,
    who doth her sins lament,
    the timely grief for errors past
    shall future woe prevent.

5   Then see the sorrows of my heart,
    ere yet it be too late;
    and hear my Saviour's dying groans,
    to give those sorrows weight.

6   For never shall my soul despair
    of mercy at thy throne,
    who knows thine only Son has dy'd
    thy justice to atone.

4

1 Blest morning! whose first
      dawning rays
   beheld the Son of God
   arise triumphant from the grave,
   and leave his dark abode.

2 Wrapt in the silence of the tomb
   the great Redeemer lay,
   till the revolving skies had brought
   the third, th' appointed day.

3 Hell and the grave combin'd their
      force
   to hold our Lord in vain;
   sudden the Conqueror arose,
   and burst their feeble chain.

4 To thy great name, Almighty Lord!
   we sacred honours pay,
   and loud hosannas shall proclaim
   the triumphs of the day.

5 Salvation and immortal praise
   to our victorious King!
   Let heav'n and earth, and rocks and
      seas,
   with glad hosannas ring.

6 To Father, Son, and Holy Ghost,
   the God whom we adore,
   be glory, as it was, and is,
   and shall be evermore.

5

1 The hour of my departure's come;
   I hear the voice that calls me home;
   at last, O Lord! let trouble cease,
   and let thy servant die in peace.

2 The race appointed I have run;
   the combat's o'er, the prize is won;
   and now my witness is on high,
   and now my record's in the sky.

3 Not in mine innocence I trust;
   I bow before thee in the dust;
   and through my Saviour's blood alone
   I look for mercy at thy throne.

4 I leave the world without a tear,
   save for the friends I held so dear;
   to heal their sorrows, Lord, descend,
   and to the friendless prove a friend.

5 I come, I come, at thy command,
   I give my spirit to thy hand;
   stretch forth thine everlasting arms,
   and shield me in the last alarms.

6 The hour of my departure's come:
   I hear the voice that calls me home:
   now, O my God! let trouble cease;
   now let thy servant die in peace.

THE HYMNS AND SONGS

CREATION MORNING

1

1 Awake, my soul, and with the sun
   your daily stage of duty run;
   shake off your sleep, and joyful
      rise
   to make your morning sacrifice.

2 Redeem your mis-spent time
      that's past
   and live this day as if your last;
   improve your talent with due
      care,
   for God's great Day yourself
      prepare.

3 Let all your speaking be sincere,
   your conscience as the noonday
      clear;
   think how all-seeing God surveys
   your secret thoughts and all your
      ways.

4 Give praise to God, who safely
      kept
   and well refreshed me while I
      slept:
   grant, Lord, that when from
      death I wake
   I may of endless life partake.

5 To You my vows I here renew:
   disperse my sins as morning
      dew;
   guard my first springs of thought
      and will
   and with Yourself my spirit fill.

6 Direct, control, suggest this day
   all I desire or do or say;
   that all my powers with all their
      might
   for Your sole glory may unite.

7 Praise God, from whom all
      blessings flow
   in heaven above and earth
      below;
   one God, three persons, we
      adore —
   to Him be praise for evermore!

Thomas Ken, 1637–1711
adapted Jubilate Hymns

MORNING

2

1 Lord, as I wake I turn to You,
Yourself the first thought of my
day;
my King, my God, whose help is
sure,
Yourself the help for which I
pray.

2 There is no blessing, Lord, from
You
for those who make their will
their way,
no praise for those who will not
praise,
no peace for those who will not
pray.

3 Your loving gifts of grace to me,
those favours I could never earn,
call for my thanks in praise and
prayer,
call me to love You in return.

4 Lord, make my life a life of love,
keep me from sin in all I do;
Lord, make Your law my only
law,
Your will my will, for love of You.

William Brian Foley, 1919–2000
from Psalm 5

3

1 Lord of all hopefulness, Lord of
all joy,
whose trust, ever childlike, no
cares could destroy,
be there at our waking, and give
us, we pray,
Your bliss in our hearts, Lord, at
the break of the day.

2 Lord of all eagerness, Lord of all
faith,
whose strong hands were skilled
at the plane and the lathe,
be there at our labours, and give
us, we pray,
Your strength in our hearts, Lord,
at the noon of the day.

3 Lord of all kindliness, Lord of all
grace,
Your hands swift to welcome,
Your arms to embrace,
be there at our homing, and give
us, we pray,
Your love in our hearts, Lord, at
the eve of the day.

4 Lord of all gentleness, Lord of all
calm,
whose voice is contentment,
whose presence is balm,
be there at our sleeping, and give
us, we pray,
Your peace in our hearts, Lord, at
the end of the day.

Jan Struther, 1901–1953

4

1 Lord, for tomorrow and its needs
I do not pray.
Keep me, my God, from stain of
sin
just for today.

2 Let me both diligently work
and duly pray.
Let me be kind in word and deed
just for today.

3 Let me no wrong or idle word
unthinking say;
but set a seal upon my lips
just for today.

4 And if today my tide of life
should ebb away,
give me the grace of peace
divine,
dear Lord, today.

5 So for tomorrow and its needs
I do not pray;
but keep me, guide me, love me,
Lord,
just for today.

Sybil Farish Partridge, 1856–1917
altered

5

1 Morning has broken
like the first morning;
blackbird has spoken
like the first bird.
Praise for the singing!
Praise for the morning!
Praise for them, springing
fresh from the Word!

2 Sweet the rain's new fall
sunlit from heaven,
like the first dewfall
on the first grass.
Praise for the sweetness
of the wet garden,
sprung in completeness
where His feet pass.

3 Mine is the sunlight!
  Mine is the morning
  born of the one light
  Eden saw play!
  Praise with elation,
  praise every morning,
  God's re-creation
  of the new day!

Eleanor Farjeon, 1881–1965

6

1 New every morning is the love
  our waking and our rising prove:
  through sleep and darkness
    safely brought,
  restored to life and power and
    thought.

2 New mercies, each returning day,
  surround Your people as they
    pray:
  new perils past, new sins
    forgiven,
  new thoughts of God, new hopes
    of heaven.

3 If in our daily life our mind
  be set to hallow all we find,
  new treasures still, of countless
    price,
  God will provide for sacrifice.

4 The trivial round, the common
    task,
  will furnish all we ought to ask:
  room to deny ourselves — a road
  to bring us daily nearer God.

5 Prepare us, Lord, in Your dear
    love
  for perfect rest with You above,
  and help us, this and every day,
  to grow more like You as we pray.

John Keble, 1792–1866

7

1 When morning gilds the skies,
  my heart awaking cries:
  may Jesus Christ be praised!
  Alike at work and prayer
  I find my Lord is there;
  may Jesus Christ be praised!

2 To God, the Word, on high
  the hosts of angels cry:
  may Jesus Christ be praised!
  Let mortals, too, upraise
  their voice in hymns of praise:
  may Jesus Christ be praised!

3 Let earth's wide circle round
  in joyful notes resound:
  may Jesus Christ be praised!
  Let air and sea and sky
  from depth to height reply:
  may Jesus Christ be praised!

4 The night becomes as day
  when from the heart we say:
  may Jesus Christ be praised!
  The powers of darkness fear
  when this glad song they hear,
  may Jesus Christ be praised!

5 Does sadness fill my mind?
  My strength in Him I find;
  may Jesus Christ be praised!
  When earthly hopes grow dim
  my comfort is in Him:
  may Jesus Christ be praised!

6 Be this, while life is mine,
  my hymn of love divine:
  may Jesus Christ be praised!
  Be this the eternal song
  through all the ages long:
  may Jesus Christ be praised!

German, 19th century
translated Edward Caswall, 1814–1878
adapted Jubilate Hymns †

Also suitable:
Holy, Holy, Holy, Lord God Almighty   161

CREATION
EVENING

8

1 Day is done, but Love unfailing
  dwells ever here;
  shadows fall, but hope,
    prevailing,
  calms every fear.
  Loving Father, none forsaking,
  take our hearts of Love's own
    making,
  watch our sleeping, guard our
    waking,
  be always near!

2 Dusk descends, but Light
    unending
  shines through our night;
  You are with us, ever lending
  new strength to sight;
  one in love, Your truth
    confessing,
  one in hope of heaven's blessing,
  may we see, in love's possessing,
  love's endless light!

3 Eyes will close, but You,
    unsleeping,
watch by our side;
death may come, in Love's safe
    keeping
still we abide.
God of love, all evil quelling,
sin forgiving, fear dispelling,
stay with us, our hearts
    indwelling,
this eventide!

James Quinn, b. 1919

9

1 Glory to You, my God, this night
for all the blessings of the light;
keep me, O keep me, King of
    kings,
beneath Your own almighty
    wings.

2 Forgive me, Lord, through Your
    dear Son,
the wrong that I this day have
    done,
that peace with God and man
    may be,
before I sleep, restored to me.

3 Teach me to live, that I may
    dread
the grave as little as my bed;
teach me to die, that so I may
rise glorious at the awesome day.

4 O may my soul on You repose
and restful sleep my eyelids
    close;
sleep that shall me more
    vigorous make
to serve my God when I awake.

5 If in the night I sleepless lie,
my mind with peaceful thoughts
    supply;
let no dark dreams disturb my
    rest,
no powers of evil me molest.

6 Praise God from whom all
    blessings flow
in heaven above and earth
    below;
one God, three persons, we
    adore —
to Him be praise for evermore!

Thomas Ken, 1637–1711
adapted Jubilate Hymns

10

1 Holy Father, cheer our way
with Your love's perpetual ray;
grant us every closing day
light at evening time.

2 Holy Saviour, calm our fears
when earth's brightness
    disappears;
grant us in our latter years
light at evening time.

3 Holy Spirit, from on high
when in mortal pains we lie;
grant us, as we come to die,
light at evening time.

4 Holy God, no dark shall be
round the blessèd Trinity;
those You keep shall always see
light at evening time.

Richard Hayes Robinson, 1842–1882

11

1 Jesus, tender Shepherd, hear me;
bless Your little lamb tonight;
through the darkness please be
    near me;
watch my sleep till morning light.

2 All this day Your hand has led
    me,
and I thank You for Your care;
You have clothed me, warmed
    and fed me;
listen to my evening prayer.

3 Let my sins be all forgiven;
bless the friends I love so well;
take me, when I die, to heaven,
happy there with You to dwell.

Mary Lundie Duncan, 1814–1840

12

1 Now the day is over,
night will soon be here,
help me to remember
You are always near.

2 As the darkness gathers,
stars shine overhead,
creatures, birds and flowers
rest their weary heads.

3 Father, give all people
calm and peaceful rest,
through Your gracious presence
may our sleep be blessed.

CREATION

4 Comfort every sufferer
watching late in pain;
those who plan some evil
from their sin restrain.

5 When the morning wakes me,
ready for the day,
help me, Lord, to serve You,
walking in Your way.

6 Glory to the Father,
glory to the Son;
and to the Holy Spirit
blessing everyone.

> Sabine Baring-Gould, 1834–1924
> *adapted* Peter J. Horrobin, *b.* 1943
> and Greg P. Leavers, *b.* 1952

13

1 Praise the Lord, all you servants
of the Lord,
who minister by night within His
house.
Lift up your hands within the
sanctuary,
and praise the Lord.

2 May this Lord, the maker of
heaven and earth,
may this Lord bless you from
Zion.
Lift up your hands within the
sanctuary,
and praise the Lord.

> *adapted* Ian White, *b.* 1956
> from Psalm 134, *New International Version*

14

1 Saviour, again to Your dear name
we raise
with one accord our parting
hymn of praise;
we give You thanks before our
worship cease;
then, in the stillness, hear Your
word of peace.

2 Grant us Your peace, Lord, on
our homeward way:
with You began, with You shall
end the day;
guard all the lips from sin, the
hearts from shame,
that in this place have called
upon Your name.

3 Grant us Your peace, Lord,
through the coming night,
turn all our darkness into perfect
light;

from harm and danger keep us
all night through,
for dark and light are both alike
to You.

4 Grant us Your peace throughout
our earthly life:
comfort in sorrow, courage in the
strife;
then, when Your voice shall
make our conflict cease,
call us, O Lord, to Your eternal
peace.

> John Ellerton, 1826–1893
> *altered*

15

1 Sun of my soul, my Saviour dear,
it is not night if You are near;
O may no earth-born cloud arise
to hide You from Your servant's
eyes.

2 When the soft dews of kindly
sleep
my wearied eyelids gently steep,
be my last thought, how sweet to
rest
for ever on my Saviour's breast!

3 Abide with me from morn till
eve,
for without You I cannot live;
abide with me when night is
nigh,
for without You I dare not die.

4 If some poor wandering child of
Yours
has spurned today Your holy
voice,
now, Lord, the gracious work
begin;
let them no more be ruled by sin.

5 Watch by the sick; enrich the
poor
with blessings from Your
boundless store;
be every mourner's bed tonight,
like infant's slumbers, pure and
light.

6 Come near and bless us when we
wake,
ere through the world our way
we take;
till in the ocean of Your love
we lose ourselves in heaven
above.

> John Keble, 1792–1866

EVENING

16

1 The day You gave us, Lord, is
   ended,
   the darkness falls at Your behest;
   to You our morning hymns
   ascended,
   Your praise shall sanctify our rest.

2 We thank You that Your Church,
   unsleeping
   while earth rolls onward into
   light,
   through all the world her watch
   is keeping,
   and rests not now by day or
   night.

3 As to each continent and island
   the dawn leads on another day,
   the voice of prayer is never
   silent,
   nor dies the strain of praise away.

4 The sun that bids us rest is
   waking
   Your Church beneath the western
   sky,
   and hour by hour fresh lips are
   making
   Your wondrous doings heard on
   high.

5 So be it, Lord: Your throne shall
   never,
   like earth's proud empires, pass
   away;
   Your kingdom stands, and grows
   for ever,
   till all Your creatures own Your
   sway.

John Ellerton, 1826–1893
adapted Jubilate Hymns

Also suitable:
Abide with me   661
At evening, when the sun had set   364
God is always near me   82
Hushed was the evening hymn   172
I lift my eyes to the quiet hills   119
O God, You are my God alone   185

CREATION
GOD'S WORLD

17

1 All creatures of our God and
   King
   lift up your voice and with us
   sing
   alleluia, alleluia.
   O burning sun with golden beam,
   and silver moon with softer
   gleam,
      O praise Him, O praise Him,
      Alleluia! Alleluia! Alleluia!

2 O rushing wind that is so strong,
   and clouds that sail in heaven
   along,
   O praise Him, alleluia.
   O rising morn, in praise rejoice,
   and lights of evening, find a
   voice:

3 O flowing water, pure and clear,
   make music for your Lord to hear,
   alleluia, alleluia.
   O fire so masterful and bright,
   giving to all both warmth and
   light,

4 Dear mother earth, who day by
   day
   unfolds rich blessings on our way,
   O praise Him, alleluia.
   The flowers and fruits that bloom
   and grow,
   let them His glory also show:

5 People and nations take your
   part,
   love and forgive with all your
   heart,
   sing praise now, alleluia.
   All who long pain and sorrow
   bear,
   praise God and on Him cast your
   care:

6 And now, most kind and gentle
   death,
   waiting to hush our fading
   breath,
   O praise him, alleluia.
   And leading home the child of
   God,
   along the way our Lord has trod:

16 Words: © in this version Jubilate Hymns, 4 Thorne Park Road, Chelston, Torquay TQ2 6RX <enquiries@jubilate.co.uk> Used by permission.

CREATION

7   Let all things their Creator bless,
    and worship Him in
       humbleness;
    O praise Him, alleluia.
    Praise, praise the Father, praise
       the Son,
    and praise the Spirit, Three
       in One;

St Francis of Assisi, 1182–1226
translated William Henry Draper, 1855–1933

18

1   *All things bright and beautiful,*
    all creatures great and small,
    all things wise and wonderful —
    the Lord God made them all.

2   Each little flower that opens,
    each little bird that sings, —
    He made their glowing colours,
    He made their tiny wings.

3   The purple-headed mountain,
    the river running by,
    the sunset, and the morning
    that brightens up the sky,

4   The cold wind in the winter,
    the pleasant summer sun,
    the ripe fruits in the garden, —
    He made them every one:

5   He gave us eyes to see them,
    and lips that we might tell
    how great is God Almighty,
    who has made all things well.

Cecil Frances Alexander, 1818–1895

19

1   Fairest Lord Jesus,
    Lord of all creation,
    Jesus, of God and man the Son;
    You will I cherish,
    You will I honour,
    You are my soul's delight and
       crown.

2   Fair are the rivers,
    meadows and forests
    clothed in the fresh green robes
       of spring;
    Jesus is fairer,
    Jesus is purer,
    He makes the saddest heart to
       sing.

3   Fair is the sunrise,
    starlight and moonlight
    spreading their glory across the
       sky;

Jesus shines brighter,
Jesus shines clearer,
than all the heavenly host on
   high.

4   All fairest beauty,
    heavenly and earthly,
    Jesus, my Lord, in You I see;
    none can be nearer,
    fairer or dearer,
    than You, my Saviour, are to me.

Münster Gesangbuch, 1677
translated Lilian Stevenson, 1870–1960
and Jubilate Hymns

20

1   For the beauty of the earth,
    for the beauty of the skies,
    for the love which from our birth
    over and around us lies,
       Christ our God, to You we raise
       this our sacrifice of praise.

2   For the beauty of each hour
    of the day and of the night,
    hill and vale, and tree and
       flower,
    sun and moon and stars of light,

3   For the joy of ear and eye,
    for the heart and mind's delight,
    for the mystic harmony
    linking sense to sound and sight,

4   For the joy of human love,
    brother, sister, parent, child,
    friends on earth and friends
       above,
    pleasures pure and undefiled,

5   For each perfect gift divine
    to our race so freely given,
    joys bestowed by love's design,
    flowers of earth and buds of
       heaven,

Folliott Sandford Pierpoint, 1835–1917

21

Refrain (sung twice):
God is good, God is great,
He's the one who did create
everything that there is by His
power.

1   Thank You, Lord, for the things I
       can see,
    thank You, thank You, Lord.
    Thank You, Lord, for the sounds I
       can hear,
    thank You, thank You, Lord.

2 Thank You, Lord, for my family,
 thank You, thank You, Lord.
 Thank You, Lord, for all my
  friends.
 thank You, thank You, Lord.

3 Thank You, Lord, for the birds in
  the sky,
 thank You, thank You, Lord.
 Thank You, Lord, for the ants on
  the ground,
 thank You, thank You, Lord.

4 Thank You, Lord, for Your love to
  me,
 thank You, thank You, Lord.
 Thank You, Lord, that You're
  always near,
 thank You, thank You, Lord.

Captain Alan J. Price, CA

22

1 He gave me eyes so I could see
 the wonders of the world.
 Without my eyes I could not see
 the other boys and girls.
 He gave me ears so I could hear
 the wind and rain and sea.
 I've got to tell it to the world,
 He made me.

2 He gave me lips so I could speak
 and say what's in my mind.
 Without my lips I could not speak
 a single word or line.
 He made my mind so I could
  think,
 and choose what I should be.
 I've got to tell it to the world,
 He made me.

3 He gave me hands so I could
  touch,
 and hold a thousand things.
 I need my hands to help me
  write,
 to help me fetch and bring.
 These feet He made so I could
  run,
 He meant me to be free.
 I've got to tell it to the world,
 He made me.

Alan Pinnock, fl. 1970

23

1 He made the water wet,
 He made the land stay dry.
 He put twinkle in the stars
 and blue in the sky.

And when He was sure
it worked as it should,
God looked at His world and
 said,
'That's good!'
 Good, good, good! He said,
  'That's good!'
 Good, good, good! God looked at
  His world and said,
 'That's good!'

2 He put a touch of wag
 in a puppy dog's tail,
 then put a little slow
 in a silly old snail.
 And when He was sure
 it worked as it should,
 God looked at His world and
  said,
 'That's good!'

Dennis Allen and Nan Allen

24

1 I have seen the golden sunshine,
 I have watched the flowers grow,
 I have listened to the song birds
 and there's one thing now I
  know,
 they were all put there for us to
  share
 by someone so divine,
 and if you're a friend of Jesus,
 you're a friend of mine.
  I've seen the light, I've seen the
   light,
  and that's why my heart sings.
  I've known the joy, I've known the
   joy
  that loving Jesus brings.

2 I have seen the morning
  sunshine,
 I have heard the oceans roar,
 I have seen the flowers of
  springtime,
 and there's one thing I am sure,
 they were all put there for us to
  share
 by someone so divine,
 and if you're a friend of Jesus,
 you're a friend of mine.

Cecil V. Chester, 1914–1997
and Benny Litchfield

22 Words and Music: © High Fye Music / Music Sales Ltd, 8/9 Frith Street, London W1D 3JB
23 Words and Music: © 1988 Lillenas Publishing Company. Administered by CopyCare Ltd, PO Box 77, Hailsham, East Sussex. BN27 3EF
24 Words and Music: © 1970 High Fye Music Ltd / Music Sales Ltd, 8/9 Frith Street, London W1D 3JB

CREATION

25

1 Immortal, invisible,
   God only wise,
   in light inaccessible,
   hid from our eyes,
   most blessed and glorious,
   the Ancient of Days,
   almighty, victorious,
   Your great name we praise.

2 Unresting, unhasting,
   and silent as light,
   nor wanting or wasting,
   You rule in Your might,
   Your justice like mountains
   high soaring above,
   like torrents your fountains
   of goodness and love.

3 To all things, life giving,
   to great and to small,
   in all ever-living,
   the true life of all;
   we blossom, then perish,
   as leaves on a tree,
   but You ever flourish
   and always shall be.

4 Great Father of Glory,
   pure Father of Light,
   Your angels adore you,
   all veiling their sight;
   all praise we shall render,
   make this Your decree:
   that You in Your splendour
   we ever shall see.

Walter Chalmers Smith, 1824–1908
based on 1 Timothy 1: 17
adapted Gaetano Raphael (Anthony) Petti,
1932–1985

26

1 Let us with a gladsome mind
   praise the Lord, for He is kind:
   For His mercy shall endure,
   ever faithful, ever sure.

2 Let us blaze His Name abroad,
   for of gods He is the God:

3 He with all-commanding might
   filled the new-made world with
   light.

4 He has caused the golden sun
   all the day his course to run.

5 And the moon to shine by night
   with her starry sisters bright.

6 All things living He can feed,
   His full hand supplies their need.

7 Let us then with gladsome mind
   praise the Lord, for He is kind:

John Milton, 1608–1674
from Psalm 136
altered

27

1 Lord of all being, throned afar,
   Your glory flames from sun and
   star;
   centre and soul of every sphere,
   and yet to loving hearts how
   near.

2 Sun of our life, Your living ray
   sheds on our path the glow of
   day;
   star of our hope, Your gentle light
   shall ever cheer the longest night.

3 Our midnight is Your smile
   withdrawn,
   our noontide is Your gracious
   dawn,
   our rainbow arch Your mercy's
   sign;
   all, but the clouds of sin, divine.

4 Lord of all life, below, above,
   whose light is truth, whose
   warmth is love;
   before the brilliance of Your
   throne
   we ask no lustre of our own.

5 Give us Your grace to make us
   true,
   and kindling hearts that burn for
   You,
   till all Your living altars claim
   one holy light, one heavenly
   flame.

Oliver Wendell Holmes, 1809–1894
adapted Gaetano Raphael (Anthony) Petti,
1932–1985

28

1 Lord of beauty, Yours the
   splendour
   shown in earth and sky and sea,
   burning sun and moonlight
   tender,
   hill and river, flower and tree:
   lest we fail our praise to render
   touch our eyes that we may see.

25 Words: © 1971 Faber Music Ltd, 3 Queen Square, London. WC1N 3AU Reprinted from *New Catholic Hymnal* by permission.
27 Words: © 1971 Faber Music Ltd, 3 Queen Square, London. WC1N 3AU Reprinted from *New Catholic Hymnal* by permission.
28 Words: © Sir Richard Mynors, Hereford

2 Lord of wisdom, whom obeying
mighty waters ebb and flow,
while unhasting, undelaying,
planets on their courses go:
in Your laws Yourself displaying,
teach our minds Your truth to
know.

3 Lord of life, alone sustaining
all below and all above,
Lord of love, by whose ordaining
sun and stars sublimely move:
in our earthly spirits reigning,
lift our hearts that we may love.

4 Lord of beauty, bid us own You,
Lord of truth, our footsteps guide,
till as love our hearts enthrone
You,
and, with vision purified,
Lord of all, when all have known
You,
You in all are glorified.

Cyril Argentine Alington, 1872–1955
altered

29

1 My God is so big, so strong and so
mighty,
there's nothing that He cannot
do.
My God is so big, so strong and so
mighty,
there's nothing that He cannot
do.
The rivers are His, the mountains
are His,
the stars are His handiwork too.
My God is so big, so strong and so
mighty,
there's nothing that He cannot
do.

2 My God is so big, so strong and so
mighty,
there's nothing that He cannot
do.
My God is so big, so strong and so
mighty,
there's nothing that He cannot
do.
He's called you to live, for Him
every day,
in all that you say and you do.
My God is so big, so strong and so
mighty,
He can do all things through you.

Anonymous

30

1 'O bless the Lord, my soul!' I
sing,
and worship day and night;
my God arrayed in majesty
and robed in glorious light:

2 For like a tent You spread the sky,
on chariot-clouds You ride;
and by the wind, Your messenger,
Your truth is prophesied.

3 You bind the sea, or loose the
storm
in lightning's primal flame;
the rising spring and flowing
stream
cry glory to Your name.

4 O mighty Lord of every land,
You know our human need,
and all the creatures of the earth
You guide and tend and feed.

5 The sun and moon appear and
set
controlled by hidden force;
the stars declare Your
faithfulness,
consistent in their course.

6 Yet what You give, O sovereign
Lord,
Your power can take away;
our life and death belong to You
until our dying day.

7 So let me sing Your worthy
praise,
Your matchless grace extol
till all creation join the hymn:
'O bless the Lord, my soul!'

Michael Arnold Perry, 1942–1996
from Psalm 104

31

1 O Lord of every shining
constellation
that wheels in splendour through
the midnight sky:
grant us Your Spirit's true
illumination
to read the secrets of Your work
on high.

2 You, Lord, have made the atom's
hidden forces;
Your laws its mighty energies
fulfil:

teach us, to whom You give such
    rich resources,
in all we use, to serve Your holy
    will.

3   O Life, awaking life in cell and
      tissue;
   from flower to bird, from beast to
      humankind:
   help us to trace, from birth to
      final issue,
   the sure unfolding purpose of
      Your mind.

4   You, Lord, have stamped Your
      image on Your creatures
   and, though they mar that image,
      love them still:
   lift up our eyes to Christ, that in
      His features
   we may discern the beauty of
      Your will.

5   Great Lord of nature, shaping
      and renewing,
   You made us more than nature's
      child to be;
   You help us tread, with grace our
      souls enduring,
   the road to life and immortality.

Albert Frederick Bayly, 1901–1984
altered Compilers of
Hymns for Today's Church, 1982

32

1   O Lord of heaven and earth and
      sea,
   to You all praise and glory be,
   who loved us from eternity
   and gave us all.

2   The golden sunshine, gentle air,
   sweet flowers and fruit, Your love
      declare;
   when harvests ripen You are
      there —
   You give us all.

3   For peaceful homes and healthful
      days,
   for all the blessings earth
      displays,
   we owe You thankfulness and
      praise —
   You give us all.

4   Freely You gave Your only Son,
   who on the cross salvation won;
   and in the life through Him
      begun
   You give us all.

5   You sent Your Spirit from above
   as wind and fire and gentle
      dove;
   and in His gifts of power and
      love
   You gave us all.

6   For souls redeemed, for sins
      forgiven,
   for means of grace and hopes of
      heaven,
   to You, O Lord, what can be
      given?
   You give us all.

7   We lose what on ourselves we
      spend;
   we have as treasure without end
   whatever, Lord, to You we
      lend —
   You give us all.

8   Father, from whom we all derive
   our life, our gifts, our power to
      give:
   O may we ever with You live;
   You give us all.

Christopher Wordsworth, 1807–1885
adapted Jubilate Hymns

33

1   O worship the King,
      all-glorious above;
   O gratefully sing
      His power and His love:
   our shield and defender,
      the Ancient of Days,
   pavilioned in splendour
      and girded with praise!

2   O tell of His might!
      O sing of His grace,
   whose robe is the light,
      whose canopy space!
   His chariots of wrath the
      deep thunder clouds form,
   and dark is His path on
      the wings of the storm.

3   The earth, with its store
      of wonders untold,
   Almighty, Your power
      has founded of old,
   established it fast by
      a changeless decree,
   and round it has cast, like
      a mantle, the sea.

GOD'S WORLD

4 Your bountiful care
     what tongue can recite?
It breathes in the air,
     it shines in the light,
it streams from the hills, it
     descends to the plain,
and sweetly distils in
     the dew and the rain.

5 Frail children of dust
     and feeble as frail,
in You do we trust,
     nor find You to fail;
Your mercies how tender,
     how firm to the end;
our maker, defender,
     redeemer and friend!

6 O measureless might!
     O infinite love!
While angels delight
     to praise You above,
Your ransomed creation,
     with glory ablaze,
with true adoration
     shall sing to Your praise!

Robert Grant, 1779–1838
from Psalm 104
adapted Compilers of *Praise!* 2000

34

1 There are hundreds of sparrows,
     thousands, millions,
they're two a penny, far too many
     there must be;
there are hundreds and
     thousands, millions of
     sparrows,
but God knows every one and
     God knows me.

2 There are hundreds of flowers,
     thousands, millions,
and flowers fair the meadows
     wear for all to see;
there are hundreds and
     thousands, millions of flowers,
but God knows every one and
     God knows me.

3 There are hundreds of planets,
     thousands, millions,
way out in space each has a place
     by God's decree;
there are hundreds and
     thousands, millions of planets,
but God knows every one and
     God knows me.

4 There are hundreds of children,
     thousands, millions,
and yet their names are written
     on God's memory,
there are hundreds and
     thousands, millions of
     children,
but God knows every one and
     God knows me,
but God knows every one and
     God knows me.

John Gowans, *b.* 1934

35

PART ONE

1 Think of a world without any
     flowers,
think of a wood without any
     trees,
think of a sky without any
     sunshine,
think of the air without any
     breeze:
we thank You, Lord, for flowers
     and trees and sunshine;
we thank You, Lord, and praise
     Your holy name.

2 Think of a world without any
     animals,
think of a field without any herd,
think of a stream without any
     fishes,
think of a dawn without any
     bird:
we thank You, Lord, for all Your
     living creatures;
we thank You, Lord, and praise
     Your holy name.

PART TWO

3 Think of a world without any
     paintings,
think of a room where all the
     walls are bare,
think of a rainbow without any
     colours,
think of the earth with darkness
     everywhere:
we thank You, Lord, for paintings
     and for colours;
we thank You, Lord, and praise
     Your holy name.

34 Words and Music: © 1970 Salvationist Publishing and Supplies Ltd, London
35 Words: © 1969 Stainer & Bell Ltd, PO Box 110, Victoria House, 23 Gruneisen Road, London N3 1DZ

4   Think of a world without any
  poetry,
  think of a book without any
  words,
  think of a song without any
  music,
  think of a hymn without any
  verse:
  we thank You, Lord, for poetry
  and music;
  we thank You, Lord, and praise
  Your holy name.

5   Think of a world without any
  science,
  think of a journey with nothing to
  explore,
  think of a quest without any
  mystery,
  nothing to seek and nothing left
  in store:
  we thank You, Lord, for miracles
  of science;
  we thank You, Lord, and praise
  Your holy name.

6   Think of a world without any
  people,
  think of a street with no-one
  living there,
  think of a town without any
  houses,
  no-one to love and nobody to
  care:
  we thank You, Lord, for families
  and friendships;
  we thank You, Lord, and praise
  Your holy name.

PART THREE

7   Think of a world without any
  worship,
  think of a God without His only
  Son,
  think of a cross without a
  resurrection,
  only a grave and not a victory
  won:
  we thank You, Lord, for showing
  us our Saviour;
  we thank You, Lord, and praise
  Your holy name.

8   Thanks to our Lord for being here
  among us,
  thanks be to Him for sharing all
  we do,
  thanks for our Church and all the
  love we find here,
  thanks for this place and all its
  promise true:

we thank You, Lord, for life in all
  its richness;
we thank You, Lord, and praise
  Your holy name.

Doreen E. Newport, b. 1927

36

1   Who put the colours in the
  rainbow?
  Who put the salt into the sea?
  Who put the cold into the
  snowflake?
  Who made you and me?
  Who put the hump upon the
  camel?
  Who put the neck on the giraffe?
  Who put the tail upon the
  monkey?
  Who made hyenas laugh?
  Who made whales and snails
  and quails?
  Who made hogs and dogs and
  frogs?
  Who made bats and rats and
  cats?
  Who made everything?

2   Who put the gold into the
  sunshine?
  Who put the sparkle in the stars?
  Who put the silver in the
  moonlight?
  Who made Earth and Mars?
  Who put the scent into the roses?
  Who taught the honey bee to
  dance?
  Who put the tree inside the
  acorn?
  It surely can't be chance!
  Who made seas and leaves and
  trees?
  Who made snow and winds that
  blow?
  Who made streams and rivers
  flow?
  God made all of these!

J.A. Paul Booth, 1931–1995

Also suitable:
A little child may know   109
God who made the earth   88
Morning has broken   5

36 Words: © Paul Booth. Administered by CopyCare Ltd, PO Box 77, Hailsham, East Sussex. BN27 3EF

CREATION
THE ENVIRONMENT

37

1 God in His love for us lent us
    this planet,
  gave it a purpose in time and in
    space:
  small as a spark from the fire of
    creation,
  cradle of life and the home of our
    race.

2 Thanks be to God for its bounty
    and beauty,
  life that sustains us in body and
    mind:
  plenty for all, if we learn how to
    share it,
  riches undreamed of to fathom
    and find.

3 Long have our human wars
    ruined its harvest;
  long has earth bowed to the
    terror of force;
  long have we wasted what others
    have need of,
  poisoned the fountain of life at its
    source.

4 Earth is the Lord's: it is ours to
    enjoy it,
  ours, as His stewards, to farm and
    defend.
  From its pollution, misuse and
    destruction,
  good Lord, deliver us, world
    without end!

Frederick Pratt Green, 1903–2000

38

1 Lord, bring the day to pass
  when forest, rock and hill,
  the beasts, the birds, the grass,
  will know Your finished will:
  when we attain our destiny
  and nature its lost unity.

2 Forgive our careless use
  of water, ore and soil —
  the plenty we abuse
  supplied by others' toil:
  save us from making self our
    creed,
  turn us towards each other's
    need.

3 Give us, when we release
  creation's secret powers,
  to harness them for peace,
  our children's peace and ours:
  teach us the art of mastering
  which makes life rich and draws
    death's sting.

4 Creation groans, travails,
  futile its present plight,
  bound — till the hour it hails
  God's children born of light
  who enter on their true estate.
  Come, Lord: new heavens and
    earth create.

Ian Masson Fraser, b. 1917

39

1 Sing praise to God on mountain
    tops
  and in earth's lowest places,
  from blue lagoon to polar waste,
  from ocean to oasis.
  No random rock produced this
    world
  but God's own will and wonder.
  Thus hills rejoice and valleys
    sing
  and clouds concur with thunder.

2 Sing praise to God where grasses
    grow
  and flowers display their beauty,
  where nature weaves her myriad
    web
  through love as much as duty.
  The seasons in their cycle speak
  of earth's complete provision.
  Let nothing mock inherent good
  nor treat it with derision.

3 Sing praise to God where fishes
    swim
  and birds fly in formation,
  where animals of every kind
  diversify creation.
  All life that finds its home on
    earth
  is meant to be respected.
  Let nothing threaten, for base
    ends,
  what God through grace
    perfected.

4 Sing praise to God where
    humankind
  its majesty embraces,
  where different races, creeds and
    tongues
  distinguish different faces.

God's image in each child of
earth
shall never pale or perish.
So treat with love each human
soul
and thus God's goodness cherish.

John Lamberton Bell, *b.* 1949
and Graham Alexander Maule, *b.* 1958

40

1 We cannot own the sunlit sky,
the moon, the wild flowers
growing,
for we are part of all that is
within life's river flowing.
With open hands receive and
share
the gifts of God's creation,
that all may have abundant life
in every earthly nation.

2 When bodies shiver in the night
and weary, wait for morning,
when children have no bread but
tears,
and war-horns sound their
warning,
God calls humanity to wake,
to join in common labour,
that all may have abundant life
in oneness with their neighbour.

3 God calls humanity to join
as partners in creating
a future free from want or fear,
life's goodness celebrating.
That new world beckons from
afar,
invites our shared endeavour,
that all may have abundant life
and peace endure for ever.

Ruth C. Duck, *b.* 1947

CREATION
SEASONS OF THE YEAR

41

1 All beautiful the march of days,
as seasons come and go;
the hand that shaped the rose
has wrought
the crystal of the snow,
has sent the silvery frost of
heaven,
the flowing waters sealed,
and laid a silent loveliness
on hill and wood and field.

2 O'er white expanses sparkling
pure
the radiant morns unfold;
the solemn splendours of the
night
burn brighter through the cold;
life mounts in every throbbing
vein,
love deepens round the hearth,
and clearer sounds the angel
hymn,
'Good will to all on earth.'

3 O God, from whose unfathomed
law
the year in beauty flows,
Yourself the vision passing by
in crystal and in rose;
day unto day declare thro'
speech,
and night to night proclaim
in ever-changing words of light
the wonder of Your name.

Frances Whitmarsh Wile, 1878–1939
altered

42

1 Fill your hearts with joy and
gladness,
sing and praise your God and
mine!
Great the Lord in love and
wisdom,
might and majesty divine!
He who framed the starry
heavens
knows and names them as they
shine.

2 Praise the Lord, His people,
    praise Him!
  Wounded souls His comfort
    know;
  those who fear Him find His
    mercies,
  peace for pain and joy for woe;
  humble hearts are high exalted,
  human pride and power laid low.

3 Praise the Lord for times and
    seasons,
  cloud and sunshine, wind and
    rain;
  spring to melt the snows of
    winter
  till the waters flow again;
  grass upon the mountain
    pastures,
  golden valleys thick with grain.

4 Fill your hearts with joy and
    gladness,
  peace and plenty crown your
    days;
  love His laws, declare His
    judgements,
  walk in all His words and ways;
  He the Lord and we His
    children:
  praise the Lord, all people,
    praise!

Timothy Dudley-Smith, b. 1926
from Psalm 147

43

1 Lord of the changing year,
  patterns and colours bright;
  all that we see and hear,
  sunrise and starlit night:
  the seasons, Lord, in splendour
    shine,
  Your never-failing wise design.

2 Lord of the winter scene,
  hard-frozen ice and snow;
  death where once life has been,
  nothing is seen to grow;
  few creatures roam, few birds
    will fly
  across the clouded Christmas sky:

3 Lord of unfolding spring,
  promise of life to come;
  nature begins to sing
  where once her tongue was
    dumb;
  the crocus blooms, the hedgerows
    wake,
  and Easter day is soon to break:

4 Lord of the summer days,
  spreading and green the trees;
  songthrush lifts high Your praise,
  gulls light on deep-blue seas;
  the warmth and welcome of the
    sun
  brings happiness to everyone:

5 Lord of the autumn gold,
  reaping and harvest-home,
  sheep safely in the fold,
  turn of the year has come:
  the seasons, Lord, in splendour
    shine,
  Your never-failing wise design.

David Mowbray, b. 1938

44

1 Mercy, blessing, favour, grace,
  saving power to us be shown;
  brightness of the Father's face
  to the nations now be known.

2 Shout in triumph, sing in praise!
  Peoples all, proclaim His worth:
  just and righteous are His ways,
  sovereign Lord of all the earth.

3 Harvests year by year proclaim
  blessings new in plenty poured;
  all the earth shall fear His name,
  all His people praise the Lord.

Timothy Dudley-Smith, b. 1926
based on Psalm 67

45

1 Spring has now unwrapped the
    flowers,
  day is fast reviving,
  life in all her growing powers
  towards the light is striving:
  gone the iron touch of cold,
  winter time and frost time,
  seedlings, working through the
    mould,
  now make up for lost time.

2 Herb and plant that, winter long,
  slumbered at their leisure,
  now bestirring, green and strong,
  find in growth their pleasure:
  all the world with beauty fills,
  gold the green enhancing;
  flowers make merry on the hills,
  set the meadows dancing.

3 Through each wonder of fair days
  God Himself expresses;
  beauty follows all His ways,
  as the world He blesses:

43 Words: © David Mowbray / Jubilate Hymns, 4 Thorne Park Road, Chelston, Torquay TQ2 6RX <enquiries@jubilate.co.uk> Used by permission.
44 Words: © Timothy Dudley-Smith in Europe and all territories not controlled by Hope Publishing Company
45 Words: © 1928 Oxford University Press, from *Oxford Book of Carols*. Reproduced by permission., Great Clarendon Street, Oxford OX2 6DP

CREATION

so, as He renews the earth,
Artist without rival,
in His grace of glad new birth
we must seek revival.

Tempus adest floridum, German, 16th century
translated Percy Dearmer, 1867–1936

46

1   The earth is Yours, O God —
    You nourish it with rain;
    the streams and rivers overflow,
    the land bears seed again.

2   The soil is Yours, O God —
    the shoots are moist with dew;
    and ripened by the burning sun
    the corn grows straight and true.

3   The hills are Yours, O God —
    their grass is lush and green,
    providing pastures for the flocks
    which everywhere are seen.

4   The whole rich land is Yours
    for fodder or for plough;
    and so, for rain, sun, soil and
        seed,
    O God, we thank You now.

Michael Saward, *b.* 1932
paraphrased from Psalm 65: 9-13

47

1   The spring again is here,
    life wakes from winter's gloom;
    in field and forest far and near
    sweet opening flowerets bloom.

2   O mystery strange and sweet,
    that life so dumbly bound
    should rise, our thankful gaze to
        greet,
    and break from underground.

3   The morn is fresh and bright,
    the slow dark hours depart:
    let days unstained and pure
        delight
    bring sunshine to the heart.

4   Lord, touch our careless eyes;
    new life, new ardour bring,
    that we may read Your mysteries,
    the wonder of Your spring.

Arthur Christopher Benson, 1862–1925

48

1   The summer days are come
        again;
    once more the glad earth yields
    her golden wealth of ripening
        grain
    and breath of clover fields
    and deepening shade of summer
        woods
    and glow of summer air
    and winging thoughts and happy
        moods
    of love and joy and prayer.

2   The summer days are come
        again;
    the birds are on the wing;
    God's praises, in their loving
        strain,
    unconsciously they sing.
    We know who gives us all the
        good
    that makes our cup o'erbrim;
    for summer joy in field and
        wood,
    we lift our song to Him.

Samuel Longfellow, 1819–1892
altered

49

1   Summer suns are glowing
    over land and sea,
    happy light is flowing
    bountiful and free;
    everything rejoices
    in the mellow rays,
    all earth's thousand voices
    swell the psalm of praise.

2   God's free mercy streaming
    over all the world,
    and His banner gleaming
    everywhere unfurled.
    Broad and deep and glorious
    as the heaven above,
    shines in might victorious
    His eternal love.

3   Lord, upon our blindness
    Your pure radiance pour;
    for Your loving-kindness
    make us love You more.
    And when clouds are drifting
    dark across the sky,
    then, the veil uplifting,
    Father, be close by.

46   Words: © Michael Saward / Jubilate Hymns, 4 Thorne Park Road, Chelston, Torquay TQ2 6RX <enquiries@jubilate.co.uk> Used by permission.

4 We will never doubt You,
though You veil Your light;
life is dark without You,
death with You is bright.
Light of light, shine o'er us
on our pilgrim way;
still go on before us
to the endless day.

William Walsham How, 1823–1897
altered

Also suitable:
Great is Your faithfulness   89
Great is Thy faithfulness   89

CREATION
HARVEST

50

1 At harvest-time we celebrate
God's gift to us of food and drink.
We thank Him for the care He's
shown
for farmers and the seeds they've
sown.

Praise the Lord! Praise the Lord!
Praise the Lord! Praise the Lord!
Praise the Lord! Praise the Lord!
Thank Him for harvest.

2 God's watched the fields through
day and night,
He's given the seeds both dark
and light.
He's watered them with fresh
cool rain
and now there's fields and fields
of grain.

3 God helps the farmers cut the
corn,
He keeps the weather dry and
warm,
until it's baled and brought
inside,
before the start of wintertide.

4 Now once the crops are in their
barns
there's work to do still on the
farms.
It's time to put the crops to use
to make the different kinds of
foods.

5 At harvest-time we celebrate
God's gifts to us of food and
drink.
Let's sing and clap to show our
thanks
for all the care God takes of us.

S. Lesley Scott

51

1 Come, you thankful people, come,
raise the song of harvest home!
all is safely gathered in
now before the storms begin:
God our maker will provide
for our needs to be supplied;
come, with all His people, come,
raise the song of harvest home!

2 All the world is God's own field,
harvests for His praise to yield;
wheat and weeds together sown
here for joy or sorrow grown:
first the blade and then the ear,
then the full corn shall appear —
Lord of harvest, grant that we
wholesome grain and pure may
be.

3 For the Lord our God shall come
and shall bring His harvest
home;
He Himself, on that great day,
worthless things shall take away,
give His angels charge at last
in the fire the weeds to cast,
but the fruitful ears to store
in His care for evermore.

4 Even so, Lord, quickly come —
bring Your final harvest home!
Gather all Your people in
free from sorrow, free from sin,
there together purified,
ever thankful at Your side —
come, with all Your angels, come,
bring that glorious harvest home!

Henry Alford, 1810–1871
adapted Jubilate Hymns

52

1 For the fruits of His creation,
thanks be to God;
for His gifts to every nation,
thanks be to God;
for the ploughing, sowing,
reaping,

CREATION

silent growth while we are
    sleeping,
future needs in earth's safe-
    keeping,
thanks be to God.

2   In the just reward of labour,
    God's will is done;
    in the help we give our
        neighbour,
    God's will is done;
    in our worldwide task of caring
    for the hungry and despairing,
    in the harvests we are sharing,
    God's will is done.

3   For the harvests of the Spirit,
    thanks be to God;
    for the good we all inherit,
    thanks be to God;
    for the wonders that astound us,
    for the truths that still confound
        us,
    most of all that love has found us,
    thanks be to God.

Frederick Pratt Green, 1903–2000

53

1   Fountain of mercy, God of love,
    how rich Your bounties are!
    The rolling seasons, as they
        move,
    proclaim Your constant care.

2   When in the bosom of the earth
    the sower hid the grain,
    Your goodness marked its secret
        birth,
    and sent the early rain.

3   You gave the influence of spring;
    the plants in beauty grew;
    the summer came its sun to
        bring,
    and mild refreshing dew.

4   These various mercies from
        above
    matured the swelling grain;
    a yellow harvest crowns Your
        love,
    and plenty fills the plain.

5   Seed-time and harvest, Lord,
        alone
    Your love on us bestows;
    let us not then forget to own
    from whom such blessing flows.

6   Fountain of love, our praise we
        bring;
    to You our songs we'll raise;
    and all created nature sing
    in glad exultant praise.

Alice Flowerdew, 1759–1830
altered

54

1   God whose farm is all creation,
    take the gratitude we give;
    take the finest of our harvest,
    crops we grow that all may live.

2   Take our ploughing, seeding,
        reaping,
    hopes and fears of sun and rain,
    all our thinking, planning,
        waiting,
    ripened in this fruit and grain.

3   All our labour, all our watching,
    all our calendar of care
    in these crops of Your creation,
    take, O God — they are our
        prayer.

L. T. John Arlott, 1914–1991

55

1   Harvest-time is the time when all
        the crops are high,
    all the food must be cut and
        stored up in the dry.
    Harvest-time — see the fruit, the
        maize and wheat,
    all the food for us to eat,
    it must be harvest-time.

2   Harvest-time, we have always got
        so much to eat,
    but for some just a little is a real
        feast.
    Harvest-time — let's remember
        all the poor,
    and let's try to give them more
    after this harvest-time.

3   Harvest-time is the time when
        we should all thank God
    for each grain, every apple and
        the green pea pod.
    Harvest-time — see the fruit, the
        maize and wheat,
    so much food for us to eat.
    Thank God for harvest-time.

Nick Harding

54 Words: © Trustees of L. T. J. Arlott
55 Words and Music: © 1995 Daybreak Music Ltd, PO Box 2848, Eastbourne, East Sussex. BN20 7XP. All rights reserved. <info@daybreakmusic.co.uk>
    International copyright secured. Used by permission.

HARVEST

56

*It takes an almighty hand, to make
your harvest grow.
It takes an almighty hand, however
you may sow.
It takes an almighty hand, the
world around me shows.
It takes the almighty hand of God.*

1   It takes His hand to grow your
garden,
all from a secret in a seed;
part of a plan He spoke and
started,
and said is 'very good indeed!'

2   It takes His hand to turn the
seasons,
to give the sun and snow their
hour;
and in this plan we learn His
reason,
His nature and eternal power.

3   It took His hands to carry sorrow,
for every sin that we have done;
and on a cross He bought
tomorrow,
a world of good, like He'd begun.

4   And in His hands there is
perfection,
that in this land we only taste;
for now we see a poor reflection,
then we shall see Him face to
face.

Ian White, *b.* 1956

57

1   Lord of the harvest, once again
we thank You for the ripened
grain;
for crops safe carried, sent to
cheer
Your servants through another
year:
for all sweet holy thoughts,
supplied
by seed-time, and by harvest-tide.

2   The bare dead grain, in autumn
sown,
its robe of vernal green puts on;
glad from its wintry grave it
springs,
fresh garnished by the King of
kings:
so, Lord, to those who sleep in
You
shall bodies glorious be and new.

3   Daily, O Lord, our prayers be
said,
as You have taught, for daily
bread;
but not alone our bodies feed, —
supply our fainting spirits' need.
O Bread of Life, from day to day
be all their comfort, food and
stay!

Joseph Anstice, 1808–1836
altered

58

1   Praise God for the harvest of
orchard and field,
praise God for the people who
gather their yield,
the long hours of labour, the skills
of a team,
the patience of science, the power
of machine.

2   Praise God for the harvest that
comes from afar,
from market and harbour, the sea
and the shore:
foods packed and transported,
and gathered and grown
by God-given neighbours, unseen
and unknown.

3   Praise God for the harvest that's
quarried and mined,
then sifted, and smelted, or
shaped and refined;
for oil and for iron, for copper
and coal,
praise God, who in love has
provided them all.

4   Praise God for the harvest of
science and skill,
the urge to discover, create and
fulfil:
for dreams and inventions that
promise to gain
a future more hopeful, a world
more humane.

5   Praise God for the harvest of
mercy and love,
from leaders and peoples who
struggle and serve
with patience and kindness, that
all may be led
to freedom and justice, and all
may be fed.

Brian Arthur Wren, *b.* 1936

59

1 We plough the fields, and scatter
the good seed on the land;
but it is fed and watered
by God's almighty hand:
He sends the snow in winter,
the warmth to swell the grain;
the breezes and the sunshine
and soft refreshing rain.

*All good gifts around us
are sent from heaven above:
then thank the Lord, O thank the
Lord
for all His love.*

2 He only is the maker
of all things near and far;
He paints the wayside flower,
He lights the evening star:
the winds and waves obey Him,
by Him the birds are fed;
much more, to us His children
He gives our daily bread.

3 We thank You, then, our Father,
for all things bright and good;
the seed-time and the harvest,
our life, our health, our food:
accept the gifts we offer
for all Your love imparts;
and that which You most
welcome
our humble, thankful hearts!

Matthias Claudius, 1740–1815
translated Jane Montgomery Campbell, 1817–1878
altered Compilers of
Hymns for Today's Church, 1982

60

1 We thank You, Lord, for all Your
gifts
of sunshine warm, and showers
of rain
that ripened all the lovely fruits
and fields of golden grain.

2 We thank You for the joy that
comes
to us, when harvest gifts we
bring —
that others, too, may know Your
love,
which speaks through everything.

3 O give us loving, thankful hearts,
for all Your goodness, love and
care;
and help us always to be glad
to give away and share.

Jessie Margaret Macdougall Ferguson, 1895–1964
altered

Also suitable:
When Zion's fortunes God restored   130
God 's World section   17–36
Environment section   37–40

THE FALL
THE HUMAN
CONDITION

61

1 Approach, my soul, the mercy-
seat,
where Jesus answers prayer;
and humbly fall before His feet
for none can perish there.

2 Your promise is my only plea;
to You alone I cry,
for burdened souls in You are
free
and such, O Lord, am I.

3 Bowed down beneath the weight
of sin,
by Satan sorely pressed,
from outward foes and fears
within,
I come to You for rest.

4 Lord, be my shield and hiding-
place,
that, sheltered near Your side,
I may my fierce accuser face
and tell him You have died.

5 Amazing love, to bleed and die,
to bear the cross and shame,
that guilty sinners such as I
might plead Your gracious name!

John Newton, 1725–1807
altered Compilers of *Praise!* 2000

62

1 Father of heaven, whose love
profound
a ransom for our souls has found,
before Your throne we sinners
bend;
to us Your pardoning love
extend.

2 Almighty Son, incarnate Word,
   our Prophet, Priest, Redeemer,
      Lord,
   before Your throne we sinners
      bend;
   to us Your saving grace extend.

3 Eternal Spirit, by whose breath
   the soul is raised from sin and
      death,
   before Your throne we sinners
      bend;
   to us Your living power extend.

4 Jehovah — Father, Spirit, Son —
   mysterious Godhead, Three-in-
      One,
   before Your throne we sinners
      bend;
   grace, pardon, life to us extend.

Edward Cooper, 1770–1833

63

1 God, be merciful to me,
   let Your love my refuge be;
   my offences wash away,
   cleanse me from my sin today.
   My transgressions I confess,
   grief and guilt my soul oppress;
   I have sinned against Your grace
   and provoked You to Your face.

2 Wash me, wash me pure within,
   cleanse, O cleanse me from my
      sin;
   in Your righteousness I trust,
   in Your judgements You are just.
   Come, salvation to impart,
   teach Your wisdom to my heart;
   make me pure, Your grace
      bestow,
   that Your mercy I may know.

3 Gracious God, my heart renew,
   make my spirit right and true;
   from my sins O hide Your face,
   blot them out in boundless grace.
   Cast Your servant not away,
   let Your Spirit with me stay;
   make me joyful, willing, strong,
   teach me Your salvation's song!

Michael Arnold Perry, 1942–1996
from Psalm 51, adapted from *The Psalter*, 1912

64

1 Help me, O God, and hear my
      cry,
   extend to me Your saving hand,
   the waters rise, the floods are
      high,
   my feet have found no place to
      stand:
   now, lest the depths become my
      grave,
   O God of hosts, draw near and
      save.

2 My secret faults, my sin and
      shame,
   lie open, Lord, before Your face,
   yet in my heart I love Your name
   and all my hope is in Your grace:
   Lord, in Your mercy, think on
      me;
   speak but the word, and set me
      free.

3 So shall I praise the God of love,
   with heaven and earth and sea
      and sky,
   who hears us from His throne
      above
   and lifts His ransomed people
      high,
   to sound His praise in ceaseless
      song
   where all who love His name
      belong.

Timothy Dudley-Smith, *b.* 1926
from Psalm 69

65

1 How can we sing with joy to God,
   how can we pray to Him,
   when we are far away from God
   in selfishness and sin?

2 How can we claim to do God's
      will
   when we have turned away
   from things of God to things of
      earth,
   and willed to disobey?

3 How can we praise the love of
      God
   which all His works make known,
   when all our works turn from His
      love
   to choices of our own?

4   God knows the sinful things we
    do,
    the godless life we live,
    yet in His love He calls to us,
    so ready to forgive.

5   So we will turn again to God —
    His ways will be our ways,
    His will our will, His love our
    love,
    and He Himself our praise!

William Brian Foley, 1919–2000
altered Compilers of *Glory to God*, 1994

66

1   How glad are those with peace of
    mind,
    their past wrongdoings left
    behind;
    their sins forgiven by the Lord —
    they stand, rejoicing in their
    God!

2   While every wrong lay
    unconfessed,
    their spirits knew no lasting rest;
    but shedding tears of honesty
    they reached the place of
    heartfelt joy.

3   With Your great wisdom, Lord,
    we pray,
    help us to walk life's path today!
    How glad are those with peace of
    mind,
    their past wrongdoings left
    behind!

David Mowbray, b. 1938
after Psalm 32

67

1   Jesus, lover of my soul,
    let me to Your presence fly,
    while the gathering waters roll,
    while the tempest still is high.
    Hide me, O my Saviour, hide,
    till the storm of life is past;
    safe into the haven, guide
    and receive my soul at last.

2   Other refuge have I none,
    all my hope in You I see:
    leave, O leave me, not alone;
    still support and comfort me.
    All my trust on You is stayed,
    all my help from You I bring:
    cover my defenceless head
    with the shadow of Your wing.

3   You, O Christ, are all I want,
    more than all in You I find:
    raise the fallen, cheer the faint,
    heal the sick and lead the blind.
    Just and holy is Your name,
    I am all unworthiness;
    false and full of sin I am,
    You are full of truth and grace.

4   Plenteous grace with You is
    found,
    grace to wash away my sin:
    let the healing streams abound;
    make and keep me clean within.
    Living Fountain, now impart
    all Your life and purity;
    spring for ever in my heart,
    rise to all eternity!

Charles Wesley, 1707–1788
adapted Jubilate Hymns

68

1   Just as I am, without one plea
    but that You died to set me free,
    and at Your bidding, 'Come to
    me!'
    O Lamb of God, I come.

2   Just as I am, without delay
    Your call of mercy I obey —
    Your blood can wash my sins
    away:
    O Lamb of God, I come.

3   Just as I am, though tossed about
    with many a conflict, many a
    doubt,
    fightings within and fears
    without:
    O Lamb of God, I come.

4   Just as I am, poor, wretched,
    blind!
    Sight, riches, healing of the
    mind —
    all that I need, in You to find:
    O Lamb of God, I come.

5   Just as I am! You will receive,
    will welcome, pardon, cleanse,
    relieve:
    because Your promise I believe,
    O Lamb of God, I come.

6   Just as I am! Your love unknown
    has broken every barrier down:
    now to be Yours, yes, Yours alone,
    O Lamb of God, I come.

7   Just as I am! Of that free love
the breadth, length, depth and
    height to prove,
here for a time and then above,
O Lamb of God, I come.

Charlotte Elliott, 1789–1871
adapted Jubilate Hymns

69

1   Lord Jesus, think on me,
and purge away my sin;
from earthborn passions set me
    free,
and make me pure within.

2   Lord Jesus, think on me,
with care and woe oppressed;
let me Your loving servant be,
and taste Your promised rest.

3   Lord Jesus, think on me,
amid the bitter strife;
through all my pain and misery
become my health and life.

4   Lord Jesus, think on me,
nor let me go astray;
through darkness and perplexity
point out the heavenly way.

5   Lord Jesus, think on me,
when tempests round me roll,
when onward comes the enemy
O Saviour, guard my soul.

6   Lord Jesus, think on me,
that when the flood is past,
I may the eternal brightness see,
and share Your joy at last.

Synesius of Cyrene, c. 365–c. 414
translated Allen William Chatfield, 1808–1896
and others

70

1   Lord, will You turn from Your
    anger and hear me?
Guilt and remorse are the
    burdens I bear;
when I acknowledge my sin and
    my folly,
show Your compassion, Your love
and Your care.

2   Lord, though my friends and
    companions desert me,
You will not leave me — I know
    You are near.
Hear my deep sighing, and see
    my great sorrow —

You know each secret, each
    longing, each fear.

3   Lord, will You answer with
    words of forgiveness?
Then shall my joy and my peace
    be restored:
faithful Redeemer and God of all
    comfort,
You are my Saviour, my King and
    my Lord!

Mollie Knight, 1917–1993
from Psalm 38

71

Merciful God and Father,
loving us like no other,
hear our prayer, the cry of our
    hearts,
as we come to You.
We acknowledge our
    transgressions,
we confess to You our sins;
show us mercy and compassion,
touch our lives with Your healing
    grace again.

Release us from the past,
as we seek Your face.
Wash us free at last,
we receive Your love,
we receive Your healing grace.
We receive Your love,
we receive Your healing grace.

Merciful God …

John Chisum and Gary Sadler

72

1   My faith looks up to Thee,
Thou Lamb of Calvary,
Saviour divine:
now hear me while I pray;
take all my guilt away;
O let me from this day
be wholly Thine.

2   May Thy rich grace impart
strength to my fainting heart,
my zeal inspire;
as Thou hast died for me,
O may my love to Thee
pure, warm, and changeless be,
a living fire.

3   While life's dark maze I tread,
and griefs around me spread,
be Thou my guide;
bid darkness turn to day,
wipe sorrow's tears away,

70   Words: © Trevor Knight/Jubilate Hymns, 4 Thorne Park Road, Chelston, Torquay TQ2 6RX <enquiries@jubilate.co.uk> Used by permission.

71   Words and Music: © 1994 Integrity's Hosanna Music/Sovereign Lifestyle Music Ltd, P.O. Box 356, Leighton Buzzard LU7 3WP <sovereignmusic@aol.com>

nor let me ever stray
from Thee aside.

4   When ends life's transient
        dream,
    when death's cold, sullen stream
        shall o'er me roll,
    blest Saviour, then, in love,
    fear and distrust remove;
    O bear me safe above,
    a ransomed soul.

Ray Palmer, 1808–1887

73

1   O Lord, the clouds are gathering,
    the fire of judgement burns,
    how we have fallen!
    O Lord, You stand appalled to
        see
    Your laws of love so scorned
    and lives so broken.

MEN: *Have mercy, Lord,*
WOMEN: *Have mercy, Lord,*
MEN: *forgive us, Lord,*
WOMEN: *forgive us, Lord,*
ALL: *restore us, Lord,*
        revive Your Church again.

MEN: *Let justice flow*
WOMEN: *Let justice flow*
MEN: *like rivers*
WOMEN: *like rivers*
ALL: *and righteousness*
        like a never-failing stream.

2   O Lord, over the nations now
    where is the dove of peace?
    Her wings are broken.
    O Lord, while precious children
        starve
    the tools of war increase;
    their bread is stolen.

3   O Lord, dark powers are poised
        to flood
    our streets with hate and fear;
    we must awaken!
    O Lord, let love reclaim the lives
    that sin would sweep away
    and let Your kingdom come.

4   Yet, O Lord, Your glorious cross
        shall tower
    triumphant in this land,
    evil confounding.
    Through the fire Your suffering
        Church displays
    the glories of her Christ:
    praises resounding!

Graham Andrew Kendrick, *b.* 1950

74

1   Rock of Ages, cleft for me,
    hide me now, my refuge be;
    let the water and the blood
    from Your wounded side which
        flowed,
    be for sin the double cure,
    cleanse me from its guilt and
        power.

2   Not the labours of my hands
    can fulfil Your law's demands;
    could my zeal no respite know,
    could my tears for ever flow,
    all for sin could not atone:
    You must save and You alone.

3   Nothing in my hand I bring,
    simply to Your cross I cling;
    naked, come to You for dress,
    helpless, look to You for grace;
    stained by sin, to You I cry:
    'Wash me, Saviour, or I die!'

4   While I draw this fleeting breath,
    when my eyelids close in death,
    when I soar through realms
        unknown,
    bow before the judgement
        throne:
    hide me then, my refuge be,
    Rock of Ages, cleft for me.

Augustus Montague Toplady, 1740–1778
adapted Jubilate Hymns

75

1   Today Your mercy calls us
    to wash away our sin,
    however great our trespass,
    whatever we have been;
    however long from mercy
    our hearts have turned away,
    Your blood, O Christ, can cleanse
        us
    and set us free today.

2   Today Your gate is open,
    and all who enter in
    shall find a father's welcome
    and pardon for their sin;
    the past shall be forgotten,
    a present joy be given,
    a future grace be promised,
    a glorious crown in heaven.

3 Today the Father calls us;
the Holy Spirit moves;
the Son has given His lifeblood
for every soul He loves.
No question will be asked us
why we so late have come,
or why we always wandered:
this is our Father's home!

4 O all-embracing mercy!
O ever-open door!
What shall we do without You,
how can we ask for more?
When all things seem against us,
to drive us to despair,
we know one gate is open,
and You will hear our prayer.

Oswald Allen, 1816–1878
adapted Compilers of *Praise!* 2000

76

1 Up from the depths I cry to God:
O listen, Lord, to me;
O hear my voice in this distress,
this mire of misery.
I wait for God with all my heart,
my hope is in His word;
and more than watchmen for the
dawn
I'm longing for the Lord.

2 If You, my God, should measure
guilt
who then could ever stand?
But those who fear Your name
will find
forgiveness from Your hand.

3 O Israel, set your hope on God
whose mercy is supreme:
the nation mourning for its sin
He surely will redeem.

Christopher Martin Idle, *b.* 1938
from Psalm 130

Also suitable:
And can it be that I should gain 487
Eternal Light! Eternal Light! 166
Jesus! name of wondrous love 350
O Father of the fatherless 96
Such love, pure as the whitest snow 191

GOD THROUGH
THE YEARS
HIS FAITHFULNESS

77

1 A gladsome hymn of praise we
sing,
and thankfully we gather
to bless the love of God above,
our everlasting Father.

2 In Him rejoice with heart and
voice,
His glory fading never,
whose providence is our defence,
who lives and loves for ever.

3 Full in His sight His children
stand,
by His strong arm defended,
and He whose wisdom guides
the world
our footsteps has attended.

4 For nothing falls unknown to
Him —
or care or joy or sorrow;
and He, whose mercy ruled the
past,
will be our stay tomorrow.

Ambrose Nichols Blatchford, 1842–1924

78

1 All my hope on God is founded,
all my trust He shall renew;
He, my guide through changing
order,
only good and only true:
God unknown,
He alone,
calls my heart to be His own.

2 Human pride and earthly glory,
sword and crown betray His
trust;
what with care and toil we
fashion,
tower and temple, fall to dust;
but God's power
hour by hour
is my temple and my tower.

3   God's great goodness lasts for
       ever,
    deep His wisdom, passing
       thought;
    splendour, light and life attend
       Him,
    beauty springing out of naught;
    evermore
    from His store
    countless stars rise and adore.

4   Day by day the almighty Giver
    grants to us His gifts of love;
    in His will our souls find
       pleasure,
    leading to our home above:
    love shall stand
    at His hand,
    joy shall wait on His command.

5   Still from man to God eternal
    sacrifice of praise be done;
    high above all praises praising
    for the gift of Christ His Son:
    hear Christ's call,
    one and all —
    those who follow shall not fall.

                    Robert Bridges, 1844–1930
          based on Joachim Neander 1650-1680
            adapted Compilers of Praise! 2000

79

1   Be still, my soul: the Lord is on
       your side;
    bear patiently the cross of grief
       and pain;
    leave to your God to order and
       provide;
    in every change He faithful will
       remain.
    Be still, my soul: your best, your
       heavenly Friend
    through thorny ways leads to a
       joyful end.

2   Be still, my soul: your God will
       undertake
    to guide the future as He has the
       past.
    Your hope, your confidence let
       nothing shake,
    all now mysterious shall be clear
       at last.
    Be still, my soul: the tempests
       still obey
    His voice, who ruled them once
       on Galilee.

3   Be still, my soul: when dearest
       friends depart

and all is darkened in the vale of
   tears,
then you shall better know His
   love, His heart,
who comes to soothe your sorrow,
   calm your fears.
Be still, my soul: for Jesus can
   repay
from His own fullness all He
   takes away.

4   Be still, my soul: the hour is
       hastening on
    when we shall be forever with
       the Lord,
    when disappointment, grief and
       fear are gone,
    sorrow forgotten, love's pure joy
       restored.
    Be still, my soul: when change
       and tears are past,
    all safe and blessèd we shall
       meet at last.

Katharina Amalia Dorothea von Schlegel, b. 1697
    translated Jane Laurie Borthwick, 1813–1897

80

1   For the might of Your arm we
       bless You,
    our God, our fathers' God;
    You have kept Your pilgrim
       people
    by the strength of Your staff and
       rod;
    You have called us to the journey
    which faithless feet ne'er trod:
    for the might of Your arm we
       bless You,
    our God, our fathers' God.

2   For the love of Christ
       constraining
    that bound their hearts as one;
    for the faith in truth and freedom
    in which their work was done;
    for the peace of God's evangel
    wherewith their feet were shod:
    for the might of Your arm we
       bless You,
    our God, our fathers' God.

3   We are watchers of a beacon
    whose light must never die;
    we are guardians of an altar
    that shows You ever nigh;
    we are children of the ransomed
    who sleep beneath the sod:
    for the might of Your arm we
       bless You,
    our God, our fathers' God.

4   May the shadow of Your presence
    around our camp be spread;
    baptise us with the courage
    with which You blessed our
        dead;
    O keep us in the pathway
    their saintly feet have trod:
    for the might of Your arm we
        bless You,
    our God, our fathers' God.

Charles Silvester Home, 1865–1914

81

1   God has made me, and He
        knows me,
    He will listen to my prayer.
    Understanding, ever loving,
    He's the God who's always there.
    Even though He made the world,
        He
    knows my name and cares for
        me.
    He will hear me when I call
        Him;
    in His heart I'll always be.

2   Help me, Lord to understand
    that I'm a child who's loved by
        You.
    You'll protect me, and be with
        me
    in the things I have to do.
    Thank You Lord, that I can trust
        You,
    thank You for the love You bring.
    Thank You that You'll never
        leave me;
    Father God, Your praise I sing.

Gillian E. Hutchinson

82

1   God is always near me,
    hearing what I say,
    knowing all my thoughts and
        deeds,
    all my work and play.

2   God is always near me;
    in the darkest night
    He can see me just the same
    as by mid-day light.

3   God is always near me,
    though so young and small;
    not a look or word or thought,
    but God knows it all.

Philipp Paul Bliss, 1838–1876

83

1   God is love: let heaven adore
        Him;
    God is love: let earth rejoice;
    let creation sing before Him,
    and exalt Him with one voice.
    He who laid the earth's
        foundation,
    He who spread the heavens
        above,
    He who breathes through all
        creation,
    He is love, eternal love.

2   God is love, and is enfolding
    all the world in one embrace;
    His unfailing grasp is holding
    every child of every race;
    and when human hearts are
        breaking
    under sorrow's iron rod,
    that same sorrow, that same
        aching
    wrings with pain the heart of
        God.

3   God is love: and though with
        blindness
    sin afflicts and clouds the will,
    God's eternal loving-kindness
    holds us fast and guides us still.
    Sin and death and hell shall
        never
    o'er us final triumph gain;
    God is love, so Love for ever
    o'er the universe must reign.

Timothy Rees, 1874–1939
altered

84

1   God is my strong salvation —
    what foe have I to fear?
    In darkness and temptation
    my light, my help is near:

2   Though hosts encamp around
        me,
    firm to the fight I stand!
    What terror can confound me,
    with God at my right hand?

3   Place on the Lord reliance,
    my soul, with courage wait —
    His truth my reassurance
    when faint and desolate:

81   Words and Music © By permission of the arranger.
83   Words: © Continuum International Publishing Group, The Tower Building, 11 York Road, London SE1 7NZ

4 His might my heart shall
     strengthen,
His love my joy increase;
mercy my days shall lengthen,
the Lord will give me peace.

James Montgomery, 1771–1854
from Psalm 27

85

1 God is our strength and refuge,
our present help in trouble;
and we therefore will not fear,
though the earth should change!
Though mountains shake and
     tremble,
though swirling floods are raging,
God the Lord of hosts is with us
     evermore!

2 There is a flowing river,
within God's holy city;
God is in the midst of her —
she shall not be moved!
God's help is swiftly given,
thrones vanish at His presence —
God the Lord of hosts is with us
     evermore!

3 Come, see the works of our
     maker,
learn of His deeds all-powerful:
wars will cease across the world
when He shatters the spear!
Be still and know your creator,
uplift Him in the nations —
God the Lord of hosts is with us
     evermore!

Richard Thomas Bewes, b. 1934
after Psalm 46

86

1 God is so good,
God is so good,
God is so good,
He's so good to me.

2 He took my sin,
He took my sin,
He took my sin,
He's so good to me.

3 Now I am free,
now I am free,
now I am free,
He's so good to me.

4 God is so good,
He took my sin,
now I am free,
He's so good to me.

Anonymous

87

God loves you, and I love you,
and that's the way it should be.
God loves you, and I love you,
and that's the way it should be.

1 You can be happy, and I can be
     happy,
and that's the way it should be.
You can be happy, and I can be
     happy,
and that's the way it should be.

2 You can be very sad, I can be
     very sad:
that's not the way it should be.
You can be very sad, I can be
     very sad:
that's not the way it should be,
     'cos …

3 We can love others like sisters
     and brothers;
and that's the way it should be.
We can love others like sisters
     and brothers;
and that's the way it should be.

Anonymous

88

1 God, who made the earth,
the air, the sky, the sea,
who gave the light its birth:
He cares for me.

2 God, who made the grass,
the flower, the fruit, the tree,
the day and night to pass:
He cares for me.

3 God, who made the sun,
the moon, the stars, is He
who, when life's clouds come on,
will care for me.

4 God, who made all things,
on earth, in air, in sea,
who changing seasons brings:
He cares for me.

5 God, who sent His Son
to die on Calvary,
He, if I lean on Him,
will care for me.

Sarah Betts Rhodes, 1829–1904

85   Words: © Richard Bewes/Jubilate Hymns, 4 Thorne Park Road, Chelston, Torquay TQ2 6RX <enquiries@jubilate.co.uk> Used by permission.
89   Words and Music: © 1925, 1951 Hope Publishing. Administered by CopyCare Ltd, PO Box 77, Hailsham, East Sussex. BN27 3EF

89

1 Great is Thy faithfulness, O God
   my Father,
there is no shadow of turning
   with Thee;
Thou changest not, Thy
   compassions they fail not,
as Thou hast been Thou for ever
   wilt be.

   Great is Thy faithfulness!
   Great is Thy faithfulness!
   Morning by morning new mercies
   I see;
   all I have needed Thy hand hath
   provided —
   great is Thy faithfulness, Lord,
   unto me!

2 Summer and winter, and springtime and harvest,
sun, moon and stars in their
   courses above,
join with all nature in manifold
   witness
to Thy great faithfulness, mercy
   and love.

3 Pardon for sin and a peace that
   endureth,
Thine own dear presence to
   cheer and to guide;
strength for today and bright
   hope for tomorrow,
blessings all mine, with ten
   thousand beside!

ALTERNATIVE VERSION

1 Great is Your faithfulness, O God
   my Father,
You have fulfilled all Your
   promise to me;
You never fail and Your love is
   unchanging;
all You have been You for ever
   will be.

   Great is Your faithfulness,
   great is Your faithfulness,
   morning by morning new mercies
   I see;
   all I have needed Your hand has
   provided;
   great is Your faithfulness, Father,
   to me.

2 Summer and winter, and
   springtime and harvest,
sun, moon and stars in their
   courses above

join with all nature in eloquent
   witness
to Your great faithfulness, mercy
   and love.

3 Pardon for sin, and a peace
   everlasting,
Your living presence to cheer and
   to guide;
strength for today, and bright
   hope for tomorrow,
these are the blessings Your love
   will provide.

Thomas O. Chisholm, 1866–1960
adapted Jubilee Hymns

90

1 How strong and sure my
   Father's care
that 'round about me, like the air,
is with me always, everywhere!
He cares for me, He cares for me.

2 O Father, help me then each day
to follow always Your good way,
and show, in all I do and say,
Your care for me, Your care for
   me.

Johann David Neyer
and Blanche Hake

91

1 I'll lift my voice, O Lord,
to glorify Your name,
for You have lifted me
above defeat and shame;
You heard my cry to heal and
   save,
and stooped to raise me from the
   grave.

2 Then to His holy name
let all His saints give praise:
His wrath is brief, His grace
is with us all our days,
for grief and tears may last a
   night,
but joy will come with morning
   light.

3 In easy times I'd felt
secure from all life's ills:
Your hand upheld me, Lord,
like Zion's timeless hills;
but with Your smile no longer
   there
assurance plunged to deep
   despair.

89 Words: 1981, Augsburg Fortress Press
90 Words: 1948, Presbyterian Board of Christian Education / Westminster John Knox Press, 100 Witherspoon Street, Louisville, KY 40202, USA
91 Words: © David Preston / Jubilee Hymns, 4 Thorne Park Road, Chelston, Torquay TQ2 6RX <enquiries@jubilate.co.uk> Used by permission.

4   To You, O Lord, I cried:
    'What can my death achieve?
    From bones among the dust
    what praise will You receive?
    O Lord, be merciful to me!
    Come quickly, help me — hear
      my plea!'

5   O how I leapt for joy
    as grief was put to flight!
    My sackcloth You removed
    and clothed me with delight,
    that You, O Lord, I might adore
    and give You thanks for
      evermore.

David G. Preston, b. 1939
from Psalm 30

92

1   Listen to my prayer, Lord,
    hear my humble cry;
    when my heart is fainting,
    to Your throne I fly.

2   In earth's farthest corner
    You will hear my voice:
    set me on Your rock, Lord,
    then I shall rejoice.

3   You have been my shelter
    when the foe was near,
    as a tower of refuge
    shielding me from fear.

4   I will rest for ever
    in Your care and love,
    guarded and protected
    as by wings above.

5   All that I have promised,
    help me to fulfil;
    and in all who love You
    work Your perfect will.

6   May Your truth and mercy
    keep me all my days;
    let my words and actions
    be my songs of praise!

James Edward Seddon, 1915–1983
after Psalm 61

93

1   Lord, I come before Your throne
    of grace;
    I find rest in Your presence, and
    fullness of joy.
    In worship and wonder I behold
    Your face,
    singing what a faithful God
    have I.

What a faithful God have I,
what a faithful God.
What a faithful God have I,
faithful in every way.

2   Lord of mercy, You have heard
    me cry;
    through the storm You're the
    beacon, my song in the night.
    In the shelter of Your wings, hear
    my heart's reply,
    singing what a faithful God
    have I.

3   Lord all sovereign, granting
    peace from heaven,
    let me comfort those who suffer
    with the comfort You have
    given.
    I will tell of Your great love for as
    long as I live,
    singing what a faithful God
    have I.

Robert Critchley, b. 1959
and Dawn Critchley, b. 1965

94

1   Lord, I would own Your tender
    care,
    and all Your love I see;
    the food I eat, the clothes I wear,
    are all Your gift to me.

2   Lord, You preserve my life from
    death
    and dangers every hour;
    I cannot draw another breath
    unless You give me power.

3   Kind angels guard me every
    night,
    as round my bed they stay;
    nor am I absent from Your sight
    in darkness or by day.

4   My health and friends and
    parents dear
    to me by God are given;
    I have not any blessing here
    but what is sent from heaven.

5   Such goodness, Lord, and
    constant care
    a child cannot repay;
    but may it be my daily prayer
    to love You and obey.

Jane Taylor, 1783–1824
altered Compilers

HIS FAITHFULNESS

95

1 Now thank we all our God
with hearts and hands and
voices;
such wonders He has done!
In Him the world rejoices,
who, from our mothers' arms,
has blessed us on our way
with countless gifts of love
and still is ours today.

2 So may this generous God
through all our life be near us:
to fill our hearts with joy
and with His peace to cheer us;
to keep us in His grace
and guide us when perplexed;
to free us from all ills
in this world and the next.

3 All praise and thanks to God
who reigns in highest heaven,
to Father and to Son
and Spirit now be given —
the one eternal God,
whom earth and heaven
adore —
for so it was, is now
and shall be evermore. Amen.

Martin Rinkart, 1586–1649
translated Catherine Winkworth, 1827–1878
adapted Compilers of *Praise!* 2000

96

1 O Father of the fatherless
in whom all families are blessed,
I love the way You father me.
You gave me life, forgave the
past;
now in Your arms I'm safe at
last —
I love the way You father me.

*Father me, for ever You'll father
me;
and in Your embrace I'll be for
ever secure.
I love the way You father me,
I love the way You father me.*

2 When bruised and broken I draw
near,
You hold me close and dry my
tears,
I love the way You father me.
At last my fearful heart is still,
surrendered to Your perfect
will —
I love the way You father me.

3 If in my foolishness I stray,
returning empty and ashamed,
I love the way You father me.
Exchanging for my wretchedness
Your radiant robes of
righteousness —
I love the way You father me.

4 And when I look into Your eyes,
from deep within my spirit cries:
I love the way You father me.
Before such love, I stand amazed,
and ever will through endless
days —
I love the way You father me.

Graham Andrew Kendrick, *b.* 1950

97

1 Praise our God with shouts of joy,
sing the glory of His name;
join to lift His praises high,
through the world His love
proclaim.

2 Come and see what God has
done
by the power of His right hand;
see the battles He has won
by His word of swift command.

3 God has tamed the raging seas,
carved a highway through the
tide,
paid the cost of our release,
come Himself to be our guide.

4 God has put us to the test,
bringing us through flood and
fire
into freedom, peace, and rest,
for our good is His desire.

5 He has not despised my prayer
nor kept back His love from me;
He has raised me from
despair —
to our God all glory be!

Christopher Martin Idle, *b.* 1938
from Psalm 66

98

1 The King of Love my shepherd
is,
whose goodness fails me never;
I nothing lack if I am His
and He is mine for ever.

2 Where streams of living water
flow
a ransomed soul, He leads me;
and where the fertile pastures
grow,
with food from heaven feeds me.

3 Perverse and foolish I have
strayed,
but in His love He sought me;
and on His shoulder gently laid,
and home, rejoicing, brought me.

4 In death's dark vale I fear no ill,
with You, dear Lord, beside me;
Your rod and staff my comfort
still,
Your cross before to guide me.

5 You spread a banquet in my sight
of love beyond all knowing;
and O the gladness and delight
from Your pure chalice flowing!

6 And so through all the length of
days
Your goodness fails me never:
Good Shepherd, may I sing Your
praise
within Your house for ever!

Henry Williams Baker, 1821–1877
from Psalm 23
adapted Jubilee Hymns

99

1 The Lord my shepherd rules my
life
and gives me all I need;
He leads me by refreshing
streams,
in pastures green I feed;
He leads me by refreshing
streams,
in pastures green I feed.

2 The Lord revives my failing
strength,
He makes my joy complete;
and in right paths, for His name's
sake,
He guides my faltering feet;
and in right paths, for His name's
sake,
He guides my faltering feet.

3 Though in a valley dark as death,
no evil makes me fear;
Your shepherd's staff protects my
way,
for You are with me there;
Your shepherd's staff protects my
way,
for You are with me there.

4 While all my enemies look on
You spread a royal feast;
You fill my cup, anoint my head,
and treat me as Your guest;
You fill my cup, anoint my head,
and treat me as Your guest.

5 Your goodness and Your gracious
love
pursue me all my days;
Your house, O Lord, shall be my
home —
Your name, my endless praise;
Your house, O Lord, shall be my
home —
Your name, my endless praise.

6 To Father, Son and Spirit, praise!
To God, whom we adore,
be worship, glory, power and
love,
both now and evermore;
be worship, glory, power and
love,
both now and evermore!

Christopher Martin Idle, *b.* 1938
from Psalm 23

100

1 Timeless love! We sing the story,
praise His wonders, tell His
worth;
love more fair than heaven's
glory,
love more firm than ancient
earth!
Tell His faithfulness abroad:
who is like Him? Praise the
Lord!

2 By His faithfulness surrounded,
north and south His hand
proclaim;
earth and heaven formed and
founded,
skies and seas, declare His name!
Wind and storm obey His word:
who is like Him? Praise the
Lord!

3 Truth and righteousness enthrone
Him,
just and equal are His ways;
more than happy, those who own
Him,
more than joy, their songs of
praise!

99 Words: © Christopher Idle / Jubilate Hymns, 4 Thorne Park Road, Chelston, Torquay TQ2 6RX <enquiries@jubilate.co.uk> Used by permission.
100 Words: © Timothy Dudley-Smith in Europe and all territories not controlled by Hope Publishing Company

Sun and shield and great
    reward:
who is like Him? Praise the
    Lord!

Timothy Dudley-Smith, b. 1926
from Psalm 89

101

1 When all Your mercies, O my
    God,
my thankful soul surveys,
uplifted by the view, I'm lost
in wonder, love and praise.

2 Unnumbered blessings on my
    soul
Your tender care bestowed
before my infant heart perceived
from whom these blessings
    flowed.

3 Ten thousand thousand precious
    gifts
my daily thanks employ;
nor is the least a cheerful heart
that takes those gifts with joy.

4 In health and sickness, joy and
    pain,
Your goodness I'll pursue;
and after death, in distant worlds,
the glorious theme renew.

5 Throughout eternity, O Lord,
a joyful song I'll raise;
but all eternity's too short
to utter all Your praise!

Joseph Addison, 1672–1719
adapted Jubilate Hymns

102

1 You're my light and my
    salvation,
I won't be afraid!
You're the stronghold of my life
by You all things were made.
Foes attack me, hassle me
but I will never fade,
for I move in the strength of the
    Lord.

Do Lord, O, do Lord, O, do
*   remember me.*
Do Lord, O, do Lord, O, do
*   remember me.*
Do Lord, O, do Lord, O, do
*   remember me,*
look away beyond the blue.

2 Though a host encamp against
    me,
I will never fear!
Even though a war surrounds me
You are always near.
One thing I have asked of You
that I will seek for sure
is to live in the house of the Lord.

3 You will hide me in Your shelter
in the day of strife;
You'll conceal me in Your tent
or set me on the height.
Now my head is lifted up
above the storms of night,
so I'll sing to the name of the
    Lord.

John Carl Ylvisaker, b. 1937
from Psalm 27

Also suitable:
Can you be sure that the rain will fall?   112
Deep in the shadows of the past   267
Heavenly Father, You have brought us   133
Let us with a gladsome mind   26
My God is so big   29
New every morning is the love   6
Your hand, O God, has guided   155,156

GOD THROUGH
THE YEARS
HIS GUIDANCE

103

1 Father, hear the prayer we
    offer —
not for ease our prayer shall be,
but for strength that we may ever
live our lives courageously.

2 Not for ever in green pastures
do we ask our way to be;
but the steep and rugged
    pathway
may we tread rejoicingly.

3 Not for ever by still waters
would we idly rest and stay;
but would strike the living
    fountains
from the rocks along our way.

4 Be our strength in hours of
    weakness,
in our wanderings be our guide;
through endeavour, failure,
    danger,
Father, be there at our side.

Love Maria Willis, 1824–1908

104

1 Guide me, O my great Redeemer,
   pilgrim through this barren land;
   I am weak, but You are mighty,
   hold me with Your powerful
      hand:
   Bread of heaven, Bread of
      heaven,
   feed me now and evermore!
   Feed me now and evermore!

2 Open now the crystal fountain
   where the healing waters flow;
   let the fiery, cloudy pillar
   lead me all my journey through:
   strong Deliverer, strong
      Deliverer,
   ever be my strength and shield,
   ever be my strength and shield.

3 When I tread the verge of Jordan
   bid my anxious fears subside;
   Death of death, and hell's
      Destruction,
   land me safe on Canaan's side:
   songs of praises, songs of praises,
   I will ever sing to You,
   I will ever sing to You.

                    William Williams, 1717–1791
              translated Peter Williams, 1727–1796

105

1 Jesus, draw me ever nearer
   as I labour through the storm.
   You have called me to this
      passage,
   and I'll follow though I'm worn.
   May this journey bring a blessing,
   may I rise on wings of faith;
   and at the end of my heart's
      testing,
   with Your likeness let me wake.

2 Jesus, guide me through the
      tempest,
   keep my spirit staid and sure.
   When the midnight meets the
      morning,
   let me love You even more.

3 Let the treasures of the trial
   form within me as I go.
   And at the end of this long
      passage,
   let me leave them at Your throne.

                         Margaret Becker

106

1 Lead, kindly light, amid the
      encircling gloom,
   O lead me on;
   the night is dark, and I am far
      from home;
   O lead me on.
   Keep firm my feet; I do not ask to
      see
   the distant scene; one step
      enough for me.

2 I was not ever thus, nor prayed
      that You
   should lead me on;
   I loved to choose, and see my
      path; but now
   O lead me on.
   I loved the broader way, and,
      spite of fears,
   pride ruled my will: remember
      not past years.

3 So long Your power has blessed
      me, sure it still
   will lead me on,
   o'er moor and fen, o'er crag and
      torrent, till
   the night is gone,
   and with the morn those angel
      faces smile,
   which I have loved long since,
      and lost awhile.

                    John Henry Newman, 1801–1890
                         altered Compilers

107

1 Lead us, heavenly Father, lead us
   over life's tempestuous sea;
   guard and guide us, keep and
      feed us,
   help from You alone have we,
   yet possessing every blessing
   in our God eternally.

2 Saviour, breathe forgiveness on
      us,
   all our sins You surely know;
   You did tread this earth before
      us,
   You did feel all earthly woe;
   lone and dreary, faint and weary,
   through the desert You did go.

3 Spirit of our God descending,
   fill our hearts with heavenly joy,
   love with every passion blending,
   pleasure that can never cloy:
   thus provided, pardoned, guided,
   nothing can our peace destroy.

James Edmeston, 1791–1867
adapted Gaetano Raphael (Anthony) Petti,
1932–1985

108

1 O God of Bethel, by whose hand
   Your children still are fed;
   who through this earthly
       pilgrimage
   Your people safely led:

2 Our vows, our prayers, we now
       present
   before Your gracious throne;
   as You have been their faithful
       God,
   so always be our own!

3 Through each perplexing path of
       life
   our wandering footsteps guide;
   give us today our daily bread,
   and for our needs provide.

4 O spread Your covering wings
       around
   till all our wanderings cease,
   and at our heavenly Father's
       home
   we shall arrive in peace.

Philip Doddridge, 1702–1751
Paraphrase 2, Genesis 28: 20-22
adapted Jubilate Hymns †

GOD THROUGH
THE YEARS
HIS PROVIDENCE

109

1 A little child may know
   our Father's name of Love;
   'tis written on the earth below,
   and on the sky above.

2 Around me when I look,
   His handiwork I see;
   this world is like a picture-book
   to teach His name to me.

3 The thousand little flowers
   within our garden found,
   the rainbow and the soft spring
       showers,
   and every pleasant sound;

4 The birds that sweetly sing,
   the moon that shines by night,
   with every tiny living thing
   rejoicing in the light;

5 And every star above,
   set in the deep blue sky,
   all tell me that our God is love,
   and tell me He is nigh.

Jane Elizabeth Leeson, 1809–1881

110

All the ends of the earth, all you
*   creatures of the sea,*
lift up your eyes to the wonders of
*   the Lord.*
For the Lord of the earth, the
*   master of the sea,*
has come with justice for the
*   world.*

1 Break into song at the deeds of
       the Lord,
   the wonders God has done in
       every age.

2 Heaven and earth shall rejoice in
       His might;
   every heart, every nation call
       Him Lord.

3 The Lord has made salvation
       known,
   faithful to the promises of old.
   Let the ends of the earth,
   let the sea and all it holds
   make music before our King!

Robert John Dufford, *b.* 1943
Psalm 98

111

1 When Noah built a great big boat,
   his neighbours thought it would
       never float.
   The rain came down and flooded
       the land,
   but God used it for good.

2 When Joseph was a young man,
   his brothers saw a caravan;
   he went to Egypt as a slave,
   but God used it for good.

3 When God called Jonah to come
   and serve,
   then Jonah ran without a word.
   The big fish came and saved his
   life,
   and God used it for good.

4 When Jesus came to Bethlehem,
   He came to give His life for men:
   He hung and died upon the
   cross,
   but God used it for good.

5 We too have troubles come our
   way,
   we too have problems every day;
   we never know and we don't
   understand,
   but God will use it for good.

                        Kathryn Ehlen

112

1 Can you be sure that the rain will
   fall?
   Can you be sure that birds will
   fly?
   Can you be sure that rivers will
   flow?
   Or that the sun will light the sky?
   God has promised.
   God never breaks a promise He
   makes.
   His Word is always true.

2 Can you be sure that the tide will
   turn?
   Can you be sure that grass will
   grow?
   Can you be sure that night will
   come,
   or that the sun will melt the
   snow?

3 You can be sure that God is near;
   you can be sure He won't let you
   down;
   you can be sure He'll always
   hear;
   and that He's given Jesus, His
   Son.

                   Geoffrey Marshall-Taylor, *b.* 1943

113

1 Come, sing praises to the Lord
   above,
   Rock of our salvation, God of
   love;
   with delight into His presence
   move,
   for the Lord our God is King!

He's the King above the
   mountains high,
   the sea is His, the land and sky;
   mighty continents and islands lie
   within the hollow of His hand.

2 Come to worship Him and bow
   the knee,
   for the shepherd of the flock is
   He;
   humble creatures in His hand are
   we —
   sing the praise of God the King!

3 Hear the story of His people now,
   you with stubborn hearts who
   will not bow;
   learn what happened long ago
   and how
   God can show you He is King!

4 Forty years He kept the prize
   away,
   made them wander till they
   walked His way,
   exiled all of them until the day
   they should honour Him as King.

                   Michael Arnold Perry, 1942–1996
                            after Psalm 95

114

1 God everlasting, at Your word
   the hills in splendour rise;
   they overshadow human life
   whose glory swiftly dies.

2 Our days like dreams come to an
   end,
   our story soon is told —
   when strength is spent, and
   beauty fades,
   and bodies have grown old.

3 Teach us, good Lord, to count our
   days,
   to cherish every hour;
   to seek Your will, to do Your
   work,
   and trust Your mighty power.

4 Lord, at Your hand we have
   received
   the cup of joy and pain:
   pour out the fullness of Your
   grace
   and we shall sing again!

                        David Mowbray, *b.* 1938
                            after Psalm 90

112 Words: © Geoffrey Marshall-Taylor, The ASPA Trust, PO Box 418. Amersham, Buckinghamshire. HP6 6WG
113 Words: © Mrs B. Perry/Jubilate Hymns, 4 Thorne Park Road, Chelston, Torquay TQ2 6RX <enquiries@jubilate.co.uk> Used by permission.
114 Words: © David Mowbray/Jubilate Hymns, 4 Thorne Park Road, Chelston, Torquay TQ2 6RX <enquiries@jubilate.co.uk> Used by permission.

115

1 God is love, His mercy brightens
all the path in which we rove;
bliss He wakes, and woe He
lightens:
God is wisdom, God is love.

2 Chance and change are busy
ever,
man decays, and ages move;
but His mercy waning never:

3 Even the hour the darkest
seeming
will His changeless goodness
prove;
from the mist His brightness
streaming:

4 He with earthly cares entwining
hope and comfort from above;
everywhere His glory shining:

John Bowring, 1792–1872

116

1 God moves in a mysterious way,
His wonders to perform;
He plants His footsteps in the sea
and rides upon the storm.

2 Deep in unfathomable mines
of never-failing skill
He treasures up His bright
designs
and works His sovereign will.

3 You fearful saints, fresh courage
take;
the clouds you so much dread
are big with mercy, and shall
break
in blessings on your head.

4 Judge not the Lord by feeble
sense,
but trust Him for His grace;
behind a frowning providence
He hides a smiling face.

5 His purposes will ripen fast,
unfolding every hour;
the bud may have a bitter taste,
but sweet will be the flower.

6 Blind unbelief is sure to err
and scan His work in vain;
God is His own interpreter
and He will make it plain.

William Cowper, 1731–1800

117

1 God's love is deeper than the
deepest ocean,
God's love is wider than the
widest sea,
God's love is higher than the
highest mountain,
deeper, wider, higher is God's
love to me.

2 God's grace is deeper than the
deepest ocean,
God's grace is wider than the
widest sea,
God's grace is higher than the
highest mountain,
deeper, wider, higher is God's
grace to me.

3 God's joy is deeper than the
deepest ocean,
God's joy is wider than the
widest sea,
God's joy is higher than the
highest mountain,
deeper, wider, higher is God's joy
to me.

4 God's peace is deeper than the
deepest ocean,
God's peace is wider than the
widest sea,
God's peace is higher than the
highest mountain,
deeper, wider, higher is God's
peace to me.

after last verse
Deeper, wider, higher,
deeper, wider, higher,
deeper, wider, higher is God
to me.

Iain D. Craig

118

1 He's got the whole wide world
in His hands,
He's got the whole wide world
in His hands,
He's got the whole wide world
in His hands,
He's got the whole world
in His hands.

2 He's got everybody here,
in His hands,
He's got everybody here,
in His hands,

He's got everybody here,
in His hands,
He's got the whole world
in His hands.

3   He's got the tiny little baby,
in His hands,
He's got the tiny little baby,
in His hands,
He's got the tiny little baby,
in His hands,
He's got the whole world
in His hands.

4   He's got you and me brother,
in His hands,
He's got you and me sister,
in His hands,
He's got you and me brother,
in His hands,
He's got the whole world
in His hands.

Anonymous

119

1   I lift my eyes to the quiet hills
in the press of a busy day;
as green hills stand in a dusty
    land
so God is my strength and stay.

2   I lift my eyes to the quiet hills
to a calm that is mine to share;
secure and still in the Father's
    will
and kept by the Father's care.

3   I lift my eyes to the quiet hills
with a prayer as I turn to sleep;
by day, by night, through the dark
    and light
my shepherd will guard His
    sheep.

4   I lift my eyes to the quiet hills
and my heart to the Father's
    throne;
in all my ways to the end of days
the Lord will preserve His own.

Timothy Dudley-Smith, *b.* 1926
from Psalm 121

120

1   In heavenly love abiding,
no change my heart shall fear:
and safe is such confiding,
for nothing changes here:
the storm may roar around me,
my heart may low be laid;
my Father's arms surround me,
how can I be afraid?

2   Wherever He may guide me
no want shall turn me back;
my Shepherd is beside me
and nothing can I lack:
His wisdom is for ever,
His sight is never dim;
His love deserts me never
and I will walk with Him.

3   Green pastures are before me,
which yet I have not seen;
bright skies will with glory
where threatening clouds have
        been:
my hope I cannot measure,
my path to life is free;
my Saviour has my treasure
and He will walk with me.

Anna Laetitia Waring, 1823–1910
adapted Jubilate Hymns

121

1   In heavenly love abiding,
no change my heart shall fear;
and safe is such confiding,
for nothing changes here:
the storm may roar without me,
my heart may low be laid;
but God is round about me,
and can I be dismayed?

2   Wherever He may guide me,
no want shall turn me back;
my Shepherd is beside me,
and nothing can I lack.
His wisdom ever waketh,
His sight is never dim:
He knows the way He taketh,
and I will walk with Him.

3   Green pastures are before me,
which yet I have not seen;
bright skies will soon be over me,
where the dark clouds have been.
My hope I cannot measure:
my path to life is free;
my Saviour has my treasure,
and He will walk with me.

My hope I cannot measure:
my path to life is free;
my Saviour has my treasure,
and He will walk with me.

In heavenly love abiding,
no change my heart shall fear;
and safe is such confiding,
for nothing changes here.

Anna Laetitia Waring, 1823–1910
altered Christopher Alan Bowater, *b.* 1947

122

1 Like a mighty river flowing,
   like a flower in beauty growing,
   far beyond all human knowing
   is the perfect peace of God.

2 Like the hills serene and even,
   like the coursing clouds of
      heaven,
   like the heart that's been forgiven
   is the perfect peace of God.

3 Like the summer breezes playing,
   like the tall trees softly swaying,
   like the lips of silent praying
   is the perfect peace of God.

4 Like the morning sun ascended,
   like the scents of evening
      blended,
   like a friendship never ended
   is the perfect peace of God.

5 Like the azure ocean swelling,
   like the jewel all-excelling,
   far beyond our human telling
   is the perfect peace of God.

                Michael Arnold Perry, 1942–1996

123

1 Like a river glorious
   is God's perfect peace,
   over all victorious,
   in its bright increase:
   perfect, yet still flowing
   fuller every day;
   perfect, yet still growing
   deeper all the way.
      Trusting in the Father
      hearts are fully blessed,
      finding as He promised
      perfect peace and rest.

2 Hidden in the hollow
   of His mighty hand
   where no harm can follow,
   in His strength we stand:
   we may trust Him fully
   all for us to do;
   those who trust Him wholly
   find Him wholly true.

                Frances Ridley Havergal, 1836–1879
                adapted Jubilate Hymns

124

1 Look and learn from the birds of
      the air,
   flying high above worry and fear;
   neither sowing nor harvesting
      seed,
   yet they're given whatever they
      need.
   If the God of earth and heaven
   cares for birds as much as this,
   won't He care much more for
      you,
   if you put your trust in Him?

2 Look and learn from the flowers
      of the field,
   bringing beauty and colour to
      life;
   neither sewing nor tailoring cloth,
   yet they're dressed in the finest
      attire.
   If the God of earth and heaven
   cares for flowers as much as this,
   won't He care much more for
      you,
   if you put your trust in Him?

3 What God wants should be our
      will;
   where God calls should be our
      goal.
   When we seek the kingdom first,
   all we've lost is ours again.
   Let's be done with anxious
      thoughts,
   set aside tomorrow's cares,
   live each day that God provides
   putting all our trust in Him.

                Young-Soo Nah
                translated John Lamberton Bell, *b.* 1949
                from Matthew 6, 23–24

125

1 Lord, for the years Your love has
      kept and guided,
   urged and inspired us, cheered
      us on our way,
   sought us and saved us,
      pardoned and provided,
   Lord of the years, we bring our
      thanks today.

2 Lord, for that Word, the Word of
      life which fires us,
   speaks to our hearts and sets our
      souls ablaze,
   teaches and trains, rebukes us
      and inspires us,
   Lord of the Word, receive Your
      people's praise.

3 Lord, for our land in this our
    generation,
  spirits oppressed by pleasure,
    wealth and care;
  for young and old, for this and
    every nation,
  Lord of our land, be pleased to
    hear our prayer.

4 Lord, for our world; when we
    disown and doubt Him,
  loveless in strength, and
    comfortless in pain;
  hungry and helpless, lost indeed
    without Him,
  Lord of the world, we pray that
    Christ may reign.

5 Lord, for ourselves; in living
    power remake us,
  self on the cross and Christ upon
    the throne;
  past put behind us, for the future
    take us,
  Lord of our lives, to live for
    Christ alone.

Timothy Dudley-Smith, *b.* 1926

126

1 Sing to the Lord a joyful song,
  lift up your hearts, your voices
    raise;
  to us His gracious gifts belong,
  to Him our songs of love and
    praise;

2 For life and love, for rest and
    food,
  for daily help and nightly care,
  sing to the Lord, for He is good,
  and praise His name, for it is fair.

3 For strength to those who on Him
    wait
  His truth to prove, His will to do,
  O praise our God, for He is great,
  trust in His name, for it is true.

4 For joys untold, that from above
  cheer those who love His sweet
    employ,
  sing to our God, for He is love,
  exalt His name, for it is joy.

5 For He is Lord of heaven and
    earth,
  whom angels serve and saints
    adore,
  the Father, Son, and Spirit blest,
  to whom be praise for evermore.
  Amen.

John Samuel Bewley Monsell, 1811–1875

127

1 There is no moment of my life,
  no place where I may go,
  no action which God does not
    see,
  no thought He does not know.

2 Before I speak, my words are
    known,
  and all that I decide.
  To come or go? God knows my
    choice,
  and makes Himself my guide.

3 If I should close my eyes to Him,
  He comes to give me sight;
  if I should go where all is dark,
  He makes my darkness light.

4 He knew my days before all days,
  before I came to be;
  He keeps me, loves me, in my
    ways —
  no lover such as He.

William Brian Foley, 1919–200[?]
from Psalm 139

128

1 Though troubles assail
  and dangers affright,
  though friends should all fail
  and foes all unite,
  yet one thing secures us,
  however we're tried:
  the Scripture assures us,
  'The Lord will provide.'

2 The birds without barn
  or storehouse are fed;
  from them let us learn
  to trust for our bread:
  His saints what is fitting
  shall not be denied;
  we know it is written:
  'The Lord will provide.'

3 His call we obey
  like Abram of old,
  not knowing our way,
  but faith makes us bold;
  for though we are strangers
  we have a good guide,
  and trust, in all dangers,
  'The Lord will provide.'

4 When Satan appears
  and hinders our path
  and fills us with fears,
  we triumph by faith;

he cannot take from us,
though often has tried,
this heart-cheering promise,
'The Lord will provide.'

5 No strength of our own
or goodness we claim;
yet since we have known
the Saviour's great name,
in this our strong tower
for safety we hide,
the Lord is our power,
'The Lord will provide.'

6 When life sinks apace,
and death is in view,
this word of His grace
shall carry us through:
not fearing or doubting,
with Christ on our side,
we hope to die shouting,
'The Lord will provide.'

John Newton, 1725–1807
revised Compilers of *Praise!* 2000

129

1 Through all the changing scenes
of life,
in trouble and in joy,
the praises of my God shall still
my heart and tongue employ.

2 Of His deliverance I will boast,
till all that are distressed,
from my example comfort take,
and charm their griefs to rest.

3 The hosts of God encamp around
the dwellings of the just;
protection He affords to all
who make His name their trust.

4 O magnify the Lord with me,
with me exalt His name;
when in distress to Him I called
He to my rescue came.

5 O make but trial of His love,
experience will decide
how blest are they, and only they,
who in His truth confide.

6 Fear Him, you saints, and you
will then
have nothing else to fear;
make but His service your
delight;
your wants shall be His care.

Nahum Tate, 1652–1715
and Nicholas Brady, 1659–1726
from Psalm 34

130

1 When Zion's fortunes God
restored,
it was a dream come true.
Our mouths were then with
laughter filled,
our tongues with songs anew.

2 The nations said, 'The Lord has
done
great things for Israel.'
The Lord did mighty things for
us,
and joy our hearts knew well.

3 Restore our fortunes, gracious
Lord,
like streams in desert soil.
A joyful harvest will reward
the weeping sower's toil.

4 The man who, bearing seed to
sow,
goes out with tears of grief,
will come again with songs of joy,
bearing his harvest sheaf.

Free Church of Scotland Psalmody Committee
from Psalm 126

Also suitable:
Praise, my soul, the King of heaven   227
Praise to the Lord, the Almighty   233

GOD THROUGH
THE YEARS
NEW YEAR   OLD YEAR

131

1 Christ be the Lord of all our days,
the swiftly-passing years:
Lord of our unremembered birth,
heirs to the brightness of the
earth;
Lord of our griefs and fears.

2 Christ be the source of all our
deeds,
the life our living shares;
the fount which flows from
worlds above
to never-failing springs of love;
the ground of all our prayers.

3 Christ be the goal of all our
hopes,
the end to whom we come;
guide of each pilgrim Christian
soul

which seeks, as compass seeks the
    pole,
our many-mansioned home.

4   Christ be the vision of our lives,
    of all we think and are;
    to shine upon our spirits' sight
    as light of everlasting light,
    the bright and morning star.

Timothy Dudley-Smith, *b.* 1926

132

1   Great God, we sing Your mighty
        hand
    by which supported still we
        stand;
    the opening year Your mercy
        shows;
    and mercy crowns its lingering
        close.

2   By day, by night, at home, abroad,
    still are we guarded by our God;
    by His incessant bounty fed,
    by His unerring counsel led.

3   With grateful hearts the past we
        own;
    the future, all to us unknown,
    we to Your guardian care commit,
    and peaceful leave before Your
        feet.

4   In scenes exalted or depressed,
    You are our joy, You are our rest;
    Your goodness all our hopes shall
        raise,
    adored through all our changing
        days.

5   When death shall interrupt these
        songs,
    and seal in silence mortal
        tongues,
    our helper God, in whom we
        trust,
    shall keep our souls and guard
        our dust.

Philip Doddridge, 1702–1751
slightly altered

133

1   Heavenly Father, You have
        brought us
    safely to the present day,
    gently leading on our footsteps,
    watching o'er us all the way.
    Friend and guide through life's
        long journey,
    grateful hearts to You we bring;

but for love so true and
    changeless
how shall we fit praises sing?

2   Mercies new and never-failing
    brightly shine through all the
        past,
    watchful care and loving-
        kindness
    always near from first to last,
    tender love, divine protection
    ever with us day and night;
    blessings more than we can
        number
    strew the path with golden light.

3   Shadows deep have crossed our
        pathway,
    we have trembled in the storm;
    clouds have gathered round so
        darkly
    that we could not see Your form:
    yet Your love has never left us
    in our griefs to be alone,
    and the help each gave the other
    was the strength that is Your
        own.

4   Many that we loved have left us,
    reaching first their journey's
        end;
    now they wait to give us
        welcome,
    brother, sister, child, and friend.
    When at last our journey's over,
    and we pass away from sight,
    Father, take us through the
        darkness
    into everlasting light.

Hester Periam Hawkins, 1848–1928
Home Hymn Book, 1885
slightly altered

134

1   March on, my soul, with strength,
    march forward, void of fear;
    He who has led will lead,
    through each succeeding year;
    and as you go upon your way,
    His hand shall hold you day by
        day.

2   March on, my soul, with strength,
    in ease you dare not dwell;
    high duty calls you forth;
    then up, and quit you well!
    Take up your cross, take up your
        sword,
    and fight the battles of your Lord!

NEW YEAR OLD YEAR

3 March on, my soul, with strength,
with strength, but not your own;
the conquest you shall gain,
through Christ your Lord alone;
His grace shall nerve your feeble
arm,
His love preserve you safe from
harm.

4 March on, my soul, with strength,
from strength to strength march
on;
warfare shall end at length,
all foes be overthrown.
Then, O my soul, if faithful now,
the crown of life awaits your
brow.

William Wright, 1859–1924
slightly altered

135

1 O Christ the same, through all
our story's pages,
our loves and hopes, our failures
and our fears;
eternal Lord, the King of all the
ages,
unchanging still, amid the
passing years:
O living Word, the source of all
creation,
who spread the skies, and set the
stars ablaze,
O Christ the same, who wrought
our whole salvation,
we bring our thanks for all our
yesterdays.

2 O Christ the same, the friend of
sinners sharing
our inmost thoughts, the secrets
none can hide,
still as of old upon Your body
bearing
the marks of love, in triumph
glorified:
O Son of Man, who stooped for us
from heaven,
O Prince of Life, in all Your
saving power,
O Christ the same, to whom our
hearts are given,
we bring our thanks for this the
present hour.

3 O Christ the same, secure within
whose keeping
our lives and loves, our days and
years remain,

our work and rest, our waking
and our sleeping,
our calm and storm, our pleasure
and our pain:
O Lord of love, for all our joys
and sorrows,
for all our hopes, when earth
shall fade and flee,
O Christ the same, beyond our
brief tomorrows,
we bring our thanks for all that is
to be.

Timothy Dudley-Smith, *b.* 1926

136

1 O God, our help in ages past,
our hope for years to come,
our shelter from the stormy blast,
and our eternal home:

2 Beneath the shadow of Your
throne
Your people lived secure;
sufficient is Your arm alone,
and our defence is sure.

3 Before the hills in order stood,
or earth from darkness came,
from everlasting You are God,
to endless years the same.

4 A thousand ages in Your sight
are like an evening gone;
short as the watch that ends the
night,
before the rising sun.

5 Time, like an ever-rolling stream,
will bear us all away;
we pass forgotten, as a dream
dies with the dawning day.

6 O God, our help in ages past,
our hope for years to come:
be our defence while life shall
last,
and our eternal home!

Isaac Watts, 1674–1748
adapted Compilers of
Hymns for Today's Church, 1982

Also suitable:

A gladsome hymn of praise we sing   77
God everlasting, at Your word   114
Lord, for the years   125
Lord of creation, giver of gladness   577
My times are in Your hand   516
Now thank we all our God   95

THE TEMPLE
DEDICATION
OF BUILDINGS

137

1 All things are Yours; nothing of
ours,
we bring to You, Lord of all
powers;
and hence with grateful hearts
today
Your own before Your feet we lay.

2 Your will was in the builders'
thought;
Your hand unseen amidst us
wrought;
through mortal motive, scheme
and plan,
Your wise eternal purpose ran.

3 In weakness and in want we call
on You, for whom the heavens
are small;
Your glory is Your children's
good;
Your joy, Your tender fatherhood.

4 O Lord, be pleased these walls to
bless;
fill with Your love their
emptiness;
and let their door become a way
to lead us to eternal day.

John Greenleaf Whittier, 1807–1892
altered

138

1 Christ is made our sure
foundation,
Christ is head and cornerstone;
chosen of the Lord and precious,
binding all the Church in one,
holy Zion's help for ever,
and her confidence alone.

2 To this temple, we implore you,
come, great Lord of hosts, today;
come with all Your
lovingkindness,
hear Your servants as they pray,
and Your fullest benediction
shed in all its brightest ray.

3 Grant, we pray, to all Your
people,
all the grace they ask to gain;
what they gain from You for ever
with the blessèd to retain,
and hereafter in Your glory
evermore with You to reign.

4 Praise and honour to the Father,
praise and honour to the Son,
praise and honour to the Spirit,
ever Three and One:
unified in power and glory,
while unending ages run. Amen.

Urbs beata Jerusalem 7th or 8th century
translated John Mason Neale, 1818–1866
adapted Gaetano Raphael (Anthony) Petti,
1932–1985

139

1 This stone in faith, O Lord, we
lay;
and build a house for You in
love;
to guard this sanctuary night and
day
look down in mercy from above.

2 Here, when Your people seek
Your face,
and dying sinners pray to live,
hear them in heaven Your
dwelling-place,
and when You hear, O Lord,
forgive!

3 Here, when Your messengers
proclaim
the blessèd gospel of Your Son,
still, by the power of His great
name,
be mighty signs and wonders
done.

4 'Hosanna!' to their heavenly
King
when children's voices raise that
song,
'Hosanna!' let their angels sing,
and heaven, with earth, the
strain prolong.

5 But will the eternal Father deign,
here to abide, no transient guest?
Will here the world's Redeemer
reign,
and here the Holy Spirit rest?

6 That glory never hence depart!
Yet choose not, Lord, this house
alone;
Your kingdom come to every
heart:
in all the world be Yours the
throne.

James Montgomery, 1771–1854
altered Compilers

138 Words: © 1971 Faber Music Ltd, 3 Queen Square, London. WC1N 3AU Reprinted from *New Catholic Hymnal* by permission.

THE PEOPLE OF GOD

Also suitable:
How lovely is Your dwelling-place 171
We love the place O God 196

THE TEMPLE
THE PEOPLE OF GOD

140

1 All those who trust the Lord
   like Zion are secure,
   which never can be moved
   but always will endure.

2 Just as the mountains stand
   around Jerusalem,
   the Lord surrounds His own,
   for ever guarding them.

3 The rule of wicked men
   will not remain for long
   upon the just men's land,
   lest righteous men do wrong.

4 On all those who are good
   bestow Your goodness, Lord —
   to those of upright heart
   who reverence Your word.

5 But God will banish those
   who choose a crooked way;
   with sinners they will go.
   Let peace on Israel stay.

Free Church of Scotland Psalmody Committee
from Psalm 125

141

1 Christ is the King! O friends
      rejoice;
   brothers and sisters, with one
      voice
   let the world know He is your
      choice.
      Alleluia! Alleluia! Alleluia!

2 O magnify the Lord, and raise
   anthems of joy and holy praise
   for Christ's brave saints of
      ancient days.

3 They with a faith for ever new
   followed the King, and round
      Him drew
   thousands of servants brave and
      true.

4 O Christian women, Christian
      men,
   all the world over, seek again
   the way disciples followed then.

5 Christ through all ages is the
      same:
   place the same hope in His great
      name;
   with the same faith His Word
      proclaim.

6 Let love's unconquerable might
   your scattered companies unite
   in service to the Lord of light.

7 So shall God's will on earth be
      done,
   new lamps be lit, new tasks
      begun,
   and the whole church at last be
      one.

George Kennedy Allen Bell, 1883–1958

142

1 City of God, how broad and far
   outspread your walls sublime!
   The true your chartered freemen
      are
   of every age and clime:

2 One holy Church, one army
      strong,
   one steadfast, high intent;
   one working band, one harvest-
      song,
   one King omnipotent.

3 How purely has your speech
      come down
   from earth's primeval youth!
   How grandly has your empire
      grown
   of freedom, love and truth!

4 How gleam your watch-fires
      through the night
   with never-fainting ray!
   How rise your towers, serene and
      bright,
   to meet the dawning day!

5 In vain the surge's angry shock,
   in vain the drifting sands:
   unharmed upon the eternal rock
   the eternal city stands.

Samuel Johnson, 1822–1882
altered Compilers

143

1 Glorious things of you are
      spoken,
   Zion, city of our God;
   He whose Word cannot be broken
   formed you for His own abode:

141 Words: By permission of Oxford University Press, Great Clarendon Street, Oxford OX2 6DP

on the rock of ages founded,
what can shake your sure repose?
With salvation's walls
    surrounded
you may smile at all your foes.

2 See, the streams of living waters
springing from eternal love!
Well supply your sons and
    daughters
and all fear of want remove:
who can faint while such a river
ever flows their thirst to assuage?
Grace, which like the Lord the
    giver
never fails from age to age.

3 Round each habitation hovering
see the cloud and fire appear
for a glory and a covering,
showing that the Lord is near:
thus they march, the pillar
    leading,
light by night and shade by day;
daily on the manna feeding
which He gives them when they
    pray.

4 Saviour, since of Zion's city
I through grace a member am,
let the world deride or pity,
I will glory in Your name:
fading are the world's best
    pleasures,
all its boasted pomp and show;
solid joys and lasting treasures
none but Zion's children know.

John Newton, 1725–1807
altered

144

1 How good and how pleasant it is
when we all live in unity,
refreshing as dew at the dawn,
like rare anointing oil upon the
    head.
   *It's so good, so good when we live
       together in peace and harmony;*
   *it's so good, so good when we live
       together in His love.*

2 How deep are the rivers that run
when we are one in Jesus
and share with the Father and
    Son
the blessings of His everlasting
life.

Graham Andrew Kendrick, *b.* 1950

145

1 How good a thing it is,
how pleasant to behold,
when all God's people live at
    one,
the law of love uphold!

2 As perfume, by its scent,
breathes fragrance all around,
so life itself will sweeter be
where unity is found.

3 And like refreshing dew
that falls upon the hills,
true union sheds its gentle grace,
and deeper love instils.

4 God grants the choicest gifts
to those who live in peace;
to them such blessings shall
    abound
and evermore increase.

James Edward Seddon, 1915–1983
after Psalm 133

146

1 Jesus put this song into our
    hearts,
Jesus put this song into our
    hearts;
it's a song of joy no one can take
    away.
Jesus put this song into our
    hearts.

2 Jesus taught us how to live in
    harmony,
Jesus taught us how to live in
    harmony;
different faces, different races, He
    made us one —
Jesus taught us how to live in
    harmony.

3 Jesus taught us how to be a
    family,
Jesus taught us how to be a
    family;
loving one another with the love
    that He gives.
Jesus taught us how to be a
    family.

4 Jesus turned our sorrow into
    dancing,
Jesus turned our sorrow into
    dancing,

changed our tears of sadness into
rivers of joy.
Jesus turned our sorrow into a
dance. (*Hey!*)

Graham Andrew Kendrick, *b. 1950*

147

1 Lord of the Church, we pray for
our renewing:
Christ over all, our undivided
aim.
Fire of the Spirit, burn for our
enduing,
wind of the Spirit, fan the living
flame!
We turn to Christ amid our fear
and failing,
the will that lacks the courage to
be free,
the weary labours, all but
unavailing,
to bring us nearer to what a
Church should be.

2 Lord of the Church, we seek a
Father's blessing,
a true repentance and a faith
restored,
a swift obedience and a new
possessing,
filled with the Holy Spirit of the
Lord!
We turn to Christ from all our
restless striving,
unnumbered voices with a single
prayer:
the living water for our souls'
reviving,
in Christ to live, and love and
serve and care.

3 Lord of the Church, we long for
our uniting,
true to one calling, by one vision
stirred;
one cross proclaiming and one
creed reciting,
one in the truth of Jesus and His
word.
So lead us on; till toil and trouble
ended,
one Church triumphant one new
song shall sing,
to praise His glory, risen and
ascended,
Christ over all, the everlasting
King!

Timothy Dudley-Smith, *b. 1926*

148

1 Men of faith, rise up and sing
of the great and glorious King;
you are strong when you feel
weak,
in your brokenness complete.

*Shout to the north and south,
sing to the east and west:
Jesus is Saviour to all,
Lord of heaven and earth.*

2 Rise up women of the truth,
stand and sing to broken hearts,
who can know the healing power
of our glorious King of Love.

Shout to the north ...

We've been through fire,
we've been through rain;
we've been refined by the power
of His name.
We've fallen deeper in love with
You,
You've burned the truth on our
lips.

Shout to the north ...

3 Rise up Church with broken
wings;
fill this place with songs again,
of our God who reigns on high:
by His grace again we'll fly.

Shout to the north ...

Coda
Lord of heaven and earth,
Lord of heaven and earth,
Lord of heaven and earth.

Martin J. Smith

149

1 Onward, Christian soldiers!
marching as to war,
with the cross of Jesus
going on before.
Christ, the royal master,
leads His armies on:
forward into battle
till the fight is won!
*Onward, Christian soldiers,
marching as to war,
with the cross of Jesus
going on before.*

2 At the name of Jesus,
Satan's armies flee:
on then, Christian soldiers,
on to victory!

147 Words: © Timothy Dudley-Smith in Europe and all territories not controlled by Hope Publishing Company
148 Words and Music: © 1995 Curious? Music / Thankyou Music. Administered (UK and Europe) by Kingsway Music <tym@kingsway.co.uk>. Remaining territories administered by worshiptogether.com songs. Used by permission.
149 Words: © in this version Jubilate Hymns, 4 Thorne Park Road, Chelston, Torquay TQ2 6RX <enquiries@jubilate.co.uk> Used by permission.

Hell's foundations tremble
at the shout of praise —
sing the song of triumph!
loud your voices raise!

3 Like a mighty army
moves the church of God:
we are humbly treading
where the saints have trod;
Christ is not divided —
all one body we,
one in hope and calling,
one in charity.

4 Crowns and thrones may perish,
kingdoms rise and wane,
but the church of Jesus
ever shall remain;
death and hell and Satan
never shall prevail —
we have Christ's own promise
and that cannot fail.

5 Onward then, you people!
march in faith, be strong!
blend with ours your voices
in the triumph song:
Glory, praise and honour
be to Christ the king!
this through countless ages
we with angels sing.

Sabine Baring-Gould, 1834–1924
adapted Jubilate Hymns

150

1 The Church's one foundation
is Jesus Christ her Lord;
she is His new creation
by water and the Word:
from heaven He came and
sought her
to be His holy bride;
with His own blood He bought
her
and for her life He died.

2 Called out from every nation,
yet one through all the earth;
her charter of salvation —
one Lord, one faith, one birth:
one holy name she blesses,
and shares one holy food;
as to one hope she presses
with every grace endued.

3 We see her long divided
by heresy and sect;
yet she by God is guided —
one people, one elect:

her vigil she is keeping,
her cry goes up, 'How long?'
and soon the night of weeping
shall be the dawn of song.

4 In toil and tribulation,
and tumult of her war,
she waits the consummation
of peace for evermore:
till with the vision glorious
her longing eyes are blessed;
at last the Church victorious
shall be the Church at rest!

5 Yet she on earth has union
with God the Three-in-One;
and mystic, sweet communion
with those whose rest is won:
O happy ones and holy!
Lord, grant to us Your grace,
with them the meek and lowly,
in heaven to see Your face.

Samuel John Stone, 1832–1900
adapted Jubilate Hymns

151

1 Through the night of doubt and
sorrow
onward goes the pilgrim band,
singing songs of expectation,
marching to the promised land.

2 Clear before us through the
darkness
gleams and burns the guiding
light;
clasping hands with one another,
we step fearless through the
night.

3 One the light of God's own
presence
on His ransomed people shed,
chasing far the gloom and terror,
brightening all the path we
tread;

4 One the object of our journey,
one the faith which never tires,
one the eager looking forward,
one the hope our God inspires:

5 One the song that lips of
thousands
lift as from the heart of one:
one the conflict, one the peril,
one the march in God begun:

THE PEOPLE OF GOD

6   One the gladness of rejoicing
    on the far eternal shore,
    where the one almighty Father
    reigns in love for evermore.

> Bernhardt Severin Ingemann, 1789–1862
> *translated* Sabine Baring-Gould, 1834–1924
> *altered*

152

1   We are marching in the light of
    God,
    we are marching in the light of
    God.
    We are marching in the light of
    God,
    we are marching in the light of
    God.
    We are marching, oh,
    we are marching in the light of
    God.
    We are marching, oh,
    we are marching in the light of
    God.

2   We are living in the love of God,
    we are living in the love of God.
    We are living in the love of God,
    we are living in the love of God.
    We are living, oh,
    we are living in the love of God.
    We are living, oh,
    we are living in the love of God.

3   We are moving in the power of
    God,
    we are moving in the power of
    God.
    We are moving in the power of
    God,
    we are moving in the power of
    God.
    We are moving, oh,
    we are moving in the power of
    God.
    We are moving, oh,
    we are moving in the power of
    God.

> South African traditional
> *translated* Anders Nyberg, *b.* 1955

153

1   We come before our fathers' God:
    the Rock of our salvation;
    the eternal arms, their loved
    abode,
    we make our habitation;
    we bring You, Lord, the praise
    they brought;

we seek You as Your saints have
    sought
in every generation.

2   The fire divine, their steps that
    led,
    burns on and still directs us;
    the heavenly shield, around
    them spread,
    still shadows and protects us;
    the grace those sinners that
    subdued,
    the strength those weaklings that
    renewed,
    defeats and resurrects us.

3   Their joy to that same Lord we
    bring,
    their song to us descending,
    the Spirit who in them did sing
    to us His music lending:
    His song in them, in us, is one;
    we raise it high, we send it on —
    the song that has no ending.

4   You saints to come, take up the
    strain,
    the same sweet theme
    endeavour;
    unbroken be the golden chain,
    keep on the song for ever!
    Safe in that ageless dwelling-
    place,
    rich with the same eternal grace,
    bless the same boundless Giver!

> Thomas Hornblower Gill, 1819–1906
> *adapted* Compilers of *Praise!* 2000

154

1   Welcome to the family,
    we're glad that you have come
    to share your life with us,
    as we grow in love,
    and may we always be to you
    what God would have us be,
    a family always there,
    to be strong and to lean on.

2   May we learn to love each other
    more with each new day,
    may words of love be on our lips
    in everything we say.
    May the Spirit melt our hearts,
    and teach us how to pray,
    that we might be a true family.

> Debby Kerner Rettino, *b.* 1951

155

1 Your hand, O God, has guided
Your flock, from age to age;
Your faithfulness is written
on history's every page.
They knew Your perfect
goodness,
whose deeds we now record;
and both to this bear witness:
one Church, one Faith, one Lord.

2 Your heralds brought the gospel
to greatest as to least;
they summoned us to hasten
and share the great King's feast.
And this was all their teaching
in every deed and word;
to all alike proclaiming:
one Church, one Faith, one Lord.

3 Through many days of darkness,
through many scenes of strife,
the faithful few fought bravely
to guard the nation's life.
Their gospel of redemption —
sin pardoned, hope restored —
was all in this enfolded:
one Church, one Faith, one Lord.

4 And we, shall we be faithless?
Shall hearts fail, hands hang
down?
Shall we evade the conflict
and throw away the crown?
Not so! In God's deep counsels
some better thing is stored;
we will maintain, unflinching,
one Church, one Faith, one Lord.

5 Your mercy will not fail us
nor leave Your work undone;
with Your right hand to help us,
the victory shall be won.
And then by earth and heaven
Your name shall be adored;
and this shall be their anthem:
one Church, one Faith, one Lord.

Edward Hayes Plumptre, 1821–1891
considerably altered

156

1 Your hand, O God, has guided
Your Church from age to age;
the tale of love is written
for us on every page.
Our fathers knew Your goodness
and we Your works record;
and each of these bear witness:
one Church, one Faith, one Lord.

One Church, one Faith, one Lord
of life,
one Father, one Spirit, one Christ.
One Church, one Faith, one Lord
of life,
one heavenly King, Lord of all.

2 Your mercy never fails us
or leaves Your work undone;
with Your right hand to help us
the victory shall be won.
And then by all creation
Your name shall be adored;
with earth and heaven singing:
one Church, one Faith, one Lord.

Edward Hayes Plumptre, 1821–1891
adapted

Also suitable:
Forth in the peace of Christ we go   280
Stand up and bless the Lord   238

THE TEMPLE
THE TRINITY

157

1 Bright the vision that delighted
once the sight of Judah's seer;
sweet the countless tongues
united
to entrance the prophet's ear.

2 Round the Lord in glory seated,
cherubim and seraphim
filled His temple and repeated
each to each the alternate hymn:

3 'Lord, Your glory fills the heaven,
earth is with its fullness stored;
unto You be glory given:
holy, holy, Lord!'

4 Heaven is still with glory ringing,
earth takes up the angels' cry:
'Holy, holy, holy,' singing,
'Lord of hosts, the Lord most
high!'

5 With His seraphim before Him,
with His holy Church below,
thus united, we adore Him,
let our glorious anthem flow:

6 'Lord, Your glory fills the heaven,
earth is with its fullness stored;
unto You be glory given:
holy, holy, holy, Lord!'

Richard Mant, 1776–1848
adapted Jubilate Hymns

158

1   Father God, we worship You,
    make us part of all You do.
    As You move among us now
    we worship You.

2   Jesus King, we worship You,
    help us listen now to You.

3   Spirit pure, we worship You,
    with Your fire our zeal renew.

Graham Andrew Kendrick, *b.* 1950

159

1   Firmly I believe and truly
    God is Three and God is One;
    and I next acknowledge duly
    manhood taken by the Son.

2   And I trust and hope most fully
    in that manhood crucified;
    and each thought and deed
    unruly
    do to death, for He has died.

3   Simply to His grace and wholly
    light and life and strength
    belong;
    and I love supremely, solely,
    Christ the holy, Christ the strong.

4   And I make this affirmation
    for the love of Christ alone:
    holy Church is His creation
    and His teachings are her own.

5   Honour, glory, power, and merit
    to the God of earth and heaven,
    Father, Son, and Holy Spirit —
    praise for evermore be given!
    Amen.

John Henry Newman, 1801–1890
adapted Jubilee Hymns

160

1   Glory be to God the Father,
    glory be to God the Son,
    glory be to God the Spirit, —
    great Jehovah, Three-in-One!
    Glory, glory, glory, glory
    while eternal ages run!

2   Glory be to Him who loved us,
    washed us from each spot and
    stain!
    Glory be to Him who bought us,
    made us kings with Him to
    reign!
    Glory, glory, glory, glory
    to the Lamb that once was slain!

3   Glory to the King of angels,
    glory to the Church's King,
    glory to the King of nations!
    heaven and earth, your praises
    bring;
    Glory, glory, glory, glory
    to the King of glory bring!

4   'Glory, blessing, praise eternal!'
    Thus the choir of angels sings;
    'Honour, riches, power,
    dominion!'
    Thus its praise creation brings;
    Glory, glory, glory, glory,
    glory to the King of kings! Amen.

Horatius N. Bonar, 1808–1889

161

1   Holy, holy, holy, Lord God
    Almighty!
    Early in the morning our song of
    praise shall be:
    holy, holy, holy! — merciful and
    mighty,
    God in three persons, glorious
    Trinity.

2   Holy, holy, holy! All the saints
    adore You
    casting down their golden crowns
    around the glassy sea,
    cherubim and seraphim falling
    down before You:
    You were and are, and evermore
    shall be!

3   Holy, holy, holy! Though the
    darkness hide You,
    though the sinful human eye
    Your glory may not see,
    You alone are holy, there is none
    beside You,
    perfect in power, in love and
    purity.

4   Holy, holy, holy, Lord God
    Almighty!
    All Your works shall praise Your
    name, in earth and sky and
    sea:
    holy, holy, holy! — merciful and
    mighty,
    God in three persons, glorious
    Trinity.

Reginald Heber, 1783–1826

162

1. I bind myself to God today,
   the strong and holy Trinity,
   to know His name and make
        Him known,
   the Three-in-One and One-in-
        Three.

2. I bind myself to God forever,
   to Jesus in His incarnation,
   baptized for me in Jordan river
   and crucified for my salvation;
   He burst the prison of His tomb,
   ascended to the heavenly throne,
   returning at the day of doom:
   by faith I make His life my own.

3. I bind myself to God today,
   to His great power to hold and
        lead,
   His eye to watch me on my way,
   His ear to listen to my need;
   the wisdom of my God to teach,
   His hand to guide, His shield to
        ward,
   the Word of God to give me
        speech,
   His heavenly host to be my
        guard.

4. Christ be with me, Christ within
        me,
   Christ behind me, Christ before
        me,
   Christ to seek me, Christ to win
        me,
   Christ to comfort and restore me;
   Christ beneath me, Christ above
        me,
   Christ in quiet, Christ in danger,
   Christ sustaining all who love
        me,
   Christ uniting friend and
        stranger!

5. I bind myself to God today,
   the strong and holy Trinity,
   to know His name and make
        Him known,
   the Three-in-One and One-in-
        Three;
   from Him all nature has creation,
   eternal Father, Spirit, Word:
   praise God, my strength and my
        salvation;
   praise in the Spirit through
        Christ the Lord! Amen.

Atromriug indiu niurt tren
attributed to St Patrick, 372–466,
translated Cecil Frances Alexander, 1818–1895,
adapted Jubilate Hymns

163

1. We believe in God Almighty,
   maker of the earth and sky;
   all we see and all that's hidden
   is His work unceasingly:
   God our Father's loving kindness
   with us till the day we die —
   evermore and evermore.

2. We believe in Christ the Saviour,
   Son of God and Son of Man;
   born of Mary, preaching, healing,
   crucified, yet risen again:
   He ascended to the Father
   there in glory long to reign —
   evermore and evermore.

3. We believe in God the Spirit,
   present in our lives today;
   speaking through the prophets'
        writings,
   guiding travellers on their way:
   to our hearts He brings
        forgiveness
   and the hope of endless joy —
   evermore and evermore.

David Mowbray, *b.* 1938

Also suitable:

Eternal Father, strong to save	603
Father of heaven, whose love profound	62
God reveals His presence	170
Lead us, heavenly Father, lead us	107

THE TEMPLE
WORSHIP

164

1. As we seek Your face,
   may we know Your heart,
   feel Your presence, acceptance,
   as we seek Your face.

2. Move among us now,
   come, reveal Your power,
   show Your presence, acceptance,
   move among us now.

3. At Your feet we fall,
   sovereign Lord,
   we cry, 'Holy, holy,'
   at Your feet we fall.

Dave Bilborough, *b.* 1965

165

1 Be still, for the presence of the
   Lord, the Holy One, is here.
   Come, bow before Him now, with
   reverence and fear.
   In Him no sin is found, we stand
   on holy ground.
   Be still, for the presence of the
   Lord, the Holy One, is here.

2 Be still, for the glory of the Lord
   is shining all around;
   He burns with holy fire, with
   splendour He is crowned.
   How awesome is the sight, our
   radiant King of light!
   Be still, for the glory of the Lord
   is shining all around.

3 Be still, for the power of the Lord
   is moving in this place,
   He comes to cleanse and heal, to
   minister His grace.
   No work too hard for Him, in
   faith receive from Him;
   be still, for the power of the Lord
   is moving in this place.

David J. Evans, b. 1957

166

1 Eternal Light! Eternal Light!
   How pure the soul must be,
   when, placed within Your
   searching sight,
   it shrinks not, but with calm
   delight
   can face such majesty.

2 The spirits who surround Your
   throne
   may bear the burning bliss;
   but that is surely theirs alone,
   since they have never, never
   known
   a fallen world like this.

3 O how shall I, whose dwelling
   here
   is dark, whose mind is dim,
   before the face of God appear
   and on my human spirit bear
   the uncreated beam?

4 There is a way for us to rise
   to that sublime abode:
   an offering and a sacrifice,
   a Holy Spirit's energies,
   an advocate with God.

5 Such grace prepares us for the
   sight
   of holiness above;
   those once in ignorance and night
   can dwell in the eternal Light,
   through the eternal Love.

Thomas Binney, 1798–1874
revised Compilers of Praise! 2000
and Jubilate Hymns

167

1 Father, we adore You,
   we are Your children gathered
   here;
   to be with You is our delight,
   a feast beyond compare.

2 Father, in Your presence
   there is such freedom to enjoy.
   We find in You a lasting peace
   that nothing can destroy.

   You are the Fountain of life,
   You are the Fountain of life,
   and as we drink, we are more than
   satisfied
   by You, O Fountain of life.

Phil Lawson-Johnston

168

1 Focus my eyes on You, O Lord;
   focus my eyes on You.
   To worship in spirit and in truth,
   focus my eyes on You.

2 Turn round my life to You, O
   Lord;
   turn round my life to You.
   To know from this time You've
   made me new,
   turn round my life to You.

3 Fill up my heart with praise, O
   Lord;
   fill up my heart with praise.
   To speak of Your love in every
   place,
   fill up my heart with praise.

Ian White, b. 1956

169

1 God is here! As we His people
   meet to offer praise and prayer,
   may we find in fuller measure
   what it is in Christ we share.
   Here, as in the world around us,
   all our varied skills and arts
   wait the coming of His Spirit
   into open minds and hearts.

2 Here are symbols to remind us
of our lifelong need of grace;
here are table, font and pulpit;
here the cross has central place.
Here in honesty of preaching,
here in silence, as in speech,
here, in newness and renewal,
God the Spirit comes to each.

3 Here our children find a
     welcome
in the Shepherd's flock and fold.
Here, as bread and wine are
     taken,
Christ sustains us as of old.
Here the servants of the Servant
seek in worship to explore
what it means in daily living
to believe and to adore.

4 Lord of all, of Church and
     Kingdom,
in an age of change and doubt,
keep us faithful to the gospel,
help us work Your purpose out.
Here, in this day's dedication,
all we have to give, receive:
we, who cannot live without You,
we adore You! We believe!

Frederick Pratt Green, 1903–2000

170

1 God reveals His presence;
let us now adore Him,
and with awe appear before
     Him;
God is in His temple;
all within keep silence,
prostrate lie with deepest
     reverence;
Him alone
God we own,
Him our God and Saviour:
Praise His name for ever.

2 God reveals His presence:
hear the harps resounding,
see the crowds the throne
     surrounding:
'Holy, holy, holy,'
hear the hymn ascending,
angels, saints, their voices
     blending;
bow Your ear
to us here;
hear, O Christ, the praises
that Your Church now raises.

3 Lord, the fount of blessing,
purify my spirit,
trusting only in Your merit;
like the holy angels
who behold Your glory,
may I ceaselessly adore You;
let Your will,
ever still
rule Your Church terrestrial,
as the hosts celestial.

Gerhard Tersteegen, 1697–1769
translated Frederick W. Foster, 1760–1835,
William Mercer, 1811–1873
and Johannes Müller, 1756–1790
verse 3 altered

171

1 How lovely is Your dwelling-
     place,
O Lord of hosts, to me.
My soul is longing and fainting
the courts of the Lord to see;
my heart and flesh, they are
     singing
for joy to the living God:
how lovely is Your dwelling-
     place,
O Lord of hosts, to me!

2 Even the sparrow finds a home
where he can settle down;
and the swallow, she can build a
     nest
where she may lay her young
within the courts of the Lord of
     hosts,
my King, my Lord, and my God:
and happy are those
who are dwelling where
the song of praise is sung!

3 And I'd rather be a door-keeper
and only stay a day,
than live the life of a sinner
and have to stay away;
for the Lord is shining as the sun,
and the Lord, He's like a
     shield —
and no good thing does He
     withhold
from those who walk His way.

4 How lovely is Your dwelling-
     place …

Jonathan Asprey
after Psalm 84

172

1 Hushed was the evening hymn,
the temple courts were dark;
the lamp was burning dim
before the sacred ark,
when suddenly a voice divine
rang through the silence of the
shrine.

2 The old man, meek and mild,
the priest of Israel, slept;
his watch the temple child,
the little Samuel, kept:
and what from Eli's sense was
sealed
the Lord to Hannah's son
revealed.

3 O give me Samuel's ear,
the open ear, O Lord,
alive and quick to hear
each whisper of Your Word —
like him to answer at Your call,
and to obey You first of all.

4 O give me Samuel's heart,
a lowly heart, that waits
to serve and play the part
You show us at Your gates,
by day and night, a heart that still
moves at the breathing of Your
will.

5 O give me Samuel's mind,
a sweet, unmurmuring faith,
obedient and resigned
to You in life and death,
that I may read with childlike
eyes
truths that are hidden from the
wise.

James Drummond Burns, 1823–1923
adapted Peter J. Horrobin, *b.* 1943
and Greg P. Leavers, *b.* 1952

173

1 I rejoiced to hear them say,
'Come and worship God today!
Come, with heart and mind and
soul,
seek the peace that makes us
whole;
see disordered lives restored
in the presence of the Lord:
from your burdens find release;
in His presence there is peace.'

2 Here in gratitude we bring
all we are to serve our King;
His forgiveness we entreat
in whom love and justice meet:
bring our needs to Him in prayer,
ask His help, and trust His care;
join with all, in every place,
who have sought and known His
grace.

3 God, the Lord of peace, is near —
come in faith, and meet Him
here;
let each restless soul be still,
glad to know and do His will:
as a city's walls and towers
offered safety — God is ours!
Therefore we rejoice, and say,
'Come and worship God today!'

Basil Ernest Bridge, *b.* 1927
from Psalm 122

174

1 I will worship (I will worship)
with all of my heart. (with all of
my heart.)
I will praise You (I will praise
You)
with all of my strength. (all my
strength.)
I will seek You (I will seek You)
all of my days. (all of my days.)
I will follow (I will follow)
all of Your ways. (all Your ways.)
I will give You all my worship,
I will give You all my praise.
You alone I long to worship,
You alone are worthy of my praise.

2 I will bow down, (I will bow
down,)
hail You as King, (hail You as
King,)
I will serve You, (I will serve
You,)
give You everything. (give You
everything.)
I will lift up (I will lift up)
my eyes to Your throne, (my eyes
to Your throne,)
I will trust You, (I will trust You,)
I will trust You alone. (trust You
alone.)

Dave Ruis

175

1 Jesus, King of kings,
   we worship and adore You;
   Jesus, Lord of heaven and earth,
   we bow down at Your feet.
   Father, we bring to You our
        worship:
   Your sovereign will be done,
   on earth Your Kingdom come;
   through Jesus Christ, Your only
        Son.

2 Jesus, Sovereign Lord,
   we worship and adore You;
   Jesus, Name above all names,
   we bow down at Your feet.
   Father, we offer You our worship:

3 Jesus, Light of the world,
   we worship and adore You;
   Jesus, Lord Emmanuel,
   we bow down at Your feet.
   Father, for Your delight we
        worship:

Christopher Philip Rolinson, *b.* 1958

176

1 Jesus, stand among us
   in Your risen power;
   let this time of worship
   be a hallowed hour.

2 Breathe the Holy Spirit
   into every heart;
   bid the fears and sorrows
   from each soul depart.

3 Thus with quickened footsteps
   we'll pursue our way,
   watching for the dawning
   of eternal day.

William Pennefather, 1816–1873
altered

177

1 Jesus, the very thought of You
   makes every moment blessed;
   but better still Your face to view
   and in Your presence rest.

2 No ear can hear, no voice
        proclaim,
   nor can the heart recall
   a sweeter sound than Jesus'
        name,
   the Saviour of us all.

3 Hope of each contrite, humble
        mind,
   joy of the poor and meek;
   to those who falter, O how kind,
   how good to those who seek!

4 But what to those who find? Ah,
        this
   nor tongue nor pen can show!
   The love of Jesus — what it is
   none but His loved ones know.

5 Jesus, be all our joy below,
   as You our prize will be;
   Jesus, be all our glory now
   and through eternity.

Jesu dulcis memoria anonymous, 12th century
attributed to Bernard of Clairvaux, 1090–1153
translated Edward Caswall, 1814–1878
vv. 1-3, 5 *adapted* Jubilate Hymns

178

1 Jesus went to worship
   in the synagogue;
   with His friends and neighbours,
   sang His praise to God.

2 We, like Jesus, worship
   in the Church today;
   still, with friends and neighbours,
   sing our songs and pray.

3 When the service ended
   Jesus took His praise
   into streets and houses,
   spelling out God's ways.

4 People came to Jesus,
   frightened, hurt and sad;
   helping them to worship,
   Jesus made them glad.

5 Holy Spirit, help us
   when this service ends,
   still to follow Jesus,
   still to be His friends.

6 When our neighbours meet us,
   may they, with surprise,
   catch a glimpse of Jesus
   rising in our eyes.

Alan Gaunt, *b.* 1935

179

1 Let us sing to the God of
        salvation,
   let us sing to the Lord our rock;
   let us come to His house with
        thanksgiving,
   let us come before the Lord and
        sing!

175 Words and Music: © 1988 Thankyou Music. Administered (UK and Europe) by Kingsway Music <tym@kingsway.co.uk>. Remaining territories administered by worshiptogether.com songs. Used by permission.

177 Words: © in this version Jubilate Hymns, 4 Thorne Park Road, Chelston, Torquay TQ2 6RX <enquiries@jubilate.co.uk> Used by permission.

178 Words: © 1991 Stainer & Bell Ltd, PO Box 110, Victoria House, 23 Gruneisen Road, London N3 1DZ

WORSHIP

Praise our Maker,
praise our Saviour,
praise the Lord our everlasting
*   King:*
every throne must bow before
*   Him —*
God is Lord of everything!

2 In His hand are the earth's
   deepest places,
and the strength of the hills is
   His;
all the sea is the Lord's, for He
   made it —
by His hands the solid rock was
   formed.

3 Let us worship the Lord our
   Maker,
let us kneel to the Lord our God;
for we all are the sheep of His
   pasture —
He will guide us by His powerful
   hand.

4 Let today be the time when you
   hear Him!
May our hearts not be hard or
   cold,
lest we stray from the Lord in
   rebellion
as His people did in time of old.

Richard Thomas Bewes, *b.* 1934
from Psalm 95

180

1 Lord Jesus, when Your people
   meet
they come before Your mercy-
   seat;
where You are sought, You shall
   be found,
and every place is holy ground.

2 Your presence, by no walls
   confined,
is known within the humble
   mind;
the meek will bring You where
   they come,
and going take You to their home.

3 Great Shepherd of Your chosen
   few,
Your former mercies here renew;
here to our waiting hearts
   proclaim
the greatness of Your saving
   name.

4 Here may we prove the power of
   prayer
to strengthen faith and sweeten
   care;
to teach our faint desires to rise
and bring all heaven before our
   eyes.

5 Lord, we are few, but You are
   near;
Your arm can save, Your ear can
   hear:
break through the heavens, come
   quickly down,
and make a thousand hearts Your
   own!

William Cowper, 1731–1800
altered Compilers of
Hymns for Today's Church, 1982

181

1 MEN: May the fragrance of
   Jesus fill this place,
WOMEN: may the fragrance of
   Jesus fill this place,
MEN: may the fragrance of
   Jesus fill this place,
WOMEN: lovely fragrance of Jesus,
ALL: rising from the sacrifice
   of lives laid down in
   adoration.

2 MEN: May the glory of Jesus
   fill His Church,
WOMEN: may the glory of Jesus
   fill His Church,
MEN: may the glory of Jesus
   fill His Church;
WOMEN: radiant glory of Jesus,
ALL: shining from our faces
   as we gaze in adoration.

3 MEN: May the beauty of Jesus
   fill my life,
WOMEN: may the beauty of Jesus
   fill my life,
MEN: may the beauty of Jesus
   fill my life:
WOMEN: perfect beauty of Jesus,
ALL: fill my thoughts, my
   words, my deeds.
my all I give in adoration;
fill my thoughts, my words,
my deeds.

Graham Andrew Kendrick, *b.* 1950

181 Words and Music: © 1986 Thankyou Music. Administered (UK and Europe) by Kingsway Music <tym@kingsway.co.uk>. Remaining territories administered by worshiptogether.com songs. Used by permission.
179 Words: © Richard Bewes/Jubilate Hymns, 4 Thorne Park Road, Chelston, Torquay TQ2 6RX <enquiries@jubilate.co.uk> Used by permission.

THE TEMPLE

182

1. My God, how wonderful You are,
Your majesty how bright;
how beautiful Your mercy seat
in depths of burning light!

2. How awesome Your eternal
years,
O everlasting Lord,
by angel spirits day and night
incessantly adored!

3. O how I fear You, living God,
with deepest, tenderest fears,
and worship You with trembling
hope
and penitential tears!

4. Yet I may love You too, O Lord,
almighty King of kings,
for You have stooped to ask of me
the love my poor heart brings.

5. No earthly father loves like You,
no mother, e'er so mild,
is patient, Lord, as You have been
with me Your sinful child.

6. How beautiful, how beautiful
the sight of You must be,
Your endless wisdom, boundless
power,
and awesome purity!

Frederick William Faber, 1814–1863
adapted Compilers

183

1. My heart is full of admiration
for You, my Lord, my God and
King.
Your excellence, my inspiration,
Your words of grace have made
my spirit sing.
All the glory, honour and power
belong to You, belong to You.
Jesus, Saviour, anointed One,
I worship You, I worship You.

2. You love what's right and hate
what's evil,
therefore Your God sets You on
high,
and on Your head pours oil of
gladness,
while fragrance fills Your royal
palaces.

3. Your throne, O God, will last
forever,
justice will be Your royal decree.
In majesty, ride out victorious,
for righteousness, truth and
humility.

Graham Andrew Kendrick, b. 195

184

1. No-one but You, Lord,
can satisfy the longing in my
heart.
Nothing I do, Lord,
can take the place of drawing
near to You.
Only You can fill my deepest
longing,
only You can breathe in me new
life;
only You can fill my heart with
laughter,
only You can answer my heart's
cry.

2. Father, I love You,
come satisfy the longing in my
heart.
Fill me, overwhelm me,
until I know Your love deep in
my heart.

Andy Par

185

1. O God, You are my God alone,
whom eagerly I seek,
though longing fills my soul with
thirst
and leaves my body weak.
Just as a dry and barren land
awaits a freshening shower
I long within Your house to see
Your glory and Your power.

2. Your faithful love surpasses life,
evoking all my praise.
Through every day, to bless Your
name
my hands in joy I'll raise.
My deepest needs You satisfy
as with a sumptuous feast.
So, on my lips and in my heart,
Your praise has never ceased.

3. Throughout the night I lie in bed
and call You, Lord, to mind;
in darkest hours I meditate
how God, my strength, is kind.
Beneath the shadow of Your
wing,

I live and feel secure;
and daily as I follow close,
Your right hand keeps me sure.

John Lamberton Bell, *b.* 1949
from Psalm 63

186

1   O Jesus, King most wonderful
and conqueror renowned;
O sweetness inexpressible
in whom all joys are found!

2   When You draw near and touch
    the heart
then truth begins to shine;
then this world's vanities depart,
then kindles love divine.

3   O Jesus, light of all below,
the fount of living fire,
surpassing all the joys we know
and all we can desire.

4   Jesus, may all confess Your name,
Your tender love adore,
and seeking You, their hearts
    inflame
to seek You more and more.

5   O Jesus whom our voices bless,
whom we would love alone;
for ever let our lives express
the image of Your own.

Jesu dulcis memoria anonymous, 12th century
attributed to Bernard of Clairvaux, 1090–1153
translated Edward Caswall, 1814–1878
adapted Jubilate Hymns

187

1   O Lord my God, when I in
    awesome wonder
consider all the works Thy hand
    hath made,
I see the stars, I hear the mighty
    thunder,
Thy power throughout the
    universe displayed;
*Then sings my soul, my Saviour
    God, to Thee:
How great Thou art! How great
    Thou art!
Then sings my soul, my Saviour
    God, to Thee:
How great Thou art! How great
    Thou art!*

2   When through the woods and
    forest glades I wander
and hear the birds sing sweetly
    in the trees;

when I look down from lofty
    mountain grandeur,
and hear the brook, and feel the
    gentle breeze;

3   And when I think that God, His
    Son not sparing,
sent Him to die — I scarce can
    take it in,
that on the cross my burden
    gladly bearing,
He bled and died to take away
    my sin:

4   When Christ shall come with
    shout of acclamation
and take me home — what joy
    shall fill my heart!
Then shall I bow in humble
    adoration
and there proclaim, my God, how
    great Thou art!

Russian hymn
translated Stuart Wesley Keene Hine, 1899–1989

188

1   Open the gates of righteousness,
for we have come to pray;
to offer thanks for all God's gifts
within His house today.

2   When we were trapped at every
    turn,
hard-pressed on every side,
the Lord our God came to our
    help
and all our bonds untied.

3   The rock the builders had refused
became the corner-stone:
who can deny this is a thing
the Lord Himself has done?

4   Enter God's house to praise His
    name,
and all His triumphs tell;
salute the people of the Lord —
beloved, we wish you well!

David Mowbray, *b.* 1938
from Psalm 118

189

1   O send Your light forth and Your
    truth,
and let them be my guide,
to bring me to the place where
    You
in holiness abide.
Then to God's altar I will go,
and in His name rejoice.

O God, my God, I'll praise Your name,
with harp, with harp,
with harp and joyful voice,
and joyful voice.

2 Why then are you downcast my soul?
And why are you afraid?
And why with dark and anxious thoughts
are you depressed, dismayed?
Rely on God and praise His name
for all that He has done.
My trust is in the God who saves;
My hope, my hope,
my hope — in Him alone,
in Him alone.

David J. Montgomery, *b. 1963*
from Psalm 43: 3-5

190

1 Overwhelmed by love,
deeper than oceans,
high as the heavens.
Ever living God.
Your love has rescued me.

2 All my sin was laid
on Your dear Son,
Your precious One.
All my debt He paid,
great is Your love for me.

No one could ever earn Your love,
Your grace and mercy is free.
Lord, these words are true,
so is my love for You.

Noël Richards, *b. 1955*

191

1 Such love, pure as the whitest snow;
such love weeps for the shame I know;
such love, paying the debt I owe;
O Jesus, such love.

2 Such love, stilling my restlessness;
such love, filling my emptiness;
such love, showing me holiness;
O Jesus, such love.

3 Such love springs from eternity;
such love, streaming through history;
such love, fountain of life to me;
O Jesus, such love.

Graham Andrew Kendrick, *b. 195*

192

1 There is a Redeemer,
Jesus, God's own Son,
precious Lamb of God, Messiah,
Holy One.
Thank you, O my Father,
for giving us Your Son,
and leaving us Your Spirit
till the work on earth is done.

2 Jesus, my Redeemer,
Name above all names,
precious Lamb of God, Messiah,
O for sinners slain.

3 When I stand in glory,
I will see His face,
and there I'll serve my King for ever
in that holy place.

Melody Green

193

1 There's a quiet understanding
when we're gathered in the Spirit,
it's a promise that He gives us,
when we gather in His name.
There's a love we feel in Jesus,
there's a manna that He feeds us
it's a promise that He gives us,
when we gather in His name.

2 And we know when we're together,
sharing love and understanding,
that our brothers and our sisters
feel the oneness that He brings.
Thank You, thank You, thank You Jesus,
for the way You love and feed us,
for the many ways You lead us;
thank You, thank You Lord.

Tedd Smith, *b. 192*

194

1 This earth belongs to God,
the world, its wealth and all its people;

190 Words and Music: © 1994 Thankyou Music. Administered (UK and Europe) by Kingsway <tym@kingsway.co.uk>. Used by permission.
191 Words and Music: © 1988 Make Way Music, PO Box 263, Croydon. CR9 5AP International copyright secured. All rights reserved. Used by permission.
192 Words and Music: © 1982 Ears to Hear Music/Birdwing Music/BMG Songs/EMI Christian Music Publishing. Administered by CopyCare Ltd
193 Words and Music: © 1973 Hope Publishing Company. Administered by CopyCare Ltd, PO Box 77, Hailsham, East Sussex. BN27 3EF
194 Words: © Christopher Idle/Jubilate Hymns, 4 Thorne Park Road, Chelston, Torquay TQ2 6RX <enquiries@jubilate.co.uk> Used by permission.

He formed the waters wide
and fashioned every sea and
shore.

GROUP A: Who may go up the
hill of the Lord
and stand in the place of
holiness?
GROUP B: Only the one whose
heart is pure,
whose hands and lips are clean.

2 Lift high your heads, you gates,
rise up, you everlasting doors,
as here now the King of glory
enters into full command.

GROUP A: Who is the King, this
King of glory,
where is the throne He comes to
claim?
GROUP B: Christ is the King, the
Lord of glory,
fresh from His victory.

3 Lift high your heads, you gates,
and fling wide open the ancient
doors,
for here comes the King of glory
taking universal power.

GROUP A: Who is the King, this
King of glory,
what is the power by which He
reigns?
GROUP B: Christ is the King, His
cross His glory,
and by love He rules.

4 All glory be to God
the Father, Son and Holy Spirit;
from ages past it was,
is now, and ever more shall be.

Christopher Martin Idle, b. 1938
from Psalm 24

195

1 To be in Your presence,
to sit at Your feet,
where Your love surrounds me,
and makes me complete:
this is my desire, O Lord,
this is my desire;
this is my desire, O Lord,
this is my desire.

2 To rest in Your presence,
not rushing away,
to cherish each moment —
here I would stay:

Noël Richards, b. 1955

196

1 We love the place, O God,
in which Your honour dwells:
the joy of Your abode,
all earthly joy excels.

2 We love the house of prayer:
for where Christ's people meet,
our risen Lord is there
to make our joy complete.

3 We love the word of life,
the word that tells of peace,
of comfort in the strife
and joys that never cease.

4 We love the cleansing sign
of life through Christ our Lord,
where with the Name divine
we seal the child of God.

5 We love the holy feast
where, nourished with this food,
by faith we feed on Christ,
His body and His blood.

6 We love to sing below
of mercies freely given,
but O, we long to know
the triumph-song of heaven.

7 Lord Jesus, give us grace
on earth to love You more,
in heaven to see Your face
and with Your saints adore.

Henry Williams Baker, 1821–1877
after William Bullock
adapted Jubilate Hymns

197

1 When the music fades, all is
stripped away,
and I simply come;
longing just to bring something
that's of worth
that will bless Your heart.

I'll bring You more than a song,
for a song in itself
is not what You have required.
You search much deeper within
through the way things appear;
You're looking into my heart.

I'm coming back to the heart of
worship,
and it's all about You,
all about You, Jesus.
I'm sorry, Lord, for the thing I've
made it,
when it's all about You,
all about You, Jesus.

195   Words and Music: © 1991 Thankyou Music. Administered (UK and Europe) by Kingsway Music <tym@kingsway.co.uk>. Remaining territories administered by
worshiptogether.com songs. Used by permission.
196   Words: © in this version Jubilate Hymns, 4 Thorne Park Road, Chelston, Torquay TQ2 6RX <enquiries@jubilate.co.uk> Used by permission.
197   Words and Music: © 1997 Thankyou Music. Administered (UK and Europe) by Kingsway Music <tym@kingsway.co.uk>. Remaining territories administered by
worshiptogether.com songs. Used by permission.

2 King of endless worth, no one
        could express
   how much You deserve.
   Though I'm weak and poor, all I
        have is Yours,
   every single breath.

   I'll bring You more than a song,
   for a song in itself
   is not what You have required.
   You search much deeper within
   through the way things appear;
   You're looking into my heart.

                              Matt Redman, b. 1974

198

1 Worship the Lord in the beauty of
        holiness!
   Bow down before Him, His glory
        proclaim;
   gold of obedience and incense of
        lowliness,
   kneel and adore Him, the Lord is
        His name!

2 Low at His feet lay your burden
        of carefulness,
   high on His heart He will bear it
        for you,
   comfort your sorrows and answer
        your prayerfulness,
   guiding your steps in the way
        that is true.

3 Fear not to enter His courts in the
        slenderness
   of the poor wealth you would
        count as your own;
   truth in its beauty and love in its
        tenderness,
   these are the offerings to bring to
        His throne.

4 These, though we bring them in
        trembling and fearfulness,
   He will accept for the Name that
        is dear;
   mornings of joy give for evenings
        of tearfulness,
   trust for our trembling and hope
        for our fear.

5 Worship the Lord in the beauty of
        holiness!
   Bow down before Him, His glory
        proclaim;
   gold of obedience and incense of
        lowliness,
   kneel and adore Him, the Lord is
        His name!

                John Samuel Bewley Monsell, 1811–1875

Also suitable:
Christ is made our sure foundation   13
God and Father, we adore You   29
Holy Spirit, hear us   46
Look upon us, blessèd Lord   27
We come before our fathers' God   15

THE TEMPLE
PRAISE
199

1 All my days I will sing this song
        of gladness,
   give my praise to the fountain of
        delights;
   for in my helplessness You heard
        my cry,
   and waves of mercy poured
        down on my life.

2 I will trust in the cross of my
        Redeemer,
   I will sing of the blood that never
        fails,
   of sins forgiven, of conscience
        cleansed,
   of death defeated and life
        without end.

   Beautiful Saviour,
   Wonderful Counsellor,
   clothed in majesty,
   Lord of history,
   You're the Way, the Truth, the
        Life.
   Star of the morning,
   glorious in holiness,
   you're the risen one,
   heaven's champion,
   and You reign, You reign over all.

3 I long to be where the praise is
        never-ending,
   yearn to dwell where the glory
        never fades,
   where countless worshippers will
        share one song,
   and cries of 'Worthy' will honour
        the Lamb!

   Beautiful Saviour ...

                              Stuart Townend, b. 196

200

1 Bring to the Lord a glad new
        song,
   children of grace extol your King;
   your love and praise to God
        belong —

199 Words and Music: © 1998 Thankyou Music. Administered (UK and Europe) by Kingsway Music <tym@kingsway.co.uk>. Remaining territories administered by worshiptogether.com songs. Used by permission.
200 Words: © Mrs B. Perry / Jubilate Hymns, 4 Thorne Park Road, Chelston, Torquay TQ2 6RX <enquiries@jubilate.co.uk> Used by permission.

to instruments of music, sing!
Let those be warned who spurn
God's name,
let rulers all obey God's word,
for justice shall bring tyrants
shame —
let every creature praise the
Lord!

2 Sing praise within these
hallowed walls,
worship beneath the dome of
heaven;
by cymbals' sounds and
trumpets' calls
let praises fit for God be given:
with strings and brass and wind
rejoice —
then, join our song in full accord
all living things with breath and
voice;
let every creature praise the
Lord!

Michael Arnold Perry, 1942–1996
from Psalms 149 and 150

201

1 Come, children, join to sing —
Alleluia! Amen!
Loud praise to Christ our King;
Alleluia! Amen!
Let all, with heart and voice,
before His throne rejoice;
praise is His gracious choice:
Alleluia! Amen!

2 Come, lift your hearts on high;
Alleluia! Amen!
Let praises fill the sky;
Alleluia! Amen!
He is our guide and friend;
to us He'll blessing send;
His love shall never end:
Alleluia! Amen!

3 Praise yet the Lord again;
Alleluia! Amen!
Life shall not end the strain;
Alleluia! Amen!
On heaven's blissful shore
His goodness we'll adore,
singing for evermore,
Alleluia! Amen!

Christian Henry Bateman, 1813–1889

202

1 From all that dwell below the
skies
let the Creator's praise arise!
Alleluia! Alleluia!
Let the Redeemer's name be
sung
through every land, in every
tongue!
Alleluia! Alleluia!
Alleluia! Alleluia! Alleluia!

2 Eternal are your mercies, Lord;
eternal truth attends your word:
Alleluia! Alleluia!
Your praise shall sound from
shore to shore
till suns shall rise and set no
more.
Alleluia! Alleluia!
Alleluia! Alleluia! Alleluia!

Isaac Watts, 1674–1748
from Psalm 117

203

1 From where the sun rises,
even to the place it goes down —
we're giving You praise,
giving You praise.
From sun-kissed islands
and even where the cold wind
blows —
we're giving You praise,
giving You praise.

*Even in the night when the sun
goes down,
we're giving You praise;
passing it along as the world goes
round,
we're giving You praise.*

2 We're lifting our faces,
looking at the One we all love —
we're giving You praise,
giving You praise.
All colours and races
joining with the angels above —
we're giving You praise,
giving You praise.

Graham Andrew Kendrick, b. 1950

THE TEMPLE

204

1 God, we praise You! God, we
   bless You!
   God, we name You sovereign
   Lord!
   Mighty King whom angels
   worship,
   Father, by Your Church adored:
   all creation shows Your glory,
   heaven and earth draw near
   Your throne
   singing, 'Holy, holy, holy,
   Lord of hosts and God alone!'

2 True apostles, faithful prophets,
   saints who set their world ablaze,
   martyrs, once unknown,
   unheeded,
   join one growing song of praise,
   while Your Church on earth
   confesses
   one majestic Trinity:
   Father, Son, and Holy Spirit,
   God, our hope eternally.

3 Jesus Christ, the King of glory,
   everlasting Son of God,
   humble was Your virgin mother,
   hard the lonely path You trod:
   by Your cross is sin defeated,
   hell confronted face to face,
   heaven opened to believers,
   sinners justified by grace.

4 Christ, at God's right hand
   victorious,
   You will judge the world You
   made;
   Lord, in mercy help Your
   servants
   for whose freedom You have
   paid:
   raise us up from dust to glory,
   guard us from all sin today;
   King enthroned above all praises,
   save Your people, God, we pray.

                    Christopher Martin Idle, b. 1938
                                  from Te Deum

205

1 He is the Lord, and He reigns on
   high:
   He is the Lord.
   Spoke into the darkness, created
   the light.
   He is the Lord.
   Who is like unto Him, never
   ending in days?
   He is the Lord.

And He comes in power when
   we call on His name:
He is the Lord.
   Show Your power, O Lord our God
   show Your power, O Lord our God
   Our God

2 Your gospel, O Lord, is the hope
   for our nation:
   You are the Lord.
   It's the power of God for our
   salvation:
   You are the Lord.
   We ask not for riches, but look to
   the cross:
   You are the Lord.
   And for our inheritance give us
   the lost:
   You are the Lord.

                                  Kevin Prosch

206

1 How good it is to sing praise to
   our God,
   the right and pleasant thing to
   praise His name.
   The Lord is building up
   Jerusalem,
   He gathers all the lost of Israel.
   He is healing the brokenhearted,
   He is binding all their wounds,
   He determines the stars in the
   heavens
   and He calls them each by name.
   Great is the Lord in power, all
   things He knows,
   He casts the wicked down, but
   lifts the low.

                         adapted Ian White, b. 195
                from Psalm 147, New International Versio

207

1 How sweet the name of Jesus
   sounds
   in a believer's ear!
   It soothes our sorrows, heals our
   wounds
   and drives away our fear.

2 It makes the wounded spirit
   whole,
   and calms the troubled breast;
   it satisfies the hungry soul,
   and gives the weary rest.

3 Dear Name, the rock on which I
   build,
   my shield and hiding-place;
   my never-failing treasury, filled
   with boundless stores of grace!

4 Jesus, my shepherd, brother,
    friend,
  my prophet, priest, and king;
  my Lord, my life, my way, my
    end —
  accept the praise I bring.

5 Weak is the effort of my heart,
  and cold my warmest thought;
  but when I see You as You are,
  I'll praise You as I ought.

6 Till then I would Your love
    proclaim
  with every fleeting breath;
  and may the music of Your name
  refresh my soul in death.

> John Newton, 1725–1807
> *altered* Compilers of
> *Hymns for Today's Church*, 1982

208

1 How sweet the name of Jesus
    sounds
  in a believer's ear;
  it soothes his sorrows, heals his
    wounds,
  and drives away his fear.
  It makes the wounded spirit
    whole,
  and calms the troubled breast;
  'tis manna to the hungry soul,
  and to the weary rest,
  and to the weary rest.

2 Dear Name, the rock on which I
    build,
  my shield, and hiding-place;
  my never-failing treasury, filled
  with boundless stores of grace.
  Jesus, my Shepherd, Saviour,
    Friend,
  my Prophet, Priest, and King;
  my Lord, my Life, my Way, my
    End,
  accept the praise I bring,
  accept the praise I bring.

3 Weak is the effort of my heart,
  and cold my warmest thought;
  but when I see You as You are,
  I'll praise You as I ought.
  I would Your boundless love
    proclaim
  with every fleeting breath;
  so shall the music of Your name
  refresh my soul in death,
  refresh my soul in death.

> John Newton, 1725–1807
> *adapted* Christopher Alan Bowater, *b.* 1947

209

1 I am so glad that our Father in
    heaven
  tells of His love in the book He
    has given:
  wonderful things in the Bible I
    see;
  this is the dearest, that Jesus
    loves me.

  I am so glad that Jesus loves me,
  Jesus loves me, Jesus loves me,
  I am so glad that Jesus loves me,
  Jesus loves even me.

2 Though I forget Him, and wander
    away,
  He'll always love me wherever I
    stray;
  back to His dear loving arms do I
    flee,
  when I remember that Jesus
    loves me.

3 O if there's only one song I can
    sing,
  when in His beauty I see the
    great King,
  this shall my song in eternity be,
  O what a wonder that Jesus loves
    me.

4 If one should ask of me: How can
    I tell?
  Glory to Jesus, I know very well;
  God's Holy Spirit with mine does
    agree,
  constantly witnessing: Jesus loves
    me.

> Philipp Paul Bliss, 1838–1876

210

I'm special because God has
    loved me,
for He gave the best thing that
    He had to save me.
His own Son Jesus, crucified to
    take the blame,
for all the bad things I have done.
Thank You Jesus, thank You Lord,
for loving me so much.
I know I don't deserve anything,
help me feel Your love right now
to know deep in my heart that
    I'm Your special friend.

> Graham Andrew Kendrick, *b.* 1950

211

1 I will sing the wondrous story
of the Christ who died for me —
how He left the realms of glory
for the cross on Calvary.
Yes, I'll sing the wondrous story
of the Christ who died for me —
sing it with His saints in glory,
gathered by the crystal sea.

2 I was lost: but Jesus found me,
found the sheep that went astray,
raised me up and gently led me
back into the narrow way.
Days of darkness still may meet
me,
sorrow's path I oft may tread;
but His presence still is with me,
by His guiding hand I'm led.

3 He will keep me till the river
rolls its waters at my feet:
then He'll bear me safely over,
made by grace for glory meet.
Yes, I'll sing the wondrous story
of the Christ who died for me —
sing it with His saints in glory,
gathered by the crystal sea.

Francis Harold Rowley, 1854–1952
restructured Compilers of
Songs and Hymns of Fellowship, 1987

212

I will wave my hands in praise
and adoration,
I will wave my hands in praise
and adoration,
I will wave my hands in praise
and adoration,
praise and adoration to the living
God.
For He's given me hands that
just love clapping;
one, two, one, two, three,
and He's given me a voice that
just loves shouting
'Hallelujah!'
He's given me feet that just love
dancing;
one, two, one, two, three,
and He's put me in a being
that has no trouble seeing
that whatever I am feeling
He is worthy to be praised.

Ian Stuart Smale, b. 1949

213

1 I worship You, O Lord,
for You have raised me up;
I cried to You for help,
and You restored my life.
You brought me back from death
and saved me from the grave.

2 Sing praises to the Lord,
all those who know His name:
for while His wrath is brief,
His favour knows no end.
Though tears may flow at night,
the morning brings new joy.

3 I said, 'I am so strong
I never shall be moved!'
But You, Lord, shook my life —
my heart was in distress.
I cried for You to help
and pleaded for Your grace:

4 My mourning You have turned
to dancing and to joy;
my sadness You dispelled
as gladness filled my soul.
And so I'll sing Your praise,
my God, through all my days!

James Edward Seddon, 1915–19
from Psalm

214

1 Jesus is the name we honour;
Jesus is the name we praise.
Majestic Name above all other
names,
the highest heaven and earth
proclaim
that Jesus is our God.
We will glorify,
we will lift Him high,
we will give Him honour and
praise.
We will glorify …

2 Jesus is the name we worship;
Jesus is the name we trust.
He is the King above all other
kings,
let all creation stand and sing
that Jesus is our God.

3 Jesus is the Father's splendour;
Jesus is the Father's joy.
He will return to reign in
majesty,
and every eye at last will see
that Jesus is our God.

Phil Lawson-Johnsto

211 Words: © Harper Collins Religious. Administered by CopyCare Ltd, PO Box 77, Hailsham, East Sussex. BN27 3EF
212 Words and Music: © 1985 Thankyou Music. Administered (UK and Europe) by Kingsway Music <tym@kingsway.co.uk>. Used by permission.
213 Words: © Representatives of the late James Edward Seddon / Jubilee Hymns, 4 Thorne Park Road, Chelston, Torquay TQ2 6RX Used by permission.
214 Words and Music: © 1991 Thankyou Music. Administered (UK and Europe) by Kingsway Music <tym@kingsway.co.uk>. Used by permission.

215

1 Jesus is Lord! Creation's voice
proclaims it,
for by His power each tree and
flower was planned and
made.
Jesus is Lord! The universe
declares it —
sun, moon and stars in heaven
cry: 'Jesus is Lord!'
Jesus is Lord! Jesus is Lord!
Praise Him with alleluias,
for Jesus is Lord!

2 Jesus is Lord! Yet from His
throne eternal
in flesh He came to die in pain
on Calvary's tree.
Jesus is Lord! From Him all life
proceeding —
yet gave His life a ransom thus
setting us free.

3 Jesus is Lord! O'er sin the
mighty conqueror;
from death He rose, and all His
foes shall own His name.
Jesus is Lord! God sent His Holy
Spirit
to show by works of power that
Jesus is Lord!

David John Mansell, *b.* 1936

216

1 Jesus! the name high over all
in hell or earth or sky;
angels again before it fall
and devils fear and fly.

2 Jesus! The name to sinners dear,
the name to sinners given;
it scatters all their guilty fear,
it turns their hell to heaven.

3 Jesus the prisoner's fetters breaks
and bruises Satan's head;
power into strengthless souls He
speaks
and life into the dead.

4 O that the world might taste and
see
the riches of His grace!
The arms of love that welcome
me
would all mankind embrace.

5 His righteousness alone I show,
His saving grace proclaim;
this is my work on earth below,
to cry, 'Behold the Lamb!'

6 Happy if with my final breath
I may but gasp His name,
preach Him to all, and cry in
death,
'Christ Jesus is the Lamb!'

* The last line of each verse is repeated.

Charles Wesley, 1707–1788
altered Compilers of *Glory to God*, 1994

217

1 King of glory, King of peace,
I will love You;
and that love may never cease,
I will move You.
You have granted my request,
You have heard me;
You have helped me when
oppressed,
You have spared me.

2 Therefore with my utmost art
I will sing You,
deepest love within my heart
I will bring You.
Though my sins against me cried,
You did clear me;
and alone, when they replied,
You did hear me.

3 Seven whole days, not one in
seven,
I will praise You,
in my heart, though not in
heaven,
I will raise You.
Small it is, in this poor sort
to enrol You;
all eternity's too short
to extol You.

George Herbert, 1593–1633
adapted Gaetano Raphael (Anthony) Petti,
1932–1985

218

1 Let all the world in every corner
sing,
'My God and King!'
The heavens are not too high,
His praise may thither fly;
the earth is not too low,
His praises there may grow.
Let all the world in every corner
sing,
'My God and King!'

215 Words and Music: © 1979 Authentic Publishing. Administered by CopyCare Ltd, PO Box 77, Hailsham, East Sussex. BN27 3EF
217 Words: © 1971 Faber Music Ltd, 3 Queen Square, London. WC1N 3AU Reprinted from *New Catholic Hymnal* by permission.

2 Let all the world in every corner
      sing,
   'My God and King!'
   The Church with psalms must
      shout,
   no door can keep them out;
   but, above all, the heart
   must bear the longest part.
   Let all the world in every corner
      sing,
   'My God and King!'

                        George Herbert, 1593–1633

219

1 My heart will sing to You because
      of Your great love,
   a love so rich, so pure, a love
      beyond compare;
   the wilderness, the barren place,
   become a blessing in the warmth
      of Your embrace.

2 When earthly wisdom dims the
      light of knowing You,
   or if my search for understanding
      clouds Your way,
   to You I fly, my hiding-place,
   where revelation is beholding
      face to face.

   May my heart sing Your praise for
      ever,
   may my voice lift Your name, my
      God;
   may my soul know no other
      treasure
   than Your love, than Your love.

                        Robin Mark

220

1 My Jesus, my Saviour,
   Lord, there is none like You.
   All of my days I want to praise
   the wonders of Your mighty love.
   My comfort, my shelter,
   tower of refuge and strength,
   let every breath, all that I am,
   never cease to worship You.
   Shout to the Lord all the earth, let
      us sing,
   power and majesty, praise to the
      King.
   Mountains bow down and the seas
      will roar at the sound of Your
      name.

I sing for joy at the work of Your
   hands,
for ever I'll love You, for ever I'll
   stand.
Nothing compares to the promise
   have in You.

                        Darlene Zsche

221

1 O for a thousand tongues to sing
   my great Redeemer's praise,
   the glories of my God and King,
   the triumphs of His grace!

2 Jesus, the name that charms our
      fears
   and bids our sorrows cease;
   this music in the sinner's ears
   is life and health and peace.

3 He breaks the power of cancelled
      sin,
   He sets the prisoner free;
   His blood can make the foulest
      clean,
   His blood availed for me.

4 He speaks — and, listening to H
      voice,
   new life the dead receive,
   the mournful broken hearts
      rejoice,
   the humble poor believe.

5 Hear Him, you deaf! His praise,
      you dumb,
   your loosened tongues employ;
   you blind, now see your Saviour
      come;
   and leap, you lame, for joy!

6 My gracious Master and my God
   assist me to proclaim
   and spread through all the earth
      abroad
   the honours of Your name.

                        Charles Wesley, 1707–17
                                          alter

222

1 O God beyond all praising,
   we worship You today
   and sing the love amazing
   that songs cannot repay;
   for we can only wonder
   at every gift You send,
   at blessings without number
   and mercies without end:

we lift our hearts before You
and wait upon Your word,
we honour and adore You,
our great and mighty Lord.

2 Then hear, O gracious Saviour,
accept the love we bring,
that we who know Your favour
may serve You as our King;
and whether our tomorrows
be filled with good or ill,
we'll triumph through our
  sorrows
and rise to bless You still:
to marvel at Your beauty
and glory in Your ways,
and make a joyful duty
our sacrifice of praise!

Michael Arnold Perry, 1942–1996

223

1 O Lord our God, how majestic is
  Your name,
the earth is filled with Your glory.
O Lord our God, You are robed
  in majesty,
You've set Your glory above the
  heavens.
  We will magnify, we will magnify
  the Lord enthroned in Zion;
  We will magnify, we will magnify
  the Lord enthroned in Zion.

2 O Lord our God, You have
  established a throne,
You reign in righteousness and
  splendour.
O Lord our God, the skies are
  ringing with Your praise,
soon those on earth will come to
  worship.

3 O Lord our God, the world was
  made at Your command,
in You all things now hold
  together.
Now to Him who sits on the
  throne and to the Lamb,
be praise and glory and power
  for ever.

Phil Lawson-Johnston

224

1 O praise the Lord, you servants
  of the Lord:
O praise His name; His lordly
  honour sing;
let us adore; to You glad homage
  bring;

honouring You, our God to be
  adored
for Your great glory, Sovereign,
  Lord and King.

2 Father of Christ — of Him whose
  work was done,
when by His death He took our
  sins away —
to You belongs all worship, day
  by day,
yea, Holy Father, everlasting Son,
and Spirit blest, all praise be
  Yours for aye!
Amen.

Apostolic Constitutions, Greek, 3rd century
translated George Ratcliffe Woodward, 1848–1934
Songs of Syon, 1910
revised Compilers of *BBC Hymn Book*, 1951
and Compilers

225

Praise Him on the trumpet, the
  psaltery and harp,
praise Him on the timbrel and
  the dance,
praise Him with stringed
  instruments too.
Praise Him on the loud cymbals,
Praise Him on the loud cymbals,
let everything that has breath
  praise the Lord.

Hallelujah, praise the Lord,
Hallelujah, praise the Lord,
let everything that has breath
  praise the Lord.
Hallelujah, praise the Lord,
Hallelujah, praise the Lord,
let everything that has breath
  praise the Lord.

John Kennett
from Psalm 150

226

1 Praise Him, praise Him,
everybody praise Him —
He is love, He is love;
praise Him, praise Him,
everybody praise Him —
God is love, God is love!

2 Thank Him, thank Him,
everybody thank Him —
He is love, He is love;
thank Him, thank Him,
everybody thank Him —
God is love, God is love!

3   Love Him, love Him,
    everybody love Him —
    He is love, He is love;
    love Him, love Him,
    everybody love Him —
    God is love, God is love!

4   Alleluia,
    glory, alleluia!
    He is love, He is love;
    alleluia,
    glory, alleluia!
    God is love, God is love!

Anonymous, c. 1890 — 'S.P.V.'
The Hymnal for Boys and Girls, 1935
adapted Jubilate Hymns

227

1   Praise, my soul, the King of
        heaven,
    to His feet your tribute bring;
    ransomed, healed, restored,
        forgiven,
    who like me His praise should
        sing?
    Praise Him!   Praise Him!
    Praise Him!   Praise Him!
    Praise the everlasting King.

2   Praise Him for His grace and
        favour
    to our fathers in distress;
    praise Him, still the same for
        ever,
    slow to anger, swift to bless.
    Praise Him!   Praise Him!
    Praise Him!   Praise Him!
    glorious in His faithfulness.

3   WOMEN:
    Father-like He tends and spares
        us,
    well our human frame He
        knows;
    in His hands He gently bears us,
    rescues us from all our foes.
    ALL:
    Praise Him!   Praise Him!
    Praise Him!   Praise Him!
    widely as His mercy flows.

4   Frail as summer's flower we
        flourish;
    blows the wind and it is gone;
    but, while mortals rise and
        perish,
    God endures unchanging on.
    Praise Him!   Praise Him!
    Praise Him!   Praise Him!
    Praise the high eternal One.

5   Angels, help us to adore Him;
    you behold Him face to face;
    sun and moon, bow down before
        Him,
    all who dwell in time and space.
    Praise Him!   Praise Him!
    Praise Him!   Praise Him!
    Praise with us the God of grace.

Henry Francis Lyte, 1793–184
from Psalm 10
adapted Compilers of *Praise!* 200

228

1   Praise the Lord in the rhythm of
        your music,
    praise the Lord in the freedom o
        your dance,
    praise the Lord in the country
        and the city,
    praise Him in the living of your
        life!

2   Praise the Lord on the organ and
        piano,
    praise the Lord on guitar and on
        the drums,
    praise the Lord on the
        tambourine and cymbals,
    praise Him in the singing of you
        song!

3   Praise the Lord with the
        movement of your bodies,
    praise the Lord with the clapping
        of your hands,
    praise the Lord with your poetry
        and painting,
    praise Him in the acting of your
        play!

4   Praise the Lord in the feeding of
        the hungry,
    praise the Lord in the healing of
        disease,
    praise the Lord as you show His
        love in action,
    praise Him in your caring for the
        poor!

5   Praise the Lord, every nation,
        every people,
    praise the Lord, men and
        women, old and young,
    praise the Lord, let us celebrate
        together,
    praise Him everything in heaven
        and earth!

Peter Casey, b. 194
alter

PRAISE

229

1 Praise the Lord of heaven,
  praise Him in the height;
  praise Him, all His angels,
  praise Him, hosts of light.
  Sun and moon together,
  shining stars aflame,
  planets in their courses,
  magnify His name!

2 Earth and ocean praise Him;
  mountains, hills and trees;
  fire and hail and tempest,
  wind and storm and seas.
  Praise Him, fields and forests,
  birds on flashing wings,
  praise Him, beasts and cattle,
  all created things.

3 Now by prince and people
  let His praise be told;
  praise Him, men and maidens;
  praise Him, young and old.
  He the Lord of glory!
  We His praise proclaim!
  High above all heavens
  magnify His name!

Timothy Dudley-Smith, b. 1926
from Psalm 148

230

1 Praise the God of our salvation,
  all life long your voices raise,
  stir your hearts to adoration,
  set your souls to sing His praise!

2 Turn to Him, His help entreating;
  only in His mercy trust:
  human pomp and power are
      fleeting;
  mortal flesh is born for dust.

3 Thankful hearts His praise have
      sounded
  down the ages long gone by:
  happy they whose hopes are
      founded
  in the God of earth and sky!

4 Faithful Lord of all things living,
  by His bounty all are blessed;
  bread to hungry bodies giving,
  justice to the long-oppressed.

5 For the strength of our salvation,
  light and life and length of days,
  praise the King of all creation,
  set your souls to sing His praise!

Timothy Dudley-Smith, b. 1926
from Psalm 146

231

1 Praise the Lord, His glories show,
      Alleluia!
  all that lives on earth below,
      Alleluia!
  angels round His throne above,
      Alleluia!
  all who see and share His love.
      Alleluia!

2 Earth to heaven and heaven to
      earth, *Alleluia!*
  tell His wonders, sing His worth;
      Alleluia!
  age to age and shore to shore,
      Alleluia!
  praise Him, praise Him
      evermore! *Alleluia!*

3 Praise the Lord, His mercies
      trace; *Alleluia!*
  praise His providence and grace,
      Alleluia!
  all that He for us has done,
      Alleluia!
  all He gives us in His Son!
      Alleluia!

4 Strings and voices, hands and
      hearts, *Alleluia!*
  in the concert play your parts;
      Alleluia!
  all that breathe, your Lord adore,
      Alleluia!
  praise Him, praise Him
      evermore! *Alleluia!*

Henry Francis Lyte, 1793–1847

232

1 Praise the Lord, you heavens,
      adore Him,
  praise Him, angels in the height!
  Sun and moon, rejoice before
      Him;
  praise Him, all you stars and
      light!

2 Praise the Lord, for He has
      spoken:
  worlds His mighty voice obeyed;
  laws, which never shall be
      broken,
  for their guidance He has made.

3 Praise the Lord, for He is
      glorious!
  Never shall His promise fail.
  God has made His saints
      victorious,
  sin and death shall not prevail.

4   Praise the God of our salvation!
    Hosts on high, His power
        proclaim;
    heaven and earth and all
        creation,
    praise and glorify His name!

Foundling Hospital Collection 1796
from Psalm 148

233

1   Praise to the Lord,
    the Almighty, the King of
        creation!
    O my soul, praise Him,
    for He is your health and
        salvation!
    Come, all who hear;
    brothers and sisters, draw near,
    praise Him in glad adoration!

2   Praise to the Lord,
    above all things so mightily
        reigning;
    keeping us safe at His side,
    and so gently sustaining.
    Have you not seen
    all you have needed has been
    met by His gracious ordaining?

3   Praise to the Lord,
    who shall prosper our work and
        defend us;
    surely His goodness and mercy
    shall daily attend us.
    Ponder anew
    what the Almighty can do
    who with His love will befriend
        us.

4   Praise to the Lord —
    O let all that is in me adore Him!
    All that has life and breath,
    come now with praises before
        Him!
    Let the 'Amen!'
    sound from His people again —
    gladly we praise and adore Him!

Joachim Neander, 1650–1680
translated Catherine Winkworth, 1827–1878
and others

234

1   Sing of the Lord's goodness,
        Father of all wisdom,
    come to Him and bless His name.
    Mercy He has shown us, His love
        is for ever,
    faithful to the end of days.

*Come then all you nations,
sing of your Lord's goodness,
melodies of praise and thanks to
    God;
ring out the Lord's glory,
praise Him with your music,
worship Him and bless His name.*

2   Power He has wielded, honour is
        His garment,
    risen from the snares of death.
    His word He has spoken, one
        bread He has broken,
    new life He now gives to all.

3   Courage in our darkness, comfort
        in our sorrow,
    Spirit of our God most high;
    solace for the weary, pardon for
        the sinner,
    splendour of the living God!

4   Praise Him with your singing,
        praise Him with the trumpet,
    praise God with the lute and
        harp;
    praise Him with the cymbals,
        praise Him with your dancing,
    praise God till the end of days.

Ernest Sands, *b.* 1949

235

1   Sing praise to the Lord!
    Praise Him in the height;
    rejoice in His Word
    you angels of light:
    you heavens, adore Him
    by whom you were made,
    and worship Him
    in brightness arrayed.

2   Sing praise to the Lord!
    Praise Him upon earth
    in tuneful accord,
    you saints of new birth:
    praise Him who has brought you
    His grace from above;
    praise Him who has taught you
    to sing of His love.

3   Sing praise to the Lord!
    All things that give sound,
    each jubilant chord
    re-echo around:
    loud organs, His glory
    proclaim in deep tone,
    and sweet harp, the story
    of what He has done.

4 Sing praise to the Lord!
   Thanksgiving and song
   to Him be outpoured
   all ages along:
   for love in creation,
   for heaven restored,
   for grace of salvation,
   sing praise to the Lord!

* (Amen, Amen.)

* These words are sung if the unison setting
   is used for v. 4.

Henry Williams Baker, 1821–1877
from Psalm 150

236

1 Sing to God new songs of
      worship —
   all His deeds are marvellous;
   He has brought salvation to us
   with His hand and holy arm:
   He has shown to all the nations
   righteousness and saving power;
   He recalled His truth and mercy
   to His people Israel.

2 Sing to God new songs of
      worship —
   earth has seen His victory;
   let the lands of earth be joyful
   praising Him with thankfulness:
   sound upon the harp with
      praises,
   play to Him with melody;
   let the trumpets sound His
      triumph,
   show your joy to God the King!

3 Sing to God new songs of
      worship —
   let the sea now make a noise;
   all on earth and in the waters
   sound your praises to the Lord:
   let the hills rejoice together,
   let the rivers clap their hands,
   for with righteousness and justice
   He will come to judge the earth.

Michael Alfred Baughen, b. 1930
from Psalm 98

237

1 Songs of praise the angels sang,
   heaven with alleluias rang,
   when creation was begun,
   when God spoke and it was
      done.

2 Songs of praise awoke the morn
   when the Prince of Peace was
      born;
   songs of praise arose when He
   captive led captivity.

3 Heaven and earth must pass
      away,
   songs of praise shall crown that
      day;
   God will make new heavens and
      earth,
   songs of praise shall greet their
      birth.

4 And shall human voice be dumb
   till that glorious kingdom come?
   No, the Church delights to raise
   psalms and hymns and songs of
      praise.

5 Saints below, with heart and
      voice,
   still in songs of praise rejoice,
   learning here, by faith and love,
   songs of praise to sing above.

6 Borne upon their final breath,
   songs of praise shall conquer
      death;
   then, amidst eternal joy,
   songs of praise their powers
      employ.

James Montgomery, 1771–1854
altered

238

1 Stand up and bless the Lord,
   you people of His choice;
   stand up and praise the Lord
      your God
   with heart and soul and voice.

2 Though high above all praise,
   above all blessing high,
   who would not fear His holy
      name,
   give thanks and glorify?

3 O for the living flame
   from His own altar brought,
   to touch our lips, our minds
      inspire,
   and wing to heaven our thought!

4 God is our strength and song,
   and His salvation ours;
   then be His love in Christ
      proclaimed
   with all our ransomed powers.

THE TEMPLE

5 Stand up and bless the Lord,
the Lord your God adore;
stand up and praise His glorious
name
both now and evermore.

James Montgomery, 1771–1854
altered

239

1 Thank You for saving me; what
can I say?
You are my everything, I will
sing Your praise.
You shed Your blood for me;
what can I say?
You took my sin and shame, a
sinner called by name.
*Great is the Lord. Great is the
Lord.*
*For we know Your truth has set us
free;*
You've set Your hope in me.

2 Mercy and grace are mine,
forgiven is my sin;
Jesus, my only hope, the Saviour
of the world.
'Great is the Lord,' we cry; God,
let Your Kingdom come.
Your Word has let me see, thank
You for saving me.
Great is the Lord …

Thank You for saving me; what
can I say?

Martin J. Smith

240

1 The God of Abraham praise
who reigns enthroned above;
the Ancient of eternal Days
and God of love!
The Lord, the great I AM,
by earth and heaven confessed —
we bow before His holy name
for ever blessed.

2 To Him we lift our voice
at whose supreme command
from death we rise to gain the
joys
at His right hand:
we all on earth forsake —
its wisdom, fame, and power;
the God of Israel we shall make
our shield and tower.

3 He by His name has sworn —
on this we shall depend,
and as on eagle's wings upborne
to heaven ascend:
there we shall see His face,
His power we shall adore,
and sing the wonders of His
grace
for evermore.

4 There rules the Lord our King,
the Lord our righteousness,
victorious over death and sin,
the Prince of Peace:
on Zion's sacred height
His Kingdom He maintains,
and glorious with His saints in
light
for ever reigns.

5 Triumphant hosts on high
give thanks eternally
and 'Holy, holy, holy,' cry,
'great Trinity!'
Hail Abraham's God and ours!
One mighty hymn we raise,
all power and majesty be Yours
and endless praise! Amen.

Thomas Olivers, 1725–1799
based on the Jewish Yigdal
adapted Jubilate Hymns

241

1 The Lord is King! lift up your
voice,
O earth, and all you heavens,
rejoice!
From world to world the joy shall
ring,
'The Lord omnipotent is King!'

2 The Lord is King! who then
shall dare
resist His will, distrust His care
or murmur at His wise decrees,
or doubt His royal promises?

3 The Lord is King! child of the
dust,
the Judge of all the earth is just;
holy and true are all His ways;
let every creature speak His
praise!

4 Come, make your wants, your
burdens known;
Christ will present them at the
throne;
and He is at the Father's side,
the Man of love, the Crucified.

6 One Lord, one empire, all
      secures;
   He reigns, and life and death are
      Yours;
   through earth and heaven one
      song shall ring,
   'The Lord omnipotent is King!'

   Josiah Conder, 1789–1885
   adapted Compilers, and others

242

1 To God be the glory, great things
      He has done!
   so loved He the world that He
      gave us His Son,
   who yielded His life an
      atonement for sin,
   who opened the life-gate that all
      may go in:
   Praise the Lord! Praise the Lord!
   Let the earth hear His voice!
   Praise the Lord! Praise the Lord!
   Let the people rejoice!
   O come to the Father, through Jesus
      the Son;
   and give Him the glory — great
      things He has done!

2 O perfect redemption, the
      purchase of blood,
   to every believer the promise of
      God!
   For every offender who truly
      believes,
   that moment from Jesus a pardon
      receives:

3 Great things He has taught us,
      great things He has done,
   and great our rejoicing through
      Jesus the Son;
   but purer, and higher, and greater
      will be
   the joy and the wonder, when
      Jesus we see:

   Frances Jane (Fanny) Crosby, 1820–1915

243

1 To God our great salvation
   a triumph-song we raise,
   with hymns of adoration
   and everlasting praise.
   That Name beyond all naming,
   from age to age adored,
   we lift on high, proclaiming
   the greatness of the Lord.

2 Declare in song and story
   the wonders we confess,
   who hail the King of glory
   the Lord our righteousness.
   In loving kindness caring
   His mercies stand displayed,
   forgiving and forbearing
   to all His hand has made.

3 His kingdom knows no ending,
   enthroned in light sublime,
   His sovereign power extending
   beyond all space and time.
   To us and all things living
   He comes in word and deed,
   forbearing and forgiving,
   to meet us in our need.

4 The King of all creation
   is near to those who call;
   the God of our salvation
   has stooped to save us all.
   Lift high your hearts and voices,
   His praises sound again;
   in God His earth rejoices
   for evermore. Amen!

   Timothy Dudley-Smith, b. 1926
   from Psalm 145

244

1 To the name of our salvation
   praise and honour let us pay,
   which for many a generation
   hid in God's foreknowledge lay,
   but with holy exultation
   we may sing aloud today.

2 Jesus is the name we treasure,
   name beyond what words can
      tell;
   name of gladness, name of
      pleasure,
   ear and heart delighting well;
   name of sweetness passing
      measure,
   saving us from sin and hell.

3 Name that still, whoever
      preaches,
   speaks like music to the ear;
   who in prayer this name
      beseeches
   finds the strongest comfort near;
   who its perfect wisdom reaches
   heavenly joy possesses here.

4 Name of majesty, exceeding
   every other power or name;
   name of health, for sinners
      needing

rescue in a world of shame;
name in which the Church is
    pleading,
sight to blind, and feet to lame.

5   Jesus, we in love adoring,
    Your most holy name revere,
    Lord of all, Your grace imploring
    so to write it in us here
    that hereafter, heavenward
        soaring,
    we may sing with angels there.

            15th century
    translated Compilers of
    Hymns Ancient and Modern, 1861
    translated John Mason Neale, 1818–1866

245

1   We are a moment, You are
        forever,
    Lord of the ages, God before time.
    We are a vapour, You are eternal,
    love everlasting reigning on high.

    Holy, holy, Lord God Almighty,
    worthy is the Lamb who was slain:
    highest praises, honour and glory
    be unto Your name, be unto Your
        name.

2   We are the broken, You are the
        healer,
    Jesus redeemer, mighty to save.
    You are the love song we'll sing
        forever,
    bowing before You, blessing Your
        name.

    Holy, holy, Lord God Almighty,
    worthy is the Lamb who was slain:
    highest praises, honour and glory
    be unto Your name, be unto Your
        name,
    be unto Your name.

            Lynn DeShazo and Gary Sadler

246

1   You servants of God, your master
        proclaim,
    and publish abroad His
        wonderful name;
    the name all-victorious of Jesus
        extol,
    His kingdom is glorious, and
        rules over all.

2   God rules in the height, almighty
        to save —
    though hid from our sight, His
        presence we have;

the great congregation His
    triumph shall sing,
ascribing salvation to Jesus our
    King.

3   'Salvation to God who sits on the
        throne!'
    let all cry aloud, and honour the
        Son;
    the praises of Jesus the angels
        proclaim,
    fall down on their faces and
        worship the Lamb.

4   Then let us adore and give Him
        His right:
    all glory and power, all wisdom
        and might,
    all honour and blessing — with
        angels above —
    and thanks never ceasing, and
        infinite love.

*   (Amen, Amen.)

*   *These words are sung if the unison setting*
    by Parry is used for v. 4.

            Charles Wesley, 1707–1788
            altered

Also suitable:
Fairest Lord Jesus   19
Fill now my life   537
God's love is deeper   117
Name of all majesty   352
Tell out my soul   301
W are singing to You, Lord   358
What a wonderful Sabiour is Jesus   360

THE TEMPLE PRAYER

247

1   Come, my soul, your plea
        prepare,
    Jesus loves to answer prayer;
    He Himself has bid you pray,
    therefore will not turn away.

2   You are coming to a King;
    large petitions with you bring,
    for His grace and power are such,
    none can ever ask too much.

3   With my burden I begin:
    Lord, remove this load of sin;
    let Your blood, for sinners spilt,
    set my conscience free from guilt.

4 Lord, I come to You for rest,
  be my heart's most welcome
    guest;
  there Your blood-bought right
    maintain
  and without a rival reign.

5 While I am a pilgrim here,
  let Your love my spirit cheer;
  as my guide, my guard, my
    friend,
  lead me to my journey's end.

6 Show me what I have to do;
  every hour my strength renew;
  let me live a life of faith;
  let me die Your people's death.

John Newton, 1725–1807
altered

248

1 Did you ever talk to God above?
  Tell Him that you need a friend
    to love.
  Pray in Jesus' name believing
    that God answers prayer.

2 Have you told Him all your cares
    and woes?
  Every tiny little fear He knows.
  You can know He'll always hear
    and He will answer prayer.

3 You can whisper in a crowd to
    Him.
  You can cry when you're alone to
    Him.
  You don't have to pray out loud
    to Him; He knows your
    thoughts.

4 On a lofty mountain peak, He's
    there.
  In a meadow by a stream, He's
    there.
  Anywhere on earth you go He's
    been there from the start.

5 Find the answer in His Word; it's
    true.
  You'll be strong because He walks
    with you.
  By His faithfulness He'll change
    you too. God answers prayer.

Frances Towle Rath

249

1 Father God in heaven, Lord most
    high:
  hear Your children's prayer, Lord
    most high:

hallowed be Your Name, Lord
    most high —
  O Lord, hear our prayer.

2 May Your kingdom come here on
    earth;
  may Your will be done here on
    earth,
  as it is in heaven so on earth —
  O Lord, hear our prayer.

3 Give us daily bread day by day,
  and forgive our sins day by day,
  as we too forgive day by day —
  O Lord, hear our prayer.

4 Lead us in Your way, make us
    strong;
  when temptations come make us
    strong;
  save us all from sin, keep us
    strong —
  O Lord, hear our prayer.

5 All things come from You, all are
    Yours —
  kingdom, glory, power, all are
    Yours;
  take our lives and gifts, all are
    Yours —
  O Lord, hear our prayer.

James Edward Seddon, 1915–1983
The Lord's Prayer

250

1 I can talk to God,
  He will hear my prayers.
  I can talk to God,
  for I know He cares.
  He will listen when I say,
  'Thank You for Your love today,
  for Your help in every way,
  oh, thank You, God.'

2 I can talk to God,
  He will hear my prayers.
  I can talk to God,
  for I know He cares.
  He will listen when I say,
  'I have done wrong things today,
  please forgive me now I pray,
  forgive me, God.'

3 I can talk to God,
  He will hear my prayers.
  I can talk to God,
  for I know He cares.
  He will listen when I say,
  'Please help all my friends today,
  help them in their work and play,
  please help them, God.'

J. Sibley

251

1 Lord, teach us how to pray aright
with reverence and with fear:
though dust and ashes in Your sight,
we may, we must draw near.

2 We perish if we cease from prayer:
O grant us power to pray;
and when to meet You we prepare,
Lord, meet us by the way.

3 God of all grace, we bring to You
a broken contrite heart;
give what Your eye delights to view —
truth in the inward part;

4 Faith in the only sacrifice
that can for sin atone;
to place our hopes, to fix our eyes,
on Christ, and Christ alone;

5 Patience to watch and weep and wait,
whatever You may send;
courage that will not hesitate
to trust You to the end.

6 Give these, and then Your will be done;
thus, strengthened with all might,
we, through Your Spirit and Your Son,
shall pray, and pray aright.

James Montgomery, 1771–1854
altered

252

1 O God, hear me calling and answer, I pray!
No distance can silence the words that I say,
no mountain, no ocean can hinder my prayer
when deep is my sorrow and dark my despair.

2 When trouble comes near me and enemies taunt,
Lord, You are the fortress no evil can daunt;
and safe on the Rock that is higher than I
Your strength is my hope as You answer my cry.

3 For Lord You have heard all the vows I have made —
my thoughts and intentions when homage I paid;
with all who have lived by the fear of Your name,
Lord, grant all my prayers as Your praise I proclaim.

4 I long for the day when Your dwelling is mine,
Your wings for a shelter, Your presence a shrine;
I praise You on earth for Your mercy and grace:
what blessings I'll sing when I look on Your face!

Paul Wigmore, *b.* 1925
Psalm 61

253

1 Our heavenly Father, through Your Son,
all hallowed be Your Name;
Your Kingdom come, Your will be done
in heaven and earth the same.

2 You are the great provider, Lord,
of bread by which we live.
We are the great forgetters, Lord,
of thanks for all You give.

3 You are the great forgiver, Lord,
of all our constant sin.
We are the unforgivers, Lord,
of all our kith and kin.

4 You are the great deliverer, Lord,
from Satan's evil snares.
Give us the faith that trusts You, Lord,
to banish all our cares.

5 You are the great example, where
You give and You forgive;
so teach us, Lord, to live Your prayer,
that we may truly live.

Patrick Stephen, 1914–2000
The Lord's Prayer

254

*Prayer is like a telephone
for us to talk to Jesus.
Prayer is like a telephone
for us to talk to God.
Prayer is like a telephone
for us to talk to Jesus.
Pick it up and use it every day.*

PRAYER

We can shout out loud,
we can whisper softly,
we can make no noise at all;
but He'll always hear our call.

. . . . . . is like a telephone
for us to talk to Jesus.
. . . . . . is like a telephone
for us to talk to God.
. . . . . . is like a telephone
for us to talk to Jesus.
Pick it up and use it every day.

We can . . .

. . . . . . is like a . . . . . .
for us to talk to Jesus.
. . . . . . is like a . . . . . .
for us to talk to God.
. . . . . . is like a . . . . . .
for us to talk to Jesus.
Pick it up and use it every day.

We can . . .

. . . . . . is like a . . . . . .
for us to talk to . . . . . .
. . . . . . is like a . . . . . .
for us to talk to . . . . . .
. . . . . . is like a . . . . . .
for us to talk to . . . . . .
Pick it up and use it every day.
Pick it up and use it every day.
Pick it up and use it every day.

At the repeat, sing the chorus three times.
The first time, omit the word *Prayer;*
the second time, omit the words *Prayer* and
telephone;
the third time, omit the words *Prayer,*
telephone and *Jesus / God.*

Paul Crouch, *b.* 1963
and David Mudie, *b.* 1961

255

1   Prayer is the soul's supreme
        desire
    expressed in thought or word;
    the burning of a hidden fire,
    a longing for the Lord.

2   Prayer is the simplest sound we
        teach
    when children learn God's
        name;
    and yet it is the noblest speech
    that human lips can frame.

3   Prayer is the secret battleground
    where victories are won;
    by prayer the will of God is
        found
    and work for Him begun.

4   Prayer is the Christian's vital
        breath,
    the Christian's native air,
    his watchword at the gates of
        death;
    he enters heaven with prayer.

5   Prayer is the Church's glorious
        song,
    her task and joy supreme;
    we name our Lord in every
        tongue,
    and praise is all our theme.

6   Jesus, by whom we come to God,
    the true and living way,
    the humble path of prayer You
        trod,
    Lord, teach us how to pray.

James Montgomery, 1771–1854
adapted Jubilate Hymns

256

Talk to God and share with Him
the thoughts you have each day.
Let Him know what's on your
*   mind —*
He loves to hear you pray.

1   With 'Sorry', 'Please' and 'Thank
        You',
    there's such a lot to say.
    God loves to hear you praying
    at any time of day.

2   In any place you go to
    our Father God is there;
    He knows what you are thinking,
    He listens to each prayer.

Margaret V. Old, 1932–2001

257

1   What a friend we have in Jesus,
    all our sins and griefs to bear!
    What a privilege to carry
    everything to God in prayer!
    O what peace we often forfeit,
    O what needless pain we bear —
    all because we do not carry
    everything to God in prayer!

2   Have we trials and temptations?
    Is there trouble anywhere?
    We should never be discouraged:
    take it to the Lord in prayer!
    Can we find a friend so faithful,
    who will all our sorrows share?
    Jesus knows our every
        weakness —
    take it to the Lord in prayer!

3   Are we weak and heavy-laden,
    burdened with a load of care?
    Jesus only is our refuge,
    take it to the Lord in prayer!
    Do your friends despise, forsake
        you?
    Take it to the Lord in prayer!
    In His arms He'll take and shield
        you,
    you will find His comfort there.

Joseph Scriven, 1819–1886
adapted Peter J. Horrobin, *b.* 1943
and Greg P. Leavers, *b.* 1952

258

1   When our confidence is shaken
    in beliefs we thought secure;
    when the spirit in its sickness
    seeks but cannot find a cure:
    God is active in the tensions
    of a faith not yet mature.

2   Solar systems, void of meaning,
    freeze the spirit into stone;
    always our researches lead us
    to the ultimate Unknown:
    faith must die, or come full circle
    to its source in God alone.

3   In the discipline of praying,
    when it's hardest to believe;
    in the drudgery of caring,
    when it's not enough to grieve:
    faith maturing, learns acceptance
    of the insights we receive.

4   God is love; and He redeems us
    in the Christ we crucify:
    this is God's eternal answer
    to the world's eternal why;
    may we in this faith maturing
    be content to live and die!

Frederick Pratt Green, 1903–2000

259

The Lord's Prayer

Our Father who art in heaven,
hallowed be Thy Name.
Thy kingdom come.
Thy will be done,
on earth as it is in heaven.
Give us this day our daily bread,
and forgive us our trespasses
as we forgive those who trespass
    against us.
And lead us not into temptation
but deliver us from evil:

for Thine is the kingdom,
the power, and the glory,
for ever and ever. Amen.

Liturgical text

260

The Lord's Prayer

Our Father in heaven,
hallowed be Your Name,
Your kingdom come,
Your will be done,
on earth as in heaven.
Give us today our daily bread.
Forgive us our sins
as we forgive those who sin
    against us.
Lead us not into temptation
but deliver us from evil.
For the Kingdom, the power,
and the glory are yours
now and forever. Amen.

Liturgical text

THE TEMPLE
THE BIBLE

261

1   Almighty God, Your word is cast
    like seed into the ground:
    now let the dew of heaven
        descend,
    and righteous fruits abound.

2   Let not the foe of Christ and man
    this holy seed remove:
    but give it root in every heart,
    to bring forth fruits of love.

3   Let not the world's deceitful cares
    the rising plant destroy;
    but let it yield a hundredfold
    the fruits of peace and joy.

4   Oft as the precious seed is sown,
    Your quickening grace bestow;
    that all whose souls the truth
        receive
    its saving power may know.

John Cawood, 1775–1852

262

1   Blessèd are all they,
    all they who do not walk
    in the counsel of the ungodly —
    blessed by God are they,
    they who reject the way,

reject the way of sin
and who turn away from
   scoffing —
blessed by God are they:
but their delight by day and night
is the law of God Almighty.

2   They are like a tree —
a tree that flourishes
being planted by the water —
blessed by God are they,
they will bring forth fruit —
their leaves will wither not,
for in all they do they prosper —
blessed by God are they:
for their delight by day and night
is the law of God Almighty.

3   The ungodly are not so
for they are like the chaff
which the wind blows clean
   away —
the ungodly are not so;
the ungodly will not stand
upon the judgement day
nor belong to God's own
   people —
the ungodly will not stand:
but God knows the way of
   righteous men
and ungodly ways will perish.

4   Blessèd are all they,
all they who do not walk
in the counsel of the ungodly —
blessed by God are they.

Michael Alfred Baughen, b. 1930
from Psalm 1

263

1   Blessed are they
   who listen not to evil counsel,
turn aside
   from every thought of sin:
day and night,
   the law of God their maker
is their joy and meditation,
   well of life within.

2   Blessed are they,
   for as a tree by streams of water
spreads its leaves
   in bountiful displays,
bears and yields
   its ripened fruit in season —
so shall they in every calling
   prosper all their days.

3   Blessed are they
   though sinners like the chaff be
    scattered,
blessed are they
   though winds of judgement
    blow;
from the Lord,
   upon His righteous servants,
loving care and tender mercies
evermore shall flow.

Paul Wigmore, b. 1925
from Psalm 1

264

1   Book of books, our people's
    strength,
statesman's, teacher's, hero's
    treasure,
bringing freedom, spreading
    truth,
shedding light that none can
    measure —
wisdom comes to those who
    know you,
all the best we have we owe you.

2   Thank we those who toiled in
    thought,
many diverse scrolls completing,
poets, prophets, scholars, saints,
each a word from God repeating,
till they came, who told the story
of His Word and showed His
    glory.

3   Praise we God, who has inspired
those whose wisdom still directs
    us:
praise Him for the Word made
    flesh,
for the Spirit who protects us,
light of knowledge, ever burning,
shed on us your deathless
    learning.

Percy Dearmer, 1867–1936

265

1   Break forth, O living light of God,
upon the world's dark hour!
Show us the way the Master trod;
reveal His saving power.

2   Remove the veil of ancient words
their message long obscure;
restore to us Your truth, O God,
and make its meaning sure.

3   O let Your word be light anew
to every nation's life;
unite us in Your will, O Lord,
and end all sinful strife.

4 O may one Lord, one Faith, one
    Word,
  one Spirit lead us still;
  and one great Church go forth in
    might
  to work God's perfect will.

Frank von Christierson, 1900–1996

266

1 Break now the bread of life,
  dear Lord, to me,
  as once You broke the loaves
  beside the sea.
  Beyond the sacred page
  I seek You Lord;
  my spirit longs for You,
  O living Word!

2 You are the bread of life,
  O Lord, to me,
  Your holy word the truth
  that sets me free;
  give me to eat and live
  with You above;
  teach me to love Your truth,
  for You are love.

3 Bless now the truth, dear Lord,
  to me, to me,
  as You did bless the bread
  by Galilee;
  then shall all bondage cease,
  all fetters fall,
  and I shall find my peace,
  my all-in-all.

4 O send Your Spirit, Lord,
  now unto me,
  that He may touch my eyes,
  and make me see;
  show me the truth concealed
  within Your word,
  and in Your book revealed
  I see You Lord.

Mary Artemisia Lathbury, 1841–1913
and Alexander Groves, 1843–1909
altered

267

1 Deep in the shadows of the past,
  far out from settled lands,
  some nomads travelled with
    their God
  across the desert sands.
  The dawn of hope for
    humankind
  was glimpsed by them alone:
  a promise calling them ahead,
  a future yet unknown.

2 While others bowed to changeless
    gods
  they met a mystery:
  God with an uncompleted name,
  'I am what I will be';
  and by their tents, around their
    fires,
  in story, song and law
  they praised, remembered,
    handed on
  a past that promised more.

3 From Abraham to Nazareth
  the promise changed and grew,
  while some, remembering the
    past,
  recorded what they knew,
  and some, in letters or laments,
  in prophecy and praise,
  recovered, held, and re-expressed
  new hope for changing days.

4 For all the writings that survived,
  for leaders, long ago,
  who sifted, chose, and then
    preserved
  the Bible that we know,
  give thanks, and find its promise
    yet
  our comfort, strength, and call,
  the working model for our faith,
  alive with hope for all.

Brian Arthur Wren, b. 1936

268

1 God has spoken — by His
    prophets,
  spoken His unchanging word;
  each from age to age proclaiming
  God the one, the righteous Lord;
  in the world's despair and
    turmoil
  one firm anchor still holds fast:
  God is King, His throne eternal,
  God the first and God the last.

2 God has spoken — by Christ
    Jesus,
  Christ, the everlasting Son;
  brightness of the Father's glory,
  with the Father ever one:
  spoken by the Word incarnate,
  Life, before all time began,
  Light of light, to earth
    descending,
  God, revealed as Son of Man.

3 God is speaking — by His Spirit
  speaking to our hearts again;
  in the age-long word expounding

God's own message, now as then.
Through the rise and fall of
nations
one sure faith is standing fast:
God abides, His word
unchanging,
God the first and God the last.

George Wallace Briggs, 1875–1959

269

1   Heavenly Father, may Your
blessing
rest upon Your children now,
when in praise Your name they
hallow,
when in prayer to You they bow:
in the wondrous story reading
of the Lord of truth and grace,
may they see Your love reflected
in the light of His dear face.

2   May they learn from this great
story
all the arts of friendliness;
truthful speech and honest action,
courage, patience, steadfastness;
how to master self and temper,
how to make their conduct fair;
when to speak and when be
silent,
when to do and when forbear.

3   May His Spirit wise and holy
with His gifts their spirits bless,
make them loving, joyous,
peaceful,
rich in goodness, gentleness,
strong in self-control, and faithful,
kind in thought and deed; for He
teaches, 'What you do for others
you are doing unto me.'

William Charter Piggott, 1872–1943

270

1   Jesus loves me! This I know,
for the Bible tells me so;
little ones to Him belong;
they are weak, but He is strong.
Yes! Jesus loves me!
Yes! Jesus loves me!
Yes! Jesus loves me!
The Bible tells me so.

2   Jesus loves me! He who died
heaven's gate to open wide;
He will wash away my sin,
let His little child come in.

3   Jesus loves me! He will stay
close beside me all the way;
then His little child will take
up to heaven, for His dear sake.

Anna Bartlett Warner, 1820–1915

271

1   Look upon us, blessèd Lord,
take our wandering thoughts and
guide us:
we have come to hear Your
Word:
with Your teaching now provide
us,
that, from earth's distractions
turning,
we Your message may be
learning.

2   For Your Spirit's radiance bright
we, assembled here, are hoping:
if You should withhold the light,
in the dark our souls were
groping:
in word, deed, and thought direct
us:
You, none other can correct us.

3   Brightness of the Father's face,
Light of light, from God
proceeding,
make us ready in this place:
ear and heart await Your leading,
In our study, prayers, and
praising,
may our souls find their
upraising.

Tobias Clausnitzer, 1619–1684
translated Robert A. S. Macalister, 1870–1950

272

1   Lord, Your word shall guide us
and with truth provide us:
teach us to receive it
and with joy believe it.

2   When our foes are near us,
then Your word shall cheer us —
word of consolation,
message of salvation.

3   When the storms distress us
and dark clouds oppress us,
then Your word protects us
and its light directs us.

4   Who can tell the pleasure,
who recount the treasure
by Your word imparted
to the simple-hearted?

5 Word of mercy, giving
   courage to the living;
   word of life, supplying
   comfort to the dying.

6 O that we discerning
   its most holy learning,
   Lord, may love and fear You —
   evermore be near You!

Henry Williams Baker, 1821–1877
adapted Jubilate Hymns

273

1 Speak, Lord, in the stillness,
   speak Your word to me;
   help me now to listen
   in expectancy.

2 Speak, O gracious Master,
   in this quiet hour;
   let me see Your face, Lord,
   feel Your touch of power.

3 For the words You give me,
   they are life indeed;
   living bread from heaven,
   now my spirit feed.

4 Speak, Your servant listens —
   I await Your word;
   let me know Your presence,
   let Your voice be heard!

5 Fill me with the knowledge
   of Your glorious will;
   all Your own good pleasure
   in my life fulfil.

Emily Crawford, 1864–1927
adapted Jubilate Hymns

274

1 Tell me the old, old story
   of unseen things above,
   of Jesus and His glory,
   of Jesus and His love.
   Tell me the story simply,
   as to a little child;
   for I am weak and weary,
   and helpless, and defiled:

   Tell me the old, old story,
   tell me the old, old story,
   tell me the old, old story
   of Jesus and His love.

2 Tell me the story slowly,
   that I may take it in, —
   that wonderful redemption,
   God's remedy for sin.
   Tell me the story often,

for I forget too soon;
the early dew of morning
has passed away at noon:

3 Tell me the story softly,
   with earnest tones and grave;
   remember, I'm the sinner
   whom Jesus came to save.
   Tell me the story always,
   if you would really be,
   in any time of trouble,
   a comforter to me:

4 Tell me the same old story
   when you have cause to fear
   that this world's empty glory
   is costing me too dear.
   Yes, and when that world's glory
   shall dawn upon my soul,
   tell me that old, old story,
   'Christ Jesus makes thee whole.'

Arabella Catherine Hankey, 1834–1911

275

1 Thanks to God whose word was
      spoken
   in the deed that made the earth.
   His the voice that called a nation,
   His the fires that tried her worth.
   God has spoken, God has
      spoken:
   praise Him for His open word.

2 Thanks to God whose Word
      incarnate
   glorified the flesh of man.
   Deeds and words and death and
      rising
   tell the grace in heaven's plan.
   God has spoken, God has
      spoken:
   praise Him for His open word.

3 Thanks to God whose word was
      written
   in the Bible's sacred page,
   record of the revelation
   showing God to every age.
   God has spoken, God has
      spoken:
   praise Him for His open word.

4 Thanks to God whose word is
      published
   in the tongues of every race.
   See its glory undiminished
   by the change of time or place.
   God has spoken, God has
      spoken:
   praise Him for His open word.

5 Thanks to God whose word is
 answered
by the Spirit's voice within.
Here we drink of joy
 unmeasured,
life redeemed from death and
 sin.
God is speaking, God is
 speaking:
praise Him for His open word.

Reginald Thomas Brooks, 1918–1985
slightly altered

276

1 The Bible tells of God's great
 plan
for people everywhere,
that all should learn to live in
 love
and in His kingdom share.

2 He sent His Son, Lord Jesus
 Christ,
to show His love for all,
and many people followed Christ
in answer to His call.

3 As God spoke then to men of old,
so still He speaks today,
we pray that we may learn His
 will
and follow in His way.

W. L. Jenkins

277

1 With all my heart I seek
the true and living way!
Lord, guide these steps of mine
or I shall go astray.

2 Let me not waver now
from simple honesty,
or fail in my resolve
to keep integrity.

3 Your laws and Your commands
remain my great delight;
I speak of them at noon
and ponder them at night.

4 Through youth and through old
 age,
Lord, may I not forget
that in Your matchless word,
there love and truth have met.

David Mowbray, *b.* 1938
after Psalm 119

Also suitable:
Children of Jerusalem   397
Spirit of God, our hearts inspire   468
Spirit of God, unseen as the wind   478
You are the way, to You alone   363

THE TEMPLE
DEDICATION OF GIFTS
OFFERINGS

278

1 Angel voices ever singing
round Your throne of light,
angel music ever ringing
rests not day or night;
thousands only live to bless You
and confess You
Lord of might.

2 Lord, beyond our mortal sight in
 glory far away,
can it be that You delight in
sinners' songs today;
may we know that You are near
 us
and will hear us?
Yes, we may!

3 Yes, we know Your heart rejoices
in each work divine,
using minds and hands and
 voices
in Your great design;
craftsman's art and music's
 measure
for Your pleasure
all combine.

4 Here to You, great God, we offer
praise in harmony,
and for Your acceptance proffer
all unworthily
hearts and minds and hands and
 voices
in our choicest
psalmody.

5 Honour, glory, might and merit
for Your works and ways,
Father, Son and Holy Spirit,
God through endless days!
With the best that You have
 given
earth and heaven
render praise.

Francis Pott, 1832–1909
adapted Jubilate Hymns

279

1   We give You but Your own,
    whate'er the gift may be;
    all that we have is Yours alone,
    a trust, O Lord, and free.

2   May we Your bounties thus
    as stewards true receive,
    and gladly, as You give to us,
    to You our first-fruits give.

William Walsham How, 1823–1897
altered

THE TEMPLE
CLOSE OF SERVICE

280

1   Forth in the peace of Christ we
    go;
    Christ to the world with joy we
    bring;
    Christ in our minds, Christ on
    our lips,
    Christ in our hearts, the world's
    true King.

2   King of our hearts, Christ makes
    us kings;
    kingship with Him His servants
    gain;
    with Christ, the Servant-Lord of
    all,
    Christ's world we serve to share
    Christ's reign.

3   Priests of the world, Christ sends
    us forth
    the world of time to consecrate,
    the world of sin by grace to heal,
    Christ's world in Christ to
    re-create.

4   Christ's are our lips, His word we
    speak;
    prophets are we whose deeds
    proclaim
    Christ's truth in love that we
    may be
    Christ in the world, to spread
    Christ's name.

5   We are the Church; Christ bids
    us show
    that in His Church all nations
    find
    their hearth and home where
    Christ restores
    true peace, true love, to all
    mankind.

James Quinn, b. 1919

281

1   Lord, dismiss us with Your
    blessing,
    fill our hearts with joy and
    peace;
    let us each, Your love possessing,
    triumph in redeeming grace;
    O refresh us, O refresh us,
    travelling through this
    wilderness.

2   Thanks we give, and adoration,
    for Your gospel's joyful sound;
    may the fruits of Your salvation
    in our hearts and lives abound;
    may Your presence, may Your
    presence,
    with us evermore be found.

John Fawcett, 1740–1817
adapted Gaetano Raphael (Anthony) Petti,
1932–1985
altered

282

All praise and thanks to God
the Father now be given,
the Son, and Him who reigns
with them in highest heaven, —
the one, eternal God,
whom earth and heaven adore;
for thus it was, is now,
and shall be evermore. Amen.

Martin Rinkart, 1586–1649
translated Catherine Winkworth, 1827–1878

283

Laud and honour to the Father,
laud and honour to the Son,
laud and honour to the Spirit,
ever Three and ever One,
One in might, and One in glory,
while unending ages run. Amen.

7th or 8th century
translated John Mason Neale, 1818–1866

284

Now to Him who loved us, gave
us
every pledge that love could
give,
freely shed His blood to save us,
gave His life that we might live,
be the kingdom
and dominion
and the glory evermore. Amen.

Samuel Miller Waring, 1790–1827

281   Words: © 1971 Faber Music Ltd, 3 Queen Square, London. WC1N 3AU Reprinted from *New Catholic Hymnal* by permission.
280   Words: © 1969, 1987 James Quinn/Cassell plc. Continuum International Publishing Group, The Tower Building, 11 York Road, London SE1 7NZ

285

Praise God from whom all
  blessings flow
in heaven above and earth
  below;
one God, three persons, we
  adore —
to Him be praise for evermore!
  Amen.

Thomas Ken, 1637–1710
adapted Jubilate Hymns

286

Unto God be praise and honour;
to the Father, to the Son,
to the mighty Spirit, glory —
ever Three and ever One:
power and glory in the highest
while eternal ages run. Amen.

Gloria et honor Deo
translated William Mair, 1830–1920
and Arthur Wellesley Wotherspoon, 1853–1936

287

May God's blessing surround you
  each day,
as you trust Him and walk in His
  way.
May His presence within guard
  and keep you from sin,
go in peace, go in joy, go in love.

Cliff Barrows

288

The Lord bless you and keep you.
The Lord make His face to shine
  upon you
and be gracious unto you.
The Lord lift up His countenance
  upon you
and give you peace. Amen.

The Aaronic Blessing, *Numbers vi*

289

Amen. *(Various settings)*

Liturgical text

Also suitable:
Jesus, tender Shepherd, hear me   11
Saviour, again to Your dear name   14

CHRIST PROMISED HIS FIRST ADVENT

290

1 Before the world began,
   one Word was there;
   grounded in God He was,
   rooted in care;
   by Him all things were made,
   in Him was love displayed,
   through Him God spoke, and
     said,
   'I am for you.'

2 Life found in Him its source,
   death found its end;
   light found in Him its course,
   darkness its friend.
   For neither death nor doubt
   nor darkness can put out
   the glow of God, the shout,
   'I am for you.'

3 The Word was in the world
   which from Him came;
   unrecognised He was,
   unknown by name;
   one with all humankind,
   with the unloved aligned,
   convincing sight and mind,
   'I am for you.'

4 All who received the Word
   by God were blessed;
   sisters and brothers they
   of earth's fond guest.
   So did the Word of grace
   proclaim in time and space
   and with a human face,
   'I am for you.'

John Lamberton Bell, *b.* 1949
and Graham Alexander Maule, *b.* 1958
based on John 1: 1-13

291

1 Come, O long-expected Jesus,
   born to set Your people free!
   From our fears and sins release
     us,
   Christ in whom our rest shall be.

2 Israel's strength and consolation,
   born salvation to impart;
   dear desire of every nation,
   joy of every longing heart:

3 Born Your people to deliver,
   born a child and yet a king;
   born to reign in us for ever,
   now Your gracious kingdom
     bring.

4 By Your own eternal Spirit
rule in all our hearts alone;
by Your all-sufficient merit
raise us to Your glorious throne.

Charles Wesley, 1707–1788
adapted Jubilate Hymns

292

1 Faithful vigil ended,
watching, waiting cease;
Master, grant Your servant
his discharge in peace.

2 All the Spirit promised,
all the Father willed,
now these eyes behold it
perfectly fulfilled.

3 This Your great deliverance
sets Your people free;
Christ their light uplifted
all the nations see.

4 Christ, Your people's glory!
watching, doubting cease:
grant to us Your servants
our discharge in peace.

Timothy Dudley-Smith, b. 1926
Luke 2: 29-32, as in New English Bible

293

1 God and Father, we adore You
for the Son, Your image bright,
in whom all Your holy nature
dawned on our once hopeless
night.

2 Far from You our footsteps
wandered
on dark paths of sin and shame;
but our midnight turned to
morning,
when the Lord of glory came.

3 Word incarnate, God revealing,
longed-for while dim ages ran,
Love Divine, we bow before You,
Son of God and Son of Man.

4 Let our life be new-created,
ever-living Lord, in You,
till we wake with Your pure
likeness,
when Your face in heaven we
view;

5 Where the saints of all the ages,
where the martyrs, glorified,
clouds and darkness far beneath
them,
in unending day abide.

6 God and Father, now we bless
You
for the Son, Your image bright,
in whom all Your holy nature
dawns on our adoring sight.

John Nelson Darby, 1800–1882
and Hugh Falconer, 1859–1931

294

1 Hail to the Lord's Anointed,
great David's greater Son!
Hail, in the time appointed
His reign on earth begun!
He comes to break oppression,
to set the captive free,
to take away transgression
and rule in equity.

2 He comes with help most speedy
to those who suffer wrong;
to save the poor and needy,
and help the weak be strong:
to give them songs for sighing,
their darkness turn to light,
whose souls, condemned and
dying,
are precious in His sight.

3 He shall come down like showers
upon the fruitful earth;
and love, joy, hope, like flowers
spring in His path to birth:
before Him on the mountains
shall peace, the herald, go;
and righteousness in fountains
from hill to valley flow.

4 Kings shall bow down before
Him
and gold and incense bring;
all nations shall adore Him,
His praise all people sing:
to Him shall prayer unceasing
and daily vows ascend;
His kingdom still increasing,
a kingdom without end.

5 In all the world victorious,
He on His throne shall rest;
from age to age more glorious,
all-blessing and all-blessed:
the tide of time shall never
His covenant remove;
His Name shall stand for ever,
His changeless name of love.

James Montgomery, 1771–1854
slightly altered

295

1 Hark the glad sound! — the
 Saviour comes,
 the Saviour promised long;
 let every heart prepare a throne
 and every voice a song.

2 He comes the prisoners to release
 in Satan's bondage held;
 the gates of brass before Him
 burst,
 the iron fetters yield.

3 He comes the broken heart to
 bind,
 the wounded soul to cure;
 and with the treasures of His
 grace
 to enrich the humble poor.

4 Our glad hosannas, Prince of
 Peace,
 Your welcome shall proclaim;
 and heaven's eternal arches ring
 with Your beloved name.

Philip Doddridge, 1702–1751
Paraphrase 39

296

1 Hills of the north, rejoice,
 river and mountain-spring,
 hark to the advent voice;
 valley and lowland, sing.
 Christ comes in righteousness
 and love,
 He brings salvation from above.

2 Isles of the southern seas,
 sing to the listening earth;
 carry on every breeze
 hope of a world's new birth:
 In Christ shall all be made anew;
 His Word is sure, His promise
 true.

3 Lands of the east, arise!
 He is your brightest morn;
 greet Him with joyous eyes,
 let praise His path adorn:
 Your seers have longed to know
 their Lord;
 to you He comes, the final Word.

4 Shores of the utmost west,
 lands of the setting sun,
 welcome the heavenly guest
 in whom the dawn has come:
 He brings a never-ending light,
 who triumphed o'er our darkest
 night.

5 Shout, as you journey on;
 songs be in every mouth!
 Lo, from the north they come,
 from east and west and south:
 In Jesus all shall find their rest,
 in Him the universe be blest.

Charles Ernest Oakley, 1832–1865
altered Compilers of *English Praise*, 1975,
Compilers of *Hymns and Psalms*, 1983

297

1 Jesus, hope of every nation,
 light of heaven upon our way;
 promise of the world's salvation,
 spring of life's eternal day!

2 Saints by faith on God depending
 wait to see Messiah born;
 sin's oppressive night is ending
 in the glory of the dawn.

3 Look, He comes! — the long-
 awaited
 Christ, Redeemer, living Word;
 hope and faith are vindicated
 as with joy we greet the Lord.

4 Glory in the highest heaven
 to the Father, Spirit, Son;
 and on earth all praise be given
 to our God, the Three-in-One!

Michael Arnold Perry, 1942–1996
Nunc Dimittis

298

1 O bless the God of Israel,
 who comes to set us free,
 who visits and redeems us
 and grants us liberty.
 The prophets spoke of mercy,
 of rescue and release;
 God shall fulfil the promise
 to bring our people peace.

2 Now from the house of David
 a child of grace is given;
 a Saviour comes among us
 to raise us up to heaven.
 Before Him goes the herald —
 forerunner in the way,
 the prophet of salvation,
 the messenger of day.

3 Where once were fear and
 darkness
 the sun begins to rise —
 the dawning of forgiveness
 upon the sinner's eyes,

CHRIST PROMISED

to guide the feet of pilgrims
along the paths of peace:
O bless our God and Saviour,
with songs that never cease!

Michael Arnold Perry, 1942–1996
from *Benedictus*

299

1 O come, O come, Emmanuel,
and ransom captive Israel
that mourns in lonely exile here
until the Son of God appear:
*Rejoice! Rejoice! Emmanuel
shall come to you, O Israel.*

2 O come, O come, O Lord of might
who to Your tribes on Sinai's
height,
in ancient times did give the law
in cloud and majesty and awe:

3 O come, O Rod of Jesse, free
Your own from Satan's tyranny;
from depths of hell Your people
save
and give the victory o'er the
grave:

4 O come, O Dayspring, come and
cheer
our spirits by Your advent here;
disperse the gloomy clouds of
night,
and death's dark shadows put to
flight:

5 O come, O Key of David, come
and open wide our heavenly
home;
make safe the way that leads on
high
and close the path to misery:

18th century,
based on the ancient *Advent Antiphons*,
translated John Mason Neale, 1818–1866
and others

300

1 On Jordan's bank the Baptist's cry
announces that the Lord is nigh;
awake and hearken, for he brings
glad tidings of the King of kings!

2 Then cleansed be every life from
sin;
make straight the way for God
within,
and let us all our hearts prepare
for Christ to come and enter
there.

3 We hail You as our Saviour, Lord,
our refuge, and our great reward;
O let Your face upon us shine
and fill the world with love
divine.

4 All praise to You, eternal Son,
whose advent has our freedom
won,
whom with the Father we adore,
and Holy Spirit, evermore.
Amen.

Charles Coffin, 1676–1749
translated John Chandler, 1806–1876
and others

301

1 Tell out, my soul, the greatness of
the Lord!
Unnumbered blessings, give my
spirit voice;
tender to me the promise of His
Word;
in God my Saviour shall my
heart rejoice.

2 Tell out, my soul, the greatness of
His name:
make known His might, the
deeds His arm has done;
His mercy sure, from age to age
the same;
His holy name, the Lord, the
Mighty One.

3 Tell out, my soul, the greatness of
His might!
Powers and dominions lay their
glory by.
Proud hearts and stubborn wills
are put to flight,
the hungry fed, the humble lifted
high.

4 Tell out, my soul, the glories of
His word!
Firm is His promise, and His
mercy sure.
Tell out, my soul, the greatness of
the Lord
to children's children and for
evermore!

Timothy Dudley-Smith, b. 1926
based on the *Magnificat*, as in *New English Bible*

302

1 The people who in darkness
walked
have seen a glorious light:
that light shines out on those who
lived
in shadows of the night.

2 To greet You, Sun of
Righteousness,
the gathering nations come;
rejoicing as when reapers bring
their harvest treasures home.

3 For now to us a Child is born,
to us a Son is given;
and on His shoulder ever rests
all power in earth and heaven.

4 His name shall be the Prince of
Peace,
eternally adored;
most wonderful of counsellors,
the great and mighty Lord.

5 His peace and righteous
government
shall over all extend;
on judgement and on justice
based,
His reign shall never end.

John Morison, 1750–1798
Paraphrase 19, Isaiah 9: 2-8
adapted Jubilee Hymns

303

*Wake up, O sleeper, and rise from
the dead,
and Christ will shine on you.
Wake up, O sleeper, and rise from
the dead,
and Christ will shine on you.*

1 Once you were darkness, but now
you are light,
now you are light in the Lord.
So as true children of light you
must live,
showing the glory of God.

2 This is the beautiful fruit of the
light,
the good, the righteous, the true.
Let us discover what pleases the
Lord
in everything we do.

3 As days get darker, take care how
you live,
not as unwise, but as wise,

making the most of each moment
He gives,
and pressing on for the prize.

Graham Andrew Kendrick, *b.* 1950

304

1 Your kingdom come! on bended
knee
through passing years we pray:
all faithful people long to see
on earth that kingdom's day.

2 The hours of waiting through the
night
no less to God belong;
the stars declare the eternal right
and shame the creature's wrong.

3 And there already in the skies
the dawn's first rays appear:
you prophets of our God, arise,
proclaim the day is near:

4 The day in whose clear shining
light
the Lord shall stand revealed,
and every wrong be turned to
right,
and every hurt be healed,

5 When justice joined with truth
and peace
make straight the Saviour's road:
the day of perfect righteousness,
the promised day of God!

Frederick Lucian Hosmer, 1840–1929
adapted Michael Arnold Perry, 1942–1996

Also suitable:
Christ is the world's true light   615
Your kingdom come, O God   626

JESUS CHRIST
HIS BIRTH

305

1 Angels from the realms of glory,
wing your flight through all the
earth;
heralds of creation's story
now proclaim Messiah's birth!
*Come and worship
Christ, the new-born King;
come and worship
worship Christ, the new-born
King.*

JESUS CHRIST

2   Shepherds in the fields abiding,
    watching by your flocks at night,
    God with us is now residing:
    see, there shines the infant Light!

3   Wise men, leave your
      contemplations!
    Brighter visions shine afar;
    seek in Him the hope of nations,
    you have seen His rising star:

4   Though an infant now we view
      Him,
    He will share His Father's
      throne,
    gather all the nations to Him;
    every knee shall then bow down:

James Montgomery, 1771–1854
adapted Jubilate Hymns

306

1   Angel voices, richly blending,
    shepherds to the manger
      sending,
    sing of peace from heaven
      descending,
    Shepherds, greet your
      Shepherd-King!

2   Lo! a star is brightly glowing!
    Eastern kings their gifts are
      showing
    to the King whose gifts pass
      knowing!
    Gentiles, greet the Gentiles'
      King!

3   To the manger come adoring,
    hearts in thankfulness outpouring
    to the Child, true peace restoring,
    Mary's Son, our God and King!

Latin, 14th-century Germany
translated James Quinn, *b.* 1919

307

1   As with gladness men of old
    did the guiding star behold;
    as with joy they hailed its light,
    leading onward, beaming bright,
    so, most gracious God, may we
    led by You forever be.

2   As with joyful steps they sped,
    Saviour, to Your lowly bed,
    there to bend the knee before
    You whom heaven and earth
      adore,
    so may we with one accord
    seek forgiveness from our Lord.

3   As they offered gifts most rare,
    gold and frankincense and
      myrrh;
    so may we, cleansed from our sin,
    lives of service now begin,
    as in love our treasures bring,
    Christ, to You our heavenly King.

4   Holy Jesus, every day
    keep us in the narrow way;
    and, when earthly things are
      past,
    bring our ransomed souls at last
    where they need no star to guide
    where no clouds Your glory hide.

5   In the heavenly country bright
    need they no created light;
    You its light, its joy, its crown,
    You its sun which goes not down
    there for ever may we sing
    Hallelujahs to our King.

William Chatterton Dix, 1837–189?
adapted Peter J. Horrobin, *b.* 194?
and Greg P. Leavers, *b.* 195?

308

At this time of giving,
gladly now we bring
gifts of goodness and mercy
from a heavenly King.

1   Earth could not contain the
      treasures
    heaven holds for you,
    perfect joy and lasting pleasures,
    love so strong and true.

2   May His tender love surround
      you
    at this Christmastime;
    may you see His smiling face
    that in the darkness shines.

3   But the many gifts He gives
    are all poured out from one;
    come receive the greatest gift,
    the gift of God's own Son.

Graham Andrew Kendrick, b. 195?

309

1   Away in a manger, no crib for a
      bed,
    the little Lord Jesus laid down
      His sweet head;
    the stars in the bright sky looked
      down where He lay,
    the little Lord Jesus asleep on the
      hay.

306   Words: © James Quinn/Geoffrey Chapman, Cassell plc. Continuum International Publishing Group, The Tower Building, 11 York Road, London SE1 7NZ
307   Words: © Peter Horrobin and Greg Leavers/Ellel Ministries International. Used by permission.
308   Words and Music: © 1988 Make Way Music, PO Box 263, Croydon, CR9 5AP. International copyright secured. All rights reserved. Used by permission.

2   The cattle are lowing, the Baby
        awakes,
    but little Lord Jesus no crying He
        makes.
    I love You, Lord Jesus! Look
        down from the sky,
    and stay by my side until
        morning is nigh.

3   Be near me, Lord Jesus; I ask You
        to stay
    close by me for ever, and love
        me, I pray.
    Bless all the dear children in
        Your tender care,
    and fit us for heaven, to live with
        You there.

Little Children's Book Philadelphia 1885
Gabriel's *Vineyard Songs* 1892
Anonymous

310

1   Baby Jesus in the manger,
    to the world He's still a stranger.
    Wise men bring their gifts
    of gold and myrrh,
    baby Jesus in the manger.
        Noël, Noël, Noël,
        hail the Emmanuel.

2   Gentle Jesus, meek and lowly,
    full of love so pure and holy.
    He will teach and pray,
    show mankind the way,
    gentle Jesus, meek and lowly.

3   Loving Jesus, mocked and beaten,
    He the sin of man has taken.
    He has paid the price,
    He has given His life,
    loving Jesus, mocked and beaten.

4   Mighty Jesus, He is risen,
    He has broken out of prison.
    He has conquered sin,
    brought new life to men,
    mighty Jesus, He is risen.

Gill Broomhall

311

1   Bethlehem, most noble city,
    with renown beyond compare,
    you alone our loving Saviour
    did for us incarnate bear.

2   Fairer than the sun at morning
    shone the star that told His birth,
    to all nations brightly showing
    that their God had come to earth.

3   By its lambent beauty guided,
    wise men from the east draw
        near,
    come with precious gifts to offer:
    gold with frankincense and
        myrrh.

4   Solemn gifts with mystic
        meaning:
    gold for royal majesty,
    frankincense a God discloses,
    myrrh foretells mortality.

5   Holy Jesus, in Your brightness
    to the Gentile world displayed,
    with the Father and the Spirit,
    endless praise to You be paid.

Aurelius Clemens Prudentius, 348–c. 413
translated Edward Caswall, 1814–1878
adapted Gaetano Raphael (Anthony) Petti,
1932–1985

312

1   Child in the manger,
    Infant of Mary;
    outcast and stranger,
    Lord of all!
    Child who inherits
    all our transgressions,
    all our demerits
    on Him fall.

2   Once the most holy
    Child of salvation
    gentle and lowly
    lived below;
    now, as our glorious
    mighty Redeemer,
    see Him victorious
    o'er each foe.

3   Prophets foretold Him,
    Infant of wonder;
    angels behold Him
    on His throne;
    worthy our Saviour
    of all their praises;
    happy for ever
    are His own.

Mary Macdonald, 1789–1872
translated Lachlan Macbean, 1853–1931

313

1   Christians, awake! Salute the
        happy morn
    on which the Saviour of the
        world was born;
    rise to adore the mystery of love
    which hosts of angels chanted
        from above!

10 Words and Music: © 1992 Thankyou Music. Administered (UK and Europe) by Kingsway Music <tym@kingsway.co.uk>. Remaining territories administered by
/orshiptogether.com songs. Used by permission.

11 Words: © 1971 Faber Music Ltd, 3 Queen Square, London. WC1N 3AU Reprinted from *New Catholic Hymnal* by permission.

13 Words: © in this version Jubilate Hymns, 4 Thorne Park Road, Chelston, Torquay TQ2 6RX <enquiries@jubilate.co.uk> Used by permission.

With them the joyful tidings first
    begun
of God incarnate and the Virgin's
    Son.

2 First, to the watchful shepherds it
    was told,
who heard the herald angel's
    voice: 'Behold,
I bring good news of your
    Messiah's birth
to you and all the nations here on
    earth!
This day has God fulfilled His
    promised word;
this day is born a Saviour, Christ
    the Lord!'

3 To Bethlehem these eager
    shepherds ran
to see the wonder of our God
    made man;
they found, with Joseph and the
    holy maid,
Jesus, the Saviour, in a manger
    laid.
Amazed, with joy this story they
    proclaim,
the first apostles of His infant
    fame.

4 Let us, like those good shepherds,
    now employ
our grateful voices to declare the
    joy:
trace we the Babe, who has
    redeemed our loss,
from this poor manger to His
    bitter cross;
treading His steps, assisted by His
    grace,
by faith again we see the
    Saviour's face.

5 Glory to God! The skies are
    singing still,
peace on the earth to people of
    goodwill!
Christ, who was born on this
    most happy day,
round all the earth His glory
    shall display.
Saved by His love, unceasing we
    shall sing
eternal praise to heaven's
    almighty King.

John Byrom, 1692–1763
adapted Jubilee Hymns

314

Come and join the celebration,
it's a very special day;
come and share our jubilation,
there's a new King born today!

1 See the shepherds
hurry down to Bethlehem;
gaze in wonder
at the Son of God who lay before
    them.

2 Wise men journey,
led to worship by a star;
kneel in homage,
bringing precious gifts from lands
    afar, so

3 'God is with us,'
round the world the message
    bring;
He is with us,
'Welcome!' all the bells on earth
    are pealing.

Valerie Collison, b. 1933

315

1 Come and hear the joyful
    singing,
Alleluia! Gloria!
set the bells of heaven ringing:
Alleluia! Gloria!
God the Lord has shown us
    favour —
Alleluia! Gloria!
Christ is born to be our Saviour.
Alleluia! Gloria!

2 Angels of His birth are telling,
Alleluia! Gloria!
Prince of Peace all powers
    excelling;
Alleluia! Gloria!
death and hell can not defeat
    Him:
Alleluia! Gloria!
go to Bethlehem and greet Him.
Alleluia! Gloria!

3 Choir and people, shout in
    wonder,
Alleluia! Gloria!
let the merry organ thunder;
Alleluia! Gloria!
thank our God for love amazing,
Alleluia! Gloria!
Father, Son and Spirit praising.
Alleluia! Gloria!

Michael Arnold Perry, 1942–1996

316

1 Come and sing the Christmas
   story
   this holy night!
   Christ is born: the hope of glory
   dawns on our sight.
   Alleluia! earth is ringing
   with a thousand angels
   singing —
   hear the message they are
   bringing
   this holy night.

2 Jesus, Saviour, Child of Mary
   this holy night,
   in a world confused and weary
   You are our light.
   God is in a manger lying,
   manhood taking, self denying,
   life embracing, death defying
   this holy night.

3 Lord of all! let us acclaim Him
   this holy night;
   King of our salvation name Him,
   throned in the height.
   Son of Man — let us adore Him,
   all of earth is waiting for Him;
   Son of God — we bow before
   Him
   this holy night.

Michael Arnold Perry, †, 1942–1996
slightly altered Compilers

317

1 Crackers and turkeys and
   pudding and cream,
   toys in the windows that I've
   never seen.
   This is the Christmas that
   everyone sees,
   but Christmas means more to me.
   It's somebody's birthday I won't
   forget,
   as I open the things that I get.
   I'll remember the inn and the
   stable so bare,
   and Jesus who once lay there.

2 Everyone's out shopping late
   every night,
   for candles and presents and
   Christmas tree lights.
   This is the Christmas that
   everyone sees,
   but Christmas means more to me.

3 Christmas morning, the start of
   the day,
   there's presents to open and new
   games to play.
   This is the Christmas that
   everyone sees,
   but Christmas means more to me.

Ian White, *b.* 1956

318

1 God rest you merry, gentlemen,
   let nothing you dismay!
   for Jesus Christ our Saviour
   was born on Christmas Day,
   to save us all from Satan's power
   when we had gone astray:
   O tidings of comfort and joy,
   comfort and joy;
   O tidings of comfort and joy!

2 From God our heavenly Father
   a holy angel came;
   the shepherds saw the glory
   and heard the voice proclaim
   that Christ was born in
   Bethlehem —
   and Jesus is His name:

3 The shepherds at these tidings
   rejoiced in heart and mind,
   and on the darkened hillside
   they left their flocks behind,
   and went to Bethlehem
   straightway
   this holy Child to find:

4 And when to Bethlehem they
   came,
   where Christ the Infant lay,
   they found Him in a manger
   where oxen fed on hay;
   and there beside her newborn
   Child
   His mother knelt to pray:

5 Now to the Lord sing praises,
   all people in this place!
   with Christian love and
   fellowship
   each other now embrace,
   and let this Christmas festival
   all bitterness displace:

Traditional, possibly 18th-century
adapted Jubilate Hymns

319

1 Good Christians all, rejoice
with heart and soul and voice!
Listen now to what we say,
Jesus Christ is born today;
ox and ass before Him bow
and He is in the manger now!
Christ is born today;
Christ is born today!

2 Good Christians all, rejoice
with heart and soul and voice!
Hear the news of endless bliss,
Jesus Christ was born for this:
He has opened heaven's door
and we are blessed for evermore!
Christ was born for this;
Christ was born for this!

3 Good Christians all, rejoice
with heart and soul and voice!
Now you need not fear the
grave;
Jesus Christ was born to save:
come at His most gracious call
to find salvation, one and all!
Christ was born to save;
Christ was born to save!

Latin and German, 14th-century
adapted John Mason Neale, 1818–1866

320

1 Good news, good news to you we
bring,
Alleluia!
News of great joy that angels
sing,
Alleluia!
Tender mercy He has shown us,
joy to all the world;
for us God sends His only Son,
Alleluia!

2 Let earth's dark shadows fly
away,
Alleluia!
In Christ has dawned an endless
day,
Alleluia!

3 Now God with us on earth
resides,
Alleluia!
And heaven's door is open wide,
Alleluia!

Graham Andrew Kendrick, *b.* 1950

321

1 Hark! the herald angels sing
glory to the new-born King;
peace on earth and mercy mild,
God and sinners reconciled!
Joyful all you nations rise,
join the triumph of the skies;
with the angelic host proclaim,
'Christ is born in Bethlehem':
Hark! the herald angels sing
glory to the new-born King.

2 Christ, by highest heaven adored
Christ, the everlasting Lord;
late in time behold Him come,
offspring of a virgin's womb:
veiled in flesh the Godhead see,
hail the incarnate Deity!
Pleased as man with us to dwell,
Jesus, our Emmanuel:

3 Hail the heaven-born Prince of
Peace,
hail the Sun of Righteousness;
light and life to all He brings,
risen with healing in His wings:
mild, He lays His glory by,
born that we no more may die;
born to raise us from the earth,
born to give us second birth:

Charles Wesley, 1707–1788 and others

322

1 Infant holy, Infant lowly,
for His bed a cattle stall;
oxen lowing, little knowing
Christ the babe is Lord of all.
Swift are winging angels singing,
Nowells ringing, tidings bringing
Christ the babe is Lord of all;
Christ the babe is Lord of all!

2 Flocks were sleeping, shepherds
keeping
vigil till the morning new,
saw the glory, heard the story —
tidings of a gospel true.
Thus rejoicing, free from sorrow,
praises voicing greet tomorrow:
Christ the babe was born for you;
Christ the babe was born for you!

Polish mediæval carol
translated Edith Margaret Gellibrand Reed
1885–1933

23

1 In the bleak mid-winter
frosty wind made moan,
earth stood hard as iron,
water like a stone;
snow had fallen, snow on snow,
snow on snow,
in the bleak mid-winter
long ago.

2 Heaven cannot hold Him,
nor the earth sustain;
heaven and earth shall flee away
when He comes to reign:
in the bleak mid-winter
a stable-place sufficed
God, the Lord Almighty,
Jesus Christ.

3 Enough for Him whom cherubim
worship night and day —
a breastful of milk
and a manger full of hay;
enough for Him whom angels
fall down before —
the wise men and the shepherds
who adore!

4 What can I give Him,
poor as I am?
If I were a shepherd
I would give a lamb;
if I were a wise man
I would do my part;
yet what I can I give Him —
give my heart.

Christina Georgina Rossetti, 1830–1894
adapted Compilers of
Hymns for Today's Church, 1982

24

1 It came upon the midnight clear,
that glorious song of old,
from angels bending near the
earth
to touch their harps of gold:
'Through all the earth, goodwill
and peace
from heaven's all-gracious King!'
The world in solemn stillness lay
to hear the angels sing.

2 With sorrow brought by sin and
strife
the world has suffered long
and, since the angels sang, have
passed
two thousand years of wrong:

the nations, still at war, hear not
the love-song which they bring:
O hush the noise and cease the
strife,
to hear the angels sing!

3 And those whose journey now is
hard,
whose hope is burning low,
who tread the rocky path of life
with painful steps and slow:
O listen to the news of love
which makes the heavens ring!
O rest beside the weary road
and hear the angels sing!

4 And still the days are hastening
on —
by prophets seen of old —
towards the fullness of the time
when comes the age foretold:
then earth and heaven renewed
shall see
the Prince of Peace, their King;
and all the world repeat the song
which now the angels sing.

Edmund Hamilton Sears, 1810–1876
adapted Jubilate Hymns

325

1 Joy to the world — the Lord has
come:
let earth receive her King,
let every heart prepare Him
room
and heaven and nature sing,
and heaven and nature sing,
and heaven, and heaven and
nature sing!

2 Joy to the earth — the Saviour
reigns:
your sweetest songs employ,
while fields and streams and
hills and plains
repeat the sounding joy,
repeat the sounding joy,
repeat, repeat the sounding joy!

3 He rules the world with truth
and grace,
and makes the nations prove
the glories of His righteousness
and wonders of His love,
and wonders of His love,
and wonder, wonders of His love.

Isaac Watts, 1674–1748

326

1 Love came down at Christmas,
   Love all lovely, Love divine;
   Love was born at Christmas —
   star and angels gave the sign.

2 Worship we the Godhead,
   Love incarnate, Love divine;
   worship we our Jesus —
   what shall be our sacred sign?

3 Love shall be our token,
   love be yours and love be mine;
   love to God and neighbour,
   love for prayer and gift and sign.

   Christina Georgina Rossetti, 1830–1894
   adapted Jubilate Hymns

327

Mighty God, Everlasting Father,
Wonderful Counsellor,
You're the Prince of peace.
Mighty God, everlasting Father,
wonderful Counsellor,
You're the Prince of Peace.

1 You are the Lord of heaven,
   You are called Emmanuel;
   God is now with us,
   ever present to deliver.
   You are God eternal,
   You are Lord of all the earth;
   love has come to us,
   bringing us new birth.

2 A light to those in darkness,
   and a guide to paths of peace;
   love and mercy dawns,
   grace, forgiveness and salvation.
   Light for revelation,
   glory to Your people;
   Son of the Most High,
   God's love gift to all.

   Mark Johnson and Helen Johnson

328

1 O come, all you faithful,
   joyful and triumphant!
   O come now, O come now, to
      Bethlehem!
   Come and behold Him, born the
      King of angels:
      O come, let us adore Him,
      O come, let us adore Him,
      O come, let us adore Him, Christ
         the Lord!

2 God from God,
   Light from light,
   He who abhors not the Virgin's
      womb;
   very God, begotten, not created:

3 Sing, choirs of angels,
   sing in exultation!
   Sing, all you citizens of heaven
      above,
   'Glory to God in the highest!'

4 Yes, Lord, we greet You,
   born for our salvation; *
   Jesus, to You be glory given!
   Word of the Father now in flesh
      appearing:

   * *or, on Christmas morning:*
   born this happy morning

   Latin, 18th century, possibly b
   John Francis Wade, c. 1711–17
   translated Frederick Oakeley, 1802–1880 and othe
   adapted Compilers
   Hymns for Today's Church, 198

329

1 Of the Father's heart begotten
   when no world had come to be,
   He is Alpha and Omega,
   He the source, the ending He,
   of the things that are, that have
      been,
   and that future years shall see:
   evermore and evermore.

2 By His word was all created;
   He commanded; it was done:
   earth and sky and boundless
      ocean
   in their threefold order one;
   all that sees the moon's soft
      radiance,
   all that breathes beneath the sun
   evermore and evermore.

3 Happy is that day for ever
   when the Virgin, filled with
      grace,
   by the Spirit's power conceiving
   bore the Saviour of our race:
   and the Babe, the world's
      Redeemer
   first revealed His sacred face:
   evermore and evermore.

4 This is He whom priests and
      poets
   sang of old with one accord;
   whom the voices of the prophets
   promised in their faithful word:

326   Words: © in this version Jubilate Hymns, 4 Thorne Park Road, Chelston, Torquay TQ2 6RX <enquiries@jubilate.co.uk> Used by permission.
327   Words and Music: © 1991 Sovereign Lifestyle Music Ltd, P.O. Box 356, Leighton Buzzard LU7 3WP <sovereignmusic@aol.com>

HIS BIRTH

now He shines, the long-
    expected;
let creation praise its Lord:
evermore and evermore.

5 Praise Him, all you hosts of
    heaven;
praise Him, angels in the height;
powers, dominions, bow before
    Him,
and extol His glorious might;
let no tongue on earth be silent,
let each heart and voice unite:
evermore and evermore.

Aurelius Clemens Prudentius, 348–c. 413
translated John Mason Neale, 1818–1866
and Henry Williams Baker, 1821–1877
adapted Compilers of *Praise!* 2000

330

1 O little town of Bethlehem,
how still we see you lie!
Above your deep and dreamless
    sleep
the silent stars go by.
Yet, in your dark streets shining
the everlasting Light;
the hopes and fears of all the
    years
are met in you to-night.

2 O morning stars, together
proclaim the holy birth
and praises sing to God the King,
and peace to all on earth.
For Christ is born of Mary;
and, gathered all above,
while mortals sleep, the angels
    keep
their watch of wondering love.

3 How silently, how silently
the wondrous gift is given!
So God imparts to human hearts
the blessings of His heaven.
No ear may hear His coming;
but in this world of sin,
where meek souls will receive
    Him, still
the dear Christ enters in.

4 O holy Child of Bethlehem,
descend to us, we pray;
cast out our sin, and enter in,
be born in us today.
We hear the Christmas angels
the great glad tidings tell:
O come to us, abide with us,
our Lord Emmanuel.

Phillips Brooks, 1835–1893

331

1 Once in royal David's city
stood a lowly cattle-shed,
where a mother laid her Baby
in a manger for His bed:
Mary was that mother mild,
Jesus Christ her little Child.

2 He came down to earth from
    heaven
who is God and Lord of all;
and His shelter was a stable
and His cradle was a stall:
with the poor and meek and
    lowly
lived on earth our Saviour holy.

3 And through all His wondrous
    childhood
He would honour and obey,
love and watch the gentle mother
in whose tender arms He lay:
Christian children all should be
kind, obedient, good as He.

4 For He is our childhood's
    pattern:
day by day like us He grew;
He was little, weak and helpless;
tears and smiles like us He
    knew:
and He feels for all our sadness,
and He shares in all our
    gladness.

5 And our eyes at last shall see
    Him
through His own redeeming
    love;
for that Child, so dear and gentle,
is our Lord in heaven above:
and He leads His children on
to the place where He has gone.

6 Not in that poor lowly stable
with the oxen standing by,
we shall see Him, but in heaven,
set at God's right hand on high:
there His children gather round
bright like stars, with glory
    crowned.

Cecil Frances Alexander, 1818–1895
adapted Peter J. Horrobin, b. 1943
and Greg P. Leavers, b. 1952

JESUS CHRIST

332

1 On Christmas night all Christians
   sing
   to hear the news the angels
   bring:
   news of great joy, news of great
   mirth,
   news of our merciful King's birth.

2 Then why should we on earth be
   so sad,
   since our Redeemer made us
   glad,
   when from our sin He set us free,
   all for to gain our liberty?

3 When sin departs before His
   grace,
   then life and health come in its
   place;
   heaven and earth with joy may
   sing,
   all for to see the new-born King.

4 All out of darkness we have light,
   which made the angels sing this
   night:
   'Glory to God, on earth be peace;
   goodwill to all shall never cease.'

* the first two lines of each verse are sung
   twice

English traditional carol

333

1 See, amid the winter snow,
   born for us on earth below;
   see, the gentle Lamb appears,
   promised from eternal years:
   Hail, O ever-blessèd morn;
   hail, redemption's happy dawn;
   sing through all Jerusalem:
   'Christ is born in Bethlehem!'

2 Low within a manger lies
   He who built the starry skies;
   He who, throned in height
   sublime,
   reigns above the cherubim:

3 Say, you humble shepherds, say
   what's your joyful news today?
   Tell us why you left your sheep
   on the lonely mountain steep:

4 'As we watched at dead of night,
   all around us shone a light;
   angels singing "Peace on earth"
   told us of a Saviour's birth.'

5 Sacred Infant, King most dear,
   what a tender love was here,
   thus to come from highest bliss
   down to such a world as this!

6 Holy Saviour, born on earth,
   teach us by Your lowly birth;
   grant that we may ever be
   taught by such humility.

Edward Caswall, 1814–18?
adapted Jubilate Hymn

334

1 See Him lying on a bed of straw:
   a draughty stable with an open
   door;
   Mary cradling the Babe she
   bore —
   the Prince of glory is His name.
   O now carry me to Bethlehem
   to see the Lord of love again:
   just as poor as was the stable then,
   the Prince of glory when He came

2 Star of silver, sweep across the
   skies,
   show where Jesus in the manger
   lies;
   shepherds swiftly from your
   stupor rise
   to see the Saviour of the world!

3 Angels, sing the song you sang,
   sing the glory of God's gracious
   plan;
   sing that Bethl'em's little Baby
   can
   be the Saviour of us all.

4 Mine are riches, from Your
   poverty,
   from Your innocence, eternity;
   mine, forgiveness by Your death
   for me,
   Child of sorrow for my joy.

Michael Arnold Perry, 1942–199?

335

1 Silent night, holy night!
   Sleeps the world; hid from sight,
   Mary and Joseph in stable bare
   watched o'er the Child belovèd
   and fair
   sleeping in heavenly rest,
   sleeping in heavenly rest.

2 Silent night, holy night!
   Shepherds first saw the light,
   heard resounding clear and long,

333 Words: © in this version Jubilate Hymns, 4 Thorne Park Road, Chelston, Torquay TQ2 6RX <enquiries@jubilate.co.uk> Used by permission.
334 Words: © Mrs B. Perry / Jubilate Hymns, 4 Thorne Park Road, Chelston, Torquay TQ2 6RX <enquiries@jubilate.co.uk> Used by permission.

far and near, the angel-song:
'Christ the Redeemer is here,
Christ the Redeemer is here!'

3 Silent night, holy night!
Son of God, O how bright
love is smiling from Your face!
Strikes for us now the hour of
grace,
Saviour, since You are born,
Saviour, since You are born!

Joseph Mohr, 1792–1848
translated Stopford Augustus Brooke, 1832–1916

336

1 The first Nowell the angel did
say
was to Bethlehem's shepherds in
fields as they lay;
in fields where they lay keeping
their sheep
on a cold winter's night that was
so deep:
*Nowell, Nowell, Nowell, Nowell,
born is the King of Israel!*

2 Then wise men from a country
far
looked up and saw a guiding
star;
they travelled on by night and
day
to reach the place where Jesus
lay:

3 At Bethlehem they entered in,
on bended knee they worshipped
Him;
they offered there in His
presence
their gold and myrrh and
frankincense:

4 Then let us all with one accord
sing praises to our heavenly
Lord;
for Christ has our salvation
wrought
and with His blood our life has
bought:

Traditional carol, possibly 7th-century
adapted Michael Arnold Perry, 1942–1996

337

1 The Virgin Mary had a baby boy,
the Virgin Mary had a baby boy,
the Virgin Mary had a baby boy,
and they said that His name was
Jesus.

*He come from the glory
He come from the glorious
kingdom;
He come from the glory,
He come from the glorious
kingdom;
O, yes! believer.
O, yes! believer.
He come from the glory
He come from the glorious
kingdom.*

2 The angels sang when the baby
was born,
the angels sang when the baby
was born,
the angels sang when the baby
was born,
and proclaimed Him the Saviour
Jesus.

3 The wise men saw where the
baby was born,
the wise men saw where the
baby was born,
the wise men saw where the
baby was born,
and they saw that His name was
Jesus.

Trinidadian carol
Anonymous

338

1 The wise may bring their
learning,
the rich may bring their wealth,
and some may bring their
greatness,
and some their strength and
health:
we too would bring our treasures
to offer to the King;
we have no wealth or learning,
what gifts then shall we bring?

2 We'll bring the many duties
we have to do each day;
we'll try our best to please Him,
at home, at school, at play:
and better are these treasures
to offer to our King
than richest gifts without them;
yet these we all may bring.

3 We'll bring Him hearts that love
Him,
we'll bring Him thankful praise,
and lives for ever striving
to follow in His ways:

and these shall be the treasures
we offer to the King,
and these are gifts that ever
our grateful hearts may bring.

Book of Praise for Children 1881
Anonymous
adapted Compilers of *BBC Hymn Book*, 1951
and others

339

1 Unto us a boy is born!
King of all creation,
came He to a world forlorn,
the Lord of every nation,
the Lord of every nation.

2 Cradled in a stall was He
with sleepy cows and asses;
but the very beasts could see
that He all men surpasses,
that He all men surpasses.

3 Herod then with fear was filled:
'A Prince,' he said, 'in Jewry!'
All the little boys he killed
at Bethlehem in his fury,
at Bethlehem in his fury.

4 Now may Mary's son, who came
so long ago to love us,
lead us all with hearts aflame
unto the joys above us,
unto the joys above us.

5 Omega and Alpha He!
Let the organ thunder,
while the choir with songs of glee
now rend the air asunder,
now rend the air asunder!

Latin, 15th-century Germany
translated Percy Dearmer, 1867–1936
v. 5 *slightly adapted* Compilers

340

1 While shepherds watched their
flocks by night
all seated on the ground,
the angel of the Lord came down
and glory shone around.

2 'Fear not!' said he — for mighty
dread
had seized their troubled
mind —
'Glad tidings of great joy I bring
to you and all mankind.

3 'To you in Bethlehem this day
is born of David's line
a Saviour, who is Christ the Lord,
and this shall be the sign:

4 'The heavenly babe you there
shall find
to human view displayed,
all simply wrapped in swaddling
clothes
and in a manger laid.'

5 Thus spoke the seraph, and at
once
appeared a shining throng
of angels praising God, who thus
addressed their joyful song:

6 'All glory be to God on high,
and to the earth be peace!
Goodwill henceforth from highest
heaven
begin and never cease.'

Nahum Tate, 1652–1715
Paraphrase 37, Luke 2: 8-15
adapted Compilers of *Praise!* 2000

Also suitable:
Worship the Lord in the beauty of holiness   198

JESUS CHRIST
HIS LIFE
AND MINISTRY

341

1 A Man once came from Galilee,
no man so great as He.
We left our work and went with
Him,
His followers to be.
Lord Jesus, be our teacher now,
and may we learn from You
to love and serve the Father God
and other people, too.

2 We saw our Master heal the sick;
we saw His love for men.
We saw His power reach out to
touch
and bring to life again.
Lord Jesus, be our healer now,
and make us whole and strong
that we may share Your love and
power
and serve You all day long.

3 They nailed Him to a cross of
wood;
they scoffed and watched Him
die.
And we could not at first believe
that He would reign on high.

339 Words and Music: © 1928 Oxford University Press, from *Oxford Book of Carols*. Reproduced by permission., Great Clarendon Street, Oxford OX2 6DP
341 Words: © Scripture Union, 207-209 Queensway, Bletchley, Milton Keynes MK2 2EB

Lord Jesus, be our Saviour now,
and may we all repent
and hate the sin that brought You
down
to bear our punishment.

4 We saw the stone was rolled
away
before the empty grave.
We met the risen Lord of life,
the One who came to save.
Lord Jesus, You are God and
King;
Oh, may we all obey
and glorify You, risen Lord,
in all we do each day.

Margaret V. Old, 1932–2001

342

1 Before the heaven and earth
were made by God's decree,
the Son of God all-glorious dwelt
in God's eternity.

2 Though in the form of God
and rich beyond compare,
He did not stay to grasp His
prize;
nor did He linger there.

3 From heights of heaven He came
to this world full of sin,
to meet with hunger, hatred, hell,
our life, our love to win.

4 The Son became true Man
and took a servant's role;
with lowliness and selfless love
He came, to make us whole.

5 Obedient to His death —
that death upon a cross,
no son had ever shown such
love,
nor father known such loss.

6 To Him enthroned on high,
by angel hosts adored,
all knees shall bow, and tongues
confess
that Jesus Christ is Lord.

The Song of Christ's Glory, Philippians 2
Brian Colin Black, b. 1926

343

1 Forty days and forty nights
You were fasting in the wild;
forty days and forty nights
tempted and yet undefiled.

2 Burning heat throughout the day,
bitter cold when light had fled;
prowling beasts around Your way,
stones Your pillow, earth Your
bed.

3 Shall not we Your trials share,
learn Your discipline of will;
and with You by fast and prayer
wrestle with the powers of hell?

4 So if Satan, pressing hard,
soul and body would destroy:
Christ who conquered, be our
Guard;
give to us the victor's joy.

George Hunt Smyttan, 1822–1870
and Francis Pott, 1832–1909
adapted Jubilee Hymns

344

1 Have you heard the raindrops
drumming on the rooftops?
Have you heard the raindrops
dripping on the ground?
Have you heard the raindrops
splashing in the streams
and running to the rivers all
around?
There's water, water of life,
Jesus gives us the water of life;
there's water, water of life,
Jesus gives us the water of life.

2 There's a busy workman digging
in the desert,
digging with a spade that flashes
in the sun;
soon there will be water rising in
the wellshaft,
spilling from the bucket as it
comes.

3 Nobody can live who hasn't any
water,
when the land is dry then
nothing much grows;
Jesus gives us life if we drink the
living water,
sing it so that everybody knows.

Martyn Christian Tinne Strover, b. 1932

345

1 I heard the voice of Jesus say:
'Come unto me and rest;
lay down, O weary one, lay down
your head upon my breast.'
I came to Jesus as I was,
weary and worn and sad,
I found in Him a resting-place,
and He has made me glad.

2   I heard the voice of Jesus say:
'Behold, I freely give
the living water; thirsty one,
stoop down and drink and live.'
I came to Jesus, and I drank
of that life-giving stream;
my thirst was quenched, my soul
    revived,
and now I live in Him.

3   I heard the voice of Jesus say:
'I am this dark world's Light;
look unto me, the dawn shall rise,
and all your day be bright.'
I looked to Jesus, and I found
in Him my star, my sun;
and in that light of life I'll walk,
till travelling days are done.

Horatius N. Bonar, 1808–1889
altered Compilers

346

1   I love to hear the story
which angel voices tell,
how once the King of Glory
came down on earth to dwell.
I am both weak and sinful,
but this I surely know,
the Lord came down to save me,
because He loved me so.

2   I'm glad my blessèd Saviour
was once a child like me,
to show how pure and holy
His little ones might be;
and, if I try to follow
His footsteps here below,
He never will forsake me,
because He loves me so.

3   To sing His love and mercy
my sweetest songs I'll raise,
and, though I cannot see Him,
I know He hears my praise;
for He has kindly promised
that even I may go
to sing among His angels,
because He loves me so.

Emily Huntington Miller, 1833–1913

347

1   Jesus Christ is waiting,
waiting in the streets;
no one is His neighbour,
all alone He eats.
Listen, Lord Jesus,
I am lonely too.
Make me, friend or stranger,
fit to wait on You.

2   Jesus Christ is raging,
raging in the streets,
where injustice spirals
and real hope retreats.
Listen, Lord Jesus,
I am angry too.
In the kingdom's causes
let me rage with You.

3   Jesus Christ is healing,
healing in the streets;
curing those who suffer,
touching those He greets.
Listen, Lord Jesus,
I have pity too.
Let my care be active,
healing just like You.

4   Jesus Christ is dancing,
dancing in the streets,
where each sign of hatred
He, with love, defeats.
Listen, Lord Jesus,
I should triumph too.
Where good conquers evil
let me dance with You.

5   Jesus Christ is calling,
calling in the streets,
'Who will join my journey?
I will guide their feet.'
Listen, Lord Jesus,
let my fears be few.
Walk one step before me;
I will follow You.

John Lamberton Bell, *b.* 1949
and Graham Alexander Maule, *b.* 1958

348

1   Jesus, good above all other,
gentle child of gentle mother,
in a stable born our brother,
give us grace to persevere.

2   Jesus, cradled in a manger,
for us facing every danger,
living as a homeless stranger,
You we make our King most dear.

3   Jesus, for Your people dying,
risen Master, death defying,
Lord in heaven, Your grace
    supplying,
keep us to Your presence near.

4   Jesus, all our sorrows bearing,
all our thoughts and hopes still
    sharing,
to Your people truth declaring;
help us all Your truth to hear.

347   Words and Music: © 1988 *Enemy of Apathy* Wild Goose Resource Group, Iona Community, Pearce Institute, 840 Govan Road, Glasgow G51 3UU
348   Words: From *English Hymnal*, 1906, by permission of Oxford University Press, Great Clarendon Street, Oxford OX2 6DP

5   Lord, in all our doings guide us;
     pride and hate shall ne'er divide
       us;
     we'll go on with You beside us,
     and with joy we'll persevere!

> John Mason Neale, 1818–1866
> and Percy Dearmer, 1867–1936
> *altered* Compilers

349

1   Jesus' hands were kind hands,
      doing good to all,
     healing pain and sickness,
      blessing children small;
     washing tired feet, and saving
      those who fall;
     Jesus' hands were kind hands,
      doing good to all.

2   Take my hands, Lord Jesus, let
      them work for You,
     make them strong and gentle,
      kind in all I do;
     let me watch You, Jesus, till I'm
      gentle too,
     till my hands are kind hands,
      quick to work for You.

> Margaret Beatrice Cropper, 1886–1980

350

1   Jesus! name of wondrous love!
     name all other names above!
     Unto which must every knee
     bow in deep humility.

2   Jesus! name of God decreed
     for this child of David's seed,
     which the angel Gabriel
     did the maiden mother tell.

3   Jesus! name of priceless worth
     to the fallen ones of earth,
     for the promise that it gave,
     'Jesus shall His people save.'

4   Jesus! only name that's given
     to all living under heaven,
     whereby they, to sin enslaved
     burst their fetters and are saved.

5   Jesus! name of wondrous love!
     human name of God above!
     Pleading only this, we claim
     our salvation in that name.

> William Walsham How, 1823–1867
> *revised* A. P. Shepherd
> *v.4 altered*

351

1   Lord, You left Your throne and
      Your kingly crown
     when You came to this earth for
      me;
     but in Bethlehem's home there
      was found no room
     for Your holy nativity:
     O come to my heart, Lord Jesus,
     there is room when You come to
      me.

2   Heaven's arches rang when the
      angels sang
     proclaiming Your royal degree,
     but in lowly birth, Lord, You
      came to earth
     and in great humility:
     O come to my heart, Lord Jesus,
     there is room when You come to
      me.

3   The foxes found rest, and the
      birds their nest
     in the shade of the cedar tree;
     but no place was known you
      could call your own
     in the hillsides of Galilee:
     O come to my heart, Lord Jesus,
     there is room when You come to
      me.

4   When You came, O Lord, with
      the living Word
     that should set Your people free,
     then with mocking scorn and
      with crown of thorn
     they led You to Calvary:
     O come to my heart, Lord Jesus,
     Your cross is all my plea.

5   When heaven's arches ring and
      its choirs shall sing
     at Your coming to victory,
     let Your voice call me home,
      saying, 'Yes, there is room!' —
     there is room at Your side for
      me!
     Then my heart shall rejoice, Lord
      Jesus,
     when You come and You call for
      me.

> Emily Elizabeth Steele Elliott, 1836–1897
> *adapted* Compilers of *Praise!* 2000

352

1 Name of all majesty,
fathomless mystery,
King of the ages
by angels adored;
power and authority,
splendour and dignity,
bow to His mastery,
Jesus is Lord!

2 Child of our destiny,
God from eternity,
love of the Father
on sinners outpoured;
see now what God has done
sending His only Son,
Christ the belovèd One,
Jesus is Lord!

3 Saviour of Calvary,
costliest victory,
darkness defeated
and Eden restored;
born as a Man to die,
nailed to a cross on high,
cold in the grave to lie,
Jesus is Lord!

4 Source of all sovereignty,
light, immortality,
life everlasting
and heaven assured;
so with the ransomed, we
praise Him eternally,
Christ in His majesty,
Jesus is Lord!

Timothy Dudley-Smith, *b.* 1926

353

1 O love, how deep, how broad,
how high!
How passing thought and fantasy
that God, the Son of God, should
take
our mortal form for mortals' sake.

2 He sent no angel to our race
of higher or of lower place,
but wore the robe of human
frame
and He Himself to this world
came.

3 For us baptized, for us He bore
His holy fast, and hungered sore;
for us temptations sharp He
knew;
for us the tempter overthrew.

4 For us He prayed, for us He
taught,
for us His daily works He
wrought,
by words, and signs, and actions,
thus
still seeking not Himself but us.

5 For us to wicked hands betrayed,
scourged, mocked, in purple robe
arrayed,
He bore the shameful cross and
death;
for us at length gave up His
breath.

6 For us He rose from death again,
for us He went on high to reign,
for us He sent His Spirit here
to guide, to strengthen, and to
cheer.

7 To Him whose boundless love
has won
salvation for us through His Son,
to God the Father, glory be
both now and through eternity.

Latin, 15th century
translated Benjamin Webb, 1819–1885 and others

354

1 O sing a song of Bethlehem,
of shepherds watching there,
and of the news that came to
them
from angels in the air:
the light that shone on
Bethlehem
fills all the world today;
of Jesus' birth and peace on earth
the angels sing alway.

2 O sing a song of Nazareth,
of sunny days of joy;
O sing of fragrant flowers' breath,
and of the sinless Boy:
for now the flowers of Nazareth
in every heart may grow;
now spreads the fame of His dear
name
on all the winds that blow.

3 O sing a song of Galilee,
of lake and woods and hill,
of Him who walked upon the sea,
and bade its waves be still:
for though, like waves on Galilee,
dark seas of trouble roll,
when faith has heard the
Master's word,
falls peace upon the soul.

4 O sing a song of Calvary,
its glory and dismay;
of Him who hung upon the tree
and took our sins away:
for He who died on Calvary
is risen from the grave,
and Christ, our Lord, by heaven
    adored,
is mighty now to save.

Louis Fitzgerald Benson, 1855–1930

355

1 Peter, James and John in a fishing
boat, *
down by the deep, deep sea.

2 Fished all night and caught no
fishes,
down by the deep, deep sea.

3 Christ came walking down by the
water,
down by the deep, deep sea.

4 Now their nets are full and
breaking,
down by the deep, deep sea.

5 Called their friends to come and
help them,
down by the deep, deep sea.

6 We are fishers of men for Jesus,
out on life's big sea.

  * The first line of each verse is sung three
times.

Anonymous

356

1 Tell me the stories of Jesus
I love to hear;
things I would ask Him to tell me
if He were here;
scenes by the wayside,
tales of the sea,
stories of Jesus,
tell them to me.

2 First let me hear how the
children
stood round His knee;
that I may know of His blessing
resting on me;
words full of kindness,
deeds full of grace,
signs of the love found
in Jesus' face.

3 Tell me in words full of wonder,
how rolled the sea,
tossing the boat in a tempest
on Galilee;
Jesus then doing
His Father's will,
ended the storm saying
Peace, peace be still.

4 Into the city I'd follow
the children's band,
waving a branch of the palm-tree
high in my hand;
worshipping Jesus,
yes, I would sing
loudest hosannas,
for He is King.

5 Show me that scene in the
garden,
of bitter pain;
and of the cross where my
Saviour
for me was slain;
and, through the sadness,
help me to see
how Jesus suffered
for love of me.

6 Gladly I'd hear of His rising
out of the grave,
living and strong and
triumphant,
mighty to save;
and how He sends us
all men to bring
stories of Jesus,
Jesus, their King.

William Henry Parker, 1845–1929
and Hugh Martin, 1890–1964
adapted Peter J. Horrobin, b. 1943
and Greg P. Leavers, b. 1952

357

1 The wise man built his house
upon the rock.
The wise man built his house
upon the rock.
The wise man built his house
upon the rock
and the rain came tumbling
down.
And the rain came down and the
floods came up,
the rain came down and the
floods came up,
the rain came down and the
floods came up,
and the house on the rock stood
firm.

355 Words and Music: © 1957 Songspiration Music
356 Words: © Peter Horrobin and Greg Leavers/Ellel Ministries International. Used by permission.

2 The foolish man built his house
      upon the sand.
   The foolish man built his house
      upon the sand.
   The foolish man built his house
      upon the sand
   and the rain came tumbling
      down.
   And the rain came down and the
      floods came up,
   the rain came down and the
      floods came up,
   the rain came down and the
      floods came up,
   and the house on the sand fell
      flat.

Anonymous

358

1 We are singing to You, Lord, our
      thanks and our joy,
   that You love every girl and You
      love every boy.
   We worship You, Lord, for You
      made everything;
   teach us more of Yourself, till we
      make You our King.

2 We are singing to You, Lord, our
      joy at Your birth;
   You left glory in heav'n to share
      our life on earth.
   You brought us forgiveness and
      joy, so we sing;
   teach us more of Yourself, till we
      make You our King.

3 We are singing our thanks that
      You took all the shame
   for our sin when You died —
      t'was for this that You came.
   To You, dear Lord Jesus, our
      praises we bring;
   teach us more of Yourself, till we
      make You our King.

Margaret V. Old, 1932–2001

359

1 We have a gospel to proclaim,
      good news for all throughout the
      earth;
   the gospel of a Saviour's name:
   we sing His glory, tell His worth.

2 Tell of His birth at Bethlehem,
   not in a royal house or hall
   but in a stable dark and dim,
   the Word made flesh, a light for
      all.

3 Tell of His death at Calvary,
   hated by those He came to save,
   in lonely suffering on the cross;
   for all He loved His life He gave.

4 Tell of that glorious Easter morn:
   empty the tomb, for He was free.
   He broke the power of death and
      hell
   that we might share His victory.

5 Tell of His reign at God's right
      hand,
   by all creation glorified.
   He sends His Spirit on His
      Church
   to live for Him, the Lamb who
      died.

6 Now we rejoice to name Him
      King:
   Jesus is Lord of all the earth.
   This gospel-message we
      proclaim:
   we sing His glory, tell His worth.

Edward Joseph Burns, *b.* 1938

360

1 What a wonderful Saviour is
      Jesus,
   what a wonderful friend is He,
   for He left all the glory of heaven,
   came to earth to die on Calvary:
      Sing hosanna! Sing hosanna!
      Sing hosanna to the King of kings!
      Sing hosanna! Sing hosanna!
      Sing hosanna to the King.

2 He arose from the grave,
      Hallelujah!
   and He lives never more to die,
   at the Father's right hand
      interceding
   He will hear and heed our
      faintest cry:

3 He is coming some day to receive
      us,
   we'll be caught up to heaven
      above,
   what a joy it will be to behold
      Him,
   sing forever of His grace and
      love.

Anonymous

361

1 Who is He, in yonder stall,
at whose feet the shepherds fall?
'Tis the Lord! O wondrous story!
'Tis the Lord, the King of glory!
At His feet we humbly fall;
crown Him, crown Him Lord of
all!

2 Who is He in deep distress,
fasting in the wilderness?

3 Who is He the gathering throng
greet with loud triumphant song?

4 Lo! at midnight, who is He,
prays in dark Gethsemane?

5 Who is He on yonder tree
dies in shame and agony?

6 Who is He that from the grave
comes to heal and help and
save?

7 Who is He that from His throne
rules through all the world
alone?

Benjamin Russell Hanby, 1833–1867

362

1 Who is He, in yonder stall,
at whose feet the shepherds fall?
'Tis the Lord! O wondrous story!
'Tis the Lord, the King of glory!

2 Who is He in deep distress,
fasting in the wilderness?

3 Who is He the gathering throng
greet with loud triumphant song?

4 Lo! at midnight, who is He,
prays in dark Gethsemane?

5 Who is He on yonder tree
dies in shame and agony?

6 Who is He that from the grave
comes to heal and help and
save?

7 Who is He that from His throne
rules through all the world
alone?

Benjamin Russell Hanby, 1833–1867

363

1 You are the way, to You alone
from sin and death we run:
and those who would the Father
seek
must seek Him through the Son.

2 You are the truth, Your Word
alone
true wisdom can impart:
You only can inform the mind
and purify the heart.

3 You are the life, the empty tomb
proclaims Your conquering arm:
and those who put their trust in
You
nor death nor hell shall harm.

4 You are the Way, the Truth, the
Life:
grant us that way to see,
that truth to keep, that life to
know
through all eternity.

George Washington Doane, 1799–1859
altered

Also suitable:
Lord Jesus Christ, You have come to us   388

JESUS CHRIST HEALING

364

1 At evening, when the sun had
set,
the sick, O Lord, around You lay:
in what distress and pain they
met,
but in what joy they went away!

2 Once more the evening comes,
and we,
oppressed with various ills, draw
near;
and though Your form we cannot
see,
we know and feel that You are
here.

3 O Saviour Christ, our fears
dispel —
for some are sick and some are
sad,
and some have never loved You
well,
and some have lost the love they
had.

4 And none, O Lord, has perfect
rest,
for none is wholly free from sin;
and those who long to serve You
best
are conscious most of wrong
within.

5 O Saviour Christ, the Son of Man,
  You have been troubled, tested, tried;
  Your kind but searching glance can scan
  the very wounds that shame would hide.

6 Your touch has still its ancient power;
  no word from You can fruitless fall:
  meet with us in this evening hour
  and in Your mercy heal us all!

Henry Twells, 1823–1900
adapted Jubilate Hymns

365

1 From You all skill and science flow,
  all pity, care and love,
  all calm and courage, faith and hope —
  O pour them from above!

2 And share them, Lord, to each and all,
  as each and all have need;
  so let Your gifts return to You
  in noble thought and deed.

3 And hasten, Lord, that perfect day
  when pain and death shall cease,
  and Your just rule shall fill the earth
  with health and light and peace:

4 When ever green the grass shall be,
  and ever blue the skies,
  and our destruction shall no more
  deface Your paradise.

Charles Kingsley, 1819–1875
adapted Michael Arnold Perry, 1942–1996

366

1 Immortal Love, for ever full,
  for ever flowing free,
  for ever shared, for ever whole,
  a never-ebbing sea!

2 Blow, winds of God, awake and blow
  the mists of earth away:
  shine out, O Light Divine, and show
  how wide and far we stray.

3 We may not climb the heavenly steeps
  to bring the Lord Christ down;
  in vain we search the lowest deeps,
  for Him no depths can drown.

4 And not for signs in heaven above,
  or earth below, they look
  who know with John His smile of love,
  with Peter His rebuke.

5 In joy of inward peace, or sense of sorrow over sin,
  He is His own best evidence;
  His witness is within.

6 And, warm, sweet, tender, even yet
  a present help is He;
  and faith has still its Olivet,
  and love its Galilee.

7 The healing of His seamless dress
  is by our beds of pain;
  we touch Him in life's throng and press,
  and we are whole again.

John Greenleaf Whittier, 1807–1892

367

1 We cannot measure how You heal
  or answer every sufferer's prayer,
  yet we believe Your grace responds
  where faith and doubt unite to care.
  Your hands, though bloodied on the cross,
  survive to hold and heal and warn,
  to carry all through death to life
  and cradle children yet unborn.

2 The pain that will not go away,
  the guilt that clings from things long past,
  the fear of what the future holds,
  are present as if meant to last.
  But present too is love which tends
  the hurt we never hoped to find,
  the private agonies inside,
  the memories that haunt the mind.

3 So some have come who need
Your help
and some have come to make
amends,
as hands which shaped and
saved the world
are present in the touch of
friends.
Lord, let Your Spirit meet us here
to mend the body, mind and soul,
to disentangle peace from pain
and make Your broken people
whole.

John Lamberton Bell, *b.* 1949
and Graham Alexander Maule, *b.* 1958

368

1 We give God thanks for those
who knew
the touch of Jesus' healing love,
they trusted Him to make them
whole,
to give them peace, their guilt
remove.

2 We offer prayer for all who go,
relying on His grace and power,
to help the anxious and the ill,
to heal their wounds, their lives
restore.

3 We dedicate our skills and time
to those who suffer where we
live,
to bring such comfort as we can
to meet their need, their pain
relieve.

4 So Jesus' touch of healing grace
lives on within our willing care;
by thought and prayer and gift
we prove
His mercy still, His love we
share.

Michael Arnold Perry, 1942–1996

369

1 Your will for us and others, Lord,
is perfect health and wholeness,
and we must seek for nothing
less
than life in all its fullness.

2 As Jesus dealt with human ills,
Your purposes revealing,
so may Your servants in this day
be channels of Your healing.

3 For suffering bodies, minds and
souls
that long for restoration,
accept our prayers of faith and
love,
and grant us all salvation;

4 So we would claim Your
promised grace,
Your presence and protection;
and, tasting now eternal life,
press on toward perfection.

Freda Nancy Head, *b.* 1914

Also suitable:
Fill your hearts with joy and gladness	42
I'll lift my voice, O Lord	91
Jesus' hands were kind hands	349
Jesus, lover of my soul	67
Merciful God and Father	71
O for a thousand tongues	221

JESUS CHRIST
BAPTISM

370

1 A little child the Saviour came,
the Mighty God was still His
name,
and angels worshipped as He lay,
the seeming infant of a day.

2 He who, a little child, once came
the life divine here to proclaim,
declares from heaven the
message free,
'Let little children come to me.'

3 We bring them here, O Lord
divine,
with sprinkled water as the sign;
their souls with saving grace
endow;
baptize them with Your Spirit
now.

4 O give Your angels charge, good
Lord,
them safely in Your way to
guard;
Your blessing on their lives
command,
and write their names upon Your
hand.

5   O Saviour, by an infant's tongue
     You hear Your perfect glory sung,
     may these, with all the heavenly
          host,
     praise Father, Son and Holy
          Ghost.

                    William Robertson, 1820–1864
                            adapted Compilers

371

1   Child of blessing, child of
          promise,
     baptised with the Spirit's sign,
     with this water God has sealed
          you
     unto love and grace divine.

2   Child of love, our love's
          expression,
     Love's creation, loved indeed!
     Fresh from God, refresh our
          spirits,
     into joy and laughter lead.

3   Child of joy, our dearest treasure,
     God's you are, from God you
          came.
     Back to God we humbly give
          you:
     live as one who bears Christ's
          name.

4   Child of God, your loving Parent,
     learn to listen for God's call.
     Grow to laugh and sing and
          worship,
     trust and love God more than all.

                            Ronald S. Cole-Turner

372

1   Dearest Jesus, we are here,
     gladly Your command obeying.
     With this child we now draw
          near
     in response to Your own saying
     that to You it shall be given
     as a child and heir of heaven.

2   Your command is clear and plain,
     and we would obey it duly:
     "You must all be born again,
     heart and life renewing truly,
     born of water and the Spirit,
     and my kingdom thus inherit."

3   This is why we come to You,
     in our arms this infant bearing;
     Lord, to us Your glory show;

let this child, Your mercy sharing,
in Your arms be shielded ever,
Yours on earth and Yours forever.

                    Heilige Flammen, Leipzig, 1720
                    Benjamin Schmolck, 1672–1737
          translated Catherine Winkworth, 1827–1878
                    reconstructed Compilers of
                    Presbyterian Hymnal, USA

373

1   O Father, in Your father-heart
     we know our children have their
          part;
     we sign them in Your threefold
          Name,
     and by the sprinkled water claim
     Your covenant in Christ revealed,
     to us and to our children sealed.

2   Name of the Father, pledge that
          we
     in You our inmost being see;
     Name of the Son, whereby we
          know
     the Father's love to all below;
     Name of the Spirit, blessèd sign
     that now we share the life divine.

3   Fulfil Your covenant of love;
     baptise our children from above;
     Your best, Your highest gift
          impart,
     the blessing of a childlike heart,
     and mould them through life's
          strain and stress
     to the full growth of perfectness.

                    Ella Sophia Armitage, 1841–1931
                            slightly altered

374

1   O God, Your life-creating love
     this sacred trust to parents gave.
     In Christ Your power came from
          above
     Your children here to claim and
          save.

2   Help us who now our pledges
          give
     the young to cherish, guard and
          guide,
     to learn of Christ, and so to live
     that they may in Your love abide.

3   Grant, Lord, as strength and
          wisdom grow,
     that every child Your truth may
          learn.

371 Words: © 1981 Ronald Cole-Turner
374 Words: © 1988 Oxford University Press. Reproduced by permission., Great Clarendon Street, Oxford OX2 6DP

Impart Your light, that each may
know
Your will, and life's true way
discern.

4 Then home and child, kept in
Your peace,
and guarded, Father, by Your
care,
will in the grace of Christ
increase,
and all Your kingdom's blessings
share.

Albert Frederick Bayly, 1901–1984
altered Compilers of *Rejoice and Sing*, 1991

375

1 Our children, Lord, in faith and
prayer
we bring before Your face;
let them Your covenant mercies
share
and save them by Your grace.

2 In early days their hearts secure
from evil ways, we pray;
and let them to life's end endure
by walking in Your way.

3 We do not ask for wealth or fame
for them in this world's strife;
we ask, in Your almighty Name:
'Give them eternal life!'

4 Before them let their parents live
in godly faith and fear;
then, Lord, to heaven their souls
receive
and bring their children there.

Thomas Haweis, 1733–1820
and Thomas Hastings, 1784–1872
adapted Compilers of *Praise!* 2000

376

1 Our children, Lord, in faith and
prayer
we bring before Your face;
let them Your covenant mercies
share
and save them by Your grace.

2 Such little ones in Your embrace
You took while here below;
to us and ours, O God of grace,
the same compassion show.

3 O Lord, Your infant feet were
found
within Your Father's shrine:
Your years with changeless virtue
crowned
were all alike divine:

4 Dependent on Your bounteous
breath
we seek Your grace alone,
in childhood, manhood, age and
death,
to keep us still Your own.

Thomas Haweis, 1733–1820
and Reginald Heber, 1783–1826
v. 2 altered Compilers
vv. 3, 4 altered Compilers of
Church Hymnary, 3rd edition, 1973

377

The Apostles' Creed

I believe in
God the Father Almighty,
maker of heaven and earth,
and in Jesus Christ His only Son
our Lord,
who was conceived by the Holy
Spirit,
born of the virgin Mary,
suffered under Pontius Pilate,
was crucified, dead and buried:
He descended into hell.
The third day He rose again from
the dead,
He ascended into heaven
and sitteth on the right hand of
God the Father Almighty:
from thence He shall come to
judge the quick and the dead.
I believe in
the Holy Spirit;
the holy catholic Church;
the communion of saints;
the forgiveness of sins,
the resurrection of the body;
and the life everlasting. Amen.

Liturgical text

378

The Apostles' Creed

I believe in God, the Father
Almighty,
Creator of heaven and earth.
I believe in Jesus Christ,
God's only Son, our Lord,
who was conceived by the Holy
Spirit,
born of the virgin Mary,
suffered under Pontius Pilate,
was crucified, died and was
buried:
He descended to the dead.
On the third day He rose again;

He ascended into heaven,
and is seated at the right hand of
the Father,
and will come again to judge the
living and the dead.
I believe in the Holy Spirit,
the holy catholic Church,
the communion of saints,
the forgiveness of sins,
the resurrection of the body,
and the life everlasting. Amen.

Liturgical text

JESUS CHRIST
THE LORD'S SUPPER

379

1   According to Your gracious word,
    because You died for me,
    I will remember You, my Lord,
    in meek humility.

2   Your body, broken for my sake,
    my bread from heaven shall be;
    I will remember You, and take
    this cup You gave for me.

3   Can I Gethsemane forget
    or Your fierce conflict see,
    and not remember there Your
        sweat
    in blood and agony?

4   And when I look upon Your
        blood
    once shed on Calvary,
    I will remember, Lamb of God,
    Your sacrifice for me.

5   Yes, while a breath, a pulse
        remains,
    this is my only plea;
    I will remember all Your pains,
    which made me whole and free.

6   And when these failing lips grow
        dumb
    and mind and memory flee,
    when You shall in Your kingdom
        come,
    Jesus, remember me.

James Montgomery, 1771–1854
adapted Compilers of Praise! 2000

380

1   Alleluia, sing to Jesus!
    His the sceptre, His the throne:
    Alleluia! — His the triumph,
    His the victory alone.
    Hear the songs of holy Zion
    thunder like a mighty flood:
    'Jesus out of every nation
    has redeemed us by His blood!'

2   Alleluia! — not as orphans
    are we left in sorrow now:
    Alleluia! — He is near us;
    faith believes, nor questions how.
    Though the cloud from sight
        received Him
    whom the angels now adore,
    shall our hearts forget His
        promise,
    'I am with you evermore'?

3   Alleluia! — Bread of Heaven,
    here on earth our food, our stay:
    Alleluia! — here the sinful
    come to You from day to day.
    Intercessor, friend of sinners,
    earth's Redeemer, plead for me,
    where the songs of all the sinless
    sweep across the crystal sea.

4   Alleluia, sing to Jesus!
    His the sceptre, His the throne:
    Alleluia! — His the triumph,
    His the victory alone.
    Hear the songs of holy Zion
    thunder like a mighty flood:
    'Jesus out of every nation
    has redeemed us by His blood!'

William Chatterton Dix, 1837–1898
altered

381

1   All who are thirsty, come to the
        Lord,
    all who are hungry, feed on His
        word;
    buy without paying, food without
        price,
    eat with thanksgiving God's
        sacrifice.

2   Why spend your money, yet have
        no bread;
    why work for nothing? Trust
        God instead!
    He will provide you richest of
        food:
    come to the waters, drink what is
        good.

3   Call on God's mercy while He is
        near,
    turn from your evil, come
        without fear;
    ask Him for pardon — grace will
        abound!
    This is the moment He can be
        found.

4   Where once were briers, flowers
        will grow,
    where lives were barren, rivers
        will flow:
    praise to our Saviour: grace and
        renown —
    ours is the blessing, His be the
        crown!

                    Michael Arnold Perry, 1942–1996

382

1   And now, O Father, mindful of
        the love
    which bought us once for all on
        Calvary's tree,
    and having with us Christ who
        reigns above,
    we celebrate with joy for all to
        see
    that only offering perfect in Your
        eyes:
    the one true, pure, immortal
        sacrifice.

2   Look, Father, look on His
        anointed face,
    and only look on us as found in
        Him;
    look not on our misusings of Your
        grace,
    our prayer so feeble and our faith
        so dim;
    for, set between our sins and their
        reward,
    we see the cross of Christ, Your
        Son, our Lord.

3   And so we come: O draw us to
        Your feet,
    most patient Saviour, who can
        love us still;
    and by this food, so awesome and
        so sweet,
    deliver us from every touch of
        ill;
    for Your glad service, Master, set
        us free,
    and make of us what You would
        have us be.

                    William Bright, 1824–1901
                    adapted Jubilate Hymns

383

Before Communion

1   Here, O my Lord, I see You face
        to face;
    here would I touch and handle
        things unseen;
    here grasp with firmer hand the
        eternal grace,
    and all my weariness upon You
        lean.

2   Mine is the sin, but Yours the
        righteousness;
    mine is the guilt, but Yours the
        cleansing blood;
    here is my robe, my refuge, and
        my peace —
    Your blood, Your righteousness, O
        Lord my God.

3   Here would I feed upon the
        bread of God,
    here drink with You the royal
        wine of heaven;
    here would I lay aside each
        earthly load,
    here taste afresh the calm of sin
        forgiven.

4   This is the hour of banquet and of
        song;
    this is the heavenly table for us
        spread;
    here let us feast, and feasting, still
        prolong
    the fellowship of living wine and
        bread.

After Communion

5   Too soon we rise, the symbols
        disappear;
    the feast, though not the love, is
        past and gone;
    the bread and wine remove, but
        You are here,
    nearer than ever, still my Shield
        and Sun.

6   I have no help but Yours; nor do
        I need
    another arm save Yours to lean
        upon;
    it is enough. My Lord, enough
        indeed;
    my strength is in Your might,
        Your might alone.

7 Feast after feast thus comes and
   passes by,
yet passing, points to that glad
   feast above,
giving sweet foretaste of the festal
   joy,
the Lamb's great bridal feast of
   bliss and love.

Horatius N. Bonar, 1808–1889
altered Compilers

384

1 I am not worthy, holy Lord,
that You should come to me:
but speak the word! — one
   gracious word
can set the sinner free.

2 I am not worthy — cold and bare
the lodging of my soul:
how can You stoop to enter here?
Lord, speak and make me whole.

3 I am not worthy; yet, my God,
shall I turn You away,
when You have given Your flesh
   and blood
my ransom price to pay?

4 Come, feed me now with food
   divine
in the appointed hour,
and this unworthy heart of mine
fill with Your love and power!

Henry Williams Baker, 1821–1877
adapted Jubilate Hymns

385

1 Jesus, the joy of loving hearts,
Fountain of life and Light of men,
from the best bliss that earth
   imparts
we turn unfilled to You again.

2 Your truth unchanged has always
   stood;
You save all those who on You
   call:
to those who seek You, O how
   good!
To those who find You, all-in-all!

3 We taste of You, the living Bread,
and long to feast upon You still;
we drink of You, the Fountain-
   head,
and thirst our souls from You to
   fill.

4 Our restless spirits long for You,
no matter where our lot is cast,
glad when Your gracious smile
   we view,
blessed when our faith can hold
   You fast.

5 O Jesus, ever with us stay;
make all our moments calm and
   bright;
chase the dark night of sin away;
spread through the world Your
   holy light.

Jesu dulcis memoria Latin 12th century
translated Ray Palmer, 1808–1887

386

1 Let all mortal flesh keep silence,
and with fear and trembling
   stand;
set your minds on things eternal,
for with blessing in His hand
Christ our God to earth
   descending
comes our homage to command.

2 King of kings, yet born of Mary,
once upon the earth He stood;
Lord of lords we now perceive
   Him
in His body and His blood —
He will give to all the faithful
His own self for heavenly food.

3 Rank on rank the host of heaven
stream before Him on the way;
as the Light of light descending
from the realms of endless day
vanquishes the powers of evil,
clears the gloom of hell away.

4 At His feet the six-winged
   seraphs,
cherubim with sleepless eye,
veil their faces in His presence
as with ceaseless voice they cry:
'Alleluia, alleluia,
alleluia, Lord most high!'

translated Gerard Moultrie, 1829–1885
based on the Liturgy of St James
adapted Jubilate Hymns

387

1 Let us break bread together on
   our knees,
let us break bread together on our
   knees:
When I fall on my knees,
with my face to the rising sun,
O Lord, have mercy on me!

2   Let us drink wine together on our
      knees,
    let us drink wine together on our
      knees:

3   Let us praise God together on our
      knees,
    let us praise God together on our
      knees:

Anonymous Afro-American

388

1   Lord Jesus Christ, You have come
      to us,
    You are one with us, Mary's Son;
    cleansing our souls from all their
      sin,
    pouring Your love and goodness
      in:
    Jesus, our love for You we sing —
    living Lord!

2   Lord Jesus Christ, You have come
      to us,
    born as one of us, Mary's Son;
    led out to die on Calvary,
    risen from death to set us free:
    living Lord Jesus, help us see
    You are Lord!

3   Lord Jesus Christ, I would come
      to You,
    live my life for You, Son of God;
    all Your commands I know are
      true,
    Your many gifts will make me
      new:
    into my life Your power breaks
      through —
    living Lord!

4   Lord Jesus Christ, now and every
      day
    teach us how to pray, Son of God;
    You have commanded us to do
    this in remembrance, Lord, of
      You:
    into our lives Your power breaks
      through —
    living Lord!

Patrick Robert Norman Appleford, b. 1925

389

1   Lord, enthroned in heavenly
      splendour,
    first-begotten from the dead,
    You alone, our strong defender,
    now lift up Your people's head.
    Alleluia!   Alleluia!
    Jesus, true and living Bread!

2   Here our humblest homage pay
      we,
    here in loving reverence bow;
    here for faith's discernment pray
      we,
    lest we fail to know You now.
    Alleluia!   Alleluia!
    You are here, we ask not how.

3   Paschal Lamb, Your offering,
      finished
    once for all when You were slain,
    in its fullness undiminished
    shall for evermore remain.
    Alleluia!   Alleluia!
    Cleansing us from every stain.

4   Life-imparting heavenly manna,
    smitten rock with streaming side,
    heaven and earth with loud
      hosanna
    worship You, the Lamb who died.
    Alleluia!   Alleluia!
    Risen, ascended, glorified!

George Hugh Bourne, 1840–1925
slightly altered

390

1   Now let us from this table rise
    renewed in body, mind and soul;
    with Christ we die and rise
      again,
    His selfless love has made us
      whole.

2   With minds alert, upheld by
      grace,
    to spread the Word in speech and
      deed,
    we follow in the steps of Christ,
    at one with all in hope and need.

3   To fill each human house with
      love,
    it is the sacrament of care;
    the work that Christ began to do
    we humbly pledge ourselves to
      share.

4   Then grant us grace,
      Companion-God,
    to choose again the pilgrim way,
    and help us to accept with joy
    the challenge of tomorrow's day.

Frederik Herman Kaan, b. 1929

391

1 Sent forth by God's blessing, our
true faith confessing,
the people of God from His table
take leave.
The supper is ended; O now be
extended
the fruits of His service in all
who believe.
The seed of His teaching, our
hungry souls reaching,
shall blossom in action for God
and for all.
His grace shall incite us, His love
shall unite us
to further God's Kingdom and
answer His call.

2 With praise and thanksgiving to
God ever living,
the tasks of our everyday life we
will face.
Our faith ever sharing, in love
ever caring,
we claim as our neighbours the
whole human race.
One Bread that has fed us, one
Light that has led us,
unite us as one in His life that we
share.
Then may all the living, with
praise and thanksgiving,
give honour to Christ and His
name that we bear.

Omer Westendorf, 1916–1998
altered

392

1 Shout for joy! The Lord has let
us feast;
heaven's own fare has fed the
last and least;
Christ's own peace is shared
again on earth;
God the Spirit fills us with new
worth.

2 No more doubting, no more
senseless dread:
Christ's good self has graced our
wine and bread;
all the wonder heaven has kept
in store
now is ours to keep for evermore.

3 Celebrate with saints who dine
on high,
witnesses that love can never die.

'Hallelujah!' — Thus their voices
ring:
nothing less in gratitude we
bring.

4 Praise the Maker, praise the
Maker's Son,
praise the Spirit — Three yet
ever One;
praise the God whose food and
friends avow
heaven starts here! The
kingdom beckons now!

John Lamberton Bell, b. 1949

393

1 We come as guests invited
when Jesus bids us dine,
His friends on earth united
to share the bread and wine;
the bread of life is broken,
the wine is freely poured
for us, in solemn token
of Christ our dying Lord.

2 We eat and drink, receiving
from Christ the grace we need,
and in our hearts believing
on Him by faith we feed;
with wonder and thanksgiving
for love that knows no end,
we find in Jesus living
our ever-present friend.

3 One bread is ours for sharing,
one single fruitful vine,
our fellowship declaring
renewed in bread and wine:
renewed, sustained and given
by token, sign and word,
the pledge and seal of heaven,
the love of Christ our Lord.

Timothy Dudley-Smith, b. 1926

394

The Nicene Creed

We believe in one God the
Father Almighty
maker of heaven and earth, and
of all things visible and
invisible:

and in one Lord Jesus Christ, the
only begotten Son of God,
God of God, Light of Light, Very
God of Very God, begotten, not
made, being of one substance
with the Father, by whom all
things were made:

who for us, and for our salvation,
came down from heaven,
and was incarnate by the Holy
Spirit of the virgin Mary, and
was made man,
and was crucified also for us
under Pontius Pilate.
He suffered and was buried;
and the third day He rose again
according to the Scriptures, and
ascended into heaven, and sits
on the right hand of the Father.
And He shall come again with
glory to judge both the quick
and the dead,
whose Kingdom shall have no
end.

And we believe in the Holy
Spirit, the Lord the Giver of
Life, who proceeds from the
Father and the Son:
who with the Father and the Son
together is worshipped and
glorified; who spoke by the
prophets.
And we believe one holy catholic
and apostolic Church.
We acknowledge one baptism for
the remission of sins.
And we look for the resurrection
of the dead and the life of the
world to come. Amen.

Contemporary Version

We believe in One God, the
Father, the almighty, maker of
heaven and earth, of all that is,
seen and unseen.

We believe in one Lord, Jesus
Christ, the only Son of God,
eternally begotten of the Father,
God from God, Light from Light,
True God from True God,
begotten not made, of one Being
with the Father.
Through Him all things were
made.
For us and for our salvation He
came down from heaven;
by the power of the Holy Spirit
He became incarnate of the
virgin Mary, and was made
man.
For our sake He was crucified
under Pontius Pilate;
He suffered death and was
buried.
He rose again in accordance with
the Scriptures.

He ascended into heaven and is
seated at the right hand of the
Father
He will come again in glory to
judge the living and the dead,
and his kingdom shall have no
end.

We believe in the Holy Spirit, the
Lord, the Giver of Life, who
proceeds from the Father and
the Son.
With the Father and the Son He
is worshipped and glorified.
He has spoken through the
Prophets.
We believe in one holy catholic
and apostolic Church.
We acknowledge one baptism for
the forgiveness of sins.
We look for the resurrection of
the dead,
and the life of the world to come.
Amen.

Liturgical text

Also suitable:

He gave His life in selfless love   400
This earth belongs to God   194
We believe in God Almighty   163

JESUS CHRIST HIS PASSION AND DEATH

395

All glory, praise and honour,
to You, Redeemer, King,
to whom the lips of children
made sweet hosannas ring.

1 'You are the King of Israel,
   great David's greater Son;
   You ride in lowly triumph,
   the Lord's anointed One!'

2 The company of angels
   are praising You on high,
   and we with all creation
   together make reply:

3 The people of the Hebrews
   with palms before You went;
   our praise and prayer and
      anthems
   before You we present.

4 To You, before Your passion,
   they sang their hymns of praise;

to You, now high exalted,
our melody we raise.

5 As You received their praises,
accept the prayers we bring,
for You delight in goodness,
O good and gracious King!

Theodulph of Orleans, c. 750–821
translated John Mason Neale, 1818–1866
adapted Jubilate Hymns

396

1 Alone You make Your way, O
    Lord,
  in sacrifice to die;
  Your sorrow, does it matter not
  to us who just pass by?

2 Our sins, not Yours, You carry,
    Lord,
  make us Your sorrow feel,
  till through our pity and our
    shame
  love answers love's appeal.

3 This is earth's darkest hour, but
    You
  its light and life restore;
  then let all praise be given You
  alive for evermore.

4 Grant us to suffer with You, Lord,
  that, as we share this hour,
  Your cross may bring us to Your
    joy
  and resurrection power.

Peter Abelard, 1079–1142
translated Francis Bland Tucker, 1895–1984
altered Compilers

397

1 Children of Jerusalem
  sang the praise of Jesus' name:
  children, too, of modern days
  join to sing the Saviour's praise.
    Hark! Hark! Hark!
    While infant voices sing
    loud hosannas, loud hosannas,
    loud hosannas to our King.

2 We are taught to love the Lord,
  we are taught to read His word,
  we are taught the way to heaven:
  praise for all to God be given.

3 Parents, teachers, old and young,
  all unite to swell the song,
  higher and yet higher rise,
  till hosannas reach the skies.

John Henley, 1800–1842

398

1 Come and see, come and see,
  come and see the King of Love;
  see the purple robe and crown of
    thorns He wears.
  Soldiers mock, rulers sneer
  as He lifts the cruel cross;
  lone and friendless now, He
    climbs towards the hill.
    We worship at Your feet,
    where wrath and mercy meet,
    and a guilty world is washed by
    love's pure stream.
    For us He was made sin —
    O help me take it in.
    Deep wounds of love cry out,
    'Father, forgive.'
    I worship, I worship the Lamb who
    was slain.

2 Come and weep, come and
    mourn
  for your sin that pierced Him
    there;
  so much deeper than the wounds
    of thorn and nail.
  All our pride, all our greed,
  all our fallenness and shame;
  and the Lord has laid the
    punishment on Him.

3 Man of heaven, born to earth
  to restore us to Your heaven.
  Here we bow in awe beneath
    Your searching eyes.
  From Your tears comes our joy,
  from Your death our life shall
    spring;
  by Your resurrection power we
    shall rise.

Graham Andrew Kendrick, b. 1950

399

1 From heaven You came, helpless
    babe,
  entered our world, Your glory
    veiled;
  not to be served but to serve,
  and give Your life that we might
    live.
    This is our God, the Servant King,
    He calls us now to follow Him,
    to bring our lives as a daily
    offering
    of worship to the Servant King.

2 There in the garden of tears
  my heavy load He chose to bear;

His heart with sorrow was torn,
'Yet not my will but yours,' He
    said.

3 Come see His hands and His feet,
the scars that speak of sacrifice,
hands that flung stars into space
to cruel nails surrendered.

4 So let us learn how to serve
and in our lives enthrone Him;
each other's needs to prefer,
for it is Christ we're serving.

Graham Andrew Kendrick, b. 1950

400

1 He gave His life in selfless love,
for sinners once He came;
He had no stain of sin Himself
but bore our guilt and shame:
He took the cup of pain and
    death,
His blood was freely shed;
we see His body on the cross,
we share the living bread.

2 He did not come to call the good
but sinners to repent;
it was the lame, the deaf, the
    blind
for whom His life was spent:
to heal the sick, to find the lost —
it was for such He came,
and round His table all may
    come
to praise His holy name.

3 They heard Him call His Father's
    name —
then, 'Finished!' was His cry;
like them we have forsaken Him
and left Him there to die:
the sins that crucified Him then
are sins His blood has cured;
the love that bound Him to a
    cross
our freedom has ensured.

4 His body broken once for us
is glorious now above;
the cup of blessing we receive,
a sharing of His love:
as in His presence we partake,
His dying we proclaim
until the hour of majesty
when Jesus comes again.

Christopher Porteous, b. 1935

401

1 He was pierced for our
    transgressions,
and bruised for our iniquities;
and to bring us peace He was
    punished,
and by His stripes we are healed.

2 He was led like a lamb to the
    slaughter,
although He was innocent of
    crime;
and, cut off from the land of the
    living,
He paid for the guilt that was
    mine.

We like sheep have gone astray,
turned each one to their own way,
and the Lord has laid on Him
the iniquity of us all.
We like sheep ...

Maggi Dawn, b. 1959

402

1 Here is love vast as the ocean,
lovingkindness as the flood,
when the Prince of Life, our
    ransom,
shed for us His precious blood.
Who His love will not
    remember?
Who can cease to sing His praise?
He can never be forgotten,
throughout heaven's eternal
    days.

2 On the mount of crucifixion
fountains opened deep and
    wide;
through the floodgates of God's
    mercy
flowed a vast and gracious tide.
Grace and love, like mighty
    rivers,
poured incessant from above,
and heaven's peace and perfect
    justice
kissed a guilty world in love.

Dyma gariad fel y moroedd
William Rees, 1802–1883
translated William Edwards, 1848–1929

403

1 Hosanna, hosanna, hosanna in
   the highest;
   hosanna, hosanna, hosanna in the
   highest:
   Lord, we lift up Your name,
   with hearts full of praise.
   Be exalted, O Lord our God —
   hosanna, in the highest.

2 Glory, glory, glory to the King of
   kings;
   glory, glory, glory to the King of
   kings:
   Lord, we lift up Your name,
   with hearts full of praise.
   Be exalted, O Lord our God —
   glory to the King of kings.

Carl Tuttle, b. 1953

404

1 Hosanna! Hosanna!
   This is a special day.
   He's coming! He's coming!
   The King is on His way.
   Did you hear? Can it be?
   Riding on a colt is He.
   Hosanna! Hosanna!
   Blessèd be our Lord.

2 Hosanna! Hosanna!
   Oh, how the voices ring.
   We see Him! We see Him!
   He is our King of kings.
   Wave the palms, sing a song!
   We have waited for so long.
   Hosanna! Hosanna!
   Blessèd be our Lord.

Kathleen Tunseth

405

1 Hosanna, loud hosanna,
   the little children sang;
   through pillared court and
   temple
   the joyful anthem rang;
   to Jesus, who had blessed them
   close folded to His breast,
   the children sang their praises,
   the simplest and the best.

2 From Olivet they followed,
   'mid an exultant crowd,
   the victor palm branch waving,
   and chanting clear and loud;
   the Lord of earth and heaven
   rode on in lowly state,
   nor scorned that little children
   should on His bidding wait.

3 'Hosanna in the highest!'
   That ancient song we sing,
   for Christ is our Redeemer,
   the Lord of heaven our King.
   O may we ever praise Him
   with heart and life and voice,
   and in His blissful presence
   eternally rejoice.

Jennette Threlfall, 1821–1880

406

1 How can I be free from sin —
   lead me to the cross of Jesus,
   from the guilt, the power, the
   pain?
   Lead me to the cross of Jesus.
   There's no other way,
   no price that I could pay;
   simply to the cross I cling.
   This is all I need,
   this is all I plead,
   that His blood was shed for me.

2 How can I know peace within —
   lead me to the cross of Jesus,
   sing a song of joy again?
   Lead me to the cross of Jesus.
   Flowing from above,
   all-forgiving love
   from the Father's heart to me!
   What a gift of grace
   His own righteousness
   clothing me in purity!

3 How can I live day by day —
   lead me to the cross of Jesus,
   following His narrow way?
   Lead me to the cross of Jesus.

Graham Andrew Kendrick, b. 1950
and Steve Thompson

407

1 How deep the Father's love for
   us,
   how vast beyond all measure,
   that He should give His only Son
   to make a wretch His treasure.
   How great the pain of searing
   loss,
   the Father turns His face away,
   as wounds which mar the
   Chosen One
   bring many sons to glory.

2 Behold the Man upon a cross,
   my sin upon His shoulders;
   ashamed, I hear my mocking
   voice

HIS PASSION AND DEATH

call out among the scoffers.
It was my sin that held Him
  there,
until it was accomplished;
His dying breath has brought me
  life —
I know that it is finished.

3 I will not boast in anything,
no gifts, no power, no wisdom;
but I will boast in Jesus Christ,
His death and resurrection.
Why should I gain from His
  reward?
I cannot give an answer,
but this I know with all my heart,
His wounds have paid my
  ransom.

Stuart Townend, b. 1963

408

1 In Christ alone my hope is found,
He is my light, my strength, my
  song;
this cornerstone, this solid
  ground,
firm through the fiercest drought
  and storm.
What heights of love, what
  depths of peace,
when fears are stilled, when
  strivings cease!
My comforter, my all-in-all,
here in the love of Christ I stand.

2 In Christ alone — who took on
  flesh,
fullness of God in helpless babe;
this gift of love and
  righteousness,
scorned by the ones He came to
  save.
Till on that cross, as Jesus died,
the wrath of God was satisfied;
for every sin on Him was laid.
here in the death of Christ I live.

3 There in the ground His body lay,
Light of the world by darkness
  slain;
then bursting forth in glorious
  day
up from the grave He rose again!
And as He stands in victory
sin's curse has lost its grip on me,
for I am His and He is mine —
bought with the precious blood of
  Christ.

4 No guilt in life, no fear in death,
this is the power of Christ in me;
from life's first cry to final breath,
Jesus commands my destiny.
No power of hell, no scheme of
  man,
can ever pluck me from His
  hand;
till He returns or calls me home,
here in the power of Christ I'll
  stand!

Stuart Townend, b. 1963
and Keith Getty, b. 1974

409

1 In the cross of Christ I glory,
towering o'er the wrecks of time;
all the light of sacred story
gathers round its head sublime.

2 When the woes of life o'ertake
  me,
hopes deceive and fears annoy,
never shall the cross forsake me;
Lo! it glows with peace and joy.

3 When the sun of bliss is beaming
light and love upon my way,
from the cross the radiance
  streaming
adds more lustre to the day.

4 Bane and blessing, pain and
  pleasure,
by the cross are sanctified;
peace is there that knows no
  measure,
joys that through all time abide.

5 In the cross of Christ I glory,
towering o'er the wrecks of time;
all the light of sacred story
gathers round its head sublime.

John Bowring, 1792–1872

410

1 It is a thing most wonderful,
almost too wonderful to be,
that God's own Son should come
  from heaven,
and die to save a child like me.

2 And yet I know that it is true:
He came to this poor world
  below,
and wept and toiled, and
  mourned and died
only because He loved me so.

408 Words and Music: © 2001 Thankyou Music. Administered (UK and Europe) by Kingsway Music <tym@kingsway.co.uk>. Remaining territories administered by worshiptogether.com songs. Used by permission.
410 Words: © in this version Jubilate Hymns, 4 Thorne Park Road, Chelston, Torquay TQ2 6RX <enquiries@jubilate.co.uk> Used by permission.

JESUS CHRIST

3 I cannot tell how He could love
a child so weak and full of sin;
His love must be most wonderful,
if He could die my love to win.

4 And yet I want to love You, Lord:
O teach me how to grow in grace,
that I may love You more and
more,
until I see You face to face.

William Walsham How, 1823–1897
adapted Jubilate Hymns

411

1 Jesus Christ, I think upon Your
sacrifice,
You became nothing, poured out
to death.
Many times I've wondered at
Your gift of life,
and I'm in that place once again.
I'm in that place once again.
*And once again I look upon the
cross where You died,
I'm humbled by Your mercy and
I'm broken inside.
Once again I thank You, once
again I pour out my life.*

2 Now You are exalted to the
highest place,
King of the heavens, where one
day I'll bow.
But for now, I marvel at this
saving grace,
and I'm full of praise once again.
I'm full of praise once again.
And once again ...

3 Thank You for the cross, thank
You for the cross,
thank You for the cross, my
Friend.
Thank You for the cross, thank
You for the cross,
thank You for the cross, my
Friend.
And once again ...

Matt Redman, b. 1974

412

1 *Lift high the cross, the love of Christ
proclaim
till all the world adore His sacred
name.*

2 Come, Christians, follow where
the Captain trod,
the King victorious, Christ the
Son of God:

3 Each new-born soldier of the
Crucified
bears on the brow the seal of Him
who died:

4 This is the sign that Satan's
armies fear
and angels veil their faces to
revere:

5 O Lord, once lifted on the tree of
pain,
draw all the world to seek You
once again:

6 From farthest regions let them
homage bring
and on His cross adore their
Saviour King:

George William Kitchin, 1827–1912
and Michael Robert Newbolt, 1874–1956

413

1 Make way, make way, for Christ
the King
in splendour arrives.
Fling wide the gates and
welcome Him
into your lives.
*Make way! Make way
for the King of kings!
Make way! Make way
and let His kingdom in.*

2 He comes the broken hearts to
heal,
the prisoners to free;
the deaf shall hear, the lame shall
dance,
the blind shall see.

3 And those who mourn with
heavy hearts,
who weep and sigh,
with laughter, joy and royal
crown
He'll beautify.

4 We call you now to worship Him
as Lord of all,
to have no other gods but Him;
their thrones must fall.

Graham Andrew Kendrick, b. 1950

414

1 Man of Sorrows! what a name
for the Son of God, who came
ruined sinners to reclaim:
Hallelujah! what a Saviour!

2 Mocked by insults harsh and
    crude,
in my place condemned He
    stood;
sealed my pardon with His
    blood:
Hallelujah! what a Saviour!

3 Guilty, vile and helpless, we;
spotless Lamb of God was He:
full atonement — can it be?
Hallelujah! what a Saviour!

4 Lifted up was He to die,
'It is finished!' was His cry;
now in heaven, exalted high:
Hallelujah! what a Saviour!

5 When He comes, our glorious
    King,
all His ransomed home to bring;
then anew this song we'll sing:
Hallelujah! what a Saviour!

Philipp Paul Bliss, 1838–1876

415

1 Meekness and majesty,
manhood and deity,
in perfect harmony,
the Man who is God:
Lord of eternity
dwells in humanity,
kneels in humility
and washes our feet.
    Oh what a mystery, meekness and
      majesty:
    bow down and worship, for this is
      your God,
    this is your God!

2 Father's pure radiance,
perfect in innocence,
yet learns obedience
to death on a cross:
suffering to give us life,
conquering through sacrifice;
and, as they crucify,
prays, 'Father forgive.'

3 Wisdom unsearchable,
God the invisible,
Love indestructible
in frailty appears.
Lord of infinity,
stooping so tenderly,
lifts our humanity
to the heights of His throne.

Graham Andrew Kendrick, b. 1950

416

1 My Lord, what love is this
that pays so dearly,
that I, the guilty one,
may go free!
    Amazing love, O what sacrifice,
    the Son of God given for me.
    My debt He pays and my death He
      dies,
    that I might live, that I might live.

2 And so, they watched Him die,
despised, rejected;
but oh, the blood He shed
flowed for me!

3 And now this love of Christ
shall flow like rivers;
come, wash your guilt away,
live again!

Graham Andrew Kendrick, b. 1950

417

1 My song is love unknown,
my Saviour's love for me;
love to the loveless shown that
    they might lovely be:
but who am I, that for my sake
my Lord should take frail flesh
    and die?

2 He came from heaven's throne
salvation to bestow;
but they refused, and none the
    longed-for Christ would
    know:
this is my Friend, my Friend
    indeed,
who at my need His life did
    spend.

3 Sometimes they crowd His way
and His sweet praises sing,
resounding all the day hosannas
    to their King:
then 'Crucify!' is all their breath,
and for His death they thirst and
    cry.

4 Why, what has my Lord done
to cause this rage and spite?
He made the lame to run, and
gave the blind their sight:
what injuries! yet these are why
the Lord most high so cruelly
    dies.

5 They rise, and they must have
my dear Lord done away;
a murderer they save, the Prince
of Life they slay!
Yet, willingly, to shame He goes,
that He His foes from this might
free.

6 In life, no house, no home
my Lord on earth might have;
in death, no friendly tomb but
what a stranger gave.
What may I say? Heaven was
His home,
but mine the tomb wherein He
lay.

7 Here might I stay and sing
of Him my soul adores;
never was love, dear King, never
was grief like Yours!
This is my Friend, in whose
sweet praise
I all my days could gladly spend.

Samuel Crossman, c. 1624–1683
vv. 1-5, 7 *adapted* Jubilate Hymns

418

1 O come and mourn with me
awhile;
come now unto the Saviour's
side;
O come, together let us mourn:
Jesus, our Lord, is crucified.

2 Have we no tears to shed for
Him
while soldiers scoff and foes
deride?
Ah, look how patiently He hangs:
Jesus, our Lord, is crucified.

3 Seven times He spoke, seven
words of love;
and all three hours His silence
cried
for mercy on the human race:
Jesus, our Lord, is crucified.

4 O break, O break, hard heart of
mine!
Your weak self-love and guilty
pride
His Pilate and His Judas were:
Jesus, our Lord, is crucified.

5 O love divine! O human sin!
In this dread act Your strength is
tried;
and victory remains with love:
Jesus, our Lord, is crucified.

Frederick William Faber, 1814–1863

419

1 O dearest Lord, Thy sacred head
with thorns was pierced for me;
O pour Thy blessing on my head,
that I may think for Thee.

2 O dearest Lord, Thy sacred hands
with nails were pierced for me;
O shed Thy blessing on my
hands,
that they may work for Thee.

3 O dearest Lord, Thy sacred feet
with nails were pierced for me;
O pour Thy blessing on my feet,
that they may follow Thee.

4 O dearest Lord, Thy sacred heart
with spear was pierced for me:
O pour Thy Spirit in my heart,
that I may live for Thee.

Henry Ernest Hardy, 1869–1946

420

1 O sacred head once wounded,
with grief and shame weighed
down,
how scornfully surrounded
with thorns, Your only crown!
How pale You are with anguish,
with fierce abuse and scorn!
How do those features languish
which once were bright as morn!

2 What bliss was Yours in glory,
O Lord of life divine!
I read the amazing story:
I joy to call You mine.
Your grief and Your compassion
were all for sinners' gain;
mine, mine was the
transgression,
but Yours the deadly pain.

3 What language shall I borrow
to praise You, dearest Friend,
for this Your dying sorrow,
Your pity without end?
Lord, make me Yours for ever!
Nor let me faithless prove;
O let me never, never
refuse such dying love!

4 Be near me when I'm dying;
Lord, show Your cross to me!
Your death, my hope supplying,
from death shall set me free.

419 Words: Cassell plc. Continuum International Publishing Group, The Tower Building, 11 York Road, London SE1 7NZ
420 Words: © in this version Praise Trust, Praise Trust, PO Box 359, Darlington. DL3 8YD

These eyes, new faith receiving,
from Jesus shall not move;
whoever dies believing
dies safely in Your love.

Paul Gerhardt, 1607–1676
translated James Waddell Alexander, 1804–1859
adapted Compilers of Praise! 2000

421

1   Praise to the Holiest in the
        height,
    and in the depth be praise;
    in all His words most wonderful,
    most sure in all His ways!

2   O loving wisdom of our God!
    when all was sin and shame,
    a second Adam to the fight
    and to the rescue came.

3   O wisest love! that flesh and
        blood,
    which did in Adam fail,
    should strive afresh against the
        foe,
    should strive and should prevail.

4   O generous love! that He who
        came
    as Man to smite our foe,
    the double agony for us
    as man should undergo:

5   And in the garden secretly,
    and on the cross on high,
    should teach His followers, and
        inspire
    to suffer and to die.

6   Praise to the Holiest in the
        height,
    and in the depth be praise;
    in all His words most wonderful,
    most sure in all His ways!

John Henry Newman, 1801–1890
adapted Compilers of
Hymns for Today's Church, 1982

422

1   Ride on, ride on in majesty,
    as all the crowds 'Hosanna!' cry;
    through waving branches slowly
        ride,
    O Saviour, to be crucified.

2   Ride on, ride on in majesty,
    in lowly pomp ride on to die;
    O Christ, Your triumph now
        begin
    with captured death, and
        conquered sin!

3   Ride on, ride on in majesty —
    the angel armies of the sky
    look down with sad and
        wondering eyes
    to see the approaching sacrifice.

4   Ride on, ride on in majesty,
    the last and fiercest foe defy;
    the Father on His sapphire
        throne
    awaits His own anointed Son.

5   Ride on, ride on in majesty,
    in lowly pomp ride on to die;
    bow Your meek head to mortal
        pain,
    then take, O God, Your power
        and reign!

Henry Hart Milman, 1791–1868
adapted Jubilate Hymns

423

1   Thank You Jesus, thank You Jesus,
    thank You Lord for loving me.
    Thank You Jesus, thank You Jesus,
    thank You Lord for loving me.

2   You went to Calvary, there You
        died for me,
    thank You Lord for loving me.
    You went to Calvary, there You
        died for me,
    thank You Lord for loving me.

3   You rose up from the grave, to
        me new life You gave,
    thank You Lord for loving me.
    You rose up from the grave, to
        me new life You gave,
    thank You Lord for loving me.

4   You're coming back again, and
        we with You shall reign,
    thank You Lord for loving me.
    You're coming back again, and
        we with You shall reign,
    thank You Lord for loving me.

Alison Revell, (née Huntley)

424

1   There is a green hill far away,
    outside a city wall,
    where the dear Lord was
        crucified,
    who died to save us all.

2   We may not know, we cannot tell
    what pains He had to bear;
    but we believe it was for us
    He hung and suffered there.

3   He died that we might be
        forgiven,
    He died to make us good,
    that we might go at last to
        heaven,
    saved by His precious blood.

4   There was no other good enough
    to pay the price of sin;
    He only could unlock the gate
    of heaven, and let us in.

5   O dearly, dearly has He loved,
    and we must love Him too,
    and trust in His redeeming blood,
    and try His works to do.

Cecil Frances Alexander, 1818–1895

425

1   There's a wideness in God's
        mercy,
    like the wideness of the sea;
    there's a kindness in His justice
    which is more than liberty.

2   There is no place where earth's
        sorrows
    are more felt than up in heaven;
    there is no place where earth's
        failings
    have such kindly judgement
        given.

3   For the love of God is broader
    than the limits of our mind;
    and the heart of the Eternal
    is most wonderfully kind.

4   But we make His love too narrow
    by false limits of our own;
    and we magnify His strictness
    with a zeal He will not own.

5   There is plentiful redemption
    in the blood that has been shed;
    there is joy for all the members
    in the sorrows of the head.

6   If our love were but more simple
    we would take Him at His word;
    and our lives would be illumined
    by the glory of the Lord.

Frederick William Faber, 1814–1863

426

1   We sing the praise of Him who
        died,
    of Him who died upon the cross;
    the sinner's hope though all
        deride,
    for this we count the world but
        loss.

2   Inscribed upon the cross we see
    in shining letters, 'God is love';
    He bears our sins upon the tree;
    He brings us mercy from above.

3   The cross! it takes our guilt
        away;
    it holds the fainting spirit up;
    it cheers with hope the gloomy
        day,
    and sweetens every bitter cup;

4   It makes the coward spirit brave,
    and nerves the feeble arm for
        fight;
    it takes its terror from the grave,
    and gilds the bed of death with
        light;

5   The balm of life, the cure of woe,
    the measure and the pledge of
        love,
    the sinner's refuge here below,
    the angels' theme in heaven
        above.

Thomas Kelly, 1769–185

427

1   When I survey the wondrous
        cross
    on which the Prince of glory died
    my richest gain I count as loss,
    and pour contempt on all my
        pride.

2   Forbid it, Lord, that I should boas
    save in the cross of Christ my
        God;
    the very things that charm me
        most —
    I sacrifice them to His blood.

3   See from His head, His hands,
        His feet,
    sorrow and love flow mingled
        down:
    when did such love and sorrow
        meet,
    or thorns compose so rich a
        crown?

4   Were the whole realm of nature
        mine,
    that were an offering far too
        small;
    love so amazing, so divine,
    demands my soul, my life, my
        all!

Isaac Watts, 1674–174
adapted Compilers c
Hymns for Today's Church, 198

Also suitable:
I will sing the wondrous story   211

JESUS CHRIST
HIS RESURRECTION

28

1 All heaven declares
the glory of the risen Lord.
Who can compare
with the beauty of the Lord?
Forever He will be
the Lamb upon the throne.
I gladly bow the knee
and worship Him alone.

2 I will proclaim
the glory of the risen Lord
who once was slain
to reconcile us to God.
Forever You will be
the Lamb upon the throne.
I gladly bow the knee
and worship You alone.

Noël Richards, *b.* 1955
and Tricia Richards, *b.* 1960

29

1 At Your feet we fall, mighty risen
Lord,
as we come before Your throne to
worship You.
By Your Spirit's power You now
draw our hearts,
and we hear Your voice in
triumph ringing clear:
'I am He that liveth,
that liveth and was dead.
Behold, I am alive
for evermore.

2 There we see You stand, mighty
risen Lord,
clothed in garments pure and
holy, shining bright;
eyes of flashing fire, feet like
burnished bronze,
and the sound of many waters is
Your voice.

3 Like the shining sun in its noonday strength,
we now see the glory of Your
wondrous face:
once that face was marred, but
now You're glorified;
and Your words, like a two-edged
sword have mighty power.

Dave Fellingham, *b.* 1945

430

1 Christ is alive! Let Christians
sing.
The cross stands empty to the sky.
Let streets and homes with
praises ring.
Love, drowned in death, shall
never die.

2 Christ is alive! No longer bound
to distant years in Palestine,
but saving, healing, here and
now,
and touching every place and
time.

3 In every insult, rift and war,
where colour, scorn or wealth
divide,
Christ suffers still, yet loves the
more,
and lives where even hope has
died.

4 Women and men, in age and
youth,
can feel the Spirit, hear the call,
and find the way, the life, the
truth,
revealed in Jesys, friend for all.

5 Christ is alive, and comes to
bring
new life to this and every age,
till earth and sky and ocean ring
with joy, with justice, love, and
praise.

Brian Arthur Wren, *b.* 1936

431

1 'Christ, the Lord, is risen today!'
all creation join to say:
raise your joys and triumphs
high;
sing, you heavens, and earth
reply:
love's redeeming work is done!
Fought the fight, the battle won:
see, our sun's eclipse has passed,
see, the light returns at last!

2 Vain the stone, the watch, the
seal:
Christ has burst the gates of hell;
death in vain forbids Him rise —
Christ has opened Paradise:
lives again our glorious King;
where, O death, is now your
sting?

Once He died, our souls to save;
where's your victory, boasting
grave?

3 Soar we now where Christ has
led,
following our exalted head;
made like Him, like Him we rise;
ours the cross, the grave, the
skies:
hail the Lord of earth and
heaven!
Praise to You by both be given;
every knee to You shall bow,
risen Christ, triumphant now!

Charles Wesley, 1707–1788
adapted Compilers of *Praise!* 2000

432

1 Easter glory fills the sky!
Christ now lives, no more to die!
Darkness has been put to flight
by the living Lord of light!
Alleluia!

2 See, the stone is rolled away
from the tomb where once He
lay!
He has risen as He said,
glorious firstborn from the dead!

3 Seek not life within the tomb;
Christ stands in the upper room!
Risen glory He conceals,
risen body He reveals!

4 Though we see His face no more,
He is with us as before!
Glory veiled, He is our priest,
His own flesh and blood our
feast!

5 Christ, the victor over death,
breathes on us the Spirit's breath!
Paradise is our reward,
endless Easter with our Lord!

James Quinn, *b.* 1919

433

1 Good Christians all, rejoice and
sing!
Now is the triumph of our King;
to all the world glad news we
bring:
Alleluia, alleluia, alleluia.

2 The Lord of life is risen today;
death's mighty stone is rolled
away:
let every tongue rejoice and say:

3 We praise in songs of victory
that love, that life, which cannot
die,
and sing with hearts uplifted
high:

4 Your name we bless, O risen
Lord,
and sing today with one accord
the life laid down, the life
restored:

Cyril Argentine Alington, 1872–195
altere

434

1 In the tomb so cold they laid
Him,
death its victim claimed;
powers of hell, they could not
hold Him —
back to life He came!
Christ is risen,
(Christ is risen,)
death has been conquered,
(death has been conquered,)
Christ is risen,
(Christ is risen,)
He shall reign for ever!

2 Hell had spent its fury on Him,
left Him crucified;
yet by blood He boldly conquered
sin and death defied.

3 Now the fear of death is broken,
Love has won the crown.
Prisoners of the darkness —
listen,
walls are tumbling down!

4 Raised from death, to heaven
ascending,
love's exalted King:
let His song of joy unending
through the nations ring!

Graham Andrew Kendrick, *b.* 19

435

1 Jesus Christ is risen today,
Alleluia.
our triumphant holy day, *Alleluia*
who did once, upon the cross,
Alleluia.
suffer to redeem our loss.
Alleluia.

2 Hymns of joy then let us sing,
praising Christ, our heavenly
King,

432 Words: © James Quinn / Cassell plc. Continuum International Publishing Group, The Tower Building, 11 York Road, London SE1 7NZ
433 Words: © Sir Richard Mynors
434 Words and Music: © 1986 Thankyou Music. Administered (UK and Europe) by Kingsway Music <tym@kingsway.co.uk>. Remaining territories administered by worshiptogether.com songs. Used by permission.

who endured the cross and
    grave,
sinners to redeem and save.

But the pains which He endured
our salvation have procured;
now above the sky He's King,
where the angels ever sing.

Sing we to our God above
praise eternal as His love;
praise Him all the heavenly host,
Father, Son and Holy Ghost.

Lyra Davidica, 1708

36

Jesus is risen from the grave,
Jesus is risen from the grave,
Jesus is risen from the grave.
Alleluia.

Jesus was seen by Mary …

Peter will soon be smiling …

Thomas will stop his doubting …

Jesus will meet His people …

Jesus will live for ever …

John Lamberton Bell, *b.* 1949
and Graham Alexander Maule, *b.* 1958

37

Jesus lives! your terrors now
can, O death, no more appal us:
Jesus lives! — by this we know
you, O grave, can not enthral us:
Alleluia!

Jesus lives! — henceforth is
    death
but the gate of life immortal;
this shall calm our trembling
    breath
when we pass its gloomy portal:
Alleluia!

Jesus lives! — for us He died:
then, alone to Jesus living,
pure in heart may we abide,
glory to our Saviour giving:
Alleluia!

Jesus lives! — this bond of love
neither life nor death shall sever,
powers in hell or heaven above
tear us from His keeping never:
Alleluia!

5 Jesus lives! — to Him the throne
over all the world is given;
may we go where He is gone,
rest and reign with Him in
    heaven.
Alleluia!

Christian Fürchtegott Gellert, 1715–1769
translated Frances Elizabeth Cox, 1812–1897
adapted Jubilate Hymns

438

1 Jesus, Prince and Saviour,
Lord of life who died,
Christ, the friend of sinners,
mocked and crucified;
for a world's salvation
He His body gave,
lay at last death's victim,
lifeless in the grave.
    Lord of life triumphant,
    risen now to reign!
    King of endless ages,
    Jesus lives again!

2 In His power and Godhead
every victory won,
pain and passion ended,
all His purpose done:
Christ the Lord is risen!
sighs and sorrows past,
death's dark night is over,
morning comes at last!

3 Resurrection morning,
sinners' bondage freed!
Christ the Lord is risen,
He is risen indeed!
Jesus, Prince and Saviour,
Lord of life who died,
Christ the King of glory
now is glorified!

Timothy Dudley-Smith, *b.* 1926

439

1 See what a morning, gloriously
    bright
with the dawning of hope in
    Jerusalem;
folded the graveclothes, tomb-
    filled with light
as the angels announce Christ is
    risen!
See God's salvation plan,
wrought in love, borne in pain,
    paid in sacrifice,
fulfilled in Christ the man,
for He lives; Christ is risen from
    the dead.

2   See Mary weeping, 'Where is He
        laid?'
    as in sorrow she turns from the
        empty tomb;
    hears a voice speaking, calling
        her name;
    it's the Master, the Lord raised to
        life again!
    The voice that spans the years,
    speaking life, stirring hope,
        bringing peace to us,
    will sound till He appears,
    for He lives; Christ is risen from
        the dead.

3   One with the Father, Ancient of
        Days,
    through the Spirit who clothes
        faith with certainty,
    honour and blessing, glory and
        praise
    to the King crowned with power
        and authority!
    And we are raised with Him,
    death is dead, love has won,
        Christ has conquered;
    and we shall reign with Him,
    for He lives; Christ is risen from
        the dead.

Stuart Townend, b. 1963
and Keith Getty, b. 1974

440

1   The day of resurrection!
    Earth, tell it out abroad;
    the passover of gladness,
    the passover of God!
    From death to life eternal,
    from earth up to the sky,
    our Christ has brought us over
    with hymns of victory.

2   Our hearts be pure from evil,
    that we may see aright
    the Lord in rays eternal
    of resurrection light;
    and, listening to His accents,
    may hear, so clear and strong,
    His own 'All hail!' and hearing
    may raise the victors' song.

3   Now let the heavens be joyful,
    and earth her song begin,
    the round world keep high
        triumph,
    for conquered death and sin;
    let all things seen and unseen
    their notes of gladness blend,

for Christ the Lord has risen —
our Joy who has no end.

St John of Damascus, d. c. 7
translated John Mason Neale, 1818–18

441

Alleluia!   Alleluia!   Alleluia!

1   The strife is past, the battle done
    now is the Victor's triumph
        won —
    O let the song of praise be sung:
    Alleluia!

2   Death's mightiest powers have
        done their worst;
    and Jesus has His foes
        dispersed —
    let shouts of praise and joy
        outburst:
    Alleluia!

3   The three sad days have quickly
        sped,
    He rises glorious from the dead,
    all glory to our risen head:
    Alleluia!

4   He broke the chains of death and
        hell;
    the bars to heaven's entrance
        fell;
    let hymns of praise His triumph
        tell:
    Alleluia!

5   Lord over death, our wounded
        King,
    save us from Satan's deadly sting
    that we may live for You and
        sing:
    Alleluia!

Latin, 17th centu
translated Francis Pott, 1832–19
vv. 1-3, 5 adapted Jubilate Hymn
v. 4 adapted Compilers of Praise! 20

442

1   Thine be the glory, risen,
        conquering Son,
    endless is the victory Thou o'er
        death hast won;
    angels in bright raiment rolled
        the stone away,
    kept the folded grave-clothes,
        where Thy body lay.
    Thine be the glory, risen,
        conquering Son,
    endless is the victory Thou o'er
        death hast won.

441 Words: in this version (vv. 1-3, 5) Jubilate Hymns, 4 Thorne Park Road, Chelston, Torquay TQ2 6RX <enquiries@jubilate.co.uk> Used by permission.
441 Words: Praise Trust, Praise Trust, PO Box 359, Darlington. DL3 8YD
442 Words: © World Student Christian Federation, 5 route des Morillons, 1218 Grand-Saconnex, Geneva, Switzerland. Used by permission.

HIS RESURRECTION

Lo! Jesus meets us, risen from
    the tomb;
lovingly He greets us, scatters
    fear and gloom;
let the Church with gladness
    hymns of triumph sing,
for her Lord now liveth; death
    hath lost its sting.

No more we doubt Thee, glorious
    Prince of Life;
life is naught without Thee: aid
    us in our strife;
make us more than conquerors,
    through Thy deathless love:
bring us safe through Jordan to
    Thy home above.

Edmond Budry, 1854–1932
translated Richard Birch Hoyle, 1875–1939

43

Glory to Jesus, risen, conquering
    Son!
Endless is the victory over death
    You won;
angels robed in splendour rolled
    the stone away,
kept the folded grave clothes
    where Your body lay:
    Glory to Jesus, risen, conquering
      Son!
    Endless is the victory over death
      You won.

See! Jesus meets us, risen from
    the tomb;
lovingly He greets us, scatters
    fear and gloom;
let the Church with gladness
    hymns of triumph sing,
for her Lord is living, death has
    lost its sting:

No more we doubt You, glorious
    Prince of Life:
what is life without You? aid us
    in our strife;
make us more than conquerors
    through Your deathless love;
bring us safe through Jordan to
    Your home above:

Edmond Budry, 1854–1932
translated Richard Birch Hoyle, 1875–1939

44

This joyful Eastertide,
away with sin and sorrow.
My Love, the Crucified,
has sprung to life this morrow:

Had Christ, that once was slain,
ne'er burst His three-day prison,
our faith had been in vain:
but now has Christ arisen,
arisen, arisen, arisen!

2   My flesh in hope shall rest,
    and for a season slumber:
    till trump from east to west
    shall wake the dead in number:

3   Death's flood has lost his chill,
    since Jesus crossed the river:
    Lover of souls, from ill
    my passing soul deliver:

George Ratcliffe Woodward, 1848–1934

Also suitable:

Jesus stand among us	176
Open the gates of righteousness	188
There's a song for all the children	659

JESUS CHRIST
HIS ASCENSION

445

1   All hail the power of Jesus'
    name!
    Before Him angels fall,
    before Him angels fall.
    Bring forth the royal diadem
    and crown Him, crown Him,
    crown Him, crown Him,
    and crown Him Lord of all.

2   Crown Him, you martyrs of our
    God,
    who for His justice call,
    who for His justice call;
    exalt the One whose path you
    trod,

3   Descendants of His chosen race,
    redeemed from Adam's fall,
    redeemed from Adam's fall,
    hail Him who saves you by His
    grace,

4   Let every people, nation, tribe,
    on this terrestrial ball,
    on this terrestrial ball,
    to Him all majesty ascribe

Edward Perronet, 1726–1792
and John Rippon, 1751–1836
adapted Compilers of Praise! 2000

446

1 All hail the power of Jesus'
name!
Before Him angels fall,
bring forth the royal diadem
and crown Him, crown Him,
crown Him,
crown Him Lord of all.

2 Crown Him, you martyrs of our
God,
who for His justice call,
exalt the One whose path you
trod,

3 Descendants of His chosen race,
redeemed from Adam's fall,
hail Him who saves you by His
grace,

4 Let every people, nation, tribe,
on this terrestrial ball,
to Him all majesty ascribe

Edward Perronet, 1726–1792
and John Rippon, 1751–1836
adapted Compilers of *Praise!* 2000

447

1 Christ is the world's Redeemer,
the holy and the pure,
the fount of heavenly wisdom,
our trust and hope secure;
the armour of His soldiers,
the Lord of earth and sky;
our health while we are living,
our life when we shall die.

2 Christ has our host surrounded
with clouds of martyrs bright,
whose victory-palms of triumph
inspire us for the fight.
For Christ the cross ascended
to save a world undone,
and, suffering for the sinful,
our full redemption won.

3 Down in the realm of darkness
He lay a captive bound,
but at the hour appointed
He rose, a victor crowned;
and now, to heaven ascended,
He sits upon the throne,
in glorious dominion,
His Father's and His own.

4 Glory to God the Father,
the unbegotten One;
all honour be to Jesus,
His sole-begotten Son;

and to the Holy Spirit —
the perfect Trinity.
Let all the worlds give answer:
'Amen — so let it be!'

St Columba, 521–8
translated Duncan Macgregor, 1854–19

448

1 Christ triumphant, ever reigning
Saviour, Master, King!
Lord of heaven, our lives
sustaining,
hear us as we sing:
Yours the glory and the crown,
the high renown, the eternal
name!

2 Word incarnate, truth revealing,
Son of Man on earth!
Power and majesty concealing
by Your humble birth:

3 Suffering Servant, scorned, ill-
treated,
victim crucified!
Death is through the cross
defeated,
sinners justified:

4 Priestly King, enthroned for eve
high in heaven above!
Sin and death and hell shall
never
stifle hymns of love:

5 So, our hearts and voices raising
through the ages long,
ceaselessly upon You gazing,
this shall be our song:

Michael Saward, *b.* 19

449

1 Crown Him with many crowns,
the Lamb upon His throne,
while heaven's eternal anthem
drowns
all music but its own!
Awake, my soul, and sing
of Him who died to be
your Saviour and your matchless
King
through all eternity.

2 Crown Him the Lord of life,
triumphant from the grave,
who rose victorious from the
strife
for those He came to save:

446 Words: © Praise Trust, Praise Trust, PO Box 359, Darlington. DL3 8YD
448 Words: © Michael Saward / Jubilate Hymns, 4 Thorne Park Road, Chelston, Torquay TQ2 6RX <enquiries@jubilate.co.uk> Used by permission.
449 Words: © in this version Jubilate Hymns, 4 Thorne Park Road, Chelston, Torquay TQ2 6RX <enquiries@jubilate.co.uk> Used by permission.

His glories now we sing
who died and reigns on high;
He died eternal life to bring
and lives that death may die.

3 Crown Him the Lord of love,
who shows His hands and side,
those wounds yet visible above
in beauty glorified.
No angel in the sky
can fully bear that sight,
but downward bends his burning
eye
at mysteries so bright.

4 Crown Him the Lord of peace,
His kingdom is at hand;
from pole to pole let warfare
cease,
and Christ rule every land!
A city stands on high,
His glory it displays,
and there the nations 'Holy' cry
in joyful hymns of praise.

5 Crown Him the Lord of years,
the Potentate of time,
Creator of the rolling spheres,
in majesty sublime:
all hail, Redeemer, hail,
for You have died for me;
Your praise shall never, never
fail
through all eternity!

*Matthew Bridges, 1800–1894
and Godfrey Thring, 1823–1903
adapted Jubilate Hymns*

450

1 Jesus is King
and I will extol Him,
give Him the glory,
and honour His name;
He reigns on high,
enthroned in the heavens —
Word of the Father,
exalted for us.

2 We have a hope
that is steadfast and certain,
gone through the curtain
and touching the throne;
we have a Priest
who is there interceding,
pouring His grace
on our lives day by day.

3 We come to Him,
our Priest and Apostle,
clothed in His glory
and bearing His name,

laying our lives
with gladness before Him —
filled with His Spirit
we worship the King:

4 'O Holy One,
our hearts do adore You;
thrilled with Your goodness
we give You our praise!'
Angels in light
with worship surround Him,
Jesus, our Saviour,
for ever the same.

Wendy Churchill

451

1 Join all the glorious names
of wisdom, love and power,
that ever mortals knew,
that angels ever bore;
all are too poor to speak His
worth,
too poor to set my Saviour forth!

2 Great Prophet of my God,
my tongue shall bless Your
name:
by You the joyful news
of our salvation came;
the joyful news of sins forgiven,
of hell subdued and peace with
heaven.

3 Jesus, my great High Priest,
the Lamb of God who died!
My guilty conscience seeks
no sacrifice beside;
the power of Your atoning blood
has won acceptance with my
God.

4 Divine almighty Lord,
my Conqueror and my King:
Your sceptre and Your sword,
Your reigning grace I sing;
Yours is the power — and so I sit
in willing service at Your feet.

5 Now let my soul arise,
and tread the tempter down:
my Captain leads me on
to conquest and a crown;
the child of God shall win the
day,
though death and hell obstruct
the way.

Isaac Watts, 1674–1748

JESUS CHRIST

452

1 King of kings, majesty,
God of heaven living in me,
gentle Saviour, closest Friend,
strong Deliverer, Beginning and
    End,
all within me falls at Your throne.
Your majesty, I can but bow.
I lay my all before You now.
In royal robes I don't deserve
I live to serve Your majesty,
I live to serve Your majesty.

2 Earth and heaven worship You,
Love eternal, faithful and true,
who bought the nations,
    ransomed souls,
brought this sinner near to Your
    throne;
all within me cries out in praise.

Jarrod Cooper

453

1 Look, you saints, the sight is
    glorious!
See the Man of Sorrows now
from the fight returned
    victorious —
every knee to Him shall bow:
crown Him, crown Him, crown
    Him, crown Him;
crowns befit the Victor's brow.

2 Crown the Saviour, angels, crown
    Him!
Rich the trophies Jesus brings;
in the seat of power enthrone
    Him
while the vault of heaven rings:
crown Him, crown Him, crown
    Him, crown Him;
crown the Saviour King of kings.

3 Sinners in derision crowned Him,
mocked the dying Saviour's
    claim;
saints and angels crowd around
    Him,
sing His triumph, praise His
    name:
crown Him, crown Him, crown
    Him, crown Him;
spread abroad the Victor's fame.

4 Hear the shout as He is greeted,
hear those loud triumphant
    chords!
Jesus Christ in glory seated —

O what joy the sight affords!
Crown Him, crown Him, crown
    Him, crown Him;
King of kings, and Lord of lords!

Thomas Kelly, 1769–1855
adapted Jubilee Hymns

454

1 Rejoice, the Lord is King!
Your Lord and King adore:
mortals, give thanks and sing,
and triumph evermore:

Lift up your heart, lift up your
    voice:
rejoice! again I say, Rejoice!

2 Jesus, the Saviour, reigns,
the God of truth and love;
when He had purged our stains
He took His seat above:

3 His kingdom cannot fail,
He rules both earth and heaven;
the keys of death and hell
are to our Jesus given:

4 He sits at God's right hand,
till all His foes submit
and bow to His command
and fall beneath His feet:

5 Rejoice in glorious hope!
Jesus the Judge shall come
and take His servants up
to their eternal home:

We soon shall hear the archangel's
    voice;
God's trumpet-call shall sound —
    Rejoice!

Charles Wesley, 1707–1788

455

1 The head that once was crowned
    with thorns
is crowned with glory now;
a royal diadem adorns
the mighty Victor's brow.

2 The highest place that heaven
    affords
is His, is His by right;
the King of kings and Lord of
    lords
and heaven's eternal light.

3 The joy of all who dwell above,
the joy of all below;
to whom He demonstrates His
    love
and grants His name to know.

452 Words and Music: © 1996, Jarrod Cooper
453 Words: © in this version Jubilee Hymns, 4 Thorne Park Road, Chelston, Torquay TQ2 6RX <enquiries@jubilee.co.uk> Used by permission.

4 To them the cross with all its
 shame,
with all its grace is given;
their name, an everlasting name,
their joy, the joy of heaven.

5 They suffer with their Lord
 below,
they reign with Him above;
their profit and their joy to know
the mystery of His love.

6 The cross He bore is life and
 health,
though shame and death to Him;
His people's hope, His people's
 wealth,
their everlasting theme.

Thomas Kelly, 1769–1855

456

1 Where high the heavenly temple
 stands,
the house of God not made with
 hands,
a great High Priest our nature
 wears,
the guardian of our race appears.

2 He who for us our surety stood,
and poured on earth His precious
 blood,
pursues in heaven His mighty
 will,
our Saviour and our helper still.

3 Though now ascended up on
 high,
He sees us with a brother's eye;
He shares with us the human
 name
and knows the frailty of our
 frame.

4 Our fellow-sufferer yet retains
a fellow-feeling of our pains;
He still remembers in the skies
His tears, His agonies and cries.

5 With boldness therefore at His
 throne
let us make all our sorrows
 known:
to help us in the darkest hour,
we ask for Christ the Saviour's
 power.

Paraphrase 58, from *Hebrews 4: 14–end*
adapted Jubilate Hymns

Also suitable:
Alleluia, sing to Jesus! 380
The Lord is King! Lift up your voice 241

THE HOLY SPIRIT HIS WORK IN INDIVIDUAL LIVES

457

1 Breathe on me, breath of God:
fill me with life anew,
that I may love as You have
 loved,
and do as You would do.

2 Breathe on me, breath of God,
until my heart is pure,
until my will is one with Yours
to do and to endure.

3 Breathe on me, breath of God;
be all my heart's desire,
until this earthly part of me
glows with your heavenly fire.

4 Breathe on me, breath of God;
so shall I never die,
but live with You the perfect life
of Your eternity.

Edwin Hatch, 1835–1889
adapted Jubilate Hymns

458

1 Come down, O Love divine!
Seek out this soul of mine
and visit it with Your own ardour
 glowing;
O Comforter, draw near,
within my heart appear,
and kindle it, Your holy flame
 bestowing.

2 There let it freely burn
till earthly passions turn
to dust and ashes in its heat
 consuming;
and let Your glorious light
shine ever on my sight,
and make my pathway clear, by
 Your illuming.

3 Let holy charity
my outward vesture be,
and lowliness become my inner
 clothing;
true lowliness of heart
which takes the humbler part,
and for its own shortcomings
weeps with loathing.

4 And so the yearning strong
with which the soul will long
shall far surpass the power of
   human telling;
for none can guess its grace
till we become the place
in which the Holy Spirit makes
His dwelling.

Bianco da Siena, d. 1434
translated Richard Frederick Littledale, 1833–1890
adapted Jubilee Hymns

459

1 Come, gracious Spirit, heavenly
   Dove,
with light and comfort from
   above;
O be our guardian, be our guide,
o'er every thought and step
   preside.

2 The light of truth to us display,
and make us know and choose
   Your way,
plant holy fear in every heart,
that we from God may ne'er
   depart.

3 Lead us to Christ, the living Way,
nor let us from His pastures
   stray;
lead us to holiness, the road
that we must take to dwell with
   God.

4 Lead us to heaven, that we may
   share
fullness of joy for ever there;
lead us to God, our final rest,
to be with Him for ever blessed.

Simon Browne, 1680–1732 and others

460

1 Come, Holy Spirit, come:
let Your bright beams arise,
dispel the darkness from our
   minds
and open all our eyes.

2 Cheer our desponding hearts,
O heavenly Paraclete;
give us to lie with humble hope
at our Redeemer's feet.

3 Revive our drooping faith,
our doubts and fears remove,
and kindle in our hearts the
   flame
of never-dying love.

4 Convince us all of sin,
then lead to Jesus' blood:
and to our wondering view
   reveal
the secret love of God.

5 Yours, Lord, to cleanse the heart,
to sanctify the soul,
to pour fresh life on every part,
and new create the whole.

6 Dwell therefore in our hearts,
our minds from bondage free;
then we shall know and praise
   and love,
our God, the One in Three.

Joseph Hart, 1712–176?
altered Compiler

461

1 Defend me, Lord, from hour to
   hour,
and bless Your servant's way;
increase Your Holy Spirit's power
within me day by day.

2 Help me to be what I should be,
and do what I should do,
and ever with Your spirit free
my daily life renew.

3 Grant me the courage from above
which You impart to all
who hear Your word and know
   Your love
and answer to Your call.

4 So may I daily grow in grace,
continuing Yours alone,
until I come to sing Your praise
with saints around Your throne.

George D'Oyly Snow, 1903–197?
slightly altered Compiler

462

1 Each day we live the Christian
   life
we're sorely tried — without,
   within;
but God the Spirit gives us
   strength
to wage a constant war with sin.

2 It's in our weakness that we find
He gives the help we greatly
   need
to honour Christ in all our ways,
as from the power of sin we're
   freed.

3   When deep within our swelling
      hearts
    the thoughts of pride and envy
      rise,
    when bitter words are on our
      tongues
    and tears of passion in our eyes,

4   He helps us keep our self-control;
    sends grace to check the hasty
      word;
    give gentle answers back again
    and fight a battle for our Lord.

5   So far as it depends on us,
    we'll live in peace as Christians
      should;
    we'll not be overcome by wrong,
    but overcome all wrong with
      good.

6   All His disciples on this earth
    have their own painful cross to
      take
    but, in the Holy Spirit's power,
    we'll live our lives for Jesus'
      sake.

We are but little children weak
Cecil Frances Alexander, 1818–1895
adapted James Alexander McCaughan, *b.* 1954

463

1   Gracious Spirit, Holy Ghost,
    taught by You, we covet most
    of Your gifts at Pentecost,
    holy, heavenly love.

2   Faith that mountains could
      remove,
    tongues of earth or heaven above,
    knowledge, all things, empty
      prove
    without heavenly love.

3   Though I as a martyr bleed,
    give my goods the poor to feed,
    all is vain if love I need;
    therefore give me love.

4   Love is kind, and suffers long;
    love is meek, and thinks no
      wrong;
    love, than death itself more
      strong:
    therefore give us love.

5   Prophecy will fade away,
    melting in the light of day;
    love will ever with us stay:
    therefore give us love.

6   Faith, and hope, and love we see
    joining hand in hand, agree;
    but the greatest of the three,
    and the best, is love.

Christopher Wordsworth, 1807–1885

464

1   He lives in us, the Christ of God,
    His Spirit joins with ours;
    He brings to us the Father's grace
    with powers beyond our powers.
    So when enticing sin grows
      strong,
    when human nature fails,
    God's Spirit in our inner self
    fights for us, and prevails.

2   Our pangs of guilt and fears of
      death
    are Satan's stratagems —
    by Jesus Christ who died for us
    God pardons; who condemns?
    And when we cannot feel our
      faith,
    nor bring ourselves to pray,
    the Spirit pleads with God for us
    in words we could not say.

3   God gave the Son to save us
      all —
    no greater love is known!
    And shall that love abandon us
    who have become Christ's own?
    For God has raised Him from the
      grave,
    in this we stand assured;
    so none can tear us from God's
      love
    of Jesus Christ the Lord.

Michael Arnold Perry, 1942–1996
from Romans 8

465

1   Holy Spirit, hear us;
    help us while we sing;
    breathe into the music
    of the praise we bring.

2   Holy Spirit, prompt us
    when we kneel to pray;
    nearer come, and teach us
    what we ought to say.

3   Holy Spirit, shine, Lord
    on the book we read;
    to its holy pages
    bring the light we need.

4 Holy Spirit, give us
   each a lowly mind;
   make us more like Jesus,
   gentle, pure, and kind.

5 Holy Spirit, help us
   daily, by Your might,
   what is wrong to conquer;
   and to choose the right.

William Henry Parker, 1845–1929

466

1 If I could speak like an angel,
   or know what tomorrow may
       bring;
   if I had faith to move mountains,
   that wouldn't mean a thing.
   If I had all the world's
       knowledge,
   but turned away from His call,
   without His love I am nothing —
   for love is the greatest gift of all.
   Love is the greatest gift of all.
   Love is the greatest gift of all;
   with God's love in my heart
   I can be a shining light,
   for love is the greatest gift of all.

2 God's love is never demanding
   but always is gentle and kind;
   God's love is always forgiving,
   leaving the past behind.
   As I look at His reflection
   it makes me feel so small,
   without His love I am nothing —
   for love is the greatest gift of all.
   Love is the greatest gift of all.
   Love is the greatest gift of all;
   with God's love in my heart
   I can be a shining light,
   for love is the greatest gift of all.
   Love is the greatest gift of all,
   love is the greatest gift of all:
   with God's love in my heart
   I can be a shining light:
   for love is the greatest gift,
   love is the greatest gift;
   love is the greatest gift of all!

Peter Jacobs, b. 1984

467

1 O Lord, who came from realms
       above
   the pure celestial fire to impart,
   kindle a flame of sacred love
   upon the altar of my heart.

2 There let it for Your glory burn
   with inextinguishable blaze,
   and trembling to its source return
   in humble prayer and fervent
       praise.

3 Jesus, confirm my heart's desire
   to work and speak and think for
       You;
   still let me guard the holy fire,
   and still in me Your gift renew.

4 Here let me prove Your perfect
       will,
   my acts of faith and love repeat,
   till death Your endless mercies
       seal
   and make the sacrifice complete!

Charles Wesley, 1707–1788
adapted Jubilate Hymns

468

1 Spirit of God, our hearts inspire,
   let us Your influence prove,
   Source of the old prophetic fire,
   Fountain of light and love.

2 Come, Holy Spirit, Lord, by
       whom
   the prophets wrote and spoke:
   the Key to all God's truth, now
       come,
   unseal the sacred Book.

3 O spread your wings, celestial
       Dove,
   above our nature's night,
   on our disordered spirits move,
   and let there now be light.

4 God, through Himself, we then
       shall know,
   if You within us shine,
   and sound, with all Your saints
       below,
   the depths of love divine.

Charles Wesley, 1707–1788
adapted Compilers of *Praise!* 2000

469

Spirit of holiness, wisdom and
*   faithfulness,*
Wind of the Lord, blowing strongly
*   and free:*
strength of our serving and joy of
*   our worshipping —*
Spirit of God, bring Your fullness
*   to me!*

466 Words and Music: © Maranatha Praise Inc. Administered by CopyCare Ltd, PO Box 77, Hailsham, East Sussex. BN27 3EF

467 Words: © in this version Jubilate Hymns, 4 Thorne Park Road, Chelston, Torquay TQ2 6RX <enquiries@jubilate.co.uk> Used by permission.

469 Words: © Christopher Idle/Jubilate Hymns, 4 Thorne Park Road, Chelston, Torquay TQ2 6RX <enquiries@jubilate.co.uk> Used by permission.

HIS WORK IN THE LIFE OF THE CHURCH

1 You came to interpret and teach
   us effectively
all that the Saviour has spoken
   and done;
to glorify Jesus is all Your
   activity —
promise and gift of the Father
   and Son:

2 You came with Your gifts to
   supply all our poverty,
pouring Your love on the Church
   in her need;
You came with Your fruit for our
   growth to maturity,
richly refreshing the souls that
   You feed:

Christopher Martin Idle, b. 1938

Also suitable:
Heavenly Father, may Your blessing   264

THE HOLY SPIRIT
HIS WORK
IN THE LIFE OF
THE CHURCH

470

1 For Your gift of God the Spirit,
power to make our lives anew,
pledge of life and hope of glory,
Saviour, we would worship You.

2 He who in creation's dawning
brooded on a lifeless deep,
still across our nature's darkness
moves to wake our souls from
   sleep.

3 He, Himself the living author,
wakes to life the sacred word,
reads with us its holy pages
and reveals our risen Lord.

4 He it is who works within us,
teaching rebel hearts to pray,
He whose holy intercessions
rise for us both night and day.

5 He the mighty God indwells us;
His to strengthen, help, empower,
His to overcome the tempter;
Ours to call in danger's hour.

6 Fill us with Your holy fullness,
God the Father, Spirit, Son;
in us, through us, then, for ever
shall Your perfect will be done.

Margaret Clarkson, b. 1915

471

1 Freedom and life are ours
for Christ has set us free!
Never again submit to powers
that lead to slavery:
Christ is the Lord who breaks
our chains, our bondage ends,
Christ is the rescuer who makes
the helpless slaves His friends.

2 Called by the Lord to use
our freedom and be strong,
not letting liberty excuse
a life of blatant wrong:
freed from the law's stern hand
God's gift of grace to prove,
know that the law's entire
   demand
is gladly met by love.

3 Spirit of God, come, fill,
emancipate us all!
Speak to us, Word of truth, until
before His throne we fall:
glory and liberty
our Father has decreed,
and if the Son shall make us free
we shall be free indeed!

Christopher Martin Idle, b. 1938

472

1 Holy Spirit, ever living
as the Church's very life;
Holy Spirit, ever striving
through her in a ceaseless strife;
Holy Spirit, ever forming
in the Church the mind of
   Christ;
You we praise with endless
   worship
for Your fruit and gifts unpriced.

2 Holy Spirit, ever working
through the Church's ministry;
quickening, strengthening, and
   absolving,
setting captive sinners free;
Holy Spirit, ever binding
age to age, and soul to soul;
in a fellowship unending,
You we worship and extol.

Timothy Rees, 1874–1939

473

1 Holy Spirit, we welcome You,
Holy Spirit, we welcome You!
Move among us with holy fire
as we lay aside all earthly desire,
hands reach out and our hearts
aspire.
Holy Spirit, Holy Spirit,
Holy Spirit, we welcome You!

2 Holy Spirit, we welcome You,
Holy Spirit, we welcome You!
Let the breeze of Your presence
blow
that Your children here might
truly know
how to move in the Spirit's flow.
Holy Spirit, Holy Spirit,
Holy Spirit, we welcome You!

3 Holy Spirit, we welcome You,
Holy Spirit, we welcome You!
Please accomplish in us today
some new work of loving grace,
we pray —
unreservedly — have Your way.
Holy Spirit, Holy Spirit,
Holy Spirit, we welcome You!

Christopher Alan Bowater, b. 1947

474

1 Lord, come and heal Your
Church,
take our lives and cleanse with
Your fire;
let Your deliverance flow as we
lift Your name up higher.
*We will draw near and surrender
our fear:
lift our hands to proclaim, 'Holy
Father, You are here!'*

2 Spirit of God, come in
and release our hearts to praise
you;
make us whole, for holy we'll
become and serve You,

3 Show us Your power, we pray,
that we may share in Your glory:
we shall arise, and go to proclaim
Your works most holy.

Christopher Philip Rolinson, b. 1958

475

1 O Breath of life, come sweeping
through us,
revive Your Church with life and
power;
O Breath of life, come, cleanse,
renew us,
and fit Your Church to meet this
hour.

2 O Wind of God, come bend us,
break us,
till humbly we confess our need;
then in Your tenderness remake
us,
revive, restore, for this we plead.

3 O Breath of love, come breathe
within us,
renewing thought and will and
heart;
come, Love of Christ, afresh to
win us,
revive Your Church in every
part.

4 Revive us, Lord! Is zeal abating
while harvest fields are vast and
white?
Revive us, Lord, the world is
waiting,
equip Your Church to spread the
light.

Elizabeth Ann Head, 1850–1936

476

1 Our great Redeemer, as He
breathed
His tender last farewell,
a Guide, a Comforter, bequeathed
with us to dwell.

2 He came in tongues of living
flame
to teach, convince, subdue;
unseen as rushing wind He
came —
as powerful too.

3 He comes sweet influence to
impart —
a gracious, willing guest;
when He can find one humble
heart
where He may rest.

4 And every virtue we possess,
and every victory won,
and every thought of holiness
are His alone.

5   Spirit of purity and grace,
     our failing strength renew;
     and make our hearts a worthier
         place
     to welcome You.

Henriette Auber, 1773–1862
adapted Jubilate Hymns

477

1   Spirit divine, inspire our prayers,
     and make our hearts Your home;
     descend with all Your gracious
         powers —
     O come, great Spirit, come!

2   Come as the light — reveal our
         need,
     our hidden failings show,
     and lead us in those paths of life
     in which the righteous go.

3   Come as the fire, and cleanse our
         hearts
     with purifying flame;
     let our whole life an offering be
     to our Redeemer's name.

4   Come as the dew, and gently
         bless
     this consecrated hour;
     may barren souls rejoice to know
     your life-creating power.

5   Come as the dove, and spread
         Your wings,
     the wings of peaceful love,
     and let Your Church on earth
         become
     blessed as the Church above.

6   Come as the wind, with rushing
         sound
     and Pentecostal grace,
     that all the world with joy may
         see
     the glory of Your face.

Andrew Reed, 1787–1862
adapted by Jubilate Hymns

478

Spirit of God, unseen as the wind,
gentle as is the dove;
teach us the truth and help us
    believe,
show us the Saviour's love.

1   You spoke to us long, long ago,
     gave us the written word;
     we read it still, needing its truth,
     through it God's voice is heard.

2   Without Your help we fail our
         Lord,
     we cannot live His way;
     we need Your power, we need
         Your strength,
     following Christ each day.

Margaret V. Old, b. 1932
based on Acts 2: 2

479

1   The Spirit came, as promised,
     in God's appointed hour;
     and now to each believer
     He comes in love and power:
     and by His Holy Spirit,
     God seals us as His own;
     and through the Son and Spirit
     makes access to His throne.

2   The Spirit makes our bodies
     the temple of the Lord;
     He binds us all together
     in faith and true accord:
     the Spirit in His greatness,
     brings power from God above;
     and with the Son and Father
     dwells in our hearts in love.

3   He bids us live together
     in unity and peace,
     employ His gifts in blessing,
     and let base passions cease:
     we should not grieve the Spirit
     by open sin or shame;
     nor let our words and actions
     deny His holy name.

4   The Word, the Spirit's weapon,
     will bring all sin to light;
     and prayer, by His directing,
     will add new joy and might:
     be filled then with His Spirit,
     live out God's will and word;
     rejoice with hymns and singing,
     make music to the Lord!

James Edward Seddon, 1915–1983

480

1   There's a spirit in the air,
     telling Christians everywhere:
     'Praise the love that Christ
         revealed,
     living, working, in our world!'

2   Lose your shyness, find your
         tongue,
     tell the world what God has
         done:
     God in Christ has come to stay.
     Live tomorrow's life today!

3 When believers break the bread,
when a hungry child is fed,
praise the love that Christ
revealed,
living, working, in our world.

4 Still the Spirit gives us light,
seeing wrong and setting right:
God in Christ has come to stay.
Live tomorrow's life today!

5 When a stranger's not alone,
where the homeless find a home,
praise the love that Christ
revealed,
living, working, in our world.

6 May the Spirit fill our praise,
guide our thoughts and change
our ways.
God in Christ has come to stay.
Live tomorrow's life today!

7 There's a Spirit in the air,
calling people everywhere:
praise the love that Christ
revealed,
living, working, in our world.

Brian Arthur Wren, *b.* 1936

Also suitable:
Heavenly Father, may Your blessing   269
Welcome to the family   154

THE HOLY SPIRIT
ORDINATION AND
COMMISSIONING

481

1 Father, Your Church with
thankfulness
receives as from Your hand
the different gifts of heart and
mind
which different lives possess.

2 Ours is the voice, but Yours the
grace
that brings to these today
the call to mark for us the way
by which to seek Your face.

3 Give them again each day the
love
that brought them to this hour:
Your peace their ministry
empower,
Your hope their fears resolve.

4 Lord, may the team of faith each
leads
be wise to do Your will;
to speak the word that
strengthens still,
and seal its talk with deeds.

5 In heaven and earth Your folk
are one,
since all to You belong.
We'll sing Your Church's
thankful song,
and praise Your living Son.

6 Your living Son the pattern
gives:
may we His pattern trace,
and find for all the human race
the way of life that lives.

Thomas Caryl Micklem, 1925–2003

482

1 God, when I came into this life
You called me by my name;
today I come, commit myself,
responding to Your claim.

2 You give me freedom to believe;
today I make my choice
and to the worship of the Church
I add my learning voice.

3 Within the circle of the faith
as member of Your cast,
I take my place with all the saints
of future, present, past.

4 In all the tensions of my life,
between my faith and doubt,
let Your great Spirit give me
hope,
sustain me, lead me out.

5 So, help me in my unbelief
and let my life be true:
feet firmly planted on the earth,
my sights set high on You.

Frederik Herman Kaan, *b.* 1929

483

1 How clear is our vocation, Lord,
when once we heed Your call:
to live according to Your word,
and daily learn, refreshed,
restored,
that You are Lord of all
and will not let us fall.

2 But if, forgetful, we should find
Your yoke is hard to bear,
if worldly pressures fray the
mind
and love itself cannot unwind
its tangled skein of care:
our inward life repair.

3 We mark Your saints, how they
become
in hindrances more sure,
whose joyful virtues put to
shame
the casual way we wear Your
name,
and by our faults obscure
Your power to cleanse and cure.

4 In what You give us, Lord, to do,
together or alone,
in old routines or ventures new,
may we not cease to look to You.
The cross You hung upon —
all You endeavoured done.

Frederick Pratt Green, 1903–2000

484

1 Pour out Your Spirit from on
high;
Lord, Your ordained servants
bless;
graces and gifts to each supply,
and clothe Your priests with
righteousness.

2 Within the temple when they
stand,
to teach the gospel full and free,
Saviour, like stars in Your right
hand
the angels of the churches be.

3 Wisdom and zeal and faith
impart,
firmness with meekness, from
above,
to bear Your people on their
heart,
and love the souls You hold in
love.

4 To watch and pray and never
faint,
by day and night strict guard to
keep,
to warn the sinner, cheer the
saint,
nourish Your lambs and feed
Your sheep.

5 Then when their task is finished
here,
in humble hope their work is
done,
when the Chief Shepherd shall
appear,
in Him may they and we be one.

James Montgomery, 1771–1854
altered Compilers

Also suitable:

Lord and Master, You have called us   548
Lord, speak to me that I may speak   550
O Lord, who came from realms above   467

THE GROWTH
OF THE CHURCH
IN INDIVIDUAL LIVES

485

1 All I once held dear,
built my life upon,
all this world reveres,
and wars to own,
all I once thought gain
I have counted loss;
spent and worthless now,
compared to this.
*Knowing You, Jesus,
knowing You,
there is no greater thing.
You're my all, You're the best,
You're my joy, my righteousness,
and I love You, Lord.*

2 Now my heart's desire
is to know You more,
to be found in You
and known as Yours;
to possess by faith
what I could not earn,
all-surpassing gift
of righteousness.

3 Oh, to know the power
of Your risen life,
and to know You in
Your sufferings;
to become like You
in Your death, my Lord,
so with You to live
and never die.

Graham Andrew Kendrick, *b.* 1950

486

1 Amazing grace — how sweet the sound —
that saved a wretch like me!
I once was lost, but now am found,
was blind, but now I see.

2 God's grace first taught my heart to fear,
His grace my fears relieved;
how precious did that grace appear
the hour I first believed!

3 Through every danger, trial and snare
I have already come;
His grace has brought me safe thus far,
and grace will lead me home.

4 The Lord has promised good to me,
His word my hope secures;
my shield and stronghold He shall be
as long as life endures.

5 And when this earthly life is past,
and mortal cares shall cease,
I shall possess with Christ at last
eternal joy and peace.

John Newton, 1725–1807
adapted Jubilee Hymns

487

1 And can it be that I should gain
an interest in the Saviour's blood?
Died He for me, who caused His pain?
For me, who Him to death pursued?
* Amazing love! how can it be
that You, my God, should die for me?

2 What mystery here! the Immortal dies!
Who can explore His strange design?
In vain the highest angel tries
to sound the depths of love divine!
What mercy this! let earth adore;
let angel minds inquire no more.

3 He left His Father's throne above —
so free, so infinite His grace —
humbled Himself in all His love
and bled for Adam's helpless race.
What mercy this, immense and free,
for, O my God, it found out me!

4 Long my imprisoned spirit lay
fast bound in sin and nature's night:
then shone Your glorious gospel ray;
I woke! the dungeon flamed with light!
My chains fell off; my heart was new,
I rose, went forth and followed You!

5 No condemnation now I dread!
Jesus, and all in Him, is mine!
Alive in Him, my living head,
and clothed in righteousness divine,
bold I approach the eternal throne
and claim the crown, through Christ my own.

* *The last two lines of each verse are sung twice.*

Charles Wesley, 1707–1788
adapted Compilers of *Praise!* 2000

488

1 As the deer pants for the water,
so my soul longs after You.
You alone are my heart's desire
and I long to worship You.
*You alone are my strength, my shield,
to You alone may my spirit yield.
You alone are my heart's desire
and I long to worship You.*

2 I want You more than gold or silver,
only You can satisfy.
You alone are the real joy-giver
and the apple of my eye.

3 You're my friend and You are my brother,
even though You are a king.
I love You more than any other,
so much more than anything.

Martin J. Nystrom, *b.* 1956

489

1 As water to the thirsty,
as beauty to the eyes,
as strength that follows weakness,
as truth instead of lies,
as songtime and springtime
and summertime to be,
so is my Lord,
my living Lord,
so is my Lord to me.

2 Like calm in place of clamour,
like peace that follows pain,
like meeting after parting,
like sunshine after rain,
like moonlight and starlight
and sunlight on the sea,
so is my Lord,
my living Lord,
so is my Lord to me.

3 As sleep that follows fever,
as gold instead of grey,
as freedom after bondage,
as sunrise to the day,
as home to the traveller
and all we long to see,
so is my Lord,
my living Lord,
so is my Lord to me.

Timothy Dudley-Smith, *b. 1926*

490

1 Lord, be my vision, supreme in
my heart,
bid every rival give way and
depart:
You my best thought in the day
or the night,
waking or sleeping, Your
presence my light.

2 Lord, be my wisdom and be my
true word,
I ever with You and You with
me, Lord:
You my great Father and I Your
true child,
once far away, but by love
reconciled.

3 Lord, be my breastplate, my
sword for the fight:
be my strong armour, for You are
my might;
You are my shelter, and You my
high tower —
raise me to heaven, O power of
my power.

4 I need no riches, nor earth's
empty praise:
You my inheritance through all
my days;
all of Your treasure to me You
impart,
high King of heaven, the first in
my heart.

5 High King of heaven, when battle
is done,
grant heaven's joy to me, bright
heaven's Sun;
Christ of my own heart, whatever
befall
still be my vision, O Ruler of all.

Irish, 8th century
translated Mary Elizabeth Byrne, 1880–1931
revised Eleanor Henrietta Hull, 1860–1935

491

1 Be Thou my vision, O Lord of my
heart,
naught be all else to me, save
that Thou art;
Thou my best thought in the day
and the night,
waking or sleeping, Thy presence
my light.

2 Be Thou my wisdom, be Thou my
true word,
I ever with Thee, and Thou with
me, Lord;
Thou my great Father, and I Thy
true heir;
Thou in me dwelling, and I in
Thy care.

3 Be Thou my breast-plate, my
sword for the fight;
be Thou my armour, and be Thou
my might;
Thou my soul's shelter, and Thou
my high tower,
raise Thou me heavenward, O
power of my power.

4 Riches I heed not, nor vain
empty praise,
Thou mine inheritance through
all my days;
Thou, and Thou only, the first in
my heart,
High King of heaven, my
treasure Thou art!

489 Words: © Timothy Dudley-Smith in Europe and all territories not controlled by Hope Publishing Company
490 Words: © Chatto & Windus / The Random House Group Ltd, 1 Cole Street, Crown Park, Rushden, Northamptonshire NN10 6RZ
491 Words: © Estate of Eleanor Hull. From *The Poem Book of the Gael* translated by M. E. Byrne and edited by Eleanor Hull. Originally published by Chatto & Windus.
Reprinted by permission of the Random House Group Ltd.

5   High King of heaven, when the
        battle is done,
     grant heaven's joy to me, O
        bright heaven's Sun!
     Christ of my own heart, whatever
        befall,
     still be my vision, O Ruler of all.

Irish, 8th century
translated Mary Elizabeth Byrne, 1880–1931
versified Eleanor Henrietta Hull, 1860–1935

492

1   Before the throne of God above
     I have a strong, a perfect plea:
     a great High Priest, whose name
        is Love,
     who ever lives and pleads for
        me.
     My name is written on His
        hands,
     my name is hidden in His heart;
     I know that while in heaven He
        stands
     no power can force me to depart,
     no power can force me to depart.

2   When Satan tempts me to
        despair
     and tells me of the guilt within,
     upward I look, and see Him there
     who made an end of all my sin.
     Because the sinless Saviour died,
     my sinful soul is counted free;
     for God, the just, is satisfied
     to look on Him and pardon me,
     to look on Him and pardon me.

3   Behold Him there! the risen
        Lamb,
     my perfect, sinless Righteousness,
     the great unchangeable I AM,
     the King of glory and of grace!
     One with my Lord I cannot die:
     my soul is purchased by His
        blood,
     my life is safe with Christ on
        high,
     with Christ, my Saviour and my
        God,
     with Christ, my Saviour and my
        God.

Charitie L. De Chenez, 1841–1923
adapted Vikki Cook

493

1   Blessed are the pure in heart,
     for they shall see their God;
     the secret of the Lord is theirs,
     their soul is Christ's abode.

2   The Lord, who left the heavens
     our life and peace to bring,
     to dwell in lowliness with us,
     our pattern and our King;

3   Still to the lowly soul
     Himself He will impart,
     and for His dwelling and His
        throne
     chooses the pure in heart.

4   Lord, we Your presence seek —
     we ask this blessing too;
     give us a pure and lowly heart,
     a temple fit for You.

John Keble, 1792–1866 and William John Hall,
1793–1861

494

1   Christ be beside me,
     Christ be before me,
     Christ be behind me,
     king of my heart;
     Christ be within me,
     Christ be below me,
     Christ be above me,
     never to part.

2   Christ on my right hand,
     Christ on my left hand,
     Christ all around me,
     shield in the strife;
     Christ in my sleeping,
     Christ in my sitting,
     Christ in my rising,
     light of my life.

3   Christ be in all hearts
     thinking about me,
     Christ be in all tongues
     telling of me;
     Christ be the vision
     in eyes that see me,
     in ears that hear me
     Christ ever be.

from *'St Patrick's Breastplate'*, 8th century
adapted James Quinn, *b.* 1919

495

1   Christ be my leader by night as
        by day;
     safe through the darkness, for He
        is the way.
     Gladly I follow, my future His
        care,
     darkness is daylight when Jesus
        is there.

2   Christ be my teacher in age as in
      youth,
    drifting or doubting, for He is the
      truth.
    Grant me to trust Him; though
      shifting as sand,
    doubt cannot daunt me; in Jesus
      I stand.

3   Christ be my saviour in calm as
      in strife;
    death cannot hold me, for He is
      the life.
    Not darkness nor doubting nor
      sin and its stain
    can touch my salvation: with
      Jesus I reign.

Timothy Dudley-Smith, b. 1926

496

1   Christian, do you hear the Lord?
    Jesus speaks His gracious word;
    gently sounds the Saviour's call,
    'Do you love Me best of all?'

2   'I delivered you when bound,
    and when bleeding, healed your
      wound;
    saw you wandering, set you right,
    turned your darkness into light.'

3   'Can a mother's tenderness
    for her own dear child grow less?
    Though she may forgetful be,
    you are always dear to Me.'

4   'Mine is an unchanging love,
    higher than the heights above,
    deeper than the depths beneath,
    free and faithful, strong as death.'

5   'You shall see My glory soon,
    when the work of grace is done;
    crowned with splendour you
      shall be:
    Christian, come and follow Me!'

6   Lord, it is my chief complaint
    that my love is weak and faint;
    yet I love You, and adore —
    O for grace to love You more!

William Cowper, 1731–1800
adapted Jubilate Hymns

497

1   Dear Lord and Father of
      mankind,
    forgive our foolish ways:
    reclothe us in our rightful mind;
    in purer lives Your service find,
    in deeper reverence praise,
    in deeper reverence praise.

2   In simple trust like theirs who
      heard,
    beside the Syrian sea,
    the gracious calling of the Lord —
    let us, like them, obey His word:
    'Rise up and follow me,
    rise up and follow me!'

3   O Sabbath rest by Galilee!
    O calm of hills above,
    when Jesus shared on bended
      knee
    the silence of eternity
    interpreted by love,
    interpreted by love!

4   With that deep hush subduing all
    our words and works that drown
    the tender whisper of Your call,
    as noiseless let Your blessing fall
    as fell Your manna down,
    as fell Your manna down.

5   Drop Your still dews of quietness,
    till all our strivings cease;
    take from our souls the strain and
      stress,
    and let our ordered lives confess
    the beauty of Your peace,
    the beauty of Your peace.

6   Breathe through the heats of our
      desire
    Your coolness and Your balm;
    let sense be dumb, let flesh retire,
    speak through the earthquake,
      wind and fire,
    O still small voice of calm,
    O still small voice of calm!

John Greenleaf Whittier, 1807–1892
adapted Jubilate Hymns

498

1   Do no sinful action;
    speak no angry word;
    you belong to Jesus,
    children of the Lord.

2   Christ is kind and gentle,
    Christ is pure and true,
    and His little children
    must be holy too.

3   There's a wicked spirit
    watching round you still,
    and he tries to tempt you
    to all harm and ill.

4   But you must not hear him,
    though it's hard for you
    to resist the evil,
    and the good to do.

5 Christ is your own master;
   He is good and true,
   and His little children
   must be holy too.

Cecil Frances Alexander, 1818–1895
altered

499

1 For the joys and for the sorrows,
   the best and worst of times,
   for this moment, for tomorrow,
   for all that lies behind;
   fears that crowd around me,
   for the failure of my plans,
   for the dreams of all I hope to be,
   the truth of what I am:
   for this I have Jesus,
   for this I have Jesus,
   for this I have Jesus,
   I have Jesus.

2 For the tears that flow in secret,
   in the broken times,
   for the moments of elation,
   or the troubled mind;
   for all the disappointments,
   or the sting of old regrets,
   all my prayers and longings
   that seem unanswered yet:

3 For the weakness of my body,
   the burden of each day,
   for the nights of doubt and worry,
   when sleep has fled away;
   needing reassurance,
   and the will to start again,
   a steely-eyed endurance,
   the strength to fight and win:

Graham Andrew Kendrick, b. 1950

500

1 God of Grace, amazing wonder,
   irresistible and free;
   oh, the miracle of mercy
   Jesus reaches down to me.
   God of Grace, I stand in wonder
   as my God restores my soul.
   His own blood has paid my
     ransom;
   awesome cost to make me whole.

2 God of Grace who loved and
     knew me
   long before the world began;
   sent my Saviour down from
     heaven:
   perfect God and perfect man.
   God of Grace, I trust in Jesus;

I'm accepted as His own.
Every day His grace sustains me
as I lean on Him alone.

3 God of Grace, I stand astounded,
   cleansed, forgiven and secure.
   All my fears are now confounded
   and my hope is ever sure.
   God of Grace now crowned in
     glory
   where one day I'll see Your face;
   and forever I'll adore You
   in Your everlasting Grace.

Keith Getty, b. 1974
and Jonathan Rea, b. 1974

501

1 I am trusting You, Lord Jesus,
   You have died for me;
   trusting You for full salvation
   great and free.

2 I am trusting You for pardon —
   at Your feet I bow;
   for Your grace and tender mercy,
   trusting now.

3 I am trusting You for cleansing,
   Jesus, Son of God;
   trusting You to make me holy
   by Your blood.

4 I am trusting You to guide me —
   You alone shall lead;
   every day and hour supplying
   all my need.

5 I am trusting You for power —
   Yours can never fail;
   words which You Yourself shall
     give me
   must prevail.

6 I am trusting You, Lord Jesus —
   never let me fall;
   I am trusting You for ever,
   and for all.

Frances Ridley Havergal, 1836–1879
altered Compilers of
Hymns for Today's Church, 1982

502

1 I need You every hour, most
     gracious Lord:
   no tender voice like Yours can
     peace afford.
   I need You, O I need You;
   every hour I need You;
   O bless me now, my Saviour!
   I come to You.

2 I need You every hour: Lord stay
   nearby;
   temptations lose their power
   when You are nigh.

3 I need You every hour, in joy or
   pain;
   come quickly and abide, or life is
   vain.

4 I need You every hour; teach me
   Your will,
   and Your rich promises in me
   fulfil.

Annie Sherwood Hawks, 1835–1918
slightly altered

503

1 I waited for the Lord my God
   and patiently I cried.
   He heard my prayer and turned
   to me
   and in His grace replied.

2 He took me from the slimy pit
   and from the miry clay:
   He set my feet upon a rock
   and made secure my way.

3 He put a new song in my mouth;
   our God to magnify;
   many shall see this, and shall
   fear
   and on the Lord rely.

4 How blessed are those whose
   trust is in
   Jehovah, God of all.
   For arrogance and ignorance
   before His throne must fall.

David J. Montgomery, *b.* 1963
Psalm 40: 1-4

504

1 I'll watch in hope for God,
   my Saviour and my Lord;
   though evil seems to reign
   I'll trust His constant word.
   I shall not fear! Though friends
   betray,
   in faith I'll pray, my God shall
   hear!

2 Although I often fall
   or stumble in the night,
   my God shall raise me up —
   the Lord will be my light.
   Through my distress He'll plead
   for me
   and I shall see His righteousness.

3 The Lord will put to shame
   the mocker's idle boast;
   God's kingdom shall extend,
   expand from coast to coast.
   From every shore they'll come to
   sing
   of Israel's King for evermore.

4 Shepherd Your flock, O God!
   And nourish us once more;
   reveal Your wondrous acts
   as You revealed before.
   Your enemies shall see Your
   power,
   and trembling, cower, upon their
   knees.

5 There is no God like You,
   who pardons and forgives,
   whose anger does not last,
   whose mercy ever lives!
   We can be sure on history's page,
   through every age, Your word
   endures.

David J. Montgomery, *b.* 1963
from Micah 7: 7-20

505

1 Jesus, Friend of all the children,
   be my friend and guide.
   Take my hand and ever keep me
   at Your side.

2 Teach me how to grow in
   goodness
   daily as I grow;
   You have been a child, and
   surely
   You will know.

3 Do not leave me or forsake me,
   ever be my friend;
   for I need You from life's
   dawning
   to its end.

Walter John Mathams, 1853–1931
adapted Compilers

506

1 Jesus, my Lord, my God, my
   all —
   hear me, O Saviour, when I call;
   hear me, and from Your
   dwelling-place
   pour down the riches of Your
   grace:
   Jesus, my Lord, whom I adore,
   help me to love You more and
   more.

2 Jesus, too late I searched for You
to pay the debt of love I owe:
how can I sing Your worthy fame,
the glorious beauty of Your
name?

3 Jesus, how strong Your love must
be
that You should come to die for
me;
how great the joy that You have
brought,
so far exceeding hope or thought!

4 Jesus, Your love shall be my
song —
to You my heart and soul belong:
my life is Yours, O Lord divine,
and You, dear Saviour, You are
mine.

Henry Collins, 1827–1919
adapted Jubilate Hymns

507

1 Lord, You have searched and
known my ways
and understood my thought from
far;
how can I rightly sound Your
praise
or tell how great Your wonders
are?

2 Besetting me, before, behind,
upon my life Your hand is laid;
caught in the compass of Your
mind
are all the things that You have
made.

3 Such knowledge is too wonderful,
too high for me to understand —
enough that the Unsearchable
has searched my heart and held
my hand.

Peter George Jarvis, *b.* 1925
based on Psalm 139: 1-6

508

1 Lord, I come to You — let my
heart be changed, renewed,
flowing from the grace that I
found in You.
And Lord, I've come to know
the weaknesses I see in me will
be stripped away
by the power of Your love:
*Hold me close, let Your love
surround me.*

*Bring me near, draw me to Your
side.
And as I wait I'll rise up like the
eagle
and I will soar with You, Your
Spirit leads me on
in the power of Your love.*

2 Lord unveil my eyes, let me see
You face to face,
the knowledge of Your love as
You live in me.
Lord renew my mind
as Your will unfolds in my life, in
living every day
by the power of Your love:

Geoff Bullock

509

1 Love divine, all loves excelling,
joy of heaven, to earth come
down:
fix in us Your humble dwelling,
all Your faithful mercies crown.
Jesus, You are all compassion,
boundless love that makes us
whole;
visit us with Your salvation,
enter every trembling soul.

2 Come, almighty to deliver,
let us all Your grace receive;
suddenly return, and never,
nevermore Your temples leave:
You we would be always blessing,
serve You as Your hosts above,
pray and praise You without
ceasing,
glory in Your perfect love.

3 Finish then Your new creation,
pure and sinless let us be;
let us see Your great salvation
perfect in eternity:
changed from glory into glory
till in heaven we take our place,
till we lay our crowns before You,
lost in wonder, love and praise.

Charles Wesley, 1707–1788
altered

510

1 Loved with everlasting love,
led by grace that love to know;
Spirit, breathing from above,
You have taught me it is so:
O what full and perfect peace,
joy and wonder all divine!
* In a love which cannot cease,
I am His and He is mine.

2　Heaven above is softer blue,
　　earth around is richer green;
　　something lives in every hue,
　　Christless eyes have never seen:
　　songs of birds in sweetness grow,
　　flowers with deeper beauties
　　　　shine,
　　since I know, as now I know,
　　I am His and He is mine.

3　His for ever, His alone!
　　Who the Lord from me shall
　　　　part?
　　With what joy and peace
　　　　unknown
　　Christ can fill the loving heart!
　　Heaven and earth may pass
　　　　away,
　　sun and stars in gloom decline,
　　but of Christ I still shall say:
　　I am His and He is mine.

*　The last two lines of each verse are repeated
　when sung to the tune Everlasting Love.

George Wade Robinson, 1838–1877

511

1　Loving Shepherd of Your sheep,
　　may we in Your safety keep;
　　nothing can Your power
　　　　withstand;
　　none can pluck us from Your
　　　　hand.

2　Loving Shepherd, You did give
　　Your own life that we might live;
　　we shall praise You every day,
　　gladly all Your will obey.

3　Loving Shepherd, ever near,
　　teach us still Your voice to hear;
　　suffer not our steps to stray
　　from the straight and narrow
　　　　way.

4　Where You guide us we shall go,
　　in Your footsteps here below;
　　then before the Father's throne
　　Saviour, claim us for Your own.

Jane Elizabeth Leeson, 1809–1881
adapted Gaetano Raphael (Anthony) Petti,
1932–1985

512

1　May the mind of Christ my
　　　　Saviour
　　live in me from day to day,
　　by His love and power control
　　　　ling
　　all I do and say.

2　May the word of God enrich me
　　in my heart, from hour to hour,
　　so that all may see I triumph
　　only through His power.

3　May the peace of God my Father
　　in my life for ever reign,
　　that I may be calm to comfort
　　those in grief and pain.

4　May the love of Jesus fill me
　　as the waters fill the sea,
　　Him exalting, self abasing,
　　this is victory!

5　May His beauty rest upon me
　　as I seek to make Him known;
　　so that all may look to Jesus,
　　seeing Him alone.

6　May I run the race before me,
　　strong and brave to face the foe,
　　looking all the while to Jesus
　　as I onward go.

Katie Barclay Wilkinson, 1859–1928
vv. 1-5 *adapted* Jubilate Hymns
v. 6 *adapted* Compilers of *Praise! 2000*

513

1　My God, I love You; not because
　　I hope for heaven thereby,
　　nor yet because if I do not
　　I shall for ever die.

2　But You, Lord Jesus, on the cross
　　once suffered in my place;
　　for me You bore the nails and
　　　　spear,
　　the darkness and disgrace:

3　And griefs and torments
　　　　numberless
　　and sweat of agony,
　　and even death itself, for one
　　who was Your enemy.

4　Then why, O Saviour Jesus
　　　　Christ,
　　should I not love You well?
　　Not for the sake of winning
　　　　heaven
　　nor of escaping hell:

5　Not with the thought of seeking
　　　　gain
　　nor working for reward,
　　but as You gave Yourself for me,
　　O ever-loving Lord.

6   So now I love You, and will love,
    and in Your praise will sing,
    solely because You are my God
    and my eternal King.

                    Latin, 17th century
        translated Edward Caswall, 1814–1878
                adapted Jubilate Hymns

514

1   My heart is filled with
        thankfulness
    to Him who bore my pain;
    who plumbed the depths of my
        disgrace
    and gave me life again;
    who crushed my curse of
        sinfulness
    and clothed me in His light,
    and wrote His law of
        righteousness
    with power upon my heart.

2   My heart is filled with
        thankfulness
    to Him who walks beside;
    who floods my weaknesses and
        strengths
    and causes fear to fly;
    whose every promise is enough
    for every step I take,
    sustaining me with arms of love
    and crowning me with grace.

3   My heart is filled with
        thankfulness
    to Him who reigns above;
    whose wisdom is my perfect
        peace;
    whose every thought is love.
    For every day I have on earth
    is given by the King,
    so I will give my life, my all
    to love and follow Him.

                Stuart Townend, *b.* 1963
                and Keith Getty, *b.* 1974

515

1   My hope is built on nothing less
    than Jesus' blood and
        righteousness;
    no merit of my own I claim,
    but wholly trust in Jesus' name.
      On Christ, the solid rock, I stand,
      all other ground is sinking sand.

2   When darkness veils His lovely
        face,
    I rest on His unchanging grace;

in every high and stormy gale,
my anchor holds and will not fail.

3   His oath, His covenant and His
        blood
    support me in the rising flood;
    when all around my soul gives
        way,
    He then is all my hope and stay.

4   When the last trumpet's voice
        shall sound,
    O may I then in Him be found,
    clothed in His righteousness
        alone,
    faultless to stand before the
        throne!

                Edward Mote, 1797–1874
                            altered

516

1   My times are in Your hand;
    my God, I wish them there!
    My life, my friends, my soul, I
        leave
    entirely to Your care.

2   My times are in Your hand
    whatever they may be,
    pleasing or painful, dark or
        bright,
    as You know best for me.

3   My times are in Your hand;
    why should I doubt or fear?
    My Father's hand will never
        cause
    His child a needless tear.

4   My times are in Your hand,
    Jesus, the Crucified;
    those hands my cruel sins had
        pierced
    are now my guard and guide.

5   My times are in Your hand;
    such faith You give to me
    that after death, at Your right
        hand
    I shall for ever be.

            William Freeman Lloyd, 1791–1853
            adapted Compilers of *Praise!* 2000

517

1   Nearer, my God, to Thee,
    nearer to Thee!
    E'en though it be a cross
    that raiseth me,
    still all my song would be,
*   'Nearer, my God, to Thee,
    nearer to Thee!'

514 Words and Music: © 2003 Thankyou Music. Administered (UK and Europe) by Kingsway Music <tym@kingsway.co.uk>. Remaining territories administered by worshiptogether.com songs. Used by permission.

2 Though, like the wanderer,
the sun gone down,
darkness be over me,
my rest a stone,
yet in my dreams I'd be
nearer, my God, to Thee,
nearer to Thee!

3 There let the way appear
steps unto heaven,
all that Thou send'st to me
in mercy given,
angels to beckon me
nearer, my God, to Thee,
nearer to Thee!

4 Then, with my waking thoughts
bright with Thy praise,
out of my stony griefs
Bethel I'll raise,
so by my woes to be
nearer, my God, to Thee,
nearer to Thee!

5 Or if on joyful wing
cleaving the sky,
sun, moon, and stars forgot,
upwards I fly,
still all my song shall be,
'Nearer, my God, to Thee,
nearer to Thee!'

*When sung to Bethany the penultimate line of
each verse is repeated.*
*When sung to Propior Deo the last line of each
verse is repeated.*

Sarah Flower Adams, 1805–1848

518

1 O for a closer walk with God,
a constant, heavenly calm;
a light to shine upon the road
that leads me to the Lamb!

2 Where is the blessing that I knew
when first I saw the Lord?
Where is the soul-refreshing
view
of Jesus and His word?

3 What peaceful hours I once
enjoyed!
How sweet their memory still!
But they have left an aching void
the world can never fill.

4 The dearest idol I have known —
however much adored —
help me to tear it from Your
throne
and worship You as Lord.

5 So shall my walk be close with
God,
my mind serene and calm;
so purer light shall mark the road
that leads me to the Lamb.

William Cowper, 1731–1800
adapted Compilers of Praise! 2000

519

1 O for a closer walk with God,
a calm and heavenly frame;
a light that shines upon the road,
leading to the Lamb.

2 Where is the blessedness I knew
when once I saw the Lord?
Where is the soul-refreshing
view
living in His word?
*A light to be my guide,
the Father's presence at my side.
In Your will my rest I find.
O for a closer walk with God,
leading to the Lamb.*

3 So shall my walk be close with
God
with all the hopes made new.
So purer light shall mark the
road
leading to the Lamb.
A light to be …

William Cowper, 1731–1800
adapted Keith Getty, b. 1974

520

1 O for a faith that will not shrink,
though pressed by many a foe,
that will not tremble on the brink
of poverty or woe,

2 That will not murmur nor
complain
beneath the chastening rod,
but, in the hour of grief or pain,
can lean upon its God;

3 A faith that shines more bright
and clear
when tempests rage without,
that when in danger knows no
fear,
in darkness feels no doubt;

4 A faith that keeps the narrow
way
till life's last spark is fled,
and with a pure and heavenly
ray
lights up a dying bed!

519   Words and Music: © 2001 Thankyou Music. Administered (UK and Europe) by Kingsway Music <tym@kingsway.co.uk>. Remaining territories administered by worshiptogether.com songs. Used by permission.

5 Lord, give me such a faith as this,
and then, whate'er may come,
I taste even now the hallowed
    bliss
of an eternal home.

William Hiley Bathurst, 1796–1877

521

1 O for a heart to praise my God,
a heart from sin set free,
a heart that's sprinkled with the
    blood
so freely shed for me;

2 A heart resigned, submissive,
    meek,
my great Redeemer's throne,
where only Christ is heard to
    speak,
where Jesus reigns alone;

3 A humble, lowly, contrite heart,
believing, true, and clean;
which neither life nor death can
    part
from Him who dwells within;

4 A heart in every thought
    renewed,
and full of love divine;
perfect, and right, and pure, and
    good,
Your life revealed in mine.

5 Your nature, gracious Lord,
    impart;
come quickly from above,
write Your new name upon my
    heart,
Your own great name of love.

Charles Wesley, 1707–1788

522

1 O God of faith, help me believe,
help me to know You shelter me,
and though Your face I cannot
    see,
O may I feel Your strength in me.

2 O God of hope, help me to know
that hope in You is strong and
    sure,
that You raised Jesus from the
    grave,
and hope is in Your power to
    save.

3 O God of love, help me to see
that love sent Christ to die for
    me,

and though unworthy I can say
that love endures from day to
    day.

4 O God of faith, help me to
    believe,
O God of hope, my saviour be.
O God of love, show love
    through me,
and shine for all the world to see.

Ron Hopgood

523

1 O Love that wilt not let me go,
I rest my weary soul in Thee:
I give Thee back the life I owe
that in Thine ocean depths its
    flow
may richer, fuller be.

2 O Light that followest all my way,
I yield my flickering torch to
    Thee:
my heart restores its borrowed
    ray
that in Thy sunshine's blaze its
    day
may brighter, fairer be.

3 O Joy that seekest me through
    pain,
I cannot close my heart to Thee;
I trace the rainbow through the
    rain,
and feel the promise is not vain,
that morn shall tearless be.

4 O Cross that liftest up my head,
I dare not ask to fly from Thee:
I lay in dust life's glory dead,
and from the ground there
    blossoms red
life that shall endless be.

George Matheson, 1842–1906

524

1 Purify my heart,
let me be as gold and precious
    silver;
purify my heart,
let me be as gold, pure gold.
    *Refiner's fire, my heart's one
        desire
    is to be holy, set apart for You,
        Lord;
    I choose to be holy, set apart for
        You,
    my Master, ready to do Your will.*

2 Purify my heart,
   cleanse me from within and
      make me holy;
   purify my heart,
   cleanse me from my sin, deep
      within.

Brian Doerksen

525

1 Safe in the shadow of the Lord
   beneath His hand and power,
   I trust in Him,
   I trust in Him,
   my fortress and my tower.

2 My hope is set on God alone
   though Satan spreads his snare;
   I trust in Him,
   I trust in Him,
   to keep me in His care.

3 From fears and phantoms of the
      night,
   from foes about my way,
   I trust in Him,
   I trust in Him,
   by darkness as by day.

4 His holy angels keep my feet
   secure from every stone;
   I trust in Him,
   I trust in Him,
   and unafraid go on.

5 Strong in the everlasting Name,
   and in my Father's care,
   I trust in Him,
   I trust in Him,
   who hears and answers prayer.

6 Safe in the shadow of the Lord,
   possessed by love divine,
   I trust in Him,
   I trust in Him,
   and meet His love with mine.

Timothy Dudley-Smith, b. 1926
from Psalm 91

526

1 Saviour, teach me, day by day,
   love's sweet lesson to obey;
   sweeter lesson cannot be,
   loving Him who first loved me.

2 With a child's glad heart of love
   at Your bidding may I move,
   prompt to serve and follow free,
   loving Him who first loved me.

3 Teach me now Your steps to trace,
   strong to follow in Your grace,
   how to live in You I see,
   loving Him who first loved me.

4 Love in loving true and right,
   in obedience finds delight;
   ever new that joy will be,
   loving Him who first loved me.

5 So may I rejoice to show
   that I feel the love I owe;
   singing, till Your face I see,
   of His love who first loved me.

Jane Elizabeth Leeson, 1809–1881
altered Compilers

527

1 The Lord's my shepherd, I'll not
      want,
   He makes me lie in pastures
      green.
   He leads me by the still, still
      waters,
   His goodness restores my soul.

   And I will trust in You alone,
   and I will trust in You alone,
   for Your endless mercy follows me,
   Your goodness will lead me home.

2 He guides my ways in
      righteousness,
   and He anoints my head with oil,
   and my cup, it overflows with joy,
   I feast on His pure delights.

3 And though I walk the darkest
      path,
   I will not fear the evil one,
   for You are with me, and Your
      rod and staff
   are the comfort I need to know.

Stuart Townend, b. 1963
from Psalm 23

528

1 What grace, O Lord, and beauty
      shone
   around Your steps below!
   What patient love was seen in all
   Your life and death of woe!

2 For ever on Your burdened heart
   a weight of sorrow hung,
   yet no ungentle, murmuring
      word
   escaped Your silent tongue.

3 Your foes might hate, despise,
      revile,
   Your friends unfaithful prove:
   unwearied in forgiveness still,
   Your heart could only love.

4 O give us hearts to love like You,
      like You, O Lord, to grieve
   far more for others' sins than all
   the wrongs that we receive.

5 One with Yourself, may every
      eye
   in all of humankind
   behold that grace and gentleness
   which, Lord, in You we find.

                    Edward Denny, 1796–1889
                       adapted Compilers

529

1 Will your anchor hold in the
      storms of life,
   when the clouds unfold their
      wings of strife?
   When the strong tides lift, and
      the cables strain,
   will your anchor drift, or firm
      remain?
   We have an anchor that keeps the
      soul
   steadfast and sure while the
      billows roll;
   fastened to the Rock which cannot
      move,
   grounded firm and deep in the
      Saviour's love!

2 Will your anchor hold in the
      straits of fear,
   when the breakers roar and the
      reef is near?
   While the surges rave, and the
      wild winds blow,
   shall the angry waves then your
      bark o'erflow?

3 Will your anchor hold in the
      floods of death,
   when the waters cold chill your
      latest breath?
   On the rising tide you can never
      fail,
   while your anchor holds within
      the veil?

4 Will your eyes behold through
      the morning light
   the city of gold and the harbour
      bright?

Will you anchor safe by the
   heavenly shore,
when life's storms are past for
   evermore?

                    Priscilla Jane Owens, 1829–190

530

1 Yield not to temptation, for
      yielding is sin,
   each victory will help you some
      other to win;
   fight steadily onward, dark
      passions subdue,
   look ever to Jesus, He will carry
      you through.
   Ask the Saviour to help you,
   comfort, strengthen, and keep you;
   He is willing to aid you,
   He will carry you through.

2 Shun evil companions, bad
      language disdain,
   God's name hold in reverence,
      nor take it in vain;
   be thoughtful and earnest, kind-
      hearted and true,
   look ever to Jesus, He will carry
      you through.

3 To all the victorious, God's gift is
      a crown.
   Through faith we shall conquer,
      though often cast down;
   He who is our Saviour our
      strength will renew,
   look ever to Jesus, He will carry
      you through.

                    Horatio Richmond Palmer, 1834–190

Also suitable:
I hear Your welcome voice   54
The wise may bring their learning   33

THE GROWTH
OF THE CHURCH
CONFIRMATION

531

1 I'm not ashamed to own my
      Lord,
   or to defend His cause,
   maintain the glory of His cross,
   and honour all His laws.

2 Jesus, my Lord! I know His
      name,
   His name is all my boast;

CONFIRMATION

nor will He put my soul to
   shame,
nor let my hope be lost.

3 I know that safe with Him
    remains,
protected by His power,
what I've committed to His trust,
till the decisive hour.

4 Then will He own His servant's
    name
before His Father's face,
and in the new Jerusalem
appoint my soul a place.

Paraphrases 54, 2 Timothy 1: 12

532

1 My God, accept my heart this day
and make it Yours alone;
no longer let my footsteps stray
from Your belovèd Son.

2 Before the cross of Him who died
in awe and shame I fall:
let every sin be crucified
and Christ be all-in-all.

3 Anoint me with Your heavenly
    grace
and seal me as Your own,
that I may see Your glorious face
and worship at Your throne.

4 Let every thought and work and
    word
to You be ever given;
then life shall be Your service,
   Lord,
and death the gate of heaven.

5 All glory to the Father be,
the Spirit and the Son;
all love and praise eternally
to God the Three-in-One.

Matthew Bridges, 1800–1894
adapted Jubilate Hymns

533

1 Who is on the Lord's side?
Who will serve the King?
Who will be His helpers
other lives to bring?
Who will leave the world's side?
Who will face the foe?
Who is on the Lord's side?
Who for Him will go?
By Your call of mercy,
by Your grace alone,
we are on the Lord's side,
Saviour, all Your own.

2 Jesus, You have bought us,
not with gold or gem,
but with Your own life-blood,
for Your diadem.
With Your blessing filling
all who come in need,
You have made us willing,
made us free indeed.
By Your great redemption,
by Your grace alone,
we are on the Lord's side,
Saviour, all Your own.

3 Fierce may be the conflict,
strong may be the foe;
but the King's own army
none can overthrow.
Round His standard ranging,
victory is secure;
for His truth unchanging
makes the triumph sure.
Joyfully enlisting
by Your grace alone,
we are on the Lord's side,
Saviour, all Your own.

4 Chosen to be soldiers
in a hostile land,
chosen, called and faithful,
for our Captain's band.
In His service royal
let us not grow cold;
let us then be loyal,
steadfast, true and bold.
Master, You will keep us
by Your grace alone,
always on the Lord's side,
Saviour, all Your own.

Frances Ridley Havergal, 1836–1879
adapted Compilers of Praise! 2000

534

1 You who know the Lord is
    gracious,
you for whom a corner-stone
stands, of God elect and precious,
laid that you may build thereon;
see that on that sure foundation
you a living temple raise,
towers that may tell forth
   salvation,
walls that may re-echo praise.

2 Living stones, by God appointed
each to its allotted place,
kings and priests, by God
   anointed,
shall you not declare His grace?

532 Words: © in this version Jubilate Hymns, 4 Thorne Park Road, Chelston, Torquay TQ2 6RX <enquiries@jubilate.co.uk> Used by permission.
533 Words: © in this version Praise Trust, Praise Trust, PO Box 359, Darlington. DL3 8YD
534 Words: © Sir Richard Mynors

You, a royal generation,
tell the tidings of your birth,
tidings of a new creation
to an old and weary earth.

3   Tell the praise of Him who called
       you
    out of darkness into light,
    broke the fetters that enthralled
       you,
    gave you freedom, peace and
       sight:
    tell the tale of sins forgiven,
    strength renewed and hope
       restored,
    till the earth, in tune with
       heaven,
    praise and magnify the Lord!

Cyril Argentine Alington, 1872–1955
from 1 Peter 2: 3-10

Also suitable:

Father, Your church with thankfulness   481
Firmly I believe and truly   159
Glorious things of you are spoken   143
God, when I came into this life   482
How clear is our vocation, Lord   483
O Lord, who came from realms above   467
We belive in God Almighty   163

THE GROWTH
OF THE CHURCH
DEDICATION

535

All that I am I lay before You;
all I possess, Lord I confess is
   nothing without You.
Saviour and King, I now enthrone
   You;
take my life, my living sacrifice to
   You.

1   Lord, be the strength within my
       weakness;
    be the supply in every need,
    that I may prove Your promises
       to me,
    faithful and true in word and
       deed.

2   Into Your hands I place the
       future;
    the past is nailed to Calvary,
    that I may live in resurrection
       power,
    no longer I but Christ in me.

James Wright

536

1   Beneath the cross of Jesus
    I gladly take my stand;
    the shadow of a mighty rock
    within a weary land;
    a home within the wilderness,
    a rest upon the way,
    from the burning of the noontide
       heat,
    and the burden of the day.

2   O safe and happy shelter!
    O refuge tried and sweet!
    The appointed place where
       heaven's love
    and heaven's justice meet!
    As weary Jacob, in his sleep,
    that wondrous dream was given,
    so seems my Saviour's cross to
       me —
    a ladder up to heaven.

3   Upon that cross of Jesus
    my eye at times can see
    the very dying form of one
    who suffered there for me;
    and from my broken heart, with
       tears,
    two wonders I confess:
    the wonders of His glorious love,
    and my unworthiness.

4   His cross! I take its shadow
    to be my hiding-place;
    I ask no other sunshine than
    the sunshine of His face;
    content to let the world go by,
    to know no gain or loss:
    my sinful self my only shame,
    my glory all — the cross!

Elizabeth Cecilia Clephane, 1830–186
adapted Compilers of Praise! 200

537

1   Fill now my life, O Lord my God
    in every part with praise;
    that my whole being may
       proclaim
    Your being and Your ways.

2   Not for the lip of praise alone,
    nor yet the praising heart,
    I ask, but for a life made up
    of praise in every part.

3   Praise in the common things of
       life,
    its goings out and in;
    praise in each duty and each
       deed,
    exalted or unseen.

536   Words: © in this version Praise Trust, Praise Trust, PO Box 359, Darlington. DL3 8YD
535   Words and Music: © 1994 Thankyou Music. Administered (UK and Europe) by Kingsway Music <tym@kingsway.co.uk>. Remaining territories administered by worshiptogether.com songs. Used by permission.

DEDICATION

4   Fill every part of me with praise;
let all my being speak
of You and of Your love, O Lord,
poor though I be and weak.

5   Then, Lord, from me You shall receive
the praise and glory due;
and so shall I begin on earth
the song for ever new.

6   So shall no part of day or night
from sacredness be free;
but all my life, with You my God,
in fellowship shall be.

*Horatius N. Bonar, 1808–1889
adapted Compilers of
Hymns for Today's Church, 1982*

538

1   He who would valiant be
'gainst all disaster,
let him in constancy
follow the Master:
there's no discouragement
shall make him once relent
his first avowed intent
to be a pilgrim.

2   Who so beset him round
with dismal stories
do but themselves confound —
his strength the more is:
no foes shall stay his might,
though he with giants fight;
he will make good his right
to be a pilgrim.

3   Since, Lord, You now defend
us with Your Spirit,
we know we at the end
shall life inherit:
then, fancies, flee away!
I'll fear not what men say,
I'll labour night and day
to be a pilgrim.

*John Bunyan, 1628–1688
adapted Percy Dearmer, 1867–1936*

539

*Here I am, wholly available —
as for me, I will serve the Lord.*

1   The fields are white unto harvest
but oh, the labourers are so few;
so Lord I give myself to help the reaping,
to gather precious souls unto You.

2   The time is right in the nation
for works of power and authority;
God's looking for a people who are willing
to be counted in His glorious victory.

3   As salt are we ready to savour,
in darkness are we ready to be light;
God's seeking out a very special people
to manifest His truth and His might.

Christopher Alan Bowater, b. 1947

540

1   I hear Your welcome voice
that calls me by Your will,
for cleansing in Your precious blood
that flowed on Calvary's hill.
*I am coming, Lord,
coming by Your will:
wash me, cleanse me, by the blood
that flowed on Calvary's hill.*

2   'Tis Jesus calls me on
to perfect faith and love,
to perfect hope, and peace, and trust,
for earth and heaven above.

3   'Tis Jesus who confirms
the blessèd work within,
by adding grace to welcomed grace,
where reigned the power of sin.

4   All hail, atoning blood!
All hail, redeeming grace!
All hail, the gift of Christ our Lord,
our strength and righteousness!

*Louis Hartsough, 1828–1919
adapted Compilers*

541

1   I, the Lord of sea and sky,
I have heard My people cry.
All who dwell in dark or sin
My hand will save.
I, who made the stars of night,
I will make their darkness bright.
Who will bear My light to them?
Whom shall I send?

Here I am, Lord.
Is it I, Lord?
I have heard You calling in the
*   night.*
I will go, Lord,
if You lead me.
I will hold Your people in my
*   heart.*

2 I, the Lord of snow and rain,
   I have borne My people's pain.
   I have wept for love of them.
   They turn away.
   I will break their hearts of stone,
   give them hearts for love alone.
   I will speak My word to them.
   Whom shall I send?

3 I, the Lord of wind and flame,
   I will tend the poor and lame.
   I will set a feast for them.
   My hand will save.
   Finest bread I will provide
   till their hearts be satisfied.
   I will give My life to them.
   Whom shall I send?

                    Daniel L. Schutte, *b.* 1947

542

1 I will offer up my life
   in spirit and truth,
   pouring out the oil of love
   as my worship to You.
   In surrender I must give
   my every part;
   Lord, receive the sacrifice
   of a broken heart.
   Jesus, what can I give,
   what can I bring
   to so faithful a friend,
   to so loving a king?
   Saviour, what can be said,
   what can be sung
   as a praise of Your name
   for the things You have done?
   Oh, my words could not tell,
   not even in part,
   of the debt of love that is owed
   by this thankful heart.

2 You deserve my every breath
   for You've paid the great cost;
   giving up Your life to death,
   even death on a cross.
   You took all my shame away,
   there defeated my sin,
   opened up the gates of heaven,
   and have beckoned me in.

                         Matt Redman, *b.* 1974

543

Jesus, all for Jesus:
all I am and have
and ever hope to be.
Jesus, all for Jesus:
all I am and have
and ever hope to be.

All of my ambitions hopes and
    plans —
I surrender these
into Your hands.
All of my ambitions hopes and
    plans —
I surrender these
into Your hands.

For it's only in Your will that I
    am free.
For it's only in Your will that I
    am free.

Jesus, all for Jesus:
all I am and have
and ever hope to be.

             Jennifer Atkinson and Robin Mark

544

1 Jesus is greater than the greatest
       heroes,
   Jesus is closer than the closest
       friends.
   He came from heaven and He
       died to save us,
   to show us love that never ends.

2 Son of God and the Lord of glory,
   He's the light; follow in His way.
   He's the truth that we can
       believe in,
   and He's the life, He's living
       today.

                       Gillian E. Hutchinson

545

1 Jesus, Master, whose I am,
   purchased Yours alone to be,
   by Your blood, O perfect Lamb,
   shed so willingly for me:
   let my heart be all Your own,
   let me live to You alone.

2 Jesus, Master, I am Yours;
   keep me faithful, keep me near,
   shine on all my days and hours,
   all my homeward way to cheer.
   Jesus! at Your feet I fall;
   be my Lord, my all-in-all!

542 Words and Music: © 1994 Thankyou Music. Administered (UK and Europe) by Kingsway Music <tym@kingsway.co.uk>. Remaining territories administered by worshiptogether.com songs. Used by permission.

543 Words and Music: © 1991 Word's Spirit of Praise Music/Administered by CopyCare Ltd, PO Box 77, Hailsham, East Sussex. BN27 3EF

544 Words and Music: © 1992 Sea Dream Music

DEDICATION

Jesus, Master, whom I serve,
though so feebly and so ill,
strengthen hand and heart and
  nerve
all Your bidding to fulfil:
open now my eyes to see
all the work You have for me.

Jesus, Master, will You use
one who owes You more than
  all?
As You will! I would not choose;
only let me hear Your call.
Jesus, let me always be
in Your service, glad and free.

Frances Ridley Havergal, 1836–1879
altered Compilers of *Praise!* 2000

46

Just as I am, Your child to be,
friend of the young, who died for
  me;
to give my life wholeheartedly,
O Jesus Christ, I come.

While I am still a child today,
I give my life, my work and play;
to You alone, without delay,
with all my heart I come.

I see in You, O Christ the light,
with You as Lord, and in Your
  might
I turn from sin to what is right,
my Lord, to You I come.

Lord, take my dreams of fame
  and gold,
I now accept a life controlled
by faith in You as days unfold,
with my whole life I come.

Just as I am, young, strong and
  free,
to be the best that I can be,
that others may see You in me,
Lord of my life, I come.

Mary Ann Hearn, 1834–1909
adapted Peter J. Horrobin, *b.* 1943
and Greg P. Leavers, *b.* 1952

47

'Lift up your hearts!' We lift
  them to the Lord,
and give to God our thanks with
  one accord;
it is our joy and duty, all our days
to lift our hearts in grateful
  thanks and praise.

2 Above the level of the former
    years,
  the mire of sin, the slough of
    guilty fears,
  the mist of doubt, the blight of
    love's decay —
  O Lord of light, lift all our hearts
    today!

3 Lift every gift that You Yourself
    have given;
  low lies the best till lifted up to
    heaven:
  low lie the bounding heart, the
    teeming brain,
  till, sent from God, they mount to
    God again.

4 Then, as the trumpet-call, in after
    years,
  'Lift up your hearts!' rings
    pealing in our ears,
  still shall those hearts respond
    with full accord,
  'We lift them up, we lift them to
    the Lord!'

Henry Montagu Butler, 1833–1918
vv. 1, 2 *adapted* Compilers of
Hymns for Today's Church, 1982
vv. 3, 4 *adapted* Compilers of
Church Hymnary, 3rd edition, 1973

548

1 Lord and Master, You have called
    us
  all Your followers to be,
  we have heard Your clear
    commandment,
  'Bring the children unto me.'

2 So we come to You, the Teacher,
  at Your feet we kneel to pray:
  we can only lead the children
  when to us You show the way.

3 Teach us Your most wondrous
    method,
  as in Galilee of old,
  You did show Your chosen
    servants
  how to bring lambs to the fold.

4 Give us store of wit and wisdom,
  give us love which never tires,
  give us Your abiding patience,
  give us hope which aye inspires.

5 Mighty Wisdom of the Godhead,
  You the one eternal Word,
  You the Counsellor, the Teacher,
  fill us with Your fullness, Lord.

Florence Margaret Smith, 1886–1958

Words: © Peter Horrobin and Greg Leavers/Ellel Ministries International. Used by permission.
Words: © The National Society

549

1 Lord of creation, to You be all
   praise!
   Most mighty Your working, most
   wondrous Your ways!
   Your glory and might are beyond
   us to tell,
   and yet in the heart of the
   humble You dwell.

2 Lord of all power, I give You my
   will,
   in joyful obedience Your tasks to
   fulfil;
   Your bondage is freedom, Your
   service is song,
   and, held in Your keeping, my
   weakness is strong.

3 Lord of all wisdom, I give You
   my mind,
   rich truth that surpasses man's
   knowledge to find;
   what eye has not seen and what
   ear has not heard
   is taught by Your Spirit and
   shines from Your word.

4 Lord of all bounty, I give You my
   heart;
   I praise and adore You for all You
   impart,
   Your love to inspire me, Your
   counsel to guide,
   Your presence to cheer me,
   whatever betide.

5 Lord of all being, I give You my
   all;
   for if I disown You I stumble and
   fall;
   but, sworn in glad service Your
   word to obey,
   and walk in Your freedom to the
   end of the way.

Jack Copley Winslow, 1882–1974

550

1 Lord, speak to me that I may
   speak
   in living echoes of Your tone;
   as You have sought, so let me
   seek
   Your wandering children, lost,
   alone.

2 O lead me, Lord, that I may lead
   the stumbling and the straying
   feet;

and feed me, Lord, that I may
   feed
   Your hungry ones with manna
   sweet.

3 O teach me, Lord, that I may
   teach
   the precious truths which You
   impart;
   and wing my words that they
   may reach
   the hidden depths of many a
   heart.

4 O fill me with Your fullness,
   Lord,
   until my heart shall overflow
   in kindling thought and glowing
   word,
   Your love to tell, Your praise to
   show.

5 O use me, Lord, use even me,
   just as You will, and when, and
   where;
   until at last Your face I see,
   Your rest, Your joy, Your glory
   share.

Frances Ridley Havergal, 1836–18?
adapted Compilers c
Hymns for Today's Church, 198

551

1 O Jesus, I have promised
   to serve You to the end —
   be now and ever near me,
   my Master and my Friend:
   I shall not fear the battle
   if You are by my side,
   nor wander from the pathway
   if You will be my guide.

2 O let me feel You near me,
   the world is ever near;
   I see the sights that dazzle,
   the tempting sounds I hear;
   my foes are ever near me,
   around me and within;
   but Jesus, draw still nearer
   and shield my soul from sin!

3 O let me hear You speaking
   in accents clear and still;
   above the storms of passion,
   the murmurs of self-will:
   O speak to reassure me,
   to hasten or control;
   and speak to make me listen,
   O Guardian of my soul.

4 O let me see Your footmarks
   and in them place my own;
   my hope to follow truly
   is in Your strength alone:
   O guide me, call me, draw me,
   uphold me to the end;
   and then in heaven receive me,
   my Saviour and my Friend.

John Ernest Bode, 1816–1874

552

1 Take my life and let it be
   all You purpose, Lord, for me;
   consecrate my passing days,
   let them flow in ceaseless praise.

2 Take my hands, and let them
      move
   at the impulse of Your love;
   take my feet, and let them run
   with the news of victory won.

3 Take my voice, and let me sing
   always, only, for my King;
   take my lips, let them proclaim
   all the beauty of Your name.

4 Take my wealth — all I possess,
   make me rich in faithfulness;
   take my mind that I may use
   every power as You shall choose.

5 Take my motives and my will,
   all Your purpose to fulfil;
   take my heart — it is Your own,
   it shall be Your royal throne.

6 Take my love — my Lord, I pour
   at Your feet its treasure-store;
   take myself, and I will be
   Yours for all eternity.

Frances Ridley Havergal, 1836–1879
adapted Jubilate Hymns

553

LEADER: Thuma mina
ALL: Thuma mina, thuma
         mina
         thuma mina, Somandla
LEADER: Send me, Lord.
ALL: Send me Jesus, send me,
         Jesus
         send me Jesus, send me
         Lord
LEADER: Lead me, Lord.
ALL: Lead me Jesus ...
LEADER: Fill me, Lord
ALL: Fill me, Jesus ...
LEADER: Thuma mina
ALL: Thuma mina ...

South African traditional

554

1 Two little fishes, five loaves of
      bread,
   five thousand people by Jesus
      were fed.
   This is what happened when one
      little lad
   gladly gave Jesus all that he had.
   All that I have,
   all that I have,
   I will give Jesus all that I have.

2 One lonely widow, two coins
      small.
   Jesus was watching when she
      gave her all,
   and Jesus said, as His heart was
      made glad,
   that she had given all that she
      had.

Dorothy G. Montgomery

Also suitable:

Confirmation section   531-534
Father, I place into Your hands   556
Hushed was the evening hymn   172
I bind myself to God today   162
Jesus' hands were kind hands   349
King of kings, majesty   452
Lord Jesus Christ, You have come to us   388
O dearest Lord, Thy sacred head   419
The wise may bring their learning   338
When I survey the wondrous cross   427

THE GROWTH
OF THE CHURCH
DISCIPLESHIP

555

1 Courage, friend, and do not
      stumble,
   though your path be dark as
      night;
   there's a star to guide the
      humble —
   trust in God, and do the right.
   Let the road be rough and dreary,
   and its end far out of sight,
   foot it bravely, strong or weary,
   * trust in God, and do the right.

* *When this hymn is sung to Courage Brother, the*
   words 'Trust in God' must be sung three times
   in the last line of each verse.   When used with
   Norman, the tune is sung twice for each verse
   of words.

vv. 2 & 3 overleaf

2 Words: © in this version Jubilate Hymns, 4 Thorne Park Road, Chelston, Torquay TQ2 6RX <enquiries@jubilate.co.uk> Used by permission.
3 Words and Music: © Utryck, Sweden / Wild Goose Resource Group, Iona Community, Pearce Institute, 840 Govan Road, Glasgow G51 3UU
4 Words and Music: © Singspiration / Brentwood Benson Music Publishing Inc / Administered by CopyCare Ltd, PO Box 77, Hailsham, East Sussex. BN27 3EF

2 Perish policy and cunning,
   perish all that fears the light!
   Whether losing, whether
      winning,
   trust in God, and do the right.
   Some will hate you, some will
      love you,
   some will flatter, some will slight:
   lift your eyes and look above you,
   trust in God, and do the right.

3 Simple rule, and safest guiding,
   inward peace, and inward might,
   star upon our path abiding —
   trust in God, and do the right.
   Courage, friend, and do not
      stumble,
   though your path be dark as
      night;
   there's a star to guide the
      humble —
   trust in God, and do the right.

Norman Macleod, 1812–1872

556

1 Father, I place into Your hands
   the things that I can't do.
   Father, I place into Your hands
   the times that I've been through.
   Father, I place into Your hands
   the way that I should go,
   for I know I always can trust You.

2 Father, I place into Your hands
   my friends and family.
   Father, I place into Your hands
   the things that trouble me.
   Father, I place into Your hands
   the person I would be,
   for I know I always can trust You.

3 Father, we love to seek Your face,
   we love to hear Your voice.
   Father, we love to sing Your
      praise,
   and in Your name rejoice.
   Father, we love to walk with You
   and in Your presence rest,
   for we know we always can trust
      You.

4 Father, I want to be with You
   and do the things You do.
   Father, I want to speak the words
   that You are speaking too.
   Father, I want to love the ones
   that You will draw to You,
   for I know that I am one with
      You.

Jenny Hewer, b. 1945

557

1 Fight the good fight with all your
      might,
   Christ is your strength, and
      Christ your right;
   lay hold on life, and it shall be
   your joy and crown eternally.

2 Run the straight race through
      God's good grace,
   lift up your eyes, and seek His
      face:
   life with its way before you lies,
   Christ is the path and Christ the
      prize.

3 Cast care aside, lean on your
      guide,
   His boundless mercy will
      provide;
   trust, and your trusting soul shall
      prove
   Christ is its life, and Christ its
      love.

4 Faint not, nor fear, His arms are
      near;
   He does not change, and you are
      dear;
   only believe and Christ shall be
   your all-in-all eternally.

John Samuel Bewley Monsell, 1811–1875
altered

558

1 I want to walk with Jesus Christ,
   all the days I live of this life on
      earth,
   to give to Him complete control
   of body and of soul:

   *Follow Him, follow Him, yield
      your life to Him,
   He has conquered death, He is
      King of kings.
   Accept the joy which He gives to
      those
   who yield their lives to Him.*

2 I want to learn to speak to Him
   to pray to Him, confess my sin,
   to open my life and let Him in,
   for joy will then be mine:

3 I want to learn to speak of Him,
   my life must show that He lives
      in me,
   my deeds, my thoughts, my
      words must speak
   all of His love for me:

556 Words and Music: © 1975 Thankyou Music. Administered (UK and Europe) by Kingsway Music <tym@kingsway.co.uk>. Remaining territories administered by worshiptogether.com songs. Used by permission.
558 Words: © 1964 Clive Simmonds

DISCIPLESHIP

4 I want to learn to read His word,
   for this is how I know the way
   to live my life as pleases Him,
   in holiness and joy:

5 O Holy Spirit of the Lord,
   enter now into my youthful heart,
   take full control of my selfish will
   and rule in every part:

Clive Simmonds

559

1 If I come to Jesus,
   He will make me glad;
   He will give me pleasure
   when my heart is sad.
   If I come to Jesus,
   happy shall I be;
   He is gently calling
   little ones like me.

2 If I come to Jesus,
   He will hear my prayer;
   He will love me dearly;
   He my sins did bear.

3 If I come to Jesus,
   He will take my hand,
   He will kindly lead me
   to a better land.

Frances Jane (Fanny) Crosby, 1820–1915

560

1 In heavenly armour we'll enter
      the land —
   the battle belongs to the Lord;
   no weapon that's fashioned
      against us will stand —
   the battle belongs to the Lord.
   We sing glory, honour,
   power and strength to the Lord;
   we sing glory, honour,
   power and strength to the Lord!

2 When the power of darkness
      comes in like a flood,
   the battle belongs to the Lord;
   He's raised up a standard, the
      power of His blood —
   the battle belongs to the Lord.
   We sing glory, honour,
   power and strength to the Lord;
   we sing glory, honour,
   power and strength to the Lord!

3 When your enemy presses in
      hard, do not fear —
   the battle belongs to the Lord;
   take courage, my friend, your
      redemption is near —

the battle belongs to the Lord.
   We sing glory, honour,
   power and strength to the Lord;
   we sing glory, honour,
   power and strength to the Lord!
   Power and strength to the Lord!

Jamie Owens-Collins, b. 1955

561

1 Jesus bids us shine
   with a pure, clear light,
   like a little candle
   burning in the night.
   In this world is darkness;
   so let us shine,
   you in your small corner,
   and I in mine.

2 Jesus bids us shine,
   first of all for Him;
   well He sees and knows it,
   if our light grows dim.
   He looks down from heaven
   to see us shine,
   you in your small corner,
   and I in mine.

3 Jesus bids us shine,
   then, for all around;
   many kinds of darkness
   in the world are found —
   sin and want and sorrow;
   so we must shine,
   you in your small corner,
   and I in mine.

Susan Bogert Warner, 1819–1885

562

1 Jesus calls above the tumult
   of our life's wild, restless sea;
   day by day His voice re-echoes,
   saying, 'Christian, follow me!'

2 As of old, apostles heard it
   by the Galilean lake,
   turned from home and toil and
      kindred,
   leaving all for His dear sake.

3 Jesus calls us from the worship
   of the vain world's golden store,
   from each rival that would claim
      us,
   saying, 'Christian, love me more!'

4 In our joys and in our sorrows,
   days of toil and hours of ease,
   still He calls, in cares and
      pleasures,
   'Christian, love me more than
      these!'

560 Words and Music: © 1984 Fairhill Music / Administered by CopyCare Ltd, PO Box 77, Hailsham, East Sussex. BN27 3EF

5   Jesus calls us! By Your mercies,
    Saviour, make us hear Your call,
    give to You our heart's obedience,
    serve and love You best of all.

Cecil Frances Alexander, 1818–1895
altered Compilers

563

1   Make me a captive, Lord,
    and then I shall be free:
    force me to render up my sword,
    and I shall conqueror be.
    I sink in life's alarms
    when by myself I stand;
    imprison me within Your arms,
    and strong shall be my hand.

2   My heart is weak and poor
    until it master find;
    it has no spring of action sure —
    it varies with the wind.
    It cannot freely move,
    till You have forged its chain;
    enslave it with Your matchless
        love,
    and deathless it shall reign.

3   My power is faint and low
    till I have learned to serve;
    it lacks the needed fire to glow,
    it lacks the breeze to nerve;
    it cannot drive the world,
    until itself be driven;
    its flag can only be unfurled
    when You shall breathe from
        heaven.

4   My will is not my own
    until to You it's given;
    it must its earthly crown resign
    if it would reach to heaven;
    it only stands unbent,
    amid the clashing strife,
    when on Your bosom it has leant
    and found in You its life.

George Matheson, 1842–1906
altered Compilers

564

1   My hope rests firm on Jesus
        Christ,
    He is my only plea.
    Though all the world should
        point and scorn,
    His ransom leaves me free,
    His ransom leaves me free.

2   My hope sustains me as I strive
    and strain towards the goal.
    Though still I stumble into sin,
    His death paid for it all,
    His death paid for it all.

3   My hope provides me with a
        spur
    to help me run this race.
    I know my tears will turn to joy
    the day I see His face,
    the day I see His face.

4   My hope is to be with my Lord,
    to know as I am known.
    To serve Him gladly all my days
    in praise before His throne,
    in praise before His throne.

Richard Creighton, *b.* 1975

565

1   O what can little hands do
    to please the King of heaven?
    The little hands some work may
        try,
    to help all those in poverty:
    such grace to mine be given.

2   O what can little lips do
    to please the King of heaven?
    The little lips can praise and
        pray,
    and gentle words of kindness
        say:
    such grace to mine be given.

3   O what can little eyes do
    to please the King of heaven?
    The little eyes can upward look,
    can learn to read God's holy
        book:
    such grace to mine be given.

4   O what can little hearts do
    to please the King of heaven?
    Young hearts, if God His Spirit
        send,
    can love their Maker, Saviour,
        Friend:
    such grace to mine be given.

Anonymous

566

1   Over all the earth, You reign on
        high,
    every mountain stream, every
        sunset sky.
    But my one request, Lord, my
        only aim
    is that You'd reign in me again.

564   Words and Music: © 2001 Thankyou Music. Administered (UK and Europe) by Kingsway Music <tym@kingsway.co.uk>. Remaining territories administered by worshiptogether.com songs. Used by permission.
566   Words and Music: © 1998 Vineyard Songs/Administered by CopyCare Ltd, PO Box 77, Hailsham, East Sussex. BN27 3EF

DISCIPLESHIP

Lord, reign in me, reign in Your
power:
over all my dreams, in my darkest
hour.
You are the Lord of all I am,
so won't You reign in me again.

2 Over every thought, over every
word,
may my life reflect the beauty of
my Lord:
'cause You mean more to me
than any earthly thing.
So won't You reign in me again.

Brenton Brown

567

1 Rise up, O Church of God!
Have done with lesser things;
give heart and soul and mind
and strength
to serve the King of kings.

2 Rise up, O Church of God!
His kingdom tarries long;
bring in the day of righteousness
and end the night of wrong.

3 Rise up, O Church of God!
Must He for ever wait?
His strength shall make your
spirit strong
in serving to be great.

4 Lift high the cross of Christ!
Tread where His feet have trod;
as servants of the Son of Man
rise up, O Church of God.

William Pierson Merrill, 1867–1954
adapted Compilers

568

1 Seek ye first the Kingdom of God,
and His righteousness,
and all these things shall be
added unto you.
Allelu, alleluia.
Alleluia, alleluia, alleluia, alleluia!

2 Man shall not live by bread
alone,
but by every word,
that proceeds from the mouth of
God.
Allelu, alleluia.

3 Ask and it shall be given unto
you,
seek and you shall find,
knock and the door shall be
opened up to you.
Allelu, alleluia.

Karen Lafferty, b. 1948

569

1 Soldiers of Christ, arise
and put your armour on;
strong in the strength which God
supplies
through His eternal Son.
Strong in the Lord of hosts,
and in His mighty power;
who in the strength of Jesus trusts
is more than conqueror.

2 Stand then in His great might,
with all His strength endued;
and take, to arm you for the fight,
the weapons of our God.
To keep your armour bright
attend with constant care,
still walking in your captain's
sight
and keeping watch with prayer.

3 From strength to strength go on:
wrestle and fight and pray;
tread all the powers of darkness
down
and win the well-fought day:
till, having all things done
and all your conflicts past,
you overcome through Christ
alone
and stand complete at last.

Charles Wesley, 1707–1788

570

1 Stand up, stand up for Jesus,
as soldiers of the cross;
lift high His royal banner,
it must not suffer loss;
from victory on to victory
His army He shall lead
till every foe is vanquished
and Christ is Lord indeed.

2 Stand up, stand up for Jesus,
the trumpet call obey
to join the mighty conflict
in this His glorious day!
You that are His, now serve Him
against unnumbered foes;
let courage rise with danger
and strength with strength
oppose.

3   Stand up, stand up for Jesus,
    stand in His strength alone:
    for human power will fail you,
    you dare not trust your own.
    Put on the gospel armour,
    keep watch with constant prayer;
    where duty calls, or danger,
    be never failing there.

4   Stand up, stand up for Jesus,
    the strife will not be long:
    this day the noise of battle,
    the next the victor's song.
    To everyone who conquers
    a crown of life shall be;
    we with the King of glory
    shall reign eternally.

George Duffield, 1818–1888
adapted Compilers of *Praise!* 2000

571

1   'Take up your cross,' the Saviour
        said,
    'if you would My disciple be;
    deny yourself, forsake the world,
    and humbly follow after me.'

2   Take up your cross — let not its
        weight
    fill your weak soul with vain
        alarm;
    His strength shall bear your spirit
        up,
    and brace your heart, and nerve
        your arm.

3   Take up your cross, despise the
        shame,
    nor let your foolish pride rebel;
    the Lord for you endured the
        cross
    to save your soul from death and
        hell.

4   Take up your cross, then, in His
        strength,
    and calmly every danger brave;
    it guides you to a better home,
    and leads to conquest of the
        grave.

5   Take up your cross and follow
        Christ,
    nor think till death to lay it
        down;
    for only those who bear the cross
    may hope to wear the glorious
        crown.

Charles William Everest, 1814–1877
adapted Compilers of *Praise!* 2000

572

1   The journey of life may be easy,
        may be hard,
    there'll be dangers on the way;
    with Christ at my side I'll do
        battle as I ride
    'gainst the foe that would lead
        me astray.

    Will you ride, ride, ride with the
        King of kings,
    will you follow my leader true;
    will you shout hosanna to the
        lowly Son of God,
    who died for me and you?

2   My burden is light and a song is
        in my heart,
    as I travel on life's way;
    for Christ is my Lord and He's
        given me His word,
    that by my side He'll stay.

3   When doubts arise and when
        tears are in my eyes,
    when all seems lost to me,
    with Christ as my guide I can
        smile whate'er betide,
    for He my strength will be.

4   I'll follow my leader wherever
        He may go,
    for Jesus is my friend;
    He'll lead me on to the place
        where He has gone,
    when I come to my journey's
        end.

Valerie Collison, *b.* 1933

573

1   Though I feel afraid
    of territory unknown,
    I know that I can say
    that I do not stand alone.
    For Jesus, You have promised
    Your presence in my heart;
    I cannot see the ending,
    but it's here that I must start.
    And all I know
    is You have called me,
    and that I will follow
    is all I can say.
    I will go where You will send me,
    and Your fire lights my way.

2   What lies across the waves
    may cause my heart to fear;
    will I survive the day,
    must I leave what's known and
        dear?

572   Words and Music: © High-Fye Music Ltd, Music Sales

573   Words and Music: © 1996 Thankyou Music. Administered (UK and Europe) by Kingsway Music <tym@kingsway.co.uk>. Remaining territories administered by worshiptogether.com songs. Used by permission.

A ship that's in the harbour
is still and safe from harm,
but it was not built to be there,
it was made for wind and storm.
*And all I know
is You have called me,
and that I will follow
is all I can say.
I will go where You will send me,
and Your fire lights my way.
Your fire lights my way.
Your fire lights my way.*

Ian White, *b.* 1956

574

1   Will you come and follow Me
    if I but call your name?
    Will you go where you don't
        know
    and never be the same?
    Will you let My love be shown,
    will you let My name be known,
    will you let My life be grown,
    in you and you in Me?

2   Will you leave yourself behind
    if I but call your name?
    Will you care for cruel and kind
    and never be the same?
    Will you risk the hostile stare
    should your life attract or scare?
    Will you let Me answer prayer
    in you and you in Me?

3   Will you let the blinded see
    if I but call your name?
    Will you set the prisoners free
    and never be the same?
    Will you kiss the leper clean,
    and do such as this unseen,
    and admit to what I mean
    in you and you in Me?

4   Will you love the 'you' you hide
    if I but call your name?
    Will you quell the fear inside
    and never be the same?
    Will you use the faith you've
        found
    to reshape the world around,
    through My sight and touch and
        sound
    in you and you in Me?

5   Lord, Your summons echoes true
    when You but call my name.
    Let me turn and follow You
    and never be the same.

In Your company I'll go
where Your love and footsteps
    show.
Thus I'll move and live and grow
in You and You in me.

John Lamberton Bell, *b.* 1949
and Graham Alexander Maule, *b.* 1958

Also suitable:

March on, my soul, with strength   134
Wake up, O sleeper, and rise from the dead   303
When our confidence is shaken   258

THE GROWTH
OF THE CHURCH
IN SOCIETY
MARRIAGE

575

1   As man and woman we were
        made,
    that love be found and life
        begun;
    the likeness of the living God,
    unique, yet called to live as one.
    Though joy or sadness, calm or
        strife,
    come praise the love that gives
        us life.

2   Now Jesus lived and gave His
        love
    to make our life and loving new;
    so celebrate with Him today,
    and drink the joy He offers you
    that makes the simple moment
        shine
    and changes water into wine.

3   And Jesus died to live again;
    so praise the love that, come
        what may,
    can bring the dawn and clear the
        skies,
    and waits to wipe all tears away;
    and let us hope for what shall be,
    believing where we cannot see.

4   Then spread the table, clear the
        hall,
    and celebrate till day is done;
    let peace go deep between us all,
    and joy be shared by everyone:
    laugh and make merry with your
        friends,
    and praise the love that never
        ends!

Brian Arthur Wren, *b.* 1936

576

1 Jesus, the Lord of love and life,
draw near to bless this man and
wife;
as they are now in love made
one,
let Your good will for them be
done.

2 Give them each day Your peace
and joy,
let no dark clouds these gifts
destroy;
in growing trust may love
endure,
to keep their marriage-bond
secure.

3 As they have vowed to have and
hold,
each by the other be consoled;
in wealth or want, in health or
pain,
till death shall part, let love
remain.

4 Deepen, O Lord, their love for
You,
and in that love, their own
renew;
each in the other find delight,
as lives and interests now unite.

5 Be to them both a guide and
friend,
through all the years their home
defend;
Jesus, the Lord of love and life,
stay near and bless this man and
wife.

James Edward Seddon, 1915–1983

577

1 Lord of creation, giver of
gladness,
in celebration we come today;
loved ones around us, hope
shining strongly,
Your love completing our deepest
joy.

2 Lord of our past days, life's rich
surprises,
clearing our pathways You wisely
led:
through painful learning we
have moved forward,
working and earning our daily
bread.

3 Lord of tomorrow: what will it
bring us?
Blessing or sorrow, all
unexplored:
each situation calls us to trust
You,
our true salvation is Christ the
Lord.

4 Lord, in Your keeping we are safe
always;
waking or sleeping You watch us
still:
save us from losing love's
precious jewel,
help us in choosing Your gracious
will.

David Mowbray, b. 1938

578

1 O Father, all creating,
whose wisdom, love, and power
first bound to lives together
in Eden's primal hour:
the lives of these Your children
with Your best gifts endue:
a home by You made happy,
a love by You kept true.

2 O Saviour, guest most generous
in Galilee of old,
these now who call upon You
within Your love enfold;
their store of earthly gladness
transform to wine of heaven,
and teach them in the tasting
to know by You it's given.

3 O Spirit of the Father,
breathe on them from above,
so mighty in Your pureness,
so tender in Your love,
that, guarded by Your presence,
kept free from strife and sin,
their lives may own Your
guidance,
around them and within.

4 Except You build it, Father,
the house is built in vain;
except You, Saviour, bless it,
the joy will turn to pain:
no power can break the union
of hearts in You made one;
and love Your Spirit hallows
is endless love begun.

John Ellerton, 1826–189
adapted Compiler

576 Words: © Representatives of the late James Edward Seddon/Jubilate Hymns, 4 Thorne Park Road, Chelston, Torquay TQ2 6RX <enquiries@jubilate.co.uk> Used by permission.

577 Words: © David Mowbray/Jubilate Hymns, 4 Thorne Park Road, Chelston, Torquay TQ2 6RX <enquiries@jubilate.co.uk> Used by permission.

579

1 O God, whose loving hand has
     led
   Your children to this joyful day,
   we pray that You will bless them
     now
   as, one in You, they face life's
     way.

2 Grant them the will to follow
     Christ
   who graced the feast in Galilee,
   and through His perfect life of
     love
   fulfilment of their love to see.

3 Give them the power to make a
     home
   where peace and honour shall
     abide,
   where Christ shall be the
     gracious Head,
   the trusted Friend, the constant
     Guide.

4 To Father, Son and Holy Ghost
   the God whom heaven and earth
     adore,
   be glory as it was of old,
   is now and shall be evermore.
     Amen.

John Boyd Moore, 1914–1993

580

1 O Lord our God, we praise Your
     name
   on this most happy day,
   as these before us in Your love
   unite upon life's way.

2 For all that shaped and formed
     their lives,
   led them Your love to know;
   for how Your hand has guided
     them,
   and caused their love to grow.

3 For wit and wisdom, faith and
     friends,
   for tenderness and love,
   dark clouds of testing, and for
     days
   when light shone from above.

4 Grant them, we pray, a home
     that's filled
   with love and joy and peace;
   and may their gifts and talents in
   Your service, Lord, increase.

5 We celebrate their marriage,
     Lord,
   and all Your blessings given.
   Hold them and keep them in
     Your love
   and bring them safe to heaven.

A. W. Godfrey Brown, b. 1936

581

1 O perfect Love, all human
     thought transcending,
   lowly we kneel in prayer before
     Your throne,
   that theirs may be the love which
     knows no ending
   who in Your love for evermore
     are one.

2 O perfect Life, be now their full
     assurance
   of tender charity and steadfast
     faith,
   of patient hope, and quiet brave
     endurance,
   with childlike trust that fears not
     pain or death.

3 Grant them the joy which
     brightens earthly sorrow,
   grant them the peace which
     calms all earthly strife;
   and to life's day the glorious
     unknown morrow
   that dawns upon eternal love
     and life.

Dorothy Frances Gurney, 1858–1932
altered Compilers of *Hymns and Psalms*, 1983

582

1 Sing of Eve and sing of Adam,
   children in the dawn of earth,
   who with dust and death within
     them,
   yet by God were given birth.
   Side by side they named creation,
   both from Eden's peace were
     hurled,
   living in their pain and passion
   all the story of the world.

2 Sing of Abraham and Sarah
   who, in leaving home and land,
   gave themselves in faithful
     freedom,
   reaching out for Yahweh's hand.
   From their love God formed a
     people,
   chosen until time be done,
   and among their generations
   God would bring to birth a Son.

3 Sing of Mary, sing of Joseph,
   keepers of the wondrous Boy,
   called by God to high vocation,
   sharing sorrow, sharing joy,
   sharing love, and by that loving
   in their home in Nazareth,
   forming one whose grace and
       glory
   suffered, died and conquered
       death.

4 Sing of man and sing of woman,
   each the other's joy and crown,
   male and female both
       transfigured
   in the Lord of life come down.
   Called to equal co-relation,
   where their gifts, becoming one,
   bring to birth a new creation,
   and the will of God is done.

                    Herbert Thomas O'Driscoll, b. 1928

583

1 The grace of life is theirs
   who on this wedding-day
   delight to make their vows,
   and for each other pray.
   May they, O Lord, together prove
   the lasting joy of Christian love.

2 Where love is, God abides;
   and God shall surely bless
   a home where trust and care
   give birth to happiness.
   May they, O Lord, together prove
   the lasting joy of such a love.

3 How slow to take offence
   love is! How quick to heal!
   How ready in distress
   to know how others feel!
   May they, O Lord, together prove
   the lasting joy of such a love.

4 And when time lays its hand
   on all we hold most dear,
   and life, by life consumed,
   fulfils its purpose here:
   may we, O Lord, together prove
   the lasting joy of Christian love.

                        Frederick Pratt Green, 1903–2000

584

1 Unless the Lord has built the
       house
   it must be built again;
   except the Lord defends a town
   its watchmen wake in vain.

2 What value has a life of haste,
   of endless, anxious toil?
   God has for those who keep His
       law
   a garland none can spoil:

3 Among God's gifts, a happy
       home —
   a blessing rich indeed;
   a joyful, loving partnership,
   a strength to those in need.

4 That home, that house, as years
       go by
   must weather storm and strain:
   unless the Lord has built the
       house
   it must be built again.

                              David Mowbray, b. 193
                                    after Psalm 12

Also suitable:
Gracious Spirit, Holy Ghost   46
Lord of all hopefulness, Lord of all joy

THE GROWTH
OF THE CHURCH
HOME AND FAMILY

585

1 Father, in Your presence kneeling
   all our heart's desire revealing,
   to Your love, in faith appealing,
   for our children, Lord, we pray.

2 Grant us wisdom so to train them
   that no mortal evil stain them —
   young for Jesus we would gain
       them:
   for our children, Lord, we pray.

3 Keep them onward, upward
       pressing,
   courage, self-control possessing;
   bravely Christ their King
       confessing:
   for our children, Lord, we pray.

4 Strengthen them for high
       endeavour —
   to Your will unfaithful never,
   God and neighbour serving ever
   for our children, Lord, we pray.

583 Words: © 1970 Stainer & Bell Ltd, PO Box 110, Victoria House, 23 Gruneisen Road, London N3 1DZ
584 Words: © David Mowbray/Jubilate Hymns, 4 Thorne Park Road, Chelston, Torquay TQ2 6RX <enquiries@jubilate.co.uk> Used by permission.
585 Words: © F.E.V. Pilcher

5 Lord, on life's adventure guide them,
in Your secret presence hide them;
to Your love we now confide them:
for our children, Lord, we pray.

Charles Venn Pilcher, 1879–1961
altered

586

1 Happy the home that welcomes You, Lord Jesus,
truest of friends, most honoured guest of all;
where hearts and eyes are bright with joy to greet You,
Your slightest wishes eager to fulfil.

2 Happy the home where man and wife together
are of one mind, believing in Your love;
through love and pain, prosperity and hardship,
through good and evil days Your care they prove.

3 Happy the home, O loving friend of children,
where they are given to You with hands of prayer;
where at Your feet they early learn to listen
to Your own words, and thank You for Your care.

4 Happy the home where work is done to please You,
in tasks both great and small, that You may see
each family doing all as You would wish them
as members of Your household, glad and free.

5 Happy the home that knows Your healing comfort,
where, unforgotten, every joy You share;
until each one, their work on earth completed,
comes to Your Father's house to meet You there.

Karl Johann Philipp Spitta, 1801–1859
translated Honor Mary Thwaites, 1914–1993

587

1 Lord of our growing years,
with us from infancy,
laughter and quick-dried tears,
freshness and energy:
Your grace surrounds us all our days —
for all Your gifts we bring our praise.

2 Lord of our strongest years,
stretching our youthful powers,
lovers and pioneers
when all the world seems ours:

3 Lord of our middle years,
giver of steadfastness,
courage that perseveres
when there is small success:

4 Lord of our older years,
steep though the road may be,
rid us of foolish fears,
bring us serenity:

5 Lord of our closing years,
always your promise stands;
hold us, when death appears,
safely within your hands:

David Mowbray, *b.* 1938

Also suitable:

For the beauty of the earth	20
O God, Your life-creating love	374
Once in royal David's city	331
Unless the Lord has built the house	584

THE GROWTH
OF THE CHURCH
THE COMMUNITY

588

1 Brother, sister, let me serve you,
let me be as Christ to you.
Pray that I may have the grace to
let you be my servant, too.

2 We are pilgrims on a journey,
and companions on the road;
we are here to help each other
walk the mile and bear the load.

3 I will hold the Christ-light for you
in the night-time of your fear;
I will hold my hand out to you,
speak the peace you long to hear.

586 Words: © Michael R. Thwaites
587 Words: © David Mowbray / Jubilate Hymns, 4 Thorne Park Road, Chelston, Torquay TQ2 6RX <enquiries@jubilate.co.uk> Used by permission.
588 Words and Music: © Sovereign Lifestyle Music Ltd, P.O. Box 356, Leighton Buzzard LU7 3WP <sovereignmusic@aol.com>

4   I will weep when you are
      weeping;
when you laugh I'll laugh with
      you.
I will share your joy and sorrow
till we've seen this journey
      through.

5   When we sing to God in heaven
we shall find such harmony,
born of all we've known together
of Christ's love and agony.

6   Won't you let me be your servant,
let me be as Christ to you?
Pray that I may have the grace to
let you be my servant, too.

Richard A. M. Gillard, *b.* 1953

589

1   Father God, on us You shower
gifts of plenty from Your dower,
to Your people give the power
all Your gifts to use aright.

2   Give pure happiness in leisure,
temperance in every pleasure,
holy use of earthly treasure,
bodies clear and spirits bright.

3   Lift from this and every nation
all that brings us degradation;
quell the forces of temptation;
put Your enemies to flight.

4   Be with us, Your strength
      supplying,
that with energy undying,
every foe on earth defying,
we may rally to the fight.

5   Lord, You are our Captain ever,
lead us on to great endeavour;
may Your Church the world
      deliver:
give us wisdom, courage, might.

6   Father, You have sought and
      found us,
Son of God, Your love has bound
      us,
Holy Ghost, within us, round
      us —
hear us Godhead infinite.

Percy Dearmer, 1867–1936
adapted Compilers

590

1   Fold to your heart your sister and
      your brother:
where pity dwells, the peace of
      God is there;
to worship rightly is to love each
      other,
each smile a hymn, each kindly
      deed a prayer.
For he whom Jesus loved has
      truly spoken:
the holier worship which He
      deigns to bless
restores the lost, and binds the
      spirit broken,
and feeds the widow and the
      fatherless.

2   Follow with reverent steps the
      great example
of Him whose holy work was
      doing good:
so shall the wide earth seem our
      Father's temple,
each loving life a psalm of
      gratitude.
Then shall all shackles fall: the
      stormy clangour
of wild war music o'er the earth
      shall cease;
love shall tread out the baleful
      fire of anger,
and in its ashes plant the tree of
      peace.

   *   *When sung to Intercessor, the tune is sung
twice for each verse.*

John Greenleaf Whittier, 1807–1892

591

1   Forth in Your name, O Lord, I go
my daily labour to pursue;
You, Lord, alone I choose to know
in all I think or speak or do.

2   The task Your wisdom has
      assigned
here let me cheerfully fulfil;
in all my work Your presence
      find
and prove Your good and perfect
      will.

3   You I would set at my right hand
whose eyes my inmost secrets
      view;
and labour on at Your command
and offer all my work to You.

589   Words: From *English Hymnal*, 1906, by permission of Oxford University Press, Great Clarendon Street, Oxford OX2 6DP
591   Words: © in this version Jubilate Hymns, 4 Thorne Park Road, Chelston, Torquay TQ2 6RX <enquiries@jubilate.co.uk> Used by permission.

Help me to bear Your easy yoke
and every moment watch and
pray;
and still to things eternal look
and hasten to that glorious day.

Gladly for You may I employ
all that Your generous grace has
given;
and run my earthly course with
joy,
and closely walk with You to
heaven.

*Charles Wesley, 1707–1788
adapted Jubilate Hymns*

92

God of the pastures, hear our
prayer,
Lord of the growing seed,
bless now the fields, for to Your
care
we look in all our need.

God of the rivers in their course,
Lord of the swelling sea,
where we must strive with
nature's force
do there our guardian be.

God of the mine and all its toil,
Lord of its hard-won spoil,
in wresting from the dark its
spoil
Your help and strength are sure.

God of the city's throbbing heart,
Lord of its industry,
bid greed and base deceit depart,
give true prosperity.

God of authority and right,
Lord of all earthly power,
to those who rule us grant Your
light,
Your wisdom be their dower.

God of the nations, mighty King,
Lord of each humble soul,
our prayers for aid to You we
bring,
come down and make us whole.

*Thomas Charles Hunter Clare, 1910–1984
adapted Compilers*

93

God, You have given us power to
sound
depths hitherto unknown;

to probe earth's hidden
mysteries,
and make their might our own;

2 Great are Your gifts: yet greater
far
this gift, O God, bestow,
that as to knowledge we attain
we may in wisdom grow.

3 Let wisdom's godly fear dispel
all fears that hate impart;
give understanding to the mind
and with new mind new heart.

4 So for Your glory and our good
may we Your gifts employ,
lest, maddened by the lust of
power,
we shall ourselves destroy.

*George Wallace Briggs, 1875–1959
adapted Compilers*

594

1 Help us to help each other, Lord,
each other's load to bear;
that all may live in true accord,
our joys and pains to share.

2 Help us to build each other up,
Your strength within us prove;
increase our faith, confirm our
hope,
and fill us with Your love.

3 Together make us free indeed —
Your life within us show;
and into You, our living head,
let us in all things grow.

4 Drawn by the magnet of Your
love
we find our hearts made new:
nearer each other let us move,
and nearer still to You.

*Charles Wesley, 1707–1788
adapted Jubilate Hymns*

595

1 I will speak out for those who
have no voices;
I will stand up for the rights of all
the oppressed;
I will speak truth and justice;
I'll defend the poor and the
needy;
I will lift up the weak in Jesus'
name.

Words: © 1976 Stainer & Bell Ltd, PO Box 110, Victoria House, 23 Gruneisen Road, London N3 1DZ

Words: By permission of Oxford University Press, Great Clarendon Street, Oxford OX2 6DP

Words: © in this version Jubilate Hymns, 4 Thorne Park Road, Chelston, Torquay TQ2 6RX <enquiries@jubilate.co.uk> Used by permission.

Words and Music: © Word's Spirit of Praise Music / Administered by CopyCare Ltd, PO Box 77, Hailsham, East Sussex. BN27 3EF

2　I will speak out for those who
　　have no choices;
　I will cry out for those who live
　　without love;
　I will show God's compassion
　to the crushed and broken in
　　spirit;
　I will lift up the weak in Jesus'
　　name.

Dave Bankhead, Ray Goudie,
Sue Rinaldi and Steve Bassett

596

1　Make me a channel of Your
　　peace.
　Where there is hatred let me
　　bring Your love.
　Where there is injury, Your
　　pardon, Lord,
　and where there's doubt, true
　　faith in You.
　　O Master, grant that I may never
　　　seek
　　so much to be consoled as to
　　　console,
　　to be understood as to understand,
　　to be loved, as to love with all my
　　　soul.

2　Make me a channel of Your
　　peace.
　Where there's despair in life let
　　me bring hope.
　Where there is darkness, only
　　light,
　and where there's sadness, ever
　　joy.
　　O Master, grant …

3　Make me a channel of Your
　　peace.
　It is in pardoning that we are
　　pardoned,
　in giving of ourselves that we
　　receive,
　and in dying that we're born to
　　eternal life.

Sebastian Temple, 1928–1997
from the Prayer of St Francis

597

1　O Jesus, strong and pure and
　　true,
　before Your feet we bow;
　the grace of earlier years renew,
　and lead us onward now.

2　The joyous life that year by year
　within these walls is stored,

the golden hope, the gladsome
　cheer,
we bring to You, O Lord.

3　Our faith endow with keener
　　powers,
　with warmer glow our love,
　and draw these faltering hearts
　　ours
　from earth to heaven above.

4　In paths our bravest ones have
　　trod
　O make us strong to go,
　that we may give our lives to
　　God
　in serving all below.

5　Scorn we the selfish aim or
　　choice,
　and love's high precept keep:
　'Rejoice with those that do rejoi■
　and weep with them that weep.

6　So hence shall flow fresh streng■
　　and grace,
　as from a full-fed spring,
　to make the world a better place
　and life a worthier thing.

William Walsham How, 1823–18■

598

1　O Master Christ, draw near to
　　take
　Your undisputed place;
　my gifts and faculties remake,
　form and re-fashion for Your sak■
　an instrument of peace.

2　O Master Christ, I choose to sow
　in place of hatred, love;
　where wounds and injuries are
　　now
　may healing and forgiveness
　　grow
　as gifts from God above.

3　O Master Christ, I choose to plan■
　hope where there is despair;
　a warmth of joy, a shaft of light
　where darkness has diminished
　　sight,
　where sorrow leaves its scar.

4　O Master Christ, make this my
　　goal —
　less to receive than give;
　to sympathise — and to make
　　whole,
　to understand and to console
　and so, through death, to live.

David Mowbray, b. 19■

599

1 Oh the life of the world is a joy
 and a treasure,
 unfolding in beauty the green-
 growing tree,
 the changing of seasons in
 mountain and valley,
 the stars and the bright restless
 sea.

2 Oh the life of the world is a
 fountain of goodness
 overflowing in labour and
 passion and pain,
 in the sound of the city and the
 silence of wisdom,
 in the birth of a child once again.

3 Oh the life of the world is the
 source of our healing.
 It rises in laughter and wells up
 in song;
 it springs from the care of the
 poor and the broken
 and refreshes where justice is
 strong.

4 So give thanks for the life and
 give love to the Maker,
 and rejoice in the gift of the
 bright risen Son,
 and walk in the peace and the
 power of the Spirit
 till the days of our living are
 done.

Kathy Galloway, *b. 1952*

600

1 One shall tell another,
 and he shall tell his friends;
 husbands, wives and children
 shall come following on.
 From house to house in families
 shall more be gathered in,
 and lights will shine in every
 street,
 so warm and welcoming.
 *Come on in and taste the new
 wine,
 the wine of the kingdom,
 the wine of the kingdom of God.
 Here is healing and forgiveness,
 the wine of the kingdom,
 the wine of the kingdom of God.*

2 Compassion of the Father
 is ready now to flow,
 through acts of love and mercy
 we must let it show.

He turns now from His anger
to show a smiling face
and longs that all should stand
 beneath
the fountain of His grace.

3 He longs to do much more than
 our faith has yet allowed,
 to thrill us and surprise us
 with His sovereign power.
 Where darkness has been darkest
 the brightest light will shine,
 His invitation comes to us,
 it's yours and it is mine.

Graham Andrew Kendrick, *b. 1950*

601

1 We hear Your cry, Lord, in the
 hungry —
 we hear Your cry, Lord, strong
 today.
 Don't let us be, Lord, indifferent
 to You —
 we hear Your cry, Lord; help us
 obey.

2 We see Your pain, Lord, in the
 wounded —
 we see Your pain, Lord, close
 today.
 Teach us to notice and have
 compassion —
 we see Your face, Lord, amid the
 pain.

3 When we have lost You, teach us
 to look, Lord,
 to the forgotten and find You
 there.
 You made Your home, Lord, with
 the weakest:
 teach us to follow and find You
 there.

4 There is a task, Lord, that You
 have set us —
 to be Your body throughout this
 world.
 To be Your hands, Lord, to be
 Your feet, Lord,
 to have Your heart, Lord; help us
 obey.

5 We hear Your cry, Lord, in the
 hungry —
 teach us to shed Your bitter tears
 at each injustice, each one
 forgotten;
 teach us to follow and find You
 there.

Garth Hewitt

602

1 When I needed a neighbour,
    were you there, were you
    there?
    When I needed a neighbour,
    were you there?
    And the creed and the colour and
    the name won't matter,
    were you there?

2 I was hungry and thirsty, were
    you there, were you there?
    I was hungry and thirsty, were
    you there?

3 I was cold, I was naked, were
    you there, were you there?
    I was cold, I was naked, were
    you there?

4 When I needed a shelter, were
    you there, were you there?
    When I needed a shelter, were
    you there?

5 When I needed a healer, were
    you there, were you there?
    When I needed a healer, were
    you there?

6 Wherever you travel, I'll be
    there, I'll be there,
    wherever you travel, I'll be there.
    And the creed and the colour and
    the name won't matter,
    I'll be there!

Sydney Carter, 1915–2004

Also suitable:
From heaven You came, helpless babe   399
Heavenly Father, may Your blessing   269
Jesus bids us shine   561
Jesus Christ is waiting   347
Jesus went to worship   178

THE GROWTH
OF THE CHURCH
IN THE NATION

603

1 Eternal Father, strong to save,
    whose arm restrains the restless
    wave,
    who told the mighty ocean deep
    its own appointed bounds to
    keep:
    we cry, O God of majesty,
    for those in peril on the sea.

2 O Christ, whose voice the waters
    heard
    and hushed their raging at Your
    word,
    who walked across the surging
    deep,
    and in the storm lay calm in
    sleep:
    we cry, O Lord of Galilee,
    for those in peril on the sea.

3 Creator Spirit, by whose breath
    were fashioned sea and sky and
    earth;
    who made the stormy chaos
    cease,
    and gave us life and light and
    peace:
    we cry, O Spirit strong and free,
    for those in peril on the sea.

4 O Trinity of love and power,
    preserve their lives in danger's
    hour;
    from rock and tempest, flood and
    flame,
    protect them by Your holy name,
    and to Your glory let there be
    glad hymns of praise from land
    and sea.

William Whiting, 1825–1878
adapted Jubilate Hymns

604

1 God! As with silent hearts we
    bring to mind
    how hate and war diminish
    humankind,
    we pause — and seek in worship
    to increase
    our knowledge of the things that
    make for peace.

2 Hallow our will as humbly we
    recall
    the lives of those who gave and
    give their all.
    We thank You, Lord, for women,
    children, men
    who seek to serve in love, today
    as then.

3 Give us deep faith to comfort
    those who mourn,
    high hope to share with all the
    newly born,
    strong love in our pursuit of
    human worth:
    'Lest we forget' the future of this
    earth.

4 So, Prince of Peace, disarm our
trust in power,
teach us to coax the plant of
peace to flower.
May we, im-passioned by Your
living word,
remember forward to a world
restored.

Frederik Herman Kaan, b. 1929

605

1 God of grace and God of glory,
come among us in Your power;
crown Your ancient Church's
story,
bring her bud to glorious flower.
Grant us wisdom, grant us
courage
for the facing of this hour.

2 See the hosts of evil round us
scorn Your Christ, attack His
ways!
Fears and doubts too long have
bound us —
free our hearts to work and
praise.
Grant us wisdom, grant us
courage
for the living of these days.

3 Save us from weak resignation
to the evils we deplore;
let the search for Your salvation
be our glory evermore.
Grant us wisdom, grant us
courage
serving You whom we adore.

4 Heal Your children's warring
madness,
bend our pride to Your control;
shame our wanton, selfish
gladness,
rich in things and poor in soul.
Grant us wisdom, grant us
courage
lest we miss Your kingdom's goal.

Harry Emerson Fosdick, 1878–1969
altered

606

1 God save our gracious Queen,
long live our noble Queen,
God save the Queen.
Send her victorious,
happy and glorious,
long to reign over us:
God save the Queen.

2 Thy choicest gifts in store
on her be pleased to pour,
long may she reign.
May she defend our laws,
and ever give us cause
to sing with heart and voice,
God save the Queen.

Anonymous, c. 1745

607

1 God save our gracious Queen,
God bless and guard our Queen,
long live the Queen!
Guard us in liberty,
bless us with unity,
save us from tyranny:
God save the Queen!

2 Lord, be our nation's light,
guide us in truth and right:
in You we stand;
give us Your faithfulness,
keep us from selfishness,
raise us to godliness:
God save our land!

3 Spirit of love and life,
healing our nation's strife,
on You we call:
teach us Your better way,
grant us Your peace today;
God bless our Queen, we pray,
God save us all!

Anonymous, c. 1745
adapted Jubilate Hymns

608

1 Judge eternal, throned in
splendour,
Lord of lords and King of kings,
with Your living fire of judge
ment
purge this land of bitter things;
over all its wide dominion
spread the healing of Your wings.

2 Weary people still are longing
for the hour that brings release;
and the city's crowded clamour
cries aloud for sin to cease;
and the countryside and
woodlands
plead in silence for their peace.

3 Crown, O Lord, Your own
endeavour;
cleave our darkness with Your
sword;

feed the faithless and the hungry
with the richness of Your word;
cleanse the body of this nation
through the glory of the Lord.

Henry Scott Holland, 1847–1918
adapted Jubilate Hymns
vv. 1, 3 *altered* Compilers of *Praise!* 2000

609

1   Lord, while for humankind we
        pray
    of every clime and coast,
    O hear us for our native land,
    the land we love the most.

2   Our fathers' resting places here,
    and here our kindred dwell,
    our children too: how should we
        love
    another land so well?

3   O guard our shores from every
        foe,
    with peace our borders bless;
    with prosperous times our cities
        crown,
    our fields with plenteousness.

4   O may we, Lord, be one in You
    in knowledge, truth and love;
    and let our songs of freedom rise
    from earth to heaven above.

5   Lord of the nations, thus to You
    our country we commend;
    be now her refuge and her trust,
    her everlasting friend.

John Reynell Wreford, 1800–1881
adapted Compilers

610

1   Lord, You in Your perfect wisdom
    times and seasons all arrange,
    working out Your changeless
        purpose
    in a world of ceaseless change;
    You did form our ancient nation,
    guiding it through all the days,
    to unfold in it Your purpose
    to Your glory and Your praise.

2   To our shores remote, benighted,
    barrier of the western waves,
    tidings in Your love You sent us,
    tidings of the cross that saves.
    Saints and heroes strove and
        suffered
    here Your gospel to proclaim;
    we, the heirs of their endeavour,
    tell the honour of their name.

3   Still Your ancient purpose
        standing
    every change and chance above;
    still Your ancient Church
        remaining,
    witness to Your changeless love.
    Grant us vision, Lord, and
        courage
    to fulfil Your work begun;
    in the Church and in the nation,
    King of kings, Your will be done.

Timothy Rees, 1874–1939

611

1   The kingdom of God is justice
        and joy,
    for Jesus restores what sin would
        destroy;
    God's power and glory in Jesus
        we know,
    and here and hereafter the
        kingdom shall grow.

2   The kingdom of God is mercy
        and grace,
    the prisoners are freed, the
        sinners find place,
    the outcast are welcomed God's
        banquet to share,
    and hope is awakened in place of
        despair.

3   The kingdom of God is challenge
        and choice,
    believe the good news, repent
        and rejoice!
    His love for us sinners brought
        Christ to His cross,
    our crisis of judgement for gain
        or for loss.

4   God's kingdom is come, the gift
        and the goal,
    in Jesus begun, in heaven made
        whole;
    the heirs of the kingdom shall
        answer His call,
    and all things cry 'Glory!' to God
        all-in-all.

Bryn Austin Rees, 1911–1983

612

1   We entrust to the Lord all His
        children
    who, responding to duty's stern
        call
    in the wars that have ravaged
        our planet

610   Words: © Community of the Resurrection, Stocksbank Road, Mirfield, West Yorkshire. WF14 0BW Used by permission.
611   Words: © Alexander Scott
612   Words: © W. H. Moseley. Used by permission.

paid the price that is highest of
   all.
Flesh had failed them, but God
   was their Saviour;
bringing rescue from battle's
   alarms;
beyond death He is always their
   refuge,
underneath, everlasting, His
   arms.

2   We commend to Him all who
     have mourned them —
loving parents and children and
   wives,
for whom pride in their selfless
   commitment
has been countered by grief for
   lost lives.
When so many returned, theirs
   were absent,
leaving long years of anguish to
   face;
may the Lord heal the wounds of
   bereavement
with the infinite power of His
   grace.

3   We commit to the Lord now our
     own lives,
as we vow in our turn to reply
to the call of the weak and the
   friendless,
though the cost to ourselves may
   be high.
When the choosing is hard, may
   God grant us
the direction that strengthens and
   calms.
For we trust in the Lord as our
   refuge,
underneath, everlasting, His
   arms.

W. Howard Moseley, *b.* 1941
Written for opening of
Falkland Islands Memorial Chapel,
Pangbourne College, March 2000.

613

1   Who can sound the depths of
     sorrow
in the father-heart of God,
for the children we've rejected,
for the lives so deeply scarred?
And each light that we've
   extinguished
has brought darkness to our land:
   Upon our nation, upon our
     nation
   have mercy, Lord!

2   We have scorned the truth You
     gave us,
we have bowed to other lords,
we have sacrificed the children
on the altars of our gods.
O let truth again shine on us,
let Your holy fear descend:
   Upon our nation, upon our
     nation
   have mercy, Lord!

3   Who can stand before Your
     anger;
who can face Your piercing eyes?
For You love the weak and
   helpless,
and You hear the victims' cries.
Yes, You are a God of justice,
and Your judgement surely
   comes:
   Upon our nation, upon our
     nation
   have mercy, Lord!

4   Who will stand against the
     violence?
Who will comfort those who
   mourn?
In an age of cruel rejection,
who will build for love a home?
Come and shake us into action,
come and melt our hearts of
   stone:
   Upon Your people, upon Your
     people
   have mercy, Lord!

5   Who can sound the depths of
     mercy
in the father-heart of God?
For there is a Man of Sorrows
who for sinners shed His blood.
He can heal the wounds of
   nations,
He can wash the guilty clean:
   Because of Jesus, because of
     Jesus
   have mercy, Lord!

Graham Andrew Kendrick, *b.* 1950

Also suitable:

God is our strength and refuge	85
Here I am, wholly available	539
O God, our help in ages past	136
When Zion's fortunes God restored	130

THE GROWTH OF THE CHURCH AMONG THE NATIONS

614

1 Almighty Father-God, you give
  the gift of life to all who live,
  look down on all earth's sin and
      strife
  and lift us to a nobler life.

2 Lift up our hearts, O King of
      kings,
  to brighter hopes and kindlier
      things,
  to visions of a larger good,
  and holier dreams of
      brotherhood.

3 The world is weary of its pain,
  of selfish greed and fruitless gain,
  of tarnished honour, falsely
      strong,
  and all its ancient deeds of
      wrong.

4 Hear now the prayer Your
      servants pray,
  uprising from all lands today,
  and, over vanquished powers of
      sin,
  O bring Your great salvation in!

John Howard Bertram Masterman, 1867–1933
adapted Compilers

615

1 Christ is the world's true light,
  its captain of salvation,
  our daystar clear and bright,
  desire of every nation:
  new life, new hope awakes
  where we accept His way;
  freedom her bondage breaks
  and night is turned to day.

2 In Christ all races meet,
  their ancient feuds forgetting,
  the whole round world complete
  from sunrise to its setting:
  when Christ is known as Lord
  all shall forsake their fear,
  to ploughshare beat the sword,
  to pruning-hook the spear.

3 One Lord, in one great name
  unite all who have known You,
  cast out our pride and shame
  that hinder to enthrone You:

the world has waited long,
  has laboured long in pain;
  to heal its ancient wrong
  come, Prince of Peace, and reign!

George Wallace Briggs, 1875–195
altered Compilers o
Hymns for Today's Church, 198

616

1 Father eternal, Ruler of creation,
  Spirit of life, which moved ere
      form was made,
  through the thick darkness
      covering every nation,
  light to our blindness, come now
      to our aid!
  Your kingdom come, O Lord, Your
      will be done.

2 Races and peoples, still we stand
      divided,
  and, sharing not our griefs, no joy
      can share;
  by wars and tumults Love is
      mocked, derided,
  His conquering cross no kingdom
      wills to bear:

3 Envious of heart, blind-eyed, with
      tongues confounded,
  nation by nation still goes
      unforgiven;
  in wrath and fear, by jealousies
      surrounded,
  building proud towers which
      shall not reach to heaven:

4 Lust of possession working
      desolations;
  there is no meekness in the sons
      of earth.
  Led by no star, the rulers of the
      nations
  still fail to bring us to the blissful
      birth:

5 How shall we love You, holy,
      hidden Being,
  if we love not the world which
      You have made?
  Let us reach out in love, for better
      seeing
  Your Word made flesh and in a
      manger laid:

Laurence Housman, 1865–195
adapted Compiler

615 Words: From *Songs of Praise Enlarged*, 1931, by permission of Oxford University Press, Great Clarendon Street, Oxford OX2 6DP
616 Words: From *English Hymnal*, 1906, by permission of Oxford University Press, Great Clarendon Street, Oxford OX2 6DP

AMONG THE NATIONS

617

1 For the healing of the nations,
Lord, we pray with one accord;
for a just and equal sharing
of the things that earth affords.
To a life of love in action
help us rise and pledge our
word.

2 Lead us forward into freedom,
from despair Your world release;
that, redeemed from war and
hatred,
all may come and go in peace.
Show us how through care and
goodness
fear will die and hope increase.

3 All that kills abundant living,
let it from the earth be banned;
pride of status, race or schooling,
dogmas that obscure Your plan.
In our common quest for justice
may we hallow life's brief span.

4 You, Creator-God, have written
Your great Name on humankind;
for our growing in Your likeness
bring the life of Christ to mind;
that by our response and service
earth its destiny may find.

Frederik Herman Kaan, b. 1929

618

1 God, give us peace that lasts
not through the fear of might,
but through the force of love
and love of life and right.
Where costly wars and weapons
lure,
show us our Lord among the
poor.

2 God, give us love that lasts,
which makes of strangers, guests;
which startles hurt with hope
and for the weak protests:
what hate or guiltiness emboss,
confront with Jesus and the cross.

3 God, give us hope that lasts
through passion, and through
pain,
through danger, doubt and death
till life is raised again.
When dread and pessimism
loom,
direct us to the empty tomb.

4 And all these things we ask
in knowledge of Your grace
which gave the earth its birth
and bore a human face;
and with our prayers we give our
word
to serve and follow Christ our
Lord.

John Lamberton Bell, b. 1949
and Graham Alexander Maule, b. 1958

619

1 God is King — be warned, you
mighty;
God is Judge through all the
land:
order your affairs with justice,
rule with firm but gentle hand.
Help the weak, support the
needy,
take to heart the fatherless;
prove the rights of those who
suffer,
meet the poor in their distress.

2 There are lands that have no
honour,
hear no wisdom, see no light;
blind, they stumble in the
darkness,
leaderless, they shake with fright.
Tremble, all you mighty rulers;
every nation, know God's worth;
power and wealth are God's
possession,
who alone shall judge the earth!

Michael Arnold Perry, 1942–1996
after Psalm 82

620

1 In Christ there is no east or west,
in Him no south or north,
but one great fellowship of love
throughout the whole wide earth.

2 In Christ shall true hearts
everywhere
their high communion find.
His service is the golden cord
close-binding humankind.

3 Join hands, disciples of the faith,
whate'er your race may be.
All children of the living God
are surely kin to me.

4   In Christ now meet both east and
    west,
    in Him meet south and north.
    all Christlike souls are one in
    Him,
    throughout the whole wide earth.

John Oxenham, pseud., 1852–1941
William Arthur Dunkerley, 1852–1941
altered

621

1   Lord, the light of Your love is
    shining,
    in the midst of the darkness,
    shining:
    Jesus, Light of the world, shine
    upon us;
    set us free by the truth You now
    bring us —
    shine on me, shine on me:
    Shine, Jesus, shine,
    fill this land with the Father's
    glory;
    blaze, Spirit, blaze,
    set our hearts on fire.
    Flow, river, flow,
    flood the nations with grace and
    mercy;
    send forth Your word, Lord,
    and let there be light!

2   Lord, I come to Your awesome
    presence,
    from the shadows into Your
    radiance;
    by the blood I may enter Your
    brightness:
    search me, try me, consume all
    my darkness —
    shine on me, shine on me:

3   As we gaze on Your kingly
    brightness
    so our faces display Your likeness,
    ever changing from glory to
    glory:
    mirrored here, may our lives tell
    Your story —
    shine on me, shine on me:

Graham Andrew Kendrick, b. 1950

622

1   O God of love, O King of peace,
    make wars throughout the world
    to cease;
    the wrath of sinful man restrain:
    give peace, O God, give peace
    again.

2   Remember, Lord, Your deeds of
    old,
    the wonders that our fathers told;
    remember not our sin's dark
    stain:
    give peace, O God, give peace
    again.

3   Whom shall we trust but You, O
    Lord,
    where rest but on Your faithful
    word?
    None ever called on You in vain:
    give peace, O God, give peace
    again.

4   Where saints and angels dwell
    above,
    all hearts are one in holy love;
    O bind us with that heavenly
    chain:
    give peace, O God, give peace
    again.

Henry Williams Baker, 1821–1877
altered

623

1   O God of our divided world,
    light up Your way where our
    ways part.
    Restore the kinship of our birth,
    revive in us a single heart —

2   A heart that sees in Christ its goal
    and cares with Christ for every
    one,
    that seeks beyond all outward
    forms
    a fellowship in God's own Son.

3   Where we have failed to
    understand
    another's heart, O Lord forgive.
    Grant us the confidence to share
    the lights whereby our neigh
    bours live.

4   Then shall we know a richer
    world
    where all divisions are disowned,
    where heart joins heart and hand
    joins hand,
    where each is loved and Christ
    enthroned.

Alan Norman Phillips, b. 1910
adapted Compilers

624

1   Restore, O Lord,
    the honour of Your name!
    In works of sovereign power
    come shake the earth again;
    that all may see,
    and come with reverent fear
    to the living God
    whose kingdom shall outlast the
    years.

2   Restore, O Lord,
    in all the earth Your fame,
    and in our time revive
    the Church that bears Your
    name;
    and in Your anger,
    Lord, remember mercy,
    O living God,
    whose mercy shall outlast the
    years.

3   Bend us, O Lord,
    where we are hard and cold,
    in Your refiner's fire
    come purify the gold.
    Though suffering comes,
    and evil crouches near,
    still our living God
    is reigning, He is reigning here.

4   Restore, O Lord,
    the honour of Your name! ...

Graham Andrew Kendrick, b. 1950 and
Christopher Philip Rolinson, b. 1958

625

Singing, we gladly worship the
  Lord together.
Singing, we gladly worship the
  Lord.
Those who are travelling the road
  of life
sow seeds of peace and love.
(repeat)

1   Come, bringing hope into a world
    of fear,
    a world which is burdened down
    with dread,
    a world which is yearning for a
    greater love
    but needs to be shown the true
    way.

2   Come, bringing joyfully in both
    your hands
    some kindling to light the path to
    peace,
    some hope that there is a more
    human world
    where justice and truth will be
    born.

3   Whenever hatefulness and
    violence
    are banished for ever from our
    hearts,
    then will the world believe the
    day is near
    when sadness and pain shall find
    their end.

Guatemalan traditional
Christine Carson

626

1   Your kingdom come, O God,
    Your rule, O Christ, begin;
    break with Your iron rod
    the tyrannies of sin.

2   Where is Your reign of peace
    and purity and love?
    When shall all hatred cease,
    as in the realms above?

3   When comes the promised time,
    that war shall be no more,
    and lust, oppression, crime
    shall flee Your face before?

4   O Lord our God, arise
    and come in Your great might!
    Revive our longing eyes,
    which languish for Your sight.

5   Scorned is Your sacred name,
    and wolves devour Your fold;
    by many deeds of shame
    we learn that love grows cold.

6   On nations near and far
    thick darkness gathers yet:
    arise, O Morning Star,
    arise and never set!

Lewis Hensley, 1824–1905
altered

Also suitable:

All the ends of the earth	110
As a fire is meant for burning	627
Bring to the Lord a glad new song	150
Christ is alive! Let Christians sing	430
Great is the darkness the covers the earth	646
It came upon the midnight clear	324
O Lord, the clouds are gathering	73
Sing to God new songs of worship	236
Your kingdom come! on bended knee	304

624   Words and Music: © 1981 Thankyou Music. Administered (UK and Europe) by Kingsway Music <tym@kingsway.co.uk>. Remaining territories administered by worshiptogether.com songs. Used by permission.

625   Words and Music: © Wild Goose Resource Group, Iona Community, Pearce Institute, 840 Govan Road, Glasgow G51 3UU

THE GROWTH OF THE CHURCH
MISSION

627

1 As a fire is meant for burning
with a bright and warming flame,
so the Church is meant for
mission,
giving glory to God's name.
Not to preach our creeds or
customs,
but to build a bridge of care,
we join hands across the nations,
finding neighbours everywhere.

2 We are learners; we are teachers;
we are pilgrims on the way.
We are seekers; we are givers;
we are vessels made of clay.
By our gentle, loving actions,
we would show that Christ is
light.
In a humble, listening Spirit,
we would live to God's delight.

3 As a green bud in the springtime
is a sign of life renewed,
so may we be signs of oneness
'mid earth's peoples, many-hued.
As a rainbow lights the heavens
when a storm is past and gone,
may our lives reflect the radiance
of God's new and glorious dawn.

Ruth C. Duck, b. 1947

628

1 Beauty for brokenness,
hope for despair,
Lord, in Your suffering world
this is our prayer.
Bread for the children,
justice, joy, peace,
sunrise to sunset
Your kingdom increase.

2 Shelter for fragile lives,
cures for their ills,
work for the craftsmen,
trade for their skills.
Land for the dispossessed,
rights for the weak,
voices to plead the cause
of those who can't speak.
   God of the poor,
   friend of the weak,
   give us compassion, we pray,
   melt our cold hearts,

let tears fall like rain.
Come, change our love
from a spark to a flame.

3 Refuge from cruel wars,
havens from fear,
cities for sanctuary,
freedoms to share.
Peace to the killing fields,
scorched earth to green,
Christ for the bitterness,
His cross for the pain.

4 Rest for the ravaged earth,
oceans and streams,
plundered and poisoned,
our future, our dreams.
Lord, end our madness,
carelessness, greed;
make us content with
the things that we need.
   God of the poor ...

5 Lighten our darkness,
breathe on this flame,
until Your justice
burns brightly again;
until the nations
learn of Your ways,
seek Your salvation
and bring You their praise.
   God of the poor ...

Graham Andrew Kendrick, b. 1950

629

1 Church of God, elect and
glorious,
holy nation, chosen race;
called as God's own special
people,
royal priests and heirs of grace:
know the purpose of your calling,
show to all His mighty deeds;
tell of love which knows no
limits,
grace which meets all human
needs.

2 God has called you out of
darkness
into His most marvellous light;
brought His truth to life within
you,
turned your blindness into sight.
Let your light so shine around
you
that God's name is glorified;
and all find fresh hope and
purpose
in Christ Jesus crucified.

MISSION

3 Once you were an alien people,
strangers to God's heart of love;
but He brought you home in
      mercy,
citizens of heaven above.
Let His love flow out to others,
let them feel a Father's care;
that they too may know His
      welcome
and His countless blessings share.

4 Church of God, elect and holy,
be the people He intends;
strong in faith and swift to
      answer
each command your Master
      sends:
royal priests, fulfil your calling
through your sacrifice and
      prayer;
give your lives in joyful service,
sing His praise, His love declare.

James Edward Seddon, 1915–1983

630

1 Eternal God, whose power
      upholds
both flower and flaming star,
to whom there is no here nor
      there,
no time, no near nor far,
no alien race, no foreign shore,
no child unsought, unknown,
O send us forth, Your prophets
      true,
to make all lands Your own!

2 O God of love, whose spirit
      wakes
in every human breast,
whom love, and love alone, can
      know,
in whom all hearts find rest,
help us to spread Your gracious
      reign,
till greed and hate shall cease,
and kindness dwell in human
      hearts,
and all the earth find peace!

3 O God of truth, whom science
      seeks
and reverent souls adore,
enlightening every earnest mind
of every clime and shore,
dispel the gloom of error's night,
of ignorance and fear,
until true wisdom from above
shall make life's pathway clear.

4 O God of beauty, oft revealed
in dreams of human art,
in speech that flows to melody,
in holiness of heart;
teach us to ban all ugliness
from eyes You meant to see,
till all shall know the loveliness
of lives made fair and free.

5 O God of righteousness and
      grace,
seen in the Christ, Your Son,
whose life and death reveal Your
      face,
by whom Your will was done.
Inspire Your heralds of good
      news
to meet Your life's demand,
till Christ is formed in
      humankind
and Yours is every land.

Henry Hallam Tweedy, 1868–1953
adapted Compilers

631

1 Far and near hear the call,
worship Him, Lord of all;
families of nations, come,
celebrate what God has done.

2 Deep and wide is the love
heaven sent from above;
God's own Son, for sinners died,
rose again — He is alive.

Say it loud, say it strong,
tell the world what God has done:
say it loud, praise His name,
let the earth rejoice for the Lord
reigns.

3 At His name, let praise begin:
oceans roar, nature sing,
for He comes to judge the earth
in righteousness and in His truth.

Say it loud ...

Graham Andrew Kendrick, *b.* 1950

632

1 Filled with compassion for all
      creation,
Jesus came into a world that was
      lost.
There was but one way that He
      could save us,
only through suffering death on a
      cross.

God, You are waiting, Your heart
is breaking
for all the people who live on the
earth.
Stir us to action, filled with Your
passion
for all the people who live on the
earth.

2   Great is Your passion for all the
    people
    living and dying without
    knowing You.
    Having no Saviour, they're lost
    forever,
    if we don't speak out and lead
    them to You.

3   From every nation we shall be
    gathered,
    millions redeemed shall be Jesus'
    reward.
    Then He will turn and say to His
    Father:
    'Truly my suffering was worth it
    all.'

Noël Richards, *b.* 1955
and Tricia Richards, *b.* 1960

633

1   'For my sake and the gospel's, go
    and tell redemption's story!'
    His heralds answer, 'Be it so,
    and Yours, Lord, all the glory!'
    They preach His birth, His life,
    His cross,
    the love of His atonement,
    for whom they count the world
    but loss,
    His Easter, His enthronement.

2   Hark, hark, the trump of jubilee
    proclaims to every nation,
    from pole to pole, by land and
    sea,
    glad tidings of salvation:
    still on and on the anthems
    spread
    of alleluia voices,
    in concert with the holy dead
    the warrior Church rejoices.

3   He comes, whose advent trumpet
    drowns
    the last of time's evangels,
    Emmanuel, crowned with many
    crowns,
    the Lord of saints and angels:
    O Trinity, the great I AM,

the Love who changest never,
the throne of God and of the
Lamb
is Yours, and Yours for ever.

Edward Henry Bickersteth, 1825–1906
adapted Compilers

634

1   Go forth and tell! O Church of
    God, awake!
    God's saving news to all the
    nations take:
    proclaim Christ Jesus, Saviour,
    Lord, and King,
    that all the world His worthy
    praise may sing.

2   Go forth and tell! God's love
    embraces all;
    He will in grace respond to all
    who call:
    how shall they call if they have
    never heard
    the gracious invitation of His
    word?

3   Go forth and tell! where still the
    darkness lies
    in wealth or want, the sinner
    surely dies:
    give us, O Lord, concern of heart
    and mind,
    a love like Yours which cares for
    humankind.

4   Go forth and tell! the doors are
    open wide:
    share God's good gifts — let no
    one be denied;
    live out your life as Christ your
    Lord shall choose,
    your ransomed powers for His
    sole glory use.

5   Go forth and tell! O Church of
    God, arise!
    Go in the strength which Christ
    your Lord supplies;
    go till all nations His great name
    adore
    and serve Him, Lord and King
    for evermore.

James Edward Seddon, 1915–1983

634   Words: © Representatives of the late James Edward Seddon / Jubilee Hymns, 4 Thorne Park Road, Chelston, Torquay TQ2 6RX <enquiries@jubilate.co.uk> Used by permission.

635

1   God of mercy, God of grace,
    show the brightness of Your face:
    shine upon us, Saviour, shine,
    fill Your Church with light
        divine;
    and Your saving health extend
    unto earth's remotest end.

2   Let the people praise You, Lord;
    be by all that live adored:
    let the nations shout and sing
    glory to their Saviour King;
    at Your feet their tribute pay,
    and Your holy will obey.

3   Let the people praise You, Lord;
    earth shall then her fruits afford,
    God to us His blessing give,
    we to God devoted live;
    all below, and all above,
    one in joy and light and love.

                    Henry Francis Lyte, 1793–1847
                    from Psalm 67

636

1   God, whose almighty word
    chaos and darkness heard,
    and took their flight:
    hear us, we humbly pray,
    and where the gospel-day
    sheds not its glorious ray,
    let there be light!

2   Saviour, who came to bring
    on Your redeeming wing
    healing and sight,
    health to the sick in mind,
    sight to the inly blind:
    O now to all mankind
    let there be light!

3   Spirit of truth and love,
    life-giving, holy dove,
    speed on Your flight!
    Move on the waters' face,
    bearing the lamp of grace,
    and, in earth's darkest place,
    let there be light!

4   Gracious and holy Three,
    glorious Trinity,
    wisdom, love, might:
    boundless as ocean's tide
    rolling in fullest pride,
    through the world far and wide,
    let there be light!

                    John Marriott, 1780–1825
                    and Thomas Raffles, 1788–1863

637

1   Jesus shall reign where'er the
        sun
    does his successive journeys run;
    His kingdom stretch from shore
        to shore
    till moons shall rise and set no
        more.

2   People and realms of every
        tongue
    declare His love in sweetest song,
    and children's voices shall
        proclaim
    their early blessings on His name.

3   Blessings abound where Jesus
        reigns —
    the prisoner leaps to lose his
        chains,
    the weary find eternal rest,
    and all who suffer want are
        blessed.

4   To Him shall endless prayer be
        made,
    and praises throng to crown His
        head;
    His name like incense shall arise
    with every morning sacrifice.

5   Let all creation rise and bring
    distinctive honours to our King;
    angels descend with songs again
    and earth repeat the loud
    'Amen!'

                    Isaac Watts, 1674–1748
                    adapted Jubilate Hymns

638

1   Lord, Your Church on earth is
        seeking
    Your renewal from above;
    teach us all the art of speaking
    with the accent of Your love.
    We would heed Your great
        commission:
    Go you into every place —
    preach, baptise, fulfil my mission,
    serve with love and share my
        grace.

2   Freedom give to those in
        bondage,
    lift the burdens caused by sin.
    Give new hope, new strength
        and courage,
    grant release from fears within:
    light for darkness; joy for sorrow;

love for hatred; peace for strife.
These and countless blessings follow
as the Spirit gives new life.

3   In the streets of every city
where the bruised and lonely live,
we will show the Saviour's pity,
and His longing to forgive.
In all lands and with all races
we will serve, and seek to bring
all the world to render praises,
Christ, to You, Redeemer, King.

Hugh Sherlock, 1905–1998
adapted Compilers

639

1   O Spirit of the living God,
in all the fullness of Your grace,
wherever human feet have trod,
descend upon our fallen race.

2   Give tongues of fire and hearts of love
to preach the reconciling word;
anoint with power from heaven above
whenever gospel truth is heard.

3   Let darkness turn to radiant light,
confusion vanish from your path;
souls without strength inspire with might:
let mercy triumph over wrath.

4   O Spirit of our God, prepare
the whole wide world the Lord to meet;
breathe out new life, like morning air,
till hearts of stone begin to beat.

5   Baptize the nations; far and near
the triumphs of the cross record;
till Christ in glory shall appear
and every people call Him Lord!

James Montgomery, 1771–1854
slightly altered

640

1   Speak forth Your word, O Father,
our hungry minds to feed,
the people starve and perish,
and cannot name their need;
for Lord, You have so made us
that not alone by bread,
but by Your word of comfort
our hunger must be fed.

2   The secrets of the atom,
the universe of light,
all wonders of creation
proclaim Your boundless might:
but only through the witness
from one to one passed on
do You reveal in fullness
the gospel of Your Son.

3   To each one in their language
to each one in their home,
by many paths and channels
the faith of Christ may come:
the printed word on paper,
the wave that spans the air,
the screen, the stage, the picture
may all its truth declare.

4   How shall they hear Your message
if there are none to preach?
How shall they learn Your lesson
if there are none to teach?
Take us, then, Lord, and use us
to tell what we have heard,
and all the minds of millions
shall feed upon Your word.

Charles Joseph Jeffries, 1896–1972

641

1   Tell all the world of Jesus,
our Saviour, Lord and King;
and let the whole creation
of His salvation sing:
proclaim His glorious greatness
in nature and in grace;
Creator and Redeemer,
the Lord of time and space.

2   Tell all the world of Jesus,
that everyone may find
the joy of His forgiveness —
true peace of heart and mind:
proclaim His perfect goodness,
His deep, unfailing care;
His love so rich in mercy,
a love beyond compare.

3   Tell all the world of Jesus,
that everyone may know
of His almighty triumph
defeating every foe:
proclaim His coming glory,
when sin is overthrown,
and He shall reign in splendour —
the King upon His throne!

James Edward Seddon, 1915–1983

640 Words: By permission of Oxford University Press, Great Clarendon Street, Oxford OX2 6DP
641 Words: © Representatives of the late James Edward Seddon/Jubilate Hymns, 4 Thorne Park Road, Chelston, Torquay TQ2 6RX <enquiries@jubilate.co.uk> Used by permission.

642

1 The Church is wherever God's
  people are praising,
singing their thanks for joy on
  this day.
The Church is wherever disciples
  of Jesus
remember His story and walk in
  His way.

2 The Church is wherever God's
  people are helping,
caring for neighbours in sickness
  and need.
The Church is wherever God's
  people are sharing
the words of the Bible in gift and
  in deed.

Carol Rose Ikeler, b. 1920

643

1 We have heard a joyful sound:
  Jesus saves!
Spread the gladness all around:
  Jesus saves!
Bear the news to every land,
send it out across the waves;
Onward! at our Lord's
  command:
  Jesus saves!

2 Send it on the rolling tide:
  Jesus saves!
Tell to sinners far and wide,
  Jesus saves!
Sing, you islands of the sea;
echo back, you ocean caves;
earth shall keep her jubilee:
  Jesus saves!

3 Sing above the battle's strife:
  Jesus saves!
By His death and endless life
  Jesus saves!
Sing it softly through the gloom,
when the heart for mercy craves;
sing in triumph o'er the tomb:
  Jesus saves!

4 Give the winds a mighty voice:
  Jesus saves!
Let the nations now rejoice:
  Jesus saves!
Shout salvation full and free,
that every land may hear God's
  praise;
this our song of victory:
  Jesus saves!

Priscilla Jane Owens, 1829–1907
adapted Compilers

Also suitable:
Forth in the peace of Christ we go   280
He gave me eyes so I could see   22
Here I am, wholly available   539
Hills of the north, rejoice   296

THE LAST THINGS
CHRIST'S RETURN

644

1 At the name of Jesus
  every knee shall bow,
every tongue confess Him
  King of glory now;
this the Father's pleasure,
that we call Him Lord,
who from the beginning
was the mighty Word.

2 At His voice creation
  sprang at once to sight,
all the angel faces,
all the hosts of light;
thrones and dominations,
stars upon their way,
all the heavenly orders,
in their great array.

3 Humbled for a season,
  to receive a name
from the lips of sinners
unto whom He came;
faithfully He bore it
spotless to the last,
brought it back victorious
when from death He passed.

4 Bore it up triumphant
  with its human light,
through all ranks of creatures
to the central height;
to the eternal Godhead,
to the Father's throne,
filled it with the glory
of His triumph won.

5 Name Him, Christians, name
  Him,
with love strong as death,
but with awe and wonder,
and with bated breath;
He is God the Saviour,
He is Christ the Lord,
ever to be worshipped,
trusted and adored.

6   In your hearts enthrone Him;
    there let Him subdue
    all that is not holy,
    all that is not true:
    crown Him as your captain
    in temptation's hour,
    let His will enfold you
    in its light and power.

7   With His Father's glory
    Jesus comes again,
    angel hosts attend Him
    and announce His reign;
    for all wreaths of empire
    meet upon His brow,
    and our hearts confess Him
    King of glory now.

                    Caroline Maria Noel, 1817–1877
                    adapted Jubilee Hymns

645

1   Christ is surely coming, bringing
        His reward,
    Alpha and Omega, First and Last
        and Lord;
    Root and Stem of David, brilliant
        Morning Star —
    meet your Judge and Saviour,
        nations near and far;
    meet your Judge and Saviour,
        nations near and far!

2   See the holy city! There they
        enter in,
    all by Christ made holy, washed
        from every sin;
    thirsty ones, desiring all He loves
        to give:
    come for living water, freely
        drink, and live;
    come for living water, freely
        drink, and live!

3   Grace be with God's people!
        Praise His holy name!
    Father, Son, and Spirit, evermore
        the same;
    Hear the certain promise from
        the eternal home:
    'Surely I come quickly! Come,
        Lord Jesus, come;
    Surely I come quickly! Come,
        Lord Jesus, come!'

                    Christopher Martin Idle, *b.* 1938

646

1   Great is the darkness that covers
        the earth,
    oppression, injustice and pain.
    Nations are slipping in hopeless
        despair,

though many have come in Your
    name,
watching while sanity dies,
touched by the madness and lies.
    *Come, Lord Jesus, come, Lord
        Jesus,*
    pour out Your Spirit we pray.
    *Come, Lord Jesus, come, Lord
        Jesus,*
    pour out Your Spirit on us today.

2   May now Your Church rise with
        power and love,
    this glorious gospel proclaim.
    In every nation salvation will
        come
    to those who believe in Your
        name.
    Help us bring light to this world,
    that we might speed Your return.

3   Great celebrations on that final
        day
    when out of the heavens You
        come.
    Darkness will vanish, all sorrow
        will end,
    and rulers will bow at Your
        throne.
    Our great commission complete,
    then face to face we shall meet.

                    Gerald Coates, *b.* 1944
                    and Noël Richards, *b.* 195[?]

647

1   Hark! a trumpet-call is
        sounding;
    'Christ is near,' it seems to say:
    'cast away the dreams of
        darkness,
    children of the dawning day!'

2   Wakened by the solemn warning,
    let our earthbound souls arise;
    Christ, our Sun, all harm
        dispelling,
    shines upon the morning skies.

3   See! the Lamb, so long expected,
    comes with pardon down from
        heaven;
    let us haste, with tears of sorrow,
    one and all to be forgiven.

4   That, when next He comes in
        glory
    and the world is wrapped in fear,
    with His mercy He may shield
        us,
    and with words of love draw
        near.

645 Words: © Christopher Idle / Jubilate Hymns, 4 Thorne Park Road, Chelston, Torquay TQ2 6RX <enquiries@jubilate.co.uk> Used by permission.
646 Words and Music: © 1992 Thankyou Music. Administered (UK and Europe) by Kingsway Music <tym@kingsway.co.uk>. Remaining territories administered by worshiptogether.com songs. Used by permission.

5   Honour, glory, might and blessing
     to the Father, and the Son,
     with the everlasting Spirit,
     while eternal ages run!

Latin
translated Edward Caswall, 1814–1878
altered

648

1   I cannot tell why He whom
          angels worship
     should set His love upon the sons
          of men;
     or why as shepherd He should
          seek the wanderers,
     to bring them back, they know not
          how nor when.
     But this I know, that He was born
          of Mary
     when Bethlehem's manger was
          His only home,
     and that He lived at Nazareth
          and laboured;
     and so the Saviour, Saviour of the
          world, has come.

2   I cannot tell how silently He
          suffered
     as with His peace He graced this
          place of tears;
     nor how His heart upon the cross
          was broken,
     the crown of pain to three and
          thirty years.
     But this I know, He heals the
          broken-hearted
     and stays our sin and calms our
          lurking fear,
     and lifts the burden from the
          heavy-laden,
     for still the Saviour, Saviour of
          the world, is here.

3   I cannot tell how He will win the
          nations,
     how He will claim His earthly
          heritage,
     how satisfy the needs and
          aspirations
     of east and west, of sinner and of
          sage.
     But this I know, all flesh shall see
          His glory,
     and He shall reap the harvest He
          has sown,
     and some glad day His sun will
          shine in splendour
     when He the Saviour, Saviour of
          the world, is known.

4   I cannot tell how all the lands
          shall worship,
     when at His bidding every storm
          is stilled;
     or who can say how great the
          jubilation
     when all our hearts with love for
          Him are filled.
     But this I know, the skies will
          sound His praises,
     ten thousand thousand human
          voices sing,
     and earth to heaven, and heaven
          to earth, will answer:
     'At last the Saviour, Saviour of the
          world, is King!'

William Young Fullerton, 1857–1932

649

1   Jesus comes with clouds
          descending —
     see the Lamb for sinners slain!
     Thousand thousand saints
          attending
     join to sing the glad refrain:
*   Alleluia!
     God appears on earth to reign.

2   Every eye shall then behold Him
     robed in awesome majesty;
     those who jeered at Him and
          sold Him,
     pierced and nailed Him to the
          tree,
     shamed and grieving
     shall their true Messiah see.

3   All the wounds of cross and
          passion
     still His glorious body bears;
     cause of endless exultation
     to His ransomed worshippers.
     With what gladness
     we shall see the Saviour's scars!

4   Yes, Amen! let all adore You,
     high on Your eternal throne;
     crowns and empires fall before
          You —
     claim the kingdom for Your own.
     Come, Lord Jesus,
     everlasting God, come down!

*   *The penultimate line of each verse is sung*
     three times.

Charles Wesley, 1707–1788
and Martin Madan, 1726–1790
based on a hymn by John Cennick 1718-1755
adapted Jubilate Hymns

650

1 Mine eyes have seen the glory of
   the coming of the Lord;
He is trampling out the vintage
   where the grapes of wrath are
   stored;
He has loosed the fateful
   lightning of His terrible swift
   sword:
His truth is marching on.
   Glory, glory, alleluia,
   glory, glory, alleluia,
   glory, glory, alleluia,
   His truth is marching on.

2 He has sounded forth the
   trumpet that shall never call
   retreat;
He is sifting out all human hearts
   before His judgement-seat;
O be swift, my soul, to answer
   Him; be jubilant, my feet!
Our God is marching on.
   Glory, glory, alleluia,
   glory, glory, alleluia,
   glory, glory, alleluia,
   our God is marching on.

3 In the beauty of the lilies Christ
   was borne across the sea,
with a glory in His bosom that
   transfigures you and me:
as He died to make us holy, let us
   live that all be free,
while God is marching on.
   Glory, glory, alleluia,
   glory, glory, alleluia,
   glory, glory, alleluia,
   while God is marching on.

4 He is coming like the glory of the
   morning on the wave;
He is wisdom to the mighty; He
   is succour to the brave;
so the world shall be His
   footstool, and the soul of time
   His slave:
our God is marching on.
   Glory, glory, alleluia,
   glory, glory, alleluia,
   glory, glory, alleluia,
   our God is marching on.

Julia Ward Howe, 1819–1810
and others

651

1 These are the days of Elijah,
   declaring the word of the Lord;
and these are the days of your
   servant, Moses,
righteousness being restored.
And though these are days of
   great trial,
of famine and darkness and
   sword,
still we are the voice in the
   desert crying,
'Prepare ye the way of the Lord.'
   Behold, He comes riding on the
     clouds,
   shining like the sun at the
     trumpet call;
   lift your voice, it's the year of
     jubilee,
   out of Zion's hill salvation comes.

2 These are the days of Ezekiel,
   the dry bones becoming as flesh;
and these are the days of your
   servant, David,
rebuilding a temple of praise.
These are the days of the harvest,
   the fields are as white in the
   world,
and we are the labourers in Your
   vineyard,
declaring the word of the Lord.

Robin Mark

652

1 Waken, O sleeper, wake and rise,
   salvation's day is near,
and let the dawn of light and
   truth
dispel the night of fear.

2 Let us prepare to face the day
of judgement and of grace,
to live as people of the light,
and perfect truth embrace.

3 Watch, then, and pray; we cannot
   know
the moment or the hour
when Christ, unheralded, will
   come
with life-renewing power.

4 Then shall the nations gather
   round
to learn His ways of peace,
when spears to pruning-hooks
   are turned,
and all our conflicts cease.

Michael Forster, b. 1946

653

1 You servants of the Lord,
   each in your calling wait;
   observe with care His heavenly
      word —
   be watchful at His gate.

2 Let all your lamps be bright
   and trim the living flame;
   be ready always in His sight,
   for awesome is His name.

3 'Watch' is your Lord's command:
   the bridegroom shall appear,
   for His returning is at hand,
   and while we speak He's near.

4 O happy servants they
   who wide awake are found
   to greet their Master on that day,
   and be with honour crowned!

5 Christ shall the banquet spread
   with His own royal hand,
   and raise each faithful servant's
      head
   amid the angelic band.

Philip Doddridge, 1702–1751
altered

Also suitable:
Jesus is the name we honour   214
Let all mortal flesh keep silence   386
Rejoice, the Lord is King!   454
Thank You, Jesus   423
Your kingdom come! on bended knee   304

THE LAST THINGS
HEAVEN

654

1 Going home, moving on,
   through God's open door;
   hush, my soul, have no fear,
   Christ has gone before.
   Parting hurts, love protests,
   pain is not denied;
   yet, in Christ, life and hope
   span the great divide.
   Going home, moving on,
   through God's open door;
   hush, my soul, have no fear,
   Christ has gone before,
   Christ has gone before.

2 No more guilt, no more fear,
   all the past is healed:
   broken dreams now restored,
   perfect grace revealed.
   Christ has died, Christ is risen,
   Christ will come again:
   death destroyed, life restored,
   love alone shall reign.
   Going home, moving on,
   through God's open door;
   hush, my soul, have no fear,
   Christ has gone before,
   Christ has gone before.

Michael Lindsay Forster, b. 1946

655

1 Here from all nations, all tongues,
      and all peoples,
   countless the crowd but their
      voices are one;
   vast is the sight and majestic
      their singing —
   'God has the victory: He reigns
      from the throne!'

2 These have come out of the
      hardest oppression;
   now they may stand in the
      presence of God,
   serving their Lord day and night
      in His temple,
   ransomed and cleansed by the
      Lamb's precious blood.

3 Gone is their thirst and no more
      shall they hunger,
   God is their shelter, His power at
      their side:
   sun shall not pain them, no
      burning will torture,
   Jesus the Lamb is their shepherd
      and guide.

4 He will go with them to clear
      living water
   flowing from springs which His
      mercy supplies;
   gone is their grief and their trials
      are over —
   God wipes away every tear from
      their eyes.

5 Blessing and glory and wisdom
      and power
   be to the Saviour again and
      again;
   might and thanksgiving and
      honour for ever
   be to our God: Alleluia! Amen.

Christopher Martin Idle, b. 1938

THE LAST THINGS

656

1 Jerusalem the golden,
with milk and honey blest,
beneath your contemplation
sink heart and voice oppressed:
I know not, oh I know not
what social joys are there,
what radiancy of glory,
what light beyond compare.

2 They stand, those halls of Zion,
conjubilant with song,
and bright with many an angel,
and all the martyr throng:
the Prince is ever in them;
the daylight is serene;
the pastures of the blessèd
are decked in glorious sheen.

3 There is the throne of David,
and there, from pain released,
the shout of them that triumph,
the song of that that feast;
and they who, with their Leader,
have conquered in the fight,
for ever and for ever
and clad in robes of white.

4 O sweet and blessèd country,
the home of God's elect!
O sweet and blessèd country,
that eager hearts expect!
Jesus, in mercy bring us
to that dear land of rest,
with God the Father reigning,
and Spirit, ever blest. Amen.

*Bernard of Cluny, 12th century
based on Revelation 7: 14; 21: 1-7,
translated John Mason Neale, 1818–1866
and Compilers of Hymns Ancient & Modern, 1861
slightly altered Compilers*

657

1 The trumpets sound, the angels
sing,
the feast is ready to begin;
the gates of heaven are open
wide,
and Jesus welcomes you inside.

2 Tables are laden with good
things:
O taste the peace and joy He
brings!
He'll fill you up with love divine,
He'll turn your water into wine.
*Sing with thankfulness songs of
pure delight,*

come and revel in heaven's love
and light;
take your place at the table of the
King —
*the feast is ready to begin,
the feast is ready to begin.*

3 The hungry heart He satisfies,
offers the poor His paradise.
Now hear all heaven, and earth
applaud
the amazing goodness of the
Lord!
Sing with thankfulness ...

Graham Andrew Kendrick, b. 1950

658

1 There is a land of pure delight
where saints immortal reign;
eternal day excludes the night
and pleasures banish pain.

2 There everlasting spring abides,
and never-withering flowers;
death, like a narrow stream,
divides
this heavenly land from ours.

3 Sweet fields beyond the rolling
flood
stand dressed in living green,
as once to Israel Canaan stood,
while Jordan flowed between.

4 But trembling mortals fear, and
shrink
to cross the narrow sea;
they linger shivering on the
brink,
afraid to launch away.

5 If we could all our doubts
remove,
those gloomy doubts that rise,
and see the Canaan that we love
with clear unclouded eyes!

6 If we could climb where Moses
stood
and view what lies before,
not Jordan's stream, nor death's
cold flood,
would keep us from the shore.

*Isaac Watts, 1674–1748
vv. 1-4 adapted Jubilate Hymns
vv. 5-6 adapted Compilers of Praise! 2000*

657 Words and Music: © 1989 Make Way Music
658 Words in this version (vv. 1-4) Jubilate Hymns, 4 Thorne Park Road, Chelston, Torquay TQ2 6RX <enquiries@jubilate.co.uk> Used by permission.
658 Words: Praise Trust, Praise Trust, PO Box 359, Darlington. DL3 8YD

659

1 There's a song for all the children
that makes the heavens ring,
a song that even angels
can never, never sing;
they praise the Lord their Maker
and see Him glorified,
but we can call Him Saviour
because for us He died.

2 There's a place for all the
children
where Jesus reigns in love,
a place of joy and freedom
that nothing can remove,
a home that is more friendly
than any home we know,
where Jesus makes us welcome
because He loves us so.

3 There's a friend for all the
children
to guide us every day,
whose care is always faithful
and never fades away;
there's no-one else so loyal —
His friendship stays the same;
He knows us and He loves us,
and Jesus is His name.

Albert Midlane, 1825–1909
adapted Jubilate Hymns

660

1 You're the Lion of Judah, the
Lamb that was slain,
You ascended to heaven and
evermore will reign;
at the end of the age when the
earth You reclaim,
You will gather the nations before
You.
And the eyes of all men will be
fixed on the Lamb who was
crucified,
for with wisdom and mercy and
justice You'll reign at Your
Father's side.
And the angels will cry:
'Hail the Lamb that was slain for
the world, rule in power.'
And the earth will reply:
'You shall reign as the King of all
kings, and the Lord of all lords.'

2 There's a shield in our hand and
a sword at our side,
there's a fire in our spirit that
cannot be denied;

as the Father has told us, for
these You have died,
for the nations that gather before
You.
And the ears of all men need to
hear of the Lamb who was
crucified,
who descended to hell yet was
raised up to reign at the
Father's side.
And the angels ...

Robin Mark

Also suitable:
At Your feet we fall, mighty risen Lord   429
If I come to Jesus   559

THE LAST THINGS
FUNERAL HYMNS

661

1 Abide with me: fast falls the
eventide;
the darkness deepens: Lord,
with me abide!
When other helpers fail and
comforts flee,
help of the helpless, O abide with
me.

2 Swift to its close ebbs out life's
little day;
earth's joys grow dim, its glories
pass away;
change and decay in all around I
see:
You never change, O Lord; abide
with me.

3 I need Your presence every
passing hour;
what but Your grace can foil the
tempter's power?
Who like Yourself my guide and
strength can be?
Through cloud and sunshine,
Lord, abide with me.

4 I fear no foe with You at hand to
bless;
ills have no weight and tears no
bitterness.
Where is death's sting? Where,
grave, your victory?
I triumph still if You abide with
me.

5 Hold, Lord, Your cross before my
     closing eyes;
  shine through the gloom and
     point me to the skies:
  heaven's morning breaks and
     earth's vain shadows flee;
  in life, in death, O Lord, abide
     with me.

Henry Francis Lyte, 1793–1847
adapted Compilers of Praise! 2000

662

1 Lord, it is not within my care
     whether I die or live;
  to love and serve You is my
     share,
  and this Your grace must give.

2 If life is long, I shall be glad
     that I may long obey;
  if short, then why should I be sad
     to soar to endless day?

3 Christ leads me through no
     darker rooms
  than He went through before;
  whoever to God's kingdom
     comes
  must enter by this door.

4 Come, Lord, when grace has
     made me fit
  Your holy face to see;
  for if Your work on earth is sweet,
     what will Your glory be?

5 My knowledge of that life is
     small,
  the eye of faith is dim;
  it is enough that Christ knows all
     and I shall be with Him.

Richard Baxter, 1615–1691
adapted Compilers of Praise! 2000

663

1 Lord of the living, in Your name
     assembled,
  we join to thank You for the life
     remembered.
  Hold us, enfold us, to Your
     children giving
  hope in believing.

2 Help us to treasure all that will
     remind us
  of the enrichment in the days
     behind us.
  Your love has set us in the
     generations,
  God of creation.

3 May we, whenever tempted to
     dejection,
  strongly recapture thoughts of
     resurrection.
  You gave us Jesus to defeat our
     sadness
  with Easter gladness.

4 God, You can lift us from the
     grave of sorrow
  into the presence of Your own
     tomorrow:
  give to Your people for the day's
     affliction
  Your benediction.

Frederik Herman Kaan, b. 1929

664

1 The sands of time are sinking;
     the dawn of heaven breaks:
  the summer morn I've longed for,
     the fair, sweet morn awakes.
  Dark, dark has been the
     midnight,
  but sunrise is at hand
  with glory, glory dwelling
  in Emmanuel's land.

2 The King in all His beauty
     without a veil is seen;
  it were a well-spent journey
     though seven deaths lay between.
  The Lamb and all His ransomed
  upon Mount Zion stand
  with glory, glory dwelling
  in Emmanuel's land.

3 Christ Jesus is the fountain,
     the deep, sweet well of love;
  the streams on earth I've tasted
     more deep I'll drink above;
  there, to an ocean fullness,
  His mercy will expand
  with glory, glory dwelling
  in Emmanuel's land.

4 With mercy and with judgement
     my web of time He wove
  and every dew of sorrow
     was glistening with His love.
  I'll bless the hand that guided,
  I'll bless the heart that planned,
  when in His glory dwelling
  in Emmanuel's land.

5 The bride eyes not her garment
     but her dear bridegroom's face;
  I will not gaze at glory
     but on my King of grace;
  not at the crown He gives me
  but on His nail-pierced hand;

663 Words: © 1968 Stainer & Bell Ltd, PO Box 110, Victoria House, 23 Gruneisen Road, London N3 1DZ

664 Words: © in this version Praise Trust, Praise Trust, PO Box 359, Darlington. DL3 8YD

the Lamb is all the glory
of Emmanuel's land.

6   I've wrestled on towards heaven
through storm and wind and
tide;
now, like a weary traveller
who leans upon his guide,
with evening shadows closing
while sinks life's lingering sand,
I greet the glory dawning
from Emmanuel's land.

Anne Ross Cousin, 1824–1906
based on writings of
Samuel Rutherford, 1600–1661
adapted Compilers of Praise! 2000

Also suitable:
Be still, my soul: the Lord is on your side   79
Guide me, O my great Redeemer   104
Jesus lives! your terrors now   437

THE LAST THINGS
THE CHURCH
TRIUMPHANT

665

1   Come, let us join our cheerful
songs
with angels round the throne;
ten thousand thousand are their
tongues,
but all their joys are one.

2   Worthy the Lamb who died, they
cry,
to be exalted thus!
Worthy the Lamb, our lips reply,
for He was slain for us!

3   Jesus is worthy to receive
all praise and power divine;
and all the blessings we can give
with songs of heaven combine.

4   Let all who live beyond the sky,
the air and earth and seas
unite to lift His glory high
and sing His endless praise!

5   Let all creation join in one
to bless the sacred name
of Him who reigns upon the
throne,
and to adore the Lamb!

Isaac Watts, 1674–1748
adapted Compilers of
Hymns for Today's Church, 1982

666

1   For all the saints, who from their
labours rest,
who to the world by faith their
Lord confessed,
Your name, O Jesus, be for ever
blessed:
Alleluia, alleluia!

2   You were their Rock, their
Fortress and their Might;
You, Lord, their Captain in the
well-fought fight,
and in the darkness their
unfailing light:

3   So may Your soldiers, faithful,
true and bold,
fight as the saints who nobly
fought of old,
and win, with them, the victor's
crown of gold:

4   One holy people, fellowship
divine!
we feebly struggle, they in glory
shine:
in earth and heaven the saints in
praise combine:

5   And when the fight is fierce, the
warfare long,
faintly we hear the distant
triumph-song;
and hearts are brave again, and
arms are strong:

6   The golden evening brightens in
the west;
soon, soon to faithful warriors
comes their rest:
the peaceful calm of Paradise the
blessed:

7   But, look! there breaks a yet
more glorious day;
saints all-triumphant rise in
bright array;
the King of glory passes on His
way!

8   From earth's wide bounds, from
ocean's farthest shore,
through gates of pearl, ascending,
they adore
the Father, Son and Spirit
evermore:

William Walsham How, 1823–1897
adapted Jubilate Hymns

THE LAST THINGS

667

1. How bright these glorious spirits
   shine;
   whence all their white array?
   How have they come to this fair
   place
   of everlasting day?
   These have endured through
   sufferings great
   and come to realms of light,
   and through the blood of Christ
   the Lamb
   their robes are pure and white.

2. Humble they stand before the
   throne,
   palm-branches in their hands;
   here they are serving Him they
   love,
   fulfilling His commands.
   No more can hunger hurt them
   now,
   nor shall they thirst again;
   no scorching heat can do them
   harm
   nor sun shall cause them pain.

3. For at the centre of the throne,
   Jesus the Lamb who died
   feeds them with nourishment
   divine,
   their shepherd and their guide.
   In pastures green He'll lead His
   flock
   where living streams appear,
   and God the Lord from every eye
   shall wipe away each tear.

   Isaac Watts, 1674–1748
   and William Cameron, 1751–1811
   Paraphrase 66
   adapted Jubilate Hymns

668

1. Salvation belongs to our God,
   who sits on the throne,
   and unto the Lamb.
   Praise and glory, wisdom and
   thanks,
   honour and power and strength:
   Be to our God for ever and ever,
   be to our God for ever and ever,
   be to our God for ever and ever.
   Amen.

2. And we, the redeemed shall be
   strong
   in purpose and unity,
   declaring aloud,
   praise and glory, wisdom and
   thanks,
   honour and power and strength.

   Adrian Howard and Pat Turner

669

1. You holy angels bright
   who wait at God's right hand,
   or through the realms of light
   fly at your Lord's command:
   assist our song,
   or else the theme
   too high will seem
   for mortal tongue.

2. You faithful souls at rest,
   who ran this earthly race,
   and now from sin released
   behold your Saviour's face:
   His praises sound
   and all unite
   in sweet delight
   to see Him crowned.

3. You saints who serve below,
   adore your heavenly King,
   and as you onward go
   your joyful anthems sing:
   take what He gives
   and praise Him still
   through good and ill,
   who ever lives.

4. So take, my soul, your part;
   triumph in God above,
   and with a well-tuned heart
   sing out your songs of love:
   with joy proclaim
   through all your days
   in ceaseless praise
   His glorious name!

   Richard Baxter, 1615–1691 and others
   adapted Jubilate Hymns

INDEXES

AUTHORS,TRANSLATORS and SOURCES   xiv

HYMNS and SONGS based on PSALMS

or LITURGICAL TEXTS   xxii

CHILDREN'S HYMNS and SONGS   xxiv

FIRST LINES   xxvi

INDEX OF AUTHORS, TRANSLATORS
and SOURCES of WORDS

Abelard, Peter (1079-1142)   396

Adams, Sarah Flower (1805-1848)   517

Addison, Joseph (1672-1719)   101

Advent Antiphons,   299

Alexander, Cecil Frances (1818-1895)
18, 162, 331, 424, 462, 498, 562

Alexander, James Waddell (1804-1859)
420

Alford, Henry (1810-1871)   51

Alington, Cyril Argentine (1872-1955)
28, 433, 534

Allen, Dennis   23

Allen, Nan   23

Allen, Oswald (1816-1878)   75

Anonymous (c. 1745)   606, 607

Anstice, Joseph (1808-1836)   57

Apostolic Constitutions, Greek,
3rd century   224

Appleford, Patrick Robert Norman
(b. 1925)   388

Arlott, L. T. John (1914-1991)   54

Armitage, Ella Sophia (1841-1931)
373

Asprey, Jonathan   171

Atkinson, Jennifer   543

Atromriug indiu niurt tren   162

Auber, Henriette (1773-1862)   476

Baker, Henry Williams (1821-77)
98, 196, 235, 272, 329, 384, 622

Bankhead, Dave   595

Baring-Gould, Sabine (1834-1924)
12, 149, 151

Barrows, Cliff   287

Bassett, Steve   595

Bateman, Christian Henry (1813-1889)
201

Bathurst, William Hiley (1796-1877)
520

Baughen, Michael Alfred (b. 1930)
236, 262

Baxter, Richard (1615-1691)   662

Bayly, Albert Frederick (1901-1984)
31, 374

Becker, Margaret   105

Bell, George Kennedy Allen
(1883-1958)   141

Bell, John Lamberton (b. 1949)
39, 124, 185, 290, 347, 367,
392, 436, 574, 618

Benedictus   298

Benson, Arthur Christopher
(1862-1925)   47

Benson, Louis Fitzgerald (1855-1930)
354

Bernard of Clairvaux, (1090-1153)
177, 186

Bewes, Richard Thomas (b. 1934)
85, 179

Bianco da Siena, (d. 1434)   458

Bickersteth, Edward Henry
(1825-1906)   633

Bilborough, Dave (b. 1965)   164

Binney, Thomas (1798-1874)   166

Black, Brian Colin (b. 1926)   342

Blatchford, Ambrose Nichols
(1842-1924)   77

Bliss, Philipp Paul (1838-1876)   82,
209, 414

Bode, John Ernest (1816-1874)   551

Bonar, Horatius N. (1808-1889)   160,
345, 383, 537

Book of Praise for Children (1881)   33

Booth, J.A. Paul (1931-1995)   36

Borthwick, Jane Laurie (1813-1897)
79

Bourne, George Hugh (1840-1925)
389

Bowater, Christopher Alan (b. 1947)
121, 208, 473, 539

Bowring, John (1792-1872)   115, 409

Brady, Nicholas (1659-1726)   129

idge, Basil Ernest (*b.* 1927) 173

idges, Matthew (1800-1894)
449, 532

idges, Robert (1844-1930) 78

iggs, George Wallace (1875-1959)
268, 593, 615

ight, William (1824-1901) 382

ooke, Stopford Augustus
(1832-1916) 335

ooks, Phillips (1835-1893) 330

ooks, Reginald Thomas (1918-1985)
275

oomhall, Gill 310

own, A. W. Godfrey (*b.* 1936) 580

own, Brenton 566

owne, Simon (1680-1732) 459

idry, Edmond (1854-1932) 442, 443

illock, Geoff 508

inyan, John (1628-1688) 538

irns, Edward Joseph (*b.* 1938) 359

irns, James Drummond (1823-1923)
172

itler, Henry Montagu (1833-1918)
547

irne, Mary Elizabeth (1880-1931)
490, 491

irom, John (1692-1763) 313

ameron, William (1751-1811) 667

ampbell, Jane Montgomery
(1817-1878) 59

arson, Christine 625

arter, Sydney (1915-2004) 602

asey, Peter (*b.* 1948) 228

aswall, Edward (1814-1878)
7, 177, 186, 311, 333, 513, 647

awood, John (1775-1852) 261

handler, John (1806-1876) 300

hatfield, Allen William (1808-1896)
69

henez, Charitie L. De (1841-1923)
492

hester, Cecil V. (1914-1997) 24

Chisholm, Thomas O. (1866-1960)
89, 89

Chisum, John 71

Christierson, Frank von (1900-1996)
265

Churchill, Wendy 450

Clare, Thomas Charles Hunter
(1910-1984) 592

Clarkson, Margaret (*b.* 1915) 470

Claudius, Matthias (1740-1815) 59

Clausnitzer, Tobias (1619-1684) 271

Clephane, Elizabeth Cecilia
(1830-1869) 536

Coates, Gerald (*b.* 1944) 646

Coffin, Charles (1676-1749) 300

Cole-Turner, Ronald S. 371

Collins, Henry (1827-1919) 506

Collison, Valerie (*b.* 1933) 314, 572

Columba, St (521-597) 447

Conder, Josiah (1789-1885) 241

Cook, Vikki 492

Cooper, Edward (1770-1833) 62

Cooper, Jarrod 452

Cousin, Anne Ross (1824-1906) 664

Cowper, William (1731-1800)
116, 180, 496, 518, 519

Cox, Frances Elizabeth (1812-1897)
437

Craig, Iain D. 117

Crawford, Emily (1864-1927) 273

Creighton, Richard (*b.* 1975) 564

Critchley, Dawn (*b.* 1965) 93

Critchley, Robert (*b.* 1959) 93

Cropper, Margaret Beatrice (1886-1980)
349

Crosby, Frances Jane (Fanny)
(1820-1915) 242, 559

Crossman, Samuel (*c.* 1624-1683) 417

Crouch, Paul (*b.* 1963) 254

Darby, John Nelson (1800-1882) 293

Dawn, Maggi (*b.* 1959) 401

Dearmer, Percy (1867-1936)
45, 264, 339, 348, 538, 589

Denny, Edward (1796-1889)   528

DeShazo, Lynn   245

Dix, William Chatterton (1837-1898)
307, 380

Doane, George Washington
(1799-1859)   363

Doddridge, Philip (1702-1751)
108, 132, 295, 653

Doerksen, Brian   524

Draper, William Henry (1855-1933)   17

Duck, Ruth C. (b. 1947)   40, 627

Dudley-Smith, Timothy (b. 1926)
42, 44, 64, 100, 119, 125, 131, 135,
147, 229, 230, 243, 292, 301, 352,
393, 438, 489, 495, 525

Duffield, George (1818-1888)   570

Dufford, Robert John (b. 1943)   110

Duncan, Mary Lundie (1814-1840)   11

Dunkerley, William Arthur
(1852-1941)   620

Edmeston, James (1791-1867)   107

Edwards, William (1848-1929)   402

Ehlen, Kathryn   111

Ellerton, John (1826-1893)   14, 16, 578

Elliott, Charlotte (1789-1871)   68

Elliott, Emily Elizabeth Steele
(1836-1897)   351

Evans, David J. (b. 1957)   165

Everest, Charles William (1814-1877)
571

Faber, Frederick William (1814-1863)
182, 418, 425

Falconer, Hugh (1859-1931)   293

Farjeon, Eleanor (1881-1965)   5

Fawcett, John (1740-1817)   281

Fellingham, Dave (b. 1945)   429

Ferguson, Jessie Margaret
Macdougall (1895-1964)   60

Flowerdew, Alice (1759-1830)   53

Foley, William Brian (1919-2000)
2, 65, 127

Forster, Michael Lindsay (b. 1946)
652, 654

Fosdick, Harry Emerson (1878-1969)
605

Foster, Frederick W. (1760-1835)   170

Francis of Assisi, St (1182-1226)   17

Fraser, Ian Masson (b. 1917)   38

Fullerton, William Young (1857-1932)
648

Galloway, Kathy (b. 1952)   599

Gaunt, Alan (b. 1935)   178

Gellert, Christian Fürchtegott
(1715-1769)   437

Gerhardt, Paul (1607-1676)   420

Getty, Keith (b. 1974)
408, 439, 500, 514, 519

Gill, Thomas Hornblower (1819-1906)
153

Gillard, Richard A. M. (b. 1953)   58

Gloria et honor Deo   286

Goudie, Ray   595

Gowans, John (b. 1934)   34

Grant, Robert (1779-1838)   33

Green, Frederick Pratt (1903-2000)
37, 52, 169, 258, 483, 583

Green, Melody   192

Groves, Alexander (1843-1909)   266

Gurney, Dorothy Frances (1858-1932)
581

Hake, Blanche   90

Hall, William John (1793-1861)   493

Hanby, Benjamin Russell (1833-1867)
361, 362

Hankey, Arabella Catherine
(1834-1911)   274

Harding, Nick   55

Hardy, Henry Ernest (1869-1946)   41

Hart, Joseph (1712-1767)   460

Hartsough, Louis (1828-1919)   540

Hastings, Thomas (1784-1872) 375
Hatch, Edwin (1835-1889) 457
Havergal, Frances Ridley (1836-1879)
    123, 501, 533, 545, 550, 552
Haweis, Thomas (1734-1820) 375, 376
Hawkins, Hester Periam (1848-1928)
    133
Hawks, Annie Sherwood (1835-1918)
    502
Head, Elizabeth Ann (1850-1936) 475
Head, Freda Nancy (b. 1914) 369
Hearn, Mary Ann (1834-1909) 546
Heber, Reginald (1783-1826) 161, 376
Heilige Flammen, Leipzig, (1720) 372
Henley, John (1800-1842) 397
Hensley, Lewis (1824-1905) 626
Herbert, George (1593-1633) 217, 218
Hewer, Jenny (b. 1945) 556
Hewitt, Garth 601
Hine, Stuart Wesley Keene (1899-1989)
    187
Holland, Henry Scott (1847-1918) 608
Holmes, Oliver Wendell (1809-1894)
    27
Home, Charles Silvester (1865-1914)
    80
Home Hymn Book, (1885) 133
Hopgood, Ron 522
Horrobin, Peter J. (b. 1943)
    12, 172, 257, 307, 331, 356, 546
Hosmer, Frederick Lucian (1840-1929)
    304
Housman, Laurence (1865-1959) 616
How, William Walsham (1823-1897)
    49, 279, 350, 410, 597, 666
Howard, Adrian 668
Howe, Julia Ward (1819-1810) 650
Hoyle, Richard Birch (1875-1939)
    442, 443
Hull, Eleanor Henrietta (1860-1935)
    490, 491
Hutchinson, Gillian E. 81, 544

The Hymnal for Boys and Girls, (1935)
    226

Idle, Christopher Martin (b. 1938)
    76, 97, 99, 194, 204, 469, 471,
    645, 655
Ikeler, Carol Rose (b. 1920) 642
Ingemann, Bernhardt Severin
    (1789-1862) 151

Jacobs, Peter (b. 1984) 466
Jarvis, Peter George (b. 1925) 507
Jeffries, Charles Joseph (1896-1972)
    640
Jenkins, W. L. 276
Jesu dulcis memoria Latin
    12th century 177, 186, 385
John of Damascus, St (d. c. 750) 440
Johnson, Helen 327
Johnson, Mark 327
Johnson, Samuel (1822-1882) 142

Kaan, Frederik Herman (b. 1929)
    390, 482, 604, 617, 663
Keble, John (1792-1866) 6, 15, 493
Kelly, Thomas (1769-1855)
    426, 453, 455
Ken, Thomas (1637-1711) 1, 9, 285
Kendrick, Graham Andrew (b. 1950)
    73, 96, 144, 146, 158, 181, 183, 191,
    203, 210, 303, 308, 320, 398, 399,
    406, 413, 415, 416, 434, 485, 499,
    600, 613, 621, 624, 628, 631, 657
Kennett, John 225
Kingsley, Charles (1819-1875) 365
Kitchin, George William (1827-1912)
    412
Knight, Mollie (1917-1993) 70

Lafferty, Karen (b. 1948) 568
Lathbury, Mary Artemisia (1841-1913)
    266

Lawson-Johnston, Phil
167, 214, 223

Leavers, Greg P. (b. 1952)
12, 172, 257, 307, 331, 356, 546

Leeson, Jane Elizabeth (1809-1881)
109, 511, 526

Litchfield, Benny   24

Littledale, Richard Frederick
(1833-1890)   458

Lloyd, William Freeman (1791-1853)
516

Longfellow, Samuel (1819-1892)   48

The Lord's Prayer   249, 253

Lyra Davidica, (1708)   435

Lyte, Henry Francis (1793-1847)
227, 231, 635, 661

Macalister, Robert A. S. (1870-1950)
271

Macbean, Lachlan (1853-1931)   312

Macdonald, Mary (1789-1872)   312

Macgregor, Duncan (1854-1923)   447

Macleod, Norman (1812-1872)   555

Madan, Martin (1726-1790)   649

Magnificat   301

Mair, William (1830-1920)   286

Mansell, David John (b. 1936)   215

Mant, Richard (1776-1848)   157

Mark, Robin   219, 543, 651, 660

Marriott, John (1780-1825)   636

Marshall-Taylor, Geoffrey (b. 1943)
112

Martin, Hugh (1890-1964)   356

Masterman, John Howard Bertram
(1867-1933)   614

Mathams, Walter John (1853-1931)
505

Matheson, George (1842-1906)
523, 563

Maule, Graham Alexander (b. 1958)
39, 290, 347, 367, 436, 574, 618

Mercer, William (1811-1873)   170

Merrill, William Pierson (1867-1954)
567

Micklem, Thomas Caryl (1925-2003)
481

Midlane, Albert (1825-1909)   659

Miller, Emily Huntington (1833-1913)
346

Milman, Henry Hart (1791-1868)   422

Milton, John (1608-1674)   26

Mohr, Joseph (1792-1848)   335

Monsell, John Samuel Bewley
(1811-1875)   126, 198, 557

Montgomery, David J. (b. 1963)
189, 503, 504

Montgomery, Dorothy G.   554

Montgomery, James (1771-1854)
84, 139, 237, 238, 251, 255, 294, 305,
379, 484, 639

Moore, John Boyd (1914-1993)   579

Morison, John (1750-1798)   302

Moseley, W. Howard (b. 1941)   612

Mote, Edward (1797-1874)   515

Moultrie, Gerard (1829-1885)   386

Mowbray, David (b. 1938)   43, 66,
114, 163, 188, 277, 577, 584, 587, 598

Mudie, David (b. 1961)   254

Müller, Johannes (1756-1790)   170

Münster Gesangbuch, (1677)   19

Nah, Young-Soo   124

Neale, John Mason (1818-1866)
138, 244, 283, 299, 319, 329, 348,
395, 440, 656

Neander, Joachim (1650-1680)   233

New English Bible   292

New International Version   13, 206

Newbolt, Michael Robert (1874-1956)
412

Newman, John Henry (1801-1890)
106, 159, 421

Newport, Doreen E. (b. 1927)   35

Newton, John (1725-1807)
61, 128, 143, 207, 208, 247, 486

Neyer, Johann David   90
Noel, Caroline Maria (1817-1877)   644
Nunc Dimittis   297
Nyberg, Anders (b. 1955)   152
Nystrom, Martin J. (b. 1956)   488

Oakeley, Frederick (1802-1880)   328
Oakley, Charles Ernest (1832-1865)   296
O'Driscoll, Herbert Thomas (b. 1928)   582
Old, Margaret V. (1932-2001)   256, 341, 358, 478
Olivers, Thomas (1725-1799)   240
Owens-Collins, Jamie (b. 1955)   560
Owens, Priscilla Jane (1829-1907)   529, 643
Oxenham, John, pseud. (1852-1941)   620

Palmer, Horatio Richmond (1834-1907)   530
Palmer, Ray (1808-1887)   72, 385
Park, Andy   184
Parker, William Henry (1845-1929)   356, 465
Partridge, Sybil Farish (1856-1917)   4
Patrick, St (372-466)   162
Pennefather, William (1816-1873)   176
Perronet, Edward (1726-1792)   445, 446
Perry, Michael Arnold (1942-1996)   30, 63, 113, 122, 200, 222, 297, 298, 304, 315, 316, 334, 336, 365, 368, 381, 464, 619
Petti, Gaetano Raphael (Anthony) (1932-1985)   25, 27, 107, 138, 217, 281, 311, 511
Phillips, Alan Norman (b. 1910)   623
Pierpoint, Folliott Sandford (1835-1917)   20
Piggott, William Charter (1872-1943)   269

Pilcher, Charles Venn (1879-1961)   585
Pinnock, Alan (fl. 1970)   22
Plumptre, Edward Hayes (1821-1891)   155, 156
Porteous, Christopher (b. 1935)   400
Pott, Francis (1832-1909)   278, 343, 441
Prayer of St Francis   596
Preston, David G. (b. 1939)   91
Price, Captain Alan J., CA   21
Prosch, Kevin   205
Prudentius, Aurelius Clemens (348-c. 413)   311, 329
The Psalter, (1912)   63

Quinn, James (b. 1919)   8, 280, 306, 432, 494

Raffles, Thomas (1788-1863)   636
Rath, Frances Towle   248
Rea, Jonathan (b. 1974)   500
Redman, Matt (b. 1974)   197, 411, 542
Reed, Andrew (1787-1862)   477
Reed, Edith Margaret Gellibrand (1885-1933)   322
Rees, Bryn Austin (1911-1983)   611
Rees, Timothy (1874-1939)   83, 472, 610
Rees, William (1802-1883)   402
Rettino, Debby Kerner (b. 1951)   154
Revell, Alison   423
Rhodes, Sarah Betts (1829-1904)   88
Richard Baxter (1615-1691)   669
Richards, Noël (b. 1955)   190, 195, 428, 632, 646
Richards, Tricia (b. 1960)   428, 632
Rinaldi, Sue   595
Rinkart, Martin (1586-1649)   95, 282
Rippon, John (1751-1836)   445, 446
Robertson, William (1820-1864)   370
Robinson, George Wade (1838-1877)   510

Robinson, Richard Hayes (1842-1882)
10

Rolinson, Christopher Philip
(b. 1958) 175, 474, 624

Rossetti, Christina Georgina
(1830-1894) 323, 326

Rowley, Francis Harold (1854-1952)
211

Ruis, Dave 174

Rutherford, Samuel (1600-1661) 664

Sadler, Gary 71, 245

'St Patrick's Breastplate', 8th century
494

Sands, Ernest (b. 1949) 234

Saward, Michael (b. 1932) 46, 448

Schlegel, Katharina Amalia
Dorothea von (b. 1697) 79

Schmolck, Benjamin (1672-1737) 372

Schutte, Daniel L. (b. 1947) 541

Scott, S. Lesley 50

Scriven, Joseph (1819-1886) 257

Sears, Edmund Hamilton (1810-1876)
324

Seddon, James Edward (1915-1983)
92, 145, 213, 249, 479, 576, 629,
634, 641

Shepherd, A. P. 350

Sherlock, Hugh (1905-1998) 638

Sibley, J. 250

Simmonds, Clive 558

Smale, Ian Stuart (b. 1949) 212

Smith, Edward Russell (b. 1927) 193

Smith, Florence Margaret (1886-1958)
548

Smith, Martin J. 148, 239

Smith, Walter Chalmers (1824-1908)
25

Smyttan, George Hunt (1822-1870)
343

Snow, George D'Oyly (1903-1977) 461

The Song of Christ's Glory, 342

Songs of Syon, (1910) 224

Spitta, Karl Johann Philipp
(1801-1859) 586

Stephen, Patrick (1914-2000) 253

Stevenson, Lilian (1870-1960) 19

Stone, Samuel John (1832-1900) 150

Strover, Martyn Christian Tinne
(b. 1932) 344

Struther, Jan (1901-1953) 3

Synesius of Cyrene, (c. 365-c. 414) 69

Tate, Nahum (1652-1715) 129, 340

Taylor, Jane (1783-1824) 94

Te Deum 204

Temple, Sebastian (1928-1997) 596

Tempus adest floridum, 45

Tersteegen, Gerhard (1697-1769) 170

Theodulph of Orleans, (c. 750-821)
395

Thompson, Steve 406

Threlfall, Jennette (1821-1880) 405

Thring, Godfrey (1823-1903) 449

Thwaites, Honor Mary (1914-1993)
586

Toplady, Augustus Montague
(1740-1778) 74

Townend, Stuart (b. 1963)
199, 407, 408, 439, 514, 527

Tucker, Francis Bland (1895-1984) 396

Tunseth, Kathleen 404

Turner, Pat 668

Tuttle, Carl (b. 1953) 403

Tweedy, Henry Hallam (1868-1953)
630

Twells, Henry (1823-1900) 364

Urbs beata Jerusalem 138

Wade, John Francis (c. 1711-1786) 328

Waring, Anna Laetitia (1823-1910)
120, 121

Waring, Samuel Miller (1790-1827)
284

Warner, Anna Bartlett (1820-1915) 270

Warner, Susan Bogert (1819-1885) 561

Watts, Isaac (1674-1748) 136, 202, 325, 427, 451, 637, 658, 665, 667

Webb, Benjamin (1819-1885) 353

Wesley, Charles (1707-1788) 67, 216, 221, 246, 291, 321, 431, 454, 467, 468, 487, 509, 521, 569, 591, 594, 649

Westendorf, Omer (1916-1998) 391

White, Ian (b. 1956) 13, 56, 168, 206, 317, 573

Whiting, William (1825-1878) 603

Whittier, John Greenleaf (1807-1892) 137, 366, 497, 590

Wigmore, Paul (b. 1925) 252, 263

Wile, Frances Whitmarsh (1878-1939) 41

Wilkinson, Katie Barclay (1859-1928) 512

Williams, Peter (1727-1796) 104

Williams, William (1717-1791) 104

Willis, Love Maria (1824-1908) 103

Winkworth, Catherine (1827-1878) 95, 233, 282, 372

Winslow, Jack Copley (1882-1974) 549

Woodward, George Ratcliffe (1848-1934) 224, 444

Wordsworth, Christopher (1807-1885) 32, 463

Wotherspoon, Arthur Wellesley (1853-1936) 286

Wreford, John Reynell (1800-1881) 609

Wren, Brian Arthur (b. 1936) 58, 267, 430, 480, 575

Wright, James 535

Wright, William (1859-1924) 134

Yigdal 240

Ylvisaker, John Carl (b. 1937) 102

Zschech, Darlene 220

INDEX of HYMNS and SONGS based on PSALMS or other LITURGICAL TEXTS

Aaronic Blessing	The Lord bless you and keep you	288
Apostles' Creed	I believe in God	377
Apostles' Creed	I believe in God (Contemporary version)	378
Benedictus	O bless the God of Israel	298
Doxology	Praise God from whom all blessings flow	285
Lord's Prayer	Father God in heaven, Lord most high	249
Lord's Prayer	Our Father who art in heaven	259
Lord's Prayer	Our Father in heaven	260
Magnificat	Tell out, my soul, the greatness of the Lord!	301
Micah 7: 7-20	I'll watch in hope for God	504
Nicene Creed	We believe in one God the Father Almighty	394
Nunc Dimittis	Faithful vigil ended	292
Paraphrase 2	O God of Bethel, by whose hand	108
Paraphrase 19	The people who in darkness walked	302
Paraphrase 37	While shepherds watched their flocks by night	340
Paraphrase 39	Hark the glad sound! – the Saviour comes	295
Paraphrase 54	I'm not ashamed to own my Lord	531
Paraphrase 58	Where high the heavenly temple stands	456
Paraphrase 66	How bright these glorious spirits shine	667
Psalm 1	Blessèd are all they	262
Psalm 1	Blessed are they	263
Psalm 5	Lord, as I wake I turn to You	2
Psalm 22	How glad are those with peace of mind	66
Psalm 23	The King of Love my shepherd is	98
Psalm 23	The Lord my shepherd rules my life	99
Psalm 23	The Lord's my shepherd, I'll not want	527
Psalm 24	This earth belongs to God	194
Psalm 27	God is my strong salvation –	84
Psalm 27	You're my light and my salvation	102
Psalm 30	I'll lift my voice, O Lord	91
Psalm 30	I worship You, O Lord	213
Psalm 34	Through all the changing scenes of life	129
Psalm 38	Lord, will You turn from Your anger and hear me?	70
Psalm 43	O send Your light forth and Your truth	189
Psalm 46	God is our strength and refuge	85
Psalm 51	God, be merciful to me	63
Psalm 61	Listen to my prayer, Lord	92
Psalm 63	O God, You are my God alone	185
Psalm 65: 9-13	The earth is Yours, O God –	46

Psalm 66	Praise our God with shouts of joy	97
Psalm 67	God of mercy, God of grace	635
Psalm 69	Help me, O God, and hear my cry	64
Psalm 82	God is King – be warned, you mighty	619
Psalm 84	How lovely is Your dwelling-place	171
Psalm 89	Timeless love! We sing the story	100
Psalm 90	God everlasting, at Your word	114
Psalm 91	Safe in the shadow of the Lord	525
Psalm 95	Come, sing praises to the Lord above	113
Psalm 95	Let us sing to the God of salvation	179
Psalm 98	Sing to God new songs of worship –	236
Psalm 103	Praise, my soul, the King of heaven	227
Psalm 104	'O bless the Lord, my soul!' I sing	30
Psalm 104	O worship the King, all-glorious above	33
Psalm 117	From all that dwell below the skies	202
Psalm 118	Open the gates of righteousness	188
Psalm 119	With all my heart I seek	277
Psalm 121	I lift my eyes to the quiet hills	119
Psalm 122	I rejoiced to hear them say	173
Psalm 125	All those who trust the Lord	140
Psalm 126	When Zion's fortunes God restored	130
Psalm 127	Unless the Lord has built the house	584
Psalm 130	Up from the depths I cry to God	76
Psalm 133	How good a thing it is	145
Psalm 134	Praise the Lord, all you servants of the Lord	13
Psalm 136	Let us with a gladsome mind	26
Psalm 139	There is no moment of my life	127
Psalm 145	To God our great salvation	243
Psalm 146	Praise the God of our salvation	230
Psalm 147	Fill your hearts with joy and gladness	42
Psalm 147	How good it is to sing praise to our God	206
Psalm 148	Praise the Lord of heaven	229
Psalm 148	Praise the Lord, you heavens, adore Him	232
Psalms 149, 150	Bring to the Lord a glad new song	200
Psalm 150	Praise Him on the trumpet, the psaltery and harp	225
Psalm 150	Sing praise to the Lord!	235
Te Deum	God, we praise You! God, we bless You!	204

INDEX of HYMNS and SONGS for CHILDREN

A little child may know	109
A Man once came from Galilee	341
All things bright and beautiful	18
At harvest-time we celebrate	50
Away in a manger, no crib for a bed	309
Can you be sure that the rain will fall?	112
Children of Jerusalem	397
Christ be my leader by night as by day	495
Come and join the celebration	314
Come, children, join to sing –	201
Crackers and turkeys and pudding and cream	317
Did you ever talk to God above?	248
Do no sinful action	498
Father, I place into Your hands	556
From where the sun rises	203
God has made me, and He knows me	81
God is always near me	82
God is so good	86
God loves you, and I love you	87
God, who made the earth	88
God's love is deeper than the deepest ocean	117
Harvest-time is the time when all the crops are high	55
Have you heard the raindrops drumming on the rooftops?	344
He gave me eyes so I could see	22
He made the water wet	23
He's got the whole wide world in His hands	118
Holy Spirit, hear us	465
How strong and sure my Father's care	90
I am so glad that our Father in heaven	209
I can talk to God	250
I have seen the golden sunshine	24
I love to hear the story	346
I want to walk with Jesus Christ	558
I will wave my hands in praise and adoration	212
If I come to Jesus	559
If I could speak like an angel	466
I'm special because God has loved me	210
It is a thing most wonderful	410
It takes an almighty hand, to make your harvest grow	56

Jesus bids us shine	561
Jesus, Friend of all the children	505
Jesus' hands were kind hands, doing good to all	349
Jesus is greater than the greatest heroes	544
Jesus is risen from the grave	436
Jesus loves me! This I know	270
Jesus, tender Shepherd, hear me	11
Jesus went to worship	178
Just as I am, Your child to be	546
Look and learn from the birds of the air	124
Lord, I would own Your tender care	94
My God is so big, so strong and so mighty	29
O what can little hands do	565
Peter, James and John in a fishing boat, *	355
Praise Him, praise Him	226
Prayer is like a telephone	254
Saviour, teach me, day by day	526
See Him lying on a bed of straw	334
Seek ye first the Kingdom of God	568
Talk to God and share with Him	256
Tell me the stories of Jesus	356
Thank You Jesus, thank You Jesus	423
The Bible tells of God's great plan	276
The Church is wherever God's people are praising	642
The journey of life may be easy, may be hard	572
The Virgin Mary had a baby boy	337
The wise man built his house upon the rock	357
The wise may bring their learning	338
There are hundreds of sparrows, thousands, millions	34
There's a song for all the children	659
Two little fishes, five loaves of bread	554
We are singing to You, Lord, our thanks and our joy	358
We thank You, Lord, for all Your gifts	60
Welcome to the family	154
What a wonderful Saviour is Jesus	360
When Noah built a great big boat	111
Who put the colours in the rainbow?	36
You're my light and my salvation	102

INDEX of FIRST LINES

A gladsome hymn of praise we sing 77
A little child may know 109
A little child the Saviour came 370
A Man once came from Galilee 341
Abide with me: fast falls the eventide 661
According to Your gracious word 379
All beautiful the march of days 41
All creatures of our God and King 17
All glory, praise and honour 395
All hail the power of Jesus' name! 445
All hail the power of Jesus' name! 446
All heaven declares 428
All I once held dear 485
All my days I will sing this song of gladness 199
All my hope on God is founded 78
All praise and thanks to God 282
All that I am I lay before You 535
All the ends of the earth, all you creatures of the sea 110
All things are Yours; nothing of ours 137
All things bright and beautiful 18
All those who trust the Lord *(Psalm 125)* 140
All who are thirsty, come to the Lord 381
Alleluia, sing to Jesus! 380
Almighty Father-God, you give 614
Almighty God, Your word is cast 261
Alone You make Your way, O Lord 396
Amazing grace – how sweet the sound 486
Amen 289
And can it be that I should gain 487
And now, O Father, mindful of the love 382
Angel voices ever singing 278
Angel voices, richly blending 306
Angels from the realms of glory 305
Approach, my soul, the mercy-seat 61
As a fire is meant for burning 627
As man and woman we were made 575
As the deer pants for the water 488
As water to the thirsty 489
As we seek Your face 164
As with gladness men of old 307
At evening, when the sun had set 364
At harvest-time we celebrate 50
At the name of Jesus 644
At this time of giving 308
At Your feet we fall, mighty risen Lord 429

Awake, my soul, and with the sun 1
Away in a manger, no crib for a bed 309

Baby Jesus in the manger 310
Be still, for the presence of the Lord, the Holy One, is here 165
Be still, my soul: the Lord is on your side 79
Be Thou my vision, O Lord of my heart 491
Beauty for brokenness 628
Before the heaven and earth 342
Before the throne of God above 492
Before the world began 290
Beneath the cross of Jesus 536
Bethlehem, most noble city 311
Blessèd are all they (Psalm 1) 262
Blessed are they (Psalm 1) 263
Blessed are the pure in heart 493
Book of books, our people's strength 264
Break forth, O living light of God 265
Break now the bread of life 266
Breathe on me, breath of God 457
Bright the vision that delighted 157
Bring to the Lord a glad new song (Psalms 149, 150) 200
Brother, sister, let me serve you 588

Can you be sure that the rain will fall? 112
Child in the manger 312
Child of blessing, child of promise 371
Children of Jerusalem 397
Christ be beside me 494
Christ be my leader by night as by day 495
Christ be the Lord of all our days 131
Christ is alive! Let Christians sing 430
Christ is made our sure foundation 138
Christ is surely coming, bringing His reward 645
Christ is the King! O friends rejoice 141
Christ is the world's Redeemer 447
Christ is the world's true light 615
Christ, the Lord, is risen today!' 431
Christ triumphant, ever reigning 448
Christian, do you hear the Lord? 496
Christians, awake! Salute the happy morn 313
Church of God, elect and glorious 629
City of God, how broad and far 142
Come and hear the joyful singing 315
Come and join the celebration 314
Come and see, come and see 398

Come and sing the Christmas story 316
Come, children, join to sing – 201
Come down, O Love divine! 458
Come, gracious Spirit, heavenly Dove 459
Come, Holy Spirit, come 460
Come, let us join our cheerful songs 665
Come, my soul, your plea prepare 247
Come, O long-expected Jesus 291
Come, sing praises to the Lord above *(Psalm 95)* 113
Come, you thankful people, come 51
Courage, friend, and do not stumble 555
Crackers and turkeys and pudding and cream 317
Crown Him with many crowns 449

Day is done, but Love unfailing 8
Dear Lord and Father of mankind 497
Dearest Jesus, we are here 372
Deep in the shadows of the past 267
Defend me, Lord, from hour to hour 461
Did you ever talk to God above? 248
Do no sinful action 498

Each day we live the Christian life 462
Easter glory fills the sky! 432
Eternal Father, strong to save 603
Eternal God, whose power upholds 630
Eternal Light! Eternal Light! 166

Fairest Lord Jesus 19
Faithful vigil ended *(Nunc Dimittis)* 292
Far and near hear the call 631
Father eternal, Ruler of creation 616
Father God in heaven, Lord most high *(Lord's Prayer)* 249
Father God, on us You shower 589
Father God, we worship You 158
Father, hear the prayer we offer – 103
Father, I place into Your hands 556
Father, in Your presence kneeling 585
Father of heaven, whose love profound 62
Father, we adore You 167
Father, Your Church with thankfulness 481
Fight the good fight with all your might 557
Fill now my life, O Lord my God 537
Fill your hearts with joy and gladness *(Psalm 147)* 42
Filled with compassion for all creation 632
Firmly I believe and truly 159

Focus my eyes on You, O Lord 168
Fold to your heart your sister and your brother 590
For all the saints, who from their labours rest 666
For my sake and the gospel's, go 633
For the beauty of the earth 20
For the fruits of His creation 52
For the healing of the nations 617
For the joys and for the sorrows 499
For the might of Your arm we bless You 80
For Your gift of God the Spirit 470
Forth in the peace of Christ we go 280
Forth in Your name, O Lord, I go 591
Forty days and forty nights 343
Fountain of mercy, God of love 53
Freedom and life are ours 471
From all that dwell below the skies *(Psalm 117)* 202
From heaven You came, helpless babe 399
From where the sun rises 203
From You all skill and science flow 365

Glorious things of you are spoken 143
Glory be to God the Father 160
Glory to Jesus, risen, conquering Son! 443
Glory to You, my God, this night 9
Go forth and tell! O Church of God, awake! 634
God and Father, we adore You 293
God! As with silent hearts we bring to mind 604
God, be merciful to me *(Psalm 51)* 63
God everlasting, at Your word *(Psalm 90)* 114
God, give us peace that lasts 618
God has made me, and He knows me 81
God has spoken – by His prophets 268
God in His love for us lent us this planet 37
God is always near me 82
God is good, God is great 21
God is here! As we His people 169
God is King – be warned, you mighty *(Psalm 82)* 619
God is love, His mercy brightens 115
God is love: let heaven adore Him 83
God is my strong salvation – *(Psalm 27)* 84
God is our strength and refuge *(Psalm 46)* 85
God is so good 86
God loves you, and I love you 87
God moves in a mysterious way 116
God of Grace, amazing wonder 500
God of grace and God of glory 605

God of mercy, God of grace *(Psalm 67)* 635
God of the pastures, hear our prayer 592
God rest you merry, gentlemen 318
God reveals His presence 170
God save our gracious Queen 607
God save our gracious Queen 606
God, we praise You! God, we bless You! *(Te Deum)* 204
God, when I came into this life 482
God, who made the earth 88
God, whose almighty word 636
God whose farm is all creation 54
God, You have given us power to sound 593
God's love is deeper than the deepest ocean 117
Going home, moving on 654
Good Christians all, rejoice 319
Good Christians all, rejoice and sing! 433
Good news, good news to you we bring 320
Gracious Spirit, Holy Ghost 463
Great God, we sing Your mighty hand 132
Great is the darkness that covers the earth 646
Great is Thy faithfulness, O God my Father 89
Guide me, O my great Redeemer 104

Hail to the Lord's Anointed 294
Happy the home that welcomes You, Lord Jesus 586
Hark! a trumpet-call is sounding 647
Hark the glad sound! – the Saviour comes *(Paraphrase 39)* 295
Hark! the herald angels sing 321
Harvest-time is the time when all the crops are high 55
Have you heard the raindrops drumming on the rooftops? 344
He gave His life in selfless love 400
He gave me eyes so I could see 22
He is the Lord, and He reigns on high 205
He lives in us, the Christ of God 464
He made the water wet 23
He was pierced for our transgressions 401
He who would valiant be 538
Heavenly Father, You have brought us 133
Heavenly Father, may Your blessing 269
Help me, O God, and hear my cry *(Psalm 69)* 64
Help us to help each other, Lord 594
Here from all nations, all tongues, and all peoples 655
Here I am, wholly available – 539
Here is love vast as the ocean 402
Here, O my Lord, I see You face to face 383
He's got the whole wide world in His hands 118

Hills of the north, rejoice 296
Holy Father, cheer our way 10
Holy, holy, holy, Lord God Almighty! 161
Holy Spirit, ever living 472
Holy Spirit, hear us 465
Holy Spirit, we welcome You 473
Hosanna, hosanna, hosanna in the highest 403
Hosanna! Hosanna! 404
Hosanna, loud hosanna 405
How bright these glorious spirits shine (Paraphrase 66) 667
How can I be free from sin – 406
How can we sing with joy to God 65
How clear is our vocation, Lord 483
How deep the Father's love for us 407
How glad are those with peace of mind (Psalm 22) 66
How good a thing it is (Psalm 133) 145
How good and how pleasant it is 144
How good it is to sing praise to our God (Psalm 147) 206
How lovely is Your dwelling-place (Psalm 84) 171
How strong and sure my Father's care 90
How sweet the name of Jesus sounds 207
How sweet the name of Jesus sounds 208
Hushed was the evening hymn 172

I am not worthy, holy Lord 384
I am so glad that our Father in heaven 209
I am trusting You, Lord Jesus 501
I believe in (Apostles' Creed) 377
I believe in God, the Father Almighty (Apostles' Creed) 378
I bind myself to God today 162
I can talk to God 250
I cannot tell why He whom angels worship 648
I have seen the golden sunshine 24
I hear Your welcome voice 540
I heard the voice of Jesus say 345
I lift my eyes to the quiet hills (Psalm 121) 119
I love to hear the story 346
I need You every hour, most gracious Lord 502
I rejoiced to hear them say (Psalm 122) 173
I, the Lord of sea and sky 541
I waited for the Lord my God 503
I want to walk with Jesus Christ 558
I will offer up my life 542
I will sing the wondrous story 211
I will speak out for those who have no voices 595
I will wave my hands in praise and adoration 212

I will worship (I will worship) 174
I worship You, O Lord *(Psalm 30)* 213
If I come to Jesus 559
If I could speak like an angel 466
I'll lift my voice, O Lord *(Psalm 30)* 91
I'll watch in hope for God *(Micah 7: 7-20)* 504
I'm not ashamed to own my Lord *(Paraphrase 54)* 531
I'm special because God has loved me 210
Immortal, invisible, God only wise 25
Immortal Love, for ever full 366
In Christ alone my hope is found 408
In Christ there is no east or west 620
In heavenly armour we'll enter the land – 560
In heavenly love abiding 120
In heavenly love abiding 121
In the bleak mid-winter 323
In the cross of Christ I glory 409
In the tomb so cold they laid Him 434
Infant holy, Infant lowly 322
It came upon the midnight clear 324
It is a thing most wonderful 410
It takes an almighty hand, to make your harvest grow 56

Jerusalem the golden 656
Jesus, all for Jesus 543
Jesus bids us shine 561
Jesus calls above the tumult 562
Jesus Christ, I think upon Your sacrifice 411
Jesus Christ is waiting 347
Jesus Christ is risen today, Alleluia. 435
Jesus comes with clouds descending 649
Jesus, draw me ever nearer 105
Jesus, Friend of all the children 505
Jesus, good above all other 348
Jesus' hands were kind hands, doing good to all 349
Jesus, hope of every nation 297
Jesus is greater than the greatest heroes 544
Jesus is King 450
Jesus is Lord! Creation's voice proclaims it 215
Jesus is risen from the grave 436
Jesus is the name we honour 214
Jesus, King of kings 175
Jesus lives! your terrors now 437
Jesus, lover of my soul 67
Jesus loves me! This I know 270
Jesus, Master, whose I am 545

Jesus, my Lord, my God, my all 506
Jesus! name of wondrous love! 350
Jesus, Prince and Saviour 438
Jesus put this song into our hearts 146
Jesus shall reign where'er the sun 637
Jesus, stand among us 176
Jesus, tender Shepherd, hear me 11
Jesus, the joy of loving hearts 385
Jesus, the Lord of love and life 576
Jesus! the name high over all 216
Jesus, the very thought of You 177
Jesus went to worship 178
Join all the glorious names 451
Joy to the world – the Lord has come 325
Judge eternal, throned in splendour 608
Just as I am, without one plea 68
Just as I am, Your child to be 546

King of glory, King of peace 217
King of kings, majesty 452

Laud and honour to the Father 283
Lead, kindly light, amid the encircling gloom 106
Lead us, heavenly Father, lead us 107
Let all mortal flesh keep silence 386
Let all the world in every corner sing 218
Let us break bread together on our knees 387
Let us sing to the God of salvation (Psalm 95) 179
Let us with a gladsome mind (Psalm 136) 26
Lift high the cross, the love of Christ proclaim 412
'Lift up your hearts!' We lift them to the Lord 547
Like a mighty river flowing 122
Like a river glorious 123
Listen to my prayer, Lord (Psalm 61) 92
Look and learn from the birds of the air 124
Look upon us, blessèd Lord 271
Look, you saints, the sight is glorious! 453
Lord and Master, You have called us 548
Lord, as I wake I turn to You (Psalm 5) 2
Lord, be my vision, supreme in my heart 490
Lord, bring the day to pass 38
Lord, come and heal Your Church 474
Lord, dismiss us with Your blessing 281
Lord, enthroned in heavenly splendour 389
Lord, for the years Your love has kept and guided 125
Lord, for tomorrow and its needs 4

Lord, I come before Your throne of grace 93
Lord, I come to You – let my heart be changed, renewed 508
Lord, I would own Your tender care 94
Lord, it is not within my care 662
Lord Jesus Christ, You have come to us 388
Lord Jesus, think on me 69
Lord Jesus, when Your people meet 180
Lord of all being, throned afar 27
Lord of all hopefulness, Lord of all joy 3
Lord of beauty, Yours the splendour 28
Lord of creation, to You be all praise! 549
Lord of creation, giver of gladness 577
Lord of our growing years 587
Lord of the changing year 43
Lord of the Church, we pray for our renewing 147
Lord of the harvest, once again 57
Lord of the living, in Your name assembled 663
Lord, speak to me that I may speak 550
Lord, teach us how to pray aright 251
Lord, the light of Your love is shining 621
Lord, while for humankind we pray 609
Lord, will You turn from Your anger and hear me? *(Psalm 38)* 70
Lord, You have searched and known my ways 507
Lord, You in Your perfect wisdom 610
Lord, You left Your throne and Your kingly crown 351
Lord, Your Church on earth is seeking 638
Lord, Your word shall guide us 272
Love came down at Christmas 326
Love divine, all loves excelling 509
Loved with everlasting love 510
Loving Shepherd of Your sheep 511

Make me a captive, Lord 563
Make me a channel of Your peace 596
Make way, make way, for Christ the King 413
Man of Sorrows! what a name 414
March on, my soul, with strength 134
May God's blessing surround you each day 287
May the fragrance of Jesus fill this place 181
May the mind of Christ my Saviour 512
Meekness and majesty 415
Men of faith, rise up and sing 148
Merciful God and Father 71
Mercy, blessing, favour, grace 44
Mighty God, Everlasting Father 327
Mine eyes have seen the glory of the coming of the Lord 650

Morning has broken 5
My faith looks up to Thee 72
My God, accept my heart this day 532
My God, how wonderful You are 182
My God, I love You; not because 513
My God is so big, so strong and so mighty 29
My heart is filled with thankfulness 514
My heart is full of admiration 183
My heart will sing to You because of Your great love 219
My hope is built on nothing less 515
My hope rests firm on Jesus Christ 564
My Jesus, my Saviour 220
My Lord, what love is this 416
My song is love unknown 417
My times are in Your hand 516

Name of all majesty 352
Nearer, my God, to Thee 517
New every morning is the love 6
No-one but You, Lord 184
Now let us from this table rise 390
Now thank we all our God 95
Now the day is over 12
Now to Him who loved us, gave us 284

O bless the God of Israel (Benedictus) 298
O bless the Lord, my soul!' I sing (Psalm 104) 30
O Breath of life, come sweeping through us 475
O Christ the same, through all our story's pages 135
O come, all you faithful 328
O come and mourn with me awhile 418
O come, O come, Emmanuel 299
O dearest Lord, Thy sacred head 419
O Father, all creating 578
O Father, in Your father-heart 373
O Father of the fatherless 96
O for a closer walk with God 519
O for a closer walk with God 518
O for a faith that will not shrink 520
O for a heart to praise my God 521
O for a thousand tongues to sing 221
O God beyond all praising 222
O God, hear me calling and answer, I pray! 252
O God of Bethel, by whose hand (Paraphrase 2) 108
O God of faith, help me believe 522
O God of love, O King of peace 622

O God of our divided world 623
O God, our help in ages past 136
O God, whose loving hand has led 579
O God, You are my God alone *(Psalm 63)* 185
O God, Your life-creating love 374
O Jesus, I have promised 551
O Jesus, King most wonderful 186
O Jesus, strong and pure and true 597
O little town of Bethlehem 330
O Lord my God, when I in awesome wonder 187
O Lord of every shining constellation 31
O Lord of heaven and earth and sea 32
O Lord our God, how majestic is Your name 223
O Lord our God, we praise Your name 580
O Lord, the clouds are gathering 73
O Lord, who came from realms above 467
O love, how deep, how broad, how high! 353
O Love that wilt not let me go 523
O Master Christ, draw near to take 598
O perfect Love, all human thought transcending 581
O praise the Lord, you servants of the Lord 224
O sacred head once wounded 420
O send Your light forth and Your truth *(Psalm 43)* 189
O sing a song of Bethlehem 354
O Spirit of the living God 639
O what can little hands do 565
O worship the King, all-glorious above *(Psalm 104)* 33
Of the Father's heart begotten 329
Oh the life of the world is a joy and a treasure 599
On Christmas night all Christians sing 332
On Jordan's bank the Baptist's cry 300
Once in royal David's city 331
One shall tell another 600
Onward! Christian soldiers! 149
Open the gates of righteousness *(Psalm 118)* 188
Our children, Lord, in faith and prayer 375
Our children, Lord, in faith and prayer 376
Our Father in heaven *(Lord's Prayer)* 260
Our Father who art in heaven *(Lord's Prayer)* 259
Our great Redeemer, as He breathed 476
Our heavenly Father, through Your Son 253
Over all the earth, You reign on high 566
Overwhelmed by love 190

Peter, James and John in a fishing boat 355
Pour out Your Spirit from on high 484

FIRST LINES

Praise God for the harvest of orchard and field 58
Praise God from whom all blessings flow (Doxology) 285
Praise Him on the trumpet, the psaltery and harp (Psalm 150) 225
Praise Him, praise Him 226
Praise, my soul, the King of heaven (Psalm 103) 227
Praise our God with shouts of joy (Psalm 66) 97
Praise the God of our salvation (Psalm 146) 230
Praise the Lord, all you servants of the Lord (Psalm 134) 13
Praise the Lord in the rhythm of your music 228
Praise the Lord of heaven (Psalm 148) 229
Praise the Lord, His glories show, Alleluia! 231
Praise the Lord, you heavens, adore Him (Psalm 148) 232
Praise to the Holiest in the height 421
Praise to the Lord 233
Prayer is like a telephone 254
Prayer is the soul's supreme desire 255
Purify my heart 524

Rejoice, the Lord is King! 454
Restore, O Lord 624
Ride on, ride on in majesty 422
Rise up, O Church of God! 567
Rock of Ages, cleft for me 74

Safe in the shadow of the Lord (Psalm 91) 525
Salvation belongs to our God 668
Saviour, again to Your dear name we raise 14
Saviour, teach me, day by day 526
See, amid the winter snow 333
See Him lying on a bed of straw 334
See what a morning, gloriously bright 439
Seek ye first the Kingdom of God 568
Sent forth by God's blessing, our true faith confessing 391
Shout for joy! The Lord has let us feast 392
Silent night, holy night! 335
Sing of Eve and sing of Adam 582
Sing of the Lord's goodness, Father of all wisdom 234
Sing praise to God on mountain tops 39
Sing praise to the Lord! (Psalm 150) 235
Sing to God new songs of worship (Psalm 98) 236
Sing to the Lord a joyful song 126
Singing, we gladly worship the Lord together 625
Soldiers of Christ, arise 569
Songs of praise the angels sang 237
Speak forth Your word, O Father 640
Speak, Lord, in the stillness 273

Spirit divine, inspire our prayers 477
Spirit of God, our hearts inspire 468
Spirit of God, unseen as the wind 478
Spirit of holiness, wisdom and faithfulness 469
Spring has now unwrapped the flowers 45
Stand up and bless the Lord 238
Stand up, stand up for Jesus 570
Such love, pure as the whitest snow 191
Summer suns are glowing 49
Sun of my soul, my Saviour dear 15

Take my life and let it be 552
'Take up your cross,' the Saviour said 571
Talk to God and share with Him 256
Tell all the world of Jesus 641
Tell me the old, old story 274
Tell me the stories of Jesus 356
Tell out, my soul, the greatness of the Lord! *(Magnificat)* 301
Thank You for saving me; what can I say? 239
Thank You Jesus, thank You Jesus 423
Thanks to God whose word was spoken 275
The Bible tells of God's great plan 276
The Church is wherever God's people are praising 642
The Church's one foundation 150
The day of resurrection! 440
The day You gave us, Lord, is ended 16
The earth is Yours, O God *(Psalm 65: 9-13)* 46
The first Nowell the angel did say 336
The God of Abraham praise 240
The grace of life is theirs 583
The head that once was crowned with thorns 455
The journey of life may be easy, may be hard 572
The King of Love my shepherd is *(Psalm 23)* 98
The kingdom of God is justice and joy 611
The Lord bless you and keep you *(Aaronic Blessing)* 288
The Lord is King! lift up your voice 241
The Lord my shepherd rules my life *(Psalm 23)* 99
The Lord's my shepherd, I'll not want *(Psalm 23)* 527
The people who in darkness walked *(Paraphrase 19)* 302
The sands of time are sinking 664
The Spirit came, as promised 479
The spring again is here 47
The strife is past, the battle done 441
The summer days are come again 48
The trumpets sound, the angels sing 657
The Virgin Mary had a baby boy 337

The wise man built his house upon the rock 357
The wise may bring their learning 338
There are hundreds of sparrows, thousands, millions 34
There is a green hill far away 424
There is a land of pure delight 658
There is a Redeemer 192
There is no moment of my life *(Psalm 139)* 127
There's a quiet understanding 193
There's a song for all the children 659
There's a spirit in the air 480
There's a wideness in God's mercy 425
These are the days of Elijah 651
Thine be the glory, risen, conquering Son 442
Think of a world without any flowers 35
This earth belongs to God *(Psalm 24)* 194
This joyful Eastertide 444
This stone in faith, O Lord, we lay 139
Though I feel afraid 573
Though troubles assail 128
Through all the changing scenes of life *(Psalm 34)* 129
Through the night of doubt and sorrow 151
Thuma mina 553
Timeless love! We sing the story *(Psalm 89)* 100
To be in Your presence 195
To God be the glory, great things He has done! 242
To God our great salvation *(Psalm 145)* 243
To the name of our salvation 244
Today Your mercy calls us 75
Two little fishes, five loaves of bread 554

Unless the Lord has built the house *(Psalm 127)* 584
Unto God be praise and honour 286
Unto us a boy is born! 339
Up from the depths I cry to God *(Psalm 130)* 76

Wake up, O sleeper, and rise from the dead 303
Waken, O sleeper, wake and rise 652
We are a moment, You are forever 245
We are marching in the light of God 152
We are singing to You, Lord, our thanks and our joy 358
We believe in God Almighty 163
We believe in one God the Father Almighty *(Nicene Creed)* 394
We cannot measure how You heal 367
We cannot own the sunlit sky 40
We come as guests invited 393
We come before our fathers' God 153

We entrust to the Lord all His children 612
We give God thanks for those who knew 368
We give You but Your own 279
We have a gospel to proclaim 359
We have heard a joyful sound 643
We hear Your cry, Lord, in the hungry 601
We love the place, O God 196
We plough the fields, and scatter 59
We sing the praise of Him who died 426
We thank You, Lord, for all Your gifts 60
Welcome to the family 154
What a friend we have in Jesus 257
What a wonderful Saviour is Jesus 360
What grace, O Lord, and beauty shone 528
When all Your mercies, O my God 101
When I needed a neighbour, were you there, were you there? 602
When I survey the wondrous cross 427
When morning gilds the skies 7
When Noah built a great big boat 111
When our confidence is shaken 258
When the music fades, all is stripped away 197
When Zion's fortunes God restored (Psalm 126) 130
Where high the heavenly temple stands (Paraphrase 58) 456
While shepherds watched their flocks by night (Paraphrase 37) 340
Who can sound the depths of sorrow 613
Who is He, in yonder stall 361
Who is He, in yonder stall 362
Who is on the Lord's side? 533
Who put the colours in the rainbow? 36
Will you come and follow Me 574
Will your anchor hold in the storms of life 529
With all my heart I seek (Psalm 119) 277

Worship the Lord in the beauty of holiness! 198
Yield not to temptation, for yielding is sin 530
You are the way, to You alone 363
You holy angels bright 669
You servants of God, your master proclaim 246
You servants of the Lord 653
You who know the Lord is gracious 534
Your hand, O God, has guided 155
Your hand, O God, has guided 156
Your kingdom come! on bended knee 304
Your kingdom come, O God 626
Your will for us and others, Lord 369
You're my light and my salvation (Psalm 27) 102
You're the Lion of Judah, the Lamb that was slain 660